Soft & Cuddly Toys

Soft & Cuddly Toys

by Robin Tarnoff

Sedgewood® Press

For CBS, Inc.:
Editorial Director: *Dina von Zweck*
Project Coordinator: *Jacqueline Weinbach*

For Sedgewood® Press:
Director: *Elizabeth P. Rice*
Associate Editor: *Leslie Gilbert*
Production Manager: *Bill Rose*
Book Design: *Bentwood Studio/Jos. Trautwein*
Photography: *Robert Epstein*

ACKNOWLEDGMENTS

I'd like to thank the following people for their help in making this project become a reality: Dina von Zweck and Jackie Weinbach of CBS for their patience and expertise; Robert Epstein for putting his special touch to the photographs; Theresa Capuana and Lina Morielli for their enthusiasm and support for all my doll making efforts; Noel Trapp, Weegee and Alfred for not sitting on the dolls before they were photographed.

Distributed by Macmillan Publishing Company, a division of Macmillan, Inc.

ISBN: 0-02-616170-2

Library of Congress Catalog Card Number: 85-50564

Printed in the United States of America
10 9 8 7 6 5 4 3 2 1

TO

HARRIET, JOSEPH and DAVID

*for their never-ending support,
encouragement, and enthusiasm.*

Contents

Introduction

What a lot of fun it was to create the characters in this book! I've been making soft dolls since I was a little girl, but working on this book has given me an opportunity to create the dolls, and all the different doll-size "worlds" in which they appear.

One thing I find so intriguing about dollmaking is that suddenly I'm in charge of all the decisions. If a doll has red hair, it's because I choose it; if a doll is happy or sad, it's because I decide it should be. It's certainly rare to be able to decide so many important matters!

I hope you'll find making the dolls in this book easy and rewarding. I *also hope you'll find the decision-making a loving and fun task, and enjoy every single step of the process. But a word of warning: Long before you've completed one of these characters, it's apt to begin forming a personality and become much more than an assemblage of fabric and stuffing. If you're not careful, it may just make some of those important decisions on its own!*

Of course, some steps in dollmaking are more fun than others. And nothing is better than putting on a smile, because that, to me, is when the doll is complete and ready to meet the world!

General Directions

HOW TO USE THIS BOOK

Before you begin making any of the dolls in this book, read all the General Directions. These guidelines apply to every project, so being familiar with them before you begin will be helpful.

Individual project instructions include a list of materials (to make your shopping easy), patterns, and lettered diagrams. For best results, do one step at a time, in the correct order.

BASIC EQUIPMENT

The following is a list of common sewing tools you will need to get the best results. After the list, specific tools and some of the "optional extras" that will make your job easier are highlighted.

Sewing

Sewing machine
Thimble

Assorted needles
Assorted threads
Dressmaker's pins
Pincushions
Embroidery hoop
Bodkin

Pattern Making

Tracing wheel
Dressmaker's tracing paper

Measuring

Tape measure
12"–18" ruler
5"–6" ruler
Circle template

Cutting

Dressmaker's shears
Small scissors
Pinking shears (optional)

Marking

Tailor's chalk
Indelible marker
Soft pencil (#1 or #2)

Pressing

Steam iron
Ironing board

Miscellaneous

Long, blunt crochet hook
or knitting needle

TOOLS FOR MEASURING. These are among the most important things in your sewing kit. The right assortment of good-quality equipment will help you resist the temptation to guess at measurements. I recommend having at least one see-through plastic ruler with clearly marked numbers. Measure often and accurately for the best results.

Circle template. Since you'll be cutting out a lot of small circles for eyes and other features, a clear plastic circle template with various-size circles will be a great aid in making shapes that are consistently round and the right size. If it's not carried in your sewing store, try a good stationery store.

TOOLS FOR CUTTING. Sewing scissors should be kept only for sewing, so that you will always have sharp blades to make a clean edge.

Dressmaker's shears are bent-handle shears with 7″ or 8″ blades hinged with a screw. The bent handles let you keep the fabric flat on the table while you're cutting.

Small scissors with round handles are used for delicate trimming. It's best to keep a pair with 5″–6″ blades and another with 3″–4″ blades.

Pinking shears (optional) are great for finishing raw edges of fabrics that don't ravel too easily.

Other useful cutting tools. A *seam ripper* is a penlike device that allows careful ripping for adjustments and mistakes. A razor blade is no substitute! *Thread clips*, a scissors variation with short blades and a spring mechanism, cut stray threads quickly and easily.

TOOLS FOR MARKING. Incorrect marking can cause haphazard stitching of seams and facial features. Accurate, careful marking will make construction easier and keep mistakes to a minimum. Here are the best marking tools for the fabrics you'll be using.

Tracing wheels come in many shapes and sizes. I recommend one with a dull-serrated edge for use on most fabrics. Delicate fabrics require a wheel with a plain, unserrated edge; heavier fabrics should be marked with a needle-point wheel.

Dressmaker's tracing paper is similar to carbon paper and is used with a tracing wheel to transfer pattern markings. Choose a color that resembles your fabric color—contrasting marks can show through. Always mark on the wrong side of the fabric.

Thread for marking should be matched to the fabric. Glazed mercerized cotton is best for thread tracing, general basting, and tacking. A contrasting color aids removal.

Dressmaker's marking pencil is good for hard-surfaced fabrics. Have one with a brush for erasing the markings.

TOOLS FOR SEWING. These items are particularly useful for hand sewing.

Needles should be sharp and of good quality. The most commonly used sizes range from #1 to #10, with #1 for coarse work and #10 for finest sewing. Use *embroidery* or *crewel needles* for embroidering features.

Pins should be rustproof stainless steel or brass dressmaker's silk pins. Pins with colored heads are easiest to see and remove.

Thread should be a matching shade or one shade darker than your fabric. The numbers printed on the spool denote the weight of the thread—the higher the number, the finer the thread. Mercerized cotton is best for most tasks. Use button and carpet thread for heavy-duty work. Use nylon and cotton-covered Dacron® polyester for permanent press fabrics. Buy specialty threads, such as embroidery floss or elastic thread, as needed.

Magnets are handy when you spill a box of pins.

Thimbles can make sewing painless—but only if they fit!

Pincushions come in several sizes. Use a large one for the bulk of your work and a wrist type for sewing and fitting.

Beeswax can be used to coat your hand-sewing threads. It adds strength and reduces tangling and knotting.

Transparent tape is helpful as a topstitching guide, for mending a torn pattern and for various other tasks.

Bodkins are used to draw elastic and cording through a casing. For small casings, you can make your own bodkin from a bobby pin, using tape to secure the thread.

Tissue paper is used for stitching fabrics that need special handling to go through the feed dog and presser foot of the sewing machine.

Needle threader is a handy little tool that can save you plenty of frustration.

Tweezers are useful for removing gathering threads and basting threads.

Embroidery hoops are available in wood or metal—both are good. Select a hoop with a spring mechanism that allows adjustment to the weight of the fabric. A cork-lined inner hoop holds fabric more securely.

TOOLS FOR PRESSING. You will need to press seams frequently in each project. Be ready!

Steam/dry iron. Steam vents should be located at the head of the soleplate for concentrated steam where you need it. A wide temperature range will suit more kinds of fabric. A spray mechanism is also helpful.

Ironing board. Just about any type will do, as long as it's sturdy, level, and adjustable to a height that's comfortable for you.

HOW TO ENLARGE PATTERNS

Here are a few methods for enlarging the patterns that appear in this book. Find the one that suits you best.

Basic method: enlarging drawings. To enlarge a drawing from this book (or any other), first trace the artwork onto a piece of paper. Then mark a grid of equal-size squares over the tracing. Next, make a grid of larger squares (but of equal proportion) on another piece of paper that is large enough to accommodate your final pattern. For example, draw a grid of 1/4" squares over the original tracing. To make your enlargement twice the size, draw 1/2" squares in your second grid. (Try to pick grid-square measurements that will be easy to work with, such as 1/4", 1/2", 1".)

Looking carefully at the original tracing, mark on the enlargement grid the points at which lines of the original drawing cross lines on the grid. You will be left with a dot pattern. Simply connect the dots on the enlargement grid and add any remaining pattern markings to get your final pattern.

Using grid or quadrille paper. Instead of making your own grids, you can buy sheets of blue graph paper. Also, sewing-supply stores often carry grid paper designed especially for enlarging patterns, or dressmaker's pattern paper with markings spaced 1" apart which you can connect to form a grid.

Using a master grid. If you are making several different patterns that will use grids of the same scale, make a master grid on heavy paper or grid paper. Tape tracing paper securely over the grid paper and work as described above, directly on the tracing paper. Reserve the master grid for your next pattern.

Pantagraph. This is a mechanical device for reducing and enlarging drawings. It's available in good art-supply stores and is moderately priced.

Photostats of patterns can be made with photocopy equipment, using the scale noted on the pattern (a usual photostat enlargement is 50% or 75%). This method can be costly, and it may be necessary to have the enlargement made in sections. But it's definitely a time-saving method.

Changing the specified size. You may choose to make a doll larger or smaller than called for in the instructions. To do this, enlarge or reduce all the dimensions by the same proportion. For example, if you want to make a doll that's one-fourth smaller than the pattern specifies, reduce all the measurements by 25%, remembering to figure the distances along seam lines and cutting lines and measurements for all accessory pieces. Also, try to work with simple reduction or enlargement proportions.

HOW TO CUT OUT PATTERNS AND TRANSFER MARKINGS

Cutting out patterns. Label each paper pattern piece and cut along the outer edges of the pattern. Place the pieces on the wrong side of the fabric, allowing at least 1" between each piece for seams. If one pattern is to be used for cutting two pieces of fabric, reverse the pattern before cutting the second fabric piece. **Note**: If the fabric has a nap, be sure to position pattern pieces so the nap will run in the same direction.

Pin each pattern piece in place. With a soft pencil or dressmaker's wheel, outline each pattern piece on the fabric. This will be your stitching line. Now cut out the pattern pieces, adding 1/4" all around as your seam allowance.

Transferring markings. Transfer all designs and markings onto the wrong side of the fabric. Place dressmaker's carbon between the design and the fabric and trace the design with a pencil or tracing wheel. This works well with any fabric, particularly heavier and deep-pile materials.

For close-weave fabrics that require lighter markings, use tracing paper and a soft pencil. If the pattern piece is symmetrical, trace the markings onto tissue paper. Turn the paper over, place it on the fabric, and retrace so that the markings transfer onto the fabric. If the pattern piece is not symmetrical, turn the paper over after the first tracing and trace the markings again. Place the paper right side up on the fabric and retrace once more so that markings are correctly located.

Still another way of transferring pattern markings is by using a light box or a sunny window. Tape the pattern piece against the glass, then tape the fabric (wrong side out) over it. The pattern markings will be visible through the fabric weave, and you can simply trace over them with a soft pencil or marker.

STITCHING, CLIPPING CURVES, TRIMMING, AND TURNING

STITCHING

The dolls in this book were made mostly with a sewing machine, with some hand stitching. I recommend using a sewing machine as often as possible, because machine stitching is generally stronger than hand sewing. However, if a doll is for display only, wear and tear may not be a significant factor. Therefore, it is possible to construct any of these dolls by hand.

Add strength to stress pieces by reinforcing seams: use small backstitches, then reinforce the seam with a pair of running stitches.

Here are the basic stitches you will be using:

Running stitch is a simple hand stitch used for gathering, tucking, and mending. Weave the point of the needle in and out of the fabric a few times and pull thread through. Repeat. Stitches should be small and evenly spaced.

Basting is a larger and looser version of the running stitch, used to hold pieces of fabric together until the final stitching. Leave long ends of thread hanging free so that stitches may be removed easily.

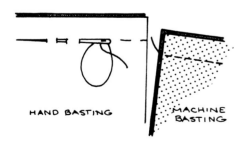

HAND BASTING   MACHINE BASTING

Overcast stitch is a hand stitch used for finishing edges on fabrics that ravel. Make even diagonal stitches over the edge of the fabric.

Whipstitch (Slipstitch) is similar to the overcast stitch and is used for basic construction and attaching body parts. Insert the needle straight up and down, close to the edge of the fabric you are joining. This will produce a series of diagonal stitches.

To make stitches perpendicular to the edges of the fabric insert needle through the fabric on a slant.

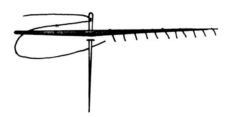

Zigzag stitching is best done by machine. It is used to join two pieces of fabric or to finish a seam allowance, and for some embroidery stitches. Follow the directions that come with your sewing machine to select the right setting.

Hemstitch should be used whenever hemming is indicated in this book. Properly done, it will show only on the wrong side.

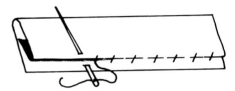

Backstitching, made by hand or machine, is excellent for anchoring fabric in place.

By hand: Push the needle up from the underside of the fabric and insert it $1/16"-1/8"$ behind the point where the thread emerged. Bring the needle out again the same distance in front of the first stitch. Repeat.

By machine: Stitch backward at the beginning and/or end of the seam to reinforce it.

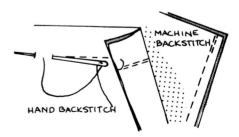

HAND BACKSTITCH   MACHINE BACKSTITCH

Tacking can be done by hand or machine for added strength and to join two pieces of fabric at a single spot.

By hand: Make two or three close parallel stitches, then cover with closely spaced tacking stitches that catch the fabric underneath.

By machine: Make a row of closely spaced zigzag stitches.

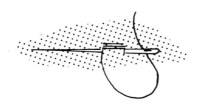

Gathering is also done by hand or machine.

By hand: Anchor the thread with a knot at one end. Make one or two parallel rows of ⅛"— to ½"—long running stitches. Leave the other end of the thread free for gathering.

By machine: Make one or two parallel rows of ⅛"— to ¼"—long running stitches. Pull the thread ends on the top side of the fabric to gather it.

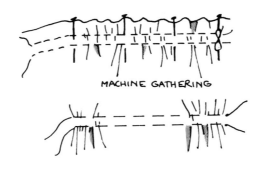

MACHINE GATHERING

Topstitching is used both decoratively and to hold two pieces of fabric together. By hand or machine, make a row of straight stitches on the right side of the fabric along the seam or in a line along the edge of a fold.

CLIPPING CURVES AND SEAMS

Throughout this book, you'll see the instructions "clip seams and curves closely." This may involve either "clipping" or "notching."

Generally, you'll want to trim seam allowances ¼" from the stitching line, but don't hesitate to trim more closely in places where less bulk is desired. At seam ends, trim diagonal corners for neat assembly, especially when seams will be meeting or crossing others. When using lightweight or loose-weave fabrics, *do not* trim too closely to the seam line, as the fabric will fray.

Clip seams that curve inward so that the fabric will spread when turned right side out. *Notch* seams that curve outward to eliminate bulkiness.

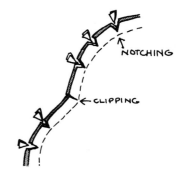

NOTCHING

CLIPPING

TURNING

Use care when you're turning pieces right side out. Tiny pieces may need a little help from a long, blunt crochet hook or knitting needle to make turning smooth and complete.

STUFFING FIGURES

The dolls in this book are stuffed with loose polyester fiberfill, sold in large 1-pound bags. Unless otherwise indicated, dolls should be stuffed firmly and evenly all around so they won't be limp and lopsided or tip over when you try to stand them up. Be careful to avoid leaving lumps here and there. Follow the stuffing tips here for firm yet huggable dolls.

Begin by stuffing all irregular and hard-to-reach places. For example, when you're working the head, stuff the nose first. On arms and legs, stuff hands or feet first, then work your way up.

For small areas, work with tiny wads of fiberfill and ease the stuffing in place firmly and evenly. On some of these areas, such as fingers, toes, or noses, you may need to use the eraser end of a pencil or the wrong end of a crochet hook to poke the stuffing firmly in place. Do not use a sharp instrument that could puncture the fabric.

When stuffing larger areas, such as body, arms, and legs, avoid lumping by using healthy handfuls of stuffing (about the size of a dinner roll). Leave the stuffing in arms and legs slightly loose in the area that gets attached to the body. Always stuff the neck tightly.

Continuously mold the shape of each part with your hands as you stuff. This will help you get the perfect shape and minimize the chance of lumps. If lumps and bumps develop, try massaging that part of the doll before you resort to removing the stuffing.

Before you stitch up an opening, pin the opening shut and squeeze the body part to test for even firmness. When you sew openings closed, try not to let stuffing catch in the seams. If this problem does occur, closely clip stray fiberfill pieces with small scissors.

EMBROIDERY STITCHES

Embroidery stitches are used mostly for facial features for these dolls. Be sure to use a needle suited to the purpose and an embroidery hoop, as described on page 11. In most cases, it is advisable to embroider the features before cutting out pattern pieces. Here are the basic stitches called for in this book.

Outline stitch is also called a "crewel stitch" or "stem stitch." Use it for outlining and making fine-detail lines. Work backward along the design line and make equal-length stitches, each time bringing the needle through the fabric where the previous stitch began. Keep the thread on the same side of the needle at all times.

Straight stitches are worked along design lines. Poke the needle up through the fabric at one end of the line and down through the other end.

Satin stitch is used for filling in areas and making special shapes. It consists of a series of straight stitches that are worked close together, side by side.

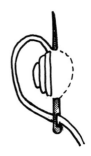

French knot seems a little complicated at first and takes a bit of practice, but adds wonderful texture in desired areas.

First, poke the needle up from the underside of the fabric. Wrap embroidery floss around the point enough times to get the size knot you desire. Then poke the point of the needle back down through the fabric close to—but not in—the hole you started with. As you pull the needle down through the fabric, use one hand to keep even tension on the thread while forming the knot.

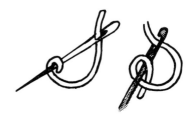

HINTS AND SHORTCUTS

These are some suggestions that will make your job easier, help you work with "difficult" fabrics, and generally give your dolls the neat, finished look you want them to have.

Losing an end. When working embroidery stitches on a stuffed piece, "losing the end" will give you the right finished look. Work your embroidery stitch as usual, then knot the floss by overstitching. Stick the needle back through the fabric and into the stuffing and bring it out about 1" from the edge of the area being worked. Clip the floss closely, then press it in. The end will get "lost" in the stuffing.

Cutting out small shapes. Many of the instructions call for cutting small pieces of felt or other fabric for facial features or decorations. Cutting these small shapes will be much easier if you back the fabric with masking tape or fusible interfacing.

Making fabrics heavier. You may choose a fabric that's a bit flimsy or too stretchy to handle easily. In either event, back the fabric with fusible interfacing. This gives a flimsy fabric more "body" and makes stretchy fabrics less so.

You can also use fusible interfacing for backing lightweight skin-tone fabrics often specified for faces or body parts. If you back the face pieces before embroidering features, knots or ends on the wrong side of the fabric will not show through.

Applying watercolor or Dr. Ph. Martin's® dye for cheek color. It is best to apply the color before stitching pieces together. Place a piece of nonabsorbent tissue paper or wax paper behind the face before applying color. Be sure to allow watercolor or dye to dry completely before proceeding.

HOW TO MAKE POMPONS

Once you've tried this simple method, you may never again lose time shopping around for the right size or color pompon. These fuzzy little balls aren't for dolls only—you'll find dozens of other uses for them, such as decorating gift wrappings, enhancing fashion accessories, and adding to center-pieces for your table.

1. Cut about 100 pieces of yarn to a length 1" longer than the desired diameter of the pompon. This is easy if you cut a strip of cardboard to match the desired yarn length, and wrap yarn evenly around it about 50 times. Secure yarn with a piece of masking tape around the middle, back to front. Then cut the yarn at the top and the bottom to yield about 100 same-size pieces.

2. Cut a piece of yarn about 18" long. Lay the short pieces of yarn evenly across the long piece. See Diagram A.

3. Tie the long piece of yarn very tightly in a triple knot around the midpoint of the small pieces.

4. Fluff out the ends to make a ball. See Diagram B. Trim the ends to make the pompon perfectly round and even.

Pompon maker kits are also available at craft and needlework stores.

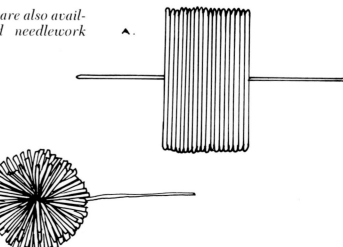

Projects

BOOM–BOOM the Clown

Boom-Boom may not impress you with his juggling skills, but a more cheerful and colorful friend is hard to find. Dress him in your brightest cottons or in grown-up silks and velvets.

SIZE: about 19″ tall

MATERIALS

Fabrics: ⅔ yard of 45″ white cotton or cotton-blend muslin for body

6½″ × 6½″ square of fusible white interfacing for face backing

1⅓ yards of 45″ bright-color cotton or cotton blend for top and bottom of outfit

¼ yard of 45″ solid-color cotton or cotton blend for boots and hat

¼ yard of 45″ solid-color cotton or cotton blend for collar

Threads: sewing threads to match green, brown, and red embroidery floss for face

Yarn: 3 yards for hair

Trim: 13″ of ⅛″ elastic for waistband

Stuffing: 1 lb. of loose polyester fiberfill

Special Material: pink watercolor or Dr. Ph. Martin's® dye for cheeks

INSTRUCTIONS

See General Directions. Enlarge patterns, adding ¼″ seam allowance all around unless otherwise indicated.

Use fusible white interfacing as a backing for Boom-Boom's face. Embroider features before cutting out pattern. Use a satin stitch for mouth and eyes, and a backstitch for the nose. Then add cheeks with watercolor or dye. Allow to dry. Cut out all pattern pieces. Make ¼″ seams throughout.

Boots: Stitch fronts and backs to body with right sides facing.

Body: Stitch front to back with right sides facing, leaving 4½″ opening for stuffing. Clip seams and curves closely. Turn right side out. Stuff tightly except where joints will be machine stitched, as indicated by dashed lines at hip and shoulder.

Top: Stitch front to back, with right sides facing. Clip seams and corners closely. Turn in ¼″ of fabric on hem and wrists. Topstitch to secure.

Collar: For first collar, fold fabric in half (as indicated on pattern on top) and, using small stitches, run a row of gathers through double layer at neck. Place top on doll. Pull in gathers until collar fits closely to neck. See Diagram A.

For second collar, sew short ends together with wrong sides facing, forming a circle as shown in Diagram B. Fold in half and gather ¼″ in from raw edges. Place on top of first collar. Pull gathers to fit closely. Fasten gathering threads. Center seam of second collar should face upward on doll's back.

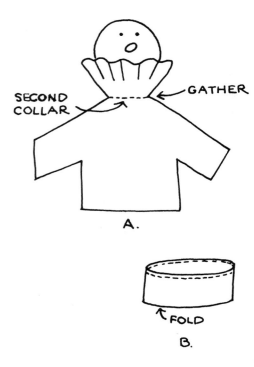

SECOND COLLAR   GATHER

A.

FOLD

B.

20

Pants: With right sides facing, stitch back to front. Clip curves and seam closely. Turn right side out and press. Turn under ¼″ of fabric at waistband. Topstitch in place, leaving 1″ opening for inserting elastic waistband. Insert elastic and topstitch closed. Turn under ¼″ at pants bottoms. Topstitch in place. Using small stitches, gather ankles of pants bottoms. Pull, and secure with a knot.

Hair: To form bangs, loop yarn 10 times around a pencil or slender cylinder. Stitch at top with overcast stitches. Slide off yarn and pin to forehead. Use slip stitches to hold yarn in place.

For each side of hair, wrap yarn eight times around a 2½″-wide piece of cardboard. Catch loops together at top and pin to each side of head. See Diagram C. Stitch top of loops to head; cut bottom of loops open.

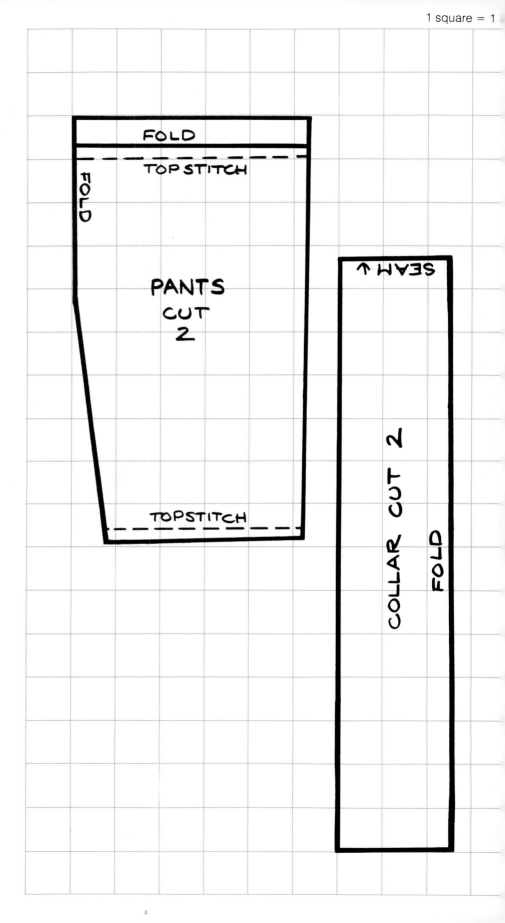

FRONT
FACE

C.

Hat: With right sides facing, stitch front and back together along stitching line. Fold fabric along fold line; press. Turn right side out. Place on doll. Tack with small stitches around sides to secure.

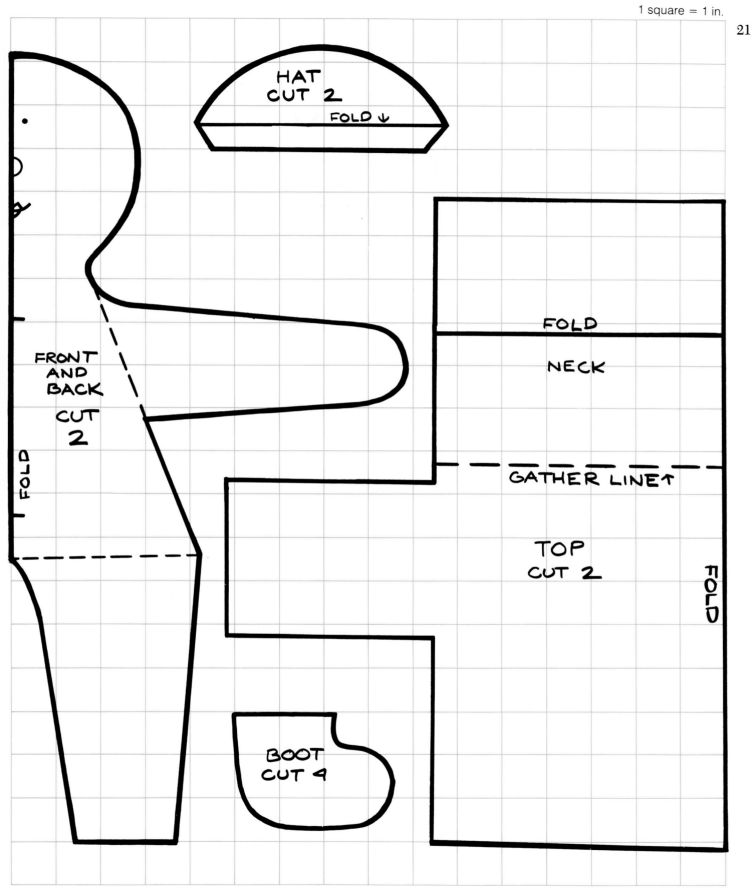

HAT
CUT 2
FOLD ↓

FOLD

NECK

GATHER LINE↑

TOP
CUT 2

FOLD

FRONT
AND
BACK

CUT
2

FOLD

BOOT
CUT 4

DANA

Decked out in the latest sweatshirt-fabric fashions, Dana is a thoroughly modern little girl. She loves to collect pillows, stuffed pigs, interesting pen pals, and anything purple.

SIZE: about 22″ tall

MATERIALS

Fabrics: ½ yard of 45″ skin-tone polyester knit for head, body and arms

1 yard of 45″ polyester/cotton fleece for skirt and top

½ yard of 36″ white cotton knit for stockings

½ yard of 45″ metallic-look fabric for boots

¼ yard of 36″ white cotton interfacing for face backing

Threads: sewing threads to match blue, brown and red embroidery floss for face

Yarn: Approximately 48 yards of mohair or soft mohairlike yarn for hair

Trims: 13″ of ⅛″ elastic for waistband and wrists

scraps of metallic-look fabric for heart appliqués

3″ of fusible mending tape (such as Stitch Witchery®) or white glue

15″ length of silver corded ribbon, bow, or barrette for hair

one ¼″ snap for dress top

Stuffing: 1 lb. of loose polyester fiberfill

Special Materials: soft, pink pastel crayon or cosmetic blusher for cheeks

shirt cardboard

INSTRUCTIONS

See General Directions. Enlarge patterns, adding ¼″ seam allowance all around unless otherwise indicated.

Use thin white cotton interfacing as backing for Dana's face. Embroider features before cutting out pattern. Use a backstitch for the nose and mouth, tiny satin stitches for eyes. Cut out all pattern pieces. Make ¼″ seams throughout.

Head: Sew back of head B to back of head C on stitching line with right sides facing. See Diagram A. With right sides facing, sew A to B and C. Clip curves and seams closely. Turn head right side out and stuff tightly.

Body: With right sides facing, stitch back to front on stitching lines, leaving openings for neck and arms; leave bottom open for stuffing.

Arms: Stitch with right sides facing. Clip curves. Turn right side out. Stuff, leaving approximately ¾″ empty at top edges of arms. Insert arms and topstitch top edges to body on both sides. See Diagram B.

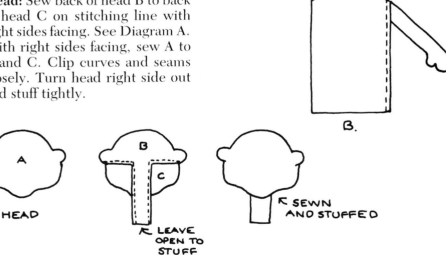

A. HEAD

B. LEAVE OPEN TO STUFF

A.

B.

SEWN AND STUFFED

Insert head into body opening and hand stitch at neckline, as indicated on pattern. See Diagram C.

ATTACH ON DOTTED LINE

C.

Stuff body tightly from bottom. Turn edges in ¼" and stitch closed.

Legs: Stitch right sides together. Clip seams and curves closely. Turn right side out. Stuff gently and shape legs evenly. Close up ends and baste to bottom of body. To secure, topstitch by machine.

Dress top: Appliqué hearts to top as follows: Cut out hearts and place on dress top as shown on pattern. Bond hearts to fabric with fusible mending tape, following directions on package. White glue (such as Elmer's®) can also be used for securing hearts.

Stitch back pieces together, leaving opening for top to fit over Dana's head. Press seam open and topstitch each side of opening, as indicated. See Diagram D. Sew

BACK
D.

back to front on stitching line with right sides facing. Clip seams and corners closely. Turn right side out. Turn neck edge under ¼" and topstitch. Turn under ⅜" at wrists and topstitch, leaving ½" opening. Insert elastic, then topstitch to close. Add snap for closure at back of neck.

Skirt: Sew short ends of hip band together on stitching line with right sides facing. Sew short ends of flounce together. Gather ¼" in from top along one flounce edge. See Diagram E. Gather flounce

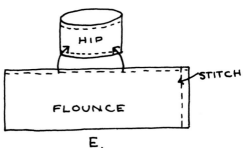

HIP

FLOUNCE

STITCH

E.

to fit width of hip band. Pin wrong sides together. Baste, and machine stitch to secure. Turn ¼" down for waistband on hip piece. Topstitch, leaving 1" open to insert 8" of elastic. Insert elastic. Topstitch closed. Hem skirt.

Boots: Stitch together with right sides facing. Clip corners and curves closely. Turn right side out. Turn under ¼" for hem. Topstitch ⅛" from edge on right sides.

Hair: Cut cardboard rectangles in the following sizes:

    1½" × 5½"—bangs
    6" × 5½"—back of hair
    4½" × 5½"—crown

Wrap yarn around cardboard, wrapping along entire 5½" length of each piece. Using small overcast stitches, sew along top of each section of hair. Slide yarn off cardboard and pin to head, as indi-

cated in Diagram F. Sew crown first, then sew back of hair, as shown in Diagram G.

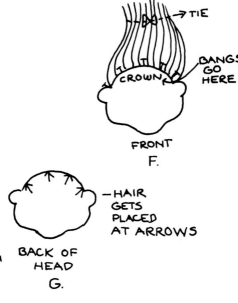

TIE

BANGS GO HERE

CROWN

FRONT
F.

HAIR GETS PLACED AT ARROWS

BACK OF HEAD
G.

For bangs, slide yarn off card. Twist yarn to create a loop effect. See Diagram H. Pin yarn to forehead and secure with overcast stitches. Tie crown hair into topknot with yarn of same color as hair, then add decorative cording, bow, or barrette. Trim hair evenly around bottom edges.

Apply pink crayon or cosmetic blusher to cheeks.

BANGS

H.

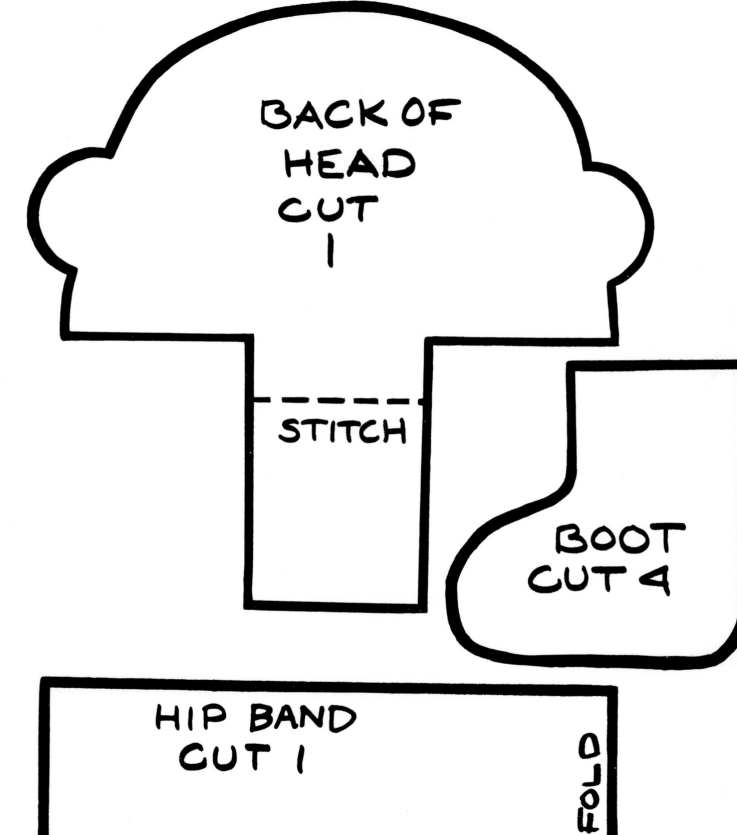

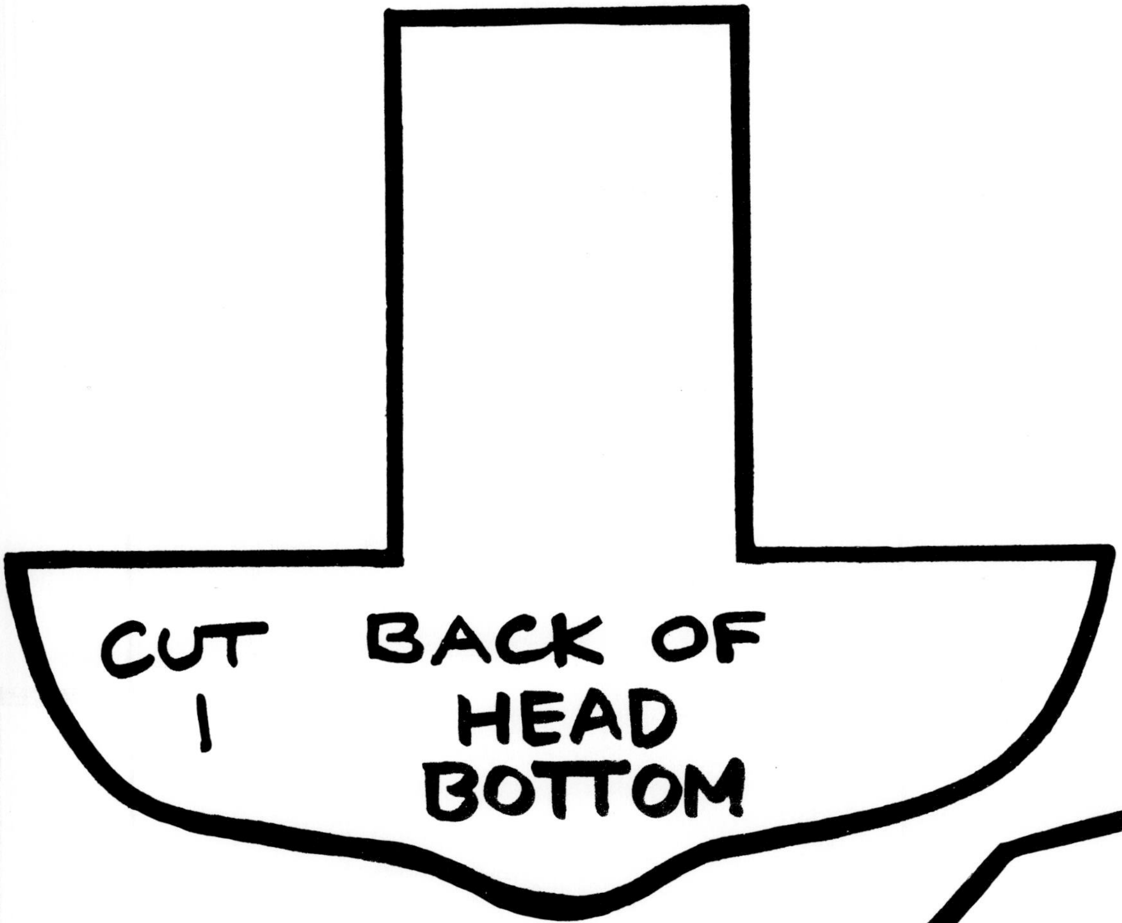

CUT 1 BACK OF HEAD BOTTOM

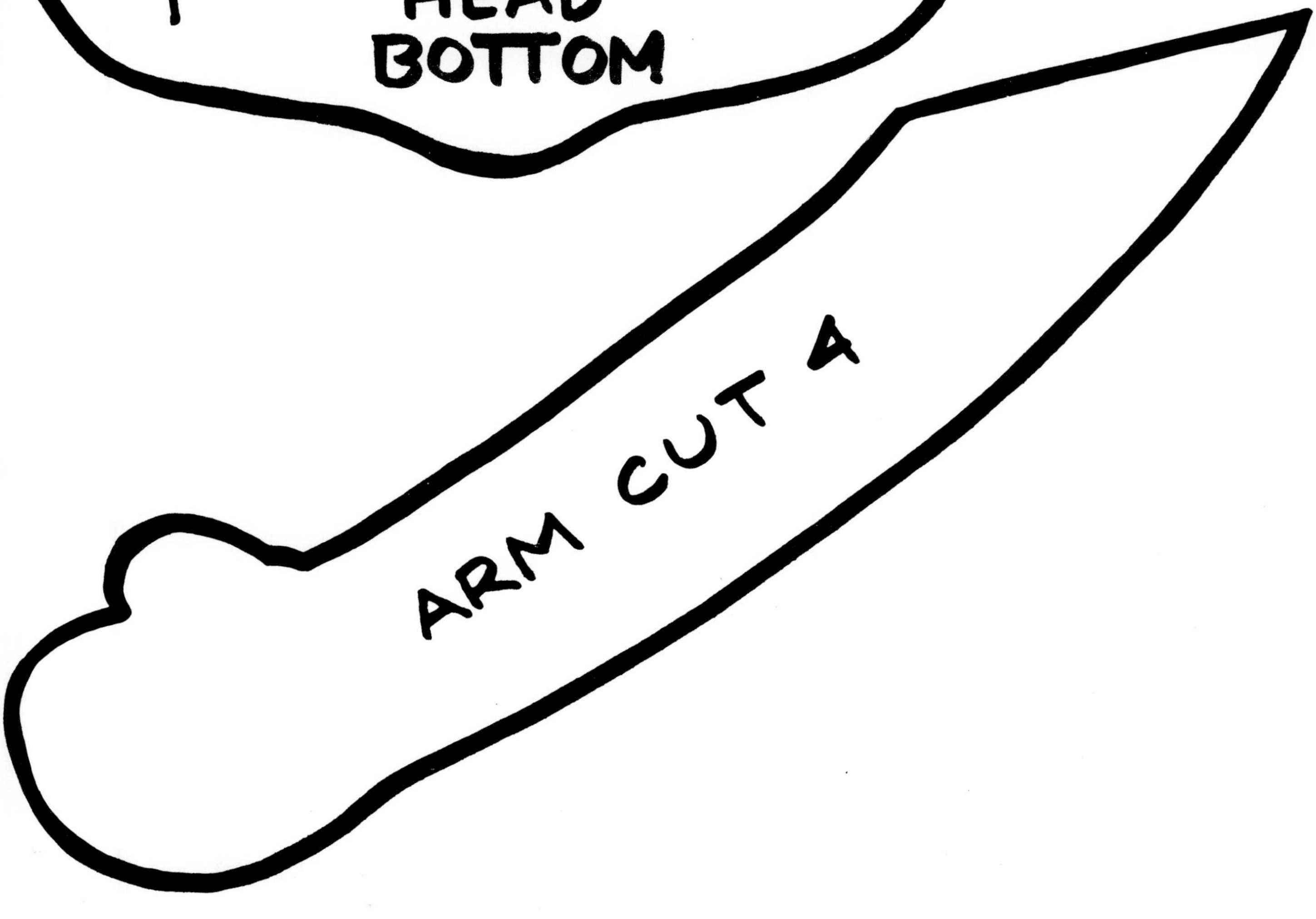

ARM CUT 4

1 square = 1 in.

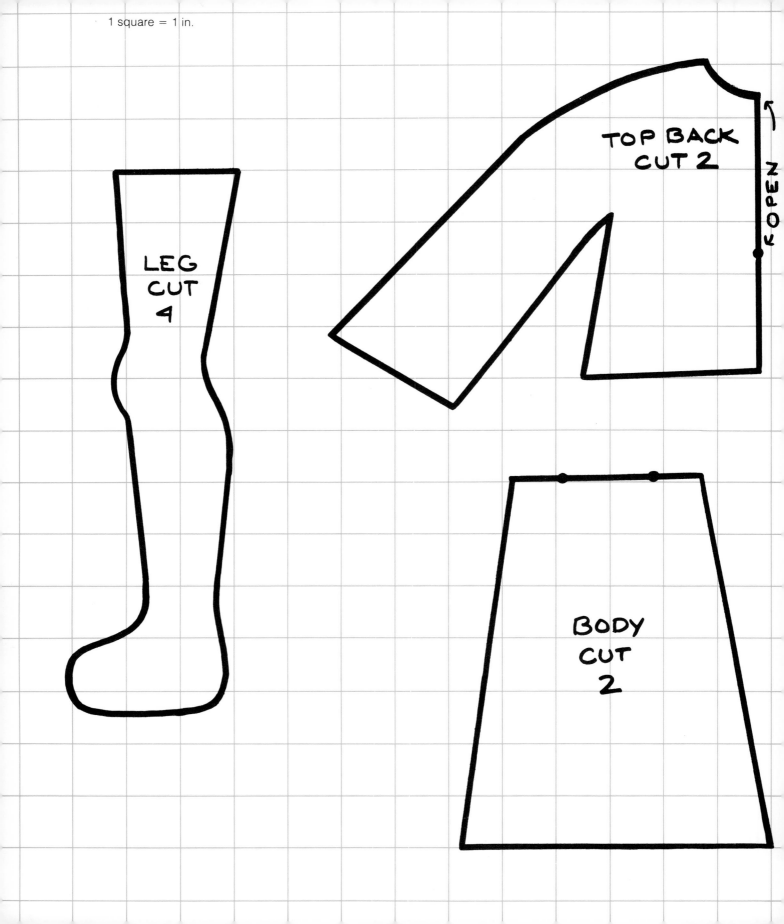

LEG
CUT
4

TOP BACK
CUT 2

OPEN

BODY
CUT
2

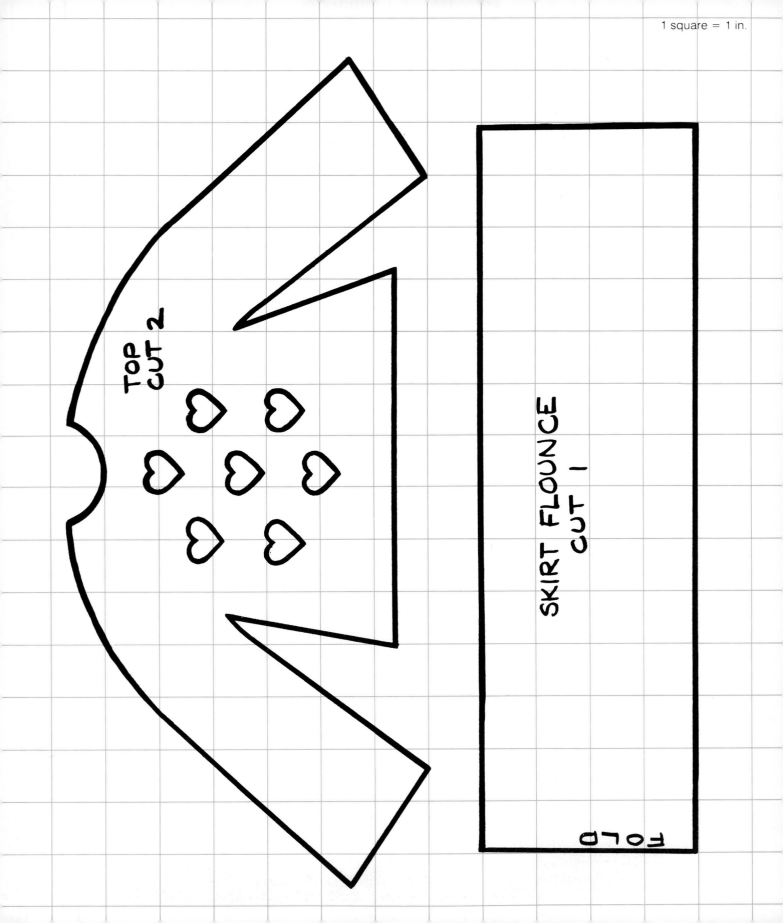

1 square = 1 in.

TOP
CUT 2

SKIRT FLOUNCE
CUT 1

FOLD

The Three Zanees

These three cookie-cutter characters are so easy and fun to make, you're liable to find yourself populating the world with Zanees. They're washable and stackable, too.

SIZE: each about 14½″ tall

MATERIALS

Enid

Fabrics: ½ yard of 36″ bright cotton or cotton blend for body

½ yard of 36″ bright cotton or cotton blend for dress

Yarn: 3 yards of worsted-weight acrylic for hair

Trim: 14″ of ¼″ ribbon for back ties on dress

Special Material: shirt cardboard

Eggbert

Fabrics: ½ yard of 36″ bright cotton or cotton blend for body

½ yard of 36″ bright cotton or cotton blend for pants

Yarn: scraps of yarn for hair

Trims: 10″ of ½″ ribbon or bias tape for suspenders

6″ of ½″ ribbon for bow tie

Egor

Fabrics: ½ yard of 36″ bright cotton or cotton blend for body

½ yard of 36″ bright cotton or cotton blend for overalls

Yarn: scraps of yarn for hair

Trims: 14″ of ¼″ ribbon for shoulder straps

11″ of ⅛″ elastic

For all

Threads: sewing threads to match

Stuffing: loose polyester fiberfill

Special Material: permanent marker for faces (test for bleeding)

INSTRUCTIONS

For all

See General Directions. Enlarge patterns, adding ¼″ seam allowance all around unless otherwise indicated. Cut out pattern pieces. Make ¼″ seams throughout unless otherwise indicated.

Enid

Body: With right sides facing, pin and stitch all around, leaving a 3″

A.

opening for stuffing. See Diagram A. Clip seams and curves closely. Turn right side out and stuff tightly. Use small slipstitches to close opening.

Dress: With right sides facing, pin back pieces A and B together. Stitch together, leaving top 3″ open. Press seam open, and topstitch on each side of opening ⅛″ from edge. See Diagram B.

With right sides facing, stitch front of dress to back. Turn under ¼″ for hem on sleeves, bottom, and neckline. Sew 7″ ribbon tie to each side at top of back opening.

Hair: Wrap yarn around 1½″ ×

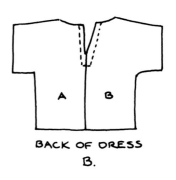

BACK OF DRESS
B.

3½" piece of cardboard. Stitch along top, and slide yarn off cardboard. Pin to head and secure with small slipstitches.

Face: Add features with permanent marker.

Bow: Cut 4" × 1⅜" scrap from dress fabric or other fabric. Gather in center. Tack securely to head.

Eggbert

Pants and suspenders: With right sides facing, stitch along center front and back crotch seams. Then pin and stitch inner leg seams. See Diagram C. Clip seams and curves closely. Turn right side out.

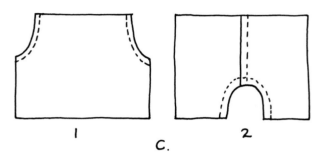

C.

Turn under ¼" of fabric at waistband and pants bottoms. Press and topstitch. Add ribbon or bias tape for suspenders, and crisscross at back. Using small hidden stitches, secure in place from wrong side.

Bow tie: Using 5" of ½"-wide ribbon, fold back ends to meet at center back. Stitch at center. Fold remaining 1" of ribbon over center of bow. Stitch ends at back, then stitch bow tie to doll. See Diagram D.

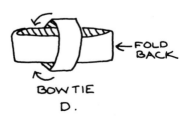

BOW TIE
D.

Short-cropped hair: Wind yarn around a pencil about 15 times. Stitch along top and slide yarn off pencil. Pin to head and stitch to secure.

Face: Add features with permanent marker.

Egor

Overalls: Follow instructions for Eggbert's pants, but cut out an extra 3½" × 3" bib piece from pants fabric. Turn under ¼" on three sides of bib; topstitch. After turning ¼" under at waistband of pants, pin bib so it's centered at waistband. See Diagram E. Topstitch ⅛" from edge at waist. Turn under ⅜" at pants bottoms. Topstitch, leaving 1" open. Insert 4" of elastic. Stitch ends of elastic together. Close opening. Add ribbon straps, and crisscross at back (about 7" for each strap).

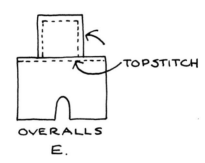

OVERALLS
E.

Hair: Wind yarn around ½" cylinder, such as marker or pen, 13 times. Stitch along top. Slide yarn off cylinder, and pin to head. Stitch in place.

Face: Add features with permanent marker.

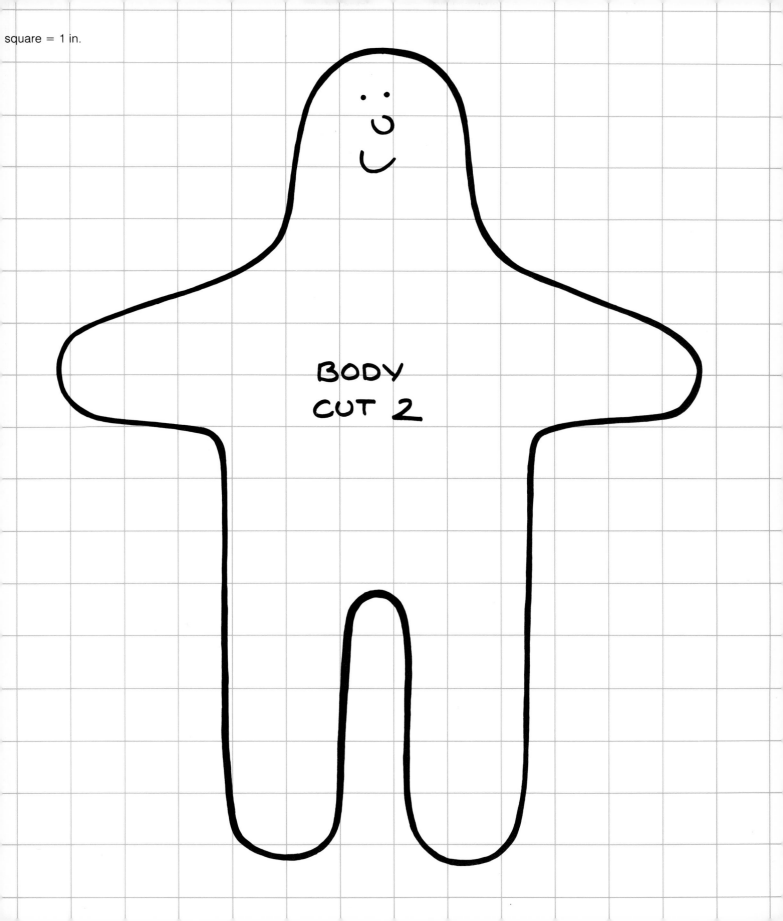

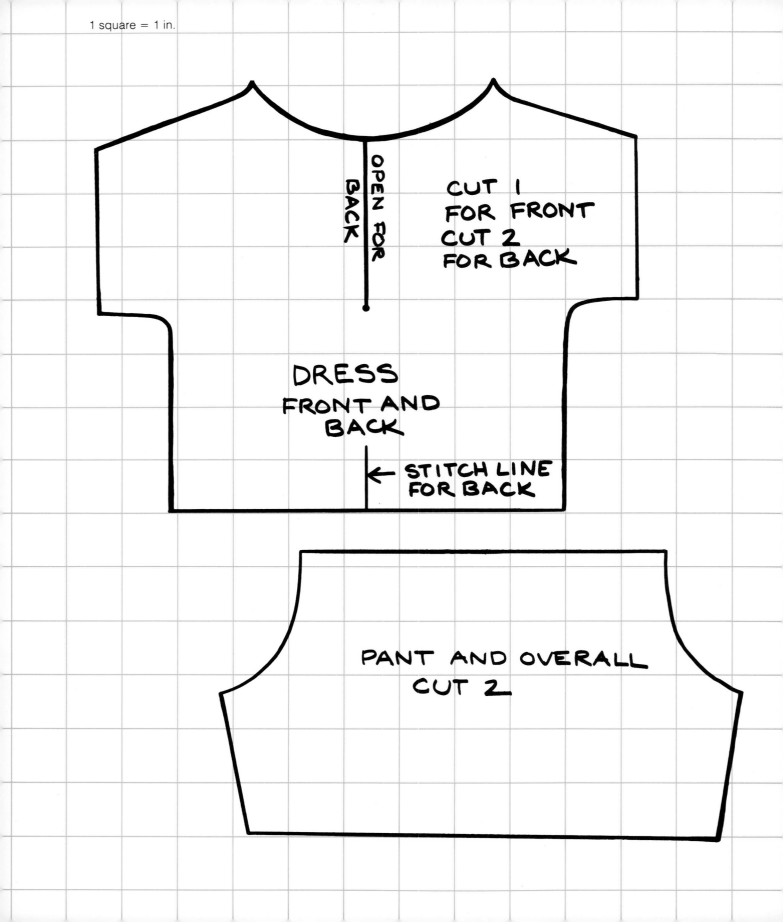

1 square = 1 in.

OPEN FOR BACK

CUT 1
FOR FRONT
CUT 2
FOR BACK

DRESS
FRONT AND
BACK

← STITCH LINE
FOR BACK

PANT AND OVERALL
CUT 2

Best Cat and Kitty of Honor

These two are very important members of the wedding, and properly dignified as they toast a purr-fect marriage. But once the Best Cat and Kitty of Honor hit the dance floor, look out—they nudge the bride and groom right out of the limelight!

SIZE: each about 14″ tall

MATERIALS

Best Cat

Fabrics: ½ yard of 45″ fake fur fabric with ³⁄₁₆″ pile for head, arms, tail, and ears

¼ yard of 36″ white cotton or cotton blend for shirt

½ yard of 36″ black wool suiting fabric, cotton, or cotton blend for jacket and pants

½ yard of 36″ black satin for shoes, jacket lining, and cummerbund

Threads: sewing threads to match black embroidery floss for face

Trims: 5″ × 3″ scrap of pale pink cotton or cotton blend for ear linings

heavy white cotton cord or nylon filament for whiskers

14″ of ¼″ white edging trim for shirt

19″ of ½″ black satin ribbon or pants and bow tie

decorative snaps (such as Western studs) for eyes

snap closure for jacket

black button for jacket

Stuffing: loose polyester fiberfill

Special Materials: thin-line permanent black marker

small dressmaker's weights

fusible interfacing

Kitty of Honor

Fabrics: ½ yard of 45″ fake fur fabric with ³⁄₁₆″ pile for head, arms, legs, tail, and ears

¾ yard of 45″ satin for hat, dress, and slippers

¼ yard of 45″ lace for skirt

8″ × 2″ scrap of lace for hat

¼ yard of 45″ lace for shawl

Threads: sewing threads to match black embroidery floss for face

Trims: 5″ × 3″ scrap of pale pink cotton or cotton blend for ear linings

heavy white cotton cord or nylon filament for whiskers

6″ of ⅜″ ribbon for slippers

artificial or dried flowers

fusible interfacing

decorative snaps (such as Western studs) for eyes

Stuffing: loose polyester fiberfill

Special Materials: thin-line permanent black marker

small dressmaker's weights

clean cap from salad dressing bottle (or similar-size) for pillbox hat

INSTRUCTIONS

For both

See General Directions. Enlarge patterns, adding ¼″ seam allowance all around unless otherwise indicated. Cut out all pattern pieces. Make ¼″ seams throughout.

Head: With right sides facing, sew back pieces A and B together along stitching line, as shown in Diagram A. Leave opening on bottom for stuffing. Turn right side out.

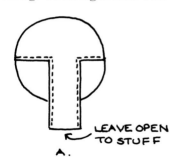

LEAVE OPEN TO STUFF

A.

Add eyes: Using only front half of decorative snaps, position snaps on face and push prongs through fabric. Fold in prongs to lie flat. Eyes will look more cat-like if you color centers with a thin-line permanent marker. See Diagram B.

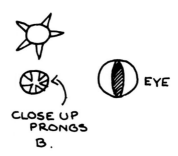

CLOSE UP
PRONGS
B.

EYE

Face: With right sides facing, stitch face front to head back. Clip seams and curves closely. Turn right side out, and stuff from bottom. Add dressmaker's weights to underside of chin for balance.

Embroider features: Use 3 or 4 strands of embroidery floss. Use outline stitch around nose area. Then fill in with satin stitch. Use one long stitch to connect nose to mouth, then create mouth with small back stitches. See Diagram C.

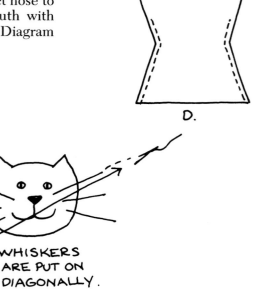

FACE

WHISKERS
ARE PUT ON
DIAGONALLY.

C.

Whiskers: Use heavy cotton cord, as shown, or nylon filament (fishing line). Thread cord through needle, and push needle gently through one side of face. Try to go through the stuffing so whisker will be secure. Bring needle out on other side of face. Cut, leaving about 6" for each whisker. Do this three times. Trim edges. Pull and even out whiskers for a realistic look.

Ears: With right sides facing, pin pink lining to ears. Stitch, leaving opening at bottom. Turn right side out. Turn under ¼" of fabric on bottom. Stitch closed. Pin to head, then secure with tiny stitches.

Kitty of Honor

Note: If the satin fabric you're using is flimsy, back it first with lightweight iron-on interfacing so it will be easier to work with.

Dress bodice: With right sides facing, stitch bodice pieces together, as indicated in Diagram D. Leave openings at neck, arms, and bottom.

D.

Arms: With right sides facing, stitch front pieces to back pieces. Turn arms right side out. Insert each arm into armhold of bodice (bodice is still wrong side out). Pin edges of arms to armholes of bodice, as for set-in sleeve. See Diagram E. Baste, then machine-

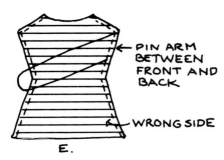

PIN ARM
BETWEEN
FRONT AND
BACK

WRONG SIDE

E.

stitch in place. Turn bodice right side out. See Diagram F. Turn under ¼" of fabric along edge of bodice neck opening. Insert neck as far as one-fourth of the way from back of head. See Diagram G. Pin to bodice neck opening, and secure with tiny stitches. Stuff bodice and arms tightly. Stitch bottom of bodice closed.

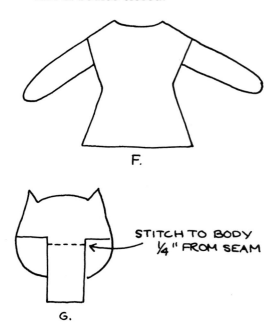

F.

STITCH TO BODY
¼" FROM SEAM

G.

Legs: With right sides facing, sew slipper A to leg B on front and back. See Diagram H. Then, with right sides facing, sew front and back of each leg together. Turn right side out and stuff. Turn down ¼″ of fabric along top edge, and stitch closed. Pin legs to body, and secure with slipstitches.

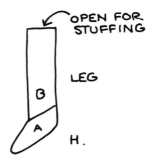

OPEN FOR STUFFING

LEG

B

A

H.

Slipper bows: Take 2¼″ piece of ribbon and fold in half to create a 1⅛″ bow. Gather center. Stitch. Then wrap ¾″ piece of ribbon over gathers, and stitch to secure. See Diagram I. Securely tack bow to slipper.

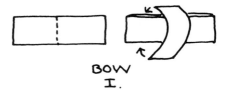

BOW
I.

Skirt: Cut 7¼″ × 40″ piece each of satin and lace. Pin lace to satin. Stitch layers together along top edge. Then, with lace sides facing, stitch side edges together, forming tube and leaving approximately 2″ opening at top edge of skirt. See Diagram J. This opening will allow tail to stick out. Fold under raw edges and topstitch around tail opening. Finished skirt should be about 6¾″ × 39½″. *Note:* If using bordered lace, allow it to hang slightly lower than satin underskirt.

With small running stitches, gather fabric ¼″ from top of skirt. Pull in gathers to correct width for waist (about 9¼″). Turn doll upside down. See Diagram K. Gather and pin skirt around body with wrong side of skirt facing out and tail opening at center back. Your stitching line should be about ½″ beneath the armhole. Use tiny running stitches to secure skirt to body. Turn doll right side up. Hem skirt.

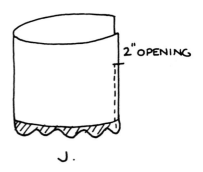

2″ OPENING

J.

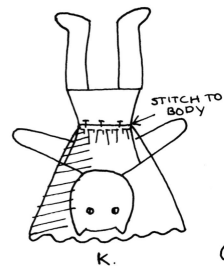

STITCH TO BODY

K.

Pillbox hat: Cut out a circle of satin 1¼″ larger all around than a salad dressing cap. See Diagram L. Place a bit of stuffing on top of the cap to create a padded look, as shown in Diagram M. Place satin circle over padding, and wrap edges to fit closely against sides. Glue edges to inside of bottle cap.

To make hatband, fold 8″ × 2″

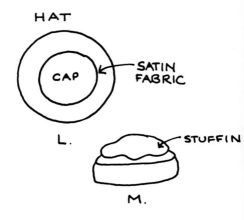

HAT

CAP — SATIN FABRIC

L.

— STUFFIN

M.

piece of lace to width of hat. Stitch ends to secure. See Diagram N. Add a flower, and stitch hat securely to head.

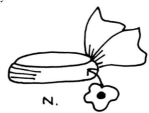

N.

Tail: With right sides facing, sew seam. Turn right side out and stuff. Turn under ¼″ at top of tail, and pin to cat at lower back. See Diagram O for tail placement. Use tiny stitches to secure tail.

1″

← TAIL PLACEMEN

O.

Shawl: Cut 29″ × 7½″ piece of lace, and drape around arms.

Optional charm bracelet: Cut a piece of gold metallic thread to fit wrist. Add charms from trimming store. Tie onto wrist.

Best Cat

Shirt: Pin parallel rows of ¼″-wide edging down center of shirt front. Baste, then machine stitch. With right sides facing, sew front of shirt to back. Add tiny black stitches down center front of shirt to resemble buttons.

Arms: See instructions for Kitty of Honor for attaching arms, legs, and head.

Tuxedo jacket: With right sides facing, stitch back piece A to back piece B. Stitch only to point C, as shown in Diagram P. Press open

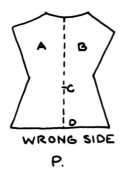

BACK OF JACKET

WRONG SIDE

P.

seam allowance between points C and D, and topstitch on right side. This vent will allow the tail to protrude. See Diagram Q. Turn under ¼″ of fabric at collar of jacket, and topstitch on right side.

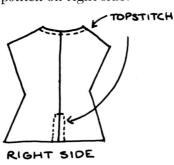

TOPSTITCH

RIGHT SIDE

Q.

Sleeves: With right sides facing, stitch underarm seams on sleeve pieces. Set aside.

Jacket front: To give lapels body, back with fusible interfacing. Pin and baste right side of satin lining to right side of jacket front. Stitch along front edge of lapel, as shown in Diagram R. Do this on both

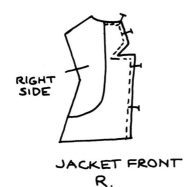

RIGHT SIDE

JACKET FRONT
R.

front pieces. Clip seams and curves closely. Turn satin lining so that right side is now on inside of jacket. Fold lapel back along dotted line indicated in Diagram S, and press.

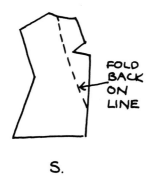

FOLD BACK ON LINE

S.

With right sides facing, pin and baste two jacket fronts to back. *Note:* The two front pieces should overlap to accommodate button and snap. Leave openings for sleeves to be set in. With sleeves right side out, push through openings. See Diagram T. Pin and baste. Stitch around arm holes, then turn jacket right side out.

Hem ¼″ along bottom of jacket and sleeves. Add snap closure to front, and sew button over it.

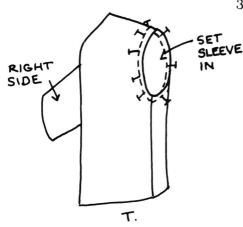

RIGHT SIDE

SET SLEEVE IN

T.

Pants: To make stripes, cut two 7½″ strips of ½″ black satin ribbon. Attach to right side of each pants leg with fusible interfacing, or machine stitch in place.

With right sides facing, stitch seams at crotch. See Diagram U. Then open and stitch inner leg seams. See Diagram V. Clip seams and curves closely. Turn right side out. At waistband, turn under ¼″ of fabric, and topstitch. Hem pants. Press center crease in pants with hot iron. Slip pants on cat and stitch at waist.

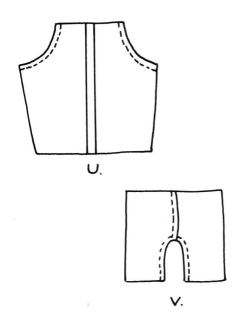

U.

V.

40

Cummerbund: Turn ¼″ of fabric under on each long edge. Top-stitch at top and bottom. Place on cat so that cummerbund overlaps waistband of pants. Pin and stitch at back to secure.

Bow tie: Cut 3¼″ length of ½″ satin ribbon. Fold back ends. Gather at center. Fold ¾″ length of ½″ satin ribbon in thirds, so that it is ¼″ wide; fold over center of bow and stitch ends at center back. See Diagram W. Position bow tie on cat 1″ below shirt neck. Tack in place. Tack flower to lapel.

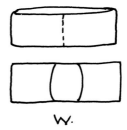

W.

Tail: With right sides facing, sew tail seam. Turn right side out and stuff. Turn under ¼″ of fabric along edge of tail opening. Pin to lower back of cat on pants. See Diagram X. Use tiny stitches to secure to pants. The tail should line up with jacket vent.

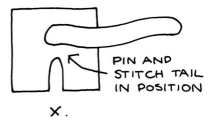

X.

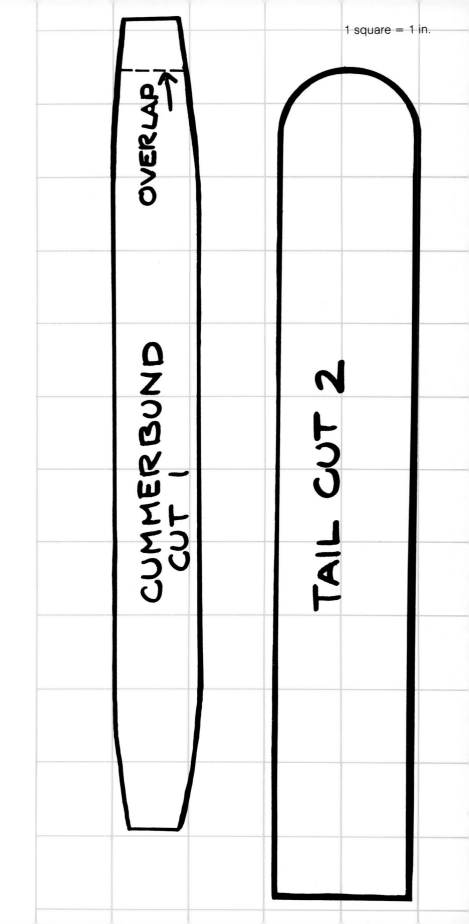

1 square = 1 in.

OVERLAP

CUMMERBUND CUT 1

TAIL CUT 2

PIN AND STITCH TAIL IN POSITION

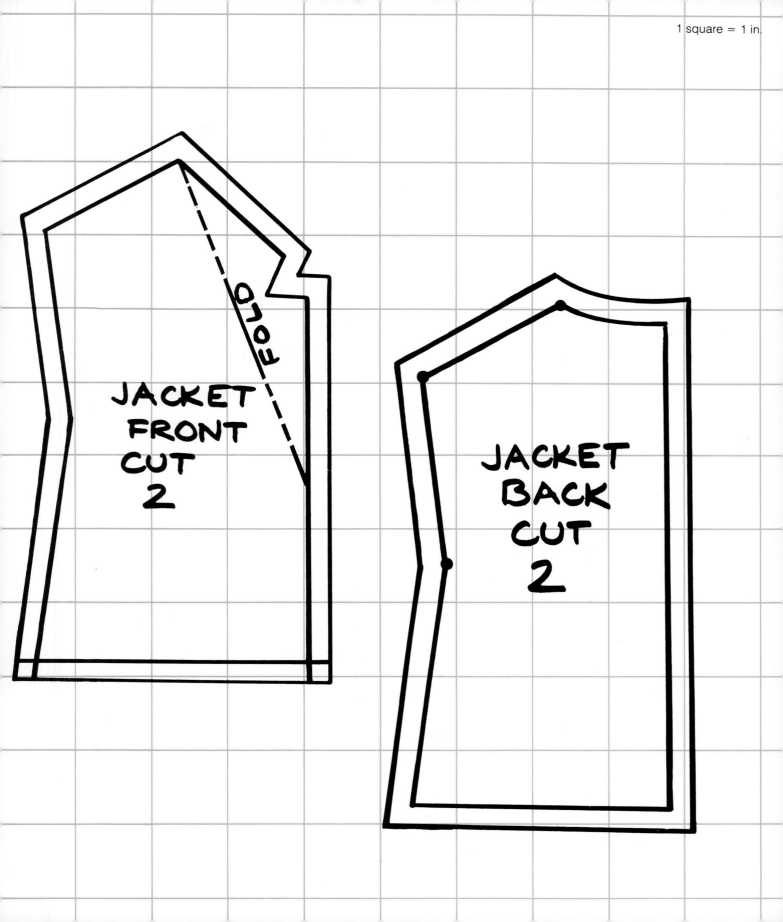

1 square = 1 in.

JACKET
FRONT
CUT
2

FOLD

JACKET
BACK
CUT
2

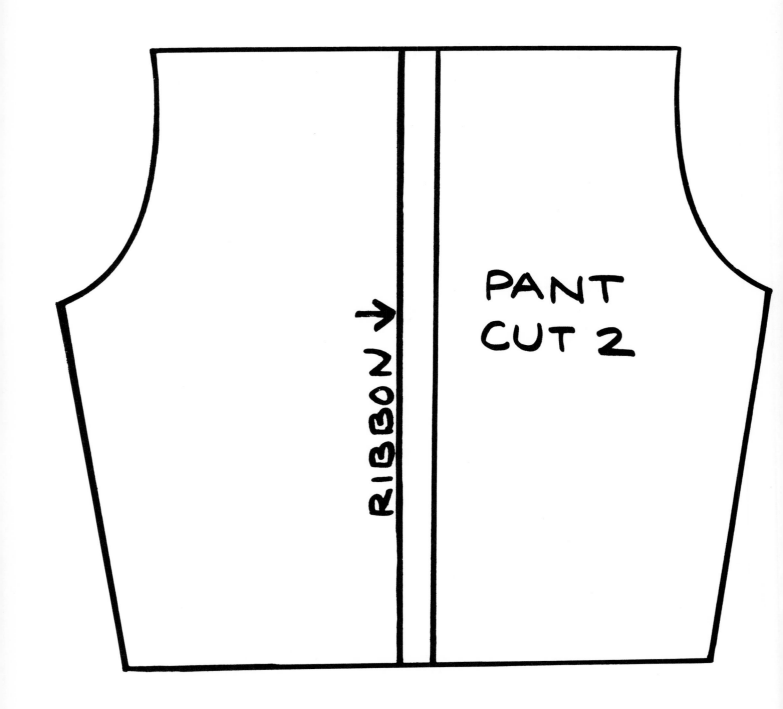

RIBBON →

PANT
CUT 2

HEAD
CUT 2

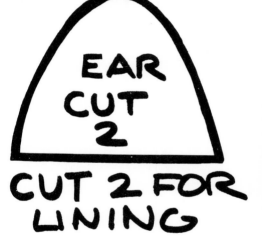

EAR
CUT
2

CUT 2 FOR
LINING

FOLD
JACKET
SLEEVE
CUT 2

SHIRT
DRESS
BODICE
CUT
2

ARM CUT 4

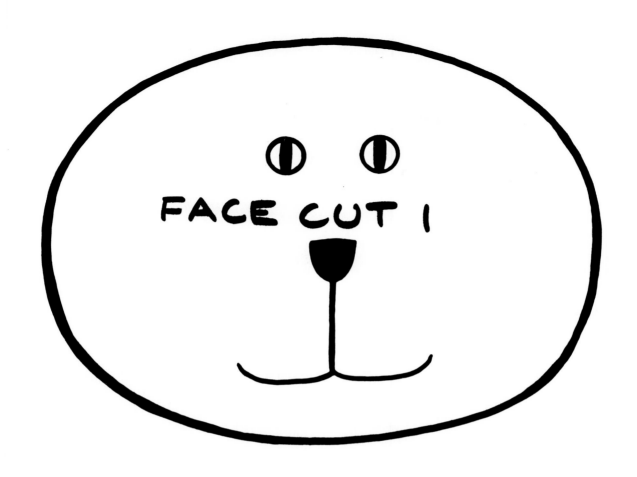

FACE CUT 1

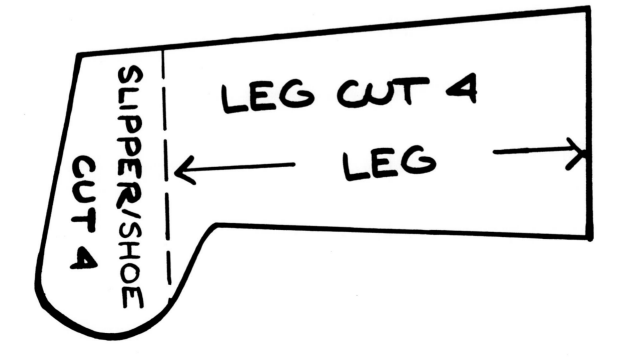

SLIPPER/SHOE CUT 4

LEG CUT 4

LEG

Goofy Puppets

This fun-fur group of goofy characters is designed to fit a troupe of little hands. They're all made from one simple pattern—try these, then create your own. The possibilities are endless for both your imagination and your favorite puppeteer's!

SIZE: each about 10″ long

MATERIALS

Randolph the Green-Nosed Reindeer

Fabrics: ½ yard of 45″ fake fur with ¼″ pile for body

½ yard of 36″ felt for antlers

Trims: scrap of stretch-knit fabric for mouth

scraps of felt for eyes

6″ square scrap of striped knit fabric for hat

1″ pompon for nose; ½″ pompon for hat (purchase, or see How to Make Pompons, page 16)

Stuffing: polyester fiberfill

Fiona Pooch

Fabrics: ½ yard of 45″ fake fur with ¼″ pile for body

¼ yard of 45″ fake fur with ¼″ pile for ears (use contrasting color)

Trims: scrap of cotton knit for mouth

scraps of felt for eyes and tongue

1″ pompon for nose (purchase, or see How To Make Pompons, page 16)

10″ × 1⅝″ cotton scrap for bow

Pinky Rabbit

Fabric: 1 yard of 45″ fake fur with ¼″ pile for body and ears

Trims: scrap of cotton knit for mouth

scraps of felt for eyes and tooth

nylon filament (fishing line) for whiskers

8″ of ribbon for headband

artificial flowers

20″ of thin floral wire for ears

Leonardo Lion

Fabric: ½ yard of 45″ fake fur with ¼″ pile for body

Trims: 11″ × 2¼″ piece of craft fur for mane

scrap of cotton knit for mouth

scraps of black, white, and turquoise felt for eyes and nose

gold-color fabric or foil paper for crown

For all

Threads: sewing threads to match

Special Material: Elmer's® Tacky Glue

INSTRUCTIONS

For all

See General Directions. Enlarge patterns, adding ¼″ seam allowance all around unless otherwise indicated. Cut out all pattern pieces. Make ¼″ seams throughout.

Body and mouth: With right sides facing, sew body piece A (bottom) to piece B (top). Do not stitch beyond dots. See Diagram A. After stitching, fold piece A down from dot. With right sides facing, pin knit mouth to bottom first, then to top, stretching fabric as you pin. See Diagram B. Baste with tiny stitches, then machine stitch. Turn right side out.

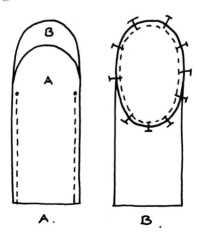

Randolph the Green-Nosed Reindeer

Antlers: With right sides facing, stitch antlers all around leaving

48

opening at bottom. Clip seams and curves closely. Turn right side out and stuff. Turn under ⅛″ of fabric around edges, and pin to puppet head approximately 4″ from corners of mouth. (Pinning will be easier if you temporarily stuff puppet with batting until you are finished working.) See Diagram C. Using tiny slipstitches, secure antlers to head.

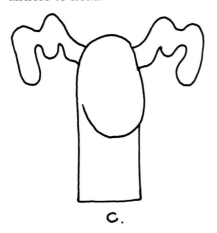

C.

Eyes: Back felt with masking tape or fusible interfacing. Cut out two ⅜″ felt circles for eyes and two ⅝″ circles of a contrasting color for pupils. With glue, secure each small circle to center of larger circle. Allow to dry, then glue eyes in place.

Nose: Glue pompon nose in place.

Hat: Fold knit fabric in half and stitch up side seam. Gather top tightly and stitch to secure, as shown in Diagram D. Turn right side out, and glue pompon in place. Turn under about ¼″ of fabric along bottom. Pin to head, then stitch in place.

HAT

D.

Fiona Pooch

Ears: With right sides facing, stitch fronts and backs together, leaving opening on top. Turn right side out. Fold under ¼″ of fabric. Pin to head, as shown in Diagram E. Stitch in place.

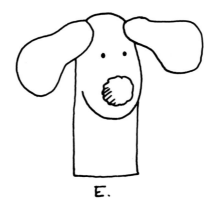

E.

Eyes: Back felt with fusible interfacing or masking tape. Cut out two ⅜″ circles for eyes and two ¼″ circles for pupils. Glue in place.

Tongue: Cut out tongue from felt. Glue in place on lower edge of mouth.

Bow: Fold 10″ × 1⅜″ cotton scrap in half lengthwise. With right sides facing, stitch as indicated in Diagram F. Turn right side out. Press, then make knot. Stitch in place.

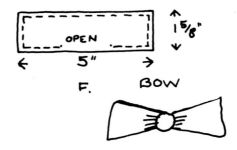

OPEN

5″

1⅝″

F.

BOW

Pinky Rabbit

Ears: With right sides facing, sew fronts and backs together, leaving bottom end open. Turn right side out. Take 10″ piece of floral wire, fold in half, and slide into ear opening. See Diagram G. Turn under ¼″ of fabric, and pin to head. Stitch to secure.

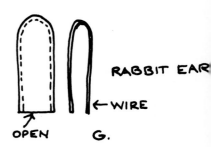

RABBIT EAR

← WIRE

OPEN

G.

Eyes: Back felt with fusible interfacing or masking tape. Cut out eyes and pupils from felt. Glue in place.

Tooth: Cut out ½″ square from white felt. Glue in place on upper edge of mouth.

Head band: Tack ribbon in place around head. Tack on artificial flowers.

Leonardo Lion

Mane: Pin craft fur to head (seam should be on bottom). Refer to photo for placement. With tiny slipstitches, stitch mane in place. Pull craft fur out to create fullness, as shown in Diagram H.

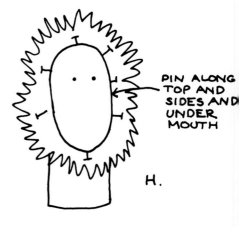

PIN ALONG TOP AND SIDES AND UNDER MOUTH

H.

Eyes: Back felt with masking tape or fusible interfacing. Cut out two ⅝″ circles from white felt, and two ⅜″ circles from black felt for pupils. Glue small circles onto large circles, then glue eyes in place on head.

Nose: Cut out nose from felt. Glue in place.

Crown: Cut out crown and curve it slightly. Glue to top of head.

1 square = 1 in.

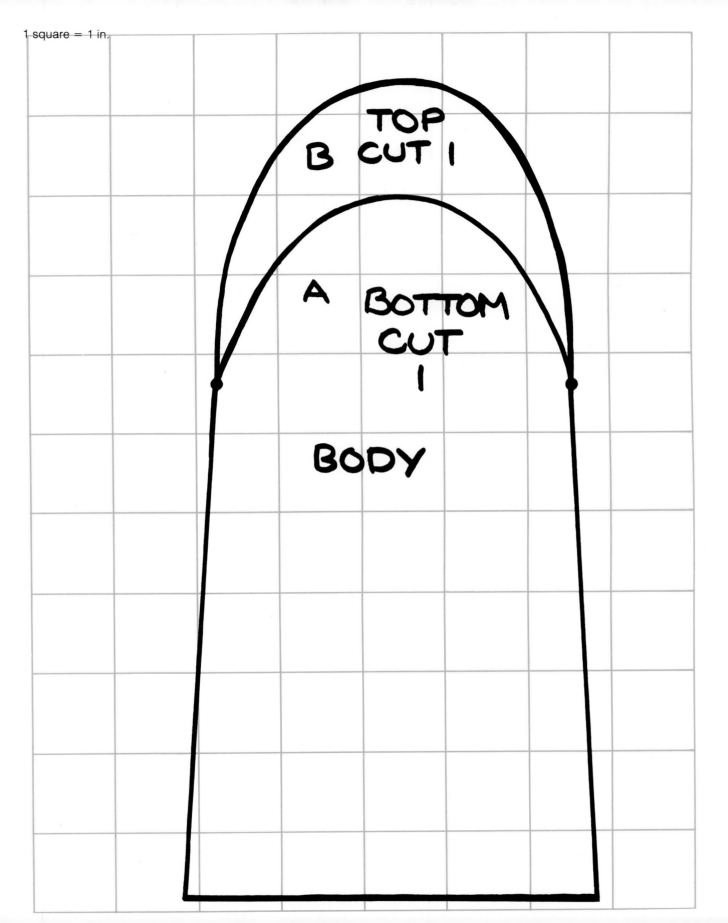

TOP
B CUT 1

A BOTTOM
CUT
1

BODY

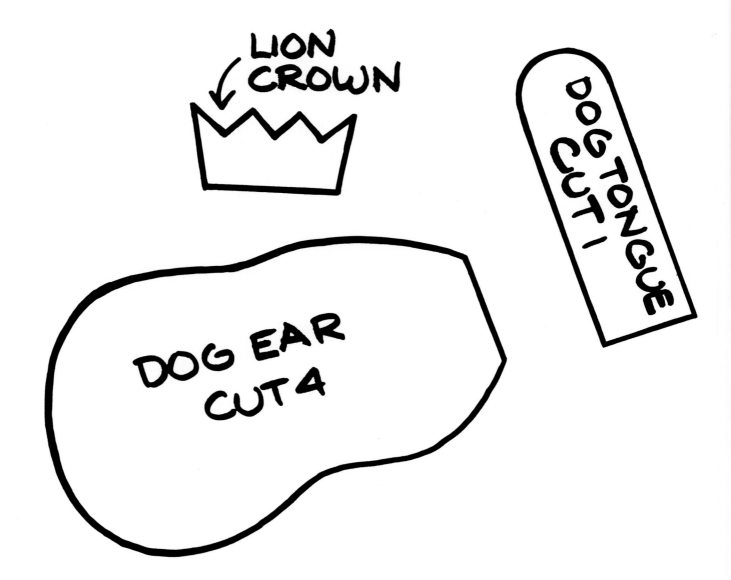

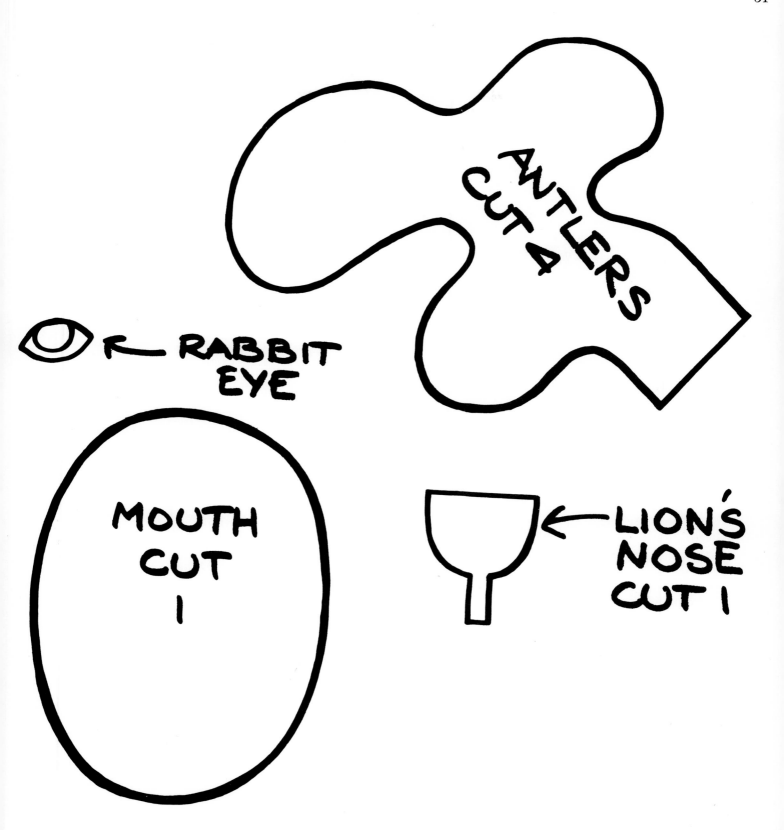

ANTLERS CUT 4

RABBIT EYE

MOUTH CUT 1

LION'S NOSE CUT 1

Emily Ann—
VICTORIAN DOLL

A bit old-fashioned and terribly proper, Emily Ann is always ready for a tea party with good friends. She's a perfect companion on rainy days, but also likes to spend some time alone with a good book.

SIZE: about 27″ tall

MATERIALS

Fabrics: ¾ yard of 36″ skin-tone cotton or cotton blend for face, body, and arms

¼ yard of 45″ striped cotton or cotton blend for legs

12″ × 12″ piece of light purple felt for boots

1½ yards of 36″ printed cotton or cotton blend for dress

Threads: sewing threads to match

black and green embroidery floss for face

Yarns: approximately 70 yards of reddish-brown knitting worsted for hair

Trims: 9″ of ⅛″ or ⅙″ elastic for wrists of dress

1½ yards of 1¼″ ruffled eyelet for neckband and hem

19″ of 1″-wide ribbon for hair bow

Stuffing: loose polyester fiberfill

Special Materials: cosmetic blusher for cheeks

shirt cardboard

INSTRUCTIONS

See General Directions. Enlarge patterns, adding ¼″ seam allowance all around unless otherwise indicated. Cut out all pattern pieces. Make ¼″ seams throughout.

Face: Transfer features onto fabric (see page 12). Using a backstitch, embroider nose, mouth, and eyelids. Use a satin stitch for embroidering eyes.

Body: With right sides facing, pin front to back, leaving openings where indicated for arms and leaving bottom open for stuffing. See Diagram A. Stitch along seam lines. Clip seams and curves closely. Turn right side out.

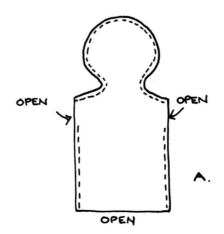

Arms: With right sides facing, stitch front and back arm pieces together. Clip curves closely. Turn right side out and stuff. Stitch across seam on each arm at elbow, as indicated on pattern, to make arms bendable. See Diagram B.

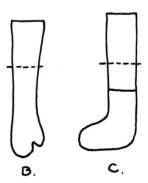

Legs and boots: With right sides facing, position boots on leg pieces, and pin. Stitch boots in place. With right sides facing, stitch leg backs to leg fronts. Clip curves closely. Turn right side out and stuff. Stitch across seam on each leg at knee, as indicated on pattern, to make legs bendable. See Diagram C.

53

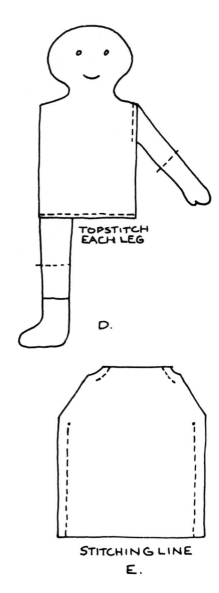

TOPSTITCH
EACH LEG

D.

STITCHING LINE

E.

RIGHT SIDES
OF SLEEVE
FACING

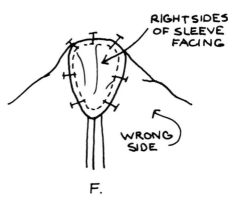

WRONG
SIDE

F.

With front of body facing you, pin arms in position so that they are angled down, with top ends inserted into arm openings of body. See Diagram D. Baste, and topstitch to secure.

Starting at head, stuff head and body. Pack stuffing tightly all the way to the bottom. Turn under ¼″ of fabric on top edge of each leg, then pin legs in position with toes facing forward, as shown in Diagram D. Baste, and topstitch across bottom of body.

Dress: With right sides facing, pin back pieces together. Stitch up center back seam line, leaving 7″ opening at top. Press seam open, and topstitch ¼″ seam allowance along each side of opening.

With right sides facing, pin back of dress to front; stitch along side seams and neck-to-shoulder seams. Leave opening for neck and sleeves, as shown in Diagram E.

Sleeves: Fold sleeve lengthwise and, with right sides facing, stitch up underarm seam. To gather top edge of each sleeve, run large gathering stitches ⅛″ from edge. Gather to fit width of sleeve opening. Leave thread ends dangling. Turn sleeve right side out. Pin sleeve to armhole with right side facing inside of dress. See Diagram F. Line up underarm seams wih dress seams. Pull gathering threads until sleeve fits armhole. Secure end threads around a pin in a figure-8 fashion. Adjust fullness to that sleeve will be fuller, with more gathers, at top of shoulder. Baste along seam line, and stitch to secure.

Neck: Run a line of gathering stitches along neckline. Leave thread ends dangling. Place dress on doll. Gather evenly to fit neck. Secure end threads around a pin in figure-8 fashion. Cut out a piece

of dress fabric 10½″ × 1″ to create a narrow neckband. Press down ¼″ on wrong side. With right sides facing, pin neckband to gathered edge. Adjust fullness, giving center of dress more gathers than sides. See Diagram G. Baste, then

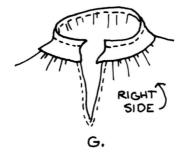

RIGHT
SIDE

G.

stitch. Trim seam edge and press toward neckband. Turn over remaining edge, and slipstitch over seam line. Topstitch pre-gathered eyelet to neckband. See Diagram H. Fold down ruffle over neckband. Add snap closure at back of dress.

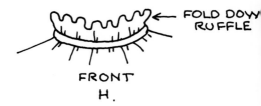

FOLD DOW
RUFFLE

FRONT
H.

Wrists: Turn fabric under 1¼″ along edge; topstitch, leaving a 1½″ opening. Insert elastic. You will need about 4″ for each wrist. Stitch opening closed.

Hem dress, and add ruffle along bottom edge.

Hair: For back of hair, wrap yarn thickly around 9″ × 8″ piece of cardboard. Stitch along top of cardboard with overcast stitches. Slide yarn off, and pin to top of head. See Diagram I. Using slip-stitches, secure yarn to head.

STITCH TO HEAD

I.

Bangs: Wrap yarn around 3½″ × 7″ piece of cardboard. Wind yarn randomly—do not fill as for back of hair. Stitch along top of card-board with overcast stitches. Slide yarn off, and pin to forehead. See Diagram J. Slipstitch to secure.

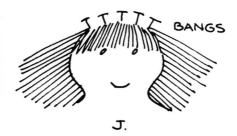

BANGS

J.

Clip ends of yarn loops open. To get the right look, you will have to open up each strand of yarn by untwisting. This is tedious and time consuming, but it looks great! After untwisting, even out the edges and bangs for a neat hair-line.

Add ribbon bow and tack in place.

As a final touch, add cosmetic blusher for cheek color.

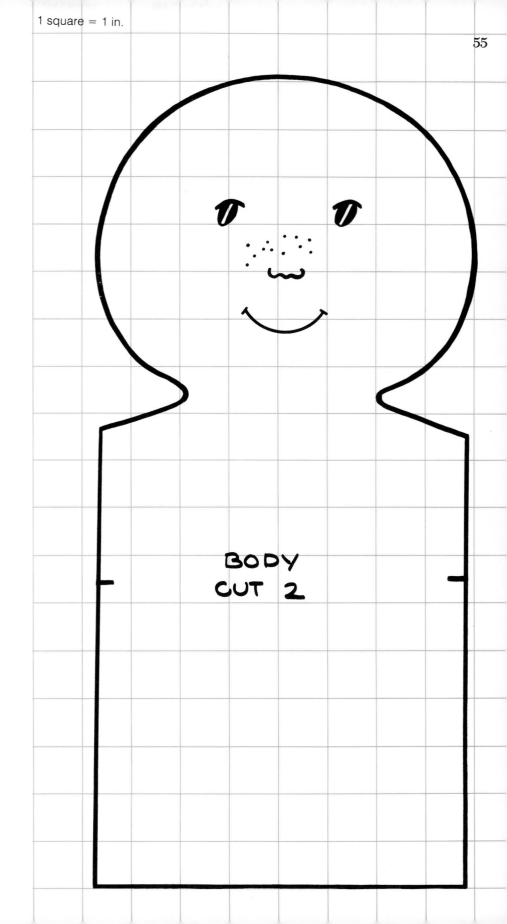

BODY
CUT 2

1 square = 1 in.

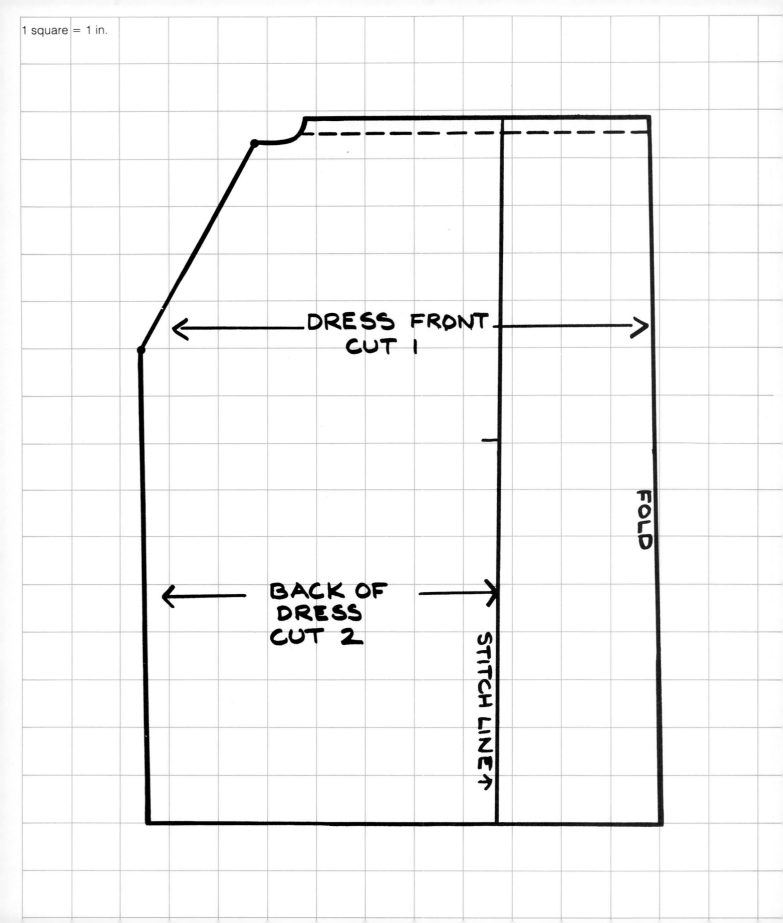

DRESS FRONT
CUT 1

BACK OF
DRESS
CUT 2

FOLD

STITCH LINE

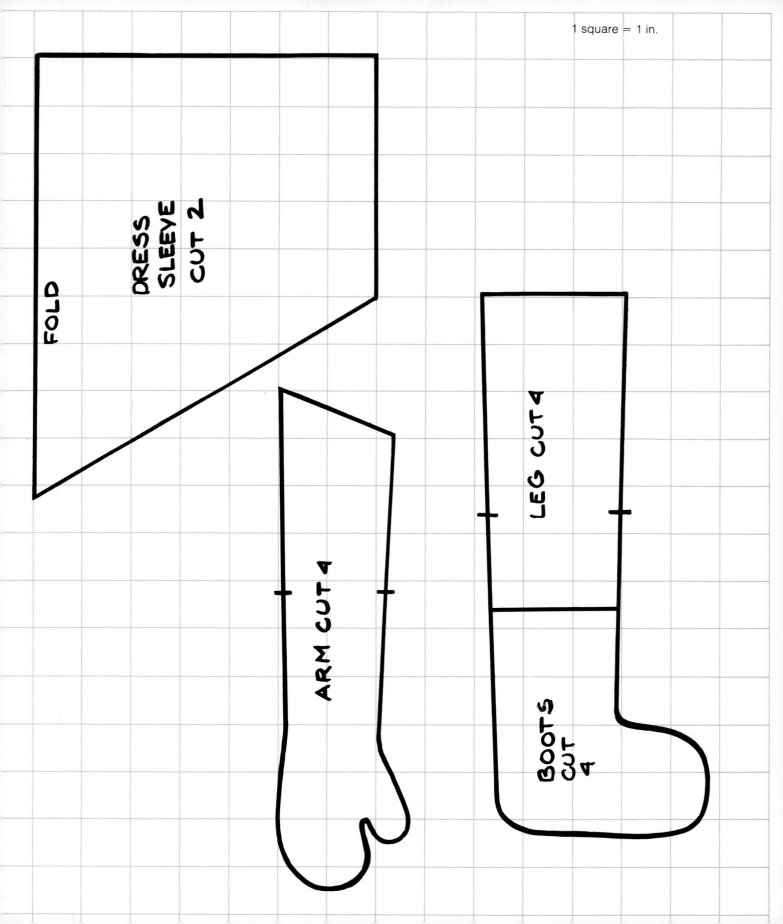

1 square = 1 in.

FOLD

DRESS SLEEVE CUT 2

ARM CUT 4

LEG CUT 4

BOOTS CUT 4

58

Outer Space Aliens and Totable Bag

One of the problems with having alien guests in the house is where to put them. Make these three friendly visitors with their totable home, and your guest room problems will be solved!

SIZE: Pink Clod: about 9″ tall
Yellow Moogy: about 9″ tall
4-Legged Snoot: about 7½″ tall
Totable Bag: 15¾″ square

MATERIALS

Pink Clod

Fabrics: ¼ yard of 45″ pink polyester fleece for body

⅛ yard of 36″ green cotton or cotton blend for legs

Trims: 2 yellow pompons (purchase, or see How To Make Pompons, page 16) for eyes

scraps of turquoise and black felt for mouth and eyes

Yellow Moogy

Fabric: ⅓ yard of 45″ yellow polyester fleece for body

Yarn: 11 yards of blue yarn, 2 yards of green yarn for hair

Trims: scraps of purple and black felt for mouth and eyes

4-Legged Snoot

Fabric: ¼ yard of 36″ striped cotton or cotton blend for body

Trims: 1 pompon (purchase, or see How To Make Pompons, page 16) for nose

scraps of white and black felt for eyes

For all Aliens

Special Material: fabric glue suitable

for 3-dimensional gluing, such as Elmer's® Tacky Glue

shirt cardboard

Totable Bag

Fabrics: ½ yard of 45″ striped cotton or cotton blend

½ yard of 45″ white or colored cotton

or cotton blend for lining

½ yard of 36″ transparent vinyl for window (preferably tinted)

Trims: 15″ × ¾″ tissue paper

Velcro® for closure

For all

Threads: sewing threads to match

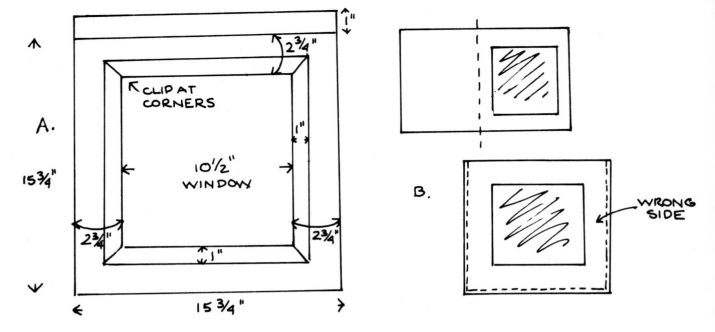

INSTRUCTIONS

For all

See General Directions. Enlarge patterns, adding ¼" seam allowance except on felt eye and mouth pieces. Cut out all pattern pieces. Make ¼" seams throughout.

Pink Clod

Body: With right sides facing, stitch back and front of body together, leaving a 2" opening for stuffing. Also leave openings for legs to be inserted.

Legs: With right sides facing, stitch backs and fronts together, leaving top open for stuffing. Turn right side out and stuff tightly. Insert legs into openings on body. Using small slipstitches, stitch around openings to secure legs.

Stuff body, and sew opening.

Face: Cut out mouth from felt and glue in place. Glue on pompon eyeballs. Cut out pupils from black felt, then glue onto pompons.

Yellow Moogy

Body: With right sides facing, stitch back and front of body together leaving a 2" opening for stuffing. Turn right side out, stuff, and sew up opening.

Hair: Wrap blue yarn around 5" × 2½" piece of cardboard. Stitch along top with overcast stitches. Slide yarn off cardboard and pin to head.

Wind green yarn around same piece of cardboard. Stitch along top. Slide yarn off and pin to head. Stitch blue and green yarn loops in place and trim ends, as shown in photograph.

Face: Cut out mouth and eyes from felt. Glue in place.

4-Legged Snoot

Body: With right sides facing, stitch back of body to front leaving a 2" opening for stuffing. Turn right side out, stuff, and sew opening.

Face: Cut out eyeballs and pupils from felt and glue in place. Glue on pompon nose.

Totable Bag

Cut out two 15¾" squares each for outside of bag and lining. From one outer-bag and one lining square, cut out center 10½" square, leaving 2¾" border all around. See Diagram A. Turn under 1" all around inner edge of window, clipping at corners on each piece. Baste turned-under edges. Cut out 12½" square of vinyl. Lay lining, wrong side down, over vinyl, centering window over vinyl. Tape basted edge to vinyl. On other side of vinyl, position outer-bag piece, wrong side toward vinyl, centering window over vinyl. Tape basted edge to vinyl. To aid machine stitching, place tissue paper on vinyl. Stitch through tissue all around, then pull off. Topstitch on right side along edge. Remove basting and tape.

Baste remaining outer-bag and lining pieces together, wrong sides facing, for back of bag. Pin back to front, with right sides facing. Sew along edges of front and back of bag on three sides. See Diagram B. Fold 1" of fabric under, around top of bag. Press, then topstitch. Add Velcro® to inside front and back.

For handle, cut piece of fabric 8" × 1½". Fold lengthwise and stitch to form strip ⅝" wide. Fold strip in half, and machine stitch ends to top of bag inside. For strength, machine stitch each end twice.

1 square = 1 in.

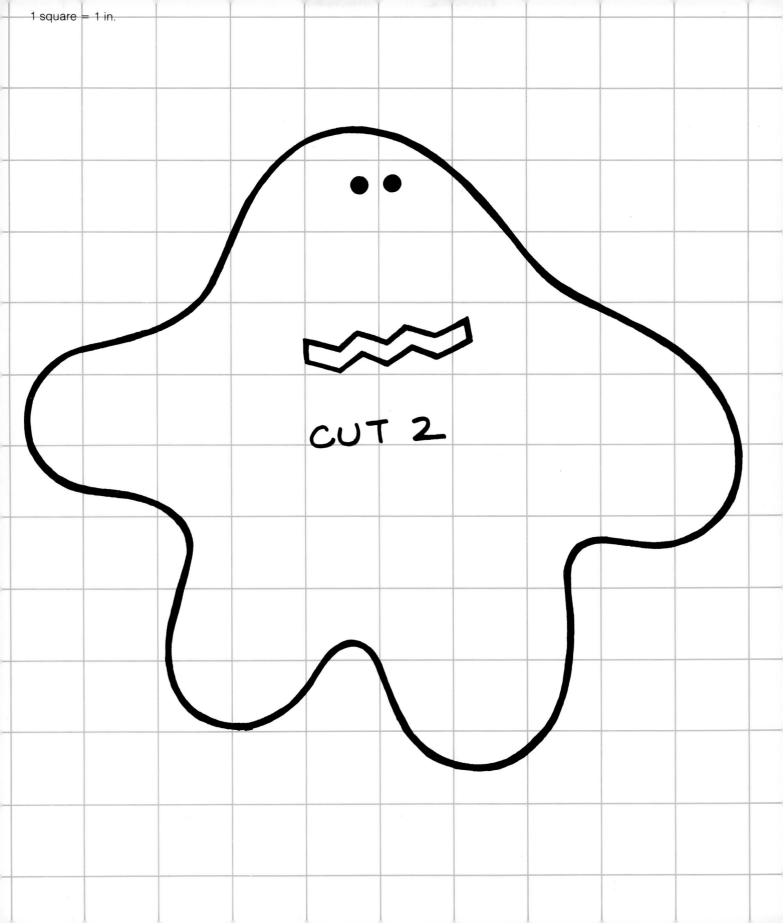

CUT 2

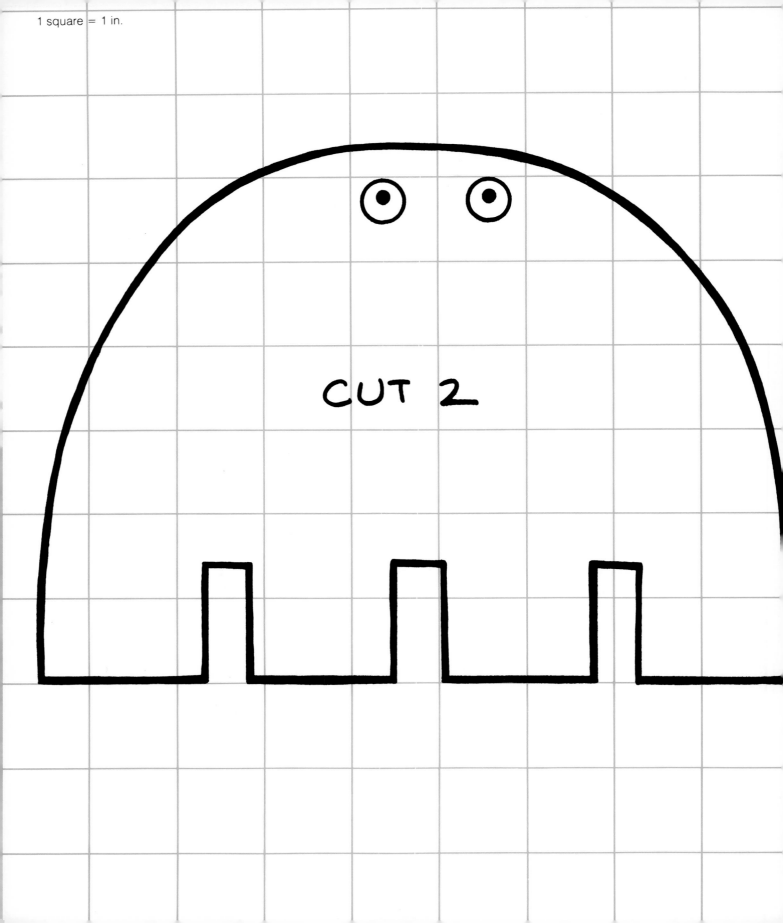

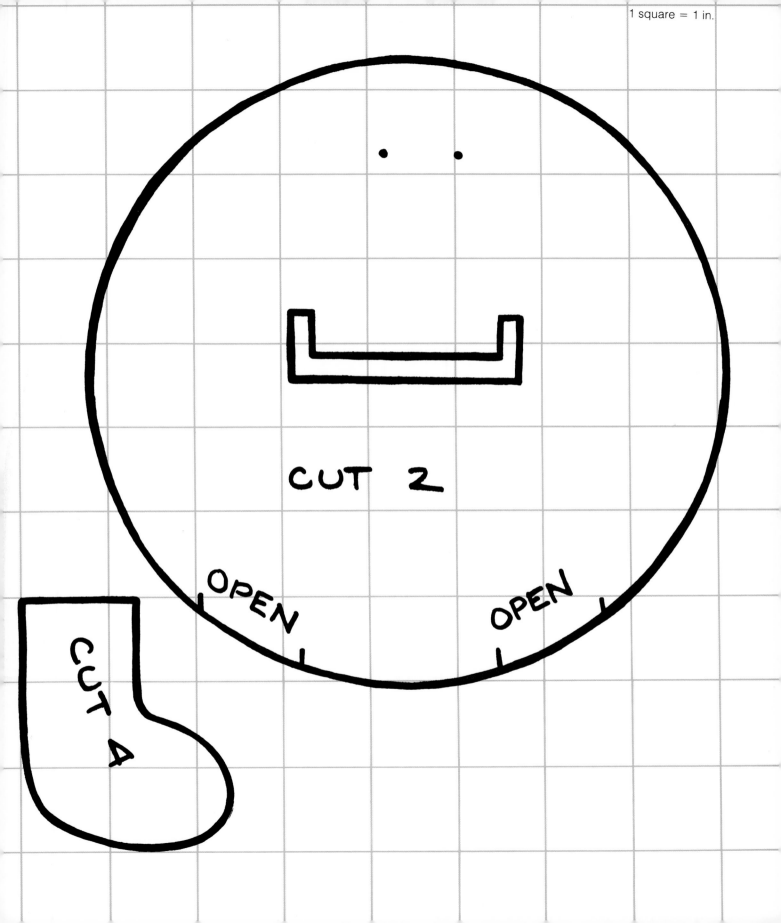

1 square = 1 in.

CUT 2

OPEN

OPEN

CUT 4

Floppy Claus

I once caught a glimpse of Santa taking a breather after he finished his rounds, and this is what he looked like. My version of Santa gets his floppiness from a combination of barley and polyester stuffing.

SIZE: about 8″ tall

MATERIALS

Fabrics: ¼ yard of 36″ cotton or cotton-blend muslin for face and hands

¾ yard of 45″ red polyester/cotton fleece for body, arms, and hat

¼ yard of 36″ black cotton or polyester/cotton blend for boots

Threads: sewing threads to match

Yarn: 2 yards of ¼″-thick white yarn for hair and beard

Trims: 1½″ of white velvet or felt for hat

1 red and 1 white pompon (purchase, or see How To Make Pompons, page 16) for nose and hat

15″ length of ⅜″-wide black ribbon for belt

scrap of felt for belt buckle

Stuffing: ¼ lb. of loose polyester fiberfill

1 lb. bag of barley

Special Materials: thin black permanent marker

hot-pink permanent marker

shirt cardboard

Elmer's® Tacky Glue

INSTRUCTIONS

See General Directions. Enlarge patterns, adding ¼″ seam allowance all around unless otherwise indicated. Be sure to place body pattern on fold of material as indicated. Cut out all pattern pieces. Make ¼″ seams throughout.

Body: With right sides facing, stitch boots to body, and stitch hands to arms. With right sides facing, sew body front piece to back, leaving 1½″ opening on each side for arms and 3″ opening at bottom for stuffing. Leave body wrong side out.

With right sides facing, sew arms together. Turn right side out. Fill arms one-quarter full with barley (a funnel makes it easy). Then stuff remainder of each arm with polyester fiberfill. Sew up openings.

On each side, slip entire stuffed arm into arm opening of body. See Diagram A. Sew up openings. Turn body right side out. Turn body upside down, and stuff first with polyester fiberfill to point indicated in Diagram B. Then fill

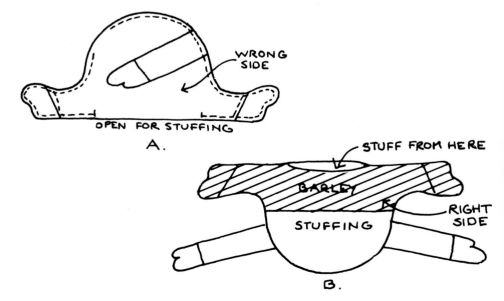

WRONG SIDE

OPEN FOR STUFFING

A.

STUFF FROM HERE

BARLEY

STUFFING

RIGHT SIDE

B.

remainder of body with barley. Close opening with tiny stitches. Now turn right side up.

Head: Draw on face with thin black marker. Highlight cheeks with pink marker. With right sides facing, stitch back and front of head together, leaving 2″ opening on top for stuffing. Clip curves closely. Turn right side out. Stuff half of head with barley, then stuff remainder with fiberfill. Close opening with small slipstitches. Attach red pompon for nose, sewing in place or using tacky glue.

Beard and hair: Reserving 13″ of yarn for mustache, wrap all remaining yarn around 9″ × 1″ piece of cardboard. Stitch along top to secure yarn. Slide yarn off cardboard. Pin yarn loops to face for beard, as shown in Diagram C. Placement should be about ½″ in from bottom seam of head.

Mustache: Fold 13″ length of yarn in half once, then fold in half again. Stitch center, then stitch to face, right under pompon nose.

Place head on body, as shown in Diagram D. Pin back of head to body and stitch with tiny slipstitches to secure.

Hat: With right sides facing, stitch cuff pieces to front and back hat pieces. With right sides facing, sew front and back of hat together. Turn right side out. Fold fabric under on fold line. Place hat on Claus's head, and tack down on sides. Sew or glue pompon to point.

Belt: Cut black ribbon to fit waist. For buckle, cut scrap of felt into 1″ square with a ⅜″ square opening with center piece. See Diagram E. Thread ribbon in and over center piece of buckle. Secure belt around waistline with glue.

ATTACHING BEARD
C.

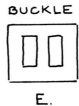

BUCKLE

E.

ATTACH HEAD
FROM HERE

D.

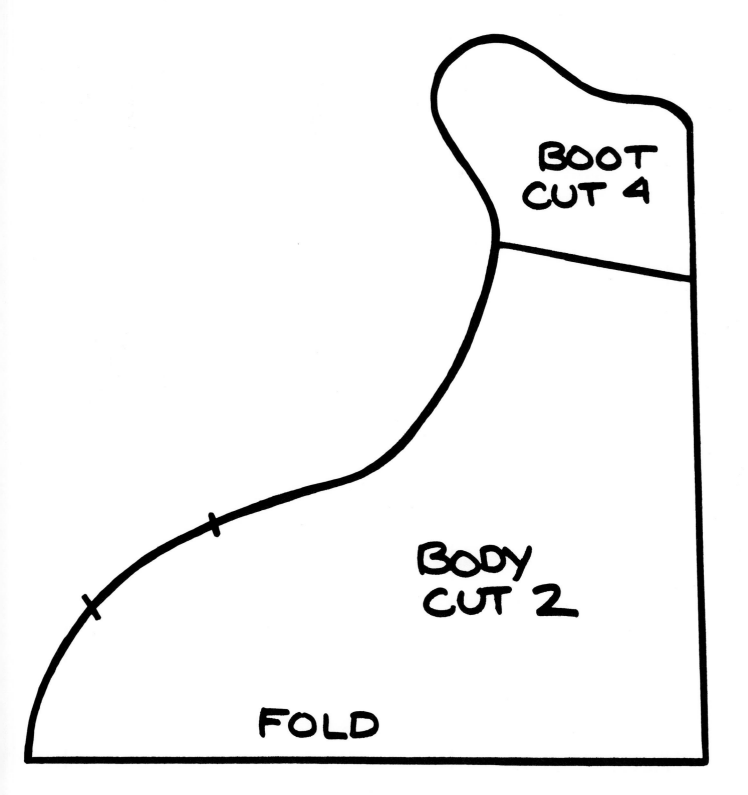

BOOT
CUT 4

BODY
CUT 2

FOLD

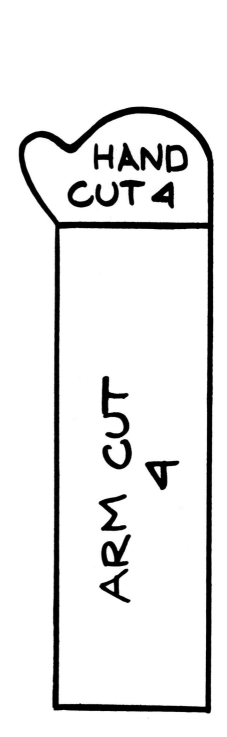

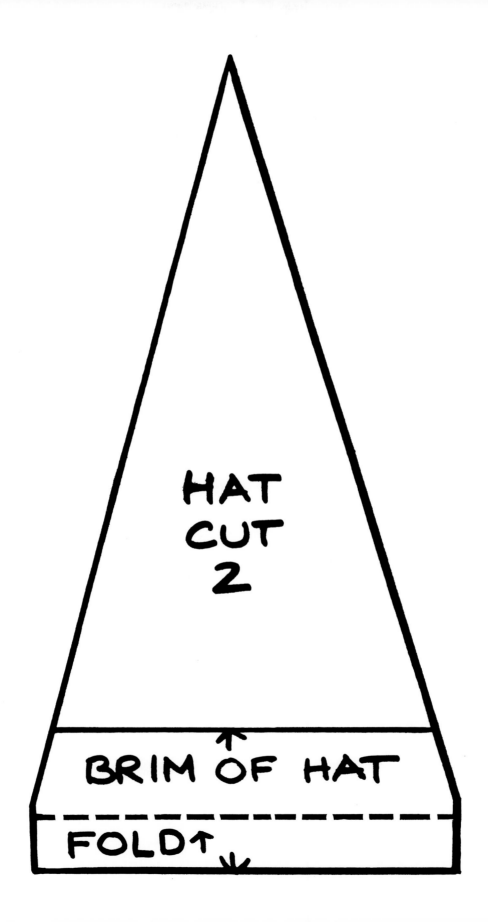

Ms. Workout

Most beanbags just sit there and do nothing . . . but you have to admire Ms. Workout's attempts to keep in shape! Made from a combination of barley and stuffing, Ms. Workout's bendability can be an inspiration to us all.

SIZE: about 8½″ tall × 14″ wide

MATERIALS

Fabrics: ½ yard of 36″ skin-tone cotton or cotton blend for face, hands, and legs

½ yard of 45″ fleece for leotard (body and arms) and headband

¼ yard of 45″ fleece for sleeveless top

¼ yard of 36″ white felt for shoes

10″ × 10″ sock or knit scrap for leg warmers

Threads: sewing threads to match

blue, brown, and red embroidery floss for face

Yarn: approximately 30 yards of mohair or soft mohairlike yarn for hair

Trim: glitter glue pen for numbers on sleeveless top

Stuffing: loose polyester fiberfill

1 lb. of barley

Special Materials: pink Dr. Ph. Martin's® dye, pink marker, or cosmetic blusher for cheeks

shirt cardboard

INSTRUCTIONS

See General Directions. Enlarge patterns, adding ¼″ seam allowance all around unless otherwise indicated. Cut out all pattern pieces. Make ¼″ seams throughout.

Head: Transfer features onto fabric being used for face (see page 12). Using backstitches, embroider eyes, nose, and mouth. If using Dr. Martin's® dye, color cheeks now and allow to dry. If using pink marker or blusher, do cheeks last.

With right sides facing, stitch face front to back along stitching line, leaving 2½″ opening at top of head for stuffing. Stuff with fiberfill, and sew up opening.

Body: Baste shoes to legs, and legs to body. Stitch. Pin front and back of body together, leaving 3″ opening at bottom and 1⅝″ opening for each arm. See Diagram A. Leave body wrong side out.

Arms: With right sides facing, pin hands to one end of arms and stitch. Sew front of arms to back of arms, leaving tops open. Turn right side out. Stuff halfway with barley, and fill the remainder with polyester fiberfill. Stitch ends closed. Slip finished arms inside arm openings of body, and sew up openings. See Diagram B.

Turn body right side out through opening in bottom. Turn body up-

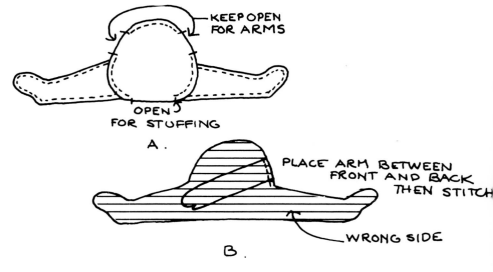

KEEP OPEN FOR ARMS

OPEN FOR STUFFING

A.

PLACE ARM BETWEEN FRONT AND BACK THEN STITCH

WRONG SIDE

B.

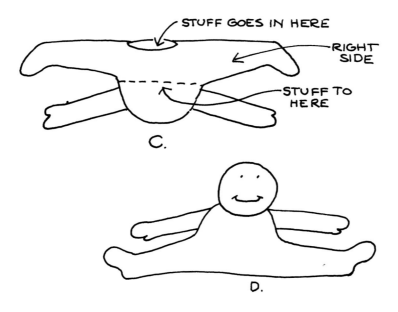

STUFF GOES IN HERE

RIGHT SIDE

STUFF TO HERE

C.

D.

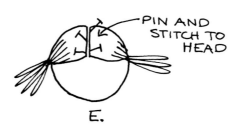

PIN AND STITCH TO HEAD

E.

side down, and stuff first with polyester fiberfill to point indicated in Diagram C. Then fill remainder of body with barley. Use very tiny slipstitches to close up bottom securely. Now turn doll right side up.

Position head on body, as shown in Diagram D. Pin back of head to body, and catch with tiny slipstitches along stitching line on pattern.

Sleeveless top: No hemming is necessary on the edges of this top. Just stitch shoulders and sides on wrong side of fabric, turn right side out, and add "1-2-3" with glitter glue pen.

Leg warmers: For each leg, cut out 5″ × 5″ piece of sock or knit fabric. Fold in half and stitch up seam. Turn right side out and place on leg. Gather the fabric a bit for a leg-warmer look.

Hair: Wrap yarn around 6″ × 6½″ piece of cardboard. Stitch along top with overcast stitches. Slide yarn off cardboard and split in half. Pin 3″ to each side of head, and make a back center part, as shown in Diagram E. Stitch yarn to head. Gather ends to make side ponytails and tie close to head.

For bangs, wind about 40 loops of yarn around ½″-diameter cylinder, such as a marker, pencil, or crayon. Stitch along top, and pull yarn off cylinder. Twist yarn for a tousled look. Pin to forehead, then stitch in place.

Headband: Cut ⅜″ × 11″ piece of fleece left from leotard. Fit around head, and tie at back. Tack down. Unhemmed fleece will roll up at edges.

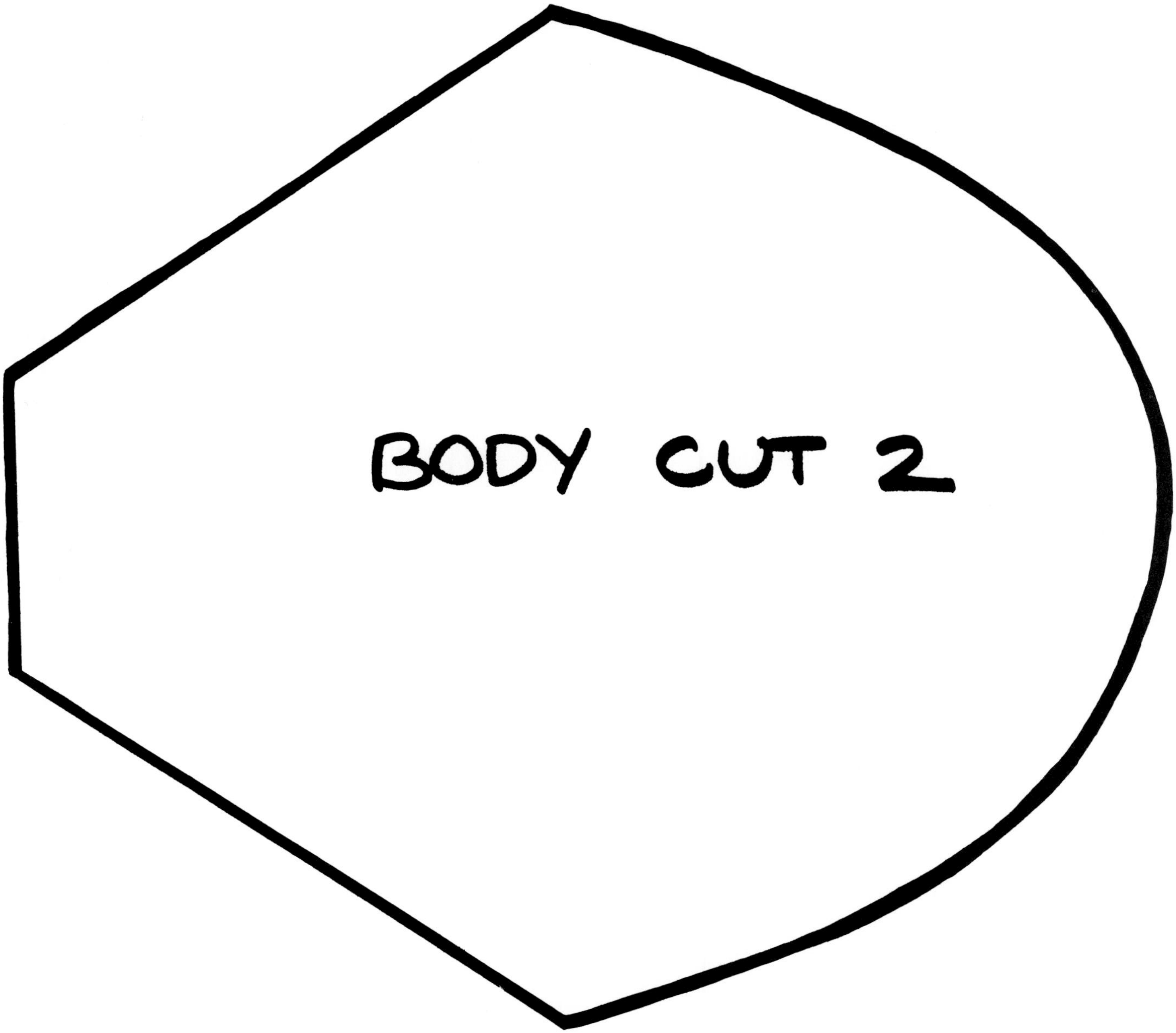

BODY CUT 2

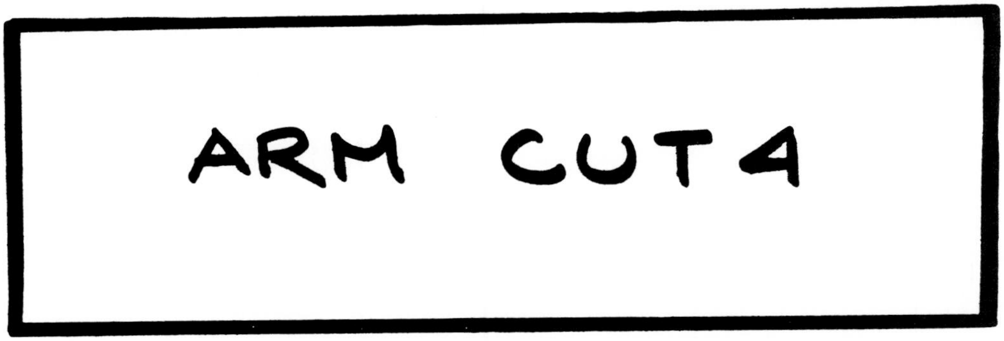

ARM CUT 4

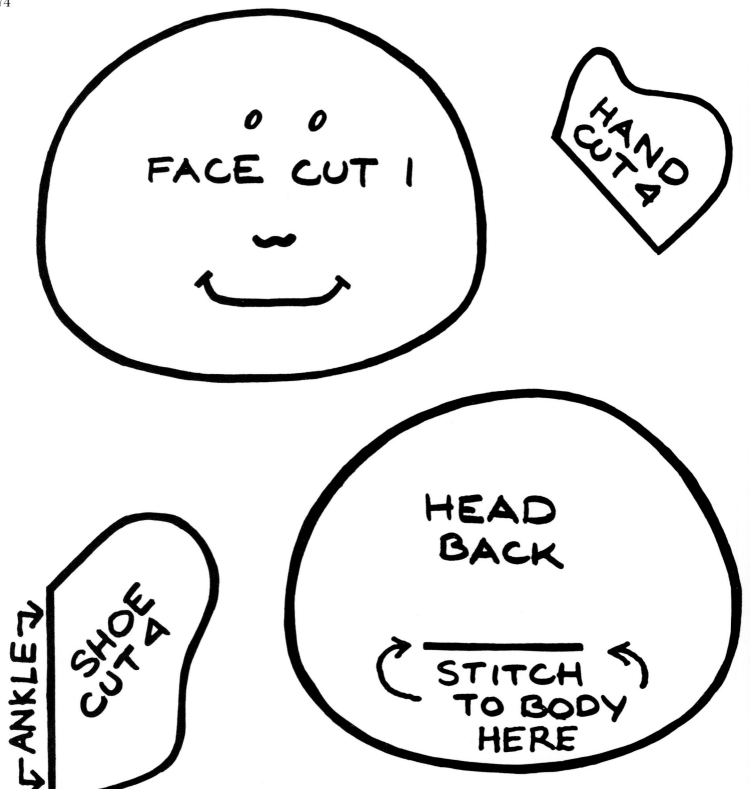

FACE CUT 1

HAND CUT 4

SHOE CUT 4

ANKLE

HEAD BACK

STITCH TO BODY HERE

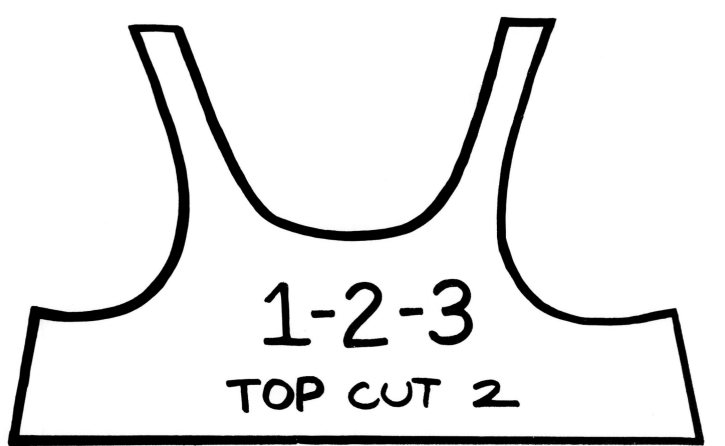

1-2-3
TOP CUT 2

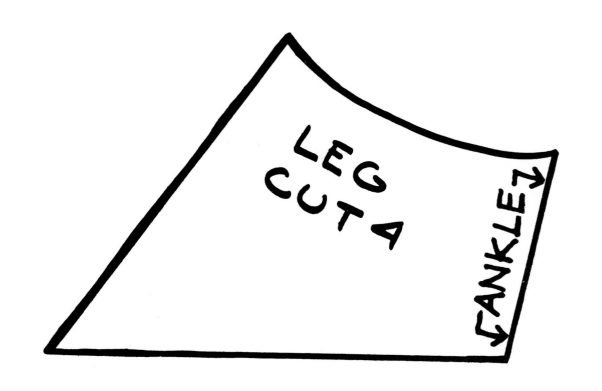

LEG
CUT 4

←ANKLE→

OGDEN BEAR

Here's a new, chunkier version of the classic Teddy. Ogden is just asking to be squeezed and hugged. Even though he's a bear, he's wise and likes school very much. And he's always ready for a family outing or a birthday party. A word of warning: Don't leave Ogden alone with a bag of cookies!

SIZE: about 20″ tall

MATERIALS

Fabrics: 1 yard of 45″ fake fur with ¼″ pile for head, back, ears, arms, underleg, and body

½ yard of 36″ colorful cotton or cotton blend for vest

Threads: sewing threads to match

medium-brown embroidery floss for nose and mouth

Trims: Two 2″-diameter bear eyes or black buttons for eyes

scrap of black felt for nose

buttons or snap closure for vest

Stuffing: loose polyester fiberfill

INSTRUCTIONS

See General Directions. Enlarge patterns, adding ¼″ seam allowance all around unless otherwise indicated. Cut out all pattern pieces for the bear. Make ¼″ seams throughout. Transfer markings (see page 12). Pin and baste.

Body: *Front:* With right sides (fur) facing, stitch front body piece A to piece B along curved center seam from neck to crotch. Then pin, baste, and stitch underleg piece to body front, around legs. See Diagram A.

Back: With right sides facing, pin body upper back C to D, leaving 5½″ opening for stuffing. See Diagam B. Then baste and machine stitch.

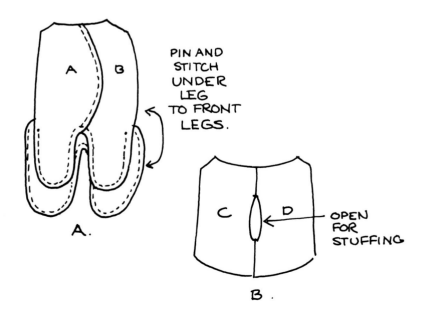

PIN AND STITCH UNDER LEG TO FRONT LEGS.

A.

OPEN FOR STUFFING

B.

Pin body back to body front, leaving an opening on each side for arms, and on top for head. See dots for placement of arm openings. Baste top of under-legs to bottom of upper back. See Diagram C. Stitch all seams. Leave body wrong side out.

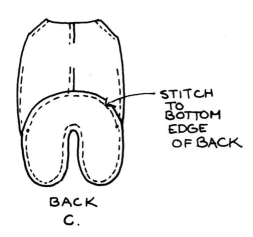

STITCH
TO
BOTTOM
EDGE
OF BACK

BACK
C.

Arms: With right sides facing, pin and stitch back and front arm pieces together. Turn right side out. Place each arm in opening on each side of body, fur sides together. Line up seams. Baste, and stitch around armhole to secure, as for set-in sleeve. See Diagram D.

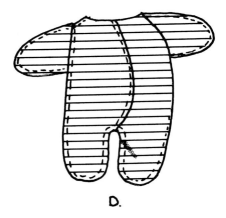

D.

Head: With right sides (fur) facing, pin head front pieces together along center seam, and machine stitch to form front of head. Follow markings for eye placement and attach plastic craft eyes or black buttons; embroidered eyes can also be used.

With right sides facing, stitch head back pieces together along curved seam to form back of head. Then stitch front of head to back of head, leaving bottom open.

Attach head in the way arms were attached to body. See Diagram E. Turn head right side out.

WRONG
SIDE

E.

Then insert head upside down into neck opening on body, with right sides facing. Line up seams. Pin, baste, then machine stitch to secure.

Turn bear right side out through opening in back. See Diagram F.

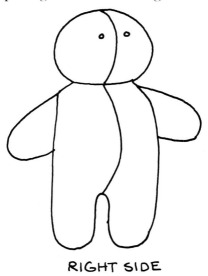

RIGHT SIDE
F.

Stuff bear from opening in back so that he is firm but squeezable. Slipstitch opening closed.

Ears: With right sides facing, pin, baste, and stitch front and back ear pieces together, leaving bottom open. Turn right side out. Turn under seam allowance of ¼″, and pin ears to head. Gather slightly to give ear a pleated look. Secure ears to head with tiny, invisible slipstitches. See Diagram G.

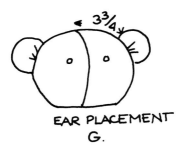

EAR PLACEMENT
G.

Face: *Nose:* Cut out black felt triangle about 1⅞″ wide by 1″ high. Secure to face with tiny tacking stitches. Slip a tiny piece of fiberfill stuffing under felt triangle to create depth. With three strands of embroidery floss, satin-stitch over felt, following triangle shape. See Diagram H.

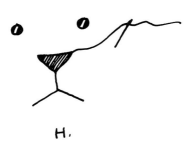

H.

Mouth: Make one long vertical stitch, approximately ⅝″ long, below nose. Then make 1⅛″ stitch to right and left. Make a tiny knot and lose the end in face fur (see page 16).

Vest: Double the fabric to give a clean line to the edge of vest. Cut out all pieces, and be sure to add ¼″ seam allowance to all pieces. With right sides facing, stitch front linings to front and back lining to back, along seams indicated in Diagrams I and J. Left and right

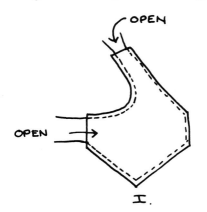

I.

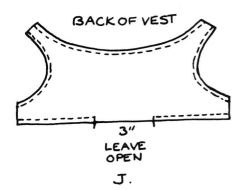

J.

sides of vest should have sides and top open for turning. Clip corners and edges closely. Turn right side out. Leave bottom of back open, as shown in Diagram J. Clip seam and turn.

Place vest on bear with wrong (lining) sides out. See Diagram K. Pin tops and sides to fit. Baste, then machine stitch. Be careful to line up edges. Turn right side out. Add buttons or snap closure.

Then hug.

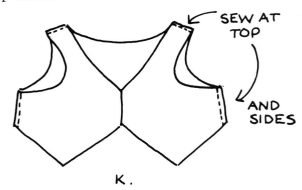

K.

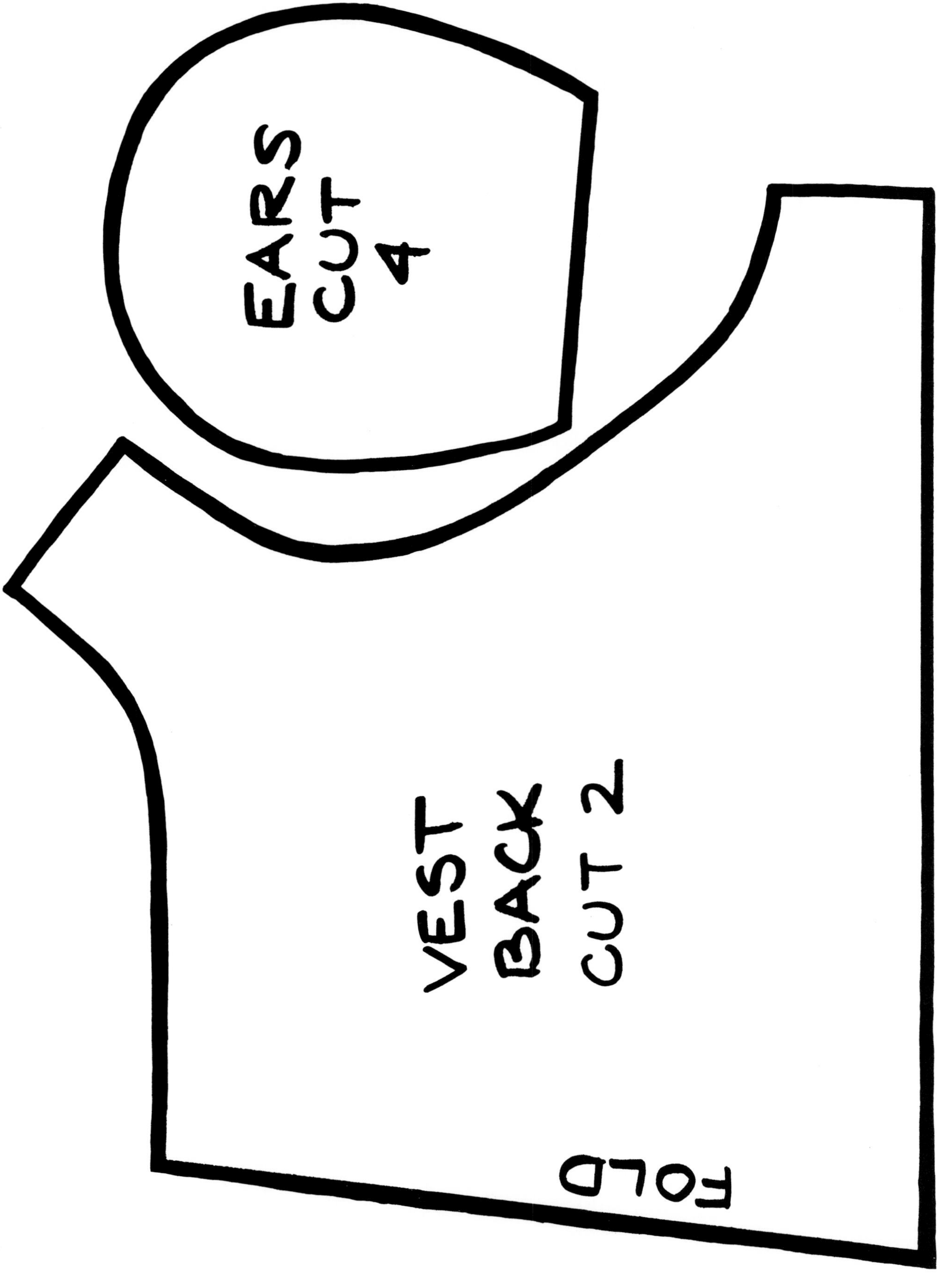

80

EARS
CUT
4

VEST
BACK
CUT 2

FOLD

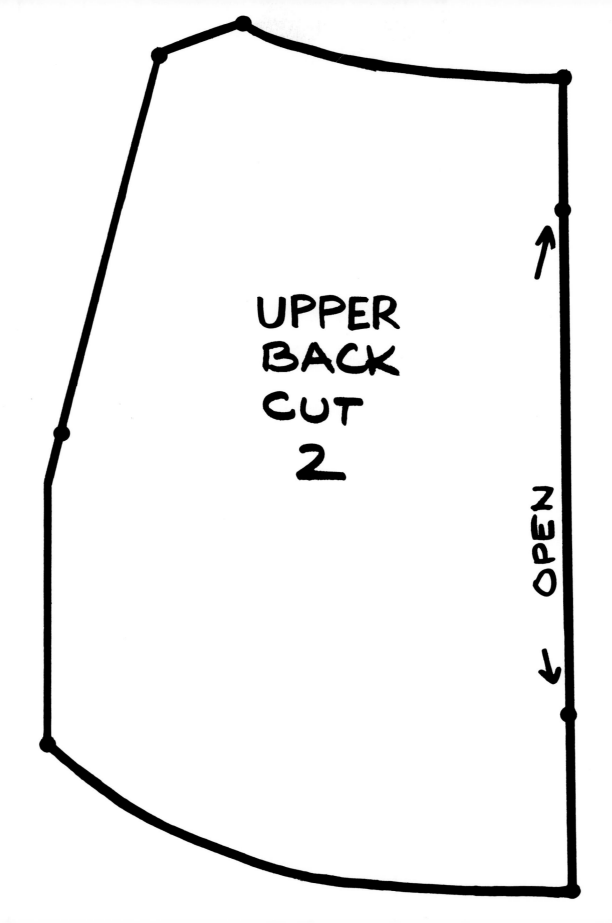

UPPER
BACK
CUT
2

OPEN

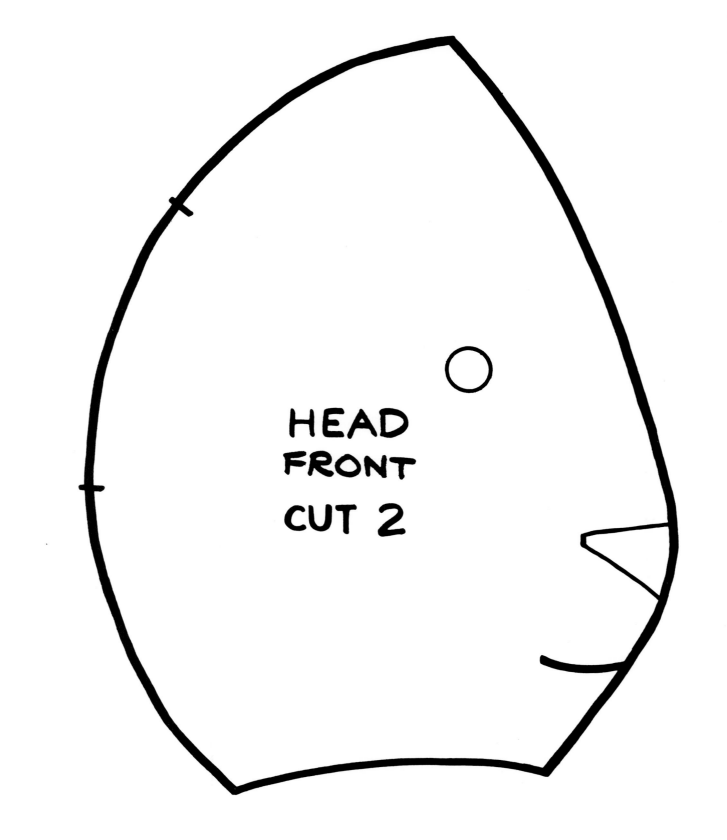

HEAD
FRONT
CUT 2

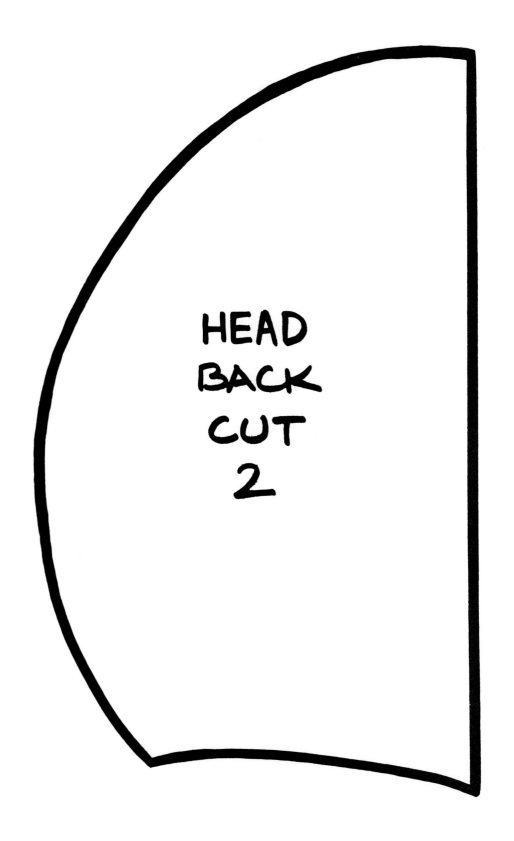

HEAD
BACK
CUT
2

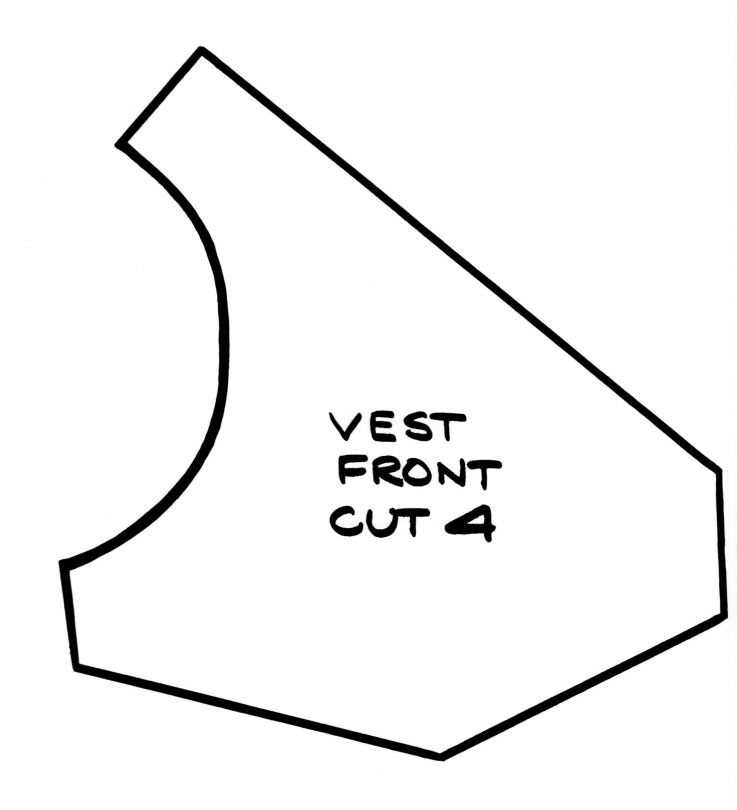

VEST
FRONT
CUT 4

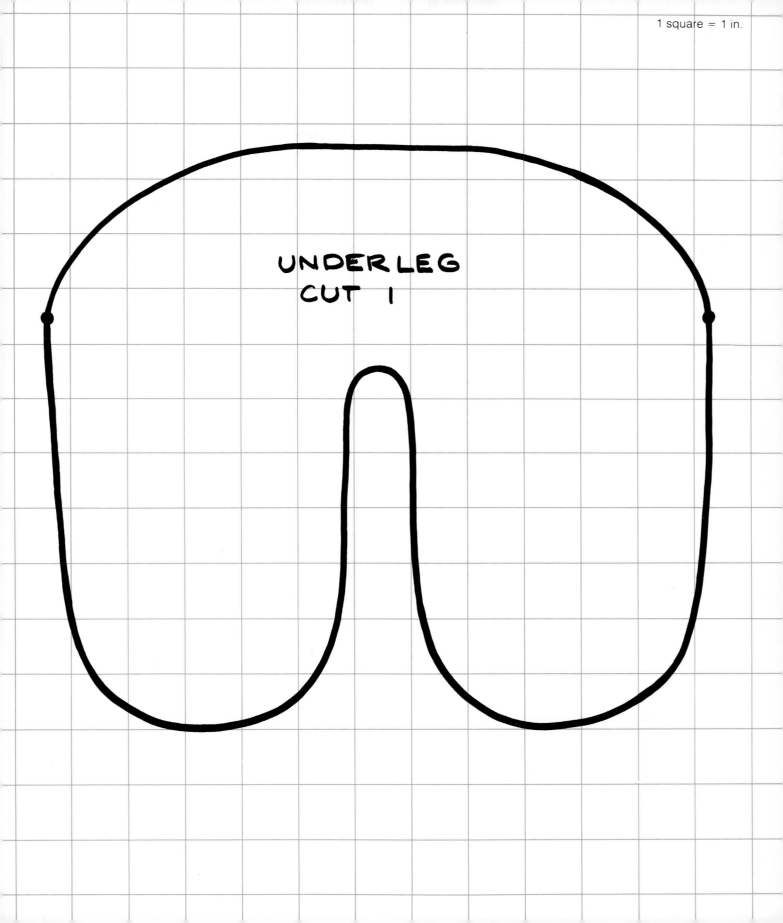

1 square = 1 in.

UNDERLEG
CUT 1

1 square = 1 in.

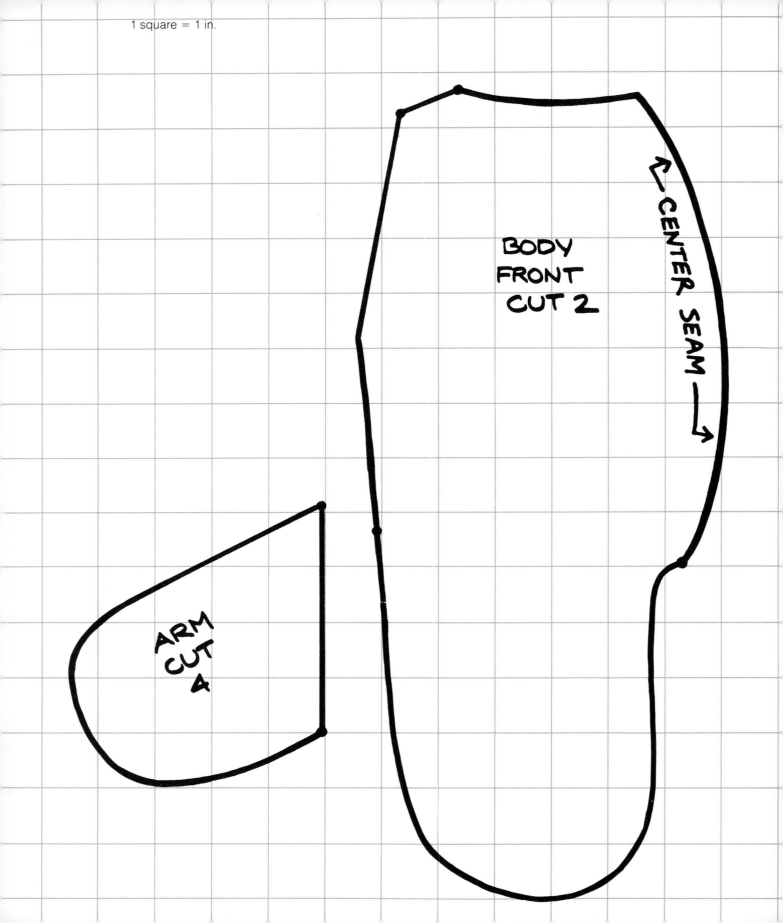

BODY
FRONT
CUT 2

CENTER SEAM →

ARM
CUT
4

MERLIN

Merlin the Magician casts a spell on everyone he meets. So don't be surprised if you find him outside one starry night, conjuring some mysterious spirit. . . . or if you catch him poking around the kitchen, looking for a jar of toad tails. Most of the time, though, just having Merlin around is magic enough.

SIZE: about 24″ tall

MATERIALS

Fabrics: ¾ yard of 45″ spandex for hat and cape

½ yard of 36″-wide silver metallic-look fabric for cape lining and star motif

½ yard of 45″ skin-tone cotton or cotton-blend fleece for head, face, hands, and nose

½ yard of 45″ satin spandex or similar fabric for shirt and pants

¼ yard of 45″ satin spandex for boots

Threads: sewing threads to match black and hot-pink embroidery floss for face

Yarn: 2 yards of orange mohair or soft mohairlike yarn for hair

Trims: 1 yard of ⅜″ ribbon for cape

29″ of ⅛″ elastic for pants

Stuffing: loose polyester fiberfill

Special Materials: cosmetic blusher for cheeks

4 small dressmaker's weights

fabric glue

INSTRUCTIONS

See General Directions. Enlarge patterns, adding ¼″ seam allowance all around unless otherwise indicated. Double material and place pattern on fold where indicated. Cut out all pattern pieces. Make ¼″ seams throughout.

Head: With right sides facing, sew back of head piece A to back of head piece B along stitching line. See Diagram A. Then sew back of head to face along stitching line. Clip curves closely. Turn right side out and stuff firmly. Do not stuff ears.

To keep head balanced forward, insert four small dressmaker's weights in underside of chin. See Diagram B.

Body: With right sides facing, sew hands to front and back of shirt at wrist. With right sides facing, sew front to back, leaving opening at bottom and at neck. Turn right side out. Turn fabric in ¼″ around neck edge and baste.

Pin head to body at stitching

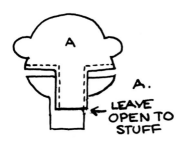

A.
←LEAVE OPEN TO STUFF

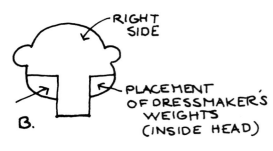

RIGHT SIDE

PLACEMENT OF DRESSMAKER'S WEIGHTS (INSIDE HEAD)

B.

line. Using tiny backstitches, sew head securely to body.

Stuff arms and shirt through bottom of body, then pin bottom closed. Now machine stitch to close.

Legs: With right sides facing, sew front and back boot pieces together, leaving top open. Turn right side out and stuff. Machine stitch closed. Using slipstitches, secure to bottom of body, as shown in Diagram C.

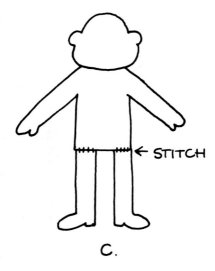

← STITCH

C.

Pants: With right sides facing, join pieces along curved stitching lines. See Diagram D. Open, and stitch inner leg seam. See Diagram E. Clip curves closely.

Turn down ½″ of fabric at waistband and stitch a casing, leaving 1″ open. Insert 16″ of elastic in opening. Stitch end of elastic at

14″ to fit waist. Topstitch opening closed.

To make cuffs, turn under ½″ of fabric at bottom of each pant leg. Topstitch around, leaving 1″ opening. Insert 6½″ of elastic, and stitch end to end at 5″. Topstitch opening closed.

Hat: With right sides facing, stitch front and back pieces together. Turn under ¼″ of fabric along bottom of hat and topstitch. Turn right side out. Stuff point and hat loosely, and pin to head. Hand sew in place with tiny, invisible stitches all around.

Cape: With right sides facing, stitch lining to outer cape, leaving 2″ opening at top for turning. Turn right side out and topstitch ¼″ from edge all around.

Arrange stars on back of cape. See Diagram F for correct placement. Secure stars with fabric glue (be sure to glue the points so they won't pop up).

F. STAR PLACEMENT

To make casing, fold ½″ along top of cape from back to front and topstitch all around, leaving opening on both ends. Insert approximately 1 yard of ⅜″ ribbon through casing, and gather. Place cape on body, gather close to neck, and tie a bow.

Nose: Sew all around nose circle with tiny running stitches, then pull and gather, leaving approximately 1″ open. See Diagram G.

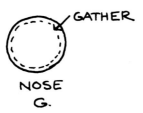

GATHER

NOSE
G.

Stuff and stitch closed. Hand stitch at back of nose to secure it to head.

Mouth and eyes: Embroider with backstitches. Hide knot for mouth under Merlin's neck; hide knots for eyes under hat.

Hair: For each side of head, loosely wind one yard of yarn into 1″ loops and stitch tops of loops together. See Diagram H. Pin to head and stitch in place.

Apply cosmetic blusher to cheeks.

SIDE HAIR

H.

D.

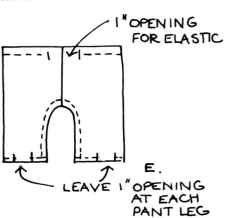

1″ OPENING FOR ELASTIC

E.

LEAVE 1″ OPENING AT EACH PANT LEG

PANT
CUT 2

FOLD

SHIRT

CUT

2

FOLD

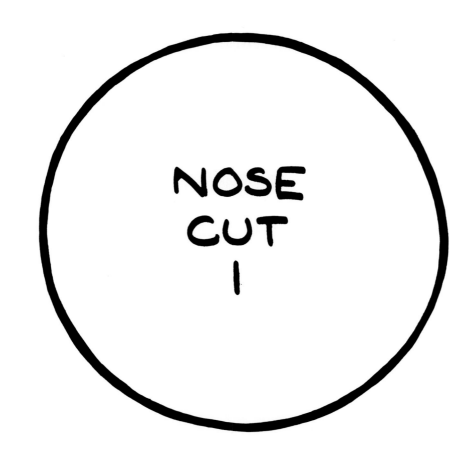

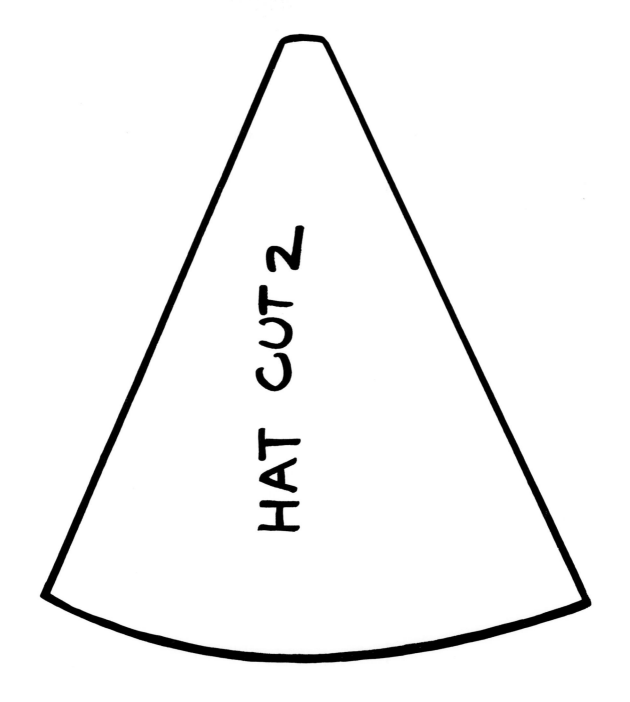

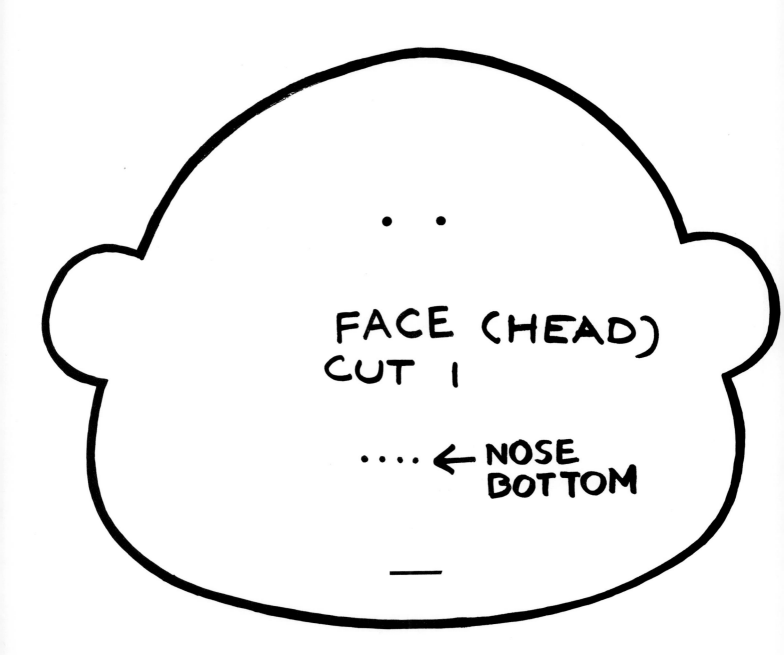

FACE (HEAD)
CUT 1

.... ← NOSE
BOTTOM

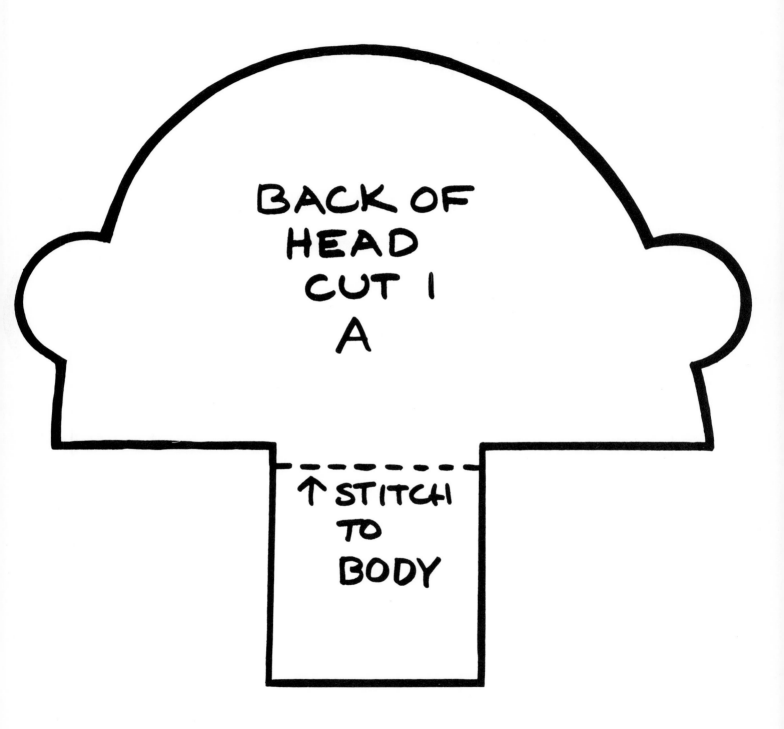

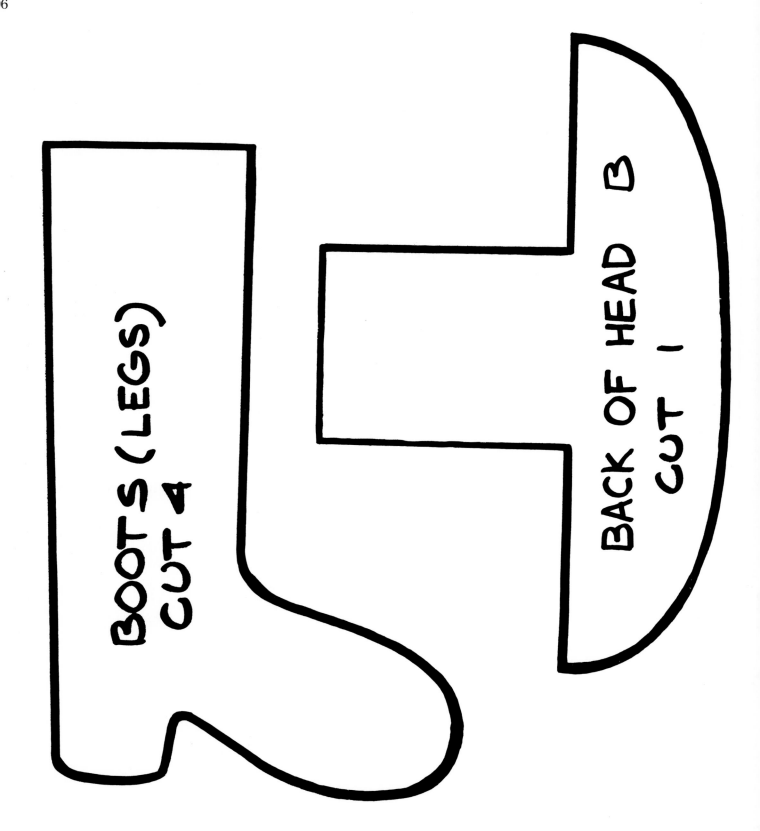

BOOTS (LEGS)
CUT 4

BACK OF HEAD B
CUT 1

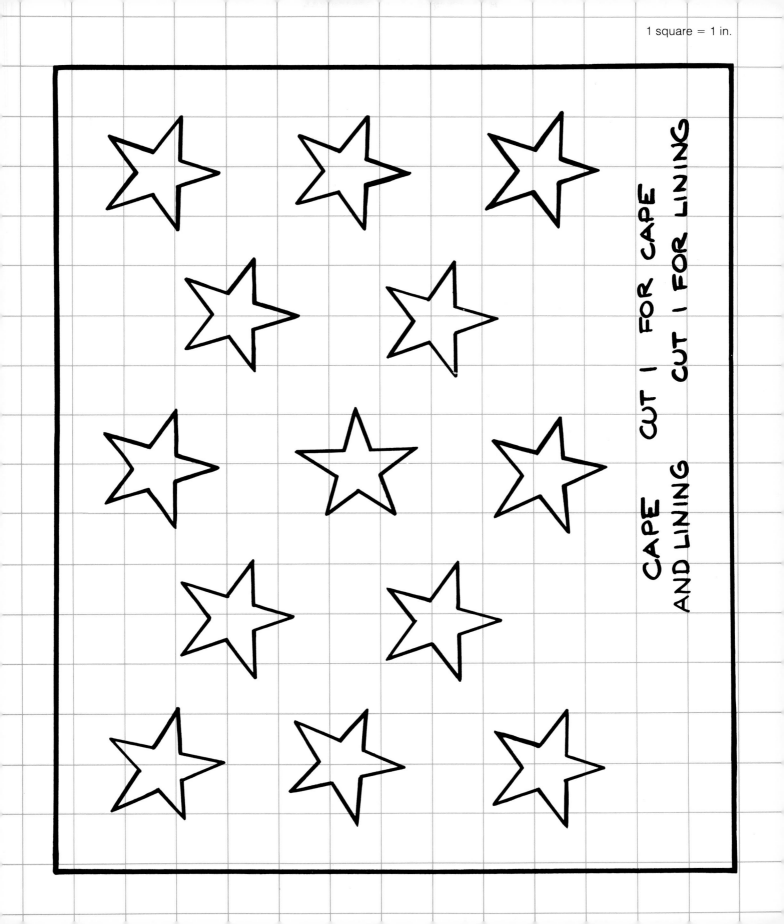

1 square = 1 in.

CAPE CUT 1 FOR CAPE

CUT 1 FOR LINING

CAPE AND LINING

Lovable Lucy

Here are the basics for making a very special Victorian doll. You'll add your own stamp of individuality to Lucy by creating her hands and dress. There are endless possible looks and uses for her: in addition to being a glamorous doll, she can also be made into a wonderful sachet or a special Christmas ornament.

SIZE: about 6½″ tall

MATERIALS

Fabrics: 8″ × 11″ piece of cotton or cotton blend for doll

6½″ × 9″ scrap or 2 scraps 4½″ × 6½″ of calico for dress

Threads: sewing threads to match

6-strand embroidery floss for gathering

Yarn: 10 to 15 yards of medium-weight (crewel or sport) yarn for hair

Trims: scrap trimmings, such as ½″-wide lace and ⅛″-wide ribbon for dress and hair

Stuffing: loose polyester fiberfill

Special Materials: waterproof, non-bleeding felt-tip markers for coloring

INSTRUCTIONS

See General Directions. Enlarge patterns, adding ¼″ seam allowance all around unless otherwise indicated.

Body: Transfer features and details onto fabric (see page 12). Color features, undies, boots, ribbons, buttons, and lace with permanent markers.

Cut out body patterns. Make ¼″ seams throughout. With right sides facing, sew pieces together along stitching lines, leaving 2″ opening along side. Clip curves, turn doll right side out, and stuff. Sew up opening.

Hair: For redhead, cut about twenty-five 8″ strands of yarn. Hold strands together and fold in half. Spread and pin folded edges over head seam at top and sides, then sew in place. Wrap more yarn around and around pencil to cover about ½″. Do not cut yarn, but slide loops from pencil and sew to front of head for curls. Make and sew 3 to 4 more bunches of curls. Cut fifteen 12″ strands of yarn. Braid at center for 4½″. Sew braid to top of head behind curls and allow ends to hang down each side, trimming to match length of back hair if necessary.

For blond, cut about forty-four 8″ strands of yarn. Divide into two bunches and fold each bunch in half. With pencil, lightly mark center-part line from center-top head seam down back to neck. Spread and pin each bunch of yarn to half of head with folded edges touching part. Sew along folds.

For brunette, cut forty-four 8″ strands of yarn and work as for redhead, omitting braid.

Dress: Double material and place pattern on fold. Cut out two dress pieces from fabric, adding ¼″ to all edges for seams and hems. Sew back and front together at sides and sleeves. Hem neck, wrist, and lower edges. Trim dress with lace and/or ribbons as shown in photograph. To gather neck, thread needle with three strands of floss and, starting at center front or back neck edge, sew running stitches around neck hem. Slip dress on doll, pull up gather, and tie floss in bow. Gather sleeves in same manner if desired.

Tie ribbons in hair as shown in photograph.

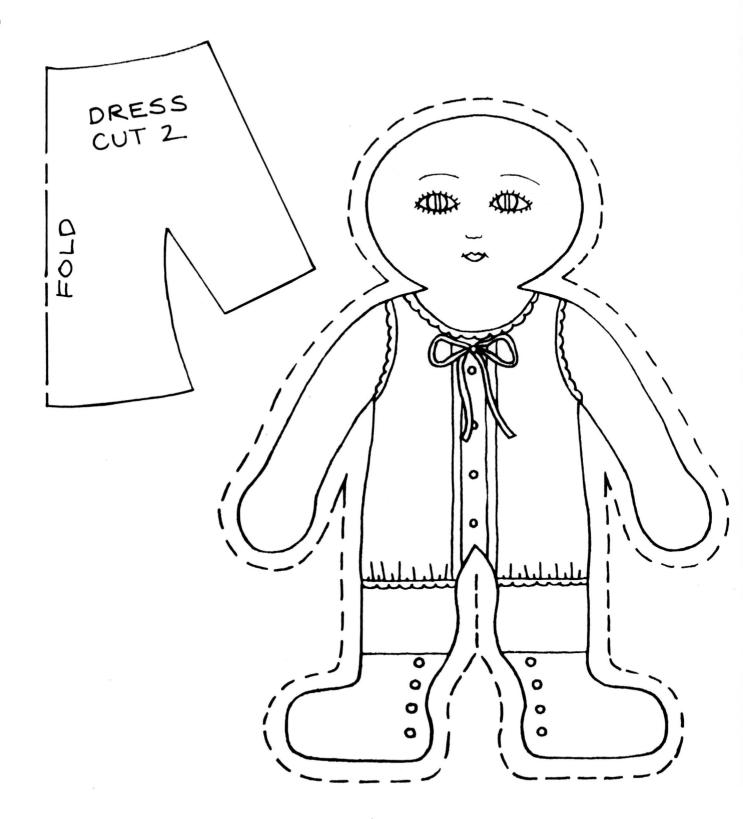

DRESS
CUT 2

FOLD

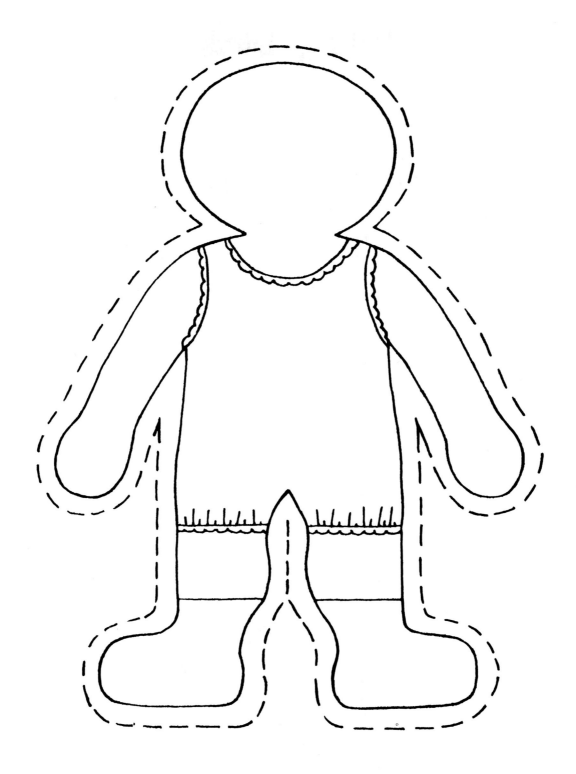

cowboy TEX

This rootin' tootin' character promises to keep any young cowhand rapt with his tales of the rodeo and the Wild West. He's also a great dancer, just in case you need a last-minute partner for the hoedown!

SIZE: about 41″ tall

MATERIALS

Fabrics: ¼ yard of 45″ skin-tone cotton or cotton blend for face and hands

¼ yard of 45″ plaid cotton or cotton blend for shirt

⅜ yard of 45″ denim for pants

¼ yard of 45″ red cotton or cotton blend for boots

scraps of brown felt for belt

Threads: sewing threads to match

embroidery floss for eyes

Yarn: 2 oz. knitting worsted yarn for hair

Trims: 1⅝″ metal belt buckle

bandana or kerchief

Stuffing: 2 lbs. of loose polyester fiberfill

INSTRUCTIONS

See General Directions. Enlarge patterns, adding ¼″ seam allowance all around unless otherwise indicated. Before cutting out patterns, embroider eyes with satin stitch. Cut out mouth from red scrap and glue to face. Place patterns on fold of material where indicated. Now cut out all pattern pieces. Make ¼″ seams throughout.

Body: For doll front, stitch head, pants, and hands to shirt. Stitch boots to pants. Now repeat these steps for back. Stitch front of body to back, with wrong sides facing. Leave about 8″ open at one side. Turn right side out, stuff, and sew up opening.

Nose: With wrong side facing, stitch front and back nose pieces together, leaving bottom open for stuffing. Clip seams and curves closely. Turn right side out, stuff, and sew up opening. Pin and stitch nose to face.

Ears: With right sides facing, stitch back and front ear pieces together, leaving straight edges open. Clip seams and curves closely. Turn right side out. Turn in open edges of ears. Pleat, topstitch along bottom edge, and sew to head.

Arms: Topstitch along stitching lines at shoulders.

Belt: Cut 1½″-wide strips of felt. Piece, if necessary, to 24″ length. Round off one end. Fold straight end over belt buckle and topstitch wih contrasting color. Work decorative topstitching onto belt.

Hair: Fold yarn in continuous 2″ loops, and stitch clumps of loops all over head. Sew a bunch of 2½″ loops below nose for mustache.

Knot kerchief or bandana around neck.

1 square = 1 in.

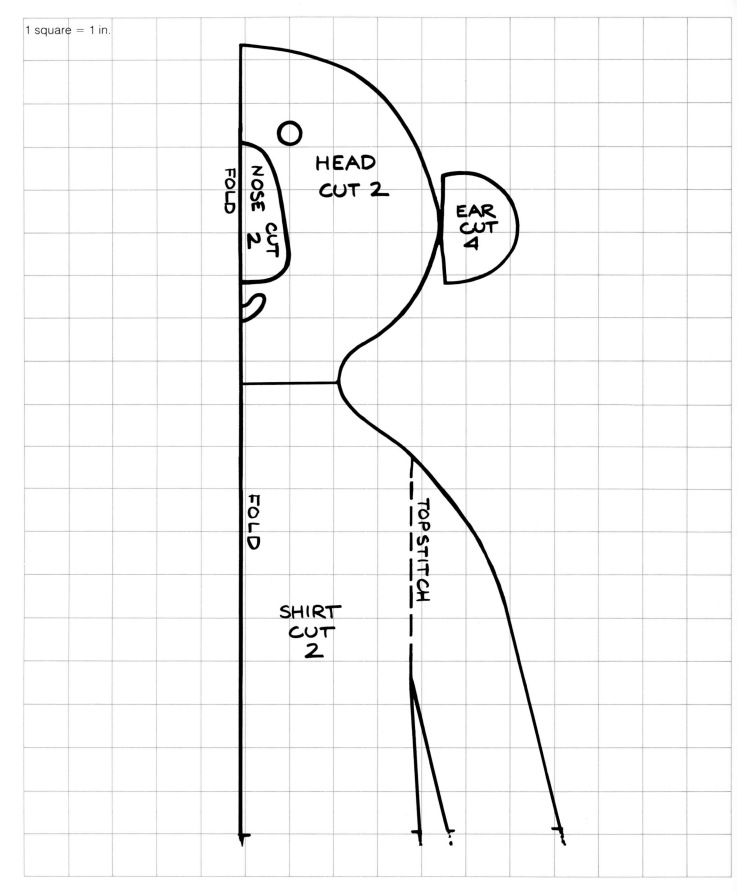

HEAD
CUT 2

NOSE
CUT
2

FOLD

EAR
CUT
4

FOLD

TOPSTITCH

SHIRT
CUT
2

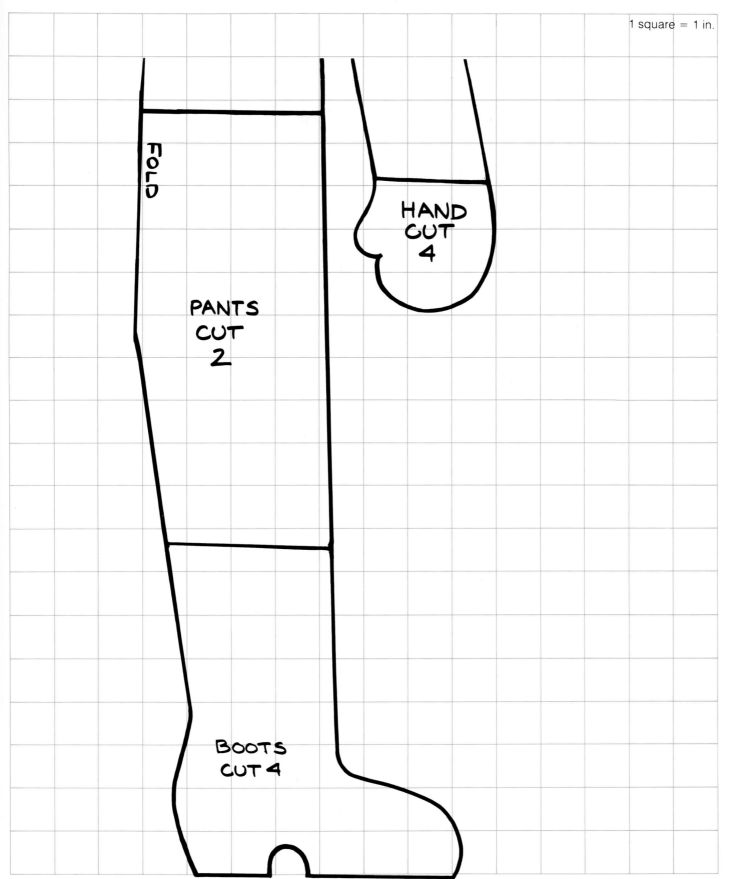

THE **Sunshine Kids**

Fresh-faced and eager to play, the Sunshine Kids can't wait to hit the sandbox. Their cheerful personalities and colorful summertime outfits are sure to keep the sun shining and chase the clouds away!

SIZE: each about 15″ tall

MATERIALS

Boy Doll

Fabrics: ½ yard of 45″ skin-tone cotton or cotton-blend fleece for face, ears, nose, legs, and hands

¼ yard of 45″ stretch terry for shirt

½ yard of 36″ bright-print cotton or cotton blend for pants

¼ yard of 36″ felt for cap

Threads: sewing threads to match

hot-pink and brown embroidery floss for face

aqua 6-strand embroidery floss for shoelaces

Yarn: approximately 20 yards of rust-color mohair or soft mohairlike yarn for hair

Trims: 6″ × 8″ felt or suedelike fabric scrap for shoes

3½″ × 3½″ scrap of white cotton for soles

2″ of ½″ ribbon for leg joints

Girl Doll

Fabrics: ¾ yard of 45″ skin-tone cotton or cotton-blend fleece for face, body, arms, and legs

¼ yard of 36″ bright heavy-weight cotton for sunhat

½ yard of 36″ cotton or cotton blend for sun dress and bloomers

¼ yard of 36″ white cotton knit for socks

Threads: sewing threads to match

Hot-pink and brown embroidery floss for face and shoelaces

Yarn: approximately 25 yards of brown mohair or mohairlike yarn for hair

Trims: 6″ × 8″ scrap of white cotton or cotton blend for shoes

3½″ × 3½″ scrap of darker cotton for soles

14″ of ¼″ ribbon for ties

2″ of ½″ ribbon for leg joints

1 yard of ¼″ eyelet trim for sun dress

13″ of ⅛″ elastic for sun dress and bloomers

For both:

Stuffing: loose polyester fiberfill

Special Materials: cosmetic blusher for cheeks

shirt cardboard

Elmer's® Tacky Glue

INSTRUCTIONS

For both

See General Directions. Enlarge patterns, adding ¼″ seam allowance all around unless otherwise indicated. Cut out all pattern pieces. Be sure to place edges of sunhat brim pattern on fold of material where indicated. Make ¼″ seams throughout.

Boy Doll

Head: With right sides facing, sew back of head pieces A and B together. With right sides facing, sew face to back of head, leaving opening at bottom. Clip seams and curves closely. Turn right side out and stuff tightly. Do not sew up bottom opening yet.

Arms: Pin hands to shirt sleeves and stitch in place. With right sides facing, sew front arm pieces to back arm pieces. Clip seams and curves closely. Turn right side out and stuff tightly, leaving opening at top. Turn under raw edges at top of arm, gather and stitch closed. See Diagram A.

A.

Body (shirt): With right sides facing, sew front of shirt to back, leaving 2″ opening at bottom for stuffing. Clip seams and curves closely. Turn right side out and stuff. Sew up opening.

Legs: With right sides facing, sew leg front and back pieces together. Clip seams and curves closely. Turn right side out and stuff. Turn under raw edges, gather ends as for arms, and stitch to secure.

Assembly: Position head so that opening fits over neck bump on top of body. Push head down, pin in place, and secure with tiny slipstitches. Head should be flush with body. See Diagram B.

B.

Push in gathered ends of arms so that they are flush with body. Pin arms in place, and stitch to body with tiny slipstitches.

For each leg, cut 1″ length of ½″ ribbon, and sew one end to gathered top of leg. Sew other end to body so that there is ½″ of ribbon between leg and body. See Diagram B. This gives leg mobility for sitting or moving.

Pants: With right sides facing, stitch along center crotch seams A and B. See Diagram C. Then open, and stitch around inner leg seam, as shown in Diagram D. Turn right side out. Turn ¼″ of fabric under at waistband, and topstitch around. Turn under ¼″ at bottom of each leg and topstitch.

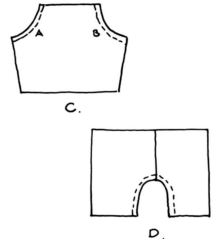

C.

D.

Straps: Press under ¼″ hem on each side of strap pieces, then topstitch. Pin straps to pants, crisscrossing in back. Secure straps to front and back of pants with tiny stitches.

Shoes: With right sides facing, stitch end D to end E along seam line. See Diagram E. With right sides facing, pin shoe to sole, and baste. Machine stitch to secure. Turn right side out and place shoe on foot. Turn under ¼″ of fabric at top of shoe. See Diagram F.

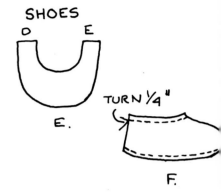

SHOES

TURN ¼″

E.

F.

There will be about ¼″ gap at front of shoe. Pinch sides 1 and 2 together to create the look of a real shoe, then secure with tacking stitch. See Diagram G.

G.

Laces: Using 6-strand embroidery floss, lace up shoe, following numbers in Diagram H. Pull needle up through fabric at #1, then work through numbers 2-7,

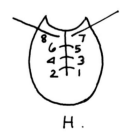

H.

as shown. Leave about 4″ of floss hanging, like a shoelace. Re-thread needle and pull floss from underneath on top left side of shoe at point number 8. Leave 4″ hanging. Knot each end of "shoelace", then tie laces in a bow.

Baseball cap (not shown): With right sides facing, stitch four pieces of crown together. Sew center seams first, then side seams. Turn crown right side out. Stitch brim to crown of cap so that right sides face. See Diagram I.

BASEBALL CAP

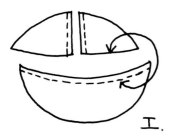

Ears: With right sides facing, stitch together along stitching line. Clip seams and curves closely. Turn right side out. Fold fabric under ¼″ along bottom edge and secure to head with tiny stitches.

Nose: Working on wrong side of fabric, run tiny gathering stitches around edge of nose. Gather, leaving ½″ opening. Stuff nose and sew up opening. Stitch to head, as indicated on pattern.

Face: *Note:* You can embroider the features before or after stuffing the head, but if you do it after, do not make knots in the embroidery floss. Instead, insert thread and lose end in stuffing (see page 16).

Use small backstitches for mouth, and small satin stitches for eyes.

Add cosmetic blusher for cheek color.

Hair: Wrap yarn around a ⅝″ cylinder, such as a marking pen, to a width of 3″. Stitch along top of loops, and slide yarn off cylinder. Twist yarn for a tousled look. Pin loops along forehead and stitch in place. Wrap and stitch enough yarn loops to fill out back of head spiraling in from edges toward center back of head. See Diagram J.

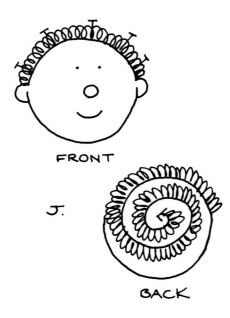

Girl Doll

Follow Boy Doll instructions for making head, body, arms, and legs, and for assembling parts. Use skin-tone fabric for Girl's body, rather than shirt fabric used for Boy.

Sun dress: Stitch short ends of strip together. Turn right side out. For casing, press under ½″ of fabric along top. Topstitch ¼″ from fold, leaving opening for elastic. Insert 13″ of elastic into casing, and sew ends together at 12″. Arrange gathers evenly. Topstitch opening closed. Hem, and edge bottom of skirt with ¼″ eyelet trim. Place sun dress on doll body.

Straps: Press under ¼″ of fabric along each long edge of strap. Fold strap in half lengthwise, stitch, and add trim to outer edges. Pin and stitch straps to front and back of sun dress.

Bloomers: Follow instructions for Boy Doll's pants, but cut pattern on "Bloomer Line," adding ¼″ seam allowance. Turn under seam allowance on each leg, and gather to fit. Secure with small stitches. Sew bloomers to legs.

Socks: Use leg pattern to cut out socks. With right sides facing, sew fronts and backs of socks together. Turn right side out. Fold raw edge under ½″. Then fold down again to make cuff. See Diagram K.

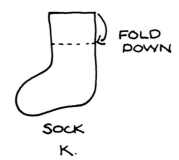

Shoes: Follow instructions for Boy Doll's shoes.

Sunhat: For brim, sew right sides together along outer edge only. Turn to right side. Press, and top-stitch along outer edge.

Crown of hat: With right sides facing, sew center seams. Then sew sides, as shown in Diagram L. Clip seams and curves closely. Turn right side out. Baste crown to inner edge of hat brim. Machine stitch crown to brim inside hat. Press seam allowance up into crown of hat. Sew ribbon-tie to each side of hat. See Diagram M.

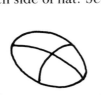

L. CROWN OF HAT

SUNHAT
M.

Hair: For bangs, wrap yarn around 2½″ × 8½″ piece of cardboard. Hand stitch along top, and slide yarn off cardboard. Pin yarn to crown of head. See Diagram N. Stitch in place.

N.

For back of hair, wrap yarn around 4½″ × 5″ piece of cardboard. Hand stitch along top, and slide yarn off cardboard. Pin to top of head, just behind bangs, and stitch in place.

To give hair a feathered look, hold scissors at an angle and trim. See Diagram O.

APPLY GLUE TO UNDERNEATH

O.

To keep hair in place, run a line of Elmer's® Tacky Glue under forehead, and another line on back of head about 2″ from top of crown.

1 square = 1 in.

SUNDRESS
CUT 1

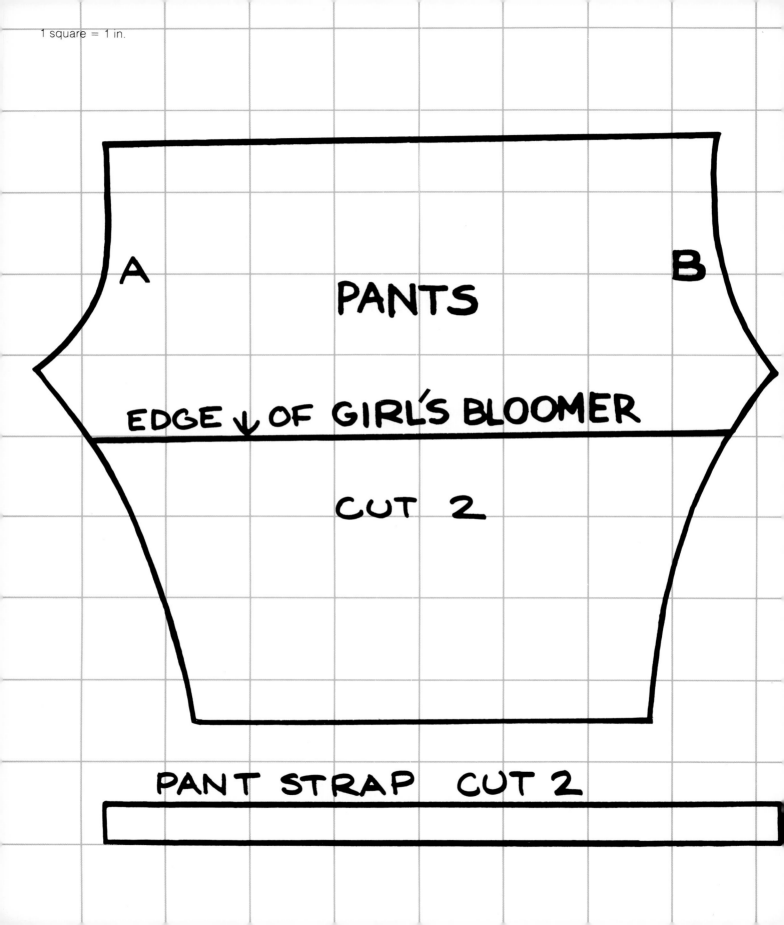

1 square = 1 in.

A

B

PANTS

EDGE ↓ OF GIRL'S BLOOMER

CUT 2

PANT STRAP   CUT 2

SUNDRESS STRAP

FOLD

CUT 2

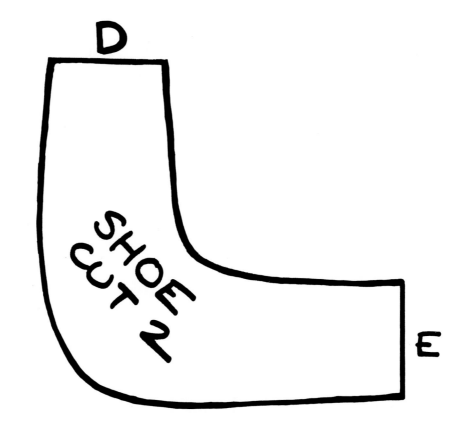

D

SHOE
CUT 2

E

114

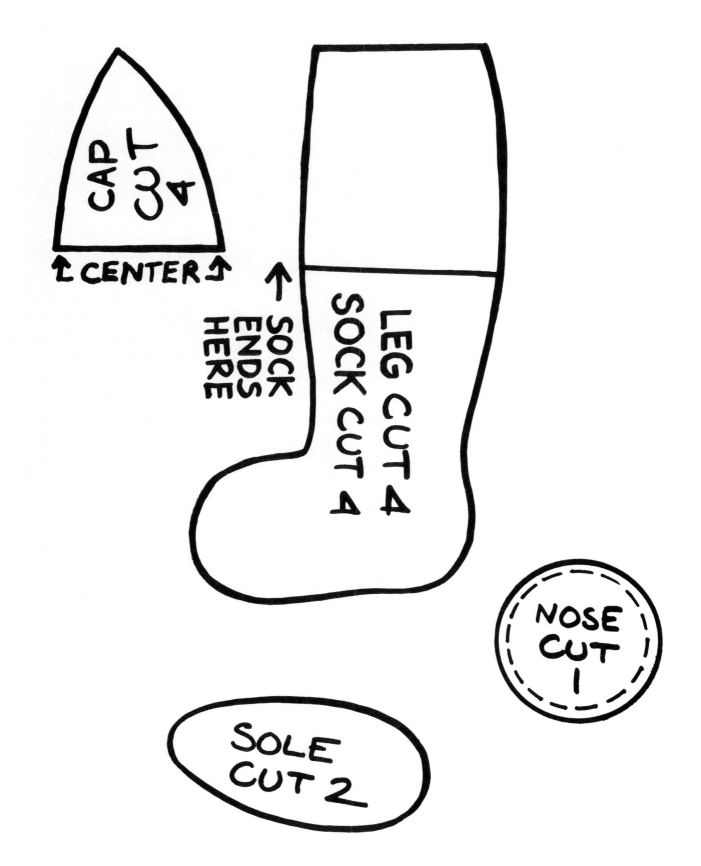

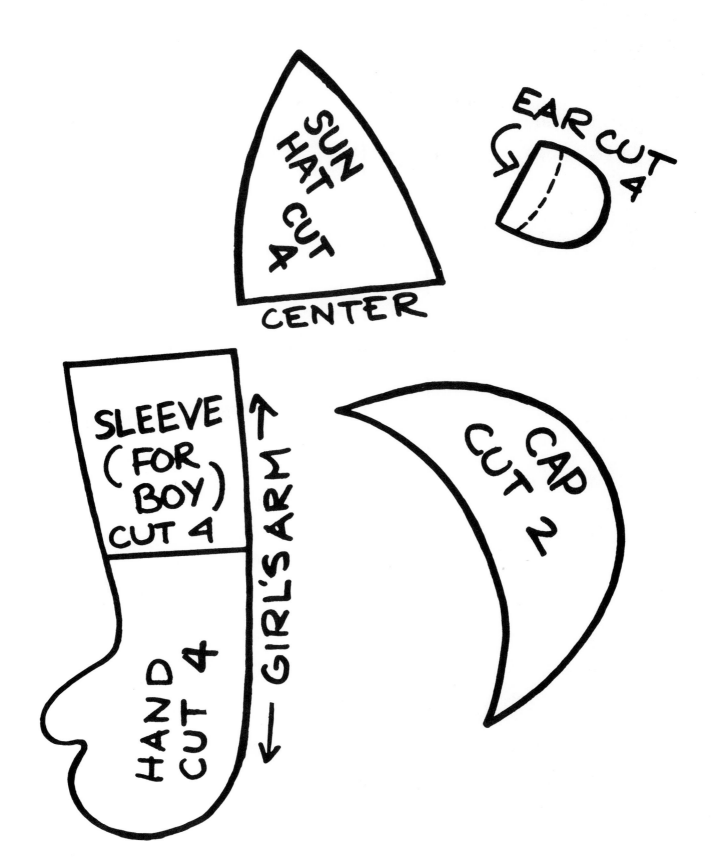

116

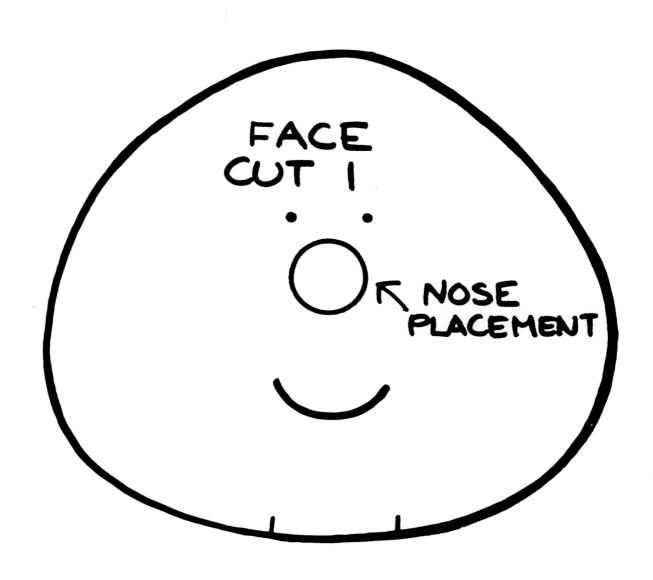

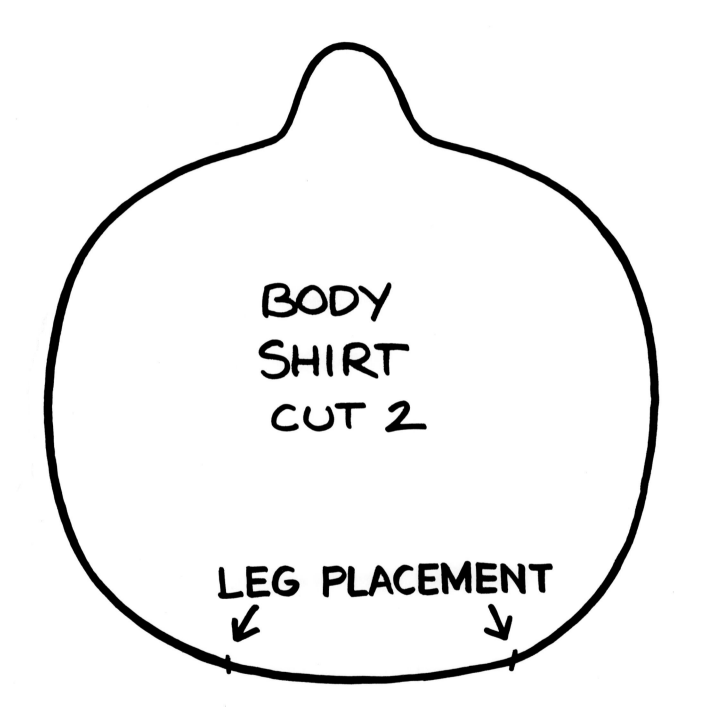

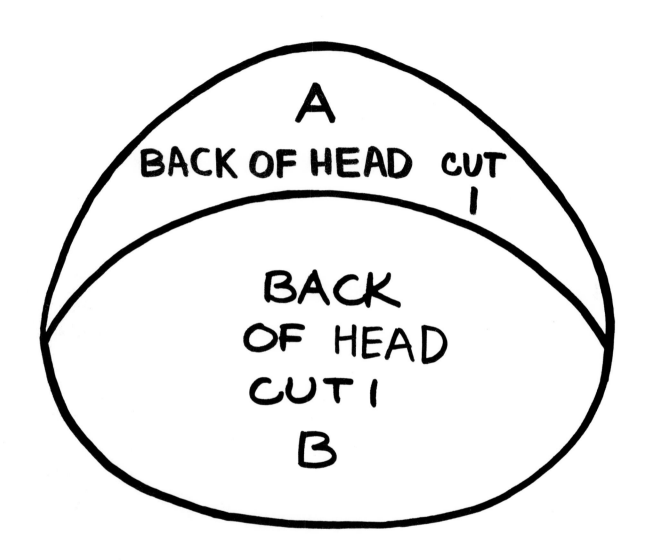

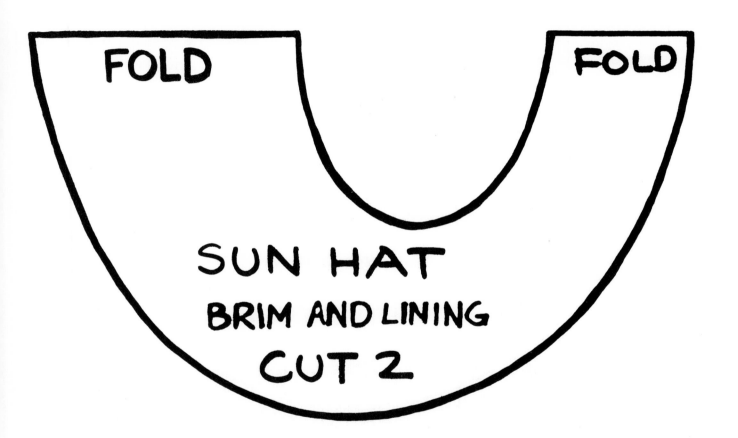

Pajama Bag Man

You can make this colorful, comical character as a cheerful reminder that the pajamas inside are being very well guarded until the next night. Fill him from a slit in the belly, and watch how he fills out!

SIZE: about 23″ tall

MATERIALS

Fabrics: ½ yard of 45″ cotton or cotton blend for hat

½ yard of 36″ skin-tone cotton for face, nose, and hands

½ yard of 45″ print cotton or cotton blend for shirt and arms

¼ yard of 36″ solid cotton or cotton blend for tie

½ yard of 36″ print cotton or cotton blend for pants

¼ yard of 36″ solid cotton or cotton blend for boots

Threads: sewing threads to match

Yarn: 4 yards of yarn for mustache

Trims: scraps of blue and white felt for eyes

2″ pompon (purchase, or see How To Make Pompons, page 16)

Stuffing: loose polyester fiberfill

Special Materials: shirt cardboard
plastic glasses (optional)
Elmer's® Tacky Glue (optional)

INSTRUCTIONS

See General Directions. Enlarge patterns, adding ¼″ seam allowance all around unless otherwise indicated. Cut out all pattern pieces. Make ¼″ seams throughout.

Body: Sew back of shirt A to back of pants A. Sew back of shirt B to back of pants B. See Diagram A.

With right sides facing, stitch back right to back left, leaving 8½″ opening in center of seam. See Diagram B. Press seam open and topstitch.

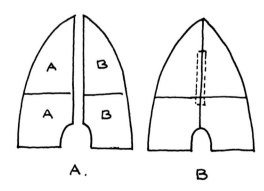

A. **B.**

Sew front of shirt to front of pants. On right side, topstitch along waist of pants. With right sides facing, stitch front and back of body together, leaving openings for arms and legs, as indicated on pattern. See Diagram C. Leave body wrong side out.

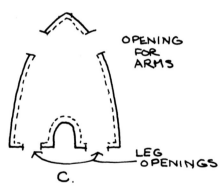

OPENING FOR ARMS

LEG OPENINGS

C.

With right sides facing, sew hands onto arms. Sew an arm front to each arm back. Clip seams closely. Turn right side out and stuff. Insert arms into arm openings of body, pin in place, and stitch on wrong side. See Diagram D (page 122). Turn body right side out.

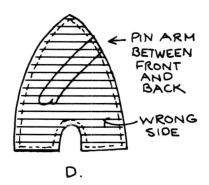

← PIN ARM BETWEEN FRONT AND BACK

← WRONG SIDE

D.

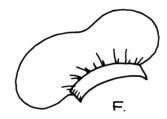

F.

Hat: Run a row of small gathering stitches around edge of circle. Sew narrow ends of band together. Fold band in half, wrong sides facing and raw edges up. Press under raw edges. Gather large circle to fit headband, as shown in Diagram F. Pin circle edge in place

between edges of headband. Stitch through all layers.

Place hat on head, then flatten, as shown in photograph. Stitch hat to head with a few tacking stitches in center. Glue or stitch pompon in place. Tack hat to head with small stitches on sides.

Tie: With right sides facing, sew front of tie to back, leaving opening on top. Turn right side out and press. Cut out 2½″ × 2½″ piece of fabric to match. Press under ½″ all around. Fold square over tie so it looks like a tie knot, and stitch on back. See Diagram G. Pin tie in place under doll's chin. Tack-stitch to secure.

Add plastic glasses if desired.

Boots: With right sides facing, stitch back and front boot pieces together, leaving opening on top. Clip corners closely. Turn right side out and stuff. Insert boots into leg openings. Pin in place, and sew up openings.

Face: With right sides facing, sew back and front pieces together, leaving 3″ opening. Clip seams and curves closely. Turn right side out and stuff. Sew up opening.

Nose: With right sides facing, sew back pieces A and B together, leaving 1″ opening at center for stuffing. With right sides facing, sew front of nose to back. Clip seams and curves closely. Turn right side out, stuff, and sew up opening. Stitch back of nose to head.

Eyes: Cut pieces out of felt scraps. Glue to face.

Mustache: Wind yarn around 2½″ × 2″ piece of cardboard. Using overcast stitches, sew along top. Slide yarn off cardboard, stitch mustache to underside of nose. Clip bottoms of yarn loops open and trim mustache.

Position head on body and stitch from underneath on back side, as shown in Diagram E.

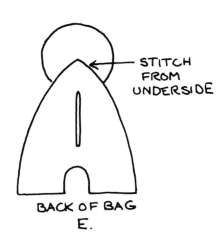

← STITCH FROM UNDERSIDE

BACK OF BAG
E.

G.

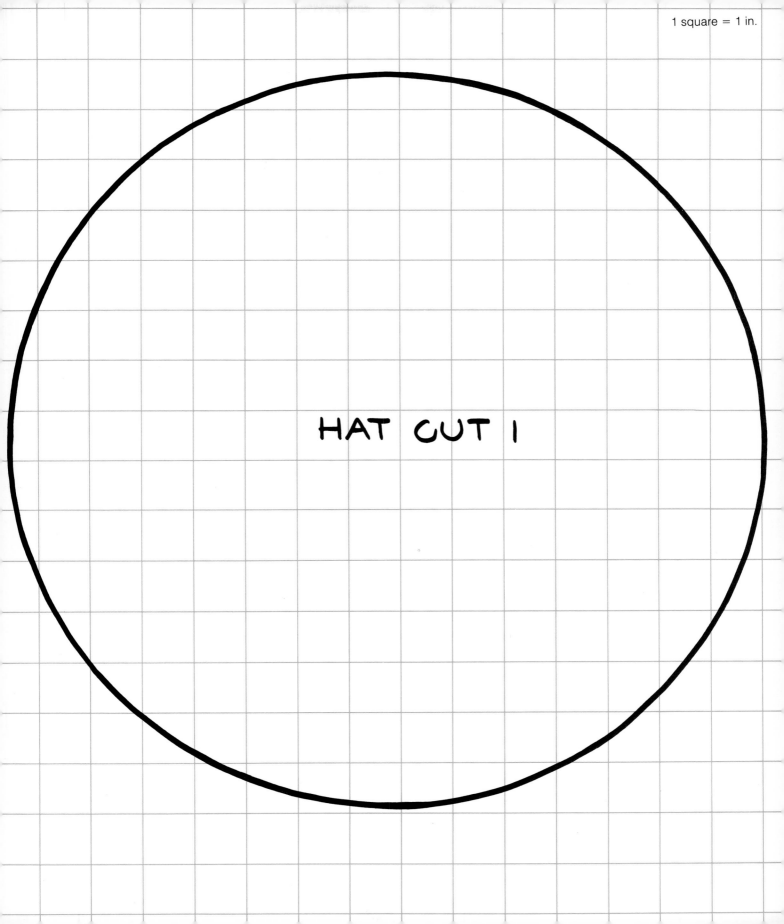

1 square = 1 in.

HAT CUT 1

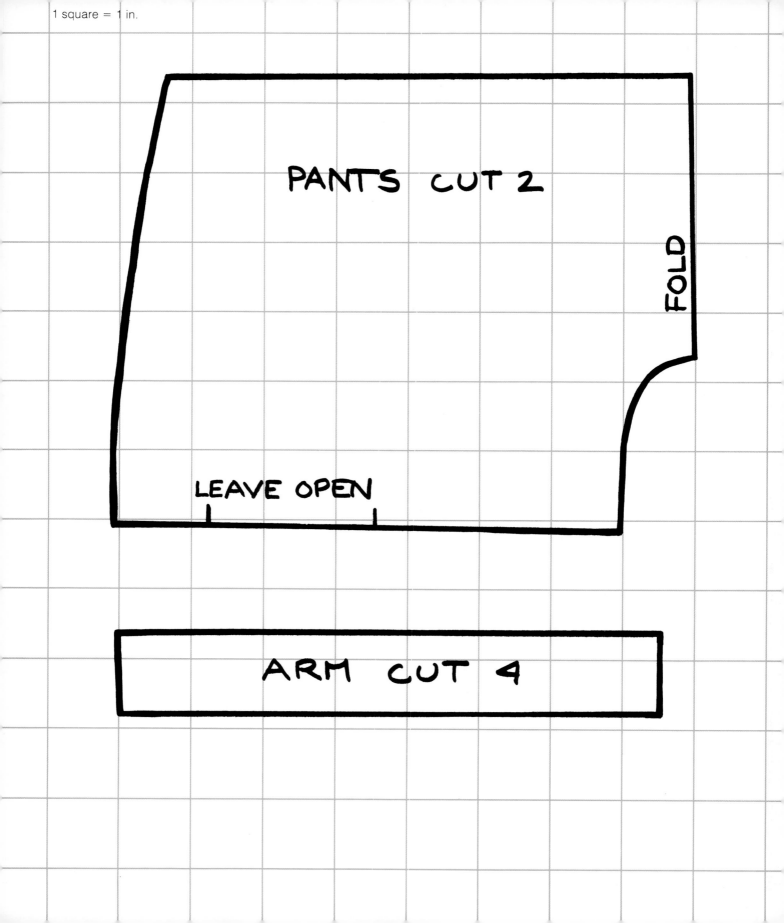

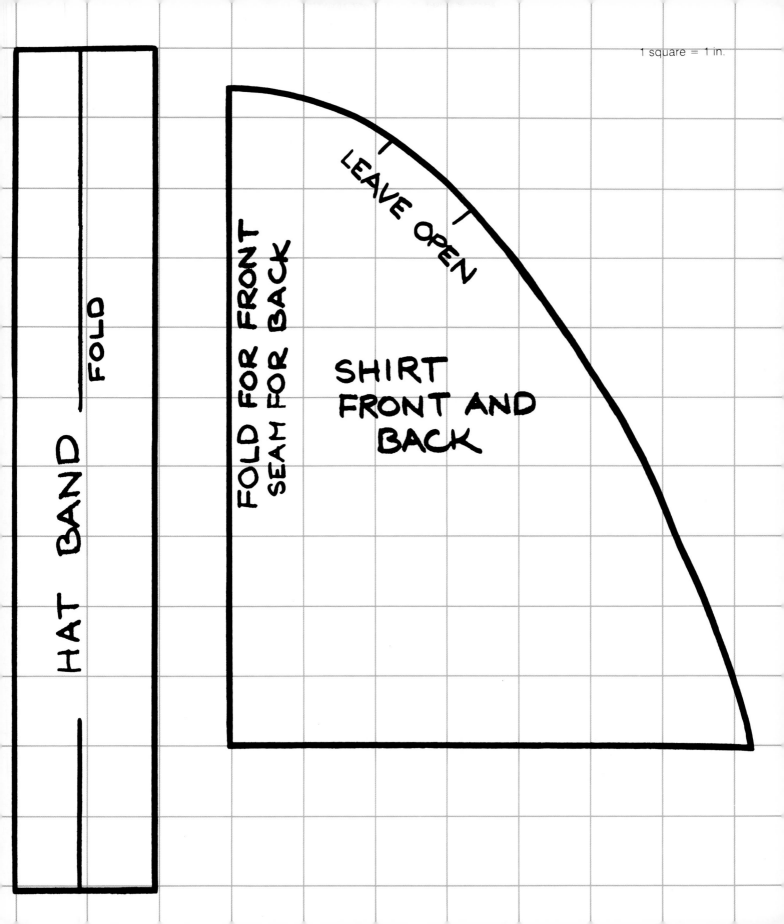

1 square = 1 in.

HAT BAND

FOLD

LEAVE OPEN

FOLD FOR FRONT
SEAM FOR BACK

SHIRT
FRONT AND
BACK

CUT PIECES
A AND B FOR
BACK. CUT CIRCLE
AS ONE PIECE
FOR FRONT

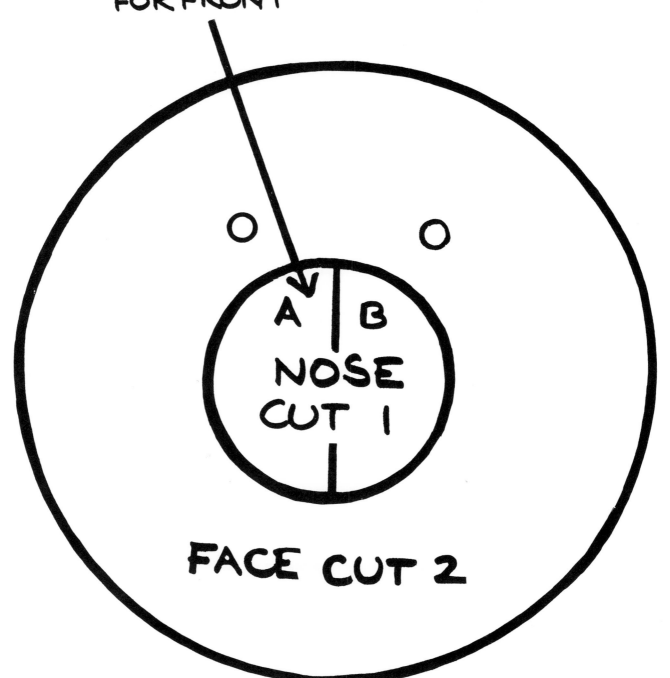

A B

NOSE
CUT 1

FACE CUT 2

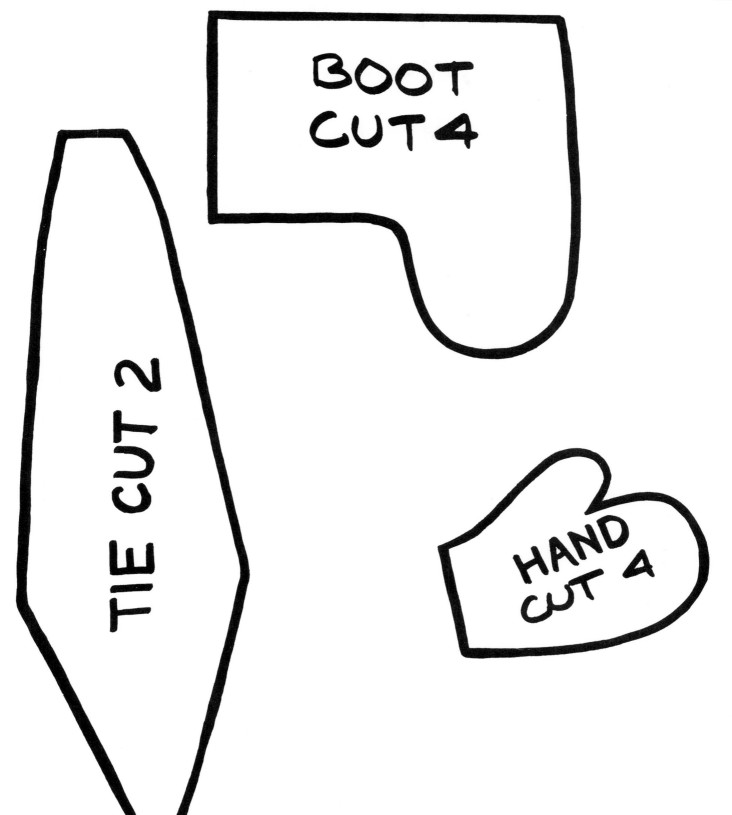

Green Grunshie

Easy to make and fun to hug. You can't deny it's great to have a Grunshie around! If he seems a bit grumpy at times, a day at the beach is all it takes to put him in the pink.

SIZE: about 18″ tall

MATERIALS

Fabrics: ¾ yard of 45″ green polyester/cotton fleece for body

½ yard of 36″ brightly colored cotton or cotton blend for shorts

2½″ × 4½″ scrap of pink stretch terry for nose

Threads: sewing threads to match

Yarn: 18 yards of bright-colored yarn for hair

Trims: 14″ of ⅛″ elastic for shorts

1″ × 1″ square of purple felt for eyes

Stuffing: loose polyester fiberfill

Special Materials: shirt cardboard

white glue (such as Elmer's®) or fabric glue

INSTRUCTIONS

See General Directions. Enlarge patterns, adding ¼″ seam allowance all around unless otherwise indicated. Place patterns on fold of material where indicated. Cut out all pattern pieces. Make ¼″ seams throughout.

Body: With right sides facing, stitch two halves of body back together, leaving 3″ opening. With right sides facing, stitch top A to bottom B. See Diagram A. Then stitch back to front. Clip corners and seams closely. Turn right side out and stuff tightly. Hand stitch back opening closed.

Nose: Stitch two halves of back together with right sides facing, leaving 1″ opening at center. Stitch front to back. Clip seams and curves closely. Turn right side out, stuff, and sew up opening. Tack to face from center back of nose.

Shorts: With right sides facing, stitch front and back crotch seams. See Diagram B. Then open, and stitch inner legs. See Diagram C. Turn down ½″ of fabric at waistband. Stitch all around, leaving 1″ opening. Insert elastic, and sew up opening. Hem and topstitch short legs.

Hair: Wrap 18 yards of yarn around 2″ × 8½″ piece of cardboard. Stitch along top. Slide yarn off cardboard, pin to head, and stitch in place. Trim hair evenly.

Eyes: Cut out ¼″-diameter felt circles. Glue in place.

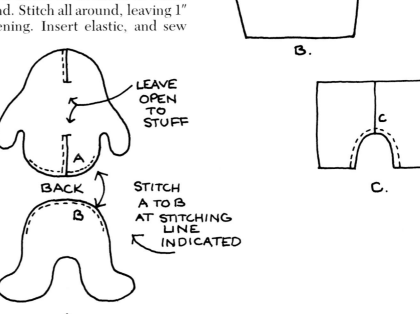

A.

B.

C.

LEAVE OPEN TO STUFF

BACK

STITCH A TO B AT STITCHING LINE INDICATED

1 square = 1 in.

TOP OF
NOSE

BODY FRONT
CUT 1

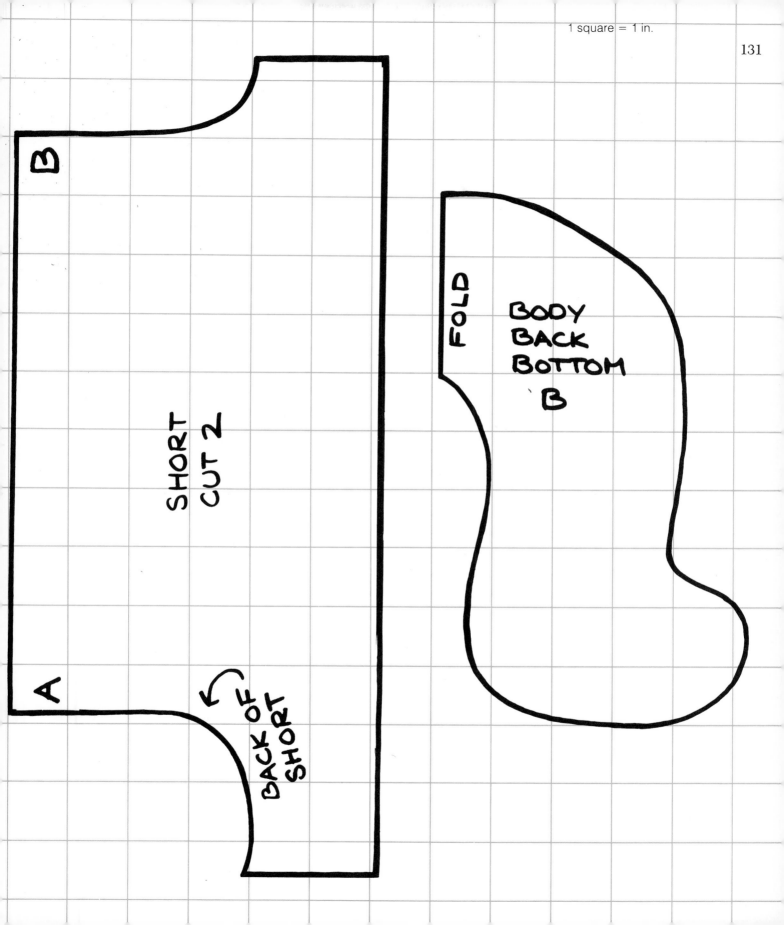

1 square = 1 in.

131

B

A

SHORT
CUT 2

BACK OF
SHORT

FOLD

BODY
BACK
BOTTOM
B

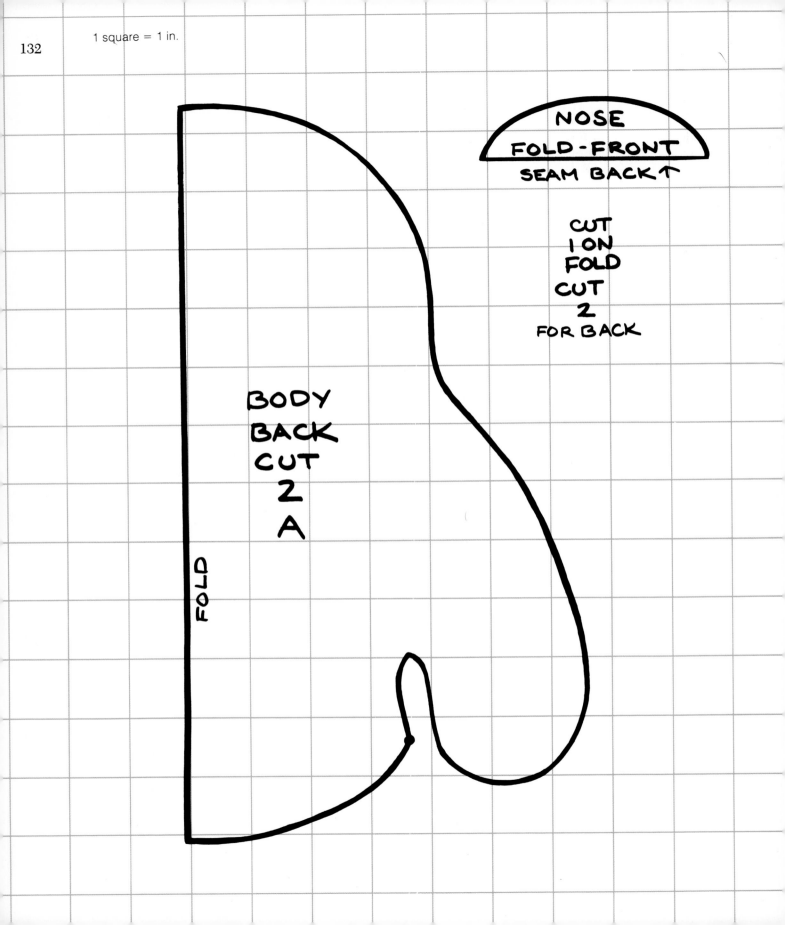

132   1 square = 1 in.

NOSE
FOLD-FRONT
SEAM BACK↑

CUT
1 ON
FOLD
CUT
2
FOR BACK

BODY
BACK
CUT
2
A

FOLD

PRIMA BALLERINA

On her toes and ready to dance, this prima ballerina does some fancy stepping! Hang her from a string and raise her leg. Then give her a push, and she'll perform a perfect pirouette.

SIZE: about 22″ tall

MATERIALS

Fabrics: ½ yard of 45″ white cotton or cotton-blend muslin for body, legs, and nose

½ yard of 36″ white cotton interfacing for face backing

¼ yard of 45″ satin for bodice and slippers

½ yard of 45″ pink tulle and ½ yard of 45″ purple tulle for tutu skirt

Threads: sewing threads to match

blue and brown embroidery floss for face

Yarn: approximately 60 yards of yarn for hair

Trims: ¾ yard of silver sequins for bodice, straps, and hair

⅜″-diameter shirt button for nose

48″ of ⅛″ ribbon for laces

Stuffing: loose polyester fiberfill

Special Materials: pink colored pencil for cheeks

shirt cardboard

INSTRUCTIONS

See General Directions. Enlarge patterns, adding ¼″ seam allowance all around unless otherwise indicated.

Use thin white cotton interfacing as a backing for Ballerina's face.

Transfer features to body front (see page 12), and embroider before cutting out pattern. Now cut out all pattern pieces. Make ¼″ seams throughout.

Body: With right sides facing, stitch front to back, leaving opening at bottom. Use small machine stitches for smooth curves. Turn right side out and stuff. Machine stitch opening closed.

Legs and slippers: With right sides facing, stitch legs to slippers, front and back. See Diagram A. Then stitch right and left half of each leg together. Clip seams closely. Turn right side out. Stuff to about

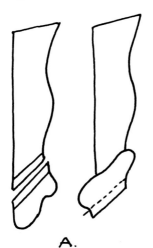

A.

¾″ from opening. Then sew up opening.

Stitch legs to body so that left leg overlaps right one. This will allow legs to move easily. See Diagram B.

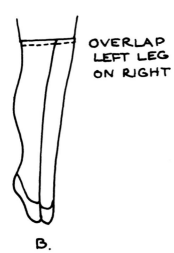

OVERLAP LEFT LEG ON RIGHT

B.

Bodice: With right sides facing, stitch two pieces of costume top together along sides and curved top, leaving opening in bottom. Turn right side out and press. Sew sequin trim along top edge.

Skirt: Cut pink and purple tulle into five pieces, each 48″ × 4½″. Lay strips one on top of the other, alternating colors. Then machine-

gather ¼″ from top. Gather to 9½″. With right sides facing, stitch skirt to satin bodice, as indicated in Diagram C. Smooth skirt down and press seam up toward bodice. Place on doll. Pin back of bodice closed, then hand stitch.

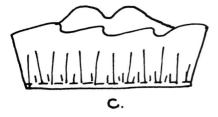

C.

Laces: Crisscross 24″ of ribbon on top of each slipper. See Diagram D. Tack ribbon in place.

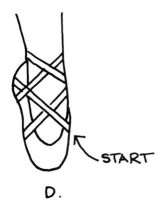

START

D.

Dress straps: Use sequin trim. Attach to front of bodice. Crisscross in back, and attach.

Nose: Cut circle of muslin ¼″ larger all around than button. Gather ⅛″ from edge. Pull fabric tightly around button and knot, then stitch button nose securely in place.

Hair: Wrap yarn around 8½″ × 6″ piece of cardboard. Stitch along top, and slide yarn off cardboard. Pin hair to back of head, as indicated in Diagram E. Pull hair forward to top and front of head. Stitch in place, and tie into topknot. Divide into four parts. Twist each part around into tight curl, and pin to create a bun on top. Stitch to secure.

BACK OF HEAD

E.

For bangs, wrap yarn around a cylinder, such as a roll of coins or a fat marking pen, about 30 times to fill 2½″. Stitch along top. Slide yarn off cylinder and twist around to create curly bangs. Pin in place. Stitch to secure.

Add sequin band to fit around base of bun. Using 8″ × 3″ piece of tulle, tie once and stitch on to create a bow.

Rouge cheeks with colored pencil.

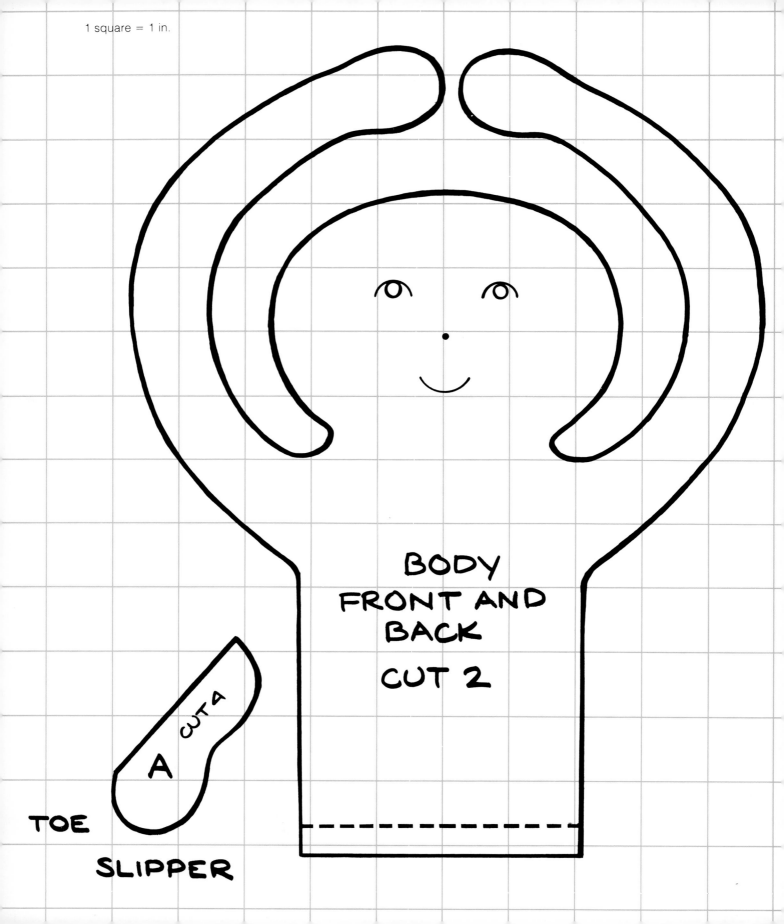

1 square = 1 in.

BODY
FRONT AND
BACK
CUT 2

CUT 4
A

TOE

SLIPPER

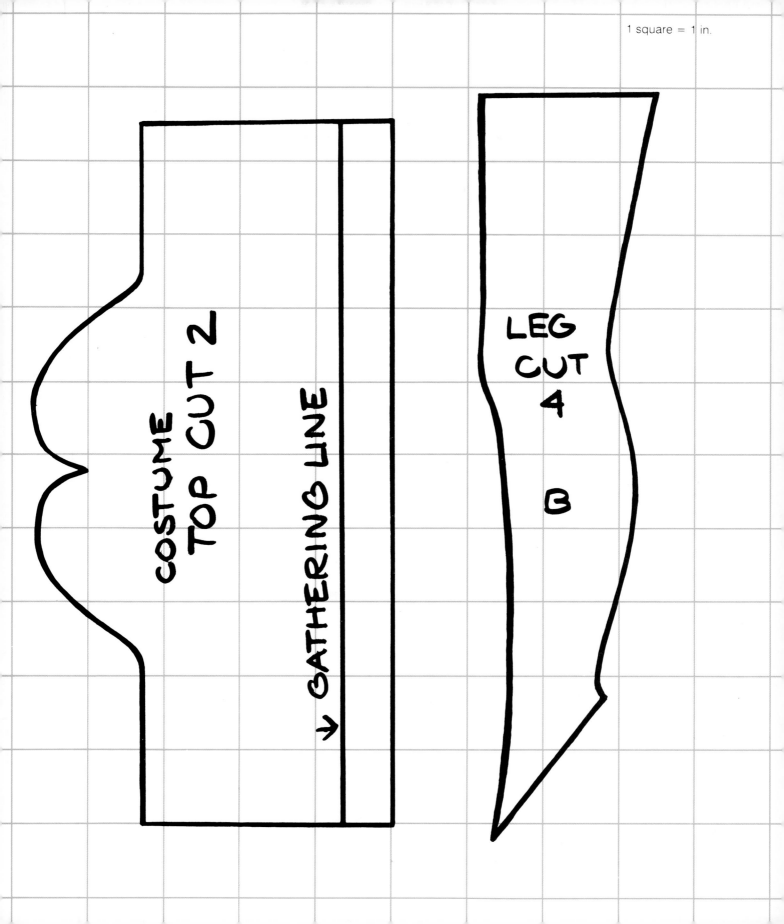

1 square = 1 in.

COSTUME
TOP CUT 2

↓ GATHERING LINE

LEG
CUT
4

B

Aunt Minna AND Uncle Gus

These days, Minna and Gus spend most of their time just holding hands and sharing memories of the old days. To look at these two now, it's hard to believe they used to be the most daring high-wire acrobats under the big top!

SIZE: about 28″ tall

MATERIALS

Aunt Minna

Fabrics: ¼ yard of 36″ unbleached muslin for head, face, and hands

⅝ yard of 45″ printed cotton or cotton blend for dress and arms

½ yard of 45″ gingham-checked cotton or cotton blend for apron

¼ yard of 45″ striped cotton or cotton blend for legs

⅜ yard of 45″ black cotton or cotton blend for boots

¼ yard of 45″ printed cotton or cotton blend for bloomers

Threads: sewing threads to match

blue and red 6-strand embroidery floss for features

Yarn: approximately 75 yards of knitting worsted for hair

Trim: 6″-diameter circle of lace fabric for snood

Uncle Gus

Fabrics: ½ yard of 36″ unbleached muslin for head, face, hands, legs, and ears

⅝ yard of 45″ denim for pants

½ yard of 45″ printed cotton or cotton blend for shirt and arms

⅜ yard of 36″ black cotton or cotton blend for boots

¼ yard of 36″ white cotton or cotton blend for shorts

Threads: sewing threads to match

blue and brown 6-strand embroidery floss for features

Yarn: approximately 33 yards of knitting worsted for hair and mustache

Trims: 8″ × 5¼″ scrap of cotton or cotton blend for bow tie

1 yard of ½″ ribbon or elastic for suspenders

Three ⅛″-diameter flat studs for pants

For both

Stuffing: loose polyester fiberfill

Special Materials: watercolor or Dr. Ph. Martin's® dye for cheeks

shirt cardboard

INSTRUCTIONS

For both

See General Directions. Enlarge patterns, adding ¼″ seam allowance all around unless otherwise indicated. Cut out all pattern pieces. Make ¼″ seams throughout.

Aunt Minna

Head: Transfer eyes to face pieces (see page 12), and embroider eyes with satin stitch. Add cheek coloring with watercolor or Dr. Ph. Martin's® dye. Allow to dry.

With right sides facing, pin and stitch head pieces A and B together for left and right sides. See Diagram A. Then stitch up center of head, joining left and right sides, leaving opening at bottom of neck for stuffing. Set aside.

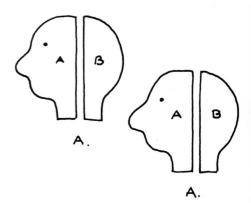

Body: Stitch front of bloomers to front of dress top. Stitch back of bloomers to back of dress top. With right sides facing, stitch front and back together, leaving openings for arms and neck, and an opening on one side for stuffing. Leave body wrong side out.

Arms: With right sides facing, pin hands to arms and stitch. For each

arm, fold piece lengthwise, right sides facing, and stitch along seam line. Leave top edge open. Turn right side out and stuff to within 1″ of top edge. Insert arms into openings at shoulders on body, and stitch in place across armhole. See Diagram B.

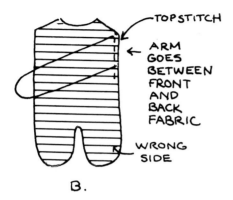

B.

Attaching head: With body wrong side out, turn head right side out and insert it upside down into neck opening of dress, as you would set in a sleeve. See Diagram C. Match

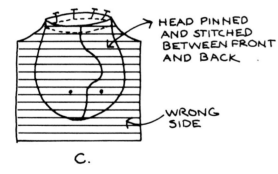

C.

up neck edges and side seams; pin, baste, and stitch around neckline to secure head to body. Turn body

right side out. See Diagram D. Stuff head and body tightly. Using small slipstitches, sew up opening.

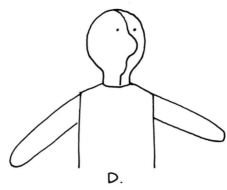

D.

Skirt: With right sides facing, stitch short ends together. Gather ½″ from skirt top to fit the width of waist. Machine stitch on gathers to secure. Turn doll upside down. With right sides facing, pin skirt to body at waist line. With your gathered stitching line ¼″ above waistline, use tiny running stitches to secure skirt to body. Turn doll right side up. Hem skirt.

Legs: Sew boot pieces to leg pieces. Fold each leg in half lengthwise with right sides facing, and stitch along seam line, leaving top edge open. Turn right side out and stuff to within 1″ of top. Turn in ¼″ of raw edge around top opening, and pin to bloomers. Make sure that toes point forward. Baste, then topstitch to secure. See Diagram E.

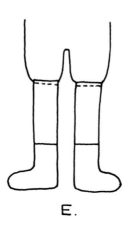

E.

Hair: Wrap yarn around 9½″ × 6″ piece of cardboard. Backstitch along top edge to make a center part. Cut yarn along bottom so that there are 6″ strands on each side of top seam. Slide yarn off cardboard. Now pin yarn to head along center seam, as shown in Diagram F. Sew hair along seam. Gather yarn at nape of neck, and tie into ponytail.

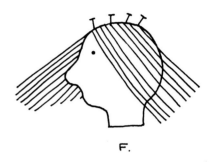

F.

Snood: Using 6″ lace circle, turn under ¼″ all around. With running stitch, gather edge of circle and pull tightly while stuffing ponytail into snood. Knot ends. With tiny stitches, sew snood edge securely to hair. See Diagram G.

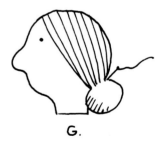

G.

Mouth: Embroider mouth with backstitch.

Apron: Turn under ¼″ on sides and top of apron bib, and topstitch ⅛″ from edge. Gather apron skirt ¼″ from top to width of apron bib. With right sides facing, stitch gathered edge to apron bib.

Straps: Turn ¼″ under on each side of neck strap and apron strings. Topstitch ⅛″ from edge. Place apron on doll. Tack on apron. Wrap neck strap around neck and tack securely in place.

Uncle Gus

Head: Transfer eyes to face pieces (see page 12), and embroider eyes with satin stitch. Add cheek coloring with watercolor or Dr. Ph. Martin's® dye. Allow to dry.

Ears: With wrong sides facing, sew back pieces to front pieces. Clip seams and curves closely. Turn right side out.

With right sides of head pieces A and B facing, pin ears into place. See Diagram H. Stitch along

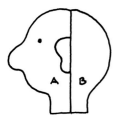

EAR PLACEMENT
H.

seams. With right sides facing, sew left side of head to right side, leaving opening at bottom of neck for stuffing. Turn right side out.

Body: Stitch front of shorts to front of shirt. Then stitch back of shorts to back of shirt. With right sides facing, sew front and back together, leaving openings at neck, armholes, and 4″ along one side of shorts for stuffing. Leave wrong side out.

Arms: With right sides facing, pin hands to arms and stitch. For each arm, fold piece lengthwise, right sides facing, and stitch along seam line, leaving top edge open. Turn right side out and stuff to within 1″ of top edge. Insert arms into openings at shoulders on body, and stitch in place across armhole. See Diagram B.

Follow instructions for Aunt Minna for attaching head to body and for stuffing.

Legs: Sew boot pieces to leg pieces. With right sides facing, fold each leg in half lengthwise and stitch along seam line, leaving top edge open. Turn right side out and stuff to within 1″ of top. Turn in ¼″ of raw edge around top opening, and pin to shorts. Make sure that toes point forward. Baste, then topstitch to secure. See Diagram E.

Pants: Before sewing pieces together, add decorative topstitching, as indicated on pattern. Attach three ⅛″ flat studs, as in picture.

With right sides facing, sew front piece to back piece. Turn right side out and roll up cuffs. Add ribbon or elastic suspenders. Tack

ends in front, crisscross in back, and tack in place.

Bow tie: With right sides facing, sew front and back pieces together, leaving 1″ opening at center. See Diagram I. Turn right

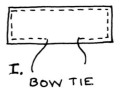

I.
BOW TIE

side out and press. Cut out piece of fabric 1″ × 3½″ for center of tie and turn under ¼″ on all sides. Press. Gather bow at center, and wrap center piece around bow. Stitch in back to secure, and tack on at neck.

Hair: Wrap yarn evenly around 9″ × 3″ piece of cardboard. Backstitch along top and bottom. Slide yarn off cardboard and pin to head (slip ears through hair). See Diagram J. Stitch to secure hair to head.

Mustache: Wrap yarn in haphazard fashion to fill 2″ × 1⅞″ piece of cardboard. Using small backhand stitches, stitch along top. Slide yarn off cardboard and cut along bottom. Pin under nose and stitch in place.

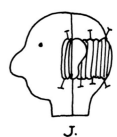

J.

1 square = 1 in.

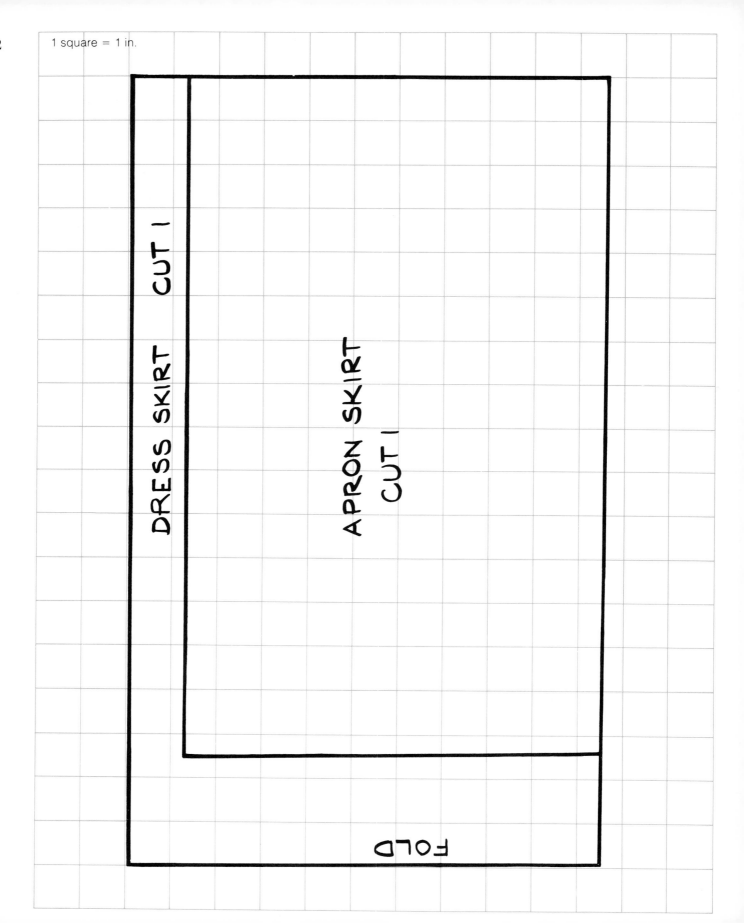

DRESS SKIRT CUT 1

APRON SKIRT CUT 1

FOLD

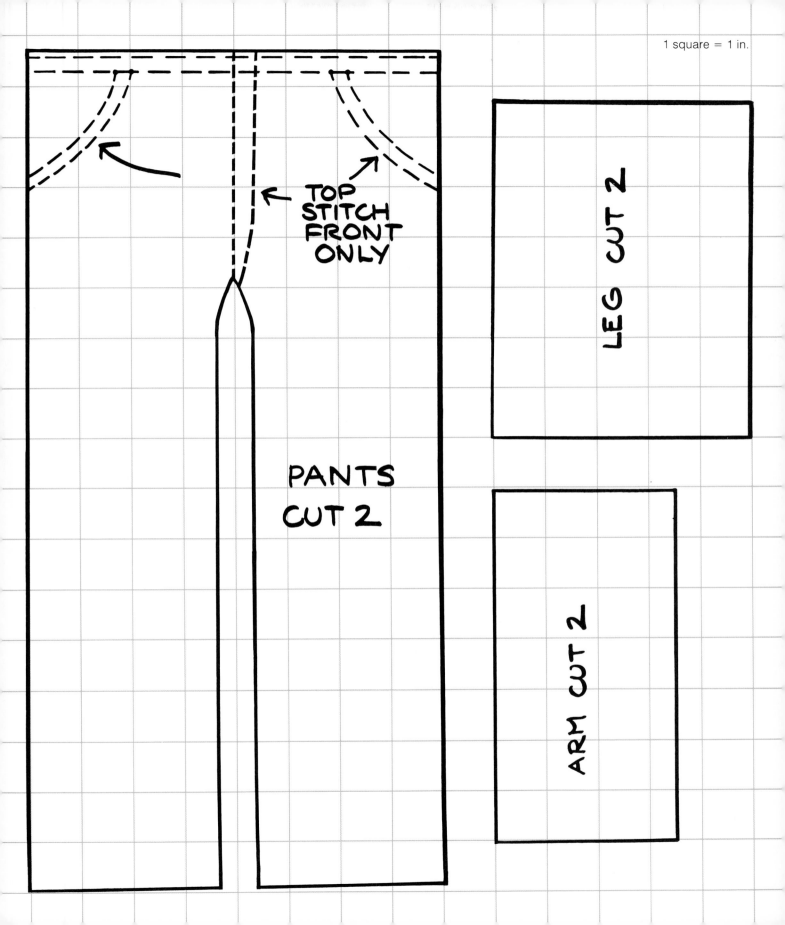

1 square = 1 in.

TOP
STITCH
FRONT
ONLY

PANTS
CUT 2

LEG CUT 2

ARM CUT 2

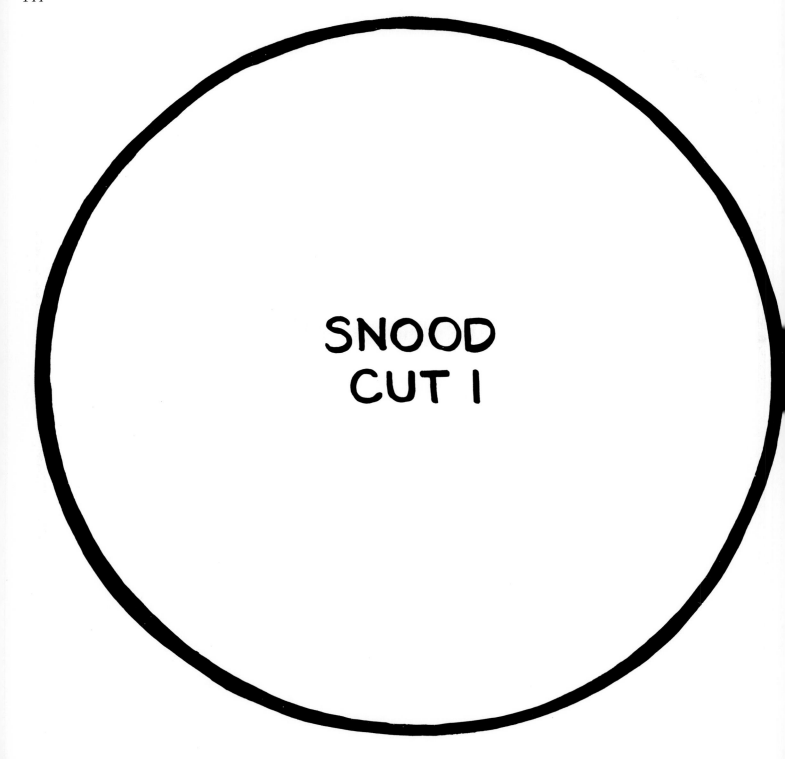

SNOOD
CUT 1

SHIRT
DRESS TOP

CUT 2
CHEST

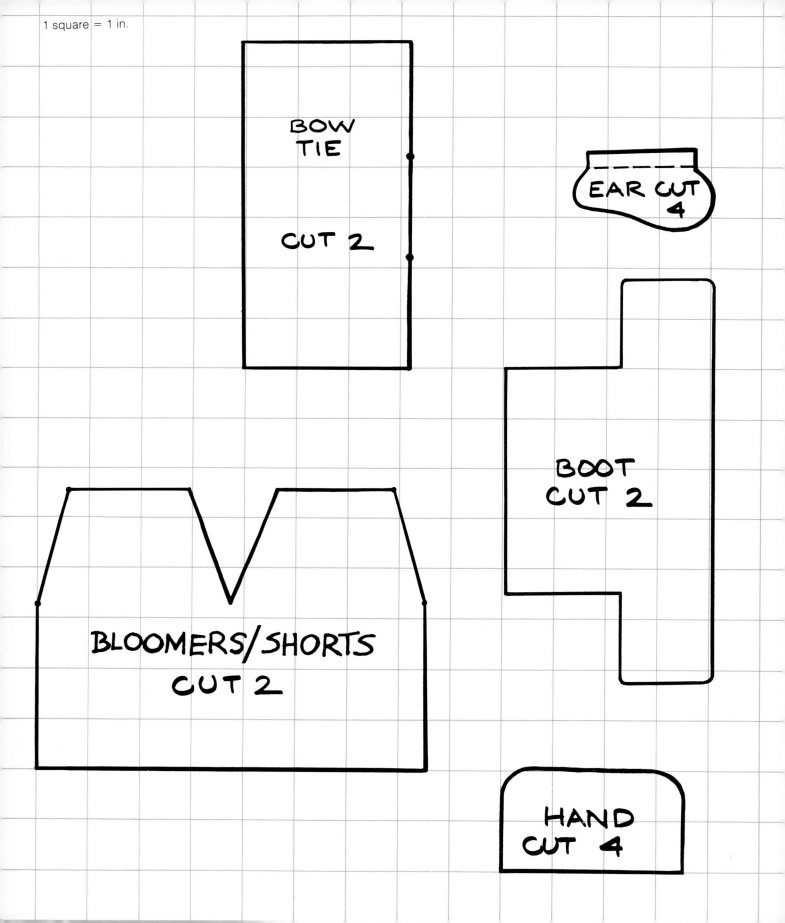

1 square = 1 in.

BOW TIE
CUT 2

EAR CUT 4

BOOT CUT 2

BLOOMERS/SHORTS
CUT 2

HAND
CUT 4

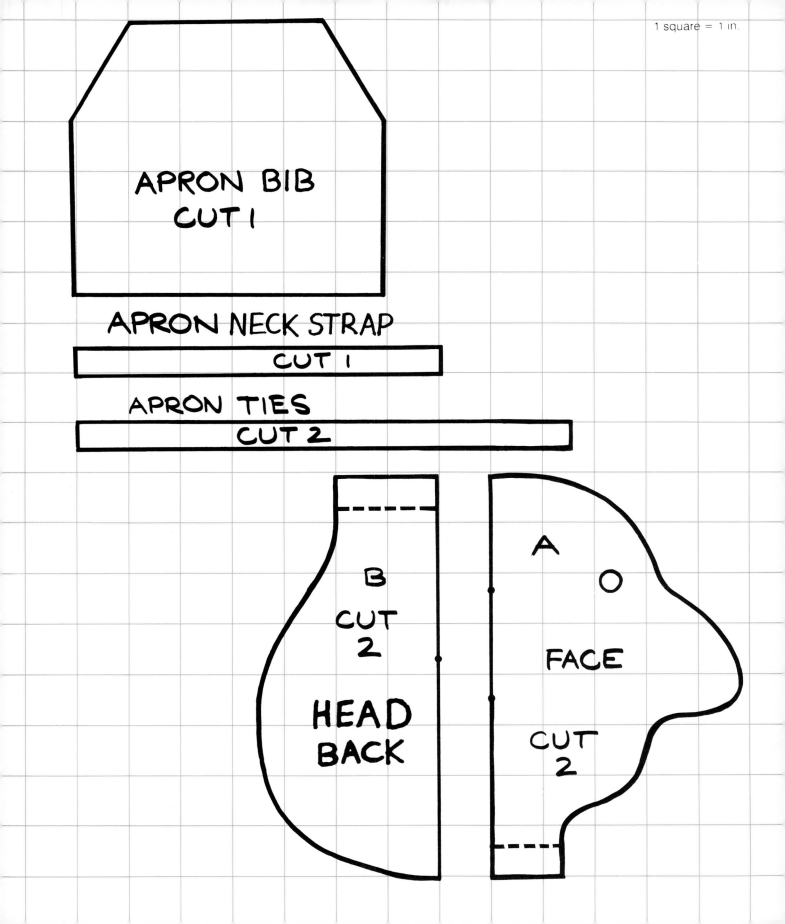

APRON BIB
CUT 1

APRON NECK STRAP
CUT 1

APRON TIES
CUT 2

B
CUT
2

HEAD
BACK

A   O

FACE

CUT
2

1 square = 1 in.

BERI, BILLY AND CRAMDEN THE DOG

A sunny day, a bunch of balloons, and—of course, Cramden the Dog. That's all Billy and Beri need for a perfect day. And they're all anyone needs for lots of fun and friendship!

SIZE: Beri and Billy: about 11″ tall
Cramden: about 6″ tall ·

MATERIALS

Beri

Fabrics: ½ yard of 36″ pink cotton or cotton blend for body

½ yard of 36″ red dotted cotton or cotton blend for skirt and top

¼ yard of 36″ bright cotton or cotton blend for hat

Yarn: approximately 9 yards of medium-weight yarn for hair

Trim: 9″ of ⅛″ elastic for skirt

Special Materials: red marker for smiling mouth

watercolor or markers for cheeks

shirt cardboard

Billy

Fabrics: ¼ yard of 36″ pink cotton or cotton blend for body

¼ yard of 36″ striped cotton or cotton blend for shirt

¼ yard of 36″ bright cotton or cotton blend for pants

¼ yard of 36″ bright cotton or cotton blend for hat

Special Materials: red marker for smiling mouth

watercolor or markers for cheeks

shirt cardboard

Cramden the Dog

Fabrics: ¼ yard of 36″ bright cotton or cotton blend for body

6″ × 2¾″ scrap of cotton or cotton blend for scarf

Trim: ½″ red pompon for nose (purchase, or see How to Make Pompons, page 16)

For all

Threads: sewing threads to match black embroidery floss for eyes

Stuffing: loose polyester fiberfill

INSTRUCTIONS

For Beri and Billy

See General Directions. Enlarge patterns, adding ¼″ seam allowance all around unless otherwise indicated.

Before cutting out patterns, embroider eyes and draw on mouths and cheeks, as shown. Place patterns on fold of material where indicated. Now cut out all pattern pieces. Make ¼″ seams throughout.

Beri

Body: With right sides facing, stitch up center seam on back of body, leaving 2″ opening in center for stuffing. See Diagram A. With right sides facing, attach front of body to back with small stitches. Clip curves and seams closely. Turn right side out and stuff. Sew up opening.

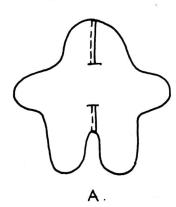

A.

Dress top: With right sides facing, sew back and front together at shoulders and underarms only. Turn right side out. Hem neck, sleeves, and bottom.

Skirt: The finished length will be 2″. Stitch short edges together. For casing, turn down ½″ on top of skirt. Topstitch around, leaving 1½″ open. Insert 9″ of elastic. Stitch elastic ends together at 8¼″. Sew up opening. Hem skirt bottom.

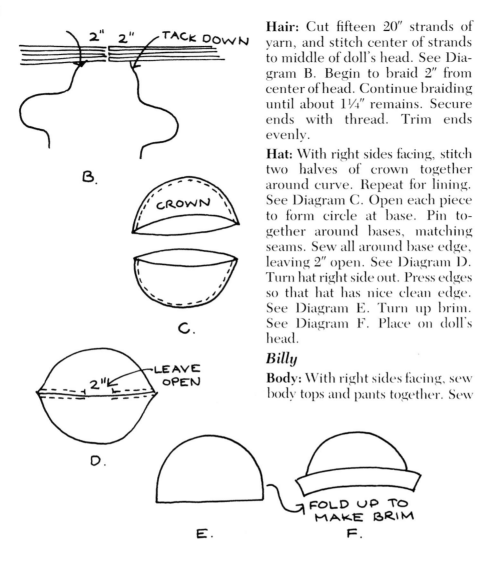

Hair: Cut fifteen 20″ strands of yarn, and stitch center of strands to middle of doll's head. See Diagram B. Begin to braid 2″ from center of head. Continue braiding until about 1¼″ remains. Secure ends with thread. Trim ends evenly.

Hat: With right sides facing, stitch two halves of crown together around curve. Repeat for lining. See Diagram C. Open each piece to form circle at base. Pin together around bases, matching seams. Sew all around base edge, leaving 2″ open. See Diagram D. Turn hat right side out. Press edges so that hat has nice clean edge. See Diagram E. Turn up brim. See Diagram F. Place on doll's head.

Billy

Body: With right sides facing, sew body tops and pants together. Sew two back pieces together, leaving 2″ opening in center for stuffing. With right sides facing, sew front and back of body together. Turn right side out, stuff, and sew up opening.

Shirt: With right sides facing, sew shoulders and underarm seams. Turn right side out. By hand or machine, hem neck, sleeves, and bottom.

Hat: Follow pattern and instructions for Beri's hat.

Cramden the Dog

Body: With right sides facing, sew body pieces together, leaving 2″ opening in back. Turn right side out, stuff, and sew up opening.

Face: Attach pompon for nose. Embroider small dots for eyes.

Scarf: Cut out and tie around neck. Hemming is optional.

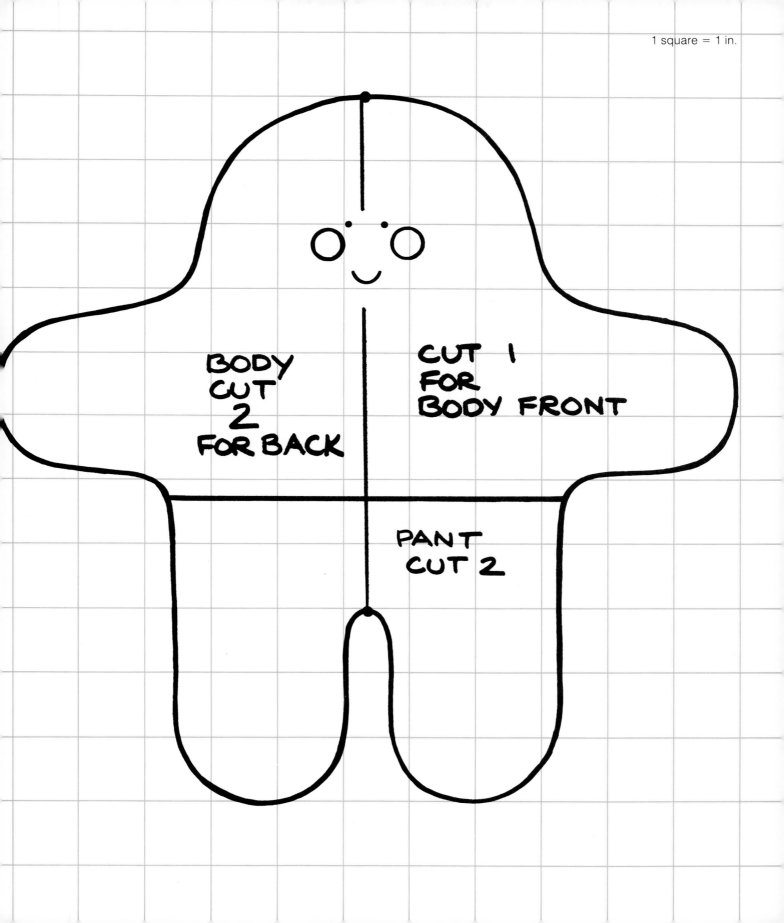

1 square = 1 in.

BODY
CUT
2
FOR BACK

CUT 1
FOR
BODY FRONT

PANT
CUT 2

1 square = 1 in.

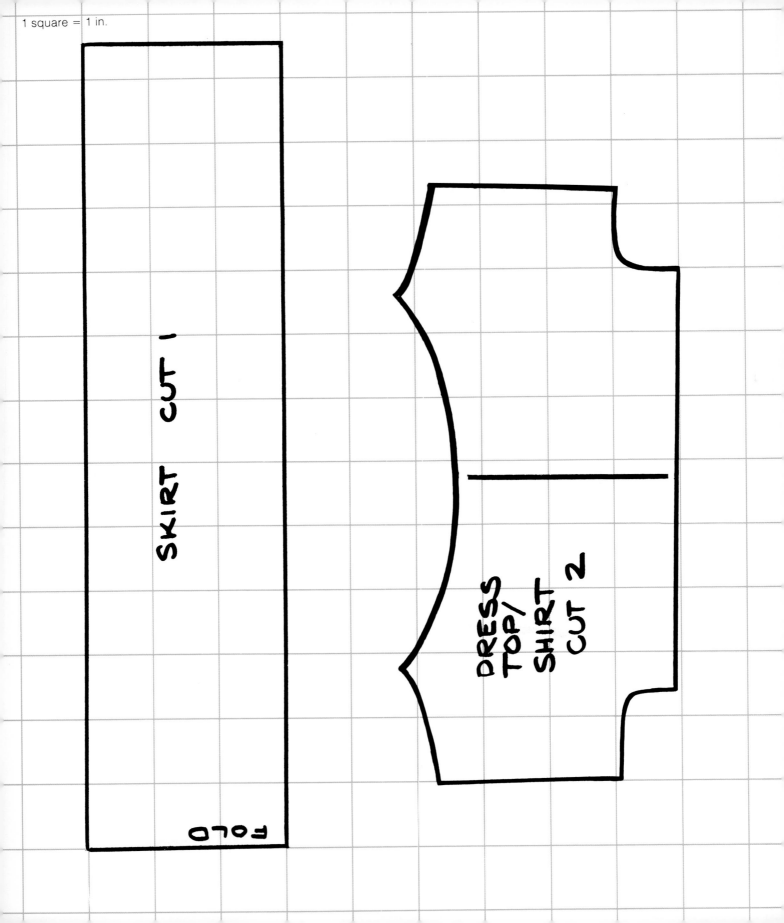

SKIRT CUT 1

FOLD

DRESS TOP/ SHIRT CUT 2

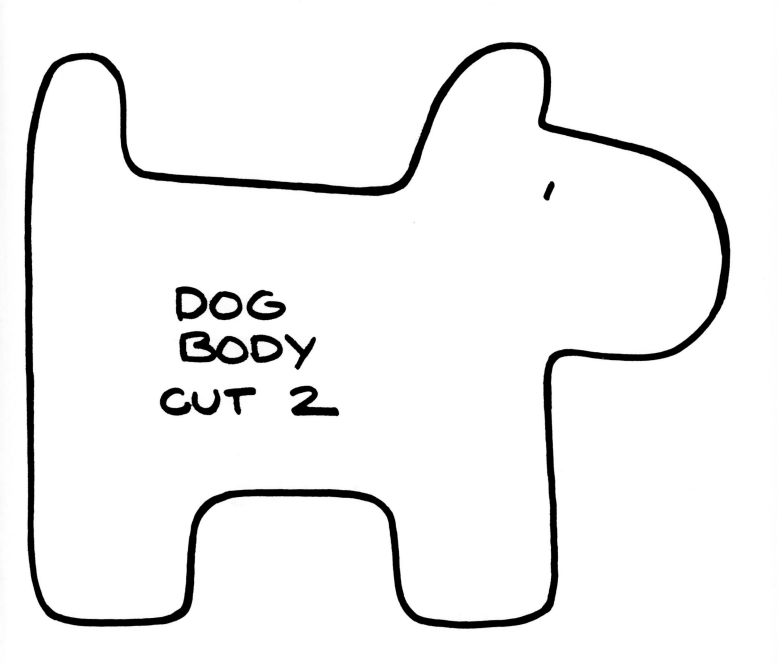

DOG
BODY
CUT 2

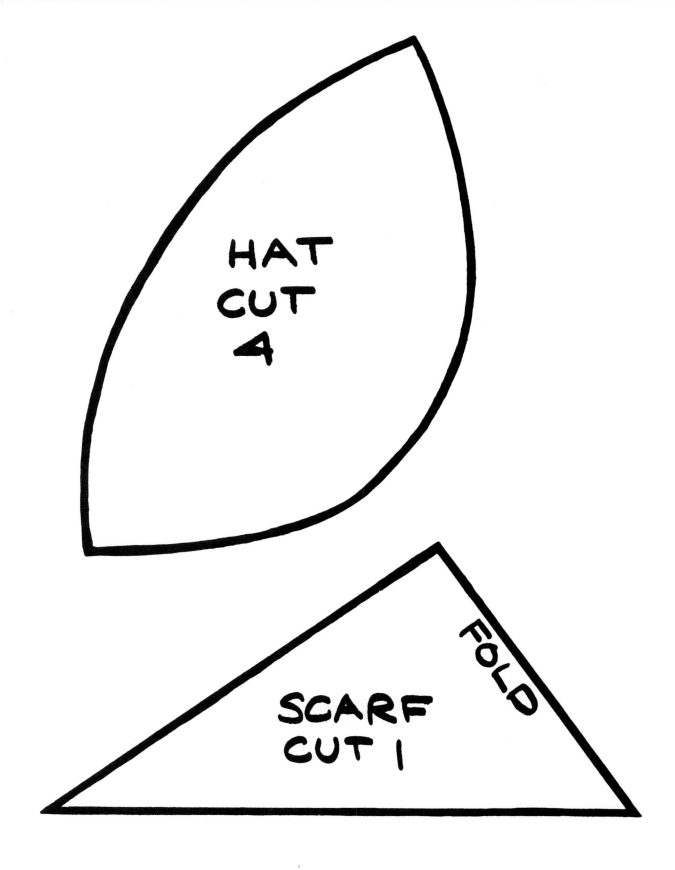

INDEX

For information on how you can have *Better Homes and Gardens* delivered to your door, write to: Mr. Robert Austin, P.O. Box 4536, Des Moines, IA 50336.

1B

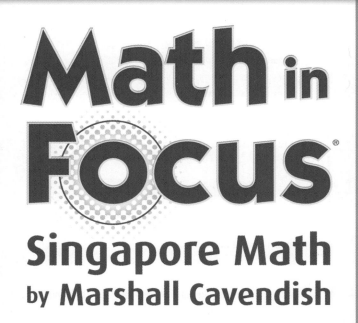

Enrichment

Consultant and Author
Dr. Fong Ho Kheong

Author
Ang Kok Cheng

Marshall Cavendish
Education

US Distributor

HOUGHTON MIFFLIN HARCOURT

COMMON
CORE

© Copyright 2009, 2013 Edition Marshall Cavendish International (Singapore) Private Limited

Published by Marshall Cavendish Education
An imprint of Marshall Cavendish International (Singapore) Private Limited
Times Centre, 1 New Industrial Road, Singapore 536196
Customer Service Hotline: (65) 6411 0820
E-mail: tmesales@sg.marshallcavendish.com
Website: www.marshallcavendish.com/education

Distributed by
Houghton Mifflin Harcourt
222 Berkeley Street
Boston, MA 02116
Tel: 617-351-5000
Website: www.hmheducation.com/mathinfocus

First published 2009
2013 Edition

Math in Focus® Enrichment 1B
ISBN 978-0-669-01575-1

Printed in Singapore

2 3 4 5 6 7 8   1401   18 17 16 15 14 13
4500373247   A B C D E

Contents

Introducing

Math in Focus®

Enrichment

Written to complement *Math in Focus®: Singapore Math* by *Marshall Cavendish* Grade 1, exercises in *Enrichment 1A* and *1B* are designed for advanced students seeking a challenge beyond the exercises and questions in the Student Books and Workbooks.

These exercises require children to draw on their fundamental mathematical understanding as well as recently acquired concepts and skills, combining problem-solving strategies with critical thinking skills.

Critical thinking skills enhanced by working on *Enrichment* exercises include classifying, comparing, sequencing, analyzing parts and whole, identifying patterns and relationships, induction (from specific to general), deduction (from general to specific), and spatial visualization.

One set of problems is provided for each chapter, to be assigned after the chapter has been completed. *Enrichment* exercises can be assigned while other students are working on the Chapter Review/Test, or while the class is working on subsequent chapters.

BLANK

CHAPTER 10 Weight

PROBLEM SOLVING
Thinking Skills

Find the weight of each object.
1 ⬜ stands for 1 unit.

Object	Weight 1 ⬜ = 1 unit
1. book	_____ units
2. pencil	_____ units
3. ruler	_____ units

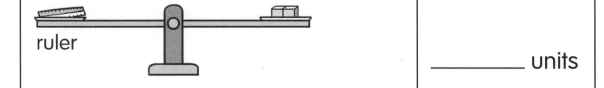

© Marshall Cavendish International (Singapore) Private Limited.

Use your answers in Exercises 1 to 3 for these exercises.
Read each sentence.
Put a check (✔) if the sentence is correct.

	Sentence	Check (✔) if correct
4.	The book is the lightest.	
5.	The pencil is heavier than the ruler.	
6.	The book is as heavy as the ruler.	
7.	The ruler is 2 units lighter than the book.	
8.	The book is as heavy as the total weight of the pencil and the ruler.	
9.	The total weight of the book, the pencil, and the ruler is 13 units.	

10. **Look at the pictures.**
Order the boxes from lightest to heaviest.
1 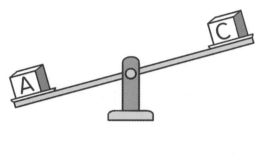 stands for 1 unit.

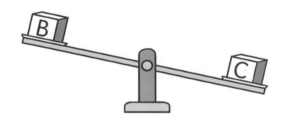

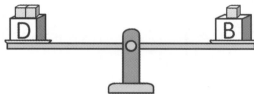

_____, _____, _____, _____
lightest   heaviest

PROBLEM SOLVING
Strategies

Solve.
Show your work.

11.   A peach has a weight of 2 units.
      An orange is 2 units heavier than the peach.
      The peach is 4 units lighter than a mango.
      What is the total weight of the three fruits?

The total weight of the three fruits is _____ units.

12. Two objects weigh 18 units in all.
One object is 8 units heavier than the other object.
What are the weights of the two objects?

A + B = 18
A − B = 8
What can A and B be?

The weights of the two objects are _____ units

and _____ units.

13. Look at the pictures.
What is the weight of the duck?
1 ▱ stands for 1 unit.

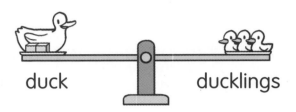

duck   ducklings

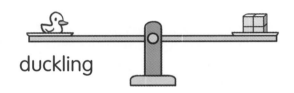

duckling

The weight of the duck is _____ units.

PROBLEM SOLVING
Exploration

Solve.

14. Adam has three toys in his toy box; a drum, a teddy bear, and a toy train.
The drum is heavier than the teddy bear.
The toy train is heavier than the teddy bear but lighter than the drum.
Which toy is the heaviest?
Which toy is the lightest?

The _____ is the heaviest.

The _____ is the lightest.

Name: _____   **Date:** _____

 **Journal Writing**

Solve and explain.

15.   Look at the picture.

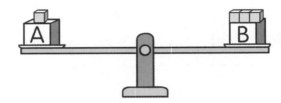

Which box is heavier, Box A or Box B?
How much heavier is it?
Explain how you know.

Look at the pictures.

16.   Arrange the boxes in order, from heaviest to lightest.

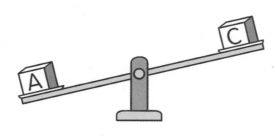

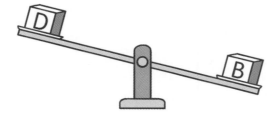

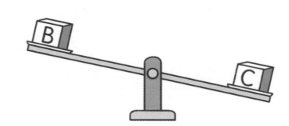

_____, _____, _____, _____

heaviest   lightest

CHAPTER 11 Picture Graphs and Bar Graphs

PROBLEM SOLVING
Thinking Skills

Look at the picture graph.
Then fill in the blanks.

This graph shows the number of apples 3 children ate.

Number of Apples Eaten

Cindy	🍎 🍎 🍎 🍎 🍎 🍎
John	🍎 🍎 🍎
Andy	🍎 🍎 🍎 🍎 🍎

Each 🍎 stands for 1 apple.

1.   Cindy ate _____ more apples than John.

2.   John ate 2 apples less than _____.

3.   John and Andy ate _____ more apples than Cindy.

Look at the picture graph.
Then fill in the blanks.

This graph shows the number of beads each child has.
The number of beads that Nancy has is missing from the graph.

Number of Beads

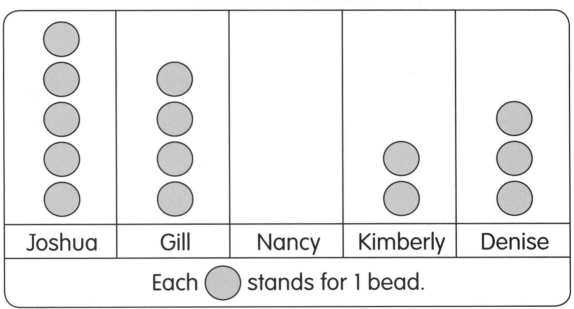

| Joshua | Gill | Nancy | Kimberly | Denise |

Each ⬤ stands for 1 bead.

4. The five children have 20 beads in all.
   How many beads does Nancy have? _____ beads

5. Joshua has 2 more beads than _____.

6. _____ has the least number of beads.

7. The total number of beads that Nancy and Kimberly
   have is greater than the total number of beads that

   _____ and _____ have.

8. A group of children share some oranges.
Tim has 5 oranges.
Lenny has 2 fewer oranges than Tim.
Josh has 4 more oranges than Lenny.
Fanny has the same number of oranges as Tim.
Susan has twice the number of oranges as Josh.

Complete the picture graph.

Number of Oranges

Fanny	Josh	Lenny	Susan	Tim

Each ◯ stands for 1 orange.

Solve.

Mr. Philip has a fruit tree farm.
He has 2 apple trees, 4 mango trees, and 5 papaya trees on his farm.

9.   Make a bar graph.

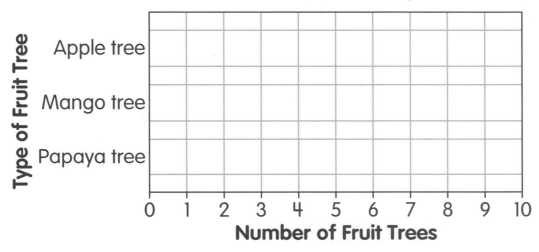

10.   After two months, 1 mango tree and 2 papaya trees were damaged.
How many trees of each type did Mr. Philip have after two months?

Mr. Philip had _____ apple trees, _____ mango

trees, and _____ papaya trees after two months.

PROBLEM SOLVING
Strategies

Look at the picture graph.
Answer the questions.

This graph shows the number of marbles 4 boys have after a game.

During the game, Riley gave 4 marbles to Logan, he got 2 marbles from Austin, and he received 1 marble from Robert.

Number of Marbles

Robert	Austin	Logan	Riley

Each 🫘 stands for 1 marble.

11. How many marbles did Riley have at first?

_____ marbles

12. How many more marbles did Robert, Austin, and Logan have in all than Riley at first? _____ marbles

● **Look at the bar graphs.**
Answer the questions.

The top bar graph shows the number of books that Tammy had at first.
The next bar graph shows the number of books that Tammy had after trading some books with her friends.

Books that Tammy Had At First

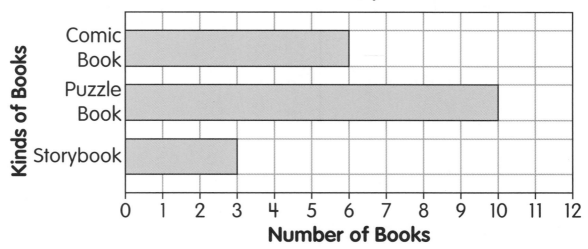

Books that Tammy Had After Trading

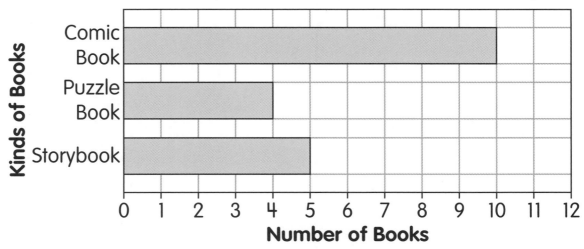

13. How many books did Tammy have at first?

14. Did she have the same number of books before and after trading books with her friends?

15. How many more comic books did she have in the end than at first?

16. Tammy had fewer _____ in the end than at first.

Complete the bar graph.

17. Mrs. Johnson baked 18 muffins for her children.
Tyler ate twice as many muffins as Emily.
Peter ate 3 more muffins than Tyler.
How many muffins did Emily eat?

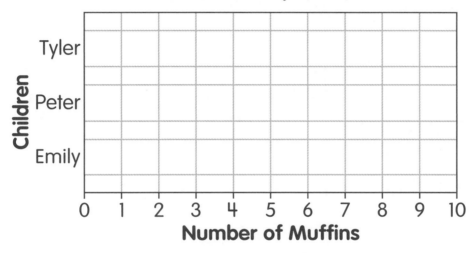

Muffins Eaten by the Children

Emily ate _____ muffins.

PROBLEM SOLVING

Exploration

Read the sentences.
Then complete the graph.

18. Lisa caught 20 butterflies of different colors: blue, black, green, red, and yellow.

Complete the bar graph to compare the number of different colored butterflies that Lisa caught.
Make your graph so that the phrases below can be used when talking about your graph.

a. 5 more than

b. 2 fewer than

c. as many as

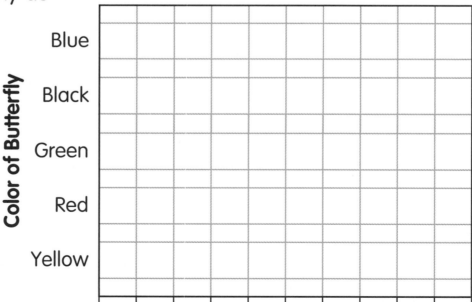

Butterflies that Lisa Caught

Color of Butterfly: Blue, Black, Green, Red, Yellow

Number of Butterflies

 **Journal Writing**

Solve.

19. Complete the picture graph based on the following
information:
Alice has 5 more ribbons than Betty.
Crystal has as many ribbons as Dawn.
Dawn has 7 fewer ribbons than Alice.
Fiona has 3 more ribbons than Dawn.
Alice has 11 ribbons.

Ribbons Owned by 5 Girls

Alice	Betty	Crystal	Dawn	Fiona

Each 🎀 stands for 1 ribbon.

20. The bar graph shows how the number of rabbits in a forest increased over 5 years.

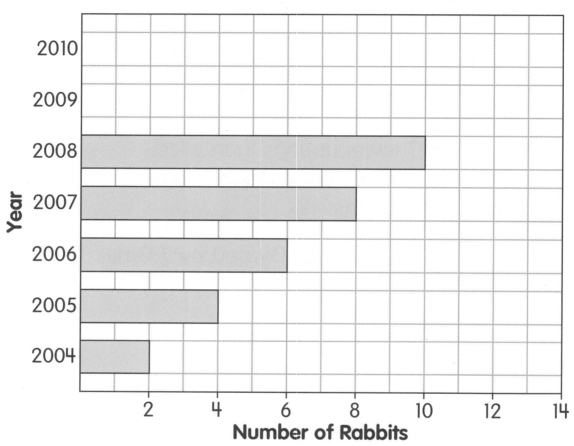

Number of Rabbits in a Forest

a. Explain the pattern in the increase in the number of rabbits from 2004 through 2008.

_____

_____

b. Using this pattern, predict the number of rabbits in the forest in 2009 and 2010.
Then complete the bar graph.

CHAPTER 12 Numbers to 40

PROBLEM SOLVING
Thinking Skills

Solve.

1. Find a number between 15 and 30 such that the reverse of its digits is 9 more than the number itself.

When you reverse the digits of 37, you get 73!

The number is _____.

2.   Each of the different shapes below has a number value. The shapes in every row and column add up to the numbers shown.
Can you find the value of each shape?

⬤	⬤	20
▭	★	27
25	22	

⬤ = _____   ★ = _____   ▭ = _____

3.   The picture shows some letters that are arranged in a pattern.
Use the key to find the missing letter.

Key:

A = 5	E = 9	I = 13	M = 17	Q = 21	U = 25	Y = 29
B = 6	F = 10	J = 14	N = 18	R = 22	V = 26	Z = 30
C = 7	G = 11	K = 15	O = 19	S = 23	W = 27	
D = 8	H = 12	L = 16	P = 20	T = 24	X = 28	

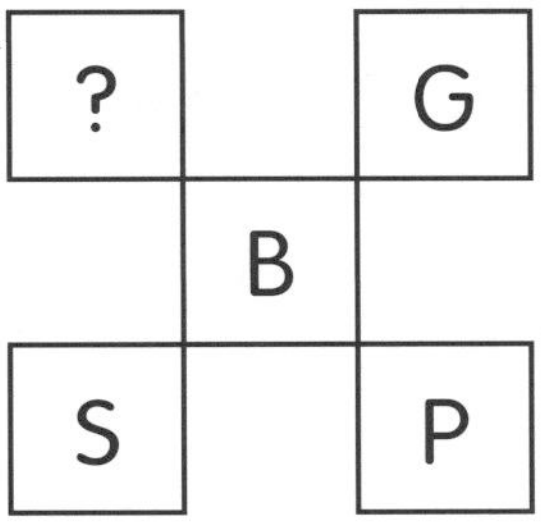

```
┌───┐   ┌───┐
│ ? │   │ G │
└───┘   └───┘
      ┌───┐
      │ B │
      └───┘
┌───┐   ┌───┐
│ S │   │ P │
└───┘   └───┘
```

The missing letter is _____.

Name: _____   Date: _____

Strategies

Solve using number lines.
Show your work.

4.   Valerie has 14 goldfish in her fish tank.
She has 8 more guppies than goldfish.
She kept some mollies in another tank.
The number of mollies is 3 less than the number
of guppies.
How many mollies does Valerie have?

Valerie has _____ mollies.

5.   Four years ago, Patrick was 15 years older than Susan.
At that time, Susan was 8 years old.
How old is Patrick now?

Patrick is _____ years old now.

Look at the number patterns.
Solve.

6. The numbers below are arranged in a pattern.
One number is incorrect.
Which number is incorrect?
What should be the correct number?

8,   9,   11,   14,   19,   23

_____ is the incorrect number.

The correct number should be _____.

7. Find the number that comes next in the pattern.

3,   6,   12,   21,   ?

The number is _____.

PROBLEM SOLVING
Exploration

Solve.
Show your work.

8. Daniel is 36 years old.
    Olivia is 10 years younger than Daniel.
    Simon is older than Olivia but younger than Daniel.
    How old can Simon be?

Simon can be _____, _____, _____, _____,

_____, _____, _____, _____,

or _____ years old.

9.   Monica has five number cards that make a pattern.
She shows three of the number cards to Louise.
Arrange the cards to make the pattern.
What can the two other number cards be?
There is more than one correct answer.

14   20

26

The two other number cards can be _____ and _____.

 **Journal Writing**

Solve and tell why.

10.   23   25   28   32   34
Do the numbers form a pattern? _____
Tell your friend why.

11.   20   24   28   32   36
Do the numbers form a pattern? _____
Tell your friend why.

Correct the mistakes.
Write the correct sentences.

12.   5 more than 19 is 14.

_____

13.   10 less than 22 is 32.

_____

Addition and Subtraction to 40

PROBLEM SOLVING

Thinking Skills

Fill in the circles.

1. Fill in the empty circles with + or – to make the sentence correct.

    (25) (   ) (7) (   ) (6) (   ) (3) = (29)

Solve.

2. The numbers in the circles are arranged in a pattern.
    Find the pattern.
    Then find the missing numbers.

    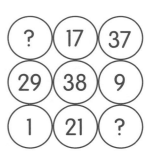

    The missing numbers are _____ and _____.

3. Look at the number sentences.

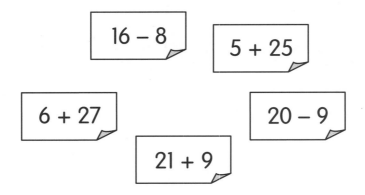

When the answers of two of these number sentences are subtracted, the result is 25.
Which are the two number sentences?

The two number sentences are _____ and

_____.

PROBLEM SOLVING

Strategies

Solve.
Show your work.

4.   20 children went to a café for lunch.
14 children ate fish burgers.
10 children ate chicken burgers.
How many children ate both fish and chicken burgers?

Number of children who ate chicken burgers	Number of children who ate fish burgers	Number of children who ate both burgers	Number of children = 20?
10	14	0	10 + 14 − 0 = 24 (No)
10	14	1	10 + 14 − 1 = 23 (No)

_____ children ate both fish and chicken burgers.

5.   Wendy has 5 more dolls than Jill.
Jill has 6 fewer dolls than Nellie.
Kiri has 3 more dolls than Jill.
Nellie has 9 dolls.
How many dolls do the four girls have in all?

The four girls have _____ dolls in all.

6.   There are 16 blue buttons on Tray A and 27 yellow buttons on Tray B.
5 blue buttons from Tray A are moved to Tray B.
9 yellow buttons from Tray B are moved to Tray A.
How many buttons are there in each tray now?

There are _____ buttons in Tray A and _____ buttons in Tray B.

PROBLEM SOLVING

Exploration

Solve.

7. Pick any three numbers shown below and complete the addition sentences.
Use a number only once in each sentence.

(4) (5) (6) (7) (8) (9)

_____ + _____ + _____ = 21

_____ + _____ + _____ = 21

_____ + _____ + _____ = 21

8. Write the number sentences.
Use three different numbers from 10 to 25.

_____ + _____ − _____ = 18

_____ − _____ + _____ = 18

There is more than one correct answer.

Name: ______________________ Date: ______________

Solve.
Show your work.

9. At an amusement park, tickets can be exchanged for toys. The chart shows the number of tickets needed for each toy.

Toy	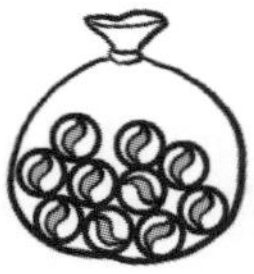 Marbles	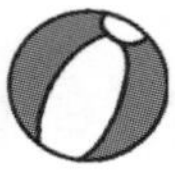 Ball	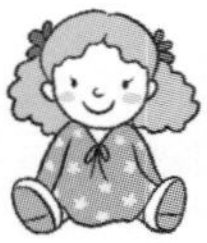 Doll	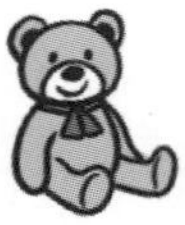 Teddy bear	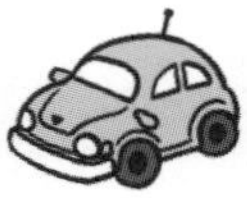 Toy car	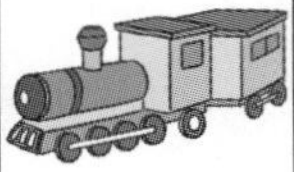 Toy Train	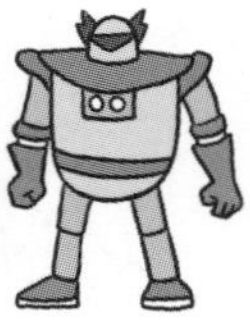 Toy robot
Number of tickets	4	7	9	13	18	25	33

Allie has 35 tickets and Ben has 40 tickets.
Each of them picks 3 toys.
What sets of toys can each child pick?

Allie can pick ______________, ______________, and ______________.

Ben can pick ______________, ______________, and ______________.

Journal Writing

Solve.

10. In the number pattern below, some numbers are covered by an ink blot.
Tell a friend how you can find the missing numbers.
Then find the missing numbers.

5,  17,   21,   25,   29,   33,   37

The missing numbers are _____.

Name: ____________________ Date: ____________

Write stories.

11. Write one addition story and one subtraction story. Use the numbers and words from the box.

Elisa	15	sandwiches	8	gives
makes	Chad	more than	23	how many

a. Addition story

____

____

____

____

b. Subtraction story

____

____

____

____

Name: _____   Date: _____

CHAPTER 14 Mental Math Strategies

PROBLEM SOLVING

Thinking Skills

Add and subtract mentally.

1. $5 + 6 + 7 =$ _____

2. $38 - 19 - 16 =$ _____

3. $16 - 5 + 11 =$ _____

4. $27 + 9 - 10 =$ _____

5. $19 - 13 + 8 =$ _____

6. $21 + 17 - 14 =$ _____

Use number bonds to help you to add and subtract mentally.

Solve.
Show your work.

7.   Find the missing number in the number bond.

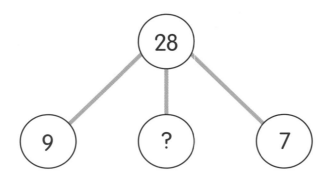

The missing number is _____.

8.   Calvin scores 36 points in a game.
Nicole scores 9 points in the same game.
How many more points does Nicole need to score to
match Calvin's points?

Nicole needs to score _____ more points.

PROBLEM SOLVING
Strategies

Solve.
Show your work.

9.   Benson and Rick went swimming.
Benson swam 8 laps of the pool.
Rick swam 3 laps more than Benson.
How many laps of the pool did they swim in all?

They swam _____ laps of the pool in all.

10.   Sandy read 14 pages of a book on Monday.
She read 4 fewer pages on Tuesday than on Monday.
How many pages of the book did Sandy read on both days?

Sandy read _____ pages of the book on both days.

11. Each shirt has 5 buttons.
Each coat has 2 more buttons than a shirt.
How many buttons are there on one shirt and two coats
in all?

There are _____ buttons on one shirt and two coats
in all.

12. Some children were at the playground.
7 children went home.
5 more children then joined the rest of the children
at the playground.
There were 15 children at the playground in the end.
How many children were there at first?

There were _____ children at first.

PROBLEM SOLVING

Exploration

Solve.
Show your work.

13. Show two ways to find the value of 5 + 8.

5 + 8 = _____

14. Show two ways to find the value of 13 − 6.

13 − 6 = _____

15. Show two ways to find the value of 9 + 8 + 7.

9 + 8 + 7 = _____

Journal Writing

Solve.

16. **a.** Order the steps to add 7 and 8.
Put the numbers 1, 2, and 3 in the boxes to show the correct order for the steps.

☐ Add to make 10; 7 + 3 = 10.

☐ Add tens and ones; 10 + 5 = 15.

☐ Use a number bond; 8 = 3 + 5.

b. Write down the steps to add 9 and 6.

Step 1 _____

_____

Step 2 _____

_____

Step 3 _____

_____

CHAPTER 15 Calendar and Time

PROBLEM SOLVING
Thinking Skills

Fill in the blanks.

1. When the clock strikes 7 o'clock, the minute hand is pointing to _____.

2. When the clock reads half past 10, the minute hand is pointing to _____.

3. When the minute hand is pointing to 12 and the hour hand is pointing to 4, the time is _____.

4. When the time is half past 2, the hour hand will be pointing between _____ and _____.

Use the calendar.

5. The events below tell about Mrs. Garcia's appointments and activities for the coming weeks.
    Help her mark the dates on the calendar.

    a. Her dental appointment is three days after March 18th.
        Circle it in red.

    b. Suzanne's birthday party is on the second Friday of April.
        Mark it with a red X.

    c. Her car will be back from the shop in 3 weeks and 3 days after March 5th.
        Circle it in blue.

    d. Grandma's birthday is on April 12th.
        Remember to buy Grandma's birthday present one week before.
        Circle it in green.

March						
S	M	T	W	T	F	S
		1	2	3	4	5
6	7	8	9	10	11	12
13	14	15	16	17	18	19
20	21	22	23	24	25	26
27	28	29	30	31		

April						
S	M	T	W	T	F	S
					1	2
3	4	5	6	7	8	9
10	11	12	13	14	15	16
17	18	19	20	21	22	23
24	25	26	27	28	29	30

Draw and solve.

6.   Pedro is meeting his friend at half past 8.

   a.   Draw the minute and hour hands to show the time on
        the clock.

   b.   This is the time shown on his watch.
        How much time does Pedro have left before he has to
        meet his friend?

        Pedro has _____ left.

PROBLEM SOLVING

Strategies

Use the calendar.

7.   Andy received an overseas package from Kelly in Singapore.
It took 1 week and 2 days for the package to arrive in the U.S. from Singapore, and another 3 days for it to reach his house.
Andy received the package on July 24ᵗʰ.
When did Kelly send the package from Singapore?
Circle it on the calendar.

S	M	T	W	T	F	S
		July				
		1	2	3	4	5
6	7	8	9	10	11	12
13	14	15	16	17	18	19
20	21	22	23	24	25	26
27	28	29	30	31		

8. Mr. Edge took his truck to the repair shop last Saturday. He was told that it would be ready two days after the third Wednesday of the month.
When will Mr. Edge be able to have his truck back?
Circle the date on the calendar for Mr. Edge.

S	M	T	W	T	F	S
		1	2	3	4	5
6	7	8	9	10	11	12
13	14	15	16	17	18	19
20	21	22	23	24	25	26
27	28	29	30	31		

To the shop

Solve.
Show your work.

9. An old cuckoo clock chimed once at 1 o'clock, twice at 2 o'clock, three times at 3 o'clock, and so on.
How many times will it have chimed in all by half past 7?

It will have chimed _____ times in all.

PROBLEM SOLVING
Exploration

Solve.

10. Study the raised knuckles on the back of your clenched fists.
In between two knuckles, there is a valley.
Imagine the first knuckle
on your left hand is
January, and the valley
is February. 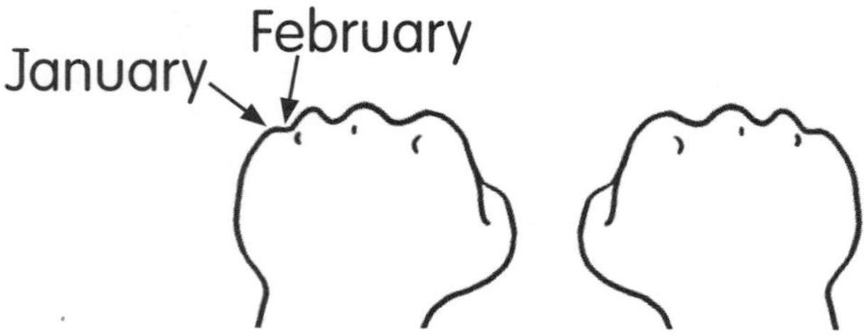
Continue to say the
months of the year in order as you move along your fists.
What do you notice?

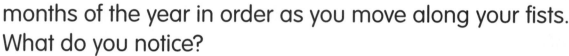

January   February

_____

_____

11. Some countries have four seasons, while others do not.
America is one of the countries that has four seasons.
Name four other countries that have four seasons.
Then name two countries that do not have four seasons.

_____

_____

Journal Writing

True or false?

12. Write *true* or *false*.
If a statement is false, explain why it is wrong.

a. All odd number months have
31 days.   _____

b. All even number months have
30 days.   _____

c. There are 7 weeks in a day.   _____

d. There are 10 months in a year.   _____

e. Guinevere was born in August.
There are 30 days in August.   _____

13. Make a diary of all the activities that you did last Sunday. Use *o'clock* or *half past* in your sentences.

My Diary of Activities

CHAPTER 16 Numbers to 100

PROBLEM SOLVING
Thinking Skills

Form 2-digit numbers by circling 2 boxes that are next to each other.

Example

Ring the number that is greater than 45 but less than 50.

5	2	0
4	6	7
1	8	3

The number 48 is greater than 45 but less than 50.

---

1. Ring the greatest number that is less than 100.

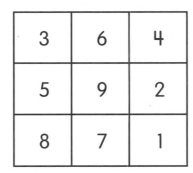

3	6	4
5	9	2
8	7	1

2. Ring the third smallest number that is greater than 10.

5	6	2
4	1	7
9	8	3

3. Arrange each number sentence, from the one with the greatest total, to the one with the least.

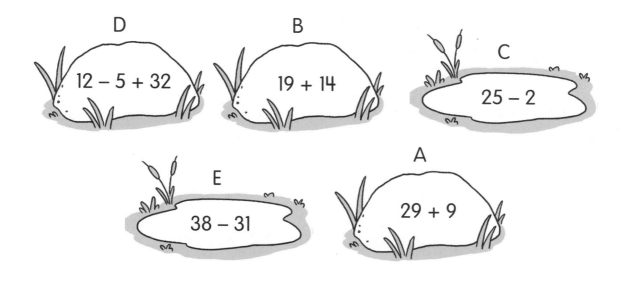

D 12 − 5 + 32

B 19 + 14

C 25 − 2

E 38 − 31

A 29 + 9

_____, _____, _____, _____, _____

greatest   least

Fill in the blanks.

4. 17 less than 84 is _____.

5. 20 more than 25 is _____.

6. _____ is 67 more than 18.

7. _____ is 43 less than 71.

PROBLEM SOLVING

Strategies

Complete the number pattern.

8.   10, 15, 25, 40, 60, _____

9.   15, 18, 16, 19, 17, 20, 18, _____, _____

10.   88, 79, _____, _____, 52, 43, 34

Look at the pattern.

11.   What are the missing numbers?

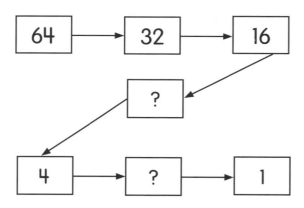

The missing numbers are _____ and _____.

Solve.
Show your work.

12. Elle is 23 years old.
Her mother is 58 years old.
In how many years will Elle's mother be twice
as old as Elle?

Elle's mother will be twice as old as Elle in _____
years.

13. Mary bought some rolls of tapes during a sale.
She gave 9 rolls to her brother, 5 rolls to her classmate,
and 7 rolls to her best friend.
Mary has 20 rolls of tape left.
How many rolls of tape did Mary buy during the sale?

Mary bought _____ rolls of tape during the sale.

PROBLEM SOLVING
Exploration

Solve.

14. Write 3 different number patterns that start with the number 55.
Each pattern must have at least 5 numbers in it that are greater than 55.

15. Write 3 different number patterns that start with the number 99.
Each pattern must have at least 5 numbers in it that are less than 99.

 **Journal Writing**

Correct the mistakes.
Write the correct sentences.

16.   7 more than 81 is 74.

_____

17.   25 less than 75 is 100.

_____

Write a word problem that involves a mystery number.
Your problem must have at least two sentences in it.
Use the numbers and words in the box.
Then find the mystery number.

18.

subtract	27	add	84	from
get	you	number	15	and

_____

_____

_____

_____

WORKING TOGETHER **Game**

Players: 2–4

Twisted Snakes!

STEP
1 Decide who will go first.

STEP
2 The second player, Player 2 says a number between 2 and 12.

6!

STEP
3 Player 1 rolls two number cubes that are numbered from 1–6.
If the total of the rolled numbers is the same as the number that Player 2 said, then Player 1's turn ends and it is Player 2's turn.

STEP
4 If Player 1 rolls a number other than the number that Player 2 said, then Player 1 moves his counter forward the number of squares shown on the cubes.

© Marshall Cavendish International (Singapore) Private Limited.

STEP 5

If the counter lands on a square that has a star on it, add the number in the star to the number of the square.

Then move the counter to the square that has the same number as the result.

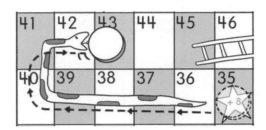

STEP 6

If the counter lands on a square that has a circle on it, subtract the number in the circle from the number of the square.

Then move the counter to the square that has the same number as the result.

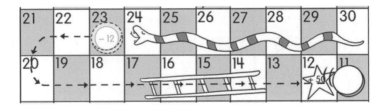

STEP 7

Take turns.

The game ends when a player reaches square 100.

The first player to reach 'Finish' wins!

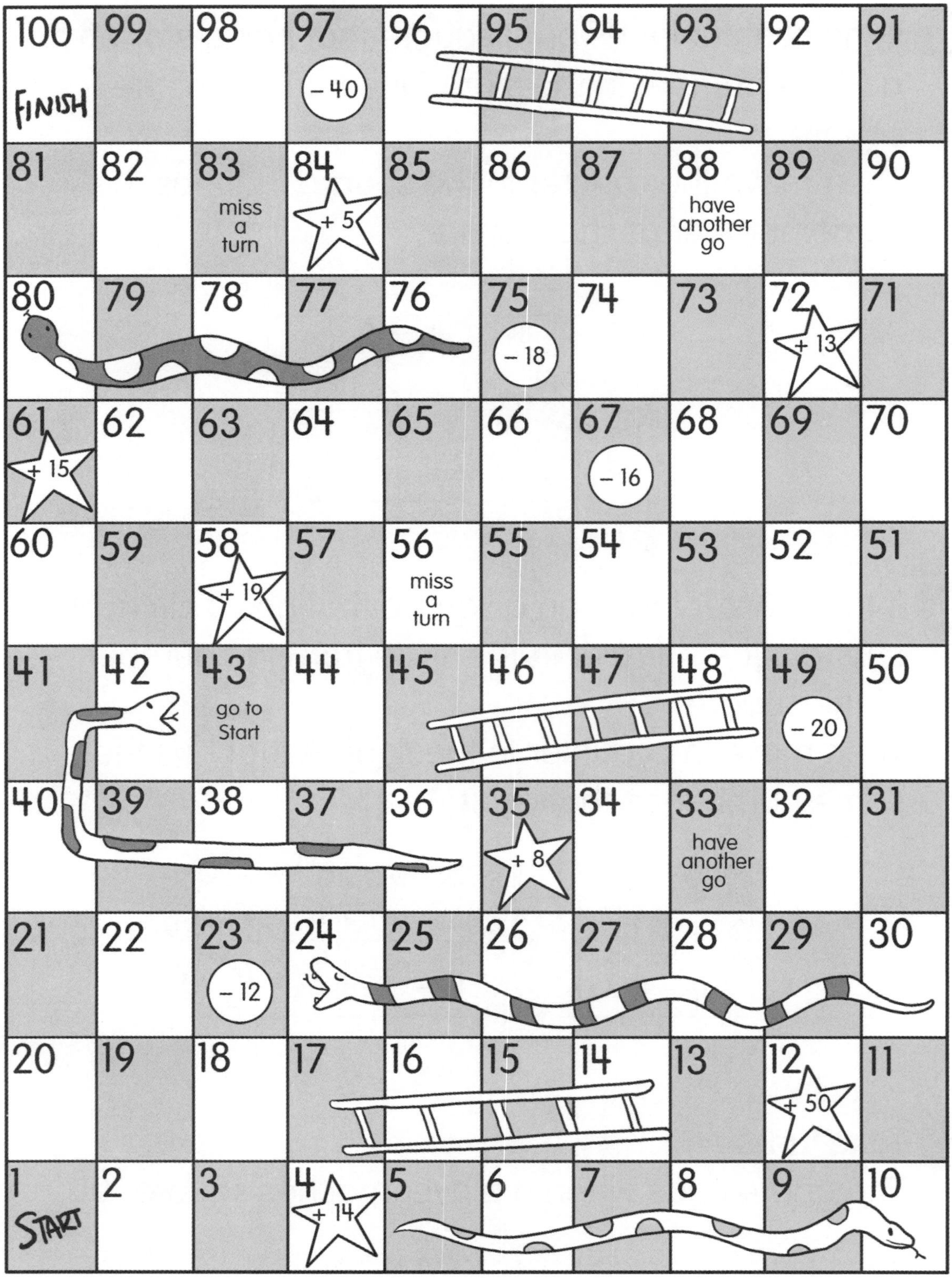

100 FINISH	99	98	97 (−40)	96	95	94	93	92	91
81	82	83 miss a turn	84 + 5	85	86	87	88 have another go	89	90
80	79	78	77	76	75 (−18)	74	73	72 + 13	71
61 + 15	62	63	64	65	66	67 (−16)	68	69	70
60	59	58 + 19	57	56 miss a turn	55	54	53	52	51
41	42	43 go to Start	44	45	46	47	48	49 (−20)	50
40	39	38	37	36	35 + 8	34	33 have another go	32	31
21	22	23 (−12)	24	25	26	27	28	29	30
20	19	18	17	16	15	14	13	12 + 50	11
1 START	2	3	4 + 14	5	6	7	8	9	10

CHAPTER 17 Addition and Subtraction to 100

Thinking Skills

Solve.
Show your work.

1. When Rodney subtracted 18 from 73, he said his answer was 65.
   This was incorrect.
   What number must be subtracted from Rodney's answer to make it correct?

The number _____ must be subtracted from Rodney's answer.

2. Jane, Matthew, and Sara each have 3 cards.
The numbers on each child's cards add up to 100.
What numbers could they have, if each number is in tens?
Each child has a different set of cards.

Jane

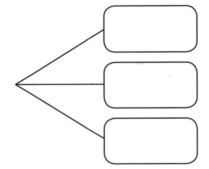

Matthew

Sara

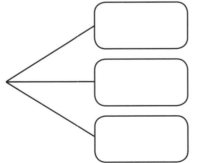

PROBLEM SOLVING
Strategies

Solve.
Show your work.

3. Penny had some gold beads and some silver beads.
    She traded 15 gold beads for 25 silver beads.
    Penny has 27 gold beads and 45 silver beads in the end.
    How many beads did Penny have at first?

    Penny had _____ beads at first.

4. Switch the positions of two numbers in the square so that
    every row and column add up to 85.
    Circle the two numbers.

19	45	16
33	24	28
33	21	36

5. Each shape stands for a different number.
Find the value of each shape.

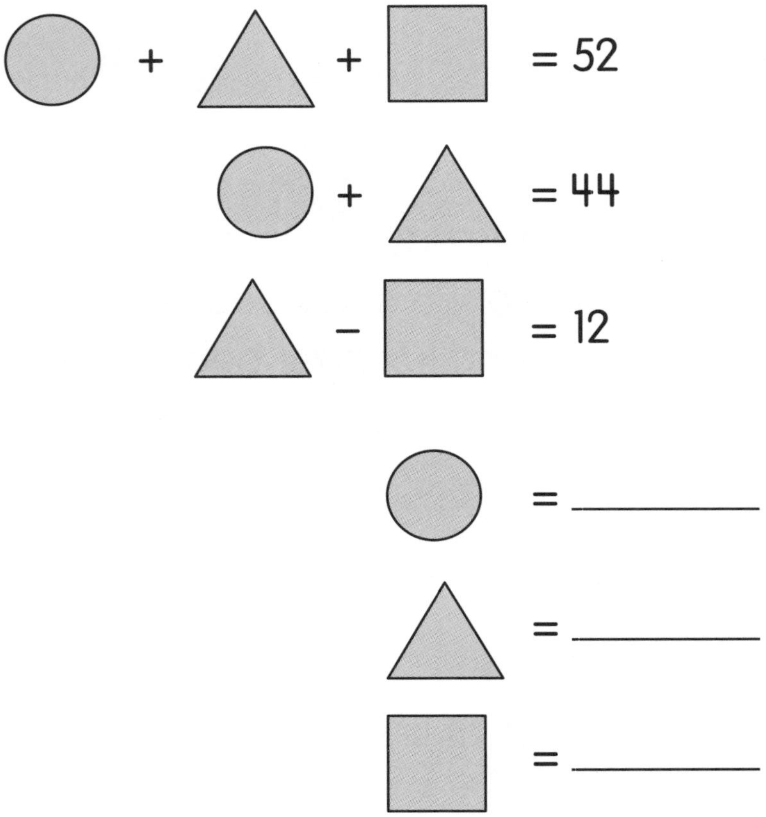

⬤ + △ + ▢ = 52

⬤ + △ = 44

△ − ▢ = 12

⬤ = _____

△ = _____

▢ = _____

Fill in the missing numbers.

6.

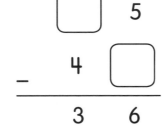

© Marshall Cavendish International (Singapore) Private Limited.

PROBLEM SOLVING

Exploration

P and R are letters that have a number value.
Find all possible values of P and R.

7.

```
    5  P
 +  2  R
 ───────
    8  2
```

8.

```
    8  P
 -  3  R
 ───────
    4  6
```

9.

```
    7  3
 -  3  P
 ───────
    3  R
```

Journal Writing

Solve.

10.   **a.**   Put the numbers 1, 2, and 3 in the boxes to show the correct order for the steps to solve:

$$\begin{array}{r} 4\;\;7 \\ +\;3\;\;8 \\ \hline \end{array}$$

☐   Add the tens.
    $1 + 4 + 3 = 8$
    Write 8 in the tens column.

☐   Add the ones.
    $7 + 8 = 15$

☐   Regroup.
    Write 5 in the ones column and 1 in the tens column.

© Marshall Cavendish International (Singapore) Private Limited.

Name: ______________________ Date: ______________

b. Write the steps to solve:

$$\begin{array}{r} 2\ 8 \\ +\ 6\ 5 \\ \hline \end{array}$$

Step 1 ______________________

____

____

Step 2 ______________________

____

____

Step 3 ______________________

____

____

18 Multiplication and Division

PROBLEM SOLVING
Thinking Skills

Draw pictures.
Then fill in the blanks.

1.   There are 6 children.
      Each child is holding 2 balloons.
      How many balloons are there in all?

6 groups of 2 = _____

© Marshall Cavendish International (Singapore) Private Limited.

Solve.

2. Helen was asked to draw 4 equal groups of triangles.
This is how she drew the triangles.

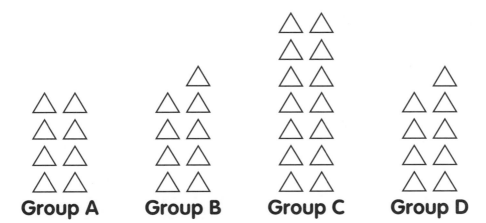

Group A   **Group B**   **Group C**   **Group D**

Her teacher said that she has drawn the groups incorrectly.
Help Helen to draw the triangles correctly.
Then fill in the blank.

Group A	**Group B**	**Group C**	**Group D**

Each group has _____ triangles.

Draw.

3. **a.** April has 6 flowers.
Diane has 4 flowers.
Pam has 8 flowers.
Draw a picture to show their flowers.

April   **Diane**   **Pam**

b. How would you share the flowers so that April, Diane, and Pam can have the same number of flowers?

April   **Diane**   **Pam**

I will take _____ flowers from _____ to

give _____.

PROBLEM SOLVING
Strategies

Solve.
Show your work.

4. Peter weighs 3 identical tables and 2 identical chairs.
Each table weighs twice as much as a chair.
Each chair has a weight of 6 pounds.
What is the total weight of the chairs and tables?

The total weight of the chairs and tables is _____.

5.   Some birds were flying south to avoid the winter cold.
Half way there, 12 of them turned back while the rest
continued.
Once they arrived south, the birds rested in 4 tall trees.
There were 8 birds in each tree.
How many birds flew together at first?

_____ birds flew together at first.

6.   There were 8 chickens and some cows in a picture.
There were 24 pairs of legs in all.
How many cows were there in the picture?

There were _____ cows in the picture.

PROBLEM SOLVING
Exploration

Study the picture.
Write three sentences with numbers or words to explain the groups in each picture.

7.

8.

Solve.

9. Arrange 18 cubes into rows so that each row has the same number of cubes.
There are 5 ways to do this.
Find all the ways.
Use the table to help you.
Then write three number sentences for each arrangement.

Arrangement	Number of rows	Number of cubes in each row	Total number of cubes

Journal Writing

Correct the mistakes.
Write the correct sentences.

10. 3 nines = 12

_____

11. Two groups of 3 is 23.

_____

12. Putting 35 into 7 equal groups is the same as
7 groups of 35.

_____

13. 5 groups of 8 is the same as 5 + 5 + 5 + 5 + 5 +
5 + 5 + 5.

_____

Name: ______________________ Date: ______________

Write stories.

14. Write one multiplication story and one division story. Use the numbers and words in the box.

4	puts	in all	24	groups	marbles
how many		each	few	6	equally

a. Adding equal groups story

____

____

____

____

b. Making equal groups story

____

____

____

____

CHAPTER 19 Money

PROBLEM SOLVING

Thinking Skills

Use the clues to match the price tags to the items.

1. Clues:

    a. The orange and the mango cost 7 dimes in all.

    b. The mango costs the most.

Price tags	Items
20¢ ●	● apple
30¢ ●	● orange
50¢ ●	● mango

2. Clues:

a. The pencil costs 25 pennies.

b. The pen costs more than the pencil.

Price tags	Items
20¢ •	• pencil
25¢ •	• pen
90¢ •	• eraser

⬤ **Solve.**
Show your work.

3. Cynthia wanted to buy some stationery.
Her mom gave her 2 quarters, 2 dimes, and 5 pennies.
If she wanted to buy 2 pencils and a notepad, how much
more money must Cynthia ask her mom for?

Item	Cost
Pencil	26¢
Pen	56¢
Ruler	20¢
Eraser	28¢
Notepad	30¢

Cynthia must ask her mom for _____ more.

4.   Jerry collected 13 empty bottles to return to the
recycling center.
Neal collected 6 fewer empty bottles less than Jerry.
Both of them were able to get 1 penny for every
two empty bottles they returned.
How many pennies did they get for their bottles?

They got _____ pennies for their bottles.

5.   Mr. Carlton bought 2 bags of oranges.
There were 8 oranges in each bag.
4 oranges cost 25¢.
How much did Mr. Carlton pay in all?

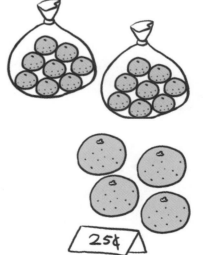

Mr. Carlton paid _____ in all.

Strategies

Fill in the blanks.

6. 9 pennies less than a quarter is equal to _____¢.

7. 2 quarters is equal to _____ pennies more than 4 nickels.

8. 5¢ more than 3 quarters is equal to _____ dimes.

Solve.
Show your work.

9. Scott had some coins.
He loaned his best buddy 4 nickels during recess, and bought an eraser from the bookshop for a dime.
Scott was left with 25¢.
How much money did he have at first?

He had _____¢ at first.

10. Rachel bought some stickers.
She received a free sticker for every 4 stickers
that she bought.
Each sticker costs 4¢, and she spent 4 dimes in all.
How many stickers did Rachel have in all?

Rachel had _____ stickers in all.

11. Lewis received a 5-penny refund for every 5 marbles
that he bought.
Each marble cost a nickel.
Lewis paid 30¢ in all.
How many marbles did he buy?

He bought _____ marbles.

PROBLEM SOLVING
Exploration

Solve.
Show your work.

12.   Sally buys a kite for 87¢.
She has 4 quarters, 5 dimes, 6 nickels, and 3 pennies.
Show three different ways that Sally can use her coins
to buy the kite.

13. The menu shows the prices of some food.

Muffin	32¢
Drink	25¢
Nuts	64¢
Crackers	20¢

Jeron has $1.
What are the possible menu items he can buy?
He must buy at least one muffin.

Journal Writing

Write a story.

14. Aaron has some coins.

Suzanne also has some coins.

Write a story using some or all of the words.

| more | quarters | in all | value |
| dimes | coins | nickels | exchange |

My story:

_____

_____

_____

_____

_____

15. Ruben has some coins in his pocket.
The coins have a total value of 55¢.
How many combinations of coins can Ruben have?
Show three combinations.

Answers

Chapter 10

Thinking skill: Comparing
Solution:

Object	Weight 1 ⬜ = 1 unit
1. book	7 units
2. pencil	4 units
3. ruler	2 units

Thinking skill: Comparing
Solution:

	Sentence	Check (✔) if correct
4.	The book is the lightest.	
5.	The pencil is heavier than the ruler.	✔
6.	The book is as heavy as the ruler.	
7.	The ruler is 2 units lighter than the book.	
8.	The book is as heavy as the total weight of the pencil and the ruler.	
9.	The total weight of the book, the pencil, and the ruler is 13 units.	✔

10. Thinking skill: Comparing
Solution: <u>D</u>, <u>B</u>, <u>C</u>, <u>A</u>
lightest   heaviest

11. Strategy: Use a diagram
Solution:

peach = 2 units

orange = peach + 2

mango = peach + 4

orange = 2 + 2 = 4 units

mango = 2 + 4 = 6 units

2 + 4 + 6 = 12 units
The total weight of the three fruits is
<u>12</u> units.

12. Strategy: Use guess and check
Solution:
List pairs of numbers that make 18 first.
Then subtract the two possible numbers to get 8.

Object A	Object B	A + B	A − B	Correct
17	1	18	16	No
16	2	18	14	No
15	3	18	12	No
14	4	18	10	No
13	5	18	8	Yes

The weights of the two objects are <u>5</u> units
and <u>13</u> units.

13. Strategy: Solve part of the problem
Solution:
1 duckling = 4 units
3 ducklings = 4 + 4 + 4
                    = 12 units
2 units + duck = 3 ducklings
2 units + duck = 12 units
                    duck = 10 units
The weight of the duck is <u>10</u> units.

14. drum; teddy bear

15. Box A is heavier. 2 unit cubes are needed
for Box B to balance Box A.
Box A is heavier by 2 units.

16.   <u>A</u>, <u>C</u>, <u>B</u>, <u>D</u>
heaviest   lightest

Chapter 11

1. Thinking skill: Comparing
    Solution: 3

2. Thinking skill: Comparing
    Solution: Andy

3. Thinking skill: Comparing
    Solution: 2

4. Thinking skill: Comparing
    Solution:
    20 − 5 − 4 − 2 − 3 = 6
    Nancy has 6 beads.

5. Thinking skill: Comparing
    Solution: Denise

6. Thinking skill: Comparing
    Solution: Kimberly

7. Thinking skill: Comparing
    Solution: Gill; Denise

8. Thinking skill: Comparing
    Solution:

Number of Oranges

Fanny	Josh	Lenny	Susan	Tim

Each ◯ stands for 1 orange.

9. Thinking skill: Comparing
    Solution:

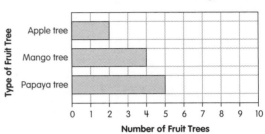

Fruit Trees on Mr. Philip's Farm

10. Thinking skill: Analyzing parts and whole
    Solution:
    2 − 0 = 2
    4 − 1 = 3
    5 − 2 = 3
    Mr. Philip had <u>2</u> apple trees, <u>3</u> mango trees, and <u>3</u> papaya trees after two months.

11. Strategy: Work backward
    Solution:
    3 + 4 − 2 − 1 = 4
    Riley had 4 marbles at first.

12. Strategy: Work backward
    Solution:
    Robert: 1 + 1 = 2
    Austin: 2 + 2 = 4
    Logan: 7 − 4 = 3
    2 + 4 + 3 − 4 = 5
    In all Robert, Austin, and Logan had 5 more marbles than Riley at first.

13. Strategy: Use before-and-after concept
    Solution:
    6 + 10 + 3 = 19
    Tammy had 19 books at first.

14. Strategy: Use before-and-after concept
    Solution: Yes

15. Strategy: Use before-and-after concept
    Solution:
    10 − 6 = 4
    She had 4 more comic books in the end.

16. Strategy: Use before-and-after concept
    Solution: puzzle books

17. Strategies: Use guess and check,
    Make a systematic list
    Solution:

Muffins Eaten by the Children

Emily ate <u>3</u> muffins.

18. Answers vary.

19.

Ribbons Owned by 5 Girls

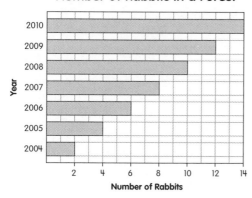

| Alice | Betty | Crystal | Dawn | Fiona |

Each 🎀 stands for 1 ribbon.

20. a. The number of rabbits increased by 2 each year from 2004 to 2008.

b.

Number of Rabbits in a Forest

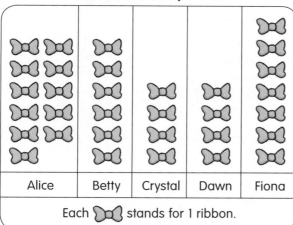

Chapter 12

1. Thinking skills: Identifying patterns and
   relationships, Comparing
   Solution:
   The number is <u>23</u>.
   Check: The reverse of 23 is 32.
   32 − 23 = 9

2. Thinking skill: Analyzing parts and whole
   Solution:

   ⬤ + ⬤ = 20

   2 ⬤ = 20

   ⬤ = 10

   ⬤ + ▬ = 25

   10 + ▬ = 25

   ▬ = 15

   ▬ + ★ = 27

   15 + ★ = 27

   ★ = 12

3. Thinking skill: Identifying patterns and
   relationships
   Solution:
   S = 23, B = 6, G = 11
   S + B + G = 23 + 6 + 11
           = 40
   P = 20
   40 − 20 − 6 = 14 (J)
   The missing letter is <u>J</u>.

4. Strategy: Use a diagram
   Solution:

   | 14 | 15 | 16 | 17 | 18 | 19 | 20 | 21 | 22 | 23 |

   Valerie has <u>19</u> mollies.

5. Strategy: Use a diagram

   Solution:

   4 years ago:

   | 8 | 9 | 10 | 11 | 12 | 13 | 14 | 15 | 16 | 17 | 18 | 19 | 20 | 21 | 22 | (23) | 24 | 25 |

   Present:

   | 20 | 21 | 22 | (23) | 24 | 25 | 26 | 27 | 28 | 29 |

   Patrick is <u>27</u> years old now.

6. Strategy: Look for patterns

   Solution:

   19; 18 (pattern is: +1, +2, +3, +4, +5)

7. Strategy: Look for patterns

   Solution:

   33 (pattern is: +3, +6, +9, +12)

8. 27, 28, 29, 30, 31, 32, 33, 34, or 35

9. Accept 2, 8; 17, 23; 8, 32; 32, 38

10. No. (correct pattern should be: +2, +3, +4, +5)

11. Yes. (pattern is: +4, +4, +4, +4)

12. Accept 5 more than 19 is 24; 5 less than 19 is 14.

13. Accept 10 less than 22 is 12; 10 more than 22 is 32.

Chapter 13

1. Thinking skill: Deduction

   Solution:

   (25) + (7) − (6) + (3) = (29)

2. Thinking skill: Identifying patterns and relationships

   Solution:

   Accept any two numbers that add up to 38. For example, 20 and 18. (pattern is: the two numbers on either side of 38 add up to 38)

3. Thinking skill: Comparing

   Solution:

   i. 16 − 8 = 8
   ii. 5 + 25 = 30
   iii. 6 + 27 = 33
   iv. 21 + 9 = 30
   v. 20 − 9 = 11

   33 − 8 = 25
   ↑ ↑
   from (iii)   from (i)

   The two number sentences are <u>16 − 8</u> and <u>6 + 27</u>.

4. Strategy: Use guess and check

   Solution:

No. of children who ate chicken burgers	No. of children who ate fish burgers	No. of children who ate both burgers	No. of children = 20?
10	14	0	10 + 14 − 0 = 24 (No)
10	14	1	10 + 14 − 1 = 23 (No)
10	14	2	10 + 14 − 2 = 22 (No)
10	14	3	10 + 14 − 3 = 21 (No)
10	14	4	10 + 14 − 4 = 20 (Yes)

   <u>4</u> children ate both fish and chicken burgers.

5. Strategy: Solve part of the problem

   Solution:

   Nellie = 9
   Jill = 9 − 6
      = 3
   Wendy = 3 + 5
        = 8
   Kiri = 3 + 3
      = 6
   Total = 9 + 3 + 8 + 6
        = 26
   The four girls have <u>26</u> dolls in all.

6. Strategy: Solve part of the problem

   Solution:

   Tray A:
   Blue buttons = 16 − 5
             = 11
   Yellow buttons = 0 + 9
               = 9
   Total = 11 + 9
        = 20
   Tray B:
   Blue buttons = 0 + 5
             = 5
   Yellow buttons = 27 − 9
               = 18
   Total = 5 + 18
        = 23
   There are <u>20</u> buttons in Tray A and <u>23</u> buttons in Tray B.

7. $\underline{8} + \underline{4} + \underline{9} = 21$
$\underline{5} + \underline{9} + \underline{7} = 21$
$\underline{6} + \underline{7} + \underline{8} = 21$

8. Answers vary.
For example,
$\underline{21} + \underline{19} - \underline{22} = 18$
$\underline{25} - \underline{20} + \underline{13} = 18$

9. Answers vary.
Allie's picks should total 35.
Ben's picks should total 40.

10. Find the pattern by subtracting any two consecutive numbers.
For example,
$21 - 17 = 4$
$33 - 29 = 4$
The pattern is +4.
$5 + 4 = 9$
$9 + 4 = 13$
The missing numbers are $\underline{9 \text{ and } 13}$.

11. Answers vary.
For example,
a. Chad makes 8 sandwiches. Elisa makes 15 more than Chad. How many sandwiches do they make in all?
b. Elisa makes 23 sandwiches. She gives 8 to Chad. How many sandwiches does she have left?

Chapter 14

1. Thinking skill: Analyzing parts and whole
Solution: 18

2. Thinking skill: Analyzing parts and whole
Solution: 3

3. Thinking skill: Analyzing parts and whole
Solution: 22

4. Thinking skill: Analyzing parts and whole
Solution: 26

5. Thinking skill: Analyzing parts and whole
Solution: 14

6. Thinking skill: Analyzing parts and whole
Solution: 24

7. Thinking skill: Analyzing parts and whole
Solution:
$28 - 9 - 7 = 12$
The missing number is $\underline{12}$.

8. Thinking skill: Comparing
Solution:
$36 - 9 = 27$
Nicole needs to score $\underline{27}$ more points.

9. Strategy: Solve part of the problem
Solution:
Rick swam: $8 + 3 = 11$ laps
$8 + 11 = 19$
They swam $\underline{19}$ laps of the pool in all.

10. Strategy: Solve part of the problem
Solution:
Tuesday: $14 - 4 = 10$ pages
$14 + 10 = 24$
Sandy read $\underline{24}$ pages of the book on both days.

11. Strategy: Solve part of the problem
Solution:
A coat has: $5 + 2 = 7$ buttons
$5 + 7 + 7 = 19$
There are $\underline{19}$ buttons on one shirt and two coats in all.

12. Strategy: Work backward
Solution:
$15 - 5 + 7 = 17$
There were $\underline{17}$ children at first.

13. Method 1
Use doubles fact (double 5).
$5 + 8 = 5 + 5 + 3$
$ = 13$

Method 2
Make 10.
$5 + 8 = 13$, with number bond: 8 splits into 3 and 2, and $5 + 5 = 10$

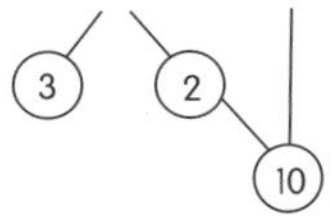

14. Method 1
Use a number bond and recall addition facts. 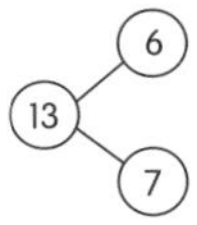
13 splits into 6 and 7
$13 - 6 = 7$

Method 2
Group into tens and ones. 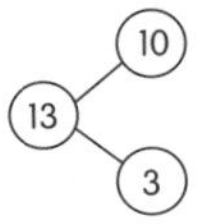
13 splits into 10 and 3
$10 - 6 = 4$
$4 + 3 = 7$

15. Method 1
Add the first two numbers first.
9 + 8 = 17
17 + 7 = 24
So, 9 + 8 + 7 = 24.

Method 2
Make 10.

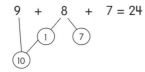

9 + 8 + 7 = 24

16. a. ② Add to make 10;
7 + 3 = 10.

③ Add tens and ones;
10 + 5 = 15.

① Use a number bond;
8 = 3 + 5.

b. **Step 1** Use a number bond;
6 = 1 + 5.

Step 2 Add to make 10;
9 + 1 = 10.

Step 3 Add tens and ones;
10 + 5 = 15.

Chapter 15

1. Thinking skill: Spatial visualization
Solution: 12

2. Thinking skill: Spatial visualization
Solution: 6

3. Thinking skill: Spatial visualization
Solution: 4 o'clock

4. Thinking skill: Spatial visualization
Solution: 2; 3

5. Thinking skill:
Solution: Classifying, Comparing

March						
S	M	T	W	T	F	S
		1	2	3	4	5
6	7	8	9	10	11	12
13	14	15	16	17	18	19
20	㉑	22	23	24	25	26
27	28	㉙	30	31		

April						
S	M	T	W	T	F	S
					1	2
3	4	⑤	6	7	8̸	9
10	11	12	13	14	15	16
17	18	19	20	21	22	23
24	25	26	27	28	29	30

6. Thinking skill: Comparing
Solution:
a.

b. Pedro has <u>half an hour</u> left.

7. Strategy: Work backward
Solution:

July						
S	M	T	W	T	F	S
		1	2	3	4	5
6	7	8	9	10	11	⑫
13	14	15	16	17	18	19
20	21	22	23	24	25	26
27	28	29	30	31		

8. Strategy: Use a diagram
Solution:

S	M	T	W	T	F	S
		1	2	3	4	5
6	7	8	9	10	11	12
13	14	15	16	17	⑱	19
20	21	22	23	24	25	26
27	28	29	30	31		

To the shop ← 5

9. Strategy: Make a systematic list,
    Look for patterns
    Solution:

Time	No. of times it sounded
1 o'clock	1
2 o'clock	2
3 o'clock	3
4 o'clock	4
5 o'clock	5
6 o'clock	6
7 o'clock	7

Total number of times
$= 1 + 2 + 3 + 4 + 5 + 6 + 7$
$= 28$
It will have chimed <u>28</u> times in all.

10. Months that land on a knuckle have 31 days.
    Months that land on a valley have 30 days.

11. Answers vary.
    For example,
    Countries that have the four seasons:
    Australia, Japan, Korea, and England
    Countries that do not have the four seasons:
    Singapore and Mexico

12. a. False
    September and November have 30 days.
    b. False
    August and October have 31 days.
    February has 28 or 29 days.
    c. False.
    There are 7 days in a week.
    d. False.
    There are 12 months in a year.
    e. False.
    There are 31 days in August.

13. Answers vary.

Chapter 16

1. Thinking skill: Comparing
    Solution:

3	6	4
5	9	2
8	7	1

2. Thinking skill: Comparing
    Solution:

5	6	2
4	1	7
9	8	3

3. Thinking skill: Comparing, Sequencing
    Solution:
    <u>D</u> , <u>A</u> , <u>B</u> , <u>C</u> , <u>E</u>
    greatest   least

4. Thinking skill: Comparing
    Solution: 67

5. Thinking skill: Comparing
    Solution: 45

6. Thinking skill: Comparing
    Solution: 85

7. Thinking skill: Comparing
    Solution: 28

8. Strategy: Look for patterns
    Solution:
    85 (pattern is: +5, +10, +15, +20, +25)

9. Strategy: Look for patterns
    Solution:
    21; 19 (pattern is: +3, −2)

10. Strategy: Look for patterns
    Solution:
    70; 61 (pattern is: −9)

11. Strategy: Look for patterns
    Solution: 8; 2

12. Strategy: Use guess and check

Solution:

Elle's age	Twice Elle's age	Mother's age	Mother = Twice Elle's age?
23	46	58	No
25	50	60	No
27	54	62	No
29	58	64	No
31	62	66	No
33	66	68	No
35	70	70	Yes

Elle's mother will be twice as old as Elle when Elle is 35 years old.
So, 35 − 23 = 12
Elle's mother will be twice as old as Elle in 12 years.

13. Strategy: Work backward

Solution:
20 + 7 + 5 + 9 = 41
Mary bought 41 rolls of tape during the sale.

14. Answers vary.
For example,
55, 57, 59, 61, 63, 65 (pattern is: +2)
55, 58, 61, 64, 67, 70 (pattern is: +3)
55, 60, 65, 70, 75, 80 (pattern is: +5)

15. Answers vary.
For example,
99, 90, 81, 72, 63, 54 (pattern is: −9)
99, 88, 77, 66, 55, 44 (pattern is: −11)
99, 79, 84, 64, 69, 49 (pattern is: −20, +5)

16. Accept 7 more than 74 is 81;
7 less than 81 is 74; 7 more than 81 is 88.

17. Accept 25 less than 100 is 75;
25 more than 75 is 100; 25 less than 75 is 50.

18. Answers vary.
For example,
Subtract 15 from the number.
Then add 27. You get 84. What is the mystery number?
84 − 27 + 15 = 72
The mystery number is 72.

Chapter 17

1. Thinking skill: Comparing

Solution:
73 − 18 = 55
65 − 55 = 10
The number 10 must be subtracted from Rodney's answer.

2. b. Thinking skill: Comparing, Analyzing parts and whole

Solution:
Answers vary.
For example,
Jane: 10, 40, 50
Matthew: 20, 70, 10
Sara: 50, 30, 20

3. Strategy: Use before-and-after concept

Solution:
Gold beads = 27 + 15
            = 42
Silver beads = 45 − 25
             = 20
Total number of beads
= 42 + 20
= 62
Penny had 62 beads at first.

4. Strategy: Look for patterns

Solution:

19	45	㉑
33	24	28
33	⑯	36

5. Strategy: Simplify the problem

Solution:

$$\bigcirc + \triangle + \square = 52$$
$$\bigcirc + \triangle = 44$$
$$44 + \square = 52$$
$$\text{So, } \square = 8$$
$$\triangle - \square = 12$$
$$\triangle - 8 = 12$$
$$\text{So, } \triangle = 20$$
$$\bigcirc + 20 = 44$$
$$\text{So, } \bigcirc = 24$$

6. Strategy: Work backward
   Solution:

   $$\begin{array}{cc} \boxed{8} & 5 \\ -\ \ 4 & \boxed{9} \\ \hline 3 & 6 \end{array}$$

7. P = 9, R = 3; P = 8, R = 4; P = 7,
   R = 5; P = 6, R = 6; P = 3, R = 9;
   P = 4, R = 8; P = 5, R = 7

8. P = 5, R = 9; P = 4, R = 8; P = 3,
   R = 7; P = 2, R = 6; P = 1, R = 5;
   P = 0, R = 4

9. P = 4, R = 9; P = 5, R = 8; P = 6,
   R = 7; P = 7, R = 6; P = 8, R = 5;
   P = 9; R = 4

10. a. ___ Add the tens.
    ⎡3⎤ 1 + 4 + 3 = 8.
        Write 8 in the tens column.

    ⎡1⎤ Add the ones.
        7 + 8 = 15.

    ⎡2⎤ Regroup.
        Write 5 in the ones column and
        1 in the tens column.

    b. **Step 1** Add the ones.
          8 + 5 = 13.

    Step 2 Regroup.
          Write 3 in the ones column and
          1 in the tens column.

    Step 3 Add the tens.
          1 + 2 + 6 = 9.
          Write 9 in the tens column.

   Chapter 18

1. Thinking skill: Comparing
   Solution:

   6 groups of 2 = <u>12</u>

2. Thinking skill: Comparing
   Solution:

   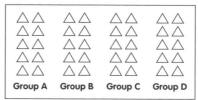

   Group A   Group B   Group C   Group D

   Each group has <u>10</u> triangles.

3. Thinking skill: Comparing
   Solution:
   a.

   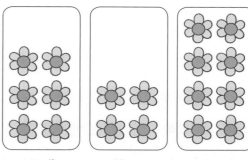

   April   **Diane**   **Pam**

   b.

   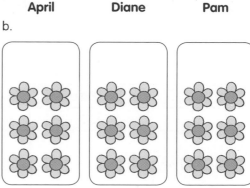

   April   **Diane**   **Pam**

   I will take <u>2</u> flowers from <u>Pam</u> to give
   <u>Diane</u>.

4. Strategy: Simplify the problem
   Solution:
   Weight of 2 chairs = 6 + 6
                     = 12
   Weight of 1 table = 6 + 6
                     = 12
   Weight of 3 tables = 12 + 12 + 12
                      = 36
   Total weight = 12 + 36
              = 48
   The total weight of the chairs and
   tables is <u>48 pounds</u>.

5. Strategy: Work backward
   Solution:
   8 + 8 + 8 + 8 = 32
   32 + 12 = 44
   <u>44</u> birds flew together at first.

6. Strategy: Analyzing parts and whole
   Solution:
   2 + 2 + 2 + 2 + 2 + 2 + 2 + 2 = 16
   24 pairs = 48
   48 − 16 = 32
   1 cow has 4 legs.
   So, 32 divided into groups of 4 = 8
   There were <u>8</u> cows in the picture.

7. 5 groups of 3 = 15
        5 threes = 15
   3 + 3 + 3 + 3 + 3 = 15

8. 4 groups of 6 = 24
        4 sixes = 24
   6 + 6 + 6 + 6 = 24

9.

Arrangement	Number of rows	Number of cubes in each row	Total number of cubes
1	1	18	18
2	2	9	18
3	3	6	18
4	6	3	18
5	9	2	18

Arrangement 1:
1 group of 18 = 18
    1 eighteen = 18

Arrangement 2:
2 groups of 9 = 18
    2 nines = 18
        9 + 9 = 18

Arrangement 3:
3 groups of 6 = 18
    3 sixes = 18
    6 + 6 + 6 = 18

Arrangement 4:
6 groups of 3 = 18
    6 threes = 18
3 + 3 + 3 + 3 + 3 + 3 = 18

Arrangement 5:
9 groups of 2 = 18
    9 twos = 18
2 + 2 + 2 + 2 + 2 + 2 + 2 + 2 + 2 = 18

10. Accept 3 fours = 12; 3 nines = 27.

11. Two groups of 3 is 6.

12. Putting 35 into 7 equal groups is the same as 35 shared into 7 equal groups.

13. Accept 5 groups of 8 is the same as 8 + 8 + 8 + 8 + 8; 8 groups of 5 is the same as 5 + 5 + 5 + 5 + 5 + 5 + 5 + 5.

14. Answers vary.
    For example,
    a. Alan has 4 bags. Each bag has 6 marbles. How many marbles does he have in all?
    b. Mrs. Cooper has 24 marbles. She puts the marbles equally into groups. Each group has 4 marbles. How many groups are there?

Chapter 19

1. Thinking skill: Comparing
   Solution:

Price tags	Items
20¢	apple
30¢	orange
50¢	mango

2. Thinking skill: Comparing
   Solution:

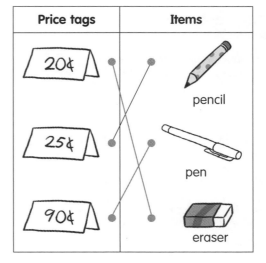

Price tags	Items
20¢	pencil
25¢	pen
90¢	eraser

3. Thinking skill: Comparing
   Solution:
   Cynthia has:
   2 quarters + 2 dimes + 5 pennies
   = 25¢ + 25¢ + 10¢ + 10¢ + 1¢ + 1¢ + 1¢ + 1¢ + 1¢
   = 75¢
   Cost of 2 pencils and 1 notepad
   = 26¢ + 26¢ + 30¢
   = 82¢
   82¢ − 75¢ = 7¢
   Cynthia must ask her mom for 7¢ more.

4. Thinking skill: Analyzing parts and whole,
                  Identifying patterns and
                  relationships
   Solution:
   Neal collected = 13 − 6
                  = 7 bottles
   Total bottles collected = 13 + 7
                           = 20

Bottles returned	No. of pennies
2	1
4	2
⋮	⋮
20	10

   They got 10 pennies for their bottles.

5. Thinking skill: Analyzing parts and whole
   Solution:
   1 bag = 8 oranges
   2 bags = 8 + 8
          = 16 oranges
   4 oranges = 25¢
   16 oranges = 25¢ + 25¢ + 25¢ + 25¢
              = 100¢
              = $1
   Mr. Carlton paid $1 in all.

6. Strategy: Use a diagram
   Solution: 16

7. Strategy: Use a diagram
   Solution: 30

8. Strategy: Use a diagram
   Solution: 8

9. Strategy: Work backward
   Solution:
   25¢ + 10¢ + 5¢ + 5¢ + 5¢ + 5¢ = 55¢
   He had 55¢ at first.

10. Strategy: Simplify the problem
    Solution:
    4 dimes = 40¢
    1 sticker costs 4¢.
    So, 10 stickers cost 40¢.

No. of stickers	No. of free stickers
4	1
8	2
12	3

    Rachel received 2 free stickers.
    10 + 2 = 12
    Rachel had 12 stickers in all.

11. Strategy: Use a diagram
    Solution:

No. of marbles	Cost of marbles	Refund	Total amount paid = 30¢?
1	5¢	No	5¢ (No)
3	15¢	No	15¢ (No)
5	25¢	Yes	25¢ − 5¢ = 20¢ (No)
7	35¢	Yes	35¢ − 5¢ = 30¢ (Yes)

    He bought 7 marbles.

12. Answers vary.
    For example,
    i.   3 quarters + 1 dime + 2 pennies
    ii. 2 quarters + 3 dimes + 1 nickel + 2 pennies
    iii. 2 quarters + 1 dime + 5 nickels + 2 pennies

13. Cost of 1 muffin = 32¢
    Amount left after buying 1 muffin
    = $1 − 32¢
    = 68¢
    Accept answers that add up to 68¢.
    For example,
    drink + 2 crackers
    = 25¢ + 20¢ + 20¢
    = 65¢
    So, he can buy 1 muffin, 2 crackers, and 1 drink.

14. Answers vary.

15. Answers vary.
    For example.
    i.   2 quarters + 1 nickel
    ii. 1 quarter + 3 dimes
    iii. 5 dimes + 1 nickel

BLANK

REALIZING THE IMPOSSIBLE

REALIZING THE IMPOSSIBLE

ART AGAINST AUTHORITY

EDITED BY
JOSH MACPHEE AND ERIK REULAND

Realizing the Impossible: Art Against Authority
© 2007 Josh MacPhee and Erik Reuland

ISBN 1-904859-32-1
ISBN-13 978-1-904859-32-1
Library of Congress Control Number: 2006924198

AK Press   AK Press
674-A 23rd St.   PO Box 12766
Oakland, CA 94612   Edinburgh EH8 9YE
USA   Scotland

akpress@akpress.org   ak@akedin.demon.co.uk
www.akpress.org   www.akuk.com

The addresses above would be delighted to provide you with the latest complete AK catalog, featuring several thousand books, pamphlets, zines, audio and video products, and stylish apparel published and distributed by AK Press. Alternately, please visit our websites for the complete catalog, latest news and updates, events, and secure ordering.

Printed with union labor in Canada on recycled, acid-free paper.

Front cover design: Josh MacPhee/justseeds.org
Front cover art: Erik Ruin
Front cover background photograph: Palle Nielsen
Interior layout and design: Josh MacPhee/justseeds.org
Indexed by Chris Dodge

TABLE OF CONTENTS

SAMPAI KETEMU DI BARIKADE

BARA MERAH SATUKAN DARAH MEMBAKAR BATAS DAN KELAS

INTRODUCTION: TOWARDS ANARCHIST ART THEORIES...

JOSH MACPHEE AND ERIK REULAND

It is said that an anarchist society is impossible. Artistic activity is the process of realizing the impossible.
—Max Blechman, "Toward an Anarchist Aesthetic"

For years we have wanted to read a book like this, and finally we have been able to produce it. As anarchists, we have seen our politics denigrated by other artists; as artists, we have had our cultural production attacked as frivolous by activists. Our interest in the intersection of these subjects is both extremely personal and intensely political. One of the goals of this book is to put forth examples, past and present, of groups and individuals that have attempted to collapse the dichotomy between pure aesthetics, unmoored from a societal context, and purely utilitarian art, slavishly beholden to politics. Much of what is explored in this collection, from Clifford Harper's focus on craft to the social experimentation of 1970s video collectives, exists in this in-between space, each in its own way refusing "art for art's sake" as well as the rigid rules of propaganda.

Even if we reject the idea that art can be boiled down to simple utility, that doesn't mean we can abandon a concern with efficacy. Although our art might be rooted in an attempt to achieve some sort of liberated self-expression, as artists we also create in order to communicate. It is not surprising, however, that we have little sense of the influence of anarchist art, since there is hardly any discussion about art within anarchist and anti-authoritarian circles (or any Left political circles beyond Marxist academia, for that matter). We want to interrogate this here: What is the impact? Who is the audience? What are anarchist artists trying to say, to whom, and why?

Of all the political philosophies, anarchism has been the most open to artistic freedom, rejecting the basis of both Marxist and capitalist conceptions of art. Both of these ideologies use different language to make the same basic claim: the former states that all art is simply a product of class antagonisms, or in other words, art is the result of the prevailing economic conditions (currently, market capitalism); and the latter demands that all cultural production should be squeezed into the market system, or in the logic of capitalism, the primary productive use of art is economic.[1]

Anarchism, the belief that human beings can and should self-organize rather than submit to top-down organizing by a state or ruling class, has had a different approach to art. Although mainstream art historians seem to want to bury this reality, any in-depth look at the last two hundred years of art can't miss the molding hands of "The Idea," as nineteenth century French artists called

Setu Legi/Taring Padi, *Bangun Kesetaraan*, linocut, 2005. Translation: Hot Coals Unite the Races and Burn Down Borders and Classes.

anarchism. Anarchism took strong root within the artistic milieu of *fin de siècle* Europe, particularly France, with some of the most innovative artists of the time regularly contributing illustrations and cartoons to anarchist publications (see Patricia Leighten's essay within). In England, William Morris' arts and crafts movement was deeply influenced by utopian and anti-authoritarian ideas. Most of the postimpressionists adhered to anarchism, in part developing their theory of pointillist paint application in accordance with their political beliefs—that tens of thousands of unique and separate points of color (or people) can exist both autonomously and harmoniously on a single canvas (or in a single society).[2] There is a long list of artists influenced by anarchism: Pablo Picasso, Camille Pissarro, Georges Seurat, Man Ray, Robert Henri, Wassily Kandinsky, Rockwell Kent, Frans Masereel, and Mark Rothko, just to list some of the more well-known ones. It has also influenced entire art and cultural movements, such as postimpressionism, Dada, surrealism, lettrisme, situationism, fluxus, and punk.

In spite of this history, and even though Marxist art theorists have been extremely prolific, there is oddly little writing readily available in English on the subject of visual art and anarchism. There are a couple of solid books on specific historical subjects (Allan Antliff's *Anarchist Modernism*, Patricia Leighten's *Reordering the Universe*, and Richard Porton's *Film and the Anarchist Imagination* come to mind), a handful of articles in obscure journals, magazines, and zines, and Max Blechman's great, yet hard-to-find, *Drunken Boat* anthologies. Because of this overall lack of written

work, we felt it was imperative to introduce a wide variety of material. *Realizing the Impossible* is the result. It is a sprawling collection, jumping from decade to decade, continent to continent, and medium to medium. Rather than a comprehensive and authoritative tome, it is an introduction to the subject. Not every aspect of art and anarchism is explored here. Hundreds of artists, projects, and political aspects aren't included, not because they are any less important, but because there is only so much we can fit in a single volume. Likewise, not everyone profiled in this book would necessarily call themselves anarchist, yet we feel that everything included emerges from a deep current of anti-authoritarianism that has consistently traversed the development and practice of modern art.

When reading these essays, it is crucial to keep in mind that anarchism is not a singular political program so much as a thorough commitment to substantive equality and the potential for human liberation.[3] It exists in opposition to the belief in taking state power by a select few (as put forward by the followers of Lenin or Mao), which in practice has lead to bureaucratic tyranny and mass starvation. As anarchists we stand against political and cultural vanguards, those self-appointed experts who claim the authority to determine what is the "correct path to revolution" or "proper role of artists." We look to alternative models and methods, engaging in the difficult work of creating a world of individuals who can all have a direct hand in the organization of society. Only when we all are empowered to organize our own lives will true liberation come.

For us, this book is the beginning of an anarchist art theory. This theory demands a place for individuals and their unique creative processes, while at the same time demanding a rigorous critique of the ruthless and competitive market individualism rampant in the art world. As political artists, we believe it is critical that we understand the history of what we are doing and think of ways we can use art for our collective liberation. It is no longer enough today to lock ourselves in our studios and produce culture. We must engage in our world in as many ways as possible. We need to

1. For a great, and much more complex, assessment of Marx's ideas toward art, see Donald Drew Egbert, *Socialism and American Art* (Princeton, NJ: Princeton University Press, 1967).

2. Robyn S. Roslak, "The Politics of Aesthetic Harmony: Neo-Impressionism, Science, and Anarchim,' *Art Bulletin* v. 73, no. 3 (September 1991): 381–90.

3. Hundreds of different strains of anarchism have been developed over the past 250 years, from more classical varieties such as anarcho-syndicalism (human liberation based in the reorganization and liberation of the working class), anarcho-communism ("from each according to their ability, to each according to their need"), and anarchist individualism/egoism (the rights of the individual are paramount, and the ego should be unfettered by societal constraints), to more contemporary developments such as anarcho-primitivism (civilization must be destroyed to free humanity), post-Left anarchy (a focus on social insurrection and a rejection of the history of Left social organization), and an anarchism that is explicitly reflective of our identities (such as anarcho-feminism, people of color anarchism, and queer anarchism).

ground our artistic production in the realities of our lives and those many others around us. Anarchism has historically attracted artists because of its steadfast commitment to the rights of the individual. We need to uphold that commitment, but as cultural creators we also need to engage with other important aspects of anarchism, particularly those of collective struggle and mutual aid. We will never create a better world simply as atomized individuals, whether workers, theorists, or artists.

With *Realizing the Impossible*, we hope to encourage artists to take their work seriously as a potential political tool. We also want to encourage political organizers and activists to think more openly about the role of creativity in social movements. As Brett Bloom says in his essay, "[Art is] about attempts to rebuild or reorder the world in ways that are more just, egalitarian, or seek to dismantle abusive, hierarchical elements of society." Because art is understood as a realm of the qualitative, where our assumptions about how the "real" world works can be temporarily put on hold, it is the very place where exciting experiments in social reorganization can take place. It is in this space that we can catch glimpses of liberation. Such experimentation offers test runs for the realization of new ways of life—ways that cannot be measured in quantities, consumer goods, or lifestyles but are instead qualitatively different, where social relations between human beings are no longer caged in by commodities and capitalism. Anarchist art can become itself a utopian instance, prefiguring a world we want to live in.

Icky A., *The Time is Now*, linocut with spraypaint, 2006.

LIFE, LABOR, ART: A DISCUSSION WITH CARLOS KOYOKUIKATL CORTÉZ

CHRISTINE FLORES-COZZA

Carlos Koyokuikatl Cortéz (1923–2005) was a poet, writer, anarchist, activist, artist, pacifist, conscientious objector, organizer, friend, husband, and "abuelo"—grandfather to all.

Carlos Cortéz was born in Milwaukee in 1923 to a Mexican Wobbly father and German socialist-pacifist mother, and followed firmly in both of their footsteps. Carlos joined the International Workers of the World (IWW) in 1947 after being released from two years of federal detention as a conscientious objector. He first pursued printmaking after he became involved with the IWW, for whom he drew cartoons and created posters throughout his life. Many of his prints and poems have been published in the IWW newspaper, the *Industrial Worker*, of which he was an editor during the 1960s and 1970s. Carlos' art has traveled beyond activist circles, and most of his woodcut prints are housed at the Mexican Fine Arts Center Museum in Chicago.

Carlos has been called a "genius at living." A construction laborer, factory worker, janitor, journalist, salesman, curator, printmaker, and poet, he was actively involved in Chicago's Mexican community, helping many in need with his skills and inspiring all through his art and poetry. He was a wise, wonderful, character of sorts and I had the great pleasure of befriending Carlos and his wife, Marianna. On one particular evening in 1999 my friend Dennis Fritz and I enjoyed a wonderful evening filled with tortillas, traditional molés, Guinness beer, and lots of amazing conversation at their home in Chicago.

In your portrait of Ricardo Flores-Magón, he is holding a manifesto which states:

> "This stuff of 'art for art's sake' is an absurdity and its defenders have always gotten on my nerves. I feel such a reverent admiration and love for art that it causes me great distress to see it prostituted by others who are incapable of having others feel what they feel nor think what they think, hide their impotence behind the slogan of 'art for art's sake.'"

Do you feel that the artist has a responsibility to convey messages in their art that make people more politically conscious?

I think that is one of the obligations the creative artist has, because art can only flourish under freedom. The artists who are strong enough and courageous enough can fight, can use their art to fight tyranny, repression and that. Of course an artist's obligation, a creative artist, whether it's a visual artist or a non-visual artist has to express what he or she feels the strongest about. And it would be useless to say to someone who has no particular sociological convictions that they should be sociological in their art. That would be something like the forced "People's Art" of the Soviet days. It has to come from the heart, from how one feels. A lot depends upon the awareness of the artist in question. If the artist is only interested in the commercial world, well, then sociological, humanitarian concerns are not for them.

Of course, the truth is that the artists who do make it on art alone are few and far between—those who are fortunate enough to have patrons and steady patronage. Usually a person who is a creative artist does it as a sideline. I am often asked by young people about making a living at art. I tell them, "Do you want to make a living off art, or do you want to make a life of art?" If you want to make a living off art, I can't help you. But if you want to make a life of art, I will give you all my encouragement. Because the truth of it is, those who make a living on art alone are few and far between. Entertainers, you know, like musicians and singers and actors can get a little steadier recompense. And that is why I think that I agree perfectly with Ricardo Magón: the concept of art for art's sake is absurd. It's like saying a hamburger for hamburger's sake. You do not disrupt the structural integrity of the hamburger by eating it.

What are your artistic influences?

My earliest influences were people like Diego Rivera, later José Clemente Orozco. And eventually José Guadelupe Posada. And then some art teacher told me I should

look at the stuff of Käthe Kollwitz. Through Käthe Kollwitz I became acquainted with the German expressionist Edvard Munch. In fact, I had a very beautiful afternoon in Oslo and I went to the Munch museum there. Marianna was saying, "You're shaking." I said, "This is a pilgrimage." Later on, I read one of Munch's remarks. When he found multiples, you know, graphics, he said, "Now I can free art from the sterile confines of the galleries and museums and the tombs of the private collectors." Well, unfortunately, the art dealers, who are at least to

me a bunch of vultures, recorded all his plots and they have catalogs that don't even list the price of his works. In other words, if you have to ask, you can't afford it. It's like these restaurants that post the menu on the outside without prices. If you have to ask, don't come in.

Please explain some of the imagery in your woodcuts and your linocuts. Like the skulls, the guitars, the manifestos, the letters...

Well, as you see, a lot of my stuff is labor heroes of the past, some not quite... Well, yes, César Chávez is unfortunately in the past now. And then, I did support work for the Pittston miners in Appalachia. As for the skeletons, that's a part of Mexican tradition. One of my inspirations was the engraver Posada. The skull has been a theme in Mexican art for four thousand years or more. In the past century the periodical cartoonist, who [used] mostly hand engraving—at that time there was no photo-electric engraving—used skeletons as caricatures, caricaturing important political people of the day, and even certain heroes. Posada did work on broadsides as well as periodicals. Broadsides that sold for a centavo or two and in which many of his graphics were skeletal. And he was only one of many engravers in Mexico who used the theme of the *calavera*, or the skeleton. Posada just happened to become known internationally and collected internationally. A few years ago, prints of his were under $100. That is, prints that were run

This page: Carlos Cortéz, *Untitled*, linocut, 1964; next page: Carlos Cortéz, *Welcome Home!*, linocut, 1965.

off at that time. The grandson of his publisher has a collection of his plates, and he runs them off and sells reproductions of the original plates. I hope that's what happens to my work if I ever become noted. Modesty is not one of my attributes! I realize the possibility that I might catch on some day, and I would not like to see my stuff selling for, you know... out of the price of the ordinary working person.

Lets talk more about art and money.

Yeah, well, money is only a medium of exchange. It's a bit more convenient for the farmer than taking his cow to the city and swapping it for an automobile, a suit of clothes, or whatever. It's a medium of exchange. But there should be, I think, you know... The present day unions that we have are too closely tied up with the domestic and foreign policy of the piece of geography they happen to be in. They are not organized on a global scale, whereas those who are organized on a global scale are the upper class, the rich people themselves. Well, as you can see, the brass hats, their soldiers were killing each other, but when everything was over it was hunky-dory. They were wining, dining, and wenching each other.

It's very important. I believe the ordinary people of this earth can do it. I think we need an equalization in buying power among the common people. Because when there is a disparity in monetary values the people on top benefit from it. They will naturally move operations to where labor is cheapest. And, at the present rate that we're going, the United States is going to be a Third World country.

How do you survive?

Well, at this late stage in my life, some of my stuff is paying the rent and putting food on the table. And paying the tax collector, which is something that rankles me. I don't turn my nose up at making money, but what is more important to me is making face. Today I received a little catalog from Spain. Some young people from [an] anarchist organization over there were here with a friend of mine who is a veteran of the struggle in Spain, from when Franco was taking over. They came to visit him, they came around, and they have some foundation that makes exhibits. They took a liking to my stuff, so I gave them copies to take back with them. Now I found they are making a traveling exhibition with a little catalog. So, it's a good ego booster.

What advice would you have for someone struggling to support themselves as they try to become and established artist?

Marianna Cortéz: You have to have someone else working for you!

Carlos Cortéz: Well, you have to have someone to put the beans and potatoes on the table. Usually most of us are working at something we ordinarily wouldn't do except that we are able to put the beans on the table. Again I say, are you going to try to make a living off art or make a life of art? Always make sure you have enough time of your own to develop the creativity within you. I took night classes in my early twenties up in Milwaukee because I was working in construction, had construction money, and was young with a lot of diversions calling. I said, "Well, there's at least a couple of times a week I can sit down and stay in practice." Later on, I'd meet some of these guys who had gotten their art degree, got a job through it, and they said all they were doing was designing soap packages or automobiles. They complained that already, if they tried to do something on their own, they had the merchandising tricks perverting what they did. So I always say, you are going to have to do some kind of work. Unfortunately, for most of us it will be something we would rather not do. Those of us who happen to have peace with our job are lucky, but we must manage to find peace one way or the other. If not, then we'd go off the hook. But always find time to develop what's in you.

Right. You know I've known so many people who have gone to art school and have gone off to work for advertising firms as graphic artists or whatever, and they don't paint anymore. They don't do what inspired them in the beginning. If I wanted to teach art in grammar school or high school, then I'd go to art school. If I want to paint, I do it or try to learn from someone who I know who inspires me or something like that...

That is about the best opportunity in art; to become an art teacher in a high school or kindergarten or what have you. And that of course is, again, peon work. Being a teacher.

But, there is also the satisfaction that you are opening doors for somebody. And I have had that satisfaction. For the past five years I've given poetry workshops at Orozco Academy in Pilsen. And apparently they like what I am doing, because they keep calling me back every spring. And it's a little extra money on the table.

I guess one of the things also is life itself. Finding peace for yourself, finding a way to live with your situation... Of course that's the situation of most people. That, I think, is what brought out our rich tradition of folklore, of folk art, of folk music, among all people. They had to have a way of making their hum-drum life bearable. Some of the most beautiful music came from the folk, which in turn influenced the classical composers. Tchaikovsky lifted directly from folk music. Bach, you listen to his stuff and

it reminds you of a folk dance. And I think culture comes up from the bottom. It never comes down from the top. The only thing that comes down from the top? There is a Mexican popular saying, "*Las gallinas de arriba siempre cagan en las de abajo.*" The chickens on the top always shit on those below.

What does Koyokuikatl mean? Why have you chosen this name?

Well, a few years ago there was a *sacerdote* (holy man) up here from Mexico. He was a practitioner of the indigenous religion, the pre-Columbian religion. He was giving baptisms and marriages. He gave Marianna and I an indigenous marriage. And then, a couple of years later, baptisms. He said he was going to give me a baptism in a Nahuatl name. He said he could choose one for me unless I had one I wanted to choose. I gave him that one and I told him the history of it. When I was up in the federal correctional during the war, it was up in the Minnesota woods, and at night, in the distance, you could hear the coyotes. And I said, "Oh, now that is beautiful. That's the sound of freedom." So I took on the name "coyote sound." And coyotes are, among the indigenous peoples of this continent, an honored animal. Honored, because of their talents of survival. They have those survival smarts. In fact, many of the pre-Columbian luminaries had "coyote" in their name, like the poet Hungry Coyote. In other words, hungry in the sense of somebody who is looking for inspiration, for ideas. The North American Indians also honored the coyote. In fact, they have a series of stories, called coyote stories, of coyotes outsmarting larger and more powerful animals

I read that you were jailed for two years when you were in Minnesota, tell me more about that?

Well, coming from an IWW father and a socialist mother (who was also a pacifist), I grew up an anti-militarist. So when World War II came along, I was about to get drafted and I had to make a decision about where I stood. I decided the only thing I could possibly do was refuse to go and suffer the consequences. Of course in some countries the consequences were you became a soldier or you were stood up against the wall by a firing squad. Well, that didn't happen here, so I could choose. In the United States, all you need to do is threaten people with jail to make them go into the army. In other countries, not so. In Germany that didn't go. There you were a soldier or "BOOM-BOOM," you faced the firing squad.

Well, I did two years. When I received my draft notice I didn't show up, and when the FBI came to pick me up they said, "What's the matter, do you like Hitler?" I said, "Look, if you guaranteed me a shot at Hitler you wouldn't have to come draft me." But to shoot at another draftee who doesn't even have the choice I have? No. I said there had been wars, a constant history of wars. The only ones who benefit are the heads of state and the rich people. Poor people always get it in the neck, which is something the American soldiers found out at the end of the war. They were living in the mud with the defeated German soldiers while the American brass hats were wining, dining, and wenching the Nazi brass hats in the palaces nearby. It showed that it's a class thing.

So tell me, what is a "wobbly"?

That's a nickname for a member of the IWW, which was founded here in Chicago in 1905. At that time there were some quite large sections of the workforce that the existing labor unions didn't bother organizing. The AF of L and other unions that grew out of the Knights of Labor and such only bothered getting big industries. Workers like agricultural workers and miners and such were not organized, so the IWW was founded with the idea of organizing those who were unorganized. But they went one step further. Instead of saying they were going to pursue the goal of better wages and better shopping conditions, the goal was to do away with the wage system altogether. The machinery of production rightfully belongs in the hands of the workers themselves. And despite the fact that we have various forms of

[elections], there was someone who said earlier in this century that if elections changed anything, they would be made illegal.

You see this in countries where socialists are elected to the presidency or prime ministership or what have you. Greece is a prime example. The machinery of production is still in the hands of a few, and it's those few who call the shots. They tell our duly elected representatives what to do. As another radical said, "The politician gets votes from the poor and money from the rich on the promise to protect one from the other." But of course, I think, you can look at this world and see who they really represent. And it doesn't matter, because it's where the jobs are, at the point of production, that calls the shots, to the presidents, prime ministers, dictators, kings, or what have you. So the logical thing is for the machinery of production to be put in the hands of the workers themselves. It was Bill Haywood who said when he was asked if he was out to overthrow the government, "No. I don't give a damn about the government." Just get the workers the right to run their own job and you can put your government in your vest pocket. Because it is the point of production that controls our society. If the workers had control over transportation, communication, who could do it better? Could the politicians do it any better? The workers have a vested interest in keeping their job running smoothly because it's their bread and butter.

To give one beautiful example, some years back, this was on...I forget whether it was May Day or Labor Day. There was a gathering at Haymarket Square and different people were asked to make speeches. Studs Terkel went around to all the speakers and said, "Look, we've got an overload of speakers. Can you keep your remarks down to five minutes?" Well, I said, "Studs, I think I can keep them down to two minutes." A fellow next to me, one of the union functionaries, had like a cord of paper in front of him. He said "How am I gonna say this in five minutes?" I said, "Throw it away and talk off the top of your head." And I said, "Well, six-hour day? We should have had the six-hour day long ago. What we really need is a four-hour day." With the excess of labor power and jobs we have I said things could be run pretty smoothly on a four-hour day, and we could put more people to work. In fact, I designed a T-shirt that said "Four hours work for eight hours pay puts more workers on the job every day." Well, I was told that my speech was the most popular that day.

I'll give another example. I was working at that time at a small chemical factory over on Belden Avenue. I was on the committee, you know, one of the union committeemen. We'd be called in to arbitrate when some employee got in trouble with manage-

JOE HILL

GÄVLE, SVERIGE
7 OKTOBER 1879
SALT LAKE CITY U.S.A.
19 NOVEMBER 1915
UNION ORGANIZER
LABOR AGITATOR
CARTOONIST. POET
MUSICIAN. COMPOSER
ITINERANT WORKER
ARBETARSÄNGAREN

MURDERED BY THE JUDICIARY IN COLLUSION WITH THE MINE OWNERS WHO WISHED TO SILENCE HIS SONGS BUT THE SONGS ARE STILL BEING SUNG!

INDUSTRIAL WORKERS OF THE WORLD
3435 N. SHEFFIELD AVENUE Suite 202
CHICAGO, ILLINOIS 60657 USA

IF WE WORKERS TAKE A NOTION
WE CAN STOP ALL SPEEDING TRAINS
EVERY SHIP UPON THE OCEAN
WE CAN TIE WITH MIGHTY CHAINS
EVERY WHEEL IN THE CREATION
EVERY MINE AND EVERY MILL
FLEETS AND ARMIES
OF ALL NATIONS
WILL AT OUR COMMAND
STAND STILL

SÖRJ EJ, ORGANISERA

ment. And, of course, each year we would negotiate a new contract with management. One time, the plant manager called us up and said there was trouble with absenteeism. Particularly after payday it seemed to be an epidemic. He said there were not enough workers; we'd have to get workers off of some other department. And if we can't fill the department, then everybody goes home with half a day's pay. But during one of the blizzards that happened in the 70s, when the city was really tied up tight, the guys showed up for work. Some of them who came up from the South Side had to get up as early as four o'clock in the morning to get to the job, and they did, they got to the job. Well, it was the early part of the year, shortly after Christmas, when the guys didn't care to see a hole in their paycheck. And the workers showed up, but the supervisory personnel, from the plant manager to the line foremen (who lived out in the suburbs), didn't make it until later in the afternoon, when there was only about, oh, less than two hours to go. And at that time we were on changeover, we were filling bottles with dishwashing [liquid] and changed bottle size, so the machine had to be adjusted. The foreman and I were just walking along pressing flesh with the workers, congratulating them. He's saying, "Proud to see that, though we weren't here, you were still carrying on." So I walk a bit behind him, and I say, "Okay guys, see? If none of us show up, the place doesn't run. If none of them show up, the plant runs beautifully. Perhaps a little better because we didn't have them breathing down our necks." So my line foreman catches up, and he says (incredulously), "Carlos, how long do you think a plant like this could operate run by workers alone, without any supervisors, foreman, or superintendents?" I said, "Well, it operated six hours very smoothly." He walked away muttering to himself!

Dennis Fritz (DF): Is the IWW that exists today the same union that "Big" Bill Haywood led in the early part of this century? That is, has the IWW's existence been continuous, or did the union cease to exist and then later reform?

No, it has been continuous, limping along. Like one of our former writers Fred Thompson said, "the doctor is always pronouncing a patient dead, but the patient is always ready for another game of cribbage." Numerically we are a ghost of what we formerly were. That I readily admit. When people ask me how many members we have, I always say "too damned few." We still have capitalism. Anyway, even in our heyday, when we had our impact on the labor movement, we were small. Never at one single time did we have a million members, although throughout the years we probably had a couple of million, of all races and ethnic groups. But that was in the early days when union organizing was a little more [well-received]. Since then, you've gotten the business unions racketeering and giving the term unionism a bad name. I think right now we are somewhere between 1000 and 2000 strong, mostly concentrated in the US and Canada. We do have some scattered memberships in Australia, England, and some of the Pacific islands. Also there are some scattered members in places like Sierra Leone, Germany, Spain, and Sweden.

DF: I have often heard the terms "anarchism," "syndicalism," and "anarcho-syndicalism" used almost interchangeably. What are the essential differences between them, and which of these terms (if any) most accurately describes the organizing philosophy of the IWW?

Well, anarchism comes from the original Greek word [anarchos] meaning "without rule." In other words, the government that governs the least governs the best. I would say the IWW falls somewhere between anarcho-syndicalism and syndicalism. Syndicalism is where society is controlled by associations of workers. As I said before, if the machinery of production was under the control of the workers who do the work, automatically society would be controlled (by workers). They would have a vested interest, a real vested interest, besides just bread and butter, if they had control of society. That's basically syndicalism. Anarcho-syndicalism is where one also believes in the philosophy of anarchy. A lot of our membership does. Also, the CNT [National Confederation of Workers, one of the most important working class organizations in Spain in the period leading up to the Spanish Civil War] are, for the most part, anarchists. Of course, in the IWW we have socialists as well. And those who are members of the Socialist Party vote Socialist in the elections. They still use their franchise, and we have no beef with that.

Once, we were asked if we were against religion. It was Bill Haywood who said, "We don't care if you worship one god or two gods." We want to know where you stand on solidarity among the workers, if you believe workers ought to have control over their own jobs and their own conditions. Your religion is your personal thing. Unless, of course, your religion interferes with your on-the-job solidarity. Like if a priest or a minister tells you, "don't join a union." Then he's talking against your class interests.

DF: One criticism often leveled at both anarchists and syndicalists is that they fail to make distinctions between different types of authority. That is, that they tend to regard all authority (or leadership) as bad, regardless of who wields it or for what purpose. Is this a fair criticism? If not, why not?

Well, let me quote long-standing Catholic anarchist Ammon Hennacy, who said that he dislikes a good leader as much as a bad leader. He said, "A good leader will find a good reason for doing something bad." It takes away from the people themselves the responsibility for their own freedom. It was Eugene Debs who said, "Do not look upon me to lead you out of the wilderness. Because if I can lead you out of the wilderness, somebody else can lead you right back in." In other words, you have to have a responsibility for your own freedom. And of course, there are going to be inevitable disagreements. You work with people on things you agree on. I have worked with Trotskyists, Stalinists, because we happened to agree on something.

DF: George Orwell wrote about that...

Orwell wrote about that in *Homage to Catalonia*. That's why the Stalinists didn't like Orwell. Even though he was not anarchist or anarcho-syndicalist himself [Orwell was a socialist], he had a good word to say about the workers' militia.

DF: The dangers inherent in centralized organization (bureaucracy, unresponsiveness, pas-

sivity of membership, etc.) are, I believe, well understood. However, it seems to me that an extremely decentralized organization might have certain problems as well. Namely, difficulty in undertaking coordinated action and a tendency towards parochialism. What are your thoughts about this?

Well, I've heard about the dangers of decentralization, and also those who beat the drum for democratic centralism. But to give you an example, during the Spanish Civil War, both the fascists and the communists were trying to find the nerve centers of the anarchists and anarcho-syndicalists. That was the CNT and the FAI [Federation of Iberian Anarchists]. But they couldn't, because there was no nerve center. It was pretty well structured so that if one group was wiped out, another group would take over. It seems to work. Again, it is the distribution of responsibility. It is not in the hands of a nuclear committee that gives directives down. There are, of course, certain conflicts there. Democracy has its inconveniences because—human beings being what they are—there are going to be differences. But as long as [we] work along together, we will work together on things we agree on. On things we don't, well, we excuse ourselves. That was the spirit of the original movement.

DF: My last question is of a more philosophical nature. If people have the power to make just, sane, and humane decisions, does it necessarily follow that they will?

I believe so. I think there is a basic survival instinct in all species. Our species are social creatures. The reasons we have wars and petty jealousies and that come from the top. We are taught to be selfish, to put ourselves above everybody else, because people divided are easily controlled. I think the very vested interest in having control is that you share that control with others. Say, for example, if you took over control of a job site, but everybody else had nothing to say, you would eventually be removed by somebody else looking to take over. This was adequately brought out in Orwell's *Animal Farm*.

Marianna Cortéz: I think when you take over you crush others. Taking over means to crush other people

DF: Well, if you look at some of the dynamics of oppression, a lot of times it is not as simple as "top-down." Sometimes people somewhere in the middle try to enlist the powers-that-be to crush the people below them.

Well, look. The armies are made of our class. The police are made of our class. The brown shirts, the storm troopers, the Klan, all are recruited from our class. The upper class never does its own dirty work.

Tell me, what does solidarity mean to you?

Well, solidarity means sticking together. Sticking together... If people go out after something, they should fight. Not say, "Okay, we're gonna go on strike," and then the boss may come along and say, "Hey, c'mon. Come work for me and you can be sure you will still have your job." That's breaking solidarity. Solidarity means being solid. Sticking together, sticking tight, being really organized. That's what broke Jim Crow down South. The people deciding that they were not going to ride segregated buses. Nobody. And, the companies felt it in the pocket. You can imagine—in some of these cities, more than half the population was Black. So when they stopped riding the busses, there was money missing...

Tell me about Charles H. Kerr publishers and your role.

¡VIVA LA HUELGA!

Ah, well. Franklin and Penelope Rosemont are friends of long standing. They have been in the IWW together for 35 years or more, and they inherited the management of Charles Kerr Publishing company. [The press was founded in 1886 by Charles H. kerr and other radical Unitarians.] They kept it going for many years, and eventually they died out. A number of socialists and Wobblies took over the operation of it, and formed the board. Well, some years back they asked me to join the board and, you know, be president of the board. And I said, "Oh yeah; you want somebody to hold the bag if the finances turn legs up!" I think it is the oldest publishing house of strictly socialist and labor publications in the country, if not the world. There may have been older ones in Germany that were suppressed during the Hitler years. But to my knowledge, it is the oldest publisher of radical books in the country, from the end of the last century.

So why do you think it is important that the general public have access to anti-establishment literature?

Well, I think education is important, and there has to be some competition with the mass media. In the olden days, before there [were] television, movies, and radio, it was simple. You would get out and put a soapbox on the sidewalk and you would have an audience. Because mostly people would be out of work, or if they did work, they would be playing their cards close to the table and enjoying an eve-

ning outside. Now, though, those who manipulate us know what they are doing. They keep people diverted with television, sports, movies, and the daily blob. To me, it's very important to keep the educational process alive. I remember one fellow, I went up to him—he was a radio repairman—he told me how in Mexico people were ignorant because there were no schools. But here, you go to school to learn how to be ignorant.

How did you start writing poetry?

In the late fifties I started writing poetry. I was sort of inspired by the Beat Generation in San Francisco. I was looking at this, I kind of liked it, and I said, "Hell, I can write shit like that too." I was initially published by the *Industrial Worker*. Later on, I found out I was being anthologized. Other periodicals were picking up my stuff. Then of course through Kerr two books came out, and through March Abrazo Press, another book.

So which of your poems in *Where Are the Voices?* still speaks to you?

They all speak to me. I am not ashamed of any of them or they would never have gotten in this book. It's like my two nieces asking, "Who's your favorite niece?" How the heck could I answer that? They are each unique in their own way. And, in this way, I think a poem is unique. Some of my work I consider my "masterpieces." Like my linocut of Magón I consider one of my masterpieces, as well as the linocut of Posada. Also, the one of the pregnant woman...

I love that one.

One time, I had my stand down at the Fiesta del Sol and this one guy came along. I was with the father of a friend, and he said, "I'm warning you, he is one of these 'art for art's sake' people." I said I thought I could handle him. And the guy looks at me and says, "Are you really proud of this stuff here?" And I said, "Well, if I were ashamed of it, you wouldn't be seeing it." I gave him the best answer I could.

I remember one time we were invited to a book fair at Circle [University of Illinois at Chicago]. I was there with my posters. So, a couple stops by. The man was a Mexican professor, his wife was white. And the wife says, "I don't like that." I said, "Well, can't win them all." And she says, "Oh, is that yours? I'm sorry." I said, "Never be sorry for an honest opinion." Like I say, you can't win them all. I can accept that without being bothered. I made her feel comfortable.

Marianna Cortéz: A fellow came here from Greece. There were about three or four people, and my brother was here, and I had food and so on. But this one particular guy was a "self-made man." He was looking around at Carlos's artwork. I liked him. He was extremely gross, but so honest. He was saying, "'Art?' What do you mean, 'art?' Artists ought to be put against the wall and shot." And everyone else was saying, "Oh, come on! You mean Carlos too?" And he said, "Why not? One less!"

What would be the one thing you would want to be known for? And tell me about the work you do in Chicago, what you are known for, and how would somebody study under you or learn from you?

Well, I am already happy to be known for what I am doing, but I think the greatest thing would be if someone in the future would say, "That's the guy who got me started." That would be the greatest thing. There are a lot of young dudes who are much better artists than I am. I recognize that, and without feeling shy about what I do. In some way some of them even claim to have been inspired by me. I think the best thing is that when you know something, you pass it on to the next person. You have to pass it on to the next person. To have something all by yourself doesn't do anything.

You don't teach art. You open doors. It's one thing to show you how to push an engraving tool, handle a brush, blend colors, and that. But that only liberates what is already inside of you.

Selected Carlos Cortéz Bibliography

Cortéz, Carlos. *Crystal-Gazing the Amber Fluid*. Chicago, IL: Charles H. Kerr, 1990.

Cortéz, Carlos. *De Kansas a Califas & Back to Chicago*. Chicago, IL: March/Abrazo Press, 1992.

Cortéz, Carlos, ed. *Viva Posada!* Chicago, IL: Charles H. Kerr, 2002.

Cortéz, Carlos. *Where Are the Voices? & Other Wobbly Poems*. Chicago, IL: Charles H. Kerr, 1997.

Cortéz, Carlos, and Dylan A.T. Miner. *Yours for the One Big Union*. Albuquerque, NM: Amoxtli Press, 2005.

Cumpian, Carlos. *Coyote Sun*. Chicago: March/Abrazo Press, 1990. Illustrated by Carlos Cortéz.

Nelson, Eugene, ed. *Pablo Cruz and the American Dream: Experiences of an Undocumented Immigrant from Mexico*. Salt Lake City, UT: Peregrine Smith, 1975. Illustrated by Carlos Cortéz.

Sorell, Víctor Alejandro, ed. *Carlos Cortéz Koyokuikatl: Soapbox Artist & Poet*. Chicago, IL: Mexican Fine Arts Center Museum, 2001.

This page: Carlos Cortéz, *May 1st*, date unknown; previous page: Photo of Carlos Cortéz by Christine Flores-Cozza, 1999.

PARLEZ
AU
CONCIERGE

FLAVIO COSTANTINI: ARTIST OF ANARCHY

BILL NOWLIN

It is hard to pass judgment on lives such as these. One stands bewildered and aghast before men capable of such deeds; and, if they defy frivolous judgment, even to explain them seems beyond the power of men who, in the presence of the same wrongs that so deeply moved them, can still remain inert.

—Robert Hunter, *Violence and the Labor Movement*

Peopled with so many daringly defiant, rebellious, and romantic individuals, the history of the anarchist movement holds a distinct fascination for many. With so many colorful and tragic incidents, attempts, and experiments in social revolution, the movement has never been easy to deal with superficially, other than by those who would dismiss it out of hand.

Writers, both anarchist and non-anarchist, have found themselves challenged to deal with the depths of commitment, insistent purity of ideals, and tragic martyrdom evident throughout the history of the anarchist movement. The movement has found its chronicler in Flavio Costantini.

Unlike some of the writers, Costantini does not deal with an incident or two in the history of anarchism and then move on to another subject but instead is intent on creating an extensive artistic documentation of the movement in his works. The first forty-three paintings in the series were presented in *The Art of Anarchy*, released in September 1975 by Cienfuegos Press.

Working from a studio in his apartment in Rapallo, Italy, he has already completed additional paintings on McKinley's assassination by Czolgosz and the martyrdom of Wobbly organizer Frank Little, and has begun several more. The originals are painted by Costantini and from each original, one hundred silkscreen prints are made by an associate in Zagreb, Yugoslavia.

One thing in Costantini's work becomes evident immediately. He is particularly drawn to the violent—the assassinations, bombings, arrests, and executions. Ravachol is clearly the figure who intrigues him the most. Ravachol symbolizes, to many, the unruly criminal element which frightens most people. This symbol of the violent anarchist—in the case of Ravachol—a figure who bombs, murders, and plunders graves, is effectively exploited by the enemies of a free and stateless society to "prove" the dangers and chaos which would descend upon us, were we to dispense with the restraining influences of party or state.

Costantini, though, involves himself with the real man, the individual character of Ravachol, not solely as a symbol—much in the way Emma Goldman showed great compassion for Leon Czolgosz, the assassin of President McKinley. And yet, Ravachol does symbolize something for Costantini—the will to act.

Kafka was a very important and early influence on Costantini's work, predating his decision to draw and paint. Costantini is the son of a professor in northern Italy, and began his professional career as a textile designer and commercial graphic artist. In a recent interview, he said, "I started to draw because I read the Kafka books, and I like them very, very much. But it was impossible to write like Kafka, so I began to draw."

The isolated, buffeted, and bewildered subjects in Kafka's works, always near the edge of

Flavio Costantini, *Paris, March 11th, 1892*, tempera, 1970s.

F. COSTANTINI

hysteria and collapse, captivated Costantini and he remained involved with them for many years. Always in mind, though, was an alternative—communism. Costantini was communist in this period until a one month visit to Russia in 1962.

Russia's Disappointment

Costantini was disappointed and disturbed by Russia. In Moscow he saw

> an endless stream of tourist peasantry who were strangely silent, neither sad nor happy, but rather canalised in a disenchanted unconscious pilgrimage. The soldiers did a lively goose step in the changing of the guard in front of Lenin's mausoleum. Sleek black cars with drawn curtains filed through the walls of the Kremlin. The revolution had ended.

He reread a book which he had hated and forgotten: *Memoirs of a Revolutionary* by Victor Serge. He felt that perhaps this was an alternative, an isolated but insistent voice. Serge's book, particularly the section on the French anarchists inspired him with new hope. Since that time, Costantini says, "I have tried, within the scope of my own possibilities, to publicize this uncompromising alternative."

Costantini agrees with Serge that the French anarchists, although "shot through with contradictions," were people who "demanded, before anything else, harmony between deeds and words." These were often very lonely

and isolated individuals, sensitive in their own way, who chose to act, and not simply wander about confused and disoriented in a bewildering world. Indeed, their reaction to confusion and bewilderment was precisely to act, to refuse to submit.

Observers of Costantini's work have said that some of his prints show a love of the decorative but that this is betrayed by an underlying feeling of loneliness bordering on morbidity.

Costantini adds:

> Before my trip to Russia I was inspired by Kafka. My drawings of that period were introverted. I don't mean to say that my work now is extroverted, but I think I've reached a greater objectivity. Kafka has grown into Ravachol. Ravachol places his explosives outside the door of his persecutors. With Kafka one remains isolated and vulnerable; with Ravachol one feels comradeship. He acts to challenge the forces which threaten us all.
>
> Then I loved Kafka but I was a communist—though a logical, rational choice, not a sentimental one. I was communist because I thought communism was the sole solution of logic and justice for humanity. Something that could replace the fraud that is Christianity. My Russian voyage made me understand the new deception of authoritarian socialism. Now, logically, I accept libertarian socialism but psychologically I am attracted by anarcho-individualism.
>
> My individualism predates my anarchism — it is inherent in my nature. The one step forward that I've made is only one: now I am able to analyze my solitude. My choice today for libertarian socialism is fully conscious.

In reply to those critics of anarchism who lump anarchists with bandits, Costantini says:

This page: Flavio Costantini, cover illustration from Albert Meltzer, ed., *The International Revolutionary Solidarity Movement*. (Orkney Islands: Cienfuegos Press, 1976.); previous page: Flavio Costantini, cover illustration from Antonio Tellez, *Sabaté: Guerrilla Extraordinary*. (Orkney Islands: Cienfuegos Press, 1974.)

"These people [Ravachol, Jacob, Bonnot] in spite of the bad consequences for the movement, have done something. They had no other choice but to fight, at that time. It was truly a class war; the workers were like slaves."

revolt in Ghibellina, deal with group struggles.

There is another element as well. Costantini says, "I feel the violence very deeply. I am very shocked by these people who gave their lives for an idea. An idea. It's terrible for me to see such people fighting in proportion to the power ranged against them."

In Costantini's work, we run up against a certain paradox of style. In almost all of his works, hardly anyone but the direct participants are portrayed, and their faces are drawn directly from available photographs—often from police files. This touch of photographic realism is played off against the increasingly stark simplicity of the backdrop.

The characters are oddly wooden, with the posed photographic faces often staring in unnatural directions, appearing distant and eerily oblivious to all that goes on around them. What is portrayed is thus like a frozen frame of film of a particular incident. A moment preserved for the viewer is presented in a startling fashion, underscoring the startling subject matter of the print itself.

Costantini's work is both documentary and artistically innovative. Increasing experimentation in technique and pattern is evident, and his exceptional talent has been widely recognized. As the scope of his work becomes more familiar to anarchists and art critics alike, we can anticipate a broad discussion of anarchism, and a deeper appreciation of the spirit of rebellion.

Individual Acts

In bourgeois ethics it is not a crime to wage war; on the contrary, it is honorable. The anarchist ethic sees war as a horrendous crime. The same goes for the accumulation of capital, etc. The same act can be considered criminal or not according to the norm by which it is judged; The bank robberies pulled off by Durruti and by Sabate are not in my opinion criminal acts.

La Bande a Bonnot—in my opinion—is symbolic in another sense: it concluded the epoch of frontal struggle of the Ravachol era between the bourgeoisie and the proletariat and initiated that of negotiations and conformism in the unions; the last surviving remnants of the irreducible ones who were isolated from the rest of the proletariat and had only the option to join the system or succumb.

Costantini's focus on individual acts rather than collective manifestations reflects his concern for the subjective. Individual courage and will dominate all his works; only a few, like the 1879 McCormick Works massacre in Chicago, and the 1894 peasant

This page: Flavio Costantini, detail of cover illustration from: Ricardo Flores Magón. *Land & Liberty: Anarchist Influences in the Mexican Revolution* (Orkney Islands: Cienfuegos Press, 1977); next page: Flavio Costantini, 1974 illustration used on the cover of L. Tifft and D. Sullivan. *The Struggle to be Human* (Orkney Islands: Cienfuegos Press, 1980).

This essay was originally published in a slightly different format in the Canadian anarchist newspaper *Open Road*, Issue 2, Spring 1977.

F. Costantini / 74

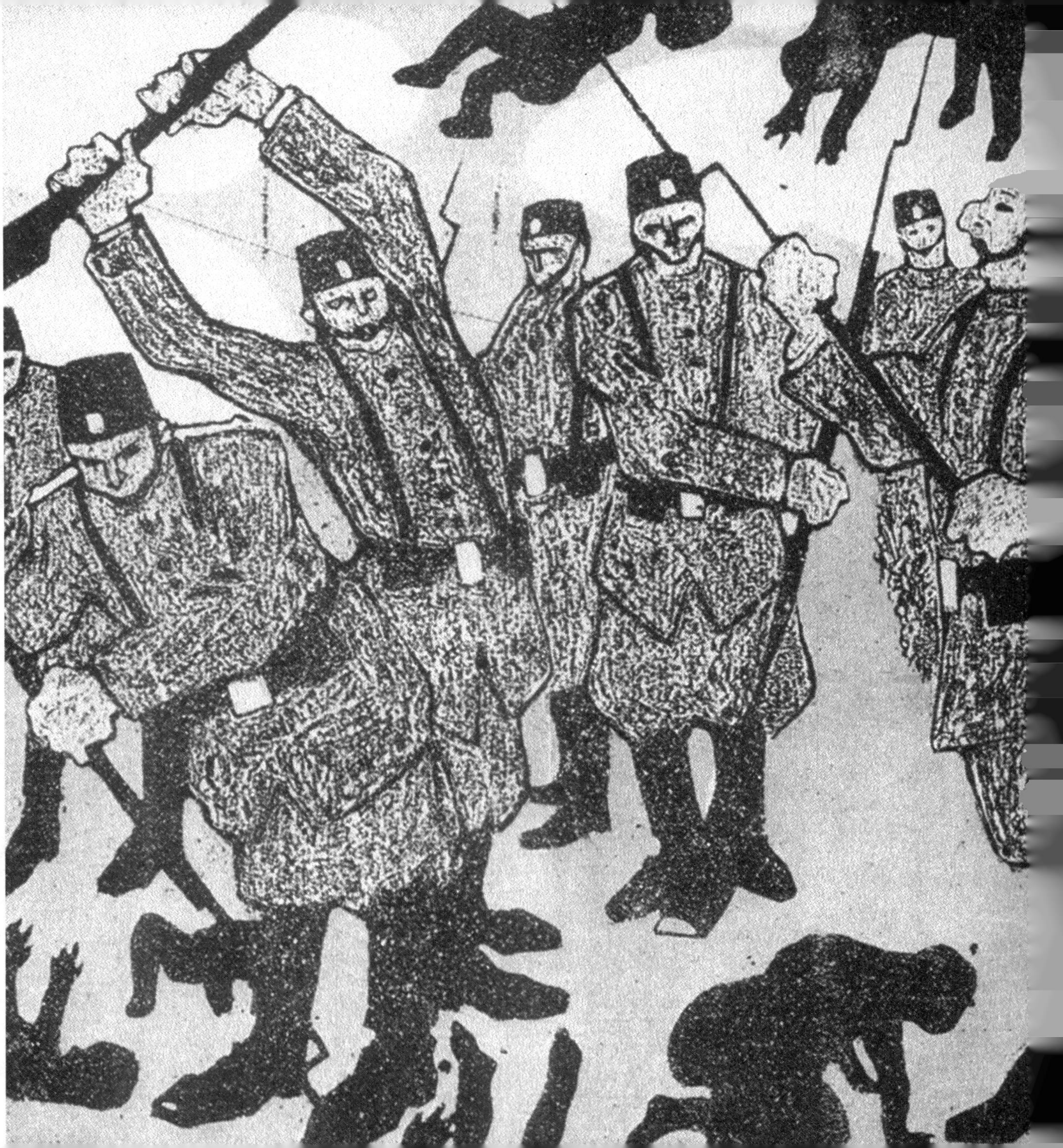

REVEIL ANARCHISTE: SALON PAINTING, POLITICAL SATIRE, MODERNIST ART

PATRICIA LEIGHTEN

Where is your exhibition?
In the magazine stands.
—Jean-Louis Forain

In pre-World War I France, many modernists—including Pablo Picasso, Maurice Vlaminck and Kees van Dongen—thought anarchist politics to be inherent in the idea of an artistic avant-garde and created new languages of form—including abrupt transitions, anti-narrative structure, and surprising juxtapositions—expressive of their desire to effect revolutionary changes in art and society.[1] Although anarchist-influenced modernist art movements such as Fauvism, Cubism, and Orphism radically altered the art of the early twentieth century, the theories that nurtured them were discredited within the art historical discourse after 1914 by the rightward swing of political discourse during and after the war, the decline of the anarchist movement, and the rise in the 1920s of a resolutely apolitical formalist art criticism. Thus a "revolutionary aesthetics"—a "politics of form"—played a crucial role in the development of modern art in pre-World War I France, but its significance was first suppressed and then forgotten.[2]

Anarchism as a political philosophy was, without question, more influential on turn-of-the-century artists than socialism, in part because anarchist theory specifically called for the participation of artists in social transformation, and in part because anarchism at one end of its spectrum stood for an absolute individualism fully compatible with a politicized bohemianism. Socialism played a smaller, though still significant, role in prewar French artistic culture.[3] Modernist artists in pre-World War I France were seriously engaged with the social and political issues of their day, and many contributed their work to anarchist journals such as *L'Assiette au beurre* and *Les Temps nouveaux*. To view the birth of modern art in this light fundamentally challenges the way modernism is popularly understood. Rather than the current galaxy of modernist giants, fixed in place by an auction system privileging "high" painted abstraction and equally high prices, an entirely different constellation of artists emerges. Artists whose work was valued for offering a variety of pictorial solutions to the problems of expression and social experience. Many artists purposely chose to work in other media—particularly satirical cartoons—with the aim of reaching a variety of audiences for specifically political purposes, including Théophile Steinlen, Félix Vallotton, and van Dongen. Such work was considered of real importance to cultural critics in this period, but their allegiance to political themes, caricatural styles, and allegorical and narrative genres disqualify them as major modernists for the willfully amnesiac culture of post-World War I.

Looking at the role of left-wing politics, and specifically anarchism, in prewar Europe corrects many myths about modernist art still in force.[4] From large-scale salon paintings to political cartoons to avant-garde abstractions, artists preoccupied with social criticism sought appropriate mediums, styles, and audiences based on their different ideas about art's influence on society.[5] They made conscious choices to employ "high" or "low" media in an attempt to reach "high" or "low" audiences. Most artists in this period, as in the previous two

1. The relation of art to politics has long been a subject of debate, though largely in fields outside art history; see Ronald Taylor, ed., *Aesthetics and Politics* (London: Verso, 1977) for key texts of Ernst Bloch, Georg Lukács, Bertolt Brecht, Walter Benjamin, and Theodor Adorno, as well as a lucid afterword by Fredric Jameson. More recently debate has centered on the issue of "modernism" vs. "avant-gardism;" see most notably Raymond Williams, *The Politics of Modernism* (London: Verso, 1989); Peter Bürger, *Theory of the Avant-garde* (Minneapolis: University of Minnesota Press, 1984) and *The Decline of Modernism* (University Park: Pennsylvania State University Press, 1992); and Thomas Crow, "Modernism and Mass Culture in the Visual Arts," in *Modernism and Modernity: The Vancouver Conference Papers*, edited by Benjamin H.D. Buchloh, Serge Guilbaut, and David Solkin (Halifax, N. S.: The Press of Nova Scotia College of Art and Design, 1983), 215–64.

2. For a consideration of the reasons for this cultural amnesia, see my "Editor's Statement: Revising Cubism," *Art Journal* 47 (winter 1988): 269–76. Fauvism was a movement characterized by bright, anti-naturalistic color, amorphous forms, and a seeming lack of linear structure, whose leading figures included Henri Matisse, André Derain, Vlaminck, van Dongen, and others. "Orphism" was not so much a movement as an evocative name coined by the poet and art critic Guillaume Apollinaire—a good friend of the artists—to account for the greater abstraction and brilliant color (seemingly used like musical notes from Orpheus' lyre) of the works of Robert Delaunay and Frantißek Kupka after 1911.

3. See Richard Sonn, *Anarchism and Cultural Politics in Fin de Siècle France* (Lincoln: University of Nebraska Press, 1989); and Eugenia Herbert, *The Artist and Social Reform: France and Belgium, 1885–1898* (New Haven: Yale University Press, 1961). For a discussion of Picasso's aesthetic politics, see my *Re-Ordering the Universe: Picasso and Anarchism, 1897–1914* (Princeton: Princeton University Press, 1989).

4. A commonplace of historical and art-historical writing asserts the decline of anarchism around 1905–1906. Following Jean Maitron in his massive *Histoire du mouvement anarchiste en France (1880–1914)* (Paris: Société Universitaire d'Editions et de Librairie, 1951), such scholars as David Cottington ("What the Papers Say: Politics and Ideology in Picasso's Collages of 1912," *Art Journal* 47 (Winter 1988): 350–59), cite the break-up that year of the leftist parliamentary alliance, *le bloc des gauches*, and the rise of the syndicalist movement as evidence of anarchism's waning appeal on both political and intellectual fronts. The history I chart here necessarily contests Maitron's and others' assertions of the disappearance of anarchist ideology and aesthetics.

centuries, were trained in the academic styles of the École des Beaux-Arts (School of Fine Arts) and exhibited their work at the annual State-sanctioned salons. In the late nineteenth century, a variety of independent salons were established, which opened more options for artists to exhibit and reach a public (most notably the Independents Salon and the Autumn Salon). Among the academic painters, socially-critical artists such as Jules Adler operated within the State-sanctioned salons, annually exhibiting naturalist paintings expressive of social concerns and addressed largely to the class in power, the bourgeoisie. Artists like Jules-Félix Grandjouan and Bernard Naudin abandoned painting altogether in favor of political satire in journals costing half a franc and addressed to both the masses and left-wing intellectuals. Others such as van Dongen divided their time between political cartooning and an outrageous avant-gardism that would, according to anarchist theory, pave the way for a new consciousness and a new society even as it abandoned (and was abandoned by) a popular audience.[6] During this unsettled period, one can see artists responding to

the dilemmas posed by contradictory anarchist ideas: art should expose the follies and iniquities of the present social order, should be addressed to the masses, yet should also be the free expression of the individual and open the path to a new social order. Most of the avant-gardists exhibited in the Independents and Autumn Salons, though some—like Picasso and Georges Braque, leading Cubists—found their way to an emerging system of entrepreneurial galleries.[7]

That French culture was thoroughly politicized in the prewar period is strikingly evident in the polemical art criticism—ranging from the extreme right to the extreme left—on art, in general, and modernism, in particular. Although historians of modernism are familiar with the relatively small body of criticism written by modernist apologists, they are largely unfamiliar with the broader range of art criticism—much of it hostile to modernism from various perspectives—in the journalistic reviews that flooded Paris in these years, evoking political issues troubling French culture at large.[8] As I will show below, this cultural criticism demonstrates that, on the one hand, politically and artistically conservative critics lauded academic and naturalist styles of art even when those styles served a thoroughly anti-establishment theme. But, on the other hand, a wide range of critics equated the overturning of traditional artistic conventions with the anarchist attack on bourgeois society. Though many anarchists stood for highly nuanced theoretical positions, fully articulated in scores of anarchist journals, the broader range of art critics were much more impressionistic and sweeping in their characterizations of politically inflected modernism. Cubism, especially, was seen as "anarchist," "revolutionary," and "an attack on the social fabric," whether for good or ill.

Leftist salon painting, adhering to naturalist style, did not inspire such criticism. Thus it was not socially-critical subject matter that offended traditionalists so much as modernist attacks on artistic form itself, on all those inherited visual conventions still taught at the École des Beaux-Arts and systematically repudiated by the modernists. For example, the art critic Maurice Robin, writing in the radical socialist journal *Les Hommes du jour* in 1909, referred to Fauvism and Cubism as "ultra-revolutionary art."[9] Coriolès in the conservative journal, *Le Gaulois* characterized the avant-garde in 1910 as manifesting "willfully revolutionary spirit, nay, anarchic tendencies."[10] J. d'Aoust, discussing Cubism and Futurism in 1912, asked, "In order to be 'of one's time' is it not necessary always to be a little 'revolutionary,' in art principally?"[11] Both right-wing newspapers like *Le Correspondant*, and left-wing journals like *Les Hommes du jour* aggressively guided their readers to respond politically to the art of this period.

A good example of this paradigm can be seen in the reception of Jules Adler, a highly successful artist associated with the anarchist movement (though less well known than his anarchist friend and rival Théophile Steinlen[12]). Through winning prizes at the annual salons, by 1898 he had achieved the status of no longer having to compete in order to exhibit his work. Thereafter, he annually submit-ted large-scale paintings to the Salon des Artistes Français on themes of work.[13] In 1900, at a time when 51% of workers made less than the one franc a day necessary for subsistence,[14] his monumental *La Grève au Creusot* (Strike at Le Creusot) depicted a recent labor upheaval in which miners and their families rose up in protest against working conditions and wage-slavery. This grandiose painting did much to cement Adler's reputation, winning public support for his depiction of the aggrieved workers. One might expect criticism from critics in such conservative art journals as the conservative *Gazette des Beaux-Arts*, but Jules Rais instead lavished praise on Adler's work, exalting its

> harmony of landscape and factory, of atmosphere and drama, of individual and crowd, of gesture and voice, of the contemporary and the heroic.

Jules Adler, *La Grève au Creusot* [Strike at Le Creusot], 1900. *Catalogue du Salon des Artistes français.* ©2006 Artists Rights Society (ARS), New York / ADAGP, Paris.

5. For various discussions—and interpretations—of the significance of these shifts in the art market, see Robert Jensen, "The Avant-Garde and the Trade in Art," *Art Journal* 47 (winter 1988): 360–67, and *Marketing Modernism in Fin-de-Siècle Europe* (Princeton: Princeton University Press, 1994); Malcolm Gee, "Dealers, Critics, and Collectors of Modern Painting: Aspects of the Parisian Art Market, 1910–1930" (Ph.D. diss., Courtauld Institute, London University, 1977); David Cottington, "Cubism and the Politics of Culture in France, 1905–1914" (Ph.D. diss., Courtauld Institute, London University, 1985) and *Cubism in the Shadow of War*; and Martha Ward, *Pissaro, Neo-Impressionism and the Spaces of the Avant-Garde* (Chicago: University of Chicago Press, 1996).

6. See my *Re-Ordering the Universe*, 14–15, 39–42, and 49–50 for discussions of anarchist aesthetic theories at the turn of the century.

7. Though it was the subject of intense debate in this historical period, the question of what constitutes an "anarchist aesthetic" has received relatively little attention in our own time. See Sonn, *Anarchism and Cultural Politics in Fin de Siècle France*; André Rezsler, *L'Esthétique anarchiste* (Paris: Presses Universitaire de France, 1973); Joan Halperin, *Félix Fénéon: Aesthete and Anarchist in Fin-de-siècle Paris* (New Haven, Conn.: Yale University Press, 1989); John Hutton, *Neo-Impressionism and the Search for Solid Ground: Art, Science, and Anarchism in Fin-de-Siècle France* (Baton Rouge: Louisiana State University Press, 1994); R. Roslak, "Scientific Aesthetics and the Aestheticized Earth: The Parallel Vision of the Neo-Impressionist Landscape and Anarcho-Communist Social Theory" (Ph.D. diss., University of California, Los Angeles, 1987) and *Neo-Impressionism and Anarchism in Fin-de-Siècle France* (Burlington, VT: Ashgate, forthcoming 2007); and my *Re-Ordering the Universe*.

8. A good example of such a dialogue is explored by Mark Antliff in "Cubism, Celtism, and the Body Politic," *The Art Bulletin* 74 (December 1992): 654–68, a detailed study of the debate between the Action Française and the Ligue celtique (whose most notable artistic supporter was the Cubist Albert Gleizes), which encoded the clash of profoundly political aesthetic positions based on France's racial "essence."

9. Maurice Robin, "Les Arts," *Les Hommes du jour* 69 (15 May 1909): n.p.

10. Coriolès, "A Propos de l'Internationalisme en Art," *Le Gaulois* (3 January 1910): 2.

11. J. d'Aoust, "La Peinture Cubiste, Futuriste... et au-delà," *Livres et art* 1 (March 1912): 153–56. The tradition for this rhetoric was already well established in the symbolist period, for example in the attack on *vers libre* by Charles Recolin--a defender of "*le vieux bon sens français*"—in his *L'Anarchie littéraire* (Paris: Perrin et cie., 1898) and in the anarchist *vers libriste* Gustave Kahn's pronouncement that "in shattering a fragment of the artistic façade [the artist] touches the social façade" (*Premiers poèmes* (Paris: Société de Mercure de France, 1897), 24; translated in Herbert, *The Artist and Social Reform*, 54). In this regard such artists as Henri Matisse, certainly no anarchist, may have attracted a form of criticism both dismaying to the artist and based on genuine misunderstanding; an artist like van Dongen was neither naive nor unprepared for politicized criticism of this sort.

12. See Phillip Denis Cate and Susan Gill, *Théophile-Alexandre Steinlen* (Salt Lake City: Gibbs M. Smith, Inc., 1982).

13. Adler (1865–1952) was a student of Adolphe William Bouguereau and Tony Robert-Fleury, though probably most influenced by Pascal Dagnan-Bouveret; he was later a founding member of the Salon d'Automne; see Gabriel P. Weisberg, *The Realist Tradition: French Painting and Drawing, 1830–1900* (Cleveland: Cleveland Museum of Art, 1980), 222, 265 and *Beyond Impressionism: The Naturalist Impulse* (New York: H.N. Abrams, 1992), 89–92; and Lucien Barbedette, *Le peintre Jules Adler* (Besançon: Editions Séquania, 1938). When an artist's painting won a Gold Medal at the Salon, that artist's work was henceforth *hors concours*, which meant that subsequent works would automatically be accepted for exhibition.

14. Leonard R. Berlanstein, *The Working People of Paris, 1871–1914* (Baltimore: Johns Hopkins University Press, 1984), 40.

15. The original reads: "*accord du paysage et des 'fabriques', du décor et du drame, de l'individu et de la foule, du geste et de la voix, du contemporain et de l'héroïque. En troupe résolue, au rythme des chants de révolte, les mineurs défilent devant l'usine. L'homme s'est dressé en face de la cheminée; la classe s'est organisée devant la machine; sous les ténèbres que déroule la fumée, la foi des drapeaux a reconquis le soleil.*" (Jules Rais, "Le Salon de 1900," *Gazette des Beaux-Arts* (3e) pér., t. XXIV, 1900): 62).

In a resolved band, to the rhythm of songs of revolt, the miners file past the factory. Man is drawn up opposite the factory smoke-stack; class organizes itself before the machine; under the shadows cast by the billowing smoke, the promise of the flags reconquers the sun."[15]

While summoning up the picture's drama, Rais neutralizes the import of the strike itself, by stating that "class organizes itself before the machine" he muffles the fact that the working class organizes in opposition not to "the machine" or the factory but to the bourgeoisie and the factory owner. He adds that the woman in the lead reminds him of Delacroix's *Liberty Leading the People*, painted following the abortive revolution of 1830, thus paying Adler's work a handsome compliment and placing it firmly in the tradition of French revolutionary painting, with its celebrations of the struggle toward the foundation of the Republic, which is now the status quo. Rather than acknowledging the threat of class war in Adler's celebration of strike action, Rais coopts the painting to republican tradition.[16] He concludes that Adler's work is "the synthesis of the most complete art that has been attempted here,

in this poor last salon of this anxious century."[17]

Art critic Henri Frantz, in his annual book reviewing the salons, raises an "aesthetic problem" in order to doubt kindly whether Adler's work isn't "*un peu trop réaliste.*" His description of the painting, however, is filled with sympathy for its subject:

> Against a somber horizon of black hills, of chimneys whose ponderous smoke darkens the atmosphere, a crowd of men and women advance singing with great banners unfurled. In the middle of all these black garments, only the flags contribute a little color. The general unity of this picture would be enough to document for us all the sadness of this scene, to show us the anguish of hunger which can be read on all the faces contracted in exasperation.
>
> But, if the painter has perfectly redeemed the heroic side, dramatic in fact in this scene, can we not ask ourselves if this representation of the worker completely accords with the plasticity of the whole work of art, and if the interpretation that M. Adler has given to it is not a little too realist[?][18]

Though there is sympathy here for the workers' "anguish of hunger," for Frantz the heroism of the theme is undermined by the unrelenting depiction of its motivating force in poverty. The painting's overabundance of detail departs from the codes of high art composition, which should subsume such misery in cathartic drama and "the plasticity of the whole." What Frantz found offensive was what Roland Barthes termed "the reality effect," that excess of descriptive detail that serves to lend all too much in the way of a realist imperative to the work's narrative, immersing viewers in the historical moment rather than providing them with the necessary "aesthetic distance" to admire the artist's compositional techniques.[19] The "reality effect" fabricates a "referential illusion" that challenges Frantz's own political position; clearly realism can also be a sign of political threat, though never as serious a one as modernist anti-traditionalism and avant-gardism.

Louis Roger's *l'Accident* (Accident) of 1910 indicts prevailing conditions of labor by depicting the body of a man brought up from the pit of a construction site by his fellow workers.[20] This was a common occurrence, judging from the few relevant statistics that survive from this period: in 1911, for example, there were 3,900 work-related injuries in Paris' 19th

arrondissement alone.[21] The Christ-like posture of the limp figure underscores the victimization of workers and suggests the artist's attitude toward labor accidents; its evocation of the realism of Caravaggio, with his plebeian models, reinforces the allusion to Christ. Given the strong social criticism implied in such works as these, one might imagine that these artists were marginalized in the government-sanctioned world of the salons and ignored by critics other than doctrinaire leftists praising them for their choice of subjects. But this was not the case. Far from this overt leftism damaging Roger's reputation, the painting resulted in a commission for a mural version in the Saint-Nazaire town hall. Such official recognition suggests that paintings like Roger's were not offensive to the salon committees as long as the style and composition of the work leaned sufficiently toward broadly readable style.

History painting, especially scenes of revolution and the Commune, also formed a powerful vehicle for political messages. The painter and cartoonist Bernard Naudin looks back to the French Revolution in such works as *Vive la Nation!* (Long Live the Nation!), shown in the Salon des Artistes Français in 1904.[22] The compositional structure is based on the directional force of an explosion detonated by the central figure, whose energy radiates outward through the

LA FÊTE DU 14 JUILLET A BRAZZAVILLE
— C'qu'on rigole aux colonies! Vive la République!

From top: Louis Roger, *l'Accident* [The Accident], 1910. *Catalogue du Salon des Artistes français*; Bernard Naudin, "La Fête du 14 Juillet à Brazzaville" [Bastille Day in Brazzaville], *L'Assiette au beurre*, March 11, 1905. ©2006 Artists Rights Society (ARS), New York/ADAGP, Paris; Bernard Naudin, *Vive la Nation!* [Long Live the Nation!], 1904. *Catalogue du Salon des Artistes français*. ©2006 Artists Rights Society (ARS), New York/ADAGP, Paris.

16. For a discussion of the nationalist and republican "official aesthetic" of the government, see Marie-Claude Genet-Delacroix, "Esthétique officielle et art national sous la Troisième République," *Le Mouvement social* 131 (April-June 1985): 105–20.

17. The original reads: "*la synthèse d'art la plus complète qu'on ait ici tentée, en ce pauvre dernier Salon du Siècle anxieux.*"

18. The original reads: "*Sur un sombre horizon de collines noires, de cheminées dont les pesantes fumées assombrissent l'atmosphère, une troupe d'hommes et de femmes s'avance en chantant avec de grandes bannières déployées. Au milieu de tous ces vêtements noirs, seuls les drapeaux apportent un peu de couleur. L'harmonie générale de ce tableau suffirait à nous documenter sur toute la tristesse de cette scène, à nous montrer l'angoisse de la faim qui se lit sur tous les visages crispés d'exaspération.*

"*Mais, si le peintre a parfaitement dégagé le côté héroïque, dramatique même de cette scène, ne pouvons-nous pas nous demander si cette représentation de l'ouvrier répond tout à fait à la plasticité de toute oeuvre d'art, et si l'interprétation que M. Adler lui a donnée n'est pas un peu trop réaliste.*" (Henri Frantz, *Le Salon de 1900: l'exposition décennale* (Paris: Goupil, 1900), 32–34)

19. Roland Barthes, "The Reality Effect," in *The Rustle of Language*. trans. Richard Howard (Berkeley: The University of California Press, 1989): 141–48.

20. Louis Roger (1874–1953) was a student of Jean-Pierre Laurens and Benjamin Constant and was *hors-concours* after 1903.

21. Berlanstein, *The Working People of Paris*, 104.

22. Jean Grave, the intellectual leader of anarchism-communism in France and the editor of *Les Temps nouveaux*, discusses Naudin as a *compagnon* in his memoir; see Jean Grave, *Quarante ans de propagande anarchiste*, the original manuscript of *Mouvement libertaire sous la Troisième République* (1930), (Paris: Flammarion, 1973), 460–61.

flags, bayonets, and other excited figures. This army struggling against the forces of monarchy combines all the laboring classes of France, revealing white heads and greybeards mingling with enthusiastic youth. Interestingly, Naudin moves away from the naturalism of the majority of these salon works toward a somewhat more modernist style. A style that never breaks with readability, suggesting the influence not only of Manet's formal simplification and open brushwork, but also of works then showing in the alternative salons by Henri de Toulouse-Lautrec, Pierre Bonnard, and the young Henri Matisse. Yet Naudin's experience as a cartoonist constitutes the strongest visual influence on his treatment of the human figure.

Naudin was an artist whose artistic decisions in many ways proceeded from political considerations, as the simple, energetic style of this painting demonstrates: the meaning easily understood, yet "modern" and folkish in style, its spirited image celebrates revolutionary action. In 1904 he made a very significant and telling decision: he stopped painting altogether, despite his initial success, in favor of a career as a political cartoonist and graphic artist.[23] His subjects shifted as well from revolutionary history—cooptable as it was to the republican tradition—to contemporary history and the images of poverty.

Some of the stylistic features of *Vive la Nation!* echo in Naudin cartoons, such as "*La Fête du 14 Juillet à Brazzaville*" from the anarchist *l'Assiette au beurre* of 1905. Naudin treated the most inflammatory subjects in his cartoons, including this infamous event of the dynamiting of an African servant on Bastille Day by French government administrators in the French Congo, a scandal that powerfully agitated both colonialists and anticolonialists at the time.[24] The simplified form, expressive line, dynamic composition, even the tricolor of the French flag common to both works suggest a stylistic dialogue between the two forms of Naudin's production. Significantly, they also share their political position: one is a celebration of the ideal of revolution, the other a damnation of the current system of Third Republic parliamentarianism for its hypocritical betrayal of the revolutionary ideals it claimed to uphold. Naudin's decision to abandon the arena of the bourgeois salon in order to devote himself to graphics and satire in the penny weeklies bespeaks a desire to reach a different audience: the working class.

Anarchist and radical socialist artists frequently manifested their political allegiances by contributing works of art and art criticism to antiparliamentary journals like the radical socialist *La Guerre sociale*, the anarcho-syndicalist *La Voix du Peuple* (the official organ of the labor union Confédération Générale du Travail [CGT]), or the anarcho-communist *Les Temps nouveaux*. Such journals also sponsored art exhibitions where anarchists could sell work on behalf of these journals and reach a sympathetic audience and clientele directly. Of the left-leaning artists exhibiting in the official salons, Naudin is exceptional in his decision to abandon not only painting for cartooning, but the Salon des Artistes français for the Salon des Indépendants and anarchist journals such as *L'Assiette au beurre*, where his drawings appeared next to the work of Steinlen, Jules-Félix Grandjouan, van Dongen, and numerous other anarchist artists. Though Naudin's choice to abandon painting was extreme, the same questions of medium and intended audience arose for a large range of artists who in their different ways, concerned themselves with the relations of politics and aesthetics.[25]

Whereas Adler et al. showed in the official salons, modernists avoided such State-sanctioned venues, exhibiting instead in independent salons

23. Naudin (1876–1946) remains obscure. See Paul Cornu, *Bernard Naudin, Dessinateur et graveur* (Nevers: Les Cahiers du Centre, 1912), which contains basic biographical information; and François Poncetton, *Catalogue des Eaux-Fortes de Bernard Naudin* (Paris: René Helleu, 1918). Neither author bothers to observe or explain the political nature of Naudin's subject matter in a large number of his etchings through at least 1910: revolutionary soldiers, beggars, executions, including that of anarchist Francisco Ferrer (1909), the persecution of unregistered prostitutes. From 1904 to 1909, Naudin published political cartoons in *L'Assiette au beurre*, *Le Témoin*, and *Cri de Paris*, and from 1905–10 he published a series of etchings entitled *Les Affligés* [The Afflicted Ones] (Cabinet des Estampes, Bibliothèque Nationale), which were exhibited at the Salon des Indépendants. According to Nancy Troy, he later worked for fashion designer Paul Poiret (see *Couture Culture: A Study in Modern Art and Fashion* (Cambridge, MA and London: The MIT Press, 2002)). By the time of the war, Naudin had become a patriot and a sergeant, doing drawings of life in the trenches; see *Croquis de campagne de Bernard Naudin, 1914–1915*, 2 vols. (Paris: René Helleu, 1915–16).

24. See Leighten, "The White Peril and l'Art nègre: Picasso, Primitivism, and Anticolonialism," *The Art Bulletin* 72 (December 1990): 609–30 for a full discussion of the Congo scandals of 1905–1906 in Paris.

25. The anarchist Kupka too made a similar decision, though his was temporary. In 1900 he wrote his friend Josef Machar that he planned to devote himself to graphic art because it was more "democratic;" see Ludmila Vachtova, *Frank Kupka, Pioneer of Abstract Art* (New York: McGraw-Hill, 1968), 41. Six years later, Kupka moved to Puteaux and thereafter devoted himself to painting instead.

26. Elisabeth and Michel Dixmier, *L'Assiette au Beurre, Revue satirique illustré, 1901–1912* (Paris: F. Maspero, 1974), 279; and Ralph Shikes, "Five Artists in the Service of Politics in the Pages of L'Assiette au Beurre," in *Art and Architecture in the Service of Politics*, edited by Henry A. Millon and Linda Nochlin. (Cambridge: Harvard University Press, 1978), 163.

and private galleries. This political choice went hand-in-hand with an aesthetic one: the pursuit of formal innovations unacceptable within the parameters of the Beaux Arts tradition and constituting an affront to critics like Rais and Frantz. The range of eccentric venues paralleled choices of "high" versus "low" genre and medium. The satirical graphics of modernist artists have too often been viewed by modern critics as irrelevant to their "real" work and dismissed either as commercial expedients, or neutral drawings given a political slant by editorial captions. To push this work off to one side is, in effect, to deny the importance for these artists of the issues and passions their cartoons addressed. In fact, their political ideals were central to their very involvement with satirical and anarchist journals, whose editors usually paid them very poorly, when they paid them at all.[26] Frequently the artists simply donated the work.[27] And these drawings were usually far from neutral: emphatically political in imagery, their thrust was unmistakable to the artists' contemporaries, even without captions. Moreover, the artists often composed the captions themselves, assuring that their intentions were clearly expressed, a fact I discovered in examining original drafts for published cartoons, with captions in the artists' own hands.[28]

The political motives of these works have been overlooked for the same reasons that the works themselves have been disregarded: the mundane and narrative preoccupations of the cartoons do not fit with conceptions of a commitment to "high" art, purely aesthetic concerns, or otherworldly spirituality. The cartoons' lithographic medium is commonly contrasted with oil-on-canvas and the more "serious" emergence of painterly abstraction. Yet the cartoons exhibit the expressive freedom, bold simplification, violent deformation, and strikingly nonliteral composition associated with paintings by the same artists. Such correspondences reveal a strong relationship in form to the development of modernism. More significantly, the formal assault on the academic tradition and the political motivations of the cartoons register a deeply adversarial impulse common to both forms of production. The cartoons are primarily addressed to the "people," eschewing the venues in place for bourgeois collectors.[29] When asked where he exhibited his works, the cartoonist Jean-Louis Forain said "in the magazine stands."[30] Thus, though cartoons necessarily remain more narrative than abstract, their posture is revealed in more than just their explicitly political captions.

The polar distance between the "low" cartoon and the "high" painted abstraction covers a subtle and complex terrain, raising questions long considered problematic by Marxist critics such as Theodor Adorno, Georg Lukács, Peter Bürger, and Thomas Crow. These are questions of fundamental importance for an understanding of the difficult relationship between art and politics for self-proclaimed leftist avant-gardists before World War I. How do artists, responding to a broadly working-class (and intellectual) liberationist movement, bring their politics into avant-garde "abstractions" that are addressed finally not to the masses but to a small circle of initiates? This central problem of modernism remained unresolved in the cultural ferment of the period, in which art could still seem to have the power, hence the obligation according to anarchist theory, to liberate consciousness and society. During the formative stages of modernism, this nagging contradiction between political realities and abstract aesthetics,

27. See Grave, *Quarante ans de propagande anarchiste*, 438–39; and Aline Dardel, "Catalogue des dessins et publications illustrés du journal anarchiste 'Les Temps Nouveaux,' 1895–1914," (Ph.D. diss., Université de Paris IV, 1980), 54–57.

28. For instance, by Jacques Villon, van Dongen, and Gris, in the Centre Georges Pompidou, Cabinet Graphique, and Bibliothèque Nationale, Cabinet des Estampes.

29. *L'Assiette au beurre*'s editors did occasionally offer cartoons published in the journal for sale, in limited runs, on better quality paper, sometimes for fund-raising purposes, suggesting that such profits accrued to the journal rather than to the artists. This contrasts with, on the one hand, the large number of artists exhibiting in the Salon des Humoristes and the Salon des Peintres-Graveurs français and, on the other, the precious editions of modernist prints and books published by such entrepreneurs as Ambroise Vollard; see Una E. Johnson, *Ambroise Vollard, Editeur* (New York: Museum of Modern Art, 1977).

30. Forain is quoted in Jacques Lethève, *La Caricature sous la IIIe République* (Paris: A. Colin, 1986), 42.

31. Frantißek Kupka too is enormously important in the anarchist avant-garde, and his complex case gets a separate chapter in my forthcoming book. Suffice it to say here that Kupka's anarchism was of central concern to him and led to a large body of vitriolic cartoons, book illustrations for a major anarchist work of theory (see Elisée Reclus, *L'Homme et la terre* (Paris: Librairie universelle, 1905–1906)), and finally—through his mingled theosophical and anarchist utopian convictions—to completely nonobjective paintings supported by his treatise of 1912, "La Création dans les arts plastiques;" see Frantißek Kupka, *La Création dans les arts plastiques* (Paris: Cercle d'art, 1989). See Virginia Spate, "L'Homme est la nature prenant conscience d'elle-même," in *Frantißek Kupka, 1871–1957, ou l'invention d'une abstraction* (Paris: Musée d'art moderne de la Ville de Paris, 1990), 15–23.

32. Villon is quoted in Dora Vallier, *Jacques Villon, Oeuvres de 1897 à 1956* (Paris: Cahiers d'art, n.d.), 116; translated in Shikes. "Five Artists in the Service of Politics in the Pages of *L'Assiette au Beurre*," 166.

33. See Dixmier, *L'Assiette au Beurre*.

34. See Shikes. "Five Artists in the Service of Politics in the pages of *L'Assiette au Beurre*," 163.

35. Cited without reference in Stanley Appelbaum, *French Satirical Drawings from "L'Assiette au Beurre"* (New York: Dover, 1978), vi; see also Shikes, "Five Artists in the Service of Politics in the pages of *L'Assiette au Beurre*," 163, who cites the testimony of Grandjouan.

36. See Dardel, "Catalogue des dessins et publications illustrés du journal anarchiste 'Les Temps Nouveaux,' 1895–1914;" Grave, *Quarante ans de propagande anarchiste*; and Louis Patsouras, "Jean Grave: French Intellectual and Anarchist, 1854–1939" (Ph.D. diss., Ohio State University, 1966).

This page: Kees van Dongen, "Le Peril Blanc" [The White Peril], *Les Temps nouveaux*, September 30, 1905. ©2006 Artists Rights Society (ARS), New York/ADAGP, Paris; next page: Kees van Dongen, *Femme Fatale*, 1905. Private collection, Paris. ©2006 Artists Rights Society (ARS), New York/ADAGP, Paris.

between demotic motives and elitist products, forced an unwanted hypocrisy on any artist aspiring to both the "political" and the "avant-garde." At the same time, in a period of structural change in the art market, with the arrival of the alternative salons and emerging galleries, cartoons may have offered a way for artists to shape their *déclassé* artistic identities for a variety of audiences and with great freedom of invention.

The careers of Kees van Dongen and Juan Gris—each for a time involved in anarchist circles—reveal different paradigms of these problems, especially compared with that of Picasso, whose path avoided the satirical journals but was nonetheless politicized.[31] The satire of Gris and van Dongen was addressed to a wide audience, from workers to intellectuals, and demanded a simplicity, readability, and directness that often resulted in highly inventive means of expression. The cartoons communicate contempt and indignation at the events depicted, and frequently register what is surely heartfelt social criticism. As even the relatively unengaged artist Jacques Villon asserted, recalling his own enormous production of satirical cartoons: "At that time the influence of the press on art was incontestable. It helped to speed up the liberation of painting from academicians."[32] Cartoons represented a powerful form of primitivism that could serve to transform artistic tradition.

Since *L'Assiette au beurre* was such a crossroads for anarchism and modernism, it is important to note that the journal did not represent a particular dogma but rather offered a great variety of anarchist approaches, from innocuous fun-making to savage criticism, from fierce individualism to

Le Peril Blanc.

outright fundraising for the CGT, sometimes coming from the same artist (for instance, Steinlen). The editors, Samuel Schwarz (1901–1903) and André de Joncières (1904–1912), had many friends among various anarchist groups, and doubtless hewed to their own political positions, but the attitudes expressed in the cartoons were by no means directed from above.[33] Both editors embarked on the journal as a (not always successful) money-making scheme rather than as a vehicle for their own ideas, clearly defined or not. They therefore gave the artists a great deal of freedom and usually paid them something, though the artists certainly did not consider it well-paying work.[34] As Steinlen put it in 1903, "If *L'Assiette au beurre* weren't the only periodical in which one can express certain things freely, we would all have abandoned it. By staying on, we make a sacrifice to Art and the [anarchist] Idea."[35] The weekly magazine—which consisted largely of full-page cartoons—was thus a vehicle for a diverse group of leftist and anarchist writers and artists whose opinions and outrage run through most of its twelve years.

Les Temps nouveaux, on the other hand, was the vehicle of its editor, Jean Grave, an anarchist-communist who in 1885 had taken over his friend Peter Kropotkin's *La Révolte* and subsequently represented Kropotkinian anarchism in France.[36] Grave ran his journal on a shoestring and frequently accepted support from artists and writers who published in the journal, including Camille Pissarro, Pierre Quillard, A. F. Hérold, and Elisée Reclus. Grave's policy was never to pay his contributors for articles or drawings; thus everything that appeared in *Les Temps nouveaux* was a donation. It is telling that from 1905 to 1907, when Grave succeeded in getting regular contributions of drawings from his pool of cartoonists, the journal increased significantly in sales, then dropped off as the artists fell away one by one.[37]

Of the hundreds of artists publishing cartoons in Paris in this period, none were as inventive or expressive as van Dongen and Gris. Kees van Dongen made his first trip to Paris from Rotterdam in 1897–1898, when he met the influential critic Félix Fénéon through anarchist contacts.[38] In 1900 he moved permanently to Paris, where he became close friends with the most committed anarchists of the neo-impressionists, Maximilien Luce and Paul Signac. In 1904 he befriended Guillaume Apollinaire, Picasso, Maurice Vlaminck, and André Derain, and in 1906 moved for a year to the Bateau-Lavoir in Montmartre, center of the Picasso circle and a building so closely associated with anarchists that it was under police surveillance.[39] As a painter passing through a wild Neo-Impressionism to a wilder Fauvism, van Dongen was

a declared anarchist and self-conscious "primitive," and his involvement with the anarchist press expressed his own political convictions. This involvement also helped him make needed money at times, although—as with all of these graphic artists—most of his income came from selling innocuous drawings to more purely "humoristic" magazines like *Le Frou-Frou*, *Le Rab'lais*, *Le Rire*, and *L'Indiscret*.[40] For the anarchist and left-wing journals, he consistently hammered on the troubling issues of bourgeois society in the Third Republic: poverty, prostitution, colonialism, and militarism.

Van Dongen's most passionate allegiance was to the anarchist movement's advocacy of sexual liberation. Dedicated male and female anarchists mounted a massive polemic on the subject of free love, entailing support for legalized abortion, attacks on the commercialization of sexuality, and the abolition of state-sanctioned marriage (anarchists supported gender equality but not suffragism, since to vote was to support the political system already in place).[41] Van Dongen strongly believed in free love and acted this out in both his art and life. The majority of his work, in his anarchist period and later, is preoccupied with celebrating sexuality in the guise of the nude female form.[42] His critique of commercialized sexuality appears in a special issue on "The Prostituted Ones" for *L'Assiette au beurre* of 26 October 1901. The series of drawings—with captions written by the artist—follows a young prostitute from her initial poverty to her inevitable death from syphilis, passing through a stage of momentary and illusory well-being.[43] Elegantly dressed and brought by carriage to the large department store *Au Printemps* after a day of work, "She ends by making 20 francs," a caption tells us, "which she spends."[44]

Van Dongen condemned colonialism through attacks on Christianity and its missionaries. In a work of 1905 for *Les Temps nouveaux* he simply and eloquently calls Christ "The White Peril;" with idiot complacency, the "Peril" stands possessively over cities, factories, armies, cannons, and ships sailing off to exploit exotic lands. Christ is here caricatured bluntly as a drunken, vainglorious fool who takes a crazy pleasure in the evil deeds perpetrated in his name. The primitivism of the drawing is brutal, and the message could not be clearer or more effective.

37. See Grave, *Quarante ans de propagande anarchiste*, 171, 438ff, 540, 547. Why the artists dropped away can only be speculated upon; in the case of Kupka, he indicated that his loyalty had been to Elisée Reclus, who died in 1905.

38. As van Dongen recalled, "I had met a curious gentleman named Félix Fénéon. I had met him because he was an anarchist. We were all anarchists without throwing bombs, we had those kinds of ideas" (quoted and translated in Donald Drew Egbert, *Social Radicalism and the Arts: Western Europe, A Cultural History from the French Revolution to 1968* (New York: Alfred A. Knopf, 1970), 254).

39. See *Re-Ordering the Universe*, chapter 2.

40. Jean Melas Kyriazi, *Van Dongen et le fauvisme* (Lausanne: La Bibliothèque des Art, 1971), 51.

41. I take issue here with John Hutton's characterization of the anarchist movement as antifeminist, in "Camille Pissarro's Turpitudes Sociales and Late Nineteenth century French Anarchist Anti-Feminism," *History Workshop* 24 (1987): 32–61. Such a reading of anarchism is too narrowly based on the reactionary elements of Proudhon's thought and does not take sufficient account of the wider discourse on feminism within the anarchist movement. See Sheila Rowbotham, *Women in Movement: Feminism and Social Action* (London: Routledge, 1992), 151–62; and Felicia Gordon, *The Integral Feminist: Madeleine Pelletier, 1874–1939: Feminism, Socialism and Medicine* (Minneapolis: University of Minnesota Press, 1990).

42. While Carol Duncan, "Virility and Domination in Early Twentieth century Vanguard Painting," in *Feminism and Art History: Questioning the Litany*, edited by Norma Broude and Mary D. Garrard (New York: Harper and Row, 1982), 293–313, is right to point out the sexist repetition of the male artist expressing himself by way of the body of the recumbent female in this period, it is also important to acknowledge the animating idea of free love, which seemed so liberating to the artists—and not only male ones—at the time.

43. Van Dongen was paid the rather generous sum of 800 francs. The original drawings for this issue show the captions in van Dongen's hand.

44. The original reads: "*Elle finit par gagner des vingt francs...qu'elle dépense.*"

45. See Sonn, *Anarchism and Cultural Politics in Fin de Siècle France*, 95–114.

46. "Liste des expositions," *Van Dongen, le peintre, 1877–1968* (Paris: Musée d'art moderne de la Ville de Paris, 1990), 237–47.

47. The original reads: "*restituent les aspects grouillants des rues pauvres et des rues chaudes de Rotterdam, la convulsive agitation des industries et les filles de Roode Zand et de Zandstraat aux prises avec les marins. Beaucoup de cette catégorie sont des dessins à l'encre de Chine que l'aquarelle bariole violemment ou colorie de nuances tendres.*" (Felix Fénéon. "Van Dongen," *Kees van Dongen, Galerie Vollard, exposition du 15 au 25 novembre 1904* (Paris: Galerie Vollard, 1904), n.p.)

Van Dongen goes further than any other artist of the period in his stark simplicity of line and form. At the same time, the setting is minimized, focusing attention on the offensively blasphemous main figure.

Other social problems occupied van Dongen as well. A cartoon of 20 June 1901 for *L'Assiette* depicts a ragged and bony street musician who confesses, "I'm not a musician or a singer... I'm starving!" The caption—"*J'suis ni musicien, ni chanteur... Je suis crève-faim!*"—is written in the *argot* of Emile Pouget's popular anarchist journal, *Le Père Peinard*, eliding the vowels to approximate underworld and street slang. The crude pictorial form, the slangy caption, and the political message are all of a piece, communicating an identification with the *lumpenproletariat*, the marginal, the starving, and the unemployed—those who inhabited the peculiar province of the anarchists.[45] Van Dongen's thick black strokes of ink evoke precisely that aspect of his later painting that offended his critics and pleased his admirers. The anarchist politics of his cartoons and the style he developed to serve them are continuous with his "audacious and violent"

high art, exhibited in the Independents' Salon and the Autumn Salon annually beginning in 1904.[46]

In his preface to van Dongen's first one-person show at the Galerie Vollard in November 1904, Fénéon sets the tone for much of the criticism of van Dongen, describing such works as *Zandstraat* (1895) as "restor[ing] the teeming appearance of the poor and heated streets of Rotterdam, the convulsive agitation of industries and the girls of Roode Zand and of Zandstraat struggling with the sailors;" he alludes also to the artist "violently" coloring some of the drawings, thus allying the traditional anarchist theme of street life with its "violence" of treatment.[47] But works like this do not come close to the primitivism evident in his later cartoons and Fauve paintings. *Femme fatale* of 1905 exhibits stark contrasts and amorphous shadows thoroughly comparable to those in his cartoons, with the addition of arbitrary and appallingly garish color. In the preface for van Dongen's exhibition at Bernheim-Jeune (where Fénéon was in charge) in 1908, Marius-Ary Leblond—actually a pair of brothers who wrote criticism as well as novels set in colonial Africa—celebrated the artist's palette as expressive of a new modernist primitivism, describing "green acidities, reds of blood-colored mandarin, phosphorous yellows, winey lilacs, electric blues;" connecting this "primitivist" sensibility with the cults of African and child art, they call the figures of such women "European idols," while van Dongen's clowns manage to "achieve human expressions in their wooden-doll faces."[48]

The offensiveness of such works resides not only in the repetition of marginal subjects like the prostitute[49] and the poor circus figure but in the ever more cartoon-like treatment of such subjects. In *Femme fatale* the garishly made-up woman joylessly advertises her breast, displaying the jewels and feathers that are the fruits of her labors. One of the jewels—a gold heart—lies above her breasts, rendering supremely ironic the "love" she offers. Both this painting's subject and its style were an affront to bourgeois morality; the buyer of the prostitute is presumably as corrupt as she, and sex for both is merely a form of commercial exchange. The style of the work counteracts the expected sexual allure of the prostitute in its departure from naturalism, emphasizing the "unnatural:" acid colors, primitivized form, and lack of spatial structure.

The unnaturalness of sex for sale is manifested in the prostitute's exaggerated lack of passion and interest in the client/viewer; in both van Dongen's cartoons and his paintings there is a corresponding awareness that such women begin and end in poverty. Through his combination of subject and style, van Dongen finds a visual equivalent to an anarchist rhetoric that encouraged sensitivity to the plight of those on the social margin, a rhetoric in which artistic daring paralleled propaganda.

Juan Gris has always been treated as a completely apolitical artist whose few cartoons supposedly represent "radicalization" by editors.[50] Yet Gris expressed pacifist convictions throughout his life. Though not provably anarchist himself, he was certainly sympathetic to it in the prewar period. The memoirs of friends like Alice Halicka and Waldemar George speak of an early "revolutionary" Gris. According to Halicka, he was very concerned with social injustice, and, naming van Dongen, Villon, Vallotton, Kupka, and her husband, artist Louis Marcoussis, "like his comrades, hate for society pushed this young rebel to substitute for vitriol and dynamite the acid of his drawings and the violence of his captions."[51] Gris, like his fellow countryman Picasso, avoided military service and, since he did not pay the exemption fee, was officially a fugitive and could not return to Spain.[52] Waldemar George called Gris "this atheist, this revolutionary, this defaulter from the Spanish army."[53] When World War I broke out in August 1914, Gris wrote to his dealer D.H. Kahnweiler that the war "does not concern me either by virtue of my nationality, character, or ideas."[54] Gris came into contact with anarchism and socialism by virtue of his antimilitarism and anticlericalism; additionally he collaborated with anarchist writers such as Charles Malato for *L'Assiette au beurre.*

In 1906 Gris also moved to the Bateau-Lavoir at the height of its reputation as an anarchist hangout, and in 1908 was eating at Picasso's every day, according to a letter that Gris wrote to a friend in Spain.[55] While his closeness to Picasso's circle alone would prove little about the influence of revolutionary rhetoric on Gris, his political cartoons testify to the importance of his brief involvement with the movement. Gris' cartoons are extraordinarily inventive in their formal means, and were for

Gris, as for van Dongen, an arena for experimentation that affected his subsequent painting. Again, as with van Dongen's, the political meanings of many of Gris' cartoons are independent of their captions; in any case numerous drawings for Gris' cartoons include manuscript captions in his own hand.[56]

Gris' political engagement is clear in a special issue of *L'Assiette au beurre* of 29 August 1908—entitled "Turkey Regenerated"—on which he collaborated with Malato and the artist d'Ostoya. More than merely criticizing Turkey, Gris uses this opportunity to devastating effect, representing a nation considered in France to be the epitome of ignorance, despotism, and backwardness (a popular attitude dating back to the Greek War of Independence of 1821–1829) as sponsoring what were, in fact, French policies, currently under bitter debate in Paris. This series constitutes a paradigmatic example of the anarchist technique of satire by inversion: Turkey is described in glowing schoolbook terms, belied in each case by the action depicted. One cartoon shows a schoolroom scene with the innocuous-sounding caption, "Instruction will be free [i.e., without

48. Marius-Ary Leblond, "Préface," Exposition van Dongen, Bernheim-Jeune, 25 novembre au 12 décembre 1908 (Paris: Bernheim-jeune, 1908).

49. See Sonn, *Anarchism and Cultural Politics in Fin de Siècle France*, 109–13, 133–34, 136–37, 153; Cate and Gill, *Théophile-Alexandre Steinlen*; and *Re-Ordering the Universe*.

50. For example, Daniel-Henry Kahnweiler in *Juan Gris: His Life and Work*, trans. Douglas Cooper, rev. ed. (New York: Abrams, 1969), 15–16, treats the cartoons as superlatively unimportant, mentioning them only in the context of how Gris made a living in Paris from 1906 to 1910. Mark Rosenthal (*Juan Gris* (Berkeley: University of California Art Museum and Abbeville Press, 1983)), expressed the same view of this body of work, though—following John Richardson in the foreword to *Juan Gris* (Dortmund: Museum am Ostwall, 1965)—he offers an astute appreciation of some of the cartoons' formal effects as "signals" of his later work: "powerful juxtapositions of shapes, foreground-background reversals, patterning, and visual rhyming" as well as "prominent wall patterns, mirrors, doors, and windows" (12). As is usual in discussions of Gris' work, none of the cartoons Rosenthal reproduces express political criticism in the drawing itself, and only one caption—of the sort that it has been easy to assume was composed by an editor—addresses a political subject; "*Bruits de guerre et bruits de paix,*" from *L'Assiette au beurre* (3 October 1908), 439, depicts two men talking in a café: "—There was a time, young man, when I was a pacifist. But with age I've realized that our country's honor must be defended. —With my blood? —Well not with mine, by Jove." Marilyn McCully and Robert Rosenblum have likewise noted the relationship between Gris' cartoons and his later paintings, though again looking only at the formal echoes between them; see McCully, "Los Comienzos de Juan Gris como Dibujante," in *Juan Gris (1887–1927)*, exhibition catalog (Madrid: Salas Pablo Ruiz Picasso, 1985), 17–32; and Rosenblum, "Cubism as Pop Art," in *Modern Art and Popular Culture: Readings in High & Low*, ed. Kirk Varnedoe and Adam Gopnik (New York: Museum of Modern Art, 1990), 123–24. Shikes makes a similar observation and rightly insists on Gris' political engagement; but he argues that to the extent that Cubist elements appear in Gris' cartoons, their expressive power as cartoons diminishes (Shikes, "Five Artists in the Service of Politics in the pages of *L'Assiette au Beurre,*" 178).

51. The original reads: "*Comme ces camarades, la haine de la société avait poussé ce jeune révolté à substituer au vitriol et à la dynamite l'acide de ses dessins et la violence de ses légendes... Il prit vite une place de premier plan servant ainsi à la fois l'art et la révolution.*" (Alice Halicka, "Quand Juan Gris travaillait à *L'Assiette au beurre,*" Arts (3 September 1948), 1, 3)

cost] and obligatory. Children will be taught respect for the law and the glorious deeds of our ancestors." The "glorious deed," however, is a beheading; the children look on in dismay. The drawing is crude, with the back wall parallel to the picture plane; cut-off forms lock the podium into place, while the blackboard appears as the only diagonal shape and the only suggested movement in an otherwise relentlessly static, nearly geometrical, construction expressive of the oppressive Ottoman state. Yet August 1908 was the midpoint of a heated five-month debate in the French Chamber of Deputies over capital punishment, so that Gris in criticizing Turkey is even more pointedly criticizing France and the supporters of the guillotine, taking the abolitionist position on the issue (France finally abolished capital punishment in 1981). In numerous ways, the drawing pushes expression to new limits, as Gris flattens space, geometrizes form, and treats figures with the utmost simplification.

He carries this stylistic radicalism as far as he would ever do in the most powerful drawing in this special issue, a cartoon posing as a comment on Turkey's imperialist ambitions in Africa. Since at least the Greek War of Independence, the French considered the Turks the most ruthless of peoples, and the Turks are here shown bayoneting the African babies they would pretend to rule. But the Turks never invaded sub-saharan Africa; the French did. Gris is evoking details of the scandals of 1905–1906 over the documented behavior of French officials and army in the French Congo. Dressing French colonial soldiers in Turkish uniforms, he criticizes the government in the severest terms. One hardly needs the caption to send the message home: "Guided by a need for expansion proper to every civilized nation, the Turks will go into the savage lands to bring civilized ways." Gris parodies the foundation of French colonial philosophy with its "civilizing mission" and turns the trope of the primitive back on the complacent French. This is possibly the starkest cartoon published in Paris in the prewar period. And Gris specifically relies on formal devices that he will use in developing his Cubism in the following years. No modulation of form or recession of space allows the viewer to escape the linear gestures of the machine-like soldiers as they intersect lethally with the soft, floppy forms of the black children. The death's-head faces are reduced to a grim simplicity, especially the prominent one in the upper center.

Such cartoons demonstrate that Gris was absorbing proto-Cubist lessons from Picasso's work in 1908, though this is not evident in his "high" art until two years later. But important elements

52. See Juan Gaya Nuño, *Juan Gris*, trans. Kenneth Lyons (Boston: New York Graphic Society, 1975), 55; and *Re-Ordering the Universe*, 22, 70.

53. The original reads: *"Cet athée, ce révolutionnaire, cet insoumis de l'armée espagnole..."* (Waldemar George, *Juan Gris* (Paris: Peintres nouveaux Gullimard, 1931), 6).

54. Juan Gris to Kahnweiler, 16 August 1914, translated in *Letters of Juan Gris* (1913–1927), edited by Douglas Cooper (London: privately printed, 1956), 8.

55. Nuño, *Juan Gris*, 259. Christopher Green. *Juan Gris* (New Haven, Conn.: Yale University Press, 1992), 16, suggests that Gris may not have moved to 13, rue Ravignan until 1908, though it seems equally possible that he occupied another studio there.

56. See Christie's sales catalogs, London, 1 April 1977, one noted; and 2 December 1980, two illustrated.

57. Juan Gris to Maurice Raynal, 17 October 1916, *Letters of Juan Gris*, ed. Cooper, 42.

58. "Picasso's Collages and the Threat of War, 1912–13," *The Art Bulletin* 67 (1985): 653–72, reprinted in *Collage: Critical Views*, edited by Katherine Hoffman (Ann Arbor: UMI Research Press, 1989).

59. See Richard Terdiman, *Discourse/Counter-Discourse: The Theory and Practice of Symbolic Resistance in Nineteenth century France* (Ithaca: Cornell University Press, 1985), for a discussion of newsprint in late-nineteenth century France; building on Mikhail Bakhtin, he maps both the dominant culture's manipulation of the daily paper and the counter-discourse of the literary avant-garde. In this light, I have explored the cultural meaning of newsprint and its resonance in Picasso's collages in "Cubist Anachronisms: Ahistoricity, Cryptoformalism, And Business-As-Usual in New York," *Oxford Art Journal* 17 (1994): 91–102.

of Gris' mature style are already in place: flatness, planarity, linearity, geometrification, repetition of lines, extreme contrast, and a fusion of abstraction and realism. All are developed in the laboratory of political satire, and all continue in his painting. Gris' graphics of 1908, with their radical primitivism and restriction of recessive space, contrast interestingly with the few surviving drawings and paintings before 1911, more realist in approach if still subtly geometrizing. Clearly Gris felt a difference in subject and aim between his cartoons and such works, and just as clearly the cartoons represented for him a more "advanced" mode of stylistic experimentation.

By 1912 Gris—studying the work of various Cubists, especially Picasso—had evolved a unique combination of abstraction and realism, as in *The Washstand*, where he creates an abstract work through the use of parallel lines that impose a grid over quite recognizable objects: washstand, bottle of cologne, and comb. And he did not forget the power of the silhouette, as is evident in *Figure in a Café* of 1914, with his hat and turned-up coat

collar, reading *Le Matin*. Such tricks of juxtaposition—Cubist geometrification (and obfuscation) and cartoon illustration—developed out of Gris' unique graphic style, invented for both visual and political punch; highly effective in his cartoons, these cartoon "tricks" constitute one of the key differences between his Cubism and that of Picasso and Braque.

As in van Dongen's work, there is a significant continuity between Gris' cartoon style and his abstract paintings. Unlike van Dongen, whose canvases developed simultaneously with his cartoons and continued to reflect his anarchist ideals and attitudes to at least 1909, Gris has self-consciously drained his paintings of political import, avoiding such anarchist subjects as prostitutes—frequent enough in his cartoons—and neutralizing his radical style. Gris' cartoon images of politically charged public events thus contrast tellingly with his frequent oil-on-canvas images of domestic interiors and privatized environments: kitchen still-lives, washstands, and views out of his own window. Of course, Gris never entirely abandoned his socially critical position. Despite the difficulty and danger of living as a noncombatant in Paris during the war, he quietly maintained his pacifist views, writing with mock *naïveté* to his friend Maurice Raynal in 1916, "I can't understand as you do this urge to massacre, to exterminate."[57] But he just as surely developed a carefully privatistic art that left his brief involvement with the anarchists behind. This operation is perhaps nowhere as visible as in his collages.

Picasso had a long history of involvement with the anarchist movement, and manipulated the subjects and styles of his art to achieve political effects in the collages of 1912–1913.[58] Given the fact that this politicized version of collage was the one that Gris inherited when he began to concentrate on *papiers-collés* in the summer and fall of 1914, on the eve of war, a comparison of his *Figure in a Café* with a work like Picasso's *Bottle of Suze* of 1912 is very revealing. Picasso's collage, also representing a café still-life with bottle, glass, and newspaper on a table, imports the gruesome facts of the Balkan War, as well as the huge anarchist and socialist peace movement gathering force in Paris. By juxtaposing articles from *Le Journal* on these subjects in the collage, Picasso evokes the topic of debate around a café table, while subverting the commodified

This page: Juan Gris, *Figure in a Café*, 1914. Acquavella Galleries, Inc., New York; previous page: Juan Gris, *The Washstand*, 1912. Private collection, Paris.

layout of newsprint common to the mass-distribution dailies he drew on. In the paper itself, the political implications of a column reporting a pacifist rally are diffused by its submersion in a patchwork of neutralizing information, from the sensationalist to the trivial to the commercial.[59] By retrieving columns from different parts of the newspaper in his collage, Picasso reunites reports that now echo meaningfully. This reorganization constitutes a counter-discourse, disrupting the original ideological formation of the newsprint. It does so furthermore in the setting of a café, that locus of friendship, argument, sedition, and police surveillance that "sustained the political, cultural and social ferment of *fin-de-siècle* and *belle époque* Paris."[60] Picasso purposefully deploys anarchist themes—war, pacifism, armaments profiteering, strike-breaking—at a moment of international crisis. By summoning the theme of state-sponsored militarism into the collage, Picasso invokes contemporary anarchist debate even as he destroys officially sanctioned artistic conventions in the work itself. Through his manipulation of current events in his collages, he establishes his own relations to the views of pacifists, socialists, and anarchists opposed to the impending war, thus placing himself in a collectivist context, a public—that is, a political—space.

The deliberation of their approaches to collage reveals Gris' careful avoidance of the political in contrast to Picasso. Gris' collage is also a café scene: a figure sits at a table drinking a beer and reading the news. Here, however, the "news" is not an intrusion from the outer political world, but a carefully selected fragment pasted just under the masthead that plays on the concept of illusion versus reality so wittily

juggled in the work itself, with its industrial artificial woodgrain paper—both "real" and carefully faked—and its literal newsprint: the headline reads, "There will be no more faking of works of art." In a collage such as *Guitar, Sheet-Music and Wineglass* of 1912, Picasso likewise invites interpretation on questions of artistic syntax, with his allusions to varying modes of visual discourse (a thoroughly conceptual guitar juxtaposed to a drawing of a glass in his earlier Cubist style, still based on visual perception); this collage plays too with an analogy between the abstraction of music and that of the work itself. Thus the "battle" announced in the headline at the bottom may metaphorically evoke artistic games comparable to Gris'. But in Picasso's collage the "battle" also inescapably refers to war. All the beauty, wit, and sheer subversiveness of the work is forced to coexist with the concrete reality of the newsprint's literal reference to the First Balkan War. In *Breakfast* (1914), Gris playfully wins this artistic contest by pasting his own name over the headline in *Le Journal*'s morning news, read over the breakfast table in the privacy of his own home.

That Gris knew perfectly well the potential of such newsprint allusions is subtly visible in numerous works produced during the war, for example in the carefully painted-in headline, "Official Communiqués," on a fictional newspaper in *Still Life with Checked Tablecloth* (1915). This at a time when he could write to Maurice Raynal, "I don't even like reading the newspapers because I am so impressed and terrified by what is happening."[61]

Spanish pacifism dies hard. Nearly alone of the avant-garde, Picasso and Gris stood by their refusal to serve in any military, stood against the forces that led Apollinaire, Moïse Kisling, Marcoussis, and so many others also from neutral countries to fight in the war.[62] When Gris used a masthead like *The Socialist*, as in *The Sun-blind* (1914),[63] he conjured up the official pacifist position of the Socialist Party before the war. And it is hard not to see Gris, in a work like *Fruit Dish, Glass, and Lemon (Still-Life with Newspaper)* (1916), commenting on his own immovable pacifism in this gloomy grey painting, its one bright, bitter spot of citron intersecting with the lighted masthead of the newspaper, *The Intransigent*. But this is a quiet sort of comment if it is one, perfectly in tune with the

60. Scott Haine, "'Café Friend:' Friendship and Fraternity in Parisian Working-Class Cafés, 1850–1914," *Journal of Contemporary History* 27 (1992): 607–26. In other works, Picasso conjures with the ideological space of another Parisian commercial institution, the department store, in relation to the commodified female; see Francis Frascina's discussion of Still-Life "Au Bon Marché" in "Realism and Ideology: An Introduction to Semiotics and Cubism," in *Primitivism, Cubism, Abstraction: The Early Twentieth Century*, edited by Charles Harrison, Francis Frascina, and Gill Perry (New Haven: Yale University Press, 1993), 95–98.

61. Juan Gris to Maurice Raynal, 20 December 1914, translated in *Letters of Juan Gris*, edited by Cooper, 20. For Gris' collages, see also Lewis Kachur, "Gris, Cubismo y Collage," in *Juan Gris (1887–1927)*, 33–44.

62. See Kenneth E. Silver, *Esprit de Corps: The Art of the Parisian Avant-Garde and the First World War, 1914–1925* (Princeton: Princeton University Press, 1989), who details the impact of the war and its patriotic rhetoric on the avant-garde, including Picasso and Gris; and *Re-Ordering the Universe*, 143–45.

63. Kenneth E. Silver discusses this work as a response to the outbreak of war in "Juan Gris y su Arte en la Gran Guerra," in *Juan Gris (1887–1927)*, 45–52.

64. Lethève points out the freer atmosphere regarding censorship following the amnesty for communards in 1880 in his *La Caricature sous la IIIe République*, 35–36.

private, inwardly-turned world of Gris' Cubist art, never parading the grand public themes of those Cubists who exhibited in the salons (such as Albert Gleizes or Fernand Léger) or playing on the world stage of public events evoked by Picasso at an earlier, and unquestionably safer, time.

The distance that Gris traveled from his cartoons to his paintings is also an index of his political evolution, and charts a very different trajectory from Naudin, van Dongen, or Picasso. Gris is an example of an artist whose radical politics, inspiring the expressive power of his cartoons, nourished his subsequent painting, but who wanted to rid his avant-garde art of those uncontrollable politics at a time when they were most intensely unacceptable. At the same time it is important to remember

that for critics hostile to modernism, the privatism and seemingly innocuous content of Gris' still-lives would not necessarily mitigate the charged import of the works' style. Gris kept a very low profile during the war, when Cubism was popularly viewed as *bôche*, the wartime slur for "German."

Thus choices of artistic venue, style, and content available to politicized artists in the period before World War I were myriad. There were numerous models provided by successful salon painters, political cartoonists, and radical modernists. Even more significantly, art criticism, which flourished in more than 250 journals available in Paris between 1881 and 1914, articulated a wide range of often politicized aesthetic positions.[64] The question of how one was likely to be received in various quarters could be grasped in advance, and thus

needs to be part of any consideration of how artists in this period fashioned their careers, addressed their audiences, and accordingly chose their mediums, genres, styles, and venues. I hope it is clearer now that avant-gardists made their choices too within this cultural discourse. Whether politically left- or right-wing, whether hostile to or supportive of modernism, art critics frequently viewed the art of the prewar period as demonstrating a political attitude toward the status quo by virtue of style alone. But readings of this sort occurred on the most superficial level; those critics who were more engaged and informed invariably addressed both style and content in their evaluation of a given artist. Of course, politicized style was not the intent of all modernists (for example, right-

wing modernists such as Roger de la Fresnaye), and we cannot assume even from an extreme radicalism of form a political posture (compare the pure abstraction of the Czech anarchist and early abstractionist Kupka with its visual counterpart in the work of the thoroughly bourgeois and "apolitical" Robert Delaunay). But we can understand that artists who saw themselves as anarchists could self-consciously play with and against the expectation of radicalism, a view that they shared with their critics. The artists' various responses to their deeply politicized culture—including satire, primitivism, and other examples of socially critical, "liberated," and "destructive" art—produced a politics of form, whose motives played an important role for such artists in encouraging the counterdiscourse of modernism.

CLIFFORD HARPER: AN ARCHIST ILLUSTRATOR

ICKY A.

In 1989, on my 16th birthday, a used copy of *Anarchy: A Graphic Guide* by Clifford Harper showed up in the mail. It was from my batty old aunt who lived in the forests of northern New York and worked in the nearby small town as a special-ed teacher. I had no idea where she got it or why she thought it would appeal to me, but it was an inspired choice. It was the only time someone in my family got me anything that I vaguely related to at that age. It took awhile, but I grew to know it well.

Anarchy: A Graphic Guide is profusely illustrated in Harper's distinctive woodcut style, featuring sharp images of rebellion, cities, and revolutionaries. As I flipped through the book I found women, men, children, guerrillas, militias, strikers, feminists, pacifists, theorists—anarchists all! The writing was straightforward and covered anarchist and anti-authoritarian movements and ideas in a way I understood. My aunt's offhand gift uncovered a secret history of the world, something that finally made sense. Here was a book made by someone, an artist, who attacked the deception and lies that I perceived as the status quo, who championed the forgotten rebels, and he did it simply with pen, paper, and a strong sense of justice.

Following this I saw Harper's work more frequently. On stickers in the streets, on book covers, as registration badges at an anarchist conference. When I moved to New Orleans in 1997 my new housemate had a copy of *The Education of Desire* (a compilation of Harper's graphics published in 1984) containing older work I had never seen before. Amongst that small group of anarchists in Louisiana there were several other people who had a similar experience with *Anarchy: A Graphic Guide*; finding a copy or having one passed onto them, having it be the first text on anarchism that spoke to them. In the infoshop we ran there we had a few of his newer releases, handsome graphics-heavy books. And then during the late 90s, with anarchism and the anti-globalization movement blooming I stopped seeing anything new by him at all. What had happened?

It wasn't until I looked for him on the internet a couple years ago that I saw he'd been busy, illustrating in the London daily *The Guardian*, doing design work and publishing his own books on Agraphia Press. His work had grown and changed since I last saw it, more greys and more subtlety in the line but still bold and distinctively his own.

Harper is currently revising *Anarchy: A Graphic Guide* for AK Press; expanding, redrawing and bringing it up to date. I keep mentioning this book not only because of its personal impact on me, but also because I believe it exemplifies what is best about Harper's work. He is a skilled illustrator whose images convey complex ideas, thoughts, and emotions in ways both beautiful and clear. Since the 1970s, Clifford Harper's artwork has represented the international anarchist movement, and he remains a tireless promoter of this cause.

Where, when and how did you start making art?

I've been drawing and making things for as long as I can remember. My pa was a carpenter (and a postman) and I got from him the practice of skill and creating.

When did making art start to coincide with your political beliefs?

I became an anarchist at 14 years and making serious drawings coincided. I was very attracted to the Bohemian practice of making drawings.

What were the politicizing factors in your life?

This is very complex, but essentially it was growing up as a worker and coming to anarchism in the early 1960s, just in time for it all to kick off in 1967.

When did you first encounter anarchism?

1963.

Who was it in 1963 that you encountered and how was it different then other lefty stuff?

I didn't come across "lefties" 'til much later. I hate the bastards. I'll rephrase that—I've a strong and natural dislike of authoritarian socialists. I lived among workers and you didn't come across many "lefties" there. Who it was that I "encountered"

were four sixth-form schoolgirls dressed all in black and wearing anti-bomb badges. They looked so cool. I asked my mate "Who are they?" and he replied "They're anarchists." And that was that. I've been an anarchist ever since and no turning back.

What was the anarchist movement like at that time period?

I don't know. I only knew the small group of anarchists I was with. Later, by 1967, I was spending a bit of time with Freedom Press and by 1968 there were anarchists just everywhere. You couldn't walk out of your front door without tripping over an anarchist. All kinds of anarchists, all kinds of ideas, activities, publications. 68! Anarchism was in the air we breathed. Hard to imagine now.

Was making art or even appreciating art considered to be part of the liberatory struggle?

Within anarchism it was a bit thin. But there were many artists who were known to be anarchists. It started to pick up in the 1970s. In the leftist movements, aesthetic ideas were under the dead, gray hands of Marxists. Not any more though.

What is the role of the artist in the anarchist movement, and what role do you think art could or should have within the movement?

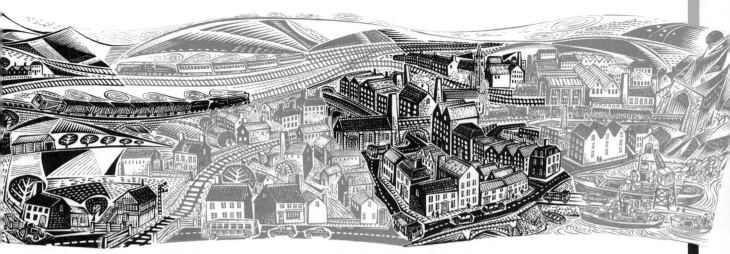

Very amusing question. Well, it's certainly changing for the better. I don't regard myself as an artist, by the way. I am a craftsman. I've an artist's mind, but that's not central to my work.

The whole art thing—artists, art works, art theorists, art critics, art galleries, art schools, art money, the whole dismal show, is so compromised, so hopelessly fucking with the state—fame, greed, wealth, prestige—that it's best left to its own degradation. I just don't want to be associated with it, it sticks to the soles of your shoes. It really stinks and you can't scrape it off. For working people like me, it's just another part of the show that has to end. Craft and skill, on the other hand, are deeply respected, and practiced, by workers, so that's where I'm at. Fuck art.

Having said that, it should be clear that I don't want artists to have any role anywhere, except at the bottom of a very deep hole. But I would like anarchists to take a good look at creative practice and thinking. If there was more of this then things would move on real quick. The principal, urgent task at this time is propaganda. The bosses have very effectively driven out of the people's minds any understanding of anarchism, and replaced it with lies. We have to counter this and creatively explain to people exactly what anarchism is and exactly what we need to do to get there. Signpost it.

I also think that creative people are good at resisting the ever-present danger of middle class leaders. We're just not interested in bullshit. You know—there's a job to be done, let's do it. In the bad old days, the last twenty-five years, most anarchists displayed an astoundingly philistine attitude to creative work. Don't ask me why. Although I do have one or two ideas about it. Things are changing, the fact that we are doing this proves it, and that can only be good. The growing anarchist creative movement will push anarchism to a better place.

Though you wrote "don't ask me why," I'm curious about what your "one or two ideas" are and if you'd care to elaborate?

You really want to know? O.K. It goes like this. Some anarchists are into control. Creativity does its thing. No matter how you try to direct it, it always surprises. I *never* know how a drawing will turn out. The drawing always, to a degree, draws itself; it pushes to where it wants to go. It's kind of... anarchist. Some anarchists fear losing control, of going to places they're not prepared for. It requires an open mind and a flexible approach. Some anarchists fear creativity contaminates the struggle. I think they think revolution is male, and creativity female, if the (male) revolution's exposed to creativity (female) it won't have a dick anymore. It won't be able to overthrow the state, because you need a dick to do that. Revolution is a dick thing. Anyway, it's just an idea and you did ask.

This page: Clifford Harper, detail from *Class War Comix #1*, 1974; next page: cover illustration for Antonio Tellez, *Sabate: Guerrilla Extraordinary (Elephant Editions, 1985.)*

Are there specific pieces of your own work that you consider to be more effective then others (politically) and what are they?

Anarchy: A Graphic Guide—the remix. You've gotta see it, it's amazing. I did drawing number 142 yesterday, Emiliano Zapata. Only 110 to go...

How do you feel about propaganda, and the term propaganda applied to some of your work?

Fine by me. I believe that "propaganda" thing is mainly a smear. It prevents people from making committed radical work.

Do you worry about issues of representation (what kind of people you draw: age, gender, race)? How do you usually decide "who" to draw?

Very much. It's quite a problem, I think. In *Anarchy: A Graphic Guide* I'm drawing as many women as I can, lots of children, dark skinned people, and animals. So far I've done elephants, horses, and dogs. A really beautiful black horse pulling a plough through a Ukrainian field. In my day-to-day work I think very hard about this.

What do you hope to achieve in your art, both personally and in a wider sense?

I don't hope. I'm doing it. The "personal" side is all about the skill, getting better at what I do, about trying new approaches, perfecting methods and also getting my work more public, which is a slow and careful road. In a "wider" sense, essentially I'm communicating to the world the urgent necessity of an anarchist revolution.

You've championed Masereel, Vallotton, and Pissarro to be remembered as anarchist artists. I was curious if you feel there is an anarchist aesthetic? If so how does this differ from a communist, fascist, or capitalist aesthetic?

Yeah, I used to wonder about this, but now I mainly think who gives a fuck about communist, fascist, capitalist, or religious art? It's all due for the scrap heap anyway, one way or another, so why bother? But as far as an anarchist aesthetic goes—You betcha! What else is there? If you're creative and you want a political position, then anarchism is the only show in town. It's creative politics. The two go together like coffee and cigarettes.

Why illustrate poetry?

Why not? Poetry and illustration are brother and sister. They've a similar scale, and they're both very much about the page, their home. They work well together and they often inhabit a lowly place, often ignored, this is a good location for subversive and questioning work to cut its teeth. In previous times all the anarchist press around the world carried a lot of poetry and illustration. There used to be a lot of major poets and illustrators who were anarchists, so it made sense. Both forms carried a lot of anarchist "ideas."

Some of your recent work has shown a vast amount of detail, complexity and wildness in nature. Is this reflective of a shift in your interests?

No. It's just what I get asked to do. Here the countryside is a big social question these days. Rural life is very important for the English, especially as we've all been driven into cities. What you call "detail" is mainly seeing what the drawing will do, where it wants to go and if it leads into difficult complexity, then seeing it through to the end.

At least in the US, the anarchist movement seems more homogenous than it once was and although I think it's growing up it is still based on youth culture. Was the movement you came up in more diverse and in what ways?

I think anarchism is in the best shape I've ever seen it. I agree it's under the boot of youth and they keep re-inventing the wheel, but this is solvable, it just requires a programme of education, but our job is telling the people what anarchism's all about. Agitation and propaganda. The anarchisms I knew in the 1960s and early 1970s were, on the one hand, good classical anarchism with the addition of ideas from Paul Goodman, the Beat poets, Colin Ward, Wilhelm Reich, the Solidarity group, and on the other, the anarchism that came from the alternative/ underground/head/ drug/music scenes. So yes, it was quite a bit broader, diverse, especially in age, and the thinking was more practical somehow—more grounded in everyday life while at the same time quite mixed up in avant garde and bohemian matters. There wasn't the thing that exists now of a kind of anarchist lifestyle, separate from everybody else. But I would say it was much less visible than now.

It also appealed to people who were non-conformist; it was, for some, quite attractive. People liked anarchists. There was a popular idea that anarchists were somehow needed, were good people to have around. Not next door, but around. When I was a kid there was a popular saying and idea, "the awkward squad." People would say, of someone who asked difficult questions or didn't follow the line, "He's one of the awkward squad..." And when I was a kid I couldn't wait to grow up, leave home, find the awkward squad and join up. Couldn't wait.

Anarchism is on the up, which I just love. It's really wonderful that this is happening exactly when it is needed. I'm fifty-seven years old, which means that I've lived through more than one resurgence of anarchism. Or rather, I used to think that

I've lived through resurgences of anarchism, more or less one every decade since the 1960s. But now, in 2006, I see this very differently. I now see through all those years there is a clear trajectory. Anarchists are increasing in numbers, working class anarchists are back, anarchism is becoming effective again.

Where have the elders gone?

In my experience elders get old. They drink, they get ill, they kill themselves, they get tired, they see the revolution as distant as ever, they retreat from this appalling world, they get ignored, sidelined, disrespected, you know... They get treated like old people. They recognize the brevity of existence—up close and personal.

This page: Clifford Harper, *Collectivised Gardens*, from Utopian Visions series, 1974; next page: illustration, *Anarchy: A Graphic Guide.* (London: Camden Press, 1987.)

Are you involved in any kind of organized political work?

At the moment I'm deeply into my own thing. Which is pretty organized and definitely political. But I always respond when anarchists ask for something.

Your *Utopian Visions* series depicts a post-revolutionary society. At the time you drew these did you feel a revolution was imminent? Was it a project of hope or dreams?

I drew those in 1974. I was part of the radical technology, radical ecology, radical science thing. The magazine *Undercurrents*, which was semi-anarchist, was asked by Wildwood House to put together a big book on all that. I did those drawings, very precisely guided by the scientists—great fun—for the wonderful book *Radical Technology* (edited by Godrey Boyle and Peter Harper and published by Wildwood House in 1977). I, and many others, felt around 1971–74 that revolution was on the cards. The *Visions* series depicted things that we thought were very imminent, aspects existed, so they were more like a summing up of where we'd reached. So they were in a sense not utopian at all, but pragmatic drawings, almost blueprints. The idea was that with those drawings in your hands, you could simply go and set it all up.

Would you undertake a project like this today?

Don't think I'd be interested. Those drawings emerged from a context. They were of their time. Now, in this time, my work is about looking back, not forward. The way I draw, the styles and so on, are all from the past. The 'Visions' were all about the here and now—then.

You've done some artwork for punk bands, how would you assess punk's influence on anarchism?

Regrettable. People go on about punk being new, shaking things up, being youthful and iconoclastic, blah-blah. But it was disrespectful of the 1960s, and it didn't earn the right to put down the efforts of an entire generation of "hippies," whatever the fuck they were. Punk took part in the reaction to the big changes that were attempted in the 1960s and it did it with the crude lies put out by the right—that the 1960s were a waste of time, ineffectual, flower-power, peace 'n' love man, let's get stoned.

How did the endpapers and more decorative work for the Rebel Press titles come about? Or the Elephant pocketbook series? Were these your ideas or theirs? What kind of working relationship do you have with anarchist presses?

Clifford Harper, *Library*, illustration for Canadian Anarchist Bookfair, 2002.

That is partly against the design/production ethos of punk. The crude DIY look. Essentially it grows from my deepening craft, I try to put everything into a drawing, to get it right and do it as best as I can, so when it comes to book design I want to maintain that process, beyond the drawing out into the whole book. Also I want to give whoever has the book, a beautiful book, and do it as cheaply as I can, to cut that rope that joins beauty to money and to join it instead to anarchy. As to anarchist presses, as long as they do what I want them to do then everything is cool.

Do you have any interest in doing comics again?

I do have an idea for a comic, which I might do later. Two stories, one short, one long. Ravachol attempted to rob a mausoleum where he thought jewelry had been interred with the corpse of a wealthy woman. All he found was a wooden crucifix. Great story, great images. The long one would be the tale of the Spanish anarchists who joined the Free French forces in 1940, so fighting from 1936 to 1945. And then what happened to them?

Your recent art work is really stunning. I wonder if with your more abstract work or the more recent stuff if the change is deliberate and focused on over time or if it's something that comes naturally and unconsciously for you?

Thanks. I think it's really about working hard at getting better. I don't find doing my work is easy, it's very hard work, very tiring, but it's all I can do.

How much time do you spend on an illustration?

How long is a piece of string? Roughly speaking, an A6 [4.13" X 5.83"] black and white drawing takes about a day, day and a half.

Do you draw from life? from your head? from photos?

Google images, praise the Lord!

Do you ever have writers'/artists' block of some sort?

Yep. Sometimes drawings are just crap and that's that. Tear it up and start again. If it's still crap then leave it for a day or two, if you can.

Have you been able to live off of making art?

All the time. I'm a professional illustrator, it's how I pay my rent and buy my grass.

Has this ever felt compromising?

Nope. If it did I wouldn't do it. People who commission me know I'm an anarchist. So I don't get the well-paid work. Boo-hoo-hoo.

What do you make of the current anarchist movement, particularly groups and movements that gained momentum out of the anti-globalization struggles?

As I've lived through forty years of anarchism I see from where we are now that what seemed like a disjointed series of stops and starts—1968, 1974, 1979, the 1980s, the 1990s and now. Now, has really been a steady growth of anarchism and it's better now than it's been in my lifetime, and the trajectory is definitely up. My own thing is what should be called classic working class anarchism and that's taken something of a knock-back in the last two decades, within anarchism itself. Which just should not be. But again that's changing a lot now. Which is how it should be. I'm not too concerned about anarchists, it's up to them to sort themselves out, but my direction is outside of the movement, out to the people. It's that time.

In the US in the late 1980s and early 1990s your graphics were all over... on fliers for demos and punk shows, on stickers, at anarchist conferences. At some point you dropped out of view over here. Was this deliberate?

Not really. I was doing work, but I was concentrating more on working in newspapers, which made me

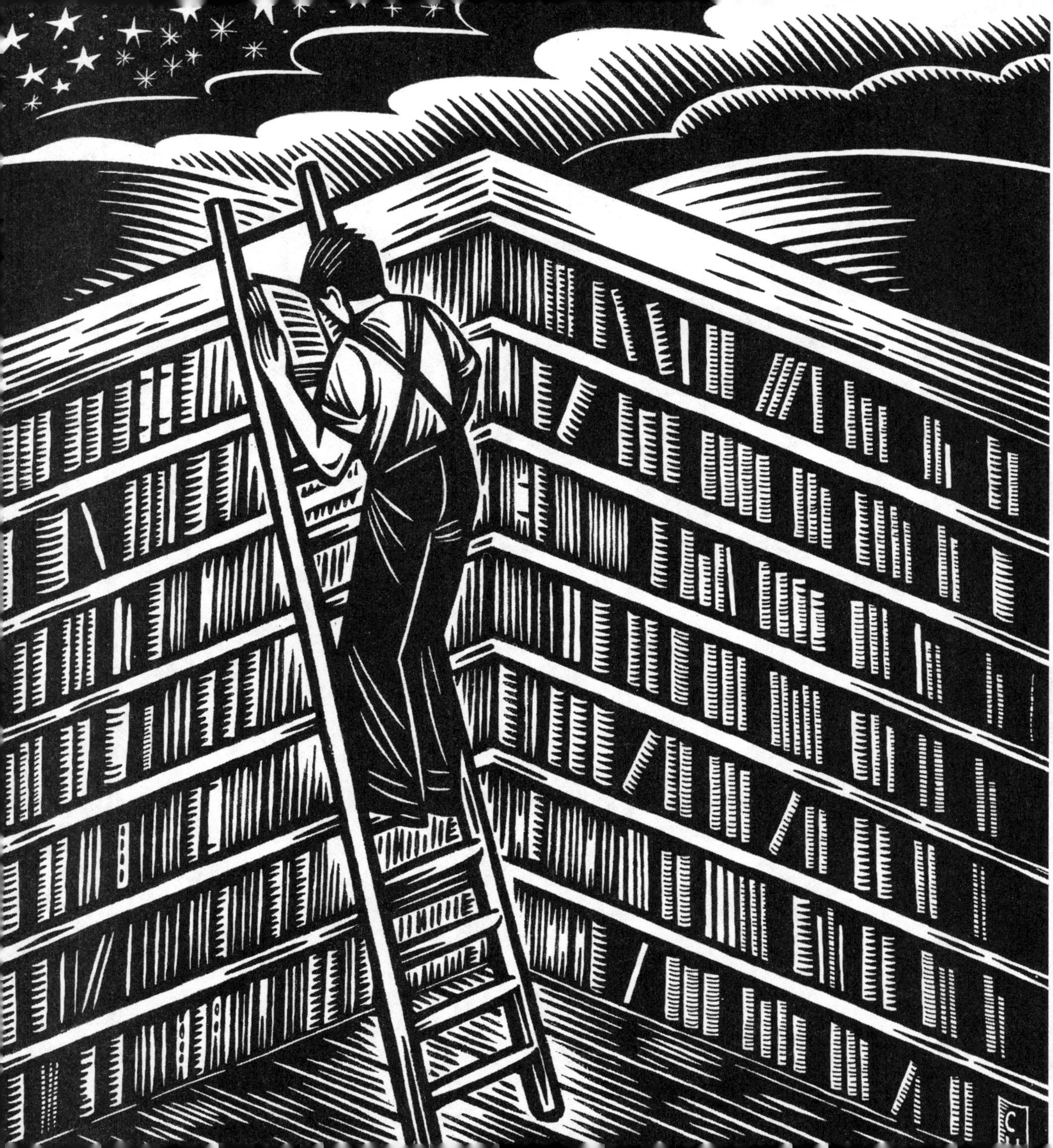

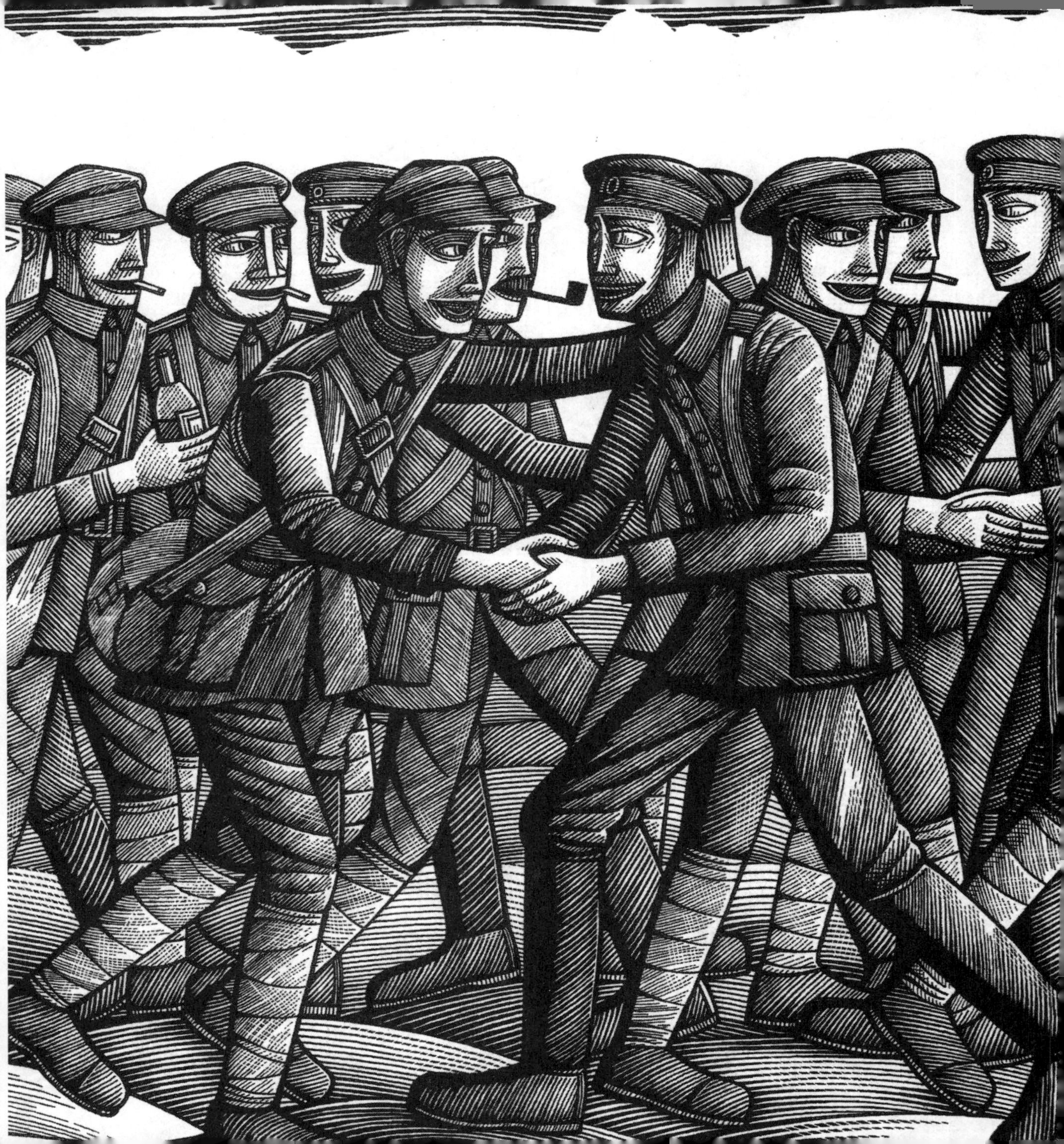

get good and professional, a really useful process. "Become the Media." Also, stuff happened and I got into trouble.

What kind of stuff?

Cigarettes and whisky and wild, wild women.

Can we expect another collection of your illustrations any time in the future?

It's not up to me. I need to get *Anarchy* delivered to AK Press first, then who knows?

Selected Bibliography

Class War Comix #1. London: Epic Productions, 1974. (Reprinted in 1979 in the US by Kitchen Sink)

The Education of Desire: The Anarchist Graphics of Clifford Harper. London: Annares Co-operative Press, 1984.

Anarchy: A Graphic Guide. London: Camden Press, 1987.

An Alphabet: Twenty Six Drawings. London: Working Press, 1990.

The Unknown Deserter: 9 Drawings. London: Working Press, 1990.

Anarchists: Thirty Six Picture Cards. London: Freedom Press, 1994.

Prolegomena: To a Study of the Return of the Repressed in History. London: Rebel Press, 1994.

Visions of Poesy: An Anthology of Twentieth Century Anarchist Poetry, edited with Dennis Gould and Jeff Cloves. London: Freedom Press, 1994.

Stamps: Designs for Anarchist Postage Stamps, introduction by Colin Ward. London: Rebel Press, 1997.

Train Journey: 1 Ticket (self published, late 90s)

The Ballad of Robin Hood and the Deer, poem by John Gallas. London: Agraphia Press, 2003.

The Ballad of Santo Caserio, poem by John Gallas. London: Agraphia Press, 2003.

The City of Dreadful Night, poem by James Thomson. London: Agraphia Press, 2003.

Country Diary: 36 Drawings. London: Agraphia Press, 2003.

Harper has also regularly designed book covers and illustrations for *Anarchismo, Anarchy Comics,* Cienfuegos Press, Elephant Editions, Freedom Press, Kate Sharpley Library, *Knockabout Comics,* the London Anarchist Bookfair, *The New Anarchist Review*, *The Raven Anarchist Quarterly*, Rebel Press, *Solidarity, Zero*, and Ellis Peters' *Cadfael* mystery series.

This page: Emiliano Zapata from *Stamps*, 1997; previous page: detail, promotional illustration, 2005.

TALLER GRAFICO

UNITED FARM WORKERS

BUTTO

MINER 54

The official voice of the United Farmworkers

EL MALCRIADO

Price 10¢

EL GRITO

Las Vegas, N.M.   Vol. VI, No.

THE MOVI

IN NU

In

EL GRITO
DEL NORTE

a cry for justice in northern

IN THIS ISSUE:

The Tijerina Trial
Pete Garcia on Trial Again
The Indians Take Back Alcatraz
Comentarios Cortos de Vicente Vigil
Inside Story on Albuquerque's Press
Addict Answers Scerese -- II
Flash Gordon is Racist

Dec. 6, 1969

Vol. II, No. 16

española, n.m.

LABOR
PRODUCES
ALL WEALTH

ORGANIZATION EDUCATION EM

Industrial

ols for the ids,
no deatl enal-
pay for thers,
as now t n for
Communt and
well-to into
hen organ d a half
of 1906, e reason
printed. t is that
tal docu is that
ill rema ne of the
of Mexi present
rs of the d. In fact,
d docum hat Mexi-
rnment p tice is still
with consitutional the-

t the Ju s only wea-
its Mex h and Ameri-
o a 20,00 man guerrilla
ments of ms to various
beaches, nched probing
up a re ution for Sept.
through huge spy net-
g Post ce scanning of
az was se r it and lowered

ellos, n

freedom-fight, how he set it down in two
tle booklets in the language of the com-
on people, how the people fought brave-
and strongly because it was clear in
eir minds exactly what they were fight-
g for, how freedom-hero Tom died penni-
s and obscure and even hated for his dan-
rous ideas.

The Mexican Revolution had its Tom
ine too—sacrificing and giving of himself
ore, but receiving no more from his
ople than his American counterpart. The
ast we can do for this freedom fighter is
hy him the tribute of celebrating his 100th
rthday this Mexican Independence Day,
pt. 16th.

Ricardo Flores Magón, born in the
axaca of his idol Benito Juarez, drew in
ith his mother's milk the ideals of liber-
democracy, and people-cooperation.
ut by his teen years, these ideas were
st the thing to get you in trouble, for the
cent was now on Law and Order and Dic-
tor Diaz's Peace-of-the-grave. Then as al-
ays Law-and-Order had

His San Luis Potosí experience sparked
a revolution in him too, for the mentor of
the Convention was Camilo Arriaga, fresh
from Paris with a big trunkful of radical
books. Ricardo roamed his library like a
kid in a candy shop. The books that pleased
him most were those of Kropotkin, Bakunin, and other Anarchists. The rest of his
life he was to be referring to their ideas in
his writings, and he'd blossomed into a full-
blown Anarchist in the first bloom of the
20th Century, referring to Anarchism as
"our saintly ideal." Ricardo returned to
Mexico City with an armful of borrowed
books. Didn't get much chance to pore over
them, though . . .

Ricardo and his brother Jesus were cast
into Belen Prison's dungeon. But not for
offending the dictator—oh goodness, no!
Diaz didn't work that way; he had his
Grand-Protector-of-the-Juarez-Constitution
image to maintain. For instance, th
pazo Liberal Cl

soned. Without n
paper, they set u
in St. Louis. Cir
30,000. But this wa
One day a Diaz
town to press libel

EL GRITO DEL DISEÑO: DISEÑO MESTIZO AND THE RADICAL VISUAL LANGUAGE IN CHICANA/O NEWSPAPERS

DYLAN MINER

During the tumultuous beginnings of *el movimiento*, the Chicana/o civil rights movement, multiple Chicana/o and labor publications functioned with the multi-dimensional goal of creating a utopian society based on equality and local/communal subsistence. In this essay I will focus on three newspapers published during the initial years of the *movimiento*, approximately 1968–1974. Despite the individual partisanship, strategies and praxis of the varying newspapers, *El Grito del Norte*, *El Malcriado* and the *Industrial Worker* all operated with the goal of abolishing the inequalities of late-capitalism, if not eliminating the entire capitalist system.

Throughout the initial years of the *movimiento*, visual and cultural practices were used to articulate the localized hybridities of Chicana/o working-class realities. *Floricanto* (poetry), *corridos* (working-class story-songs), *música* (music) and *teatro* (theater) filled the aural and oral domains, while posters and muralism were the driving force on the visual end. Somewhere between these divergent genres, radical Chicana/o newspapers educated local and national communities on current events, cultural practices, and community activities. Yet in spite of the importance of the newspapers for disseminating radical information to a certain geographic, ethnic, and class-based community, the visual iconography and rhetoric of these publications has been little studied by radical historians. By addressing these newspapers as visual documents, I will begin to analyze this complicated area of study.

The history of graphic design, much like other forms of cultural history, is a field burdened with theoretical problems. In the essay, "Good History/Bad History," designers and critics Tibor Kalman, J. Abbott Miller, and Karrie Jacobs state that

> There are two problems with design history. The first is how design history is written, for how history is written effects how the past is seen and understood. How history is written effects how the past is used. And that's the second problem: Most design history is not written, it's shown. There is a lot to look at, but not much to think about.[1]

Kalman, Miller, and Jacobs continue their argument by stating that the "study of design history is a way of filtering the past; it's a way of selecting what's important to remember, shaping it and classifying it. It's also a way of selecting what's important to forget."[2] The exclusion of certain items from design history, usually those designed using counter-hegemonic visual iconography, affects the manner that historians frame art historical and design scholarship. Design discourse, unlike that emerging from other intellectual and activist traditions, continues to argue for an objective quality to "good design." Not surprisingly, this design customarily emanates from professional designers producing large-scale campaigns for multi-national corporations or large international magazines.

Contradicting the supposed objective benefits of mainstream visual design, Chicana/o graphic design, particularly in regards to newspapers and posters, did not follow the principles of dominant (post-)modernist graphic systems. Instead, *El Grito del Norte*, *El Malcriado*, and the *Industrial Worker* articulated a design system that directly related to their revolutionary cultural and political posture. In other words, these radical newspapers did not appear as sterile as the mainstream modernist newspapers that were produced in the media centers of New York or San Francisco, and were widely available through mass circulation. Likewise, since the political perspective and visual style of these newspapers were in opposition to capitalist beliefs, structures, and images, these newspapers remain an important historical document about the radical bearing of the *movimiento*. By turning to these newspapers, we can learn much about the anti-authoritarian movement of working-class Chicanas/os.

History of *El Grito del Norte*, *El Malcriado* and *Industrial Worker*

The three newspapers discussed here, *El Grito del Norte* (1968–1973), *El Malcriado* (1964–1976), and the *Industrial Worker* (1908–present), each operate as oppositional viewpoints to those offered by the mainstream media. Through their different strategies these newspapers attempted to combat the global effects of late-capitalism and its effects on marginalized working peoples. *El Grito del Norte* was a paper operating in solidarity with the *nuevo-mexicana/o* landgrant movement in northern New Mexico. *El Malcriado* was the official voice of the

Ricardo Flores Magón article as published in *Industrial Worker*, May 1974.

PAGE 4 INDUSTRIAL WORKER MAY 1974

RICARDO FLORES MAGÓN,

Forward-looking Mexicans can literally describe their Ricardo Flores Magon as

THE MAN WHO MADE TOMORROW

by Rey Devis

Zapata and Pancho Villa, labeled respectively as "Attila" and "bandit," have been elevated to their true status as national heroes. Isn't it high time, on this, his 100th anniversary, to rehabilitate the Revolution's great precursor and philosopher, Ricardo Flores Magón, who has been painted as both (at the same time!) a dangerous leftist and a reactionary sell-out?

ALL THE WORLD knows about Tom Paine of the American Revolution—how he saw very sharply the issues of that great freedom-fight, how he set it down in two little booklets in the language of the common people, how the people fought bravely and strongly because it was clear in their minds exactly what they were fighting for, how freedom-hero Tom died penniless and obscure and even hated for his dangerous ideas.

The Mexican Revolution had its Tom Paine too—sacrificing and giving of himself more, but receiving no more from his people than his American counterpart. The least we can do for this freedom fighter is pay him the tribute of celebrating his 100th birthday this Mexican Independence Day, Sept. 16th.

Ricardo Flores Magón, born in the Oaxaca of his idol Benito Juarez, drew in with his mother's milk the ideals of liberty, democracy, and people-cooperation. But by his teen years, these ideas were just the thing to get you in trouble, for the accent was now on Law and Order and Dictator Diaz's Peace-of-the-grave. Then as always Law-and-Order had its price: thought control, crooks in government, mass poverty, guns instead of bread, prisons yes, schools no.

Ricardo fought the dictatorship inside Mexico as long as he dared: At 18 he was in the thick of a student protest against the Dictator's highhanded outmoded ways.

hopes. But even he didn't realize that he'd sparked one of the great, cleansing revolutions of our planet.

His San Luis Potosí experience sparked a revolution in him too, for the mentor of the Convention was Camilo Arriaga, fresh from Paris with a big trunkful of radical books. Ricardo roamed his library like a kid in a candy shop. The books that pleased him most were those of Kropotkin, Bakunin, and other Anarchists. The rest of his life he was to be referring to their ideas in his writings, and he'd blossomed into a full-blown Anarchist in the first bloom of the 20th Century, referring to Anarchism as "our saintly ideal." Ricardo returned to Mexico City with an armful of borrowed books. Didn't get much chance to pore over them, though . . .

Ricardo and his brother Jesus were cast into Belen Prison's dungeon. But not for offending the dictator—oh goodness, no! Diaz didn't work that way; he had his Grand-Protector-of-the-Juarez-Constitution image to maintain. For instance, the Lampazo Liberal Club wasn't closed down for opposing one-man rule, but for burning an effigy of Judas on Good Friday instead of the next day. So the Flores were jailed for libeling a Diaz official.

Belen dungeon was the perfect rehabilitation emporium for a hard-core law-and-order man: Sewers doubled as air and light vents, rats nipped the prisoners, spiders

sweetie. So back to penny-pinching . . .Super-scrimping plus help from friends finally got them their press. By November they had copies of *Regeneración* to be thankful for.

But these starry-eyed America-lovers were in for a shock. One December evening a knife-wielding Diaz agent burst into their San Antonio home. Enrique Flores jumped and disarmed him. Four American detectives, who just happened to be handy, arrested—no, not the goon, but Enrique. The judge laid a $30 fine on—no, not the attacker, but the attacked.

Must be too close to Diaz influence; better get away from the border, the staff reasoned. Without missing an issue of their paper, they set up at 107 North Avenue in St. Louis. Circulation soon rose to 30,000, But this wasn't all that rose . . .

One day a Diaz political boss came to town to press libel charges against the pap-

Toronto, then Montreal, they decided to hell with running. They would stand and fight on the ground of their own choosing, if it cost them their lives! The staff wound up operations at 2645 Lafayette St., and Los Angeles became the paper's home for the rest of its hectic days.

The young propagandists were in St. Louis only 1½ years, yet one of the important events in the whole history of Mexico took place there around them. These men and followers in and out of the U.S. set up the Revolutionary Junta (organizing committee) of the Liberal Party of Mexico, with Ricardo Flores Magón as Chairman.

This Junta carefully canvassed both leaders and humble people all over Mexico for the things that should be won from a revolution—no Sunday work, end of child labor, not having to pay debts owed by one's grandfather, right of farmers to own land and workers to have unions, minimum

United Farm Workers Union, helping to gain support for various farm worker boycotts and strikes, predominantly in California. The *Industrial Worker* has historically been a general labor newspaper published by the Industrial Workers of the World, an anarcho-syndicalist labor union. These publications, although wide-ranging in the activities they covered and supported, demonstrate the diversity of the Chicana/o movement.

By operating in opposition to mainstream capitalist-controlled media, these papers functioned analogous to those that served as the foundation for the working-class press in North America. For instance, the views espoused through the editorial, literary, and visual forms in Chicana/o activist newspapers were oppositional stances not usually being disseminated through other venues. As locally-produced independent newspapers reliant on volunteer labor, these papers were able to operate autonomously from mainstream funding. By operating autonomously from conventional media sources, working-class and activist papers confronted the racism and class-bias ubiquitous in the media. The independent Chicana/o press was able to give voice to the struggle in the fields, factories and *el norte* and challenge the monovocality of "professional" print publications. Kevin Barnhurst and John Nerone argue that

> the professional newspaper challenged multivocality. The reporter's soothing monotone overrode every other voice in the news, reducing all other speakers to sound bites and focusing attention on the unvoiced landscape behind everything else. Where voices could not be reduced, they were dumped into ghettoes... The monovocality of the modern news forms justifies itself as democratic.[3]

El Grito del Norte, *El Malcriado*, and the *Industrial Worker*, on the other hand, truly were democratic: offering a multitude of dissenting voices from a variety of perspectives. If the "professional newspaper" presents a monovocal perspective, volunteer and community publications proffer self-determination and community autonomy.

When discussing the early-nineteenth century media, Rodger Streitmatter writes that "America's mainstream newspapers had scant regard for the struggling new movement launched by the laborers, siding instead with the...capitalists

and the growth that they symbolized."[4] Streitmatter argues that the intention of working-class newspapers is to guarantee that working peoples do not spend their entire existence perspiring solely to enhance the power and prestige of the industrialist. He writes that "the common purpose of the publications was to ensure that American workers did not exist merely to enhance the power and abundance of the merchant capitalists."[5] Just as the initial labor publications performed the necessary task of silent agitator, the papers of the late 1960s and early-1970s functioned in a similar vein: offering a culture of resistance and struggle. The oppression of the farmworker, the colonialism in northern New Mexico and the exploitation of a global working-class were all harshly attacked within the pages of Chicana/o publications.

While there may appear to be a disconnect between working-class publications from the nineteenth century and Chicana/o publications from the 1960s and 1970s, they in fact have much in common. Particularly the *Industrial Worker*, which began circulation in 1908, less than three years after the incorporation of the anarcho-syndicalist labor union Industrial Workers of the World (IWW or Wobblies). As one of the most radical labor organizations in the history of the modern world, the IWW was much more than an industrial union. In fact, the IWW was (and continues to be) an anarchist-affiliated cultural and social organization. The *Industrial Worker* became one of its official mouthpieces, publishing articles, artwork, and poetry by and for a multi-ethnic working-class. The success of the *Industrial Worker*, like the other two papers, depended on the cultural production of working-class artists writers and poets (frequently rank-and-file union members). Without the submissions of working peoples as a demonstration of solidarity, the *Industrial Worker* would lack material for publication.

Unlike the racist and sexist histories of North American craft unionism, Wobbly industrial unionism has always welcomed racialized, foreign-born and female members. In fact, at the 1905 founding convention in Chicago, Lucy E. González Parsons (the wife of assassinated anarchist Albert Parsons) and *latinoamericano* Daniel de Leon, along with countless other people of color, women, and foreign-born workers, would play an instrumental role in creating IWW philosophy. In traditional Wobbly folklore, many of the oral histories, stories, and songs revolve around heroic women and people of color, so often excluded from mainstream labor discourse.[6]

During the late 1960s and early 1970s, the *Industrial Worker* was edited by Chicano artist and poet Carlos Cortéz.[7] During his shift as editor, Cortéz applied Wobbly aesthetics to Chicana/o, Latina/o, and American-Indian issues. Because of Cortéz's involvement in *movimiento* activities, during the period of his editorship, the *Industrial Worker* was just as much a Chicana/o paper as was the UFW's *Malcriado*. In turn, the readership expanded to members of the Chicana/o movement not ordinarily involved in the IWW, while the articles and visual imagery continued to address themes and ideas relevant to both Wobbly and Chicana/o communities.

For instance, something that Cortéz habitually intimated was that the anarcho-syndicalism of the IWW is unequivocally connected with the early twentieth century politics of Mexican anarchists Enrique and Ricardo Flores Magón. In many regards, the relationship between the IWW and the Flores Magón's *Partido Liberal Mexicano* (PLM) was both ideological and historical. In fact, before his assassination by the state of Utah, Wobbly martyr Joe Hill traveled to Baja California to fight with *floresmagonista* forces in the Mexican Revolution.[8] Cortéz rejuvenated this connection, beginning with a two-part essay in the spring of 1974. In this essay, Rey Devis (likely a pseudonym for Cortéz) engaged the *Industrial Worker* readership in the history and theory of the Flores Magón brothers.

In addition to the Wobbly re-connection with the PLM and the Flores Magón brothers, the *Industrial Worker* showed continued solidarity with the United Farm Workers union in nearly every issue. At this point, the newspaper also began to include illustrations borrowed from Mexico's radical printmaking collective the Taller de Gráfica Popular (TGP) and its populist predecessor José Guadalupe Posada.[9] This became a regular appearance, and the inclusion of Posada and the TGP is important as they created a radical artistic legacy unmatched in this hemisphere. In his essay "Rethinking the Accomplishments of the Taller de Gráfica Popular in Relation to *la Revolución*," anarcho-Marxist art historian David Craven states that although vague in his political motivation, "the revolutionary legacy of Posada is now an established fact."[10] For Craven, this legacy refers directly to the post-Posada graphic production of the TGP (and other radical artists) and the manner in which modern socially engaged artists look to Posada as a major influence. In recent years, many Chicana/o and US Latina/o artists have continued the revolutionary legacy of Mexican printmaking. Cortéz was himself a printmaker and he likewise drew upon Posada and the TGP as visual source material. In fact, the affinity between Cortéz and Posada was so great that in 2002 Cortéz edited a book on Posada published by North America's oldest socialist press, Charles H. Kerr.[11]

The legacy of the IWW could be seen in the political praxis and visual output of both *El Grito del Norte* and the United Farm Workers' *El Malcriado*. *El Grito del Norte* was published in Española and Las Vegas, New Mexico between 1968 and 1973 by a cadre of Chicana/o and non-Latina/o revolutionary activists. The founders and initial editors of *El Grito* were activist Elizabeth "Betita" Martínez and *movimiento* lawyer Beverly Axelrod. In addition to local insurgents, many North American revolutionaries and reformists relocated to northern New Mexico to create the newspaper in solidarity with the activi-

1. Tibor Kalman, J. Abbott Miller, and Karrie Jacobs, "Good History/Bad History." In *Looking Closer: Critical Writings on Graphic Design* edited by Michael Beirut, et al., (New York: Allworth, 1994), 25–26.

2. Ibid., 26.

3. Ibid., 303.

4. Rodger Streitmatter. "Origins of the American Labor Press." *Journalism History* 25:3 (Autumn 1999), 99.

5. Ibid., 99–100.

6. For more on the history of the IWW, see Paul Buhle and Nicole Schulman, eds. *Wobblies!: A Graphic History of the IWW* (New York: Verso, 2005), or Joyce Kornbluh, ed. *Rebel Voices: An IWW Anthology* (Ann Arbor: University of Michigan, 1964).

7. I most often refer to him as Carlos Cortéz Koyokuikatl, but since his name usually appears within the *Industrial Worker* simply as Carlos Cortéz I will use that within this essay.

8. To this date, this fact remains unverifiable according to many historians. Others place Hill in Baja California during the revolution.

9. David Craven, "Rethinking the Accomplishments of the *Taller de Gráfica Popular* in Relation to *la Revolución*," unpublished manuscript (2001). The tradition of satirizing political printmaking in Mexico (and the Latina/o US community) is usually accredited to Posada, even though his political tendencies were less than radical. Typically, radical artists and historians view Posada as acting in solidarity with their social justice movements. In fact, he created an image of anarchist revolutionary Emiliano Zapata for a counter-revolutionary newspaper. Substantial research still needs to be conducted on Posada to determine his political tendencies.

10. Ibid.

11. Carlos Cortéz. *¡Viva Posada!: A Salute to the Printmaker of the Mexican Revolution* (Chicago: Charles H. Kerr, 2002).

12. By recognizing the autonomy of *pueblos*, which translates as both communities and peoples, the Chicana/o movement in New Mexico struggled against all forms of hierarchy. This is not to say, however, that sexism and classism were not prevalent within this same movement.

El Grito del Norte masthead pre-1971 (top) and post-1971 (bottom).

ties of the *Alianza Federal de Mercedes* (Federal Landgrant Alliance), later known as the *Alianza de Pueblos Libres* (Alliance of Free Pueblos).[12] The *Alianza* was an "Indo-Hispano" movement attempting to recover communal lands lost through North American swindling after the Treaty of Guadalupe Hidalgo in 1848.

The leader of the *Alianza* was Reies López Tijerina, a working-class evangelical preacher who had conducted missionary work throughout the US-Mexico borderlands. He arrived in northern New Mexico in 1959 and formed the *Alianza* with other working-class *nuevomexicanas/os* in 1963. Within three years, a critical mass had been reached in

northern New Mexico. At this time, there were over 20,000 *Alianzistas* in the region.[13] Much like the land-based struggles of the Mexican Revolution, from which activists were drawing inspiration, *Alianzistas* rose up in arms to regain communally held lands unlawfully taken by private, state and federal means.

El Grito, unlike the other two papers under discussion, had a predominately female staff and clearly expressed a Chicana feminist voice, although definitely not the same feminist perspective that was being voiced by the Anglo-American women's movement. Early on in the *movimiento*, *El Grito del Norte* was publishing feminist texts written mainly by figures such as Enriqueta Longeaux y Vásquez and Betita Martínez. In 1971, Martínez issued a call to action for radical Chicanas, while simultaneously confronting *movimiento machismo*. In the June 5th issue of *El Grito* she writes that

> We must help Chicanas to overcome feelings of inferiority that many have, or feelings that they can perform only certain kinds of work and should not be involved in making decisions outside the home. Unfortunately, these feelings are often encouraged by machos who fail to see that we need every Chicana and Chicano in this struggle. Because many men of *El Movimiento* do this, even men who call themselves "revolutionary," there has been much talk recently about *La Chicana's* role. The fact is, nothing could be more truly Chicana than the Chicana who wants to be more than a wife, mother, housekeeper.[14]

In addition to its pro-Chicana, feminist stance, *El Grito* operated from a nonpartisan leftist position. According to a text in *Monthly Review*, also by Betita Martínez, she states that the paper

> began in 1968 as a vehicle to support the Alianza. It soon expanded to cover the Chicano movement in urban areas, workers' struggles, and Latino political prisoners, along with a broad spectrum that ranged from the black liberation movement to Mexican student protest to radical whites.[15]

For Martínez, an important goal of the paper was the expression of an international working-class solidarity. She continues by stating that it was a "combination of what could be called liberatory or revolutionary nationalism with international-ism [that] made *El Grito* very unusual among the dozens of more nationalist Chicano movement newspapers."[16] This "liberatory or revolutionary nationalism" was in fact very much oriented toward an anarchist approach. This nationalism, unlike those aligned with Stalinist or Maoist factions, was one that attempted to diminish all forms of oppression, even those tied to partisan politics. Similarly, these same activists issued the following call at a University of California MEChA (Movimiento Estudiantil Chicana/o de Aztlán) conference:

> By fighting imperialism in the US and by aligning ourselves with the progressive working class move-ment of this country, we necessarily accomplish a step towards a world solidarity of workers... We also realize the various tools and tactics that cur-rently can be applied to enhance this class struggle analysis. One such tool is cultural identity as a means of organizing and politicizing for an end to class society.[17]

By merging class status with Chicana/o identity, pub-lications such as these I am discussing broke away from narrow nationalist positions. Unfortunately, historians have fixated on those factions that more narrowly defined the Chicana/o movement.

After ceasing publication of *El Grito del Norte*, Martinez and other members of the edi-torial committee relocated from northern New Mexico to Albuquerque and launched the Chicano Communications Center (CCC). The CCC was active in a multitude of activities for working-class peoples and in 1976 published a photographic book entitled *450 Years of Chicano History*.[18] Among the countless photos and illustrations of Chicana/o working-class struggles, the book included three reproductions of Wobbly art along with a brief discussion of the role

---

This page: IWW images reproduced in Elizabeth Martinez, *450 Years of Chicano History*; next page: Andy Zermeño cartoon from *El Malcriado*.

SEEDS OF REVOLT

Ricardo Flores Magón, the Mexican revo-lutionary, had much influence on our work-ers in the U.S. When he was exiled by Díaz, he settled in Los Angeles. Because of his ra-dical activities, he was sent to prison in Lea-venworth, Kansas. On Nov. 22, 1918, a guard strangled him. Thousands of workers here and in México mourned his death.

Another big influence was the I.W.W.(In-ternational Workers of the World, called Wobblies), the only Anglo union that had success in organizing our people. Joe Hill of the IWW fought with the Magón forces in Mexico, it is said. The IWW helped to or-ganize the Wheatland, Cal. strike of hops pickers, who included many Chicanos.

Ricardo Flores Magón

A BIRD THAT LAYS SUCH ROTTEN EGGS IS LONG OVERDUE FOR EXTINCTION

SEMBRADORES

I.W.W. INDUSTRIAL CODE

WAKE UP! ... JOIN the I.W.W.

Símbolos y carteles de la IWW
IWW symbols and posters

Ricardo Flores Magón, el revolucionario mexicano, grandemente influyó a nuestros trabajadores en los E.U. Cuando fue exilado por Díaz, se estable-ció en Los Angeles. Por causa de sus actividades radicales, fue condenado a la prisión de Leavenworth, Kansas. El 22 de noviembre de 1918, un guardia lo estranguló. Miles de trabajadores lloraron su muerte.

Otra influencia fue la I.W.W. (Trabajadores Internacionales del Mundo), la única unión angla que pudo organizar a nuestra gente. Se dice que Joe Hill de la IWW luchó con las fuerzas de los Magón en México. La IWW ayudó a organizar la huelga de Wheatland, Calif. de los trabajadores de 'jape'.

that the IWW played in Chicana/o and Mexican political and social history. In *450 Years*, the editor Betita Martínez writes that "another big influence [on Chicana/o revolutionary thought] was the IWW...the only anglo union that had success organizing our people."[19]

As Martínez makes apparent, among Chicana/o working peoples the IWW was quite an influential association. Labor historian Zaragosa Vargas agrees with Martínez when he writes that alongside the anarcho-syndicalist PLM and the Texas Socialist Party, the "Industrial Workers of the World and the Western Federation of Miners [affiliated with the IWW]...drew large numbers of Mexican workers into their ranks."[20] As point of fact, as early as 1916 Carlos Cortéz's father Alfredo Cortéz was a red-card carrying Wobbly. Furthermore, the 1990 Smithsonian Folkways compilation of Joe Hill songs, aptly titled *Don't Mourn—Organize!: Songs of Labor Songwriter Joe Hill* features Alfredo Cortéz singing Joe Hill's "The White Slave."

Another Chicana/o publication, *Justicia* (1978), emerged in Albuquerque shortly thereafter and also used historic IWW graphics. As part of the September 1978 *Justicia* front page, the newspaper included one of the IWWs most circulated images: "The Hand That Will Rule the World–One Big Union." The drawing, created by Ralph Chaplin using the name Bing-O, was first printed in the June 30, 1917 edition of *Solidarity!*, an IWW periodical.[21] The resolve to use Wobbly cartoons within Chicana/o movement publications sustains an established legacy between *mexicana/o* laborers and the unique form of IWW anarchism. The connection between IWW anarcho-syndicalist utopianism and Chicana/o resistance, like that occurring in New Mexico, was sustained throughout the *movimiento* by innumerable collectives and individuals.

Just as the IWW had considerable success in organizing "unskilled" laborers in the early decades of the twentieth century, the Wobbly tradition also became associated with the *campesina/o* struggles of the United Farm Workers. Although the ideologies of industrial unionism (work-

13. Elizabeth Sutherland Martínez and Enriqueta Longeaux y Vásquez. *Viva la Raza! The Struggle of the Mexican-American People* (Garden City: Doubleday, 1974), 160.

14. Elizabeth "Betita" Martínez, "Viva la Chicana and All Brave Women of La Causa." In *Chicana Feminist Thought: The Basic Historical Writings* edited by Alma M. García, (New York: Routledge, 1997), 80.

15. Elizabeth "Betita" Martínez. "A View from New Mexico: Recollections from the Movimiento Left." *Monthly Review* (July–August 2002), 81.

16. Ibid.

17. Minority position paper presented at the 1973 University of California MEChA conference held in Riverside. As cited in George Mariscal. *Brown-eyed Children of the Sun: Lessons of the Chicano Movement, 1965–1975* (Albuquerque: University of New Mexico, 2005), 69.

18. A subsequent edition was published in 1991 with the updated title *500 Years of Chicano History*. Currently Betita Martínez is working on a similar project focusing on the role of women, similarly titled *500 Years of Chicana History*.

19. Elizabeth Martínez. *500 Years of Chicano History* (Albuquerque: Southwest Organizing Project, 1991), 92.

20. Zaragosa Vargas, "Citizen, Immigrant, and Foreign Wage Workers: The Chicana/o Labor Refrain in US Labor Historiography." In *Voices of a New Chicana/o History*, edited by Refugio I. Rochín and Dennis N. Valdés (East Lansing: Michigan State University, 2000), 155.

21. Ralph Chaplin was the most prolific Wobbly cartoonist, yet he is most well known for penning the union hymn, "Solidarity Forever." According to radical historian Franklin Rosemont, "Chaplin the cartoonist produced an impressive and many-sided body of work, for which he deserves greater recognition." This image, and other works by Chaplin, continue to frequent the pages of the *Industrial Worker*.

22. César Chávez quote in Susan Ferriss. *The Fight in the Fields: Cesar Chavez and the Farmworkers Movement* (New York: Harcourt Brace, 1997), 80.

No te necesito...aqui tengo a m'ijo

ers are organized by the "industry" in which they work—IWW) and craft unionism (workers are organized by the tasks in which they labor—UFW) are seemingly opposed, *El Malcriado* candidly recognized the historic role that IWW syndicalists played

in the organization of North American workers, especially those of Mexican-descent.

In 1964, César Chávez founded the Spanish-language paper *El Malcriado*. By the late 1960s the newspaper was being published in two separate editions: one each in Spanish and English. The paper's name, *Malcriado*, positions the farmworker struggle, like the other movements I discuss, simultaneously within both class and ethnic struggles. While "*malcriado*" simply means "ill-bred," Chávez explained in an interview with fellow union organizer and biographer Fred Ross that "during the (Mexican) *Revolución* one of the people's papers was called *El Malcriado*."[22] This antecedent struggle for *campesina/o* equality in the Mexican Revolution was sustained by the working-class struggles of the UFW. Like the visual resistance of both the *Industrial Worker* and *El Grito*, *El Malcriado* looked toward the Mexican Revolution as a source of aesthetic and ideological inspiration. The majority of the initial artwork of *El Malcriado* was cartoon drawings by UFW artist Andy Zermeño, however

Above: UFW logo printed in *El Grito*. Below: UFW story from the *Industrial Worker*, 1973. Next page, top: *El Malcriado* from 19; bottom: *El Malcriado* from 1972.

PAGE 12 INDUSTRIAL WORKER APRIL 1973

PRODUCTIVITY & CITY WORKERS

By a City Worker

In June 1972 a number of contracts were negotiated between New York City workers and the city. Unfortunately, every one of these contracts contained the following clause: The city may establish any productivity rules it wants in exchange for pay raises. Nixon's Pay Board kept all raises for '72 at 5.5% — it refused to touch the productivity clauses. They are intact to this day.

In December, 150 welfare workers were dismissed. The reasons: absenteeism and lateness. Hearings were planned for 700 more workers. District Council 37, the major union for municipal employees, was able to reduce some of the penalties. In the District 37 newspaper, an article on this issue fell short of what one would expect a "worker's" paper to supply; it didn't give a detailed breakdown of the penalty reductions and, furthermore, the piece ended by concluding that employees shouldn't take too many absences or be late too often since both make collective bargaining more difficult.

Something else happened in December that was at least twice as interesting as the aforementioned. Deputy Mayor Edward Hamilton ordered a study of average sick leave taken by city employees during the year. The results showed that the average was 9.76 days a year. The allowed sick leave is 12 days a year.

It might seem that of course employees should work an honest day's work (John DeLury, head of the NYC Sanitation Men's

get filled by a new person. The remaining workers take over the work on the old job while doing their usual work.

There is yet another way added work is passed on to existing staff. Employees without civil-service status — known as provisionals — are fired without apparent cause. The union does complain about this. It says that the ranks of the provisionals are filled with political hacks; when provisionals are let go it is always the low-paid ones, never the hacks. I know personally several politically hired at $20,000 and up after these layoffs of provisionals making $5,000 to $9,000. This was during the job freeze.

Still another problem is filling out productivity reports. In the Relocation Department where I work, workers who are supposed to be finding homes for undomiciled tenants, not to mention getting them finan-

cial benefits, don't have time for this work because they are filling out forms. All these things present the classic pattern of speedups.

What are District Council 37 and other city unions doing to fight this situation? With the new productivity clauses they negotiated "in our interest" there is very little that can be done legally. What they have been doing is negotiating for an automatic dues checkoff whether an employee wants it or not. The major issue the unions are presently fighting for is to keep civil service open only to those who pass competitive exams. This issue is basically a code for keeping minority groups out. In other words, the unions are doing nothing to stop speedups, layoffs, and dismissals which affect all employees whether they have civil-service status or not.

BOYCOTT LETTUCE

The Worth Of A Continental Dollar

The international set-up of card-sharks, dice gamblers, thieves, extortionists, and strong-arm men — sometimes called "Capitalists" and "National governments" — this whole tinker-toy structure of pitiless corruption was shaken to its sand-foundation in the last weeks of February 1973. Precipitating the chaos was the devaluation of the US dollar by 10% and the raising of the "official" (ha!) price of gold to $42.22 American an ounce. At the same time, Japan was forced to again float the yen upwards, and Switzerland, Britain,

ing against a US dollar which represents nothing more than the paper it is printed on.

At the very time the US Government was reluctantly "admitting" that 36 US bucks no longer bought an ounce of gold, but instead $42.22, the REAL price of gold on the world open market skyrocketed to a high of $95 an ounce on February 23rd, finally settling for the day on the London market at between $84 and $86.

A far cry from $42 smackers, eh Tricky Dick?

value profits from the hides of the US working class. Sure, your good buddies on the Phase III Cost of Living Council — guys like George Meany (AFL-CIO), I.W. Abel (United Steelworkers), Paul Hall (Seafarers International), Frank "the fink" Fitzsimmons (Teamsters), and Leonard "liberal" Woodcock (United Auto Workers) — these boys won't give you much trouble.

But there are some working people still around with enough brains and guts, with enough self-respect and dignity, to fight back. They won't be taken in by your jingo

Taller de Gráfica Popular linocuts were also regularly featured along with imagery borrowed from other AFL-CIO affiliated unions.

The March 7, 1967 *El Malcriado* is an exemplary model of the style, genre, and medium enacted by UFW editors and contributors. This issue includes a stylized photographic reproduction of César Chávez on the cover with interior graphics produced either by the TGP, Andy Zermeño, or borrowed from organizations such as the United Auto Workers' Education Department. It is in this 1967 issue that the UFW began an open dialogue on the history of North American labor organizing. As part of this discourse, they included a supplement on the history of labor: aptly titled "The Sacrifice of the Wobblies and the Birth of the AFL-CIO." Again, a link was established between contemporary Chicana/o working-class organizations (in this case, the UFW) and the radical legacy of the IWW.

In addition to the relationship of *El Grito del Norte* and *El Malcriado* to Wobbly traditions and imagery, each of these three publications were known to freely share graphics and illustrations with other *movimiento* publications. For example, to correspond with an article about the end to the UFW's anti-immigration policies, the May 1973 issue of *El Grito del Norte* published what appears to be an Andy Zermeño comic above the text to the article. On the other hand, *El Malcriado* also freely appropriates *El Grito*'s Zapata logo that was used throughout northern New Mexico as part of the Alianza insurgency.[23]

With the high levels of crossover imagery being printed in each of the publications, it is obvious that each organization operated within a similar visual language of resistance. Even if the strategies and goals of the organizations were divergent, the visual manner in which they were articulated was similar.

Design as *Mestiza/o* Metaphor

One of the least studied areas of radical cultural production has to be publication design. While historians and critics often focus analysis on the textual and fine art elements of the movement, little attention has been given to the manner that alternative publications have handled design (and

political) issues. Much design theory emerges from a eurocentric and bourgeois aesthetic and it is only beginning to incorporate non-elitist elements from cultural studies and postcolonial theory.

Focusing on the design issues of the radical Chicana/o press during the *movimiento* raises a multitude of questions, only some of which will be addressed here. In fact, the simplest questions have to do with the editorial intentions of the design schema of each tabloid. Do the editorial and production collectives of these radical publications care about how the visual and textual elements fit together? Are the visual elements afterthoughts in their location, or do they create an intended interplay with the text? Do *El Grito del Norte*, *El Malcriado*, or the *Industrial Worker* attempt to attack the stylistic hegemony of newspapers or merely attempt to replicate them?

North American newspaper design at the turn of the twentieth century became increasingly homogonized by a series of consistent layout constraints. Kevin Barnhurst and John Nerone write that

> by the end of the century newspapers came to share certain

design features: six columns, modular layout, a small story count, two or three front-page illustrations, sans serif and upper- and lowercase headlines, and so forth. In order to present a uniformly crisp, modernist façade, newspapers had become less diverse, not unlike the glass boxes of modernist architecture.[24]

Instead of a six column design, the "anticolonial modernism" of *El Grito del Norte*, *El Malcriado*, and the *Industrial Worker* all used a two or three column motif. Barnhurst and Nerone write that "at the height of modern newspaper design, the rules of form were widely understood and rigidly enforced in the United States... Protomodern old-timers clung to Bodoni headlines despite withering attacks from the young High Modernist bucks who pushed for Helvetica."[25] Dismissing these regulations as unim-

This page: *El Malcriado* mastheads, old (top) and new (bottom); next page: graphic used to fill white space in the *Industrial Worker*, December 1969.

portant, the designers of *El Grito*, *El Malcriado*, and the *Industrial Worker* would often run a melange of fonts (serif, sans serif, blackletter, handwritten, etc.) on the same page. While this inclusion of a number of typefaces may be viewed by mainstream designers as poor design, inversely it can be viewed as an engaged *mestiza/o* design. That is, a design that attacks the binary prescriptions of Anglo-American social structures, a hybrid incorporation of vernacular forms into modern cultural forms.

In the early twentieth century, the American Type Founders Company organized fonts into "type families." The rationale for this creation of a genealogical system for letterforms is connected to a fictitious idea of genetic purity. J. Abbott Miller and Ellen Lupton argue that "this system—still in use today—aimed to encourage printers and their clients to use genetically related characters rather than combining fonts of mixed heritage."[26] When Chicana/o designers integrated multiple typefaces within their newspapers they challenged majority beliefs on race. By choosing to evoke mixed typographical heritages, the three papers under analysis engaged their audience in a discourse on mestizaje, a dialogue prominent within the history of Chicana/o culture.[27] Consequently, *mestiza/o* design is one that combines a diversity of visual elements and strategies as a confrontation to the binary assumptions dominant in the United States.

While examining the pages of *El Grito del Norte* or the *Industrial Worker*, as well as the evocation of a mestiza/o aesthetic, it becomes obvious that the physicality involved in the design process became one of the main impetuses for how these tabloids took shape. What this means is that during the late 1960s and early 1970s newspapers were laid out using cut-and-paste techniques.[28] This time-consuming procedure often made it difficult to pre-determine page layouts until all articles and graphic elements were in the hand of the editor or production manager. There was a tendency to end up with barren space within the pages. Many of the smaller graphic elements in the design schema of these newspapers were used solely to disguise an otherwise stark location on the page.

In graphic design, unused space is often termed "white space." By placing "random" visual elements on the page publication designers were able to decrease the amount of excess white space. As if alluding to its double racial and design connotation of the term, Kalman, Miller and Jacobs ask "when and where did the term 'white space' come into use? Did they have it in the Renaissance? Did it mean the same thing?"[29] Why would Chicana/o

BOYCOTT GRAPES

journalist-designers allow a place for the "White" space to speak? Was this not already occurring in the mainstream press? Is there a relationship between the filling of white space that appears in the pages of these independent papers and the entry of Chicanas/os into the white space of American culture? By renouncing white space as a formal design element in these publications, the designers were promoting an oppositional (political) perspective.

The low technology of the cut-and-paste layout technique allowed for the unintentional non-parallel (i.e. crooked) layout of elements within the corpus of the *Industrial Worker*. In the February 1973 issue, for example, many of the columns of text, as well as graphic elements appear askew. While these visual incongruencies may partially have their origins in the constraints of an under-staffed, under-funded newspaper, I believe that these uneven elements also reflect the nitty-gritty of Wobbly cultural production and the aesthetic sensibility of Chicana/o culture. Within Chicana/o critical discourse, this hybrid artistic practice is known as *rasquache*, a nuanced term with a range of meaning. For art historian and critic Tomás Ybarra-

Frausto, its foremost proponent, *rasquachismo* is first and foremost a working-class sensibility.[30] Ybarra-Frausto believes that "*rasquachismo* draws its essence within the world of the tattered, shattered, and broken: *lo remendado*[stitched together]."[31] *Rasquachismo* is an aesthetic choice used by those who are forced to make do without proper tools, without materials, without supplies, etc. That is to say that *rasquachismo* is an underdog sensibility that allows working-class peoples the ability to counter the hegemonic forms of popular culture by creating *lo rasquache*. The crooked design elements in the *Industrial Worker*, as well as other *movimiento* publications, are the perfect example of a *rasquache* working-class Chicana/o graphic design. By making do with absence, these publications participate in a culture of resistance.

Just as the *Industrial Worker* often contained crooked columns of text, *El Malcriado* and *El Grito del Norte* made similar design choices in their layout and production. Initially *El Malcriado* was an eight by ten inch newsprint periodical. In the late 1960s it changed print formats and, like the other two papers, was published as a full-sized tabloid. This new format allowed for inexpensive printing, a large amount of surface area for text and image and once folded was easily distributed through the mail. As is the case with most alternative publications, these Chicana/o and working-class publications were usually distributed free of charge in local stores, at community events and through the mail. Therefore, inexpensive production qualities became an economic necessity.

One aspect of the publication design that was carefully considered was the logo and masthead for both *El Grito del Norte* and

23. *El Grito del Norte*, November 1968.

24. Kevin G. Barnhurst and John Nerone. *The Form of News: A History* (New York: Guilford, 2001), 213.

25. Ibid., 261.

26. J. Abbott Miller and Ellen Lupton, "A Natural History of Typography." In *Looking Closer: Critical Writings on Graphic Design* edited by Michael Beirut, et al., (New York: Allworth, 1994), 22.

27. Even though *mestizaje* translates as "miscegenation," its conventions within Latin American and Latina/o cultural history signify both racial and cultural hybridity. The complexities of the term are absent from its English-language application.

28. While working as the Advertisement Designer and Production Manager at a daily newspaper in Michigan during the late 1990s, I continued to use a cut-and-paste application until the release of the computer program Adobe InDesign.

29. Kalman, Miller, and Jacobs, 28.

30. Tomás Ybarra-Frausto, "Rasquachismo: A Chicano Sensibility." In *Chicano Art: Resistance and Affirmation, 1965–1985*, edited by Richard Griswold del castillo, Teresa McKenna, Yvonne Yarbro-Bejarano (Los Angeles: Wight Art gallery, 1991), 155–162.

31. Ibid., 156.

32. Susan Ferriss, 174.

33. Elizabeth Martinez (2002), 83.

MINER 66

LABOR
PRODUCES
ALL WEALTH

ORGANIZATION EDUCATION EMANCIPATION

ALL WEALTH
MUST GO
TO LABOR

Industrial Worker

AN INJURY TO ONE IS AN INJURY TO ALL

VOLUME 66, NUMBER 12 — W. N. 1281   CHICAGO, ILLINOIS DECEMBER 1969   10 CENTS

This page: *Industrial Worker* masthead, 1969; next page: Emanuel Martínez, Zapata, silkscreen, 1967.

El Malcriado. The initial years of *El Malcriado* featured the publication title printed in a large black san serif font with the phrase "*La Voz del Campesino*" (The Voice of the Farmworker) printed in a much smaller black serif on a solid grey background. As the *movimiento* progressed, by the early 1970s this nondescript masthead became more easily identifiable. The new masthead included the title *EL MALCRIADO* printed black in all caps floating on a grey photographic field of individuals marching in a picket line. Above the title, the text "The official voice of the United Farmworkers" now positioned the publication as an official organ. To the right of the title is situated the UFW eagle, which also identifies that the publication comes from the UFW. Placing the indigenous visual identity of the UFW (many argue that the Farmworkers' eagle was in fact the icon for the entire *movimiento)* on the cover helped to place the union as champion of both Chicana/o and working-class struggles. The added dimensions of the *Malcriado* masthead parallel the continued victories for the UFW in the union struggle. Journalists Susan Ferriss and Ricardo Sandoval write that by 1971

> Chavez and the farmworkers union had won key contracts, against all odds and without a law giving farmworkers the right to organize. Union members' lives were improving dramatically, so much so that a generation of farmworkers was for the first time able to settle down, buy modest homes, and save money.[32]

As the UFW won victories, the *rasquache* aesthetic of *El Malcriado* was abandoned in exchange for a slicker and more conventional look. Yet even with a more technically savvy appearance, *El Malcriado* remained in touch with working-class and *mexicana/o* aesthetic demands. Since modernist design systems were not universally acceptable, the paper's designers drew both from local vernacular traditions as well as hegemonic visual forms. This hybrid aesthetic is part and parcel of a *mestiza/o* design and remained on the pages of *El Malcriado*.

Just as *El Malcriado*'s logo and masthead changed over time, so did the overall formal scheme of *El Grito*'s logotype. Initially, *El Grito del Norte* included an iconic drawing of indigenous Mexican anarchist Emiliano Zapata within its masthead. However, for some reason, by 1971 Zapata had been removed from the logo. The Zapata image was taken from a popular Emanuel Martínez serigraph. This print of Zapata, typically screenprinted on used manila folders, turned up all over northern New Mexico and southern Colorado during the years of the *Alianza* anti-authoritarian resistance. The iconography of Zapata was paramount during the Chicana/o movement because his prophetic call for "*Tierra y Libertad*" was appropriated by Alianzistas as a community call to arms. This exclamation connected New Mexican activities with turn-of-the-century revolutionary struggles in Mexico. Activist-editor Betita Martínez recalls that "Emiliano Zapata, whose portrait provided the logo for *El Grito*'s masthead, had raised the cries that echoed all over northern New Mexico: '*Tierra y Libertad*' and '*Tierra, Pan y Justicia!*' [Land and Liberty; Land, Bread and Justice]."[33]

Even though she highlights Zapata's importance to New Mexican activists, Martínez does not acknowledge the fact that three years into the publication of the paper, his image was removed from the masthead. While the alterations to the logotype of *El Malcriado* speak to the acceptability of the United Farmworkers in mainstream political discourse, the changes to *El Grito del Norte* are more ellusive. Did the removal of Zapata signal the end of the *Alianza* revolutionary struggle? Did this modification signify the end of armed struggle and the move toward structural reformation? These questions, like so many others, remain unanswered. It is interesting to note that shortly after Zapata's removal from the masthead and the creation of a more "de-politicized" logo, many involved in *El Grito* would relocate to Albuquerque and the paper's production ceased.

Conclusion

During the late 1960s and early 1970s, Chicana/o community newspapers were commonplace throughout the US southwest, midwest and pacific northwest. Published in both English and Spanish, in addition to selections in working-class Spanish, English, Caló, Nahuatl, and a mixture thereof, these class-conscious publications challenged the racist manner in which Chicanas/os were being portrayed in the mainstream press. These papers, incorporating both text and image, not only countered the hegemonic vantage point of Anglo-America, but also helped articulate a radical new society in the process. It is this new society in the shell of the old, as the IWW refers to it, that makes these publications so significant.

The majority of those involved in these Chicana/o publications not only supported the Black Power and American Indian Movements in the US, they also defended Third World liberation and working-class struggles throughout the globe. Regrettably, beginning in the 1980s and expanding during the 1990s, the revolutionary and activist position of many of these papers was supplanted by the institutionalization of a mainstream Latina/o (usually referred to as Hispanic) media operating from Miami.

Auspiciously, however, the anti-capitalist perspective of many of these publications perseveres at the grassroots level and can be seen cropping up in countless current radical publications. With the rise of a youthful cohort of anti-capitalists during the late-1990s, and an explosion of new independent media, these older radical newspapers serve as a model to which we may turn. These papers are not noteworthy in so much as they formulate a unilateral and doctrinaire direction for the future, but because they reveal the complexities of the past. Most factions of the Chicana/o movement and the publications they produced did not claim a paradigmatic solution to the inequities of late-capitalist society. By properly attending to the visual and intellectual tensions of *El Grito del Norte*, *El Malcriado,* and the *Industrial Worker* we may produce, in their wake, a more complex and nuanced future.

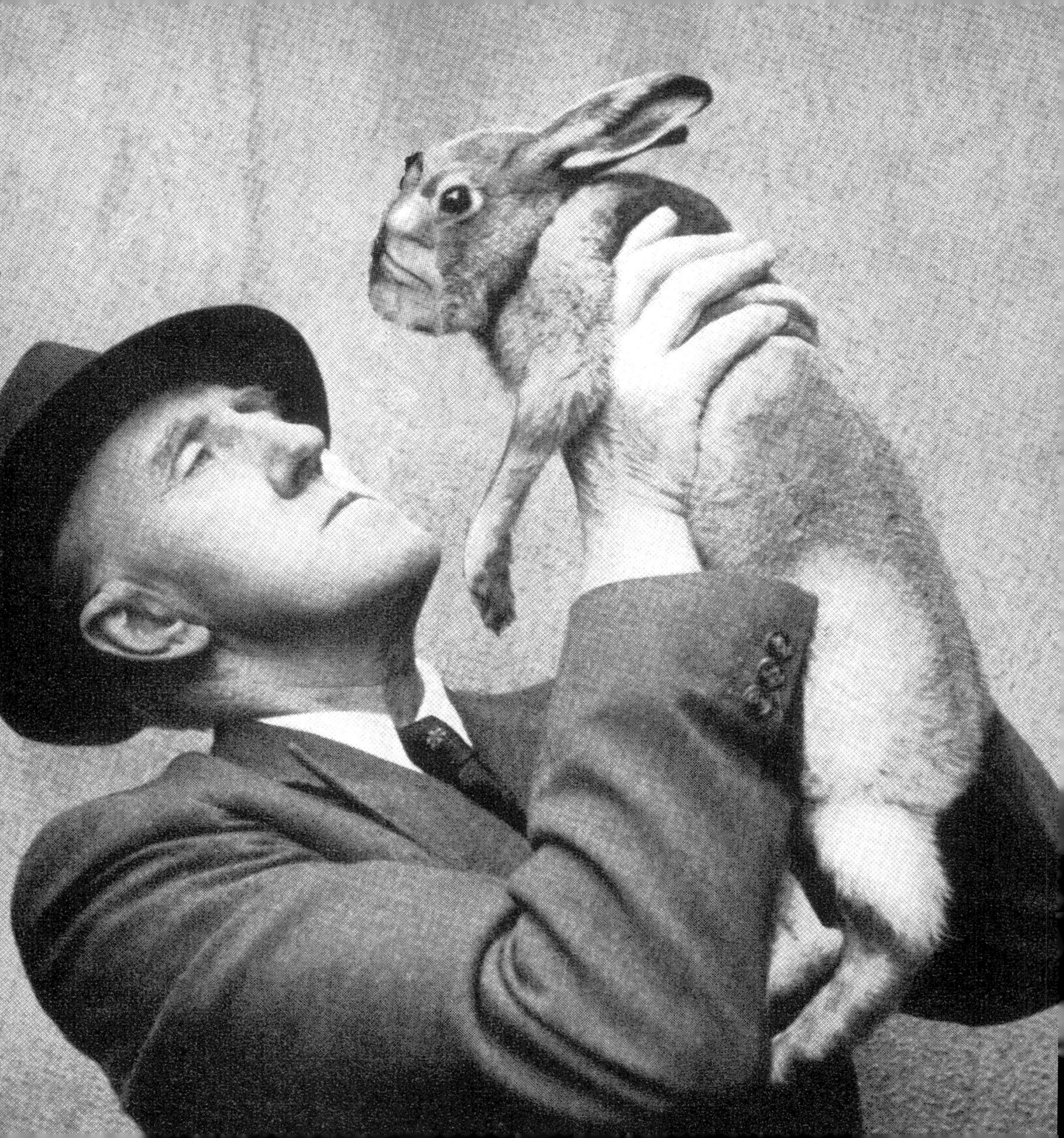

GEE VAUCHER: CRASS ART
ERIK REULAND

I encountered a strange phenomenon when I first started telling my punk rock friends I was doing an interview with Gee Vaucher. The reaction of these people, well-versed in punk music and anarchist ideology, was most often one of puzzlement. "Who?," they would ask. "Oh, you know, she did the artwork for Crass," I'd reply, and immediately their eyes would light up. They'd had her foldout poster proclaiming "YOUR COUNTRY NEEDS YOU," with its graphic of a soldier's severed hand impaled on a strand of barbed wire, tacked to their bedroom wall. They'd spent hours puzzling over her amazingly complex photorealistic collage-like paintings that adorned the covers and booklets of Crass records. They'd worn her work as t-shirts and borrowed it to illustrate zines and flyers.

Despite her association with one of anarchist punk's most enduringly popular bands, Gee's work stretches both long before and long after that band's existence. She has always been prolific as well as diverse in medium. In the mid-1970s, she and her long time collaborator Penny Rimbaud (later Crass' drummer/lyricist) performed in the experimental performance art group Exit. From 1977 to 1981, she self-published three issues of *International Anthem: A Nihilist Newspaper for the Living*, featuring her unique collage work and Penny Rimbaud's poetic typewriter texts. Throughout the late 1970s and early 1980s, she designed innumerable record covers and posters for Crass and other bands on their label, Crass Records, as well as working on films that were projected during Crass' live performances.

Since then, she has published two collections of her work, *Crass Art And Other Pre-Postmodern Monsters* (AK Press, 1999) and a recent book of collages entitled *Animal Rites-A Pictorial Study of Relationships* (Exitstencil Press, 2004), which features collages juxtaposing human faces with animal bodies. She has also continued to exhibit in various group and solo shows throughout the world.

Gee continues to live at Dial House, a collectively run "open house" she and Rimbaud helped found in 1967. Self-described as a "Centre for Dynamic Cultural Change," the house hosts permaculture workshops, Camp Idle, traveling artists, and was closely associated with the Free Festival movement of the 1960s and 1970s.

What formal arts education/training have you had, if any? What did you learn from this?

I studied painting and graphics in the early sixties at the South East Essex School of Art, in East London. It was a very radical time for the arts; in painting, the cross-over between abstract expressionism and pop art, in music, the arrival of the Beatles and modern jazz, in the written world there were the works of the British Angry Young Men, the American Beats, and the French Existentialists, and there was also the growth of the women's movement. Everything seemed to be up for questioning, up for grabs. The Second World War had left its deep scars on our parents. As students we were looking for a new way of life and the art schools in particular became centers for the new consciousness that later, in the seventies, became known as "youth culture."

What I got from my five years at art school was space, time, and free equipment to experiment with. I have never really thought that anyone can learn to be an artist by being at art school because being an artist is a deep, internal drive and commitment that can never be taught, only experienced; inspiration can come from anywhere. If you enroll at an art school with the idea that you'll somehow miraculously become an artist, you may as well give up then and there: it's not that easy.

When you were starting out there was an immense amount of experimentation going on in the art world, from pop art to happenings to neorealism. How do you feel about these movements and your relation to them?

I'm not really sure that I have ever particularly interacted with current art movements. Often what I was doing would seem to parallel them, but that certainly wasn't intentional. I particularly liked the work of David Hockney when I was at art school.

In fact, there was a time when I couldn't actually work because he seemed to paint exactly what I was attempting to do, not only in how it was observed but how it was expressed. As he seemed to be saying it better than I could at the time, I gave up because I found it all a bit uncanny and mildly depressing. On reflection, the experience drove me in another direction which I have been following ever since.

I've never really bothered to keep in touch with what is going on in the 'art world,' particularly the commercial one. That's not to say that I'm uninformed, somehow information filters through, but I've always worked pretty much in isolation. Of course there are movements that I have been drawn to. When I was an art student I loved the Mannerists; but there were lots of other schools of art which caught my eye and imagination, from the Mannerists to the Dadaists. Everything can offer some kind of inspiration at different times and in different moods. I pick up on ideas when they reflect my current thinking if I feel they might offer some mileage. Sometimes I look at the work of others, regardless of whether I consider it good or bad art, simply to get a kick-start when I need it.

Can you talk about Exit and what it was you did with them? What was a typical Exit performance like?

Exit was a project that I worked on with Penny Rimbaud and a couple of other art school friends. Initially we were what could loosely be described as an avant-garde band inspired by American free jazz and modern European classical music, but we pretty soon enlarged to include theater, images, film—in fact anything that might add dimension to what we were trying to say, which was to find a truly free form of expression. We were always looking for ways to push artistic boundaries.

There was no such thing as a typical Exit performance—what was typical was its difference every time. When we started, I played a stripped-down upright piano, not unlike a harp, which gave a sound something like John Cage's prepared pianos, but amplified. Rather than playing it upright I would lay it flat, sitting in the middle to play. Having pickups attached to the strings made it a very powerful instrument. As the band grew we would go out to perform with anything up to twenty performers, offering incredibly complex and confrontational shows, so much so that most of the audience would leave. Eventually, however, we narrowed down the project until generally speaking it was just Penny and myself performing pieces which had obvious parallels with Happenings. By then we had met various members of the New York Fluxus Movement, notably the film-maker Anthony McCall with whom we collaborated over the years. Many of the performance techniques developed with Exit later became incorporated in Crass, which is one reason why Crass sounded like no other punk band.

How and when did you start publishing *International Anthem*? How was it received?

I had always wanted to produce a newspaper that could be a vehicle for my own work and for Penny's writing, plus work by other friends who I felt had something to say, but lack of money had always prevented me from being able to do so.

In the mid-70s I went to New York City and ended up living there for a couple of years. I was very fortunate from the start as I was recognized as a political illustrator and was always given interesting commissions. In fact the first came from the *New York Times*. I had all the work I could handle, and the great result was that I managed to earn enough money to finance the first issue of *International Anthem, A Nihilist Newspaper for the Living*.

People seemed to like it, and I sold quite a few copies through Printed Matter, who distributed and encouraged small art-publishers and who are still going strong in NYC. But it was hard to find outlets, I used to carry a bundle around with me all the time, trying to sell them to bookshops that I liked the look of, or just giving them away, but that was even harder. Many people refused to take one, or would just flick through it and give it back. The usual thing. Trying to get large distributors to take it on was a dead loss—they were always saying that they couldn't carry it because it wasn't easy to categorize, which seemed pretty dumb given that that was one of its major strengths. It seems strange that old copies of the paper have now become fairly valuable artefacts advertised on the Internet. Although I eventually had to give up on the project because of the workload created by Crass, I actually managed to publish three editions. In fact I had nearly finished two more. One was in response to the Falklands War, the other was on the history of Ireland, which when it got to be twice the size of the *Sunday New York Times*, I gave up.

How did your relationship with Crass evolve? What does it mean to be a non-musical member of the group? How did your role differ from others?

Since the early 1970s, Dial House has operated as a creative center offering open space to a huge variety of creative artists, writers, film-makers, etc. Crass was a natural outcome of that situation: two people getting together to express what they felt needed saying—in this case Steve Ignorant and Penny, and then being joined by others who liked what was going on. In this respect, the creation of Crass has many parallels with Exit.

Penny and [I] lived at Dial House from the start, but Crass started up toward the end of the two years that I was living in New York. Obviously we kept in constant contact, and although in different mediums, we were saying the same kind of things. Eventually, with art editors in New York asking me to change an illustration because its content was too strong, it seemed timely and obvious to move back to Dial House and work together again more closely.

From the very start, Crass utilized a whole range of artistic expressions. They were never interested in simply being another rock 'n' roll outfit. Again, the parallels with Exit are obvious. Penny and myself had a broad experience in avant-garde expression and it was inevitable that Crass would follow that line.

Being a non-playing member of the band was never a problem for me. We all had our jobs to do and mine was different only in that I didn't have to spend hours stuck in a very stuffy, small rehearsal room, and they didn't have to spend hours alone painting in a studio. In the truest sense of the word, we shared the overall experience, and there was no separation.

Did the graphics you made for Crass evolve out of group discussion or ideas? Were they subject to group critique?

Although we would always discuss the overall themes of albums, it was always left to me as to how I should interpret them. Crass operated a veto system; if someone really strongly didn't like something it got binned without question. Although as far as I can remember that only happened twice, with a couple of songs.

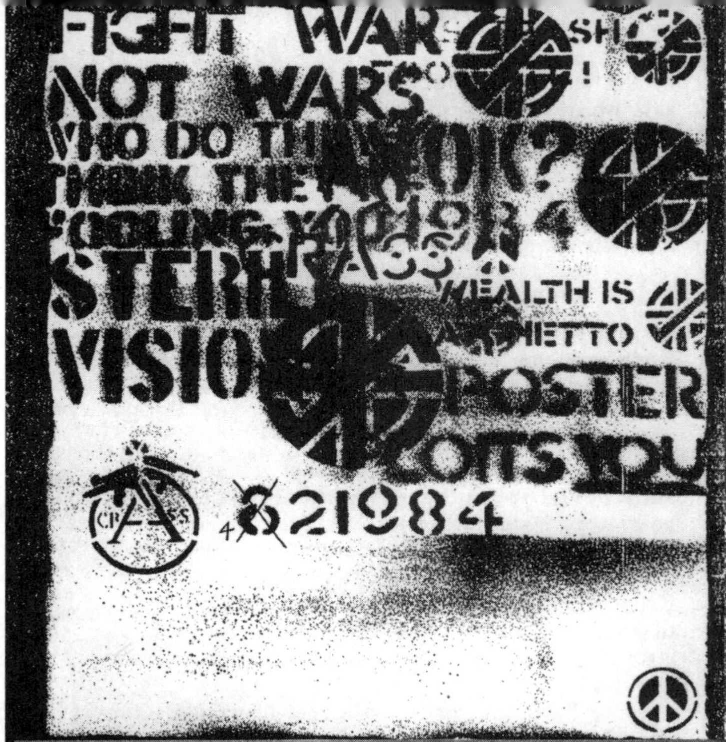
FIGHT WAR
NOT WARS
WEALTH IS
POSTER
821984

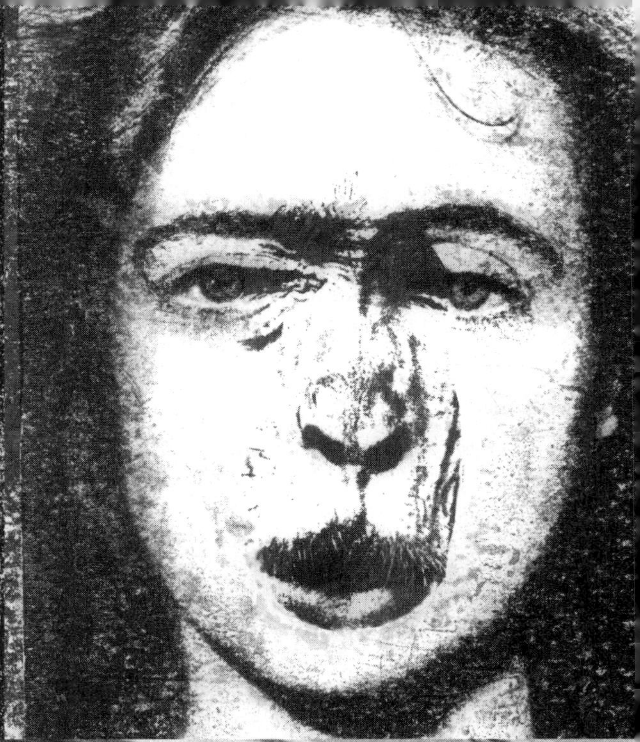

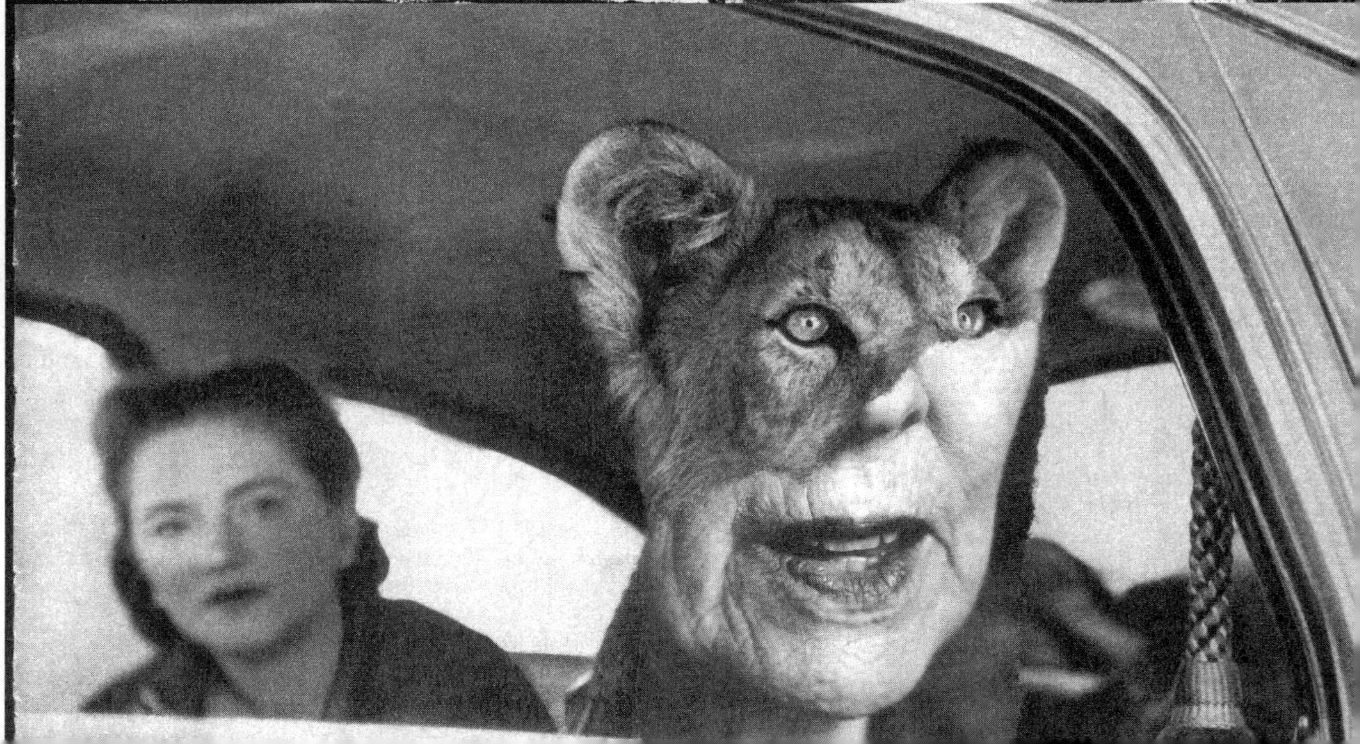

Clockwise, from top left: stencils from the back cover of Crass, *The Feeding of the 5000*, 1978; Gee Vaucher, *Self Portrait*, transfer print, from *Animal Rites*, 2004; Gee Vaucher, *Untitled*, collage from *Animal Rites*, 2004.

Where did Crass' stencil style come from? Starting on the first record, there are stenciled letters on the cover, and your drawings of people holding stenciled banners. Were you involved in Crass' stenciling on the street? Were other bands stenciling at the time? Were activists?

We happened to have some old metal stencil kits of various type size around and it seemed the most obvious and useful thing to use for what we wanted to do. I loved it anyway and the fact that you could spray large type designs without having to draw it out by hand was a real bonus. You have to remember that in the 1970s there were no photocopy machines or computers around, there was only the typewriter and designer's Letraset which was very expensive. Making stencils were free and easy.

We would also make stencils to spray on offensive advertising on the streets and especially on the London underground. Every month, we would decide who was going to spray what underground line and head out in pairs to graffiti on all the sexist and violent advertising with a very neatly placed message. The stencil sprays always looked very neat and acceptable even if what they were saying didn't. Again it was free and easy and did a great job. I don't remember other bands or activists using stencil lettering in the beginning, but it soon became popular, especially for banners at demonstrations.

How has your work changed since Crass, in terms of subject matter and style? When Crass ended, did you have to find new outlets for your work? What were they?

When Crass finished, it gave me a lot more freedom to pursue many of the ideas I had never had time to follow up before. Within three years of Crass ending though, I found myself caring for my mother for the next two years. I couldn't actually work in the studio, as looking after my mum took priority over everything else. I felt confident that when I could finally get back into the painting, rather than feeling I had lost anything during that time, that the experience of caring for her would have been an enriching one for both of us, and it was.

As for new outlets for my work, it was the same as before Crass. I would be asked to illustrate a book or CD cover and it would be the way I would earn a bit of money. This would give me enough to pursue my own more intimate work and from that would come exhibitions and books or anything else that might grab me and make me work

Over the years, my work has superficially changed, it has become freer in expression and isn't so overtly political, but of course the sentiments are fundamentally the same, caring about people and the world that I live in. When I look at the body of my work, I am aware that I have always been concerned with the psychology of events and the interactions of people within them. In that respect, nothing has changed over all these years.

It is a long journey, and luckily I still haven't arrived at its destination, and I hope I never will. Every new piece of work is unique in its demands. I hope that I will never end up thinking that I know what I am doing, because if I got into that position I reckon there wouldn't be much point in doing anything at all. Who wants to keep experiencing the thing that you think you already know?

It seems that you like to publish your work in print editions (books, newspapers, record covers) and distribute it *en masse*. Do you exhibit it in other forms and spaces? What kind of space do you prefer? Why?

I do like to work on my own books, etc., I love printed matter. As for distributing them *en masse*, that's a bit grand, but I have gotten quite a few going out over the years. I also like working on canvas, I never know what size I'm going to work with until I start, the most recent paintings are 8'x6'. I've also been messing around with sculptures, which I really like. I'm also going to have a go at casting in stone sometime soon. Really, I like trying everything and mixing it about, but I always come back to paper.

I'm often asked to exhibit and really like to show in public galleries rather than at private ones. I like the walk through nature of public buildings and the amazing range of people that visit them. Very often they are in the building for other reasons and it is only by default that they see the show and are exposed to something different. It certainly enlarges the range of public viewers and it is not just visited by friends.

REULAND 74

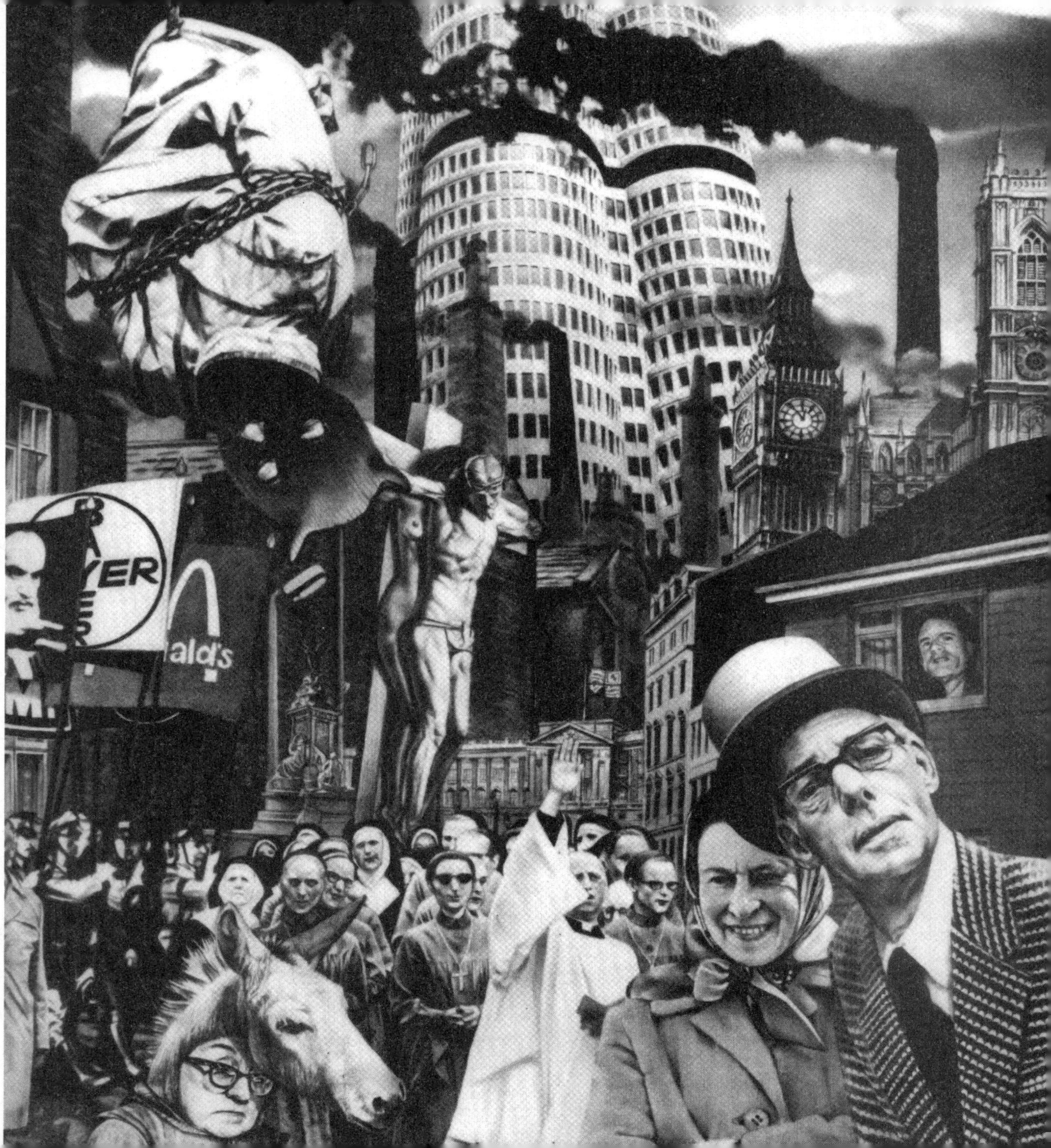

Having said that, I've shown in 96 Gillespie in London several times, and although it is a private gallery, it has the feel of a public space, probably due to the fact that is opposite the old Arsenal football ground and on home-weekends you'd have several thousands fans peering into the show. I've also had a good experience showing at Gavin Brown's in New York. I'm liking the mixing of art worlds at the moment.

Since the late 1960s, you've lived in a more or less collective/communal situation. Why are you still living that way?

Apart from my two years in New York City, I have lived all my adult life at Dial House which, being an "open house," has been and continues to be an extraordinarily broadening experience. It hasn't always been easy, but I've certainly learned a lot about how to be with myself and other people. It's back to the psychological, philosophical, and moral dilemmas that we are all faced with, but at Dial House it has always been within a very intense context. How do we live together respecting differences yet remaining ourselves? How do we take responsibility for our own actions if they conflict with another's? How can we move away from what most people seem to see as the natural human behaviour of self-interest, past and future? Dial House has been a fantastic experiment in human relationships, one that I continue to contribute to and learn through.

Can you talk about your recent collage series *Animal Rites*? What are the thoughts and intentions behind these images?

Animal Rites is a commentary on the relationship between humans and animals, about how we imbue animals with human characteristics and thereby deny them their own. Some of the pieces in the book are very dark and go beyond mere comment and become expressions of their own. I think, as usual, the work asks more questions than it gives answers, but that is the way I think it should be.

What are you working on right now?

Recently I've been working on large canvases, painting portraits of children who have seen too much and who have suffered the effects of brutality from domestic violence to war: the destruction of innocence. They are on the one hand very beautiful, but on the other very disturbing. Despite the subject matter, I want them to be positive, to show hope, to show that despite the horrors of history, especially our own, we can and do survive.

I am also working on a couple of new books, one for children, which I hope to finish soon. As usual I have so many projects going on that sometimes I'm not sure which one is which, but I guess that's what it's all about; looking for the connection, a wholeness.

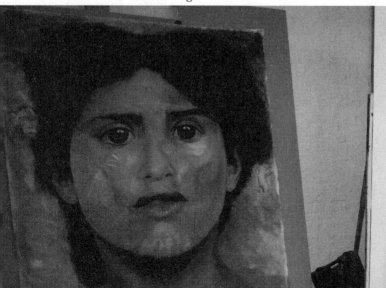
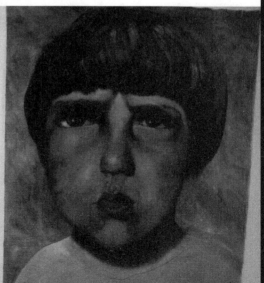

This page: Gee Vaucher, paintings in process in the studio. Photo: Gee Vaucher; previous page: Gee Vaucher, poster (detail) released with Crass, *Christ: The Album*, 1982.

DisneyWar

SHADOWS IN THE STREETS: THE STENCIL ART OF THE NEW ARGENTINA

ERICK LYLE

When I arrived in Buenos Aires, all the dailies featured front-page photos of Venezuelan President Hugo Chávez greeting Argentine President Nestor Kirchner that weekend in Caracas. This was accompanied by a new report that said Argentina had the fastest growing economy in Latin America. But there wasn't any news in the paper that had not already been spray painted on the capital's walls.

Graffiti demanding *"Bush Fuera Argentina"* (Bush get out of Argentina) was sprayed everywhere downtown. Statues of Argentine generals on their horses were tattooed with slogans like, *"Bush=imperialismo"* and terse messages like *"Chorros"* and *"Ladrones"* raced across the facades of banks around the Plaza de Mayo, like rioting protesters.

Eye-catching spray-painted stencil art also covered the city's walls—random graphics, layered into spontaneous murals by unknown artists. Scenes from famous movies, pictures of rock stars, political slogans, marijuana leaves, old ad campaigns, flying birds, dancing women, politicians' faces, running crowds, and comic strips—all fluttered ghostly and cinematic across the walls of the city, like scraps of newsprint blown down the street by the wind off the river at night.

"I think they leave it up for the tourists. Don't you?" Nicolas, a stencil artist from the group Buenos Aires (BsAs) Stencil would say to me, months later, with a wink and more than a hint of challenge in his grin. "All the Americans want to come here to see 'The Revolution.'"

It had been two full weeks since George W. Bush's humiliation at the hands of the crafty Hugo Chávez and the thousands of protesters he'd rallied against Bush at the Summit of the Americas in Argentina, but the graffiti remained. There was even spray paint on the grill pattern of the towering metal riot barricades that the Federal Police had used to seal off one end of the plaza from the Casa Rosada, the grand, sunset-pink palace that is the seat of the executive branch of the Argentine government.

I would learn later, though, that the riot barricades had not been installed for Bush's visit. They had been put there during the days of the economic crisis in December 2001, when street protests forced five governments from office in two weeks. Now, the economy was surging again and Argentina was even—with Chavez' help—about to pay off its debt to the IMF. But, the riot barricades had been there ever since. They were part of the look of the new Argentina.

Was there really a "revolution" to be seen in the spray paint on Argentina's walls? If so, what kind of revolution was it? What did the graffiti, angry political slogans, and lyrical stencil images, have to say about where Argentina was heading now after four years of political and economic crisis? I sought out Buenos Aires' stencil artists to find out.

Streets to Museum

Gonzalo of BsAs Stencil told me, "During the crisis, I remember walking home from work one day, and passing a crowd of people with masks on burning a McDonald's."

When I met Gonzalo, he had just finished painting a similar image from the crisis of 2001—a masked *piquetero*, blockading a street with a burning tire.

But the image is not on the street. It is on the wall of the Centro Cultural Borges, just off Calle Florida, Buenos Aires' main upscale shopping street. Upstairs in the museum, there are exhibits by Dali and Chagall. Here in the lobby, the street artists BsAs Stencil are showing their new stencil art in a rare indoor show, fittingly called *Adentro* (Inside).

The four years it has taken for the protests in the streets to become art in the museum have been an intensely difficult period of nonstop change for *Argentinos*. In December 2001, years of severe recession and government-imposed austerity measures that slashed health care and education spending and cut pensions and unemployment benefits, finally came to a head when middle class *Argentinos*, lacking any faith in the economy or its currency, withdrew $135 billion from their bank accounts. In response, the government introduced new restrictions limiting the amount of money *Argentinos* could withdraw. But, within weeks, Argentina defaulted on its loans to the IMF. With the economy in freefall, a general strike shut the country down.

Today, the events that began "the crisis" on December 19th are remembered simply as "19/12," a date that changed everything in Argentina, like "9/11" in the USA. Widespread looting of shops and supermarkets began across the nation, and President Fernando De La Rua, echoing the repression of the military dictatorship that "disappeared" an estimated 30,000 people between 1976 and 1983, declared a state of emergency, suspending all constitutional rights and limiting assemblies of more than three people. That night, one million people in Buenos Aires alone took to the streets, banging pots and pans, and defying the state of emergency.

Anonymous, *Ahora o Nunca*, 2001. Photo: Ryan Hollon.

The finance minister resigned, and over the next 24-hours, twenty-two protesters would be killed across the country in violent street protest. De La Rua resigned, fleeing the Casa Rosada by helicopter, and within two weeks, four more governments were installed and then fell.

What followed were two years of grinding poverty and hardship across Argentina.

"The quality of life fell until it was as low as it could go," remembers Nico of the stencil group, Vomito Attack. "During the first months, the city was in complete chaos."

"I remember coming home from work and seeing Corrientes Street all on fire. People were running everywhere, carrying shoes, carrying boxes from stores," says Nicolas, of BsAs Stencil.

In a country that once had been the IMF's "success story" in Latin America, there were suddenly homeless people everywhere and people in the streets, scavenging in the trash for bottles, cardboard, or paper to recycle.

"Not one of my friends had any work," remembers Nico. "And products started to change: the chocolate was three times smaller and three times more expensive and the paper it was wrapped in was three times worse quality. Cars quit using gas and started using ethanol, which is much cheaper. Paper became very, very expensive."

It was also a time of unprecedented grassroots political protest. The *cacerolazo* movement —named from *cacerola*, Spanish for cooking pot —birthed with the pot and pan banging of 19/12, continued to signify the spirit of the times, as enormous crowds gathered regularly to hold festive and angry protests in front of the banks and government buildings—now protected by riot shutters—at Plaza de Mayo.

"*Que se vayan todos*" (They all must go) was the rallying cry of the *asambleas populares*, a type of direct democracy neighborhood meeting that began to appear throughout the city. The crisis was so far-reaching and the breakdown of the social order so complete that people from all walks of life began to meet in their own neighborhoods to discuss ways to help provide food or health care for each other and to start up alternative media to print the truth about the popular uprising in Argentina. Demanding the end of *all* political parties, the assemblies were

regular meetings of common people in public parks or on street corners, discussing neighborhood autonomy and putting it into practice.

Indeed, what was so remarkable about the protest movements in Argentina at that time was that upper and middle class people were active participants in street protest and direct democracy. The *ahorristas*, or savers, were a movement of more or less affluent people who had lost their life's savings to the government restrictions on money withdrawal from banks. Weekly protests of these upper class folks were black bloc protest-reels of smashed windows and spray-painted bank facades—only carried out in broad daylight without masks by men with suits and briefcases or women in heels.

It was out of this new spirit of participation that the art movement of stenciling in the streets was born. "It was in the air," says Gonzalo today. "You'd see all the people in the streets and think, 'I have to do something.'"

Some images tried to make clear political points, others told jokes. Some were playful or colorful—images that captured the frenetic motion of the crowded streets. And some simply sucked you into their wonder—inscrutable, dreamlike, with a mystery life all their own, like bits of a mass subconscious, cut up and put back together.

"The stencils weren't driving the protest in any way or really even documenting it, but the protests and the assemblies and the stencils were all tied together in some way," says Nico. "The first stencil I saw summed everything up: it was a plate of food with a knife and fork and the caption 'Now or Never.'"

BsAs Stencil was one of the first groups in Buenos Aires to start painting stencils in the streets.

"I lived downtown and everything was happening all around me," says Nicolas. "The city was in the mood. It was hot and no one had any money."

The stencil was an ideal art form for a penniless grassroots democratic movement. Easily cut out of plastic—most stencilers in Buenos Aires use old x-rays scavenged from hospital trash—each image requires only a fine mist of spray paint.

"Every day, the buildings around the plaza would be attacked again and again with paint and the paint would be whitewashed a few days later, until there was no money in the budget anymore for white paint," remembers Nico. "Then the buildings stayed covered in graffiti for months."

They are still painted today. The flourishing street art has, indeed, become a tourist attraction. *Time Out Buenos Aires*, a guide book for tourists sold at every newsstand, has an article on stencil art and recommends the purchase of *Hasta La Victoria, Stencil!*, a glossy art book from late 2004 that compiles photos of stencils in the streets of the capital over the years of the crisis. The book's title is a play on Che Guevara's famous phrase from the Cuban Revolution, "Ever onward to victory," and the book clearly intends to link the stencil look with Latin American revolution. But with a hefty cover price of nearly $17 US and essays in English as well as Spanish, the book is clearly more directed toward tourists than Argentines.

Ironically, as stencil art from the streets gains fame and is increasingly shown indoors in museums, the era of mass participation in Argentine political life that the stencil represents has almost disappeared. There are still many worker-occupied and operated businesses across the country—including the tourist hotel, Hotel Baumann

in the heart of Buenos Aires on Calle Callao—but the neighborhood assemblies—once estimated as 200 separate groups meeting regularly throughout the city—have mostly ceased to exist except in name only.

One factor is that, after several years of having to take care of each aspect of their own survival, people in Argentina are just plain exhausted. But, ironically, it is most likely the government's turn to the left—along with the recovering economy—that has led to the popular assembly movement's demise.

In May 2003, Nestor Kirchner, a former governor of the province of Santa Cruz, was elected president of Argentina, defeating former President Carlos Menem, who had led the country during the spendthrift, post-dictatorship years when it amassed the enormous debt that had led to its economic collapse.

Kirchner won with only a tiny fraction of the population's support—22% of the vote in a presidential election with the lowest turnout in Argentine history—but soon became popular with a series of bold moves in the areas of the economy and human rights. Kirchner used Argentina's loan defaults as a bargaining chip, refusing to repay any of Argentina's debt until the IMF and private creditors restructured the debts to more favorable terms. Meanwhile, Kirchner made prosecution of those involved in the "Dirty War" of 1976–83 a priority. His government repealed the amnesty law that had protected former military officials who had participated in the torture and disappearances of countless thousands of Argentines, and for the first time in a generation, the country took serious steps toward coming to grips with its recent history.

Kirchner's critics point out that he is almost as in love with executive branch power as Bush, making law by presidential decree instead of sending laws to be debated in congress far more than any of his predecessors since the return of democracy. But, when I arrived in Buenos Aires, Kirchner was on a serious roll. A month before, his FPV party (Front for Victory) had swept midterm parliamentary elections across the country and many Kirchner friends and allies—even his own wife, Cristina—were elected to Senate positions. Weeks later, as host of the Summit of the Americas, Kirchner was given the stage—with the riot-filled streets as backdrop—to take his position alongside Hugo Chavez and Brazil's Lula De Silva as the strongest voices against the Free Trade Area of the Americas (FTAA) agreement while making Bush look pathetically weak and unpopular in Latin America.

On the weekend of my arrival, Kirchner was in Caracas, reveling in the success of the anti-US riots with Chavez. On the front page of all the dailies, Chavez was shown greeting Kirchner, curiously, while wearing a huge, Mexican sombrero. In the week before, Chavez had called Mexican president Vicente Fox "The puppy of the empire" for his acceptance of the FTAA agreement. Fox and officials from the USA had demanded an apology, but, instead, when Chavez met Kirchner, he wore a Mexican hat and sang him a *ranchera*, a traditional Mexican folk song. Chavez was fearless and witty and, I thought, watching his daily antics in the paper must be something of what it was like to watch the young Mohammed Ali in action. Now, Chavez was lending some of his aura of indestructibility—and a great deal of his nation's oil cash—to Kirchner. The two leaders that weekend spoke of a joint oil pipeline to be built by Venezuela, Brazil, and Argentina and Chavez promised to buy millions of dollars of Argentine debt bonds.

A month later, Argentina would, like Brazil, shock the world by paying back its IMF debt in full in a single payment with the help it received from Chavez. There were protests in Buenos Aires from the leftover fragments of the popular assembly movement who said that the government had no business paying anything to the IMF while there were still so many unemployed and homeless in Argentina. But the protests were drowned out by the cheers of the majority who hailed Kirchner's move as a step toward national—and South American—independence from the IMF, and, by extension, the USA. The "Turn to The Left" may have started with popular assemblies in the streets, but it was now symbolized by the handshake of Chavez and Kirchner. Four years after the crisis and the birth of the stencil art in the streets, it is telling that, though the overall look is the same, the spray paint on the walls of the capital, today, is more against the USA than against the Argentine government.

Santiago Run-In

The first stencil artist I met in Argentina is possibly the least known among other stencilers, but, in many ways, the most representative of the times in Argentina. Santiago Spirito, sometimes one half of the group Vomito Attack, was trained as an architect. But with Argentina's unemployment around 12%, he is lucky to be working long hours as a waiter in a sushi restaurant near Newberry Airport. Like many young adults in Argentina, Santiago, 31, has been forced to move back in with a parent.

Santiago came into my life quite accidentally. When my travel partner, Ivy, and I arrived in Buenos Aires, we spent days, walking around town, marveling at the stencil art on the walls and wondering who the artists were. Then, late one night, Santiago walked by Ivy in the street. She heard the tell-tale clink! of a spray can in his bag and started a conversation. It turned out he was an artist whose work we had seen before, and they agreed to go out stenciling together some time.

They did go out and stencil in San Telmo one time, but it still wasn't easy to meet up with Santiago. Besides attempted meetings foiled by the common Argentine problem of malfunctioning cell phones, it turned out that Santiago worked constantly and didn't get out of work most nights until after 3:00 AM.

Though Santiago was hard to find in person, I came to enjoy finding his work in the streets. One quiet Sunday afternoon, Ivy and I turned a corner of a deserted street in Recoleta to find a street scene Santiago had painted along an underpass. There were lifelike DJs and boom-boxes spray-painted on the walls in red, yellow, green, and black. The ghost-like images dancing in and out of each other as if we'd stumbled upon a live dance party in the street.

There was his stencil of the serious man in a suit, a sort of waiter, playing a big concertina, huge Pegasus wings coming out of his back. And there were the dancing people and the cranes. Santiago had painted in San Telmo a series of two-color stencils of people and cranes together so that the people appeared to be both dancing and being lifted higher and higher by the cranes. His art had a dream-like quality and he frequently would use the same image several times to give the appearance of movement. Unlike other stencilers I talked to later, who claimed they gave little thought to where they put up their images, Santiago was more likely to pick only one spot to paint a group of images and then paint the images in a series to create a larger painting out of them.

Finally, one night, past 4:00 AM, Ivy and I took a cab to the apartment Santiago lives in with his mother in the Palermo neighborhood. Santiago had a sort-of shaggy, young John Lennon haircut and drooping, exhausted eyes. He had just come from work and had to get up at 8:00 AM to pick up his two kids from his former marriage—aged nine and one and a half—for a rare chance to visit.

Santiago brought us into the living room, which had more or less been turned into a stencil-cutting workshop. Many of his larger stencils—some as tall as three- or four-feet—lay in piles around the room. He lit a joint and lay back on the carpet, staring at the ceiling and talking, while Ivy cut a stencil.

Santiago, like the other stencilers I would later talk to, said that before the crisis there was no street art in Argentina. Curiously, other Latin American nations like Brazil and Mexico have had thriving graffiti and street art scenes for years. But in highly developed Argentina, stencils were only used before 2001 by political parties to paint slogans or sometimes by rock bands to advertise themselves. When he saw the new expression in the streets, he started making stencils with Nico, the other half of Vomito Attack, in the summer of 2003.

"Making stencils is my way to express my... interior things," he said, choosing his English words carefully. "In the university, I made architecture but I didn't make art."

Nico and Santiago both worked all the time at the sushi restaurant and would go out to stencil after they got off work at

3:00 AM. They signed their work, Vomito Attack, "because you vomit all you want to say and then when you vomit it all out, you're better."

I asked him what his mother thought of his stenciling, or at least the mess. "Oh, it is so horrible living here!" he said. "My mother doesn't understand any of this. She's very right wing. She

thinks the military dictatorship was good for this country!"

As it turned out, no one in Santiago's life understood his art. His ex-wife thought his growing obsession with stenciling was crazy and none of his friends from architecture school could make any sense of it, either. "Most of my friends my age are married now, with kids. They don't know anything about my secret life, stenciling in the streets all night!"

I got a sudden picture of poor, exhausted Santiago—overworked and harassed by his nagging mom, spending every waking hour either at work or trying to see his kids—enduring all just for the rare chance to make some art in the streets. It occurred to me that what really broke through when the crisis caused so many old institutions to collapse was the dream life of Argentina. The economic crisis that had crushed so many hopes had, ironically, provided new opportunities for people like Santiago to reinvent themselves or to participate in ways they'd never imagined.

I asked him if he thought the crisis had, in some ways, been a lucky break for him. He said that it had, indeed, been "an opportunity." Out of it, he had discovered stenciling. Now there was a picture of Santiago in *Hasta La Victoria, Stencil!* and some of his art had made it into the book. Even better, Nico had been asked to do a big stencil art show at the Argentine National Library in Recoleta this coming March, and Santiago was to work with him on the project.

"If I have the possibility of continuing with stencils all my life, I would," he said.

Riding home across the city at 6:00 AM, it occurred to me that March would be the 30th anniversary of the coup that brought the military dictatorship to power. Between 1976 and 1983, hidden torture centers were set up throughout the capital on ordinary streets like the ones we were driving through right now. I thought of a generation of curiously blank, graffiti-free walls and shuddered.

Buenos Aires Stencil

I met the members of BsAs Stencil—Gonzalo, Nicolas, and Deborah—at Nicolas' apartment, downtown, on Calle Lavalle, a block from Buenos Aires' famed arena, Luna Park. When I arrived, the atmosphere was a party. There were wine and beer bottles out and a couple of extra friends around "to translate, just in case."

Most of the images that have made the stenciling movement in Buenos Aires known throughout the world have been made by BsAs Stencil. Many of the older stencil groups around the capital would tell me that they were inspired to start stenciling by seeing BsAs Stencil's work in the streets. They have participated in art shows as far away as Mexico City and, when I met them, had just exhibited a rare solo show in the Centro Cultural Borges.

The group was riding high at the moment, used to being interviewed, and they enjoyed telling stories and laughing at themselves. They seemed cocky—not necessarily pompous or arrogant, but like they knew they made good art and they were having a good time doing it.

"First of all, we are not a collective!" yelled Gonzalo, holding up his beer. "We have dictators! We have slaves!"

He started to tell me about the time Nicolas had just finished painting a huge white wall and the police came. The cops were so angry because he was painting on the back of the police station! He had to buff it all out, of course.

Then there was the time the cops showed up in Palermo while they were painting. Nicolas told them casually, "We have arrived to work. We are the decorators."

The oldest of the group at 35, Gonzalo has unruly long hair and a sort-of handle bar mustache, and he's a generous host. Before I made my way fully around the room, giving everyone present the traditional Argentine greeting of a cheek kiss, Gonzalo had already tried to give me a beer, a bottle of wine, a BsAs Stencil T-Shirt, and had offered to make me coffee. When I finally sat, it felt more like I was the guest of honor than the person there to interview them.

Nicolas is 30, the only one in the group with an art school background. The night before, he and I had talked in Spanish for a half an hour, while waiting to see if Gonzalo and Deborah would arrive. That's when he'd told me that stencils were only left up to attract tourists. Like many things Nicolas would say, I wasn't sure if he believed it himself, though it did make sense in a roundabout way. I ended up enjoying his artful way of delivering provocative questions with a careless shrug and an inscrutable smile.

"So you live in San Telmo," he had said, appraising me. "That is a tourist area, no? How can you know the *real* Buenos Aires if you don't see La Boca or Barracas?"

I started to bristle and tell him, angrily, that, of course, I knew San Telmo was full of tourists and, of course, I had visited those other neighborhoods, when I saw Nicolas was smiling somewhat mischievously. I flashed on where I was: easily the fanciest and most expensive apartment I'd been in during my stay in Buenos Aires, just down the hill from the financial district and across the street from the prefab yuppie/tourist shopping area Puerto Madero, and I let it go.

Though I did many interviews for this piece in Spanish, Gonzalo speaks the best English of the three and on that night sat opposite me and did most of the talking, while Nicolas sat or lay on the floor against the wall, drinking from a bottle of wine and smoking. He looked both comfortable and somewhat intense, like book jacket photos of the young Julio Cortazar. When he spoke, he'd direct his questions in Spanish toward the others, while all the while staring at me.

BsAs Stencil are often credited as the first group of artists to start stenciling in the streets, starting in early 2002, months after the start of the crisis. I asked about the beginning of the stencil art movement.

"There was an excess of out of work graphic designers then," shrugged Nicolas. "It could have happened anywhere."

Gonzalo laughed, but disagreed. "The air was different then. It felt like a unique time. I was working as a graphic designer and living near Congreso and I would see all these people in the streets. I'm not used to being in a political party but I felt I had to express something, too."

Deborah agreed. "The ideas were simpler then. The stencils on the wall were like a common language everyone shared."

"But it wasn't just Argentine," said Nicolas, looking at me. "The feeling was also anti-Bush. In the whole world. Our first stencil was an anti-war stencil about the US bombing Afghanistan."

Deborah showed me a book of their collected images so that she could explain any subtle references to Argentine politics, culture, or history that I may not understand. The images, seen back to back, form a scrapbook of the crisis—not a news account or a commentary, but a sort of impressionistic history of the era.

There is the sinking ship that is simply the Buenos Aires city logo of a ship on the Rio Plata, drawn so that the ship is listing to its side and sinking. There is the image of General San Martin—the Argentine George Washington—fused with a picture of Elvis. And there is the text *"Se cayo el sistema"* (The system is down).

Deborah explained, "It is common to hear 'The system is down' in Argentina. When you call the bank, when you call a government office or an airline, so often they will say, 'I'm sorry, but the system is down right now.' So we made this during the crisis, because during that time, if you saw this written in the streets, you would easily get it."

Nicolas said, "I worked in a bank during the crisis. All day, people would call me, screaming at me about their money and I would have to say, 'I'm sorry, but the system is down right now.'"

The second stencil they cut was the "Disney War" image of Bush with Mickey Mouse ears. The image is famous now, and the BsAs Stencil website features a photo of Diego Maradona, Argentina's notorious *futbol*-legend-turned-left-wing-activist-talk-show-host-friend-of-Castro—probably the biggest celebrity in Argentina today—wearing a "Disney War" T-shirt designed by the group.

Looking at stencil after stencil, it is clear that BsAs Stencil has received so much more attention than other stencil groups simply because they so consistently make smart, clever, sharp-looking images. It is interesting that their work succeeds in the same way that successful advertising does, by clever juxtaposition and quick turn of phrase and by giving the audience credit for already knowing half of the joke. BsAs Stencil's best images are ready to digest—easily viewed and immediately, satisfyingly understood.

My favorite that night was the image of a bus, speeding down the street, with *"inconsciente"* (unconscious) written on the side. Buses in Buenos

Aires are known as *colectivos*. "*Colectivo*" also means collective. All at once, I saw the bus and thought, "collective unconscious." It was both fun and evocative. I thought of the image speeding along the walls of Buenos Aires and thought of Argentina—all aboard the bus for wherever the ride takes them for these four years, as the country's collective unconscious, the common language, appears new and freshly painted each morning on the streets.

Run Don't Walk

When I first saw Run Don't Walk's website, I thought that Federico's art was a bit like the fever dreams of an overworked graphic arts designer that had come unmoored and flown across the city, combined with the doodling of a tagger kid fresh out of the Rhode Island School of Design. When I arrived at his place near Congreso, I found that I'd nailed it. Federico is a freelance graphic designer who works from home in a long room with high ceilings, punk records spilling out of the shelves lining the walls, and a work table overflowing with markers, exacto-knives, spray cans, and glossy art magazines in English and Spanish.

One half of Run Don't Walk—along with Tester, the singer of his band—Federico comes out of the DIY punk rock scene and it shows in Run Don't Walk's art. Their stencils are sometimes drawn by

hand and feature an intentional, messy drip aesthetic. They use marker drawings and traditional freehand graffiti in their displays, and their colorful, charming art is not derivative of—but could easily be said to be in the same school with—artists like Barry McGee or Chris Johanson. Their work has more of the touch of the human hand than much of the straight-off-the-computer images that mirrors the look of advertising in Buenos Aires' streets.

Having run a punk label, designed bands' record covers and silk screened band t-shirts and vinyl stickers, Federico told me he sees painting in the streets as "a natural progression," from the punk scene. He started making stencils after seeing the "Disney War" stencil. "I didn't know who was painting in the streets at first," he said. "I just knew I wanted to do it."

"It started as a kind of game," he said. "I had a map of the city in my mind and I took stickers and markers with me everywhere I went. I like the interaction with the city itself."

I asked Federico why he feels he needs to make his art

in the streets instead of trying to get into museums. He said, "A gallery show could be an opportunity to expand your ideas. But if you don't do it in the streets, it is pointless, because the real thing is what is happening in the streets."

"When you are in the streets all day, you see an invasion of the city by these ads. When you paint in the streets you are taking the streets back, making the city yours."

According to Federico, there are two main factors in the sudden explosion of both the stencil art form in the streets and the movement's popularity.

"First is technology," he said, "which is weird because the stencil itself is the most primitive technology there is. The availability of computers, digital cameras and the use of the fotolog websites have made it easy to network photos of stencils.

"Second is that the media got into it quickly and stencils hit the mainstream in a positive way. Now advertisers use stencils to get street cred and its accepted by society at large."

It would seem that technology might also have helped stenciling be accepted by society. The almost universal use of computer-generated images has consolidated stenciling's look into a slick, easily readable art form. As we talked, I thought about the art form that so cleverly mimics advertising and also seems to be a visual representation of a collective unconscious. Does it mean that the collective unconscious has been almost completely colonized by advertising and that stenciling is a form of purging it, a literal "*vomito* attack," as Santiago claims? Or do the cinematic images from US movies and culture represent an inner yearning in formerly rich Argentina for the quality products and Hollywood movies the country had grown accustomed to?

I asked Federico how the country's rapidly growing economy has affected the stencil art in the streets. I was thinking specifically of stenciling's shift away from politics and towards inclusion of more US pop culture references. But Federico surprised me by saying that the stencils themselves had become the product.

"Now, maybe stenciling is becoming co-opted by companies. We get emails to do ads. Krylon was talking to us about doing murals for them. Its weird to grow up in your ghetto and suddenly your ghetto is cool to everybody."

I assumed he was saying that he is against this commercialization, but he surprised me again when he says of the Krylon offer: "I think Run Don't Walk can do some stuff like that, like on the side. It is a good way to get free materials."

He shifted gears and asked me what I thought of the US stencil artist OBEY (Shepard Fairey), known since the 1980s for his Andre The Giant street art campaign that has ballooned into an industry of Andre The Giant products. I had been enjoying our conversation and was reluctant to answer, because I sensed that I was about to disappoint Federico. But, since he asked, I told him that I have always hated OBEY. I told him that I thought the artist Shepard Fairey had cynically turned graffiti culture into a self promoting ad campaign, turning the wonder of street art into a cheap hustle in a way that was no different than the corporate advertising that already clutters up our cities and demands that we "obey."

Federico looked pained. He said, "Well, I don't know him personally, of course. But, when I looked at his website, there was a line of shirts, there were belt buckles...I thought it was quite impressive."

It occurred to me that in this new era, four years removed from the economic crisis that gave it birth, the stencil in Buenos Aires is one step away

from BECOMING advertising. If so, advertising for what? The "new freedom?" "The Revolution" as Nicolas had snidely suggested? Stencils represented the participation people wanted, and pop culture images represented the products they will get. The stencil was the aesthetic of a new participation that had long faded.

Sadly, there was now a rift in our conversation, and Federico became defensive. "Its not possible to sell out here, in the same way that it is in the US," he says. "It is difficult to make more than thirty shirts at a time. It is hard to find places to sell them."

I fully understand wanting to make some money off of doing the art you want to do. I nodded sympathetically and said, "Of course."

Federico continued, "But it gets to the point where you have to ask yourself what you want to do. Do you want to be a romantic who painted Buenos Aires and died alone or do you want to be like OBEY?"

Nico's Place

I met Nico, the better-known half of Vomito Attack, at his apartment in the San Telmo neighborhood, where I also lived. He introduced me to the twenty-something kid from Boston who rents the spare room, so that Nico can pay his own rent, and then we went out to the streets. Nearly 30, Nico is wiry, keyed up, with a paranoid energy, and he reminded me of someone—say a Lower East Side squatter I met at an anti-police brutality rally twelve years ago or maybe a punk rock bike mechanic I'd last seen in 1997 heading to the train yard in Philly on a ten-speed. He looked over his shoulder as we walked and also pointed out his stencils here and there on the walls of Calle Defensa.

"That's one of mine," he said, grinning, pointing at a block of painted text reading, "Thi$ Is Art," a statement that summed up a major part of Vomito Attack's stencil message.

Nico enjoyed explaining his stencils and there is a sense that much of his art is motivated at gut level by a joyful search for revenge against society. Laughing, he told me that for the recent fourth anniversary of the crisis of 2001—just a couple days before Christmas—he debuted a new stencil all across the city. Instead of *Feliz Navidad*, Nico wished his fellow *porteños*, *Feliz Crisis*.

We stopped and sat against a wall in Plaza Dorrego, the heart of tourist San Telmo, the neighborhood of cobblestone streets where the tango was born. It seemed fitting. The Buenos Aires stencilers themselves had become somewhat of a tourist attraction lately. Nico told me that I was the third person to interview him that week, after a European film crew and another writer from the US.

"The first time I saw someone in the street taking pictures with my paintings, I loved it," he said. But Nico was wary of the attention, too, and he has earned his reputation as Buenos Aires' most political stencil artist. He told me about the first interview he consented to for a documentary film crew from the Netherlands. Nico refused to appear for the cameras, except anonymously, to be dragged before them, dressed in an Abu Ghraib-style hood with prisoner overalls.

Nico is often the only stenciler invited who refuses to appear at stencil art exhibitions sponsored by the government of Buenos Aires. "Art is business," he said, scowling. "When the crisis came, I saw that I didn't want to be making photos for exhibitions. I wanted to work in the shit like this," he tells me, motioning to the busy square.

In a sense, Nico had a front row seat at two major life-changing crises. In 2001, Nico was a photographer and moved to New York City, planning to stay for several months. Instead, on the morning of September 11, he was photographing the burning World Trade Center towers from the riverfront near his apartment in Queens. Soon after, terrified of the anti-immigrant hysteria brewing in the USA, Nico headed home to Argentina—just in time for the economic collapse and protests that brought down the government that December.

For a year, Nico and two women friends scraped out a living, running a vegetarian food delivery service by bike out of a home kitchen. By 2003, Nico was working until late at night at the restaurant where he met Santiago and started Vomito Attack.

"Most of the people who were painting stencils in the streets then had not been artists before the crisis," Nico says. Without money for photo paper or film, Nico also turned to stencils and to making political collages out of newspaper and trash, because he felt he had to "do *something*."

"To be in the streets gave me a new opportunity," Nico said, looking out at the tourists in the plaza eagerly capturing images with digital cameras. "I did things I never expected to be able to do because of stencils."

In 2003, the lefty daily newspaper, *Pagina 12*, started running a "stencil of the

This page: collage by Nico; previous page: stencil by Nico/Vomito Attack. Photos: Nico.

week" photo series in their Thursday supplement. "They put Vomito Attack in the paper six weeks in a row," he says. "I told them not to print the name but they did anyway."

While other stencilers in Buenos Aires have embraced opportunities to exhibit indoors, Nico prefers to organize his own illegal art events, like a stencil art party he held on a chunk of abandoned freeway with a visiting graffiti writer from Belgium.

"It went great!" he remembered, with the Argentine preoccupation with food, "we served *choripanes*!"

In December 2004, Nico was the main organizer of Argentina's first ever Reclaim the Streets party. He estimates that about 300 people came to the apparently "spontaneous" dance party that blocked off the streets in front of the famed Teatro Colon and the cops let it run late into the night.

When I met Nico, though, he had just been asked to organize a stencil show in March 2006 at the Argentine National Library. He asked Santiago to help. They remain friends, though the two have rarely stenciled together since Nico left the restaurant job.

"My topic will be 'Five years of crisis'—not just the crisis in Argentina but the wars in Afghanistan and Iraq that have come from September 11 five years ago." For Nico, the subject matter is a part of his personal history. But the timing of the show was deeply personal, too. "March 24 will be the 30th anniversary of the coup," he said, gravely. "But, also, I will turn 30 years old that week." He studied my face, as if to see if I understood what he meant.

"I was born at the same time as the dictatorship."

Skating with Cucusita

Perhaps the biggest tribute to the egalitarian nature of stencil art in Argentina is the story of Cucusita. The one stenciler that was again and again mentioned by other stencilers as the most admired of all, was not the more famous BsAs Stencil or the more political Vomito Attack, but the more elusive Cucusita—a skater kid from one of Buenos Aires' poorest neighborhoods who cuts the most intricate stencils with the tiniest lines in the city and only paints them in a hospital parking lot, where almost no one ever sees them.

"I don't know how he can do it," said Gonzalo of BsAs Stencil. "The thinnest little lines!"

"I heard that maybe he heats up the knife before he cuts the X-Rays," Valentina of Burzaco Stencil would later tell me. "But who knows what kind of knife he must be using!"

One afternoon I had a phone call from Cucusita, himself, telling me he wanted to talk to me "for the book from the USA." He told me to come to the hospital parking lot on Calle Brasil at Pinchincha where he skates all day every Saturday and Sunday to look at his stencils painted there. "I will be easy to find. I will be the thinnest one there," he said.

I rode my bike through the down and out Constitucion barrio and then past a sprawling landscape of worn out ball fields and blocky buildings so barren that it hurts the heart. The sky was open there and the lonely distances between buildings evoked the sad plazas in US postwar housing projects. As I rode, I found I was marveling at Cucusita's story already.

Cucusita had told me that he was from Villa Lugano, a neighborhood said to be *duro*, so hard that Argentines I met were astonished when I told them I'd been there to explore it. A full hour on the bus from the city center, Villa Lugano is a neighborhood of low, shabby houses that lay at the capital's southwest border beyond the vast, underused "Park of The City" and several shanty towns along the commuter train line. As I approached the particularly ugly hospital where Cucusita told me I'd find him, I thought of him riding the bus for an hour every weekend morning only to come to the same kind of worn-out ghetto decay he'd started at.

In front of the hospital, even though the sun was going down, I found a cement plaza filled with skaters, doing tricks off the monumental concrete benches. Cucusita—himself cut from the thinnest of lines—was easy to find in the crowd. He noticed me, the lone gringo, as I saw him and he skated over and told me where I could go around so I didn't have to hop the wrought iron fence.

Cucusita—or Alejandro, as he told me I could also call him—showed me the stencils that cover his skateboard and then showed me, one by one, the benches the skaters circle every weekend, while the other skaters kidded him for being "interviewed." Cucusita had decorated each bench with images from 1980s USA skate culture. Old ads from *Thrasher magazine*, Powell Peralta logos, Pushead drawings—a series of familiar images of ghoulish hands pulling dripping eyes from sockets, and skating skeletons all rendered perfectly with painstakingly razored hairline cuts.

Cucusita turned out to be not what I'd expected in a number of ways. First of all, he's not exactly a kid at all—he's twenty-nine years old. He has been stenciling for fun since he was a little kid and started stenciling in the streets—at the skaters' *old* spot—in the year 2000, a full year before the crisis gave everyone else their start.

I tried out some of the questions I had asked all the other stencilers. To each one, he said, more or less, no. He never thinks about the likely audience for his stencils, walking by in the streets. He doesn't think about "Art in the streets," or art in general. He doesn't care about politics and he doesn't have a message. He cuts stencils out of old X-Rays, like everyone else, and the X-Rays are easy to find because he only stencils at the hospital. His interests are simple and modest: skating and cutting stencils. I asked him why he chose only these images and he shrugged and laughed: "I don't have the imagination to make a drawing for a stencil, so I just make a copy of these ones."

The fact that Cucusita's practically hidden stencils are so well-known and that he was asked to take part in the first big stencil art show in the city at the Recoleta gallery shows another way that the internet has changed the formerly very site-specific world of street art. Cucusita is not attempting to communicate with random citizens in the street. Instead, his intended audience—beside the other skaters at the spot—are other stencilers from all over the city and even South America, who look at his photos on his carefully maintained website. His site, *Assholeco. com.ar*, has numerous, jaw-dropping photos of stencils made up of jungles of twisting, interwoven vines of cuts, where you can only look and think, "How did he *do* that?!?" Unmoored from their physical reality, the value of the stencils becomes not their message or aesthetic, but simply Cucusita's amazing technical virtuosity in cutting them.

Cucusita walked me through an empty lot behind the hospital, past an abandoned medieval city prison from the last century, and to a wall where he had painted some of his larger works, near enough to busy Caseras Avenue to seem as if he almost wants people to see these ones. Cucusita is a fan of punk rock and there were Misfits logos and skulls there, as well as a larger Pushead drawing that he says took him fourteen hours to cut. "I got cramps in my hand!" he said, shaking his head and laughing.

And that was that. We'd run out of stencils to talk about and the skating day was done. We walked north toward the city center, where Cucusita would embark on the aimless Saturday night of penniless punk rockers the world over. Cucusita said that after skating all day every Saturday, he skates another five miles north and east to the Retiro train station, where some of the skaters meet up to hang out, before he takes a bus home to Villa Lugano late at night. I asked him if he ever went to the punk rock record store on Calle Santa Fe or if he'd seen any good bands lately, and he looked pained. I realized he never had any money. I asked him what else he did for fun in town. He grinned. "I make stickers and put them on the police cars in the parking lot by the police station on Belgrano. Or sometimes, when I see empanada delivery guys on their motos, I see if I can skate fast enough to catch up to them and skate along side long enough to put one of my stickers on their motorcycle!"

Inside the Museum Show

As the stencil art in the streets gained more notoriety and more attention in the press, group indoor shows inevitably followed. In 2003, Stencil Attack was the first meeting of groups like Run Don't Walk, BsAs Stencil, and Burzaco Stencil all in one show. Bigger shows followed in 2004 at more prestigious venues like the University of Buenos Aires and the Cultural Center Recoleta.

Today, work from the more well known stencil groups is part of a permanent exhibition at the Cultural Center in Recoleta. Photos of the exhibit show a floor to ceiling free-for-all—colorful stencils layered on top of each other, covering almost every inch of the available walls, with each group's images playing off the other's. The group shows were wild explosions of color and feeling, a celebration of the sheer fun of stenciling, as wild and unplanned as the art form's own arrival on the streets had been.

The stencilers embraced opportunities to make stencil art indoors, as long as the shows were in the collective and non-profit spirit of the era. More controversial in the stencil community was BsAs Stencil and Run Don't Walk's decision to participate in 2004 in the annual, city-wide, high-end gallery exhibitions of ArteBA, a "contemporary art fair" very much aimed at the rich and not the stencil viewer in the street.

When I asked Nico about ArteBA, he scowled and called it "a capitalist art flea market." BsAs Stencil's website shrugs away any controversy, saying simply, "They called us. We went." The site shows pictures of the groups' biting work for the show, a series of five stenciled shopping carts, loaded to overflowing with stenciled images, as if the images had all been bought at the store. The piece was either a clever, irresistible commentary on the consumerist art world or a cynical copout, depending on how you looked at it. Either way, it bore the trademark stamp of BsAs Stencil's humor and willingness to try to put their work into new and challenging contexts.

BsAs Stencil was still setting the pace for the city's other groups. Their solo show, *Adentro*, in January 2006 at Centro Cultural Borges was significant in the Buenos Aires stencil world because it was the first time that an individual group had been singled out for a show, instead of stenciling, itself, being featured as a novel art form. When I arrived, I saw Federico and Tester across the room, and was glad to see that Cucusita had made it, too. He hadn't seemed to believe me when I told him the show would be free. It seemed like most of the stencilers in the capital—with the exception of Nico—had come to see what BsAs Stencil would do "inside."

At the show, I was introduced to Ivan of *Smnr.com*, the online clearinghouse for the street art of the Americas. Only twenty-one, and as young and excited as you might expect of someone who has spent three years running a full-time website about stencils, Ivan told me he lived just outside the capital in a town that was itself a bit of a stencil. In La Ciudad de Evita (The City of Evita), he explained, the streets had been laid out in a shape that would show Evita's face when viewed from an airplane. I wondered which part of her face he lived in, while he regaled me with information about the stencil world.

"Chile has a lot of stickers, but there are a lot of people in Santiago stenciling," he reported. "Mexico and Brazil have a lot of street art. There are all different kinds, but in Brazil they tend to spray-paint drawings and not text in the streets."

"And there is one—one!—person making stencils in Peru now!" He looked grave and lowered his voice. "But in Bolivia...*No hay nada*."

It seemed, really, as if there was nothing about graffiti that Ivan did not know. I mentioned to him that I was to go out stenciling with Nico and Santiago the following night. He said, "I know. I heard," and then he asked me to draw my tag in his scrapbook. He had looked me up online. I drew the tag and Ivan and I agreed to meet and go put up stickers sometime. Then he ran off, open scrapbook in hand, to get a tag from The London Police, a group of hotshit stencilers from England, in town to check out the Buenos Aires stencil scene and to go painting in the streets after the show with BsAs Stencil.

Cucusita came over and asked me what I thought of the show. I told him it looked good so

far. He eyed me with consternation and shook his head. He said, "But where are the STENCILS?" It was true; where most stencil art shows before had been an overlapping riot of images, for this show BsAs Stencil had elected, instead, to cover the one broad wall and the corner with three oversize stencil images that resembled traditional gallery paintings, and then had made a collage mural wrapping around the corner. The pieces, viewed left to right, told a story like a comic strip, all expounding on the show's theme, "Inside."

In the first panel, a masked bandit appeared to be crawling into the museum through a window, brandishing a gun. In the second, a gang of soccer rioters sodomized an exhausted-looking man in a suit with an alarm-clock windup mechanism sticking out of his back. In the third, a farmer surveyed a hole in his fence and gazed off toward the mural, where a stampede of Indians on horseback with spears had tramped across the museum's walls, past a *piquetero*'s blazing tire. The entire piece was painted conservatively in only two colors—orange and black—with a lot of blank space on the white walls, thus using the official colors of the city of Buenos Aires. In the corner above, the ship from the city logo was sinking as the Indians and *piqueteros* of the collage made their way past a stoic *gaucho* toward the Centro Cultural Borges' overpriced, yuppie café.

I liked the show a lot and studied it for awhile, savoring its ambiguity. Had the art form birthed by the crisis helped the ideas from the street to break into the museum, and by extension, mainstream Argentine thought? Were the concerns of the *piqueteros* in fact now represented here, "inside?" And could it be said, by extension, that after the events of the crisis, those concerns had now been allowed inside with the government of Kirchner? If so, was Kirchner the Indian or the museum?

And, now that it had broken in and shocked a few suits, what would happen? Had the art from the streets been lured "inside," only to be trapped there?

Stenciling with Vomito Attack

The night after the Centro Borges show, I went out to Nico's old apartment in Flores, a neighborhood some sixty blocks southwest of downtown Buenos Aires, to meet up with him and Santiago for a night of stenciling. On Calle San Juan, there were Orthodox Jews walking the crowded streets in the shadows of rows of modern, blocky apartment buildings of ten or more stories, and immigrants from Bolivia working the counters at Chinese-owned produce stands and kiosks. It occurred to me that Flores looked eerily like a part of Queens, uprooted and replanted here, south of the equator.

Nico had already moved all of his stuff to his new place in San Telmo, and when I stepped out of the elevator, I found him pacing around the empty rooms of his apartment like some half-mad Dostoevsky character. He greeted me with a clipping from that morning's *Clarin*, one of Argentina's leading daily papers, about BsAs Stencil's show at Centro Borges. The article mentioned the *Hasta La Victoria* book and name checked most of the more known stencil groups. BsAs Stencil had

taken care to mention Vomito Attack, but in a sort-of sideways tribute, saying, "We don't only do political work, but there are groups that only do political work, like Vomito Attack."

Nico's apartment seemed to me like a stumbled upon crime scene. The walls were completely covered to the ceilings in posters and collages made of cut up trash and newspaper. The paper had then been covered with stencils or thick swashes of colorful paint sprayed and dripped and smeared over the top.

One wall was decorated with Aerolineas Argentina promotional posters that had been turned on their sides so that the planes' noses pointed down in a straight crash. An opposite wall showed the photo Nico had taken on the morning of 9/11 of a crowd of Orthodox Jews watching the World Trade Center towers collapsing from the waterfront in Queens—the familiar image particularly jarring from this amateur camera angle.

In the rooms, Nico's artist sketchbooks are piled on the floor. I leafed through the books—page after page thick with pasted scraps of newspaper, found street trash, old photos—all cut up and rearranged. Nico's art echoed the eerie feeling I'd had since I arrived in Buenos Aires that everything here had somehow been cut up, scrambled, forced back together to make something both new and old. Buenos Aires, with its French architecture and its Spanish generals, its Italian pizza and English football—a thrift-store Europe, cobbled together from broken pieces of the Old World, carefully carried across the seas to America and planted here in the poison soil of the get-rich-scheme called "Argentina."

There were books of photos that Nico, himself, had taken and then carefully cut and reassembled. In Nico's cut-ups I saw Argentina's split European/Latin American personality and its exile separation from its origins. In the slashed and rearranged bodies, I saw the secret horrors of concentration camp Argentina in the Dirty War and the forced economic experimentation of the IMF debt years that tore the country apart, and rebuilt it again and again with such a disfiguring effect of people's lives. If the stenciling bursting forth in the streets of BA now is an effortless, playful, collective landscape of a newly free country's subconscious, then Nico's physically ripped and stuck together art seems like a willful effort to vomit up a collective horror buried deep in the country's subconscious. The art asks if a country that has gone through so much can ever be completely whole again, or if, in fact, it had been assembled wrong from the very beginning.

I told Nico I thought the art was powerful and I thought it would be great in the show at the National Library, especially because of the show's coincidence with the coup's anniversary.

He shrugged and said, "Right now, I don't know if I will do the show at the library. I have decided I want to go back to New York in April."

I suggested that he could do both, but he shook his head, "I will need to concentrate on getting my things ready to travel."

As I puzzled over Nico's disinterest in the opportunity to do the National Library show, I found some photos of Nico's Reclaim The Streets party. There were shots of confused businessmen in suits, walking wide around a pile of mannequins in the street, and in the foreground there was a trash can overflowing with pieces of cardboard and paper, each one stenciled by Nico with the word "arte." Here, I thought, was Buenos Aires stenciling at this moment: poised between the "opportunity" of government sponsored exhibitions and the indifferent "fuck you!" to the art world of Vomito Attack, with neither option completely satisfying.

Just then, Santiago arrived. He was a wreck—asleep on his feet, with the claustrophobic tension of hours of bus rides across town on BA's packed *collectivos* showing in his sweat-soaked shirt and messed up hair. He was carrying his stencils rolled up in an enormous tube of flexible cardboard, slung across his back, and he looked like an illegal graffiti artist skillfully disguised as someone on their way to yoga if anyone in Buenos Aires ever actually carried yoga mats around. Once inside the door, he slumped over in a corner and started rolling a joint.

Nico and Santiago started talking heatedly in the corner while they smoked the joint. Though Nico and I had been speaking in Spanish all night, they talked too quietly and quickly for me to make much of it out. From what I could tell, they were arguing about the exhibition at the National Library. It occurred to me that Santiago didn't feel like he would be able to do the show himself, and that he would need Nico's determination to get it done. When I had a moment later to ask Santiago how his planning for the show was going, he grimaced and looked toward Nico and said only, "I still don't know what is going to happen."

Santiago had been up all night working, and out all day with his kids. With drooping eyelids, he rolled another joint and opened a beer. And then another, and another. It wasn't until hours later that we finally gathered together our cans of paint and stencils and headed out to Flores for my first time stenciling in Buenos Aires.

We walked away from the main drag, past several darkened blocks where prostitutes stood in front of cheap, down and out looking hotels. Nico led the way, stenciling here and there as we walked, Santiago trudged along with his huge yoga roll—until we arrived at a set of train tracks, where a dirty white wall, listlessly covered in fading tags awaited us. There was no one around, nor did it feel like anyone ever *would* walk by, and the whole area smelled overwhelmingly of shit. Nevertheless, this was the spot Nico had in mind and Santiago started unrolling his stencils on the ground while Nico went quickly to work. He enthusiastically sprayed a recurring pattern of bombs, crucifixes, and TV sets in some of the untagged areas, while Santiago taped up a cardboard square with a big hole in it, and then started spraying silver paint evenly through it to make a background on the wall for his image. Next he taped up his stencil and did a mist of black across it. He took down the stencil and an image of a life-size man doing a jig with a bottle in one hand was suddenly and joyfully hopping about on the wall.

I decided it was my turn and went over and sprayed in orange and black, a couple of 3D prints of Ivy's cartoon alligator stencil, so that the gators now snapped at the man's dancing feet. We stepped back a few feet to admire the two paintings together and they looked good.

But the night ended as edgily and unsatisfyingly as it had begun. Santiago realized he had rolled his stencils out in the wrong spot and his stencils and cardboard were smeared with what was probably human shit.

This page: various stencils by Burzaco Stencil; next page: Burzaco Stencil. *The Ramones*, 2006. Photos: Burzaco Stencil.

Out in Burzaco

One Monday afternoon, I took a train from the Constitution Station south to Burzaco to meet the kids from Burzaco Stencil, the only one of the Buenos Aires stencil groups that doesn't actually live or paint in BA. The train lurched and heaved across the lifeless Riachuelo River, and the dense streets of the capital slowly gave way to the big sky and long, flat vistas of the suburbs. One hour outside BA the train stopped at a small grouping of one-story buildings sprawled along weedy empty lots. I picked Valentina and Federico out of the small crowd at the Burzaco station when I saw their matching Converse sneakers and the Los Crudos patch on Federico's sweatshirt.

Val and Fed are twenty-one and twenty-two, respectively, and have a charming, punk rock enthusiasm, as well as an interview line that sounds like a promotional ad trying to lure graffiti artists to their small town. "You will see," promised Valentina, "that it is much better to paint here in Burzaco than in Buenos Aires." We sat in the grass of the empty lot behind the station on Burzaco's listless main drag and I took notes while they finished each other's sentences.

"We think the Capital is too visually contaminated already with stencils. Don't you agree?" Valentina says. "Why would we go there when we can paint here in Burzaco?"

I agreed that Burzaco is nice, with its open space, greenery, and less hectic atmosphere, but I suggested that there might be more glory in painting in the capital where they could reach a bigger audience there.

"But we are more appreciated here," said Federico.

"There are a lot of young people here in Burzaco," Valentina declared.

"And here we can paint in the middle of the day and no one cares!"

"Sundays are the best!"

"...after the *carne asada* when everyone's asleep!"

Sure enough, they produced some stencils and paint from their backpacks and we walked over to the cinder block wall of the train station, where they started to paint in broad daylight. My head impulsively swiveled around, scanning the nearly empty streets for the cops or do-gooders, but there was simply no one around. When I turned back, Val had painted an intricately cut, six-inch tall stencil of a Bolex camera next to a bare-chested Betty Page, draped in a leopard-print sweater. "What we're doing is not vandalism. It is art!" reminded Valentina.

"One time, we were painting a little motorbike image on the train station and this guy driving by saw us. He came back a couple of minutes later with a T-shirt so we could put the image on the shirt for him!" added Fed.

"And another time, someone wanted our chainsaw on their shirt!," said Val. "The young people of Burzaco like the stencils very much!"

We walked through the quiet streets of the town, Valentina's paint audibly clinking in her bag, and talked about the sudden explosion of the BA stenciling movement and the publicity that has come with it.

"We were the second group to start stenciling, after BsAs Stencil," claimed Valentina. "We saw 'Disney War' in Buenos Aires and then sent [BsAs Stencil] stencils we made. They told us we should paint *their* stencils here in Burzaco. After that, we started making our own."

We stopped in front of a long white wall that fronts a church's courtyard. Valentina said this wall has long been one of their favorite places to paint stencils in Burzaco. "We don't like to put our ideas in other people's heads. Instead, we try to make the streets nicer and more colorful for people with images we like."

I asked them what kind of images they usually choose to uplift the people of Burzaco.

"We like to paint serial killers, or movie stuff like *Taxi Driver, Scarface*. And hot chicks!" said Valentina. "...or stuff from B-horror movies from the 1950s!" added Fed.

The church's wall was stencil-free, but was covered with cloudy, off-white splotches of paint. "Sometimes they cover them up," Valentina said, her eyes narrowing. "But we just go back and put them up again!"

Like all the stencilers I talked to, Burzaco Stencil hated the *Hasta La Victoria, Stencil!* book.

When I asked Gonzalo of BsAs Stencil about it, his eyes widened and he stammered, "This book...is...is a FUCKING SHIT! They photoshopped out all of the walls and the streets and the people and even changed some of the paint colors!"

Bringing it up to Valentina and Federico likewise triggered a rapid-fire barrage of complaint, best reprinted as a sort-of punk rock band interview:

Val: The spirit of the stencil was killed by this book!

Fed: It kills the stencil to be in the galleries and not the streets!

Val: We made a stencil about it. *"Hasta Aqui Llegue La Stencil"* [basically, "Up to here came the stencil"].

Fed: These books are only for your ego. Or for your mom. Because the stencil was born in the streets!

Val: I think it's dead!

Fed (thoughtfully): Perhaps in a couple years, it will be reborn.

Val: It's not even started yet and they killed it! We are angry!

We circled the streets of Burzaco one more time and talked of our mutual love of the Ramones.

"Dee Dee lived right here in Burzaco!" Valentina proclaimed. "Didn't you know?"

I knew that Dee Dee Ramone had, near the end, married an Argentine teenager who was, at first at least, too young to really bring back to the States, but I had always imagined that they lived in Buenos Aires together.

"They lived in La Plata and they lived here in Burzaco!" Valentina said. As we walked further down the train tracks, we passed a stencil on a traffic guard with an image of Sid Vicious' face.

"That was one of our first stencils," Fed said. I stopped and tried to imagine Dee Dee living here in Burzaco, walking down these lonely tracks, under this big sky and coming face to face with this ghostly image of his old acquaintance from the Chelsea Hotel. Where would Dee Dee score drugs in Burzaco?

They told me that their next project was to cut a life-size stencil of The Ramones, as pictured on the first record cover, and to paint The Ramones onto the cinder block wall of the train station.

We went back to Federico's parents' house, where his little brother was practicing the electric guitar in the garage. Federico rolled out the plastic with the still uncut image of The Ramones and we listened to records. Valentina said, "You have to hear this band we know. It's pathetic. They try so hard to sound exactly like The Ramones."

She put on the record for a minute and we listened. She sniffed and shook her head and said, "See what I mean? It's so embarrassing. They sound just like them!"

It is Better Not to Speak of Some Things

Late one night, Nico met me at my place on Avenida Independencia so that we could go stencil some more in San Telmo. The streets, scalding and smoky all day, were now haunted by the breeze from the Rio Plata and the sense of a nearby, remembered but always unseen ocean. The enormous mouth of the river is almost thirty miles across to Uruguay from Buenos Aires, yet, because of industry and the port, there is almost no place in the heart of the city where you can actually see the river. The city's buildings crowd inward—maybe with their back to the ocean and Europe, or maybe to the memory of the countless victims of the dictatorship that were dropped out of planes and into the river.

Nico told me not to worry about cops while we painted. They never did anything if they caught you doing graffiti. All the stencil artists here had told me the same thing. Federico had said, "Maybe they take you into the station and ask, 'How much money do you have on you?' That is the Argentine way."

But what the cops did or did not do in Argentina was one of the many subjects in Argentina I would never really feel I had learned the truth about. Just another subject that left me feeling like the exasperated Englishman, Humphries, in Graham Greene's Argentina novel, *The Honorary Consul*, who says, "One can never get at the truth (down here)."

On the one hand, just that week, two cops that had been captured on film in late 2002 killing two *piqueteros* in a protest on the bridge to the Buenos Aires suburb Avalleneda—the famed "Avalleneda Massacre"—had received sentences of life in prison, something I told Nico would never happen in the United States. But Nico shrugged and, even after saying that cops wouldn't arrest you for graffiti, had said, "The cops here just put the drugs on you anytime they want and they kill so many people everyday." It was what everybody said about the cops. Could it be that these cops got the maximum sentence, but cops still were killing people with impunity and no one notices or cares enough to write about it in the paper or to try to stop it?

I thought of a story told to me by my Buenos Aires roommate, Pepe, a Patagonian. He told me about his old friend who had been in a wild rock band in La Plata that had a dog for a singer. He was practically crying from laughter, trying to describe the dog tied up on the stage, howling while the band played. Then his eyes narrowed and his face went abruptly blank. He looked directly into my eyes and said, "The police..." and made a gun with his hand. He pulled the imaginary trigger and went, "Pfft!' through his teeth. It was exactly clear what he meant, but I asked to be sure, "You mean the police killed your friend?" Pepe's face hardened and he nodded. His friend was political, a squatter, and in a band. He had disappeared and never been found. What else could have happened?

What actually happens or has happened is never quite certain in this country still reconstructing a national memory from the long blackout of the Dirty War. In the 1980s, President Carlos Menem's amnesty law protected the coup's military officials from prosecution and stalled a national dialogue on the meaning of the Dirty War, while his profligate borrowing flooded the country with cash and new products.

In Osvaldo Soriano's post-dictatorship novel *Una Sombra Ya Pronto Seras*, this era is embodied by a drunken businessman, driving in circles, lost in the Pampas in a breaking down Mercedes with a backseat filled with booze and food and cigarettes. The businessman points at his head and says, "I have a hole right here. Ten years are just gone, just like that."

The stencilers I interviewed in Argentina are mostly around thirty years old, the kids of the generation that lived under the dictatorship, but few of them make art about the country's fascist history.

"This guy from Spain, Dr. Hoffman, who came here to make stencils wanted to make some

about the dictatorship," Federico told me. "But when you live in it everyday, you don't think about making art about it."

My Spanish wasn't working so good on this night, and we rode our bikes through the neighborhood mostly in silence, looking both ways for cops, anyway, and painting occasionally. I had made my own stencil for this night—simple, hand-lettered text, that read, "*Es Mejor No Hablar De Ciertas Cosas*" (It is better not to speak of some things) in honor of a song title by the enormously popular Argentine punk/reggae band from the early 1980s, Sumo. In the quiet, I thought back to my first conversation with Nico in Plaza Dorrego, and thought of the many questions I still wanted to ask Nico about it.

That day, Nico had blamed the 1976 military coup in Argentina on the United States' government, saying that the US had organized the military and paid everyone to pull it off. I was surprised. It is known that the US trained many Argentine military officials from the coup at the School of the Americas, but I've never heard anyone claim that the US made the coup happen in the way it did in Chile. I protested to Nico that certainly the conditions in Argentina brought about the opportunity for the coup and that many people in the country wanted the coup and directly benefited from it. And how many coups had Argentina had in the twentieth century alone, anyway? Elected democracy had always been fragile at best here.

But Nico was adamant. "The US made the coup and then they made Menem, who changed the culture of Argentina," he told me. "Before Menem there were intellectuals and after Menem, there were McDonald's and all anyone cared about was money and clothes, and the products and media of the USA."

Nico looked around the Plaza nervously, even though we were surrounded by tourists and he was speaking in English. He continued speaking quietly, telling me his theory about the truth behind last year's tragic Cromagnon incident in Buenos Aires. On New Year's Eve 2004, a packed nightclub, called Cromagnon, had caught on fire and hundreds of mostly poor kids attending a rock concert died, trapped inside, because the owner had permanently chained the fire exits shut to keep people from sneaking in without paying. The resulting scandal had a hallucinatory "Only In Argentina" quality. The nightclub owner had been arrested for murder, but, the mayor of Buenos Aires had also been forced by angry protesters—who held him directly responsible for the deaths—to resign. He was now on trial for the kids' deaths, too. Meanwhile, clubs all over the country—indeed all over South America—had been shut down for code violations.

Nico told me solemnly that the fire was not an accident. "How could it have been?" he asked, angrily. "The media was there filming while it burned and they already knew how many people were inside," he said. "And now, look: all the country is worried about security. We have to have 'Exit' signs everywhere like in the US and we don't have any clubs."

It was an astounding accusation to me. He had told me that he thought Kirchner was "the first president ever that (he) wasn't ashamed of" and now he was saying Kirchner's government burned down a club and killed hundreds of kids. Couldn't they just shut down all the clubs without killing all those people?

Nico said I didn't understand. "You see how Kirchner tells the grocery stores they have to charge a certain amount for milk. That is how it works here, like with Peron. If the grocery stores don't do what Kirchner says, maybe one of their factories will burn down. That is the Argentine way."

Nico looked around, nervously again, and warned me, "You understand, these are things I never talk about with *anyone*, except maybe my

mother, because you can't talk with anyone here about anything."

I said, "There are many subjects in Argentina, I have noticed, that no one will talk about."

He laughed and nodded. I thought of Nicolas from Buenos Aires and his equally astounding claim, only half joking, that the government left the graffiti up in the streets to promote a revolutionary look for tourists. There was a common thread here, a artist's representation of cause and effect: first the coup, then the McDonald's. The impossibility of discussion lent a mythical quality to recent Argentine history. If everyone believed it, then wasn't it as good as true? It was a hallucinatory, unverifiable history—an impressionistic history, less like a newspaper and more like a painting.

Or a stencil. We stopped at a long, high wall, surrounding a lot near Parque Lezama and Nico unrolled his stencils. He looked both ways and said under his breath, "This is a headquarters of the military police."

I looked around and saw no signs or cameras or guards or anything that would give the place's identity away. I said, "Really? Are you sure?"

But Nico was already working quickly, painting his stencils across the wall. There was much I still wanted to ask, but I went ahead and added my own stencil. I painted *Es Mejor No Hablar De Ciertas Cosas* right across the wall of what may or may not have been a military police headquarters and I didn't know whether to be afraid or to be proud.

BsAs No Future

When I met with BsAs Stencil a couple days after the museum show, I asked them about how they thought it had gone, and about the pros and cons of going "inside."

"It was a step forward for us, to focus on the difference between the streets and the gallery," said Deborah.

"People who know our work probably expected something else," said Gonzalo. "We wanted to do this show with fewer colors, more blank walls, to do something different."

"For this show, we had the time that you don't have in the streets to really think about the images and plan everything out. We picked these

images because we identify strongly with them," said Nicolas.

"Its better in the streets," he said. "But I enjoyed it."

Gonzalo shrugged. "We are street artists who go and do work in a gallery. It would be good if the usual artists brought their stuff outside for a change!"

I told them that I thought the art in the show was probably the strongest, most cohesive presentation of their political message that I had seen in their work, but I wondered if some of the radical potential of stenciling was lost by bringing it indoors. Following that line of thought, I asked them if they could remember a way that stencils themselves had actually been the instrument in any sort of political event. Could they remember a time when the emotional power and street smarts of the art itself, its surrounding buzz or hype, its power to bring people into a museum, had ever been harnessed in some way in a political cause?

Gonzalo remembered BsAs Stencil taking part in an event called "The Garage Party" in 2003 during the crisis. The event was an exhibition of stencil art work painted on site in a parking lot in Congreso and featured electronic music and dancing. It was at a time when no one had any money, so the price of admission was donated food, which was to be sent to victims of a flood in Santa Fe province.

I asked Gonzalo if they had considered putting on their own similar events as a way to control the exhibition of their art and to generate money or interest in other causes. He laughed and said, "No, we are too lazy for that."

Deborah wanted to talk about their shirt ideas, their upcoming merchandising. "Sometimes we work for ad agencies," she said. "At least, with this we are doing what we like for ourselves."

BsAs Stencil is a seriously good group of artists, but what is next for them, I wondered? Will they be able to adapt to the rapidly changing country and keep making art that is smart and relevant or will they fade out as the tension in their work between the streets and the gallery fades out? I pressed onward with Gonzalo, telling him there has to be a way for stencils to live up to the spirit of freedom they were born from. I tried to tell him about a group of artists and activists I was involved with back in San Francisco that took over an enormous abandoned building, decorated it with murals top to bottom, and turned it into a free breakfast program/punk venue/community space for four months of 2001 until the cops shut it down.

Gonzalo was smiling, but I could see he didn't really understand what I meant. As I talked, I realized that I don't really even know the words in English, let alone in Spanish, for what I was trying to describe. The nearest I could come would be the air was different, but I still don't know the words for what I want.

I asked them what the future holds for the group.

"We think if people continue to offer us shows indoors, we will do them," said Gonzalo.

"We are interested in making more shirts," Deborah said.

From the floor, Nicolas said, "We don't talk about the future."

The End

Since I left Buenos Aires, many of the stencil groups I talked to have continued to do shows together. In July 2006, the University of Buenos Aires School

of Architecture, Design, and Urbanism organized a show called *Dicen Las Paredes* (The Walls Speak), that featured favorites like BsAs Stencil, Run Don't Walk, and Burzaco Stencil, alongside newer groups like Nazza Stencil and Kid Gaucho.

Also in July, Nestor Kirchner appeared with Hugo Chavez in Caracas again and endorsed the idea of a regional military defense pact between Argentina and Venezuela and other countries.

I wrote an email to Gonzalo of BsAs Stencil asking him if he ever missed the days of the crisis, if it had seemed more possible or more exciting to make a political statement with art in those days.

He replied, "It would be childish to say that one could miss a moment in which the banks robbed the savings of the people and police shot unarmed protesters. It seems more accurate to us to say that we miss the excitement and the urge to participate that the people had in those days and that later was lost a bit at a time until we arrived at the indifference that characterizes this society."

In the online reviews of *Dicen Las Paredes*, I saw that "Santiago Spirito (of Vomito Attack)" had also taken part in the show and it made me think of my last night living in Buenos Aires, when I last saw Santiago.

I had gone to Palermo to meet him in a pizzeria after he got out of work so that we could stencil and hang out before I left the city. When I showed up, he was finishing a second beer, smoking, his exhausted eyes smiling. He proudly showed me photos of all of his stencils that he had cataloged on his new cell phone's camera.

I asked him how the exhibition at the library was going. He winced, and said, "Nico may go to New York instead. Maybe I have another friend who will do the show with me...*Vamos a ver*..." he trailed off, his eyes looking up toward his smoke curling toward the ceiling.

Sumo played their hits of the 80s on the pizzeria loudspeakers and I thought of my stencil: *Es mejor no hablar*. I told him I hoped it would work out. The exhibition would coincide with the 30th anniversary of the coup and would be a great opportunity to say something about that time in a national gallery where it would certainly get a lot of attention throughout the country.

He closed his eyes and laughed a bit and said, "Yes, I suppose so. I hadn't thought of that."

We talked about stenciling and I asked him about the future.

"I have been thinking of trying new materials," he said. "I think maybe I will try putting things up in the streets, maybe with some type of cement."

As he answered, Sumo sang along with their big hit, "Waiting for 1989...We don't want no more war..." And I had the curious feeling that we were somehow lost in Argentina's recent history, driving around in endless circles, like the amnesiac businessman in Soriano's novel.

I asked him finally about my favorite stencil of his, the image of the dancing people and the cranes. He looked up, deep in thought. Finally, he said, "I think it represented love or that people love to dance. Really, it's about doing whatever you want to, right up until you die."

I thought of the cinematic blur of the country's collective unconscious layered on Buenos Aires walls and I thought of the blur of protesters, running through its streets. I thought of Nico born with the dictatorship and I thought of Cucusita chasing down motos on his skateboard for the fun of it. And I thought of the people dancing with the cranes. Were they rising up or were they being manipulated? What was the next chapter in the whole unverifiable, unspeakable rumor of Argentina's impressionistic history?

As it turned out, the March exhibition at the Biblioteca Nacional never happened. When the anniversary of the coup happened, the week that Nico turned thirty, hundreds of thousands of marchers filled streets throughout the nation in memorial to the disappeared. Nico made thirty stencils, one for each year since the coup. Some of the stencils read:

NUNCA MAS STATE ASSASSINS,
NUNCA MAS TORTURE,
NUNCA MAS BANNED BOOKS,
NUNCA MAS ASSASSINATED STUDENTS,
NUNCA MAS THE POLICE,
NUNCA MAS THE MILITARY,
NUNCA MAS THE CHURCH,
NUNCA MAS IN THE WORLD!

He painted them in the streets all over Buenos Aires. Then he left Argentina for New York City.

Nico/Vomito Attack, *Nunca Mas*, 2006. Photo: Nico.

SUBVERSIVE MULTIPLES: A CONVERSATION BETWEEN CONTEMPORARY PRINTMAKERS

MEREDITH STERN

A couple years ago there were several political arts projects gaining national visibility which indicated that there was a growing community of radical artists. The Drawing Resistance traveling art show,[1] the Beehive Collective poster project,[2] the Celebrate People's History poster project[3] and the Street Art Workers[4] involved dozens of artists, some of whom had worked together, and others who had never met. I was living in New Orleans without a community of radical artists to share ideas with, and decided to hit the road to connect with several of these people in person to see what we could come up with together. I interviewed over a dozen folks on the East Coast and Midwest and found that we were all struggling with similar questions; such as what roles art can play in social movements, what historical groups and artists present models which inspire us, and what other possibilities exist for creative resistance?

Years later, most of the interviews were transcribed, but largely unedited, when Josh and Erik suggested that the idea be re-envisioned as a chapter for this book. We decided to choose printmakers in their mid-twenties to late-thirties, who are fairly consistent in their creative output, to talk together by way of the Internet and to share ideas. The artists involved are people who have worked together and have been inspired by each other's work. The result was over sixty pages of dialogue, which has been tightly squeezed into a handful of sound bites from each artist. It's a small window into a growing community of artists who are trying to figure out what exactly is the power of visual images.

Why do you choose to create prints? How do you consider the materials you work with?

Miriam Klein Stahl: I make prints for the populous appeal. I am in love with the idea of many people having ownership of an image. Prints are a threat to the idea that there is one precious piece of art that hangs for only a few to see.

Colin Matthes: Prints are largely accessible, can be made with simple tools, can be widely distributed, and sold inexpensively or given away. Prints also retain the beauty of a handmade object and employ a relatively low tech process that complements the craft of the printer.

Morgan F.P. Andrews: Carving and printing with wood, masonite, or linoleum appeals to me because the process is in line with how I experience the visual world: not as objects that fill up a blank white space, but as images that emerge from darkness. I have this degenerative retinal disease—Cone/Rod Dystrophy Type 5, or CORD5 for short. Basically it's like the contrast and sharpness knobs on my eyeballs are very slowly being turned askew for the rest of my life. As a kid, with my fleeting visual acuity, I was actively discouraged by peers and mentors and made to feel like I couldn't create anything visual. I delved headlong into the independent black-and-white comics explosion of the 1980s like early issues of *World War 3 Illustrated*.[5] The harsh lines and political overtones were exactly what my eyes and brain were thirsty for. Eventually I tried my hand at woodcutting as part of a regimen of visual rehabilitation. The whole grueling process of carving a block, inking it up, registering it cor-

Previous page, clockwise from top left: Meredith Stern, *Safe Sex is Hot*, reduction linocut, 2004; Nicole Schulman, *Eve and the Big Apple*, linocut, 1999; Miriam Klein Stahl, *mugshot (thank you emma goldman)*, linocut, 2002; Erik Ruin, *Checkpoints (Ten Plagues of the Occupation series)*, silkscreen, 2004; Bec Young, *The Torn Deities of Displaced People and Demolished Houses (Deities We Need series)*, stencil, 2005.

rectly, and rubbing the back of paper (or cloth) with a wooden spoon (or rolling pin) is so laborious and real and magical.

Erik Ruin: I get kicks from printmaking's modern history as painting's low-rent, unfinished cousin. When I feel like I'm a part of a continuum that stretches from Kollwitz to Frasconi to Tobocman, from the Taller de Grafica Popular's graphic campaigns to those of us who go out at night with a bucket of wheat-paste or a pocket full of stickers... It not only gives me a real lift, it also challenges me to take the potential of this thing made with crumpled paper and shoplifted ink seriously.

What do you think about art as a commodity? If you sell your work, how do you decide the price of a piece?

Courtney Dailey: I hate the idea of having to sell things. I like to give things away or trade. I have sold some work before, but now I have pretty much stopped pricing things. It always felt wrong; the prices seemed too high or too low, and didn't honor the action of making it like I needed it to. Instead, I have figured out other ways to make money, so I can trade/share art that I make with people who like it. That feels better to me.

Swoon: Right now I am supporting myself from my work. I was a waitress for a lot of years and when the opportunity started to present itself for me to be supported by the things I was already doing, and loved, I was very ready. The gallery I work with is run by an enthusiast for the slightly insane, no questions, no restrictions, and on a base level my work has always been about getting obsessed by something and following it through. I am still divided about how much it costs to support myself and the things I make, and who my work is available to, but I love being flattened tired every day from working on my own wildest dreams and not from serving brunch. I hate the idea of what I am making being narrowed down to its value as an object for investment or sale. On the other hand, selling art has allowed me to realize larger and more difficult projects, which in turn is allowing me to grow as an artist and explore more terrain, so I can't knock it that hard. I'm happy.

Josh MacPhee: Unfortunately, we live in society where the dominant economic model is one where the value of things is defined by how much you can sell them for. This isn't a good thing, but I'm not a purist. I sell art because I don't how else to survive while making it. I pretty strongly believe that art should be affordable to people that are interested in it. Because the dominant art world has become so distant from mainstream US culture, most people don't conceive of contemporary art as a part of everyday life. In order to help get art back into people's lives and homes I like to make large runs of multiples (prints, etc) and price them extremely cheaply, usually between $5–$50 so that more of them go out into the world. I would much rather sell one hundred prints for $10 to make $1000 than sell one painting for $1000. Only one person feels attached to that painting, but one hundred people get to do something with the print.

Chris Stain: I think it is good if art is used to educate, uplift, or inspire. In my opinion art becomes soulless and loses its value when produced for commercial purposes—like selling cigarettes. I understand that people need to make a living, and maybe they are artists or designers by nature. It's a personal decision based on your conscience and what you want to contribute to life. I try to price my work reasonably so that most people can afford it. There are times

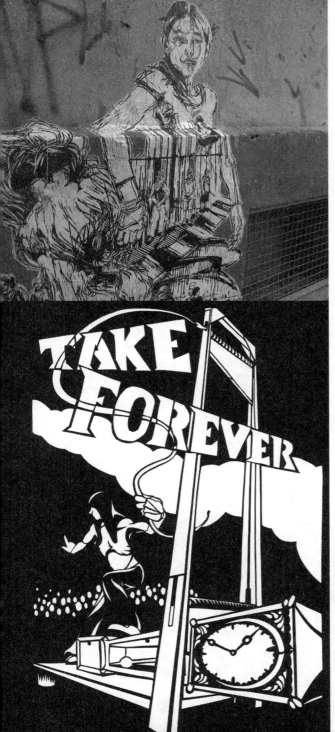

when I show at a gallery and they want 50% of the cost, and to make it worth my while I have to raise the price. The best thing to do is to put it on the street whenever I can. That way it is free for everyone and it will reach a wider audience than just those who visit a gallery.

Nicole Schulman: I work as a restorer for works on paper, where I am privileged to see some of the really sleazy art dealers in action. I once saw a beautiful large drawing by Ashcan artist Everett Shinn depicting an evicted family on the street with all their belongings in the gutter. The piece had been an illustration for *The Masses*—a left wing journal founded in 1911. The drawing was selling for something like $10,000. No one who could afford it would give a damn about the subject matter, and would probably buy it as an investment and put it into storage. It made me want to stamp "Not to be sold for the profit of scumbag art dealers after my death!" on all my artwork.

What do you think is the role(s) of an artist in society?

Miriam Klein Stahl: Troublemakers and beautifiers.

Pete Yahnke: To make amazing things that inspire and challenge people. To create a sense of possibility. I think this is a role for all people, not just those called artists.

Roger Peet: The role of an artist in society is to enrapture and enrage, if possible at the same time. The artist should also, if possible, try to make people laugh. For me artistic responsibility means respect for brutalized individuals or groups of which one is not a part of. It means serious consideration of the representations one makes of those groups and their histories. If you aren't a part of it, how can you know how to show it? I find it better to heap sarcastic vitriol on people I hate, than to extol the virtues of people I don't know.

Colin Matthes: Artists can tell stories of the forgotten, the under-represented, or the voiceless. They can tell stories not commonly told, or tell common stories with added beauty or complexity.

This page: top, Swoon, *Helena, Buenos Aires*, linocut pasted on the street, 2005; bottom, Roger Peet, *Take Forever*, cut paper, 2006; previous page: Chris Stain, *I Love NY*, stencil, 2006.

Morgan F.P. Andrews, *Stick Vs. Drum*, linocut, 2001.

Erik Ruin: I'm not entirely sure there is a role for an artist—at least not in my idyllic daydream of a future society. It's paradoxical, I know, because making art is pretty much what I live for. I guess what I'm talking about is all this nonsense I hear (in many circles) about the artist as the visionary, sacred image-maker/visual prophet whose production is so far removed from that of the craftspeople and construction workers, and is part of a "creative class," etc. So we're either all artists, or none of us are, or maybe the term needs to be redefined.

Shaun Slifer: This is like when people ask "what is art?" Even though I know what I think, I almost never know how to answer it. I'm always thinking about it because, I think, when you live a lifestyle where you surround yourself with other activists or progressive folks, there's often this underlying feeling of needing to prove that you're doing something, not just sitting around drawing shit when you could be volunteering with a group like the needle exchange. Still, I think the primary role of artists is as question-askers and tricksters, shouting forbidden questions and making things which challenge authorities and things-as-they-are. I think the best artists have shit on their shoes—they're running around in the middle of everything, they can't settle down, they can't shut up, and they can't quit fidgeting with everything.

Bec Young: My eternal dilemma is trying to make more time for my art. I always seem to fill my time with other projects, like running a community bike shop. Shaun's answer made me realize how important these things are to me, how they inform my art. I wouldn't want to be an artist without these experiences in my life, even though it takes me away from my art sometimes.

In the 1820s Comte Henri de Saint-Simon envisioned the role of the artist to "envision the future of society." In 1968 *The Black Panther* printed an article about the role of revolutionary art and wrote, "ART AS REVOLUTION: The Black Panther Party calls it revolutionary art—this kind of art enlightens the party to continue its vigorous attack against the enemy, as well as educate the masses of black people—we do this by showing them through pictures—The Correct Handling of the Revolution." What do you think of these statements applied today?

Morgan F.P. Andrews: Saint-Simon's quote puts the role of the artist in the realm of science fiction and makes me think of the gaudy pictures of a paradise imagined on the cover of some Jehovah's Witnesses pamphlet, with all these multi-colored humans rolling around in the grass with pandas and tigers. I hold these things up as a mirror to my ideals, recognizing that one person's envisioned future is not shared by all, and that the utopia that I yearn for might seem as unappealing as Hieronymus Bosch's crazed orgy of devils in the last panel of his "Garden of Earthly Delights" painting. It may be presumptuous for us to envision "the future of society," but to

APROXIME-SE DA PESSOAS COM UMA VARA

APPROACH PEOPLE WITH A STICK

ACÉRCATE A OTROS CON UN PALO

E ELAS FOGEM

AND THEY RUN AWAY

Y LA GENTE HUIRÁ

explore many possible futures via our art can stimulate a less didactic conversation about society.

Icky A.: During Saint-Simon's time I think there was an idea that increased technology and humanist enlightenment would lead to a world that got cumulatively better. We live on the other side of the A-bomb, three great wars, and the commodification of everything. So in response, I would say no. Some people have made powerful art that critiques the present day, some have made beautiful art that looks back, some make self indulgent art that laughs at any of these concepts, some people make amazing utopian art. But I think that statement is too calcified to apply today.

  As for the Panthers, I love Emory Douglas' art, and I love Chinese communist comic books, and that art style really worked for them. But that statement is really vague and vanguardist. It's important that people do political art that they are passionate about, that reflects their reality and pushes things, and it's important that art does something besides decorate a wall or go to a gallery. I think it's important that political art is understandable, its message is clear, but I have no idea what the "Correct Handling of the Revolution" would be.

Roger Peet: I think that Saint-Simon's quote today should include the word "annihilation" between the words "future" and "of."

  As to the second quote, well, one, there is no revolution. Two, there is no "correct" way to do anything, especially "revolution." With all due respect to the Panthers, I can't stand the way this preachy vanguardism sounds in any mouth.

Erik Ruin: I think both statements are exciting in their ramifications, and are thus useful constructs to compare and contrast your mission and work to, but are still pretty limiting. That said, I'd be excited to see more work either envisioning the future of our society, playing a direct instructive role in revolutionary struggle, or both.

Chris Stain: Personally, I have a hard enough time envisioning my own future and how I am going to support my family. What to speak of society? I think it's a statement based on an idealistic mentality, because if I cannot take care of myself, my family, and their needs, how am I going to be able to envision some utopia when the people around me are struggling? Art as revolution, like any other subject, needs someone who has the heart to create it, and someone who has the heart to receive it.

Bec Young: I think Chris' statement about art as revolution is really poignant. This is what I mean when I say that I don't think I can expect everyone to understand my work. Some will, some won't, and maybe some who don't now will understand it later. I just try to put pieces of my soul into my work and see if it makes sense to others.

Some activists believe art should only serve utilitarian functions. What are your thoughts on that?

ROXIME-SE
OM UM
AMBOR

PROACH
ITH A
DRUM

ÉRCATE
ON UN
AMBOR

E ELAS
CHEGAM
MAIS
PERTO

AND THEY
COME
CLOSER

Y ELLOS SE
ACERCARÁN
A TÍ

This page, from left: Courtney Dailey, *Please*, silkscreen, 2004; Colin Matthes, *Shopping and Soldiering*, silk-screen, 2006. Next page, from left: Shaun Slifer, *Arise (Moth)*, stencil, 2004; Pete Yahnke, *the flock*, linocut, 2006.

Bec Young: What is utilitarian function? Who decides what is utilitarian and what is not? Are we talking about only supporting weavers of rugs and throwers of pots that we use in our daily lives? Then tell me who these people are, because in the craft circles I've been in, most people are still trying to keep "craft" from being a dirty word of low esteem. Or are we only talking about printmaking? In that case, again, who is to judge if a print serves a utilitarian function? And even if there could be a fair way to judge that (which there isn't, because it's subjective), are artists to turn into productive automatons, churning out works that function with so much utility? I might as well do graphic design for Ford.

Shaun Slifer: I see art as a language, and as such multifaceted and diverse and encompassing anything you can get your hands on. Calling only for a more utilitarian art dismisses several decades of experimentation, the road where people challenge conventions and redefine "art." This is never utilitarian, but is necessary. Was jazz ever utilitarian? If people were concerned with music in that way, then it would never have evolved.

Josh MacPhee: Art is about representation, of either the outside world, or the inside worlds we all create in our heads and hearts. Artistic representation can be direct, an attempt to act like a camera and capture some sort of exact likeness of a person or situation, or it can be indirect, mythic, stylized, an attempt to capture a mood, feeling, movement, set of ideas, people in action. I think most people think of utility in terms of the first example, art should

purely represent a political idea, but it is often more useful if you expand the definition of what has utility...creating myths, complicating situations, getting the critical thinking process started. These are all potentially useful things

Morgan F.P. Andrews: There's this loose definition of permaculture as "anything that can serve three functions." I like to play this game where I pick up an object and determine how it fits the triple-purpose criteria of permaculture. I made these prints that had the words *Terra E Teto* on them—"Land & Roof" in Portuguese—and I sold them on this tour that raised money for an encampment outside of São Paulo. People bought hundreds of these prints and in doing so: 1. Helped to fund the building of

and some people today believe that art is a bourgeois excess. I think art can play a multitude of roles in our lives—as a form of resistance and a voice for people who are oppressed, as well as a way of recording history or as a means to bring joy and hope to people's lives. Leaders like Hitler and Stalin have understood this and have tried to instill fear into their citizens by banning art. There is a rich history of art serving to function as both a beautiful object and organizing tool. For example, some slaves in the US South sewed routes to freedom into quilts.

What do you think are the strengths and/or weaknesses of art that is explicitly political? Do you make art that is explicitly political?

Erik Ruin: I like much art that is explicitly political. I admire its clarity and lack of pretensions. Of course there is much art that is trite, clichéd, uninspired, poorly designed, or whose politics and/or framing of issues I disagree with. Too many violent images used too casually, too many images of our enemies, etc. I make art that is both explicit and implicit in its politics. One kind of work informs and strengthens the other.

Icky A.: Weaknesses—it can be alienating and dumb. Strengths—it can educate and agitate. It can move people to become aware and, hopefully, more involved. It can add a sense of beauty to a political movement. Sometimes dumb blunt messaging is what is needed.

Shaun Slifer: Political art is especially strong when it communicates on a personal level, and especially weak

a school, 2. Learned some words in another language, and 3. Had a nice piece of art to hang on their wall.

Nicole Schulman: I love anarchists who love to boss people around. Frankly I used to feel that way myself, but life is more complex than that. That way of thinking is fascistic. It's a mentality that says "if you can't eat it, you can't live in it, and you can't wear it—it's useless." I know there is art that is made to specifically be expensive wallpaper, or worse—an investment. I have no sympathy for that type of art. I believe that nonpolitical art has value, even if mine is very political.

Courtney Dailey: Art is utilitarian. I know a lot of people who cannot live without art, and without making art.

Swoon: To hell with "shoulds."

Meredith Stern: Over the years there are always people who devalue the importance of art and music; anarchists at the turn of the century, members of the Weather Underground,

when it makes people feel dumb or not hip to alternative subculture. A lot of it ends up being particularly alienating when artists use too much anger and lose the chance to empower or inspire. The immediate instinct in political work might be to scream but I don't think screaming is always the best tactic.

Pete Yahnke: I think that explicitly political art gets easily labeled as propaganda and thus gets dismissed. It is harder to pull off political work that isn't explicit and still conveys a message you hope it would, but then the viewer can bring their own experience to it.

Meredith Stern: When I was living in a dorm in my first year at college I had animal rights propaganda covering every inch of my door. Everyone thought I was insane. By the end of the year I felt like a failure in my inability to convert people to the cause of animal liberation. Meanwhile, I was working in a deli serving sandwiches and this kid, who had gotten meat sandwiches for weeks, started occasionally ordering veggie hoagies. I was so happy I overstuffed them. We started hanging out, talking about food, punk, and politics. He says through our conversations and many cooking dates he gradually decided to stop eating meat. I think there are a million methods to communicate—through direct or subtle language. It's a matter of who our audience is, and how we communicate, that determines the effect they may have.

How do you gauge the effectiveness of your work? For you, does this relate to your ability to express yourself? Does it relate to how an audience sees your work? Or are there other ways of judging your work?

Bec Young: I don't think I can really expect immediate understanding of my work. People bring as much of themselves to viewing and analyzing art as they do to anything else. This is true for everything, not just art. For example, I see a billboard for Starbucks and I think, "fascist homogenized monopoly." But that is all about me and my experiences. Other people see it and think, "the coffee there is really good." So I try not to take it personally, how people view my work. While I am working on it, I talk to people and try to get a sense of whether the message is totally lost or not.

Josh MacPhee: This is the hardest question in many ways. There's a catch-22 in here. On the one hand, by claiming

This page: Icky A., *Community Control*, linocut, 2006; next page: Swoon, *Strong*, linocut pasted on the street, 2005.

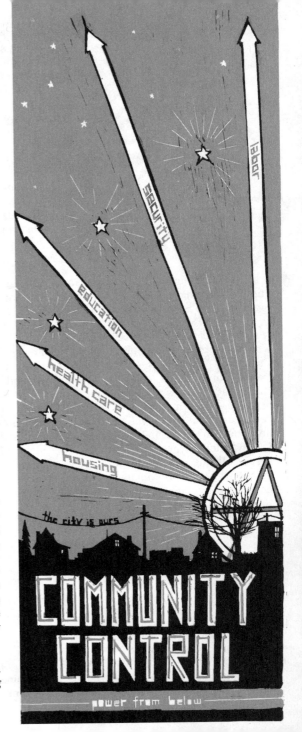

a piece of art is political, it takes it out of the realm of "pretty pictures" and adds some element of utility. Once there is a claim of utility, you can't avoid wanting to quantify that, to define what works or what doesn't. Otherwise what's the point of claiming politics? At the same time, art can't be boiled down to purely quantifiable factors; it is and always will be qualitative, that's what makes it art. And as long as it is qualitative, it is nearly impossible to define its effectiveness, because it has different effects on different people, and those effects might be extremely difficult to define. There is no doubt that 1960s counterculture, the music, art, posters, street theater, etc., played a role in the changes that happened to both individuals and the larger society, but it is almost impossible to point to one poster, or one song, that created that change. I'm not sure you can gauge the effectiveness of a single piece of art.

Shaun Slifer: It is a more or less even balance between my own screwy notions about how it looks and works, and other people's reactions to it once it's done. Some of the most fulfilling reactions are from children because they don't have a lot of baggage yet. Also, input from anyone who doesn't spend a lot of time thinking about art. I was setting up this big collaborative installation in this student center at a university a couple of years ago, and one of the janitors rolls by with all of his gear and asks if we're the artists. We said yes, he nodded, looked around for a second, and then said "So, this is about..." and basically completely nailed everything we were trying to do. It made me feel like I was not at all crazy, or in my own world. So often when we are thinking about art so much and surround ourselves with a lot of artists (and, if in school, professors), we only really get input from them on a peer to peer level, and not a lot of responses from the rest of the world.

Swoon: I hear a lot of surprising and wonderful things from some people, others walk right by without even seeing it. I don't really know what the word "effective" means here, but some people walking down the street, see it, and are affected. I get a few

boos and some pretty encouraging cheers when I am out putting up work. It's these interactions that I love. Actually the responses from people, in the form of emails and personal encounters, have meant an incredible amount to me, letting me know that I do reach some surprisingly far away corners. It's so encouraging.

Miriam Klein Stahl: I often put my work in places for free. If it all gets taken, I feel like it was successful.

I live in fear of ending up like my friend's step-mom. She was career waitress, who was diagnosed with Stage 1 breast cancer, it would have been curable... if she had been insured.

As a charity case, she received "experimental" treatment. The experiment failed, and she died.

This was not called MURDER, this was business as usual in the for-profit U.S. healthcare system.

America has the most advanced medical care in the world, and over 40 Million people can't get their hands on ANY of it.

FOR YOUR INFORMATION: Uninsured women between the ages of 50 and 64 are 40% more likely to DIE than privately insured women, and women ages 35-49 are 60% more likely to DIE than privately insured women.

-Kaiser Commission on Medicaid and the Uninsured, Uninsured in America: a Chart Book, Second Edition, May 2000.

Do you think of yourself as a part of an artistic movement? Why/why not? If yes, who are the people involved?

Swoon: I was just at a talk at the New School recently, and there was a lot of theory running in circles and it made me ill. Perhaps I'm an anti-intellectual, but the people I love build double-decker bikes and joust each other over puked-on mattresses. Everyone feels euphoric and insane, and no one stands around asking each other if it's art. This summer I am building a flotilla of rafts and taking myself and everyone I love down the Mississippi. To me it's all related—it's moving, so it must be a movement.

Roger Peet: If I am part of an artistic movement, it is a movement of the artistic lower bowel.

Chris Stain: I see myself as part of one of the many facets of the graffiti movement. It's made up largely of people who choose objects outside the house as their canvas. But not only due to placement of images, but because of the self-taught, do-it-yourself spirit that graffiti art offers.

Icky A.: There's a crew of us on the fringe of the anarcho-punk scene doing prints of a political nature, and I think things are coming together in some ways. Everyone is improving their skills and making bigger and grander prints. This group ties in vaguely to some post-art school street art scene, whose work is really exciting. I think there's a lot of intelligence and creativity in this larger group and I hope things will keep coming together.

Pete Yahnke: Sometimes it feels connected, other times it's really isolating. I think group shows like Paper Politics[6] help with the connectedness of it all. I used to be part of the *Blackthorn* Collective here in Portland and that was a huge collaborative process. I think the whole printmaking medium lends itself to collaboration. It's perfect for the co-op work shop due to all the processes and print runs.

Courtney Dailey: I feel connected to a D.I.Y. movement, on some levels, where participation is the important part, not the outcome of an action. The Bookmobile/Mobilivre is a huge collaboration in terms of people, geography, and scale of participation. I have been collaborating as curator and show organizer, as collective member of Space 1026 (communal studios and gallery in Philadelphia), as art-maker, as house-mate, for a long time, probably since high school.

Nicole Schulman: It seems there is a movement of political art and comics—perhaps it's because the internet makes communication much easier to work with people in different states and countries. I have collaborated with the *World War 3* folks—now in its twenty fifth year—both within the magazine and the activist offshoot—WW3 Arts In Action (*ww3artsinaction.org*). I owe all my artistic and personal development to them.

Chris Stain: I see myself as part of the self taught artist graffiti movement, made up largely of people who choose objects outside the house as their canvas.

What role do you think art plays in social change? What roles do you think art plays in our lives?

Swoon: I am in Mexico at the moment. I just came out of the mountains from a week in an indigenous village in the south. I was there with a couple of friends who have been working there for five years. The community has its own police force to protect themselves from government corruption and exploitation, and they are in the midst of building all kinds of other autonomous projects. My friends Abigail and Rafael went there originally to work on a mural which was supposed to take about six months but they have since lent their hands to all of these other projects which are about strengthening the indigenous communities in the area, and helping them build a slow nonviolent revolution from the inside. The other day Rafael said to me "Siqueiros and Orozco, they were good, their work documented life after the Mexican revolution, but Posada...he was the only one whose work was actually part of the process of revolution. That's what we want our work to be, part of the process." They are my favorite example of something real and working at the moment.

Roger Peet: Art has a role in social change. I know it does. Defining it is another matter. In contrast to the common dictum that holds preaching to the choir in mild contempt, I think that one thing that art does well in social movements is remind people that there are others out there [who] think as they do, or indeed, not as they do. Preaching to the unconverted is proselytizing, and I hate that.

Colin Matthes: Ideally, art can inspire hope, encourage critical thinking, capture emotion, and stimulate creativity. It can declare another way to think about and participate in living. Art can document or challenge history, create a framework for social change, and create a vision of a more just world. When art is used in activism it provides an appealing and accessible entry point to social issues and radical politics.

This page: Pete Yahnke, *who will take the mountain and give it to the sea*, linocut, 2006; previous page: Nicole Schulman, *It's Only a Matter of Time*, scratchboard, 2006.

Bec Young: The answers to this question are really interesting, because it comes down to social change versus personal change. Personal change is a microcosm of social change. I hope art does play a bigger role, I just don't know how. The question about personal change is so much easier to answer; it's one small person as opposed to a huge system. Sometimes it's easier to think of my art that way—to focus on transformation of one small space, or one person, rather than a massive, world wide change.

When creating an image how concerned are you with how an audience will interpret your image?

Colin Matthes: I am specifically concerned with how and if the audience thinks about the images, and the feelings they convey. I think my most successful work presents contradictory or complex relationships and/or personal narratives that, more than direct interpretation, encourage (hopefully critical) thought in the viewer. I am not looking to force an immediate reaction but to facilitate a thought process in a way. For instance, in one image a worker and an animal are chained together, leaving the viewer to consider their common predicament and how this situation occurs.

Meredith Stern: I recently worked a small local craft fair where I sold prints, some blatantly political and some more subtly so. One was a print with one hundred angry birds obscuring the sky over a city, grasping at buildings. It was titled *Birds of Prey: aka Real Estate Developers*. I found out later one of the buyers was this asshole downtown real estate developer who bought the print for display in a "sample loft" where new tenants can come to see how the space can be "made liveable." The idea behind my print was too subtle—it was lost with this guy. I'd like for people to be able to glean different meanings than I intend, but not to the extent that my work could be used to promote an idea opposite of its intended meaning.

Courtney Dailey: I hope that people will consider an image I make, that they will be generous enough to look at and think about it. That is all I can hope for. Where they go from there is beyond anything I can imagine.

1. Drawing Resistance was a traveling artshow featuring radical printmakers, postermakers, and painters. It was curated by Nicholas Lampert & Sue Simiensky-Bietela and travelled to over 30 cities from 2001-2005. For more info, see www.drawingresistance.org.

2. The Beehive Collective creates portable murals about globalization, based on feedback from the affected communities. For more info, see www.beehivecollective.org

3. The Celebrate People's History Poster Series is a growing collection of posters produced around people's history, points in the struggle for social justice. As of the printing of this book, 40 posters have been printed, including many by the artists in this roundtable discussion. More about the posters can be found at www.justseeds.org/cph.

4. The Street Art Workers (SAW) is a loose network of artists and designers that have a goal of using their art to communicate political ideas in public space through various forms of street art. More information about SAW can be found at www.streetartworkers.org.

5. *World War 3 Illustrated* is a political comics magazine that was started in New York City in 1980 in response to the election of Ronald Reagan as president of the US. Formed by Peter Kuper and Seth Tobocman, WW3 has served as an outlet for radical art for comics artists, graphics producers and illustrators from around the world. For more info, see www.worldwar3illustrated.org

6. Paper Politics is an exhibition of nearly 200 political prints by as many artists. It was curated by Josh MacPhee and all of the artists in this discussion have prints in the show. A catalog documenting the exhibit is available at www.justseeds.org.

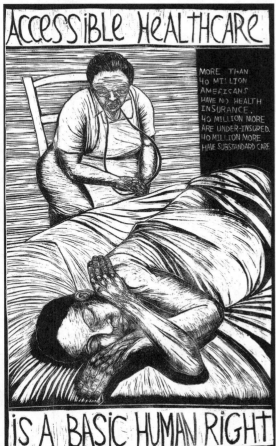

ACCESSIBLE HEALTHCARE

MORE THAN 40 MILLION AMERICANS HAVE NO HEALTH INSURANCE. 40 MILLION MORE ARE UNDER-INSURED. 40 MILLION MORE HAVE SUBSTANDARD CARE

IS A BASIC HUMAN RIGHT

laughing at clouds

This page, clockwise from top left: Bec Young, Cathartic God of Grief (Deities We Need series), 2006; Miriam Klein Stahl, unmarried, linocut, 2001; IckyA., Spring Fever, linocut, 2006; Roger Peet; Laughing at Clouds, stencil, 2006; Meredith Stern, Health Care is a Right, reduction linocut, 2006. Previous page, from top: Colin Matthes, Cells Dominance Either Burning This One Security, silkscreen, 2006; Josh MacPhee and Shaun Slifer, Winter in America, silkscreen pasted on street, 2005.

Printmaker Biographies:

Icky A. is a printmaker who lives in Portland, OR. He publishes the zine *Nosedive*.

Morgan F.P. Andrews began carving woodblock prints as a means of rehabilitation from a degenerative retinal disease and soon began using his blockprints as a vehicle for telling stories. He has made prints for numerous organizations and publications, and sometimes turns them into scenery and characters in puppet shows that tour the globe.

Courtney Dailey lives and works in Philadelphia, making things and things to do. Some are: Space 1026 (collective art studios and gallery), projet MOBILIVRE-BOOKMOBILE project (traveling book/zine exhibition), the Year of Queer (curatorial project), *the Odyssey* (video and print zine). Courtney is invested in the future (cautiously).

Josh MacPhee is an artist, curator and activist currently living in Troy, NY. His work often revolves around themes of radical politics, privatization and public space. *Justseeds.org*

Colin Matthes lives in Milwaukee, WI and makes drawings, prints, installations, and zines. Recent projects include *Everyday Transactions*, which considers connections between business, warfare, and leisure, and *Animals and Workers*, exploring relationships between animals and workers in food production. His work can be viewed at *Ideasinpictures. org*.

Roger Peet is a recluse in a log cabin on a mountainside in southern Oregon. He does some public art here and there, as well as rude and largely incomprehensible puppet shows. Write him: 37081 Tiller Trail Hwy, Tiller, OR 97484.

Erik Ruin is a Minneapolis-based, Michigan-raised printmaker and shadow-puppeteer. He is also a member of the Prison Poster Project and Barebones Productions.

Nicole Schulman is a frequent contributor, and occasional editor of the collectively-run *World War 3 Illustrated* magazine. Her comics and illustrations have been printed internationally in such publications as *The New York Times*, *The Progressive*, and *Inguine Mah!gazine* (Italy), and she is the co-editor of *Wobblies: A Graphic History of the Industrial Workers of the World*. Her work has been exhibited across the United States and Europe, as well as Tel Aviv, Hebron, and Seoul, South Korea. She was born and raised in New York City, and continues to live there. *Nicoleschuman.com*

Miriam Klein Stahl is the co-founder of the Arts and Humanities Academy at Berkeley High and Another

Country Free Press. She is committed to educational reform and creating free art.

Shaun Slifer works in whatever media he can get his fidgeting hands on. He was raised in Nebraska and Tennessee, and currently resides in Western Pennsylvania, where he tries his best to remember his dreams every morning.

Chris Stain grew up in Baltimore and got into graffiti when he was really young. His art is based on his upbringing and the common struggle of all working people.

Meredith Stern is a printmaker who recently co-curated the *Pocket Change* group show. She lives in Providence RI, where she is currently working to help establish cooperative housing.

Swoon is an artist who fell in love with printmaking about six years ago, when she discovered it to be a medium with which she could make life-sized, graphic, reproducible images with just an ink roller and her own stockinged feet dancing across the block (in lieu of a printing press), on the floor of her tiny Brooklyn apartment. She highly recommends that you try it.

Pete Yahnke was born in Milwaukee, WI in 1975 and grew up in Oconto Falls (population 2,500), an old paper mill town in the northern woods of WI. Primarilly a printmaker and musician, he has traveled across the US, Canada, Mexico, and all of Europe, by foot, bike, freight train, passenger train, plane, bus, broken down vans, boats, panel trucks running on vegetable oil, and luck. He has worked as a deconstructionist, truck driver, furniture mover, telemarketer, housepainter, beet harvester, collective café cook, dishwasher, black and white custom photo printer, personal caregiver, farmers' market seller, delivery driver, produce warehouse worker, fence builder, mechanic, grocery stock clerk, construction laborer, demolition laborer, advertising designer, gas station attendant, espresso maker, hay bale thrower, window factory press opera-

tor, diaper factory worker, and hole digger. Pete currently resides in Portland, OR.

Bec Young is an artist living in the post-everything rural city of Detroit, Michigan. Despite the current state of affairs, she still stubbornly believes in the transformative power of art. When not making art, she can usually be found performing puppet shows, running a community bike shop, practicing reiki, or tending her lovely beehives.

This page, from top: Courtney Dailey, *What We Do #1*, silkscreen, 2005; Josh MacPhee, *Buck the System*, stencil, 2006. Previous page: Erik Ruin, *Crowd Scene #3*, stencil, 2005.

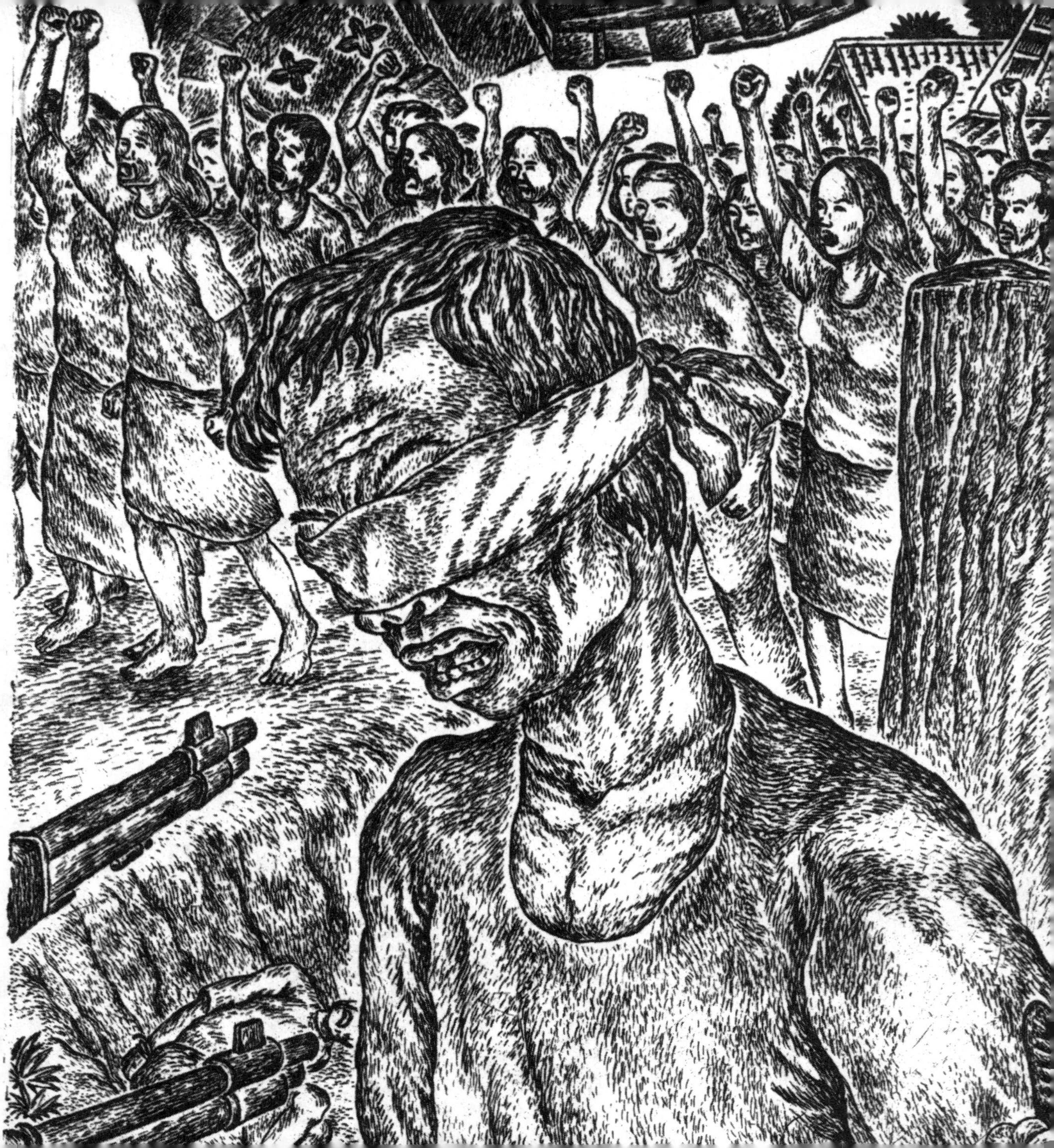

TARING PADI: UNDER SIEGE IN INDONESIA

ROGER PEET

Indonesia is many worlds in one. Tens of thousands of islands, hundreds of languages, vast mountain ranges, forests, cities, and the ocean in between. Likewise it has a multitude of histories rolling through it on a million different wheels—some small as molecules, others like an army of bulldozers.

Indonesia's colonial masters, the Dutch, left the country after World War II. For the next twenty years it was run by President Sukarno, a leader of the independence movement under whose quasi-benevolent tutelage grew a large communist party and sympathetic population, thus angering the US government.

In 1965 after an abortive coup, Sukarno was removed from power by Major General Suharto who promptly initiated what can only be called a genocide against the nation's communists. Funded, trained, and armed by the US, army and paramilitary units fanned out across the archipelago, slaughtering whomever had acquired the communist taint. The worst massacres were in Java and Bali, two of the most densely populated islands. In Bali, the massive population loss was cynically manipulated by the national government and the state departments of several western nations, notably France, to lay the foundation for the grotesque tourist industry that currently blankets the island with dilute cultural tat and desperate street-level capitalism.

Life ground on under Suharto for thirty years. Separatist rebellions in Aceh, Maluku, Papua, and East Timor received further blessings of brutality from the government. In 1998, something finally changed. Massive street protests rocked the nation's cities. The people of Indonesia let out a cry of "Enough!" heard around the world. Suharto reluctantly loosened his grip, and stepped down.

The aftermath of the regime's end is a history of political alliances forging and fracturing on a national scale. Associations emerged from beneath the corpse of authoritarian rule and clamored for power and possibility. A share of the action was suddenly within reach. In the run-up to elections in 1999, factions painted the walls and facades of the cities with exhortations to allegiance, color-coded red, yellow, and green.

Had you been walking the streets of Yogyakarta, a large city in central Java, at that time you would have seen dozens of black and white posters—block prints, woodcuts, and pen and ink drawings slapped up over the electoral color schemes. The posters would have been full of people; images of hands and faces and bodies, fighting a common enemy and defending a common interest. You'd sit down to eat in a street-side food stall and there'd be a stack of photocopied zines and comics on the bench next to you, full of imaginative skewerings of the powerful and the wannabes, something to chuckle at and ponder while you ate your *nasi gudeg*. Maybe you'd turn a corner and see a banner twenty-foot square, swarming with images of people dissatisfied with choices that meant nothing. All this art would be marked with a logo featuring a sprig of rice, a star, and a cog.

Meet Taring Padi, a loose collective of cultural fulminators based in Yogyakarta (Yogya for short). Art students, meatball sellers, bicycle-taxi drivers, propagandists par excellence. Some members of the group are writers, some are musicians. Some are puppeteers, gardeners, parking attendants. They work anonymously, reflecting their focus on *Seni Kerakyatan*, or people's art, essentially a concept that seeks to promote the social messages within the art over the individual popularity of the artist.

For eight years Taring Padi have been hacking their way out of the strictures of national culture left behind by the Suharto regime, inviting whomever has an inclination to join the fray. They are definitely not alone in their struggles—they share members, resources, tactics and strategy with counter-cultural nexi across the archipelago. For a number of years they squatted the former campus of Institut Seni Indonesia, an art university abandoned in 1997. The large campus functioned as a living space, community gathering center, and workshop for six years. There were gardens, animals, printmaking equipment, gallery areas and space to hold parties. Although recently evicted, their energy is still massive, and they continue to kick out the projects. This interview took place with Taring Padi member Tony in February of 2006.

On May 27th, 2006, a massive earthquake (6.3 on the Richter scale) struck near the city of Yogyakarta. Over 5,000 were killed, almost 40,000 were injured, and over half a million homes were destroyed or damaged. In the aftermath of the earthquake, Taring Padi have set up a "*posko*" or distribution point for food, construction, and medical supplies in their neighborhood, where 80% of the houses have been completely destroyed.

This page: Yusuf, *Multicultural of the Rich*, linocut, 2003. Next page: Surya, *Untitled*, lithograph, 2004.

Unfortunately Taring Padi does not currently have a website to collect international relief. Donations can be sent to Taring Padi, care of the author. They can be contacted directly through their member Yusuf at tajamwangi@yahoo.com.

————

How long has Taring Padi been around?

About eight years. During the period of Suharto's breakdown, there was a lot of action and art going on here in Yogya. In 1997 the art school that a number of us were attending moved campuses to a newer facility, leaving the old one vacant. We took it over and turned it into a collective space, an art factory of sorts. That was the squat. It was an amazing place. Now that we don't have it anymore, people have been saying that Taring Padi is dead. And yes, we lost a lot, but we still do a lot of work supporting farmer associations, labor associations, other collectives in Indonesia, especially Java. We're not interested in making overtures to the major media, and this makes a lot of people think that as a group we're finished. But we've had exhibitions in Malaysia, in Singapore, we toured and had exhibitions in support of actions going on in Europe. Now we've joined up with an independent arts festival in Sydney, and are doing exhibitions with friends from Bandung and Jakarta. We've also worked on a forest arts festival with some friends from up north, supported and organized an alternative media festival here in Yogya, and made a street art festival in Jakarta. We work within our communities in Yogya too. So, when people say, where is Taring Padi, is it over? No! We still go for it every day.

Recently one of our group was chatting with friends from Jakarta, they asked him what Taring Padi is now, communist, anarchist? We are free! Some people continue to study communist authors, but I think generally we are more anarchist. We had people who were very close to the Young Communist party, and we are still close to them, but not like before. We are not participants, not party members. But we can still sit down in Taring Padi, the communist and the anarchists. We don't spend much time finding out ideologically where people come from, the farmers and other people that we work with. If they're independent and want to talk about problems, subjects of interest to us, then okay, we can get together.

What happened to the squat?

We had heard that the city government wanted to use the building for some other purpose; one plan was to build a mall there, another was to use the building for a high school. The school plan was the one that they chose. They made it clear to us that they wanted us out soon, and we wanted to resist but didn't really feel up to facing the military. We asked them if we could act as caretakers for the building in the interim period, while the plans were being finalized, because plans for development like this take a long time to actually happen here. They just wanted us out. We were in Australia doing an exhibition when we heard that people from the neighbourhood had broken in and stolen everything; they took the doors, the windows, the floor tiles, all the beautiful hardwood trim. It was an old building, well built. They also took the plumbing, the wires, all the fixtures—gutted it, basically. We told the government, "you should have let us be caretakers, that's what we were already doing. Now you have a ruined building to show for it."

So Taring Padi is in a state of transition now?

Yes. Before, in this group, we had a president, a vice president, a secretary, like officers in the politburo. It was very hierarchical. All that is changed now. Taring Padi has become more of a community of people, whereas before we were a cultural institution. We don't have membership anymore, just activists. In 2003, we had a big meeting and critiqued our methods. We decided we didn't want to have a process of approval for members. Anybody who wants to can join this project and work with us.

      Inside the collective mind of Taring Padi, a lot of people started to get a hold of a more libertarian ideology—anarchism, individualism, something like that. At this point we still have a treasurer who keeps track of the money, but we're no longer centralized. You can connect directly with anyone to find out about the group. We do have a spokesperson, but that's just a central point from which to share information. Anyone who has the time or inclination can be the voice of the organization.

So, are there specific campaigns that Taring Padi is working on right now? You mentioned all those festivals, what do you do at them?

Taring Padi is a generalized machine. We try not to focus on one point, on single issues. For us, obviously, there are a lot of problems in Indonesia and the world right now. We do art campaigns about organic farming, farmer's rights, land rights, biodiversity, governmental complicity in illegal logging. We know that all this is very complicated. We try to include as much historical background in the works as possible, and to do printing and distribution ourselves. We all meet together and decide to make something, be it a

poster or a painting, something to promote the event, something to act as a sort of educational medium for the issues being discussed or celebrated.

We are currently planning new projects—we want to do something about the bombings in Bali. And we're going to make big paintings for the *warung nasi*, the street food stalls.

How so?

A lot of the food stalls that set up at night have tarps or cloths that they hang up to make an enclosed space. These are usually painted with a list of what's on the menu, and pictures, you know, chicken, goat, duck, fish, whatever. Most people use the commercial sign painters in Yogya to do their images, but we are going to get people to let us do paintings for them, and include motifs and information of our own. These will refer to various social justice issues, historical issues, the hidden things of daily life,

bring them back into the open by displaying them on the walls of the places people eat everyday.

That's brilliant. Any other projects like that?

We've made a series of stickers, anti-militarist, anti-globalist themes, that are the size and shape of the cheap matchboxes. We go around to the kiosks, get their cases of matches, and make them into little propaganda units. Everybody uses those matches. Lots of projects are underway. In Yogya right now we are planning murals, doing a lot of stencils. A lot of young people here are getting into that.

Have there been repercussions from the work you all do, from the government or police? From the Islamic fundamentalists?

Well, we try to be careful. The general political situation is moving to the right, becoming more conservative. When we were still in the squat we were attacked by the fundamentalists a couple of times. They beat people. They brought swords.

Swords? Like knives?

No! Swords, man! Big fucking swords! Very long, and sharp! And they brought clubs and came into the squat on motorcycles and attacked.

Why do the fundamentalists hate Taring Padi?

During the period of reformation, after the fall of Suharto, the political situation here in Indonesia went through a lot of polarization. People started to define themselves more clearly; who is fundamentalist, who is liberal, who is socialist, everybody took sides. After Suharto left a lot of the common people came out into the open and started to take an interest in political power. People wanted to stake claims on the available political power in specific areas, and formed militias. There was a big increase in paramilitary activity. One day, we had a run-in with this local motorcycle gang, and a friend of mine lost a kidney from the stomping they gave him. Afterwards we were trying to find out why they attacked us. We went to the head of their organization and had a meeting with him, mediated by a friend of ours from a legal NGO. The response to our question, 'Why?,'

was the classic stigma applied to us: You are communists, anti-god, you use drugs and prostitutes. We were able to use a certain degree of diplomacy in that situation, explain that we're making art for their communities, and he eventually started denying that his group had attacked us at all. Fuck you man, they had your logo on their clothes!

We discovered that the military had been talking to the various fundamentalist groups, telling them that we were atheistic communists and should be punished. So it's possible that was what was going on with the motorcycle gang as well. Some of my friends moved away after all of that.

The military is still very powerful here, and the national right wing and the fundamentalists are growing too. There's a lot of Taliban in Indonesia now, since the US invaded Afghanistan. It's traditional for the government and the army to use fundamentalist groups to do their dirty work. When South Maluku province, which is a predominantly Christian area in the east, declared independence, the government used local and imported Muslim militias to crush the provisional government. There was a terrible war there, in Ambon, which is still partitioned like Belfast or Cyprus. This tactic is a colonial legacy from the Dutch. Political desires and differences are turned into religious war.

Is Taring Padi working on anything pertaining to the recent cost-of-living increases?

It's a complicated issue, of course. There has been a recent massive rise, nearly a doubling, of the price of gas and electricity and, perhaps most importantly, rice. Gas here in Indonesia is nationalized; one state corporation is in charge of all production and distribution. They have responded to the current global situation by pegging fuel prices to the so-called free market price, with the result, of course, that prices soar, and they take massive profits in both export and domestic markets, and the people get the shaft. It's similar with the rice. A lot of rice is being exported, stockpiles are being depleted, and the price has nearly doubled here at home.

We organized some protests and made a bunch of posters. It's inspired some of us to focus on learning more about alternative energy sources, and how to communicate those possibilities.

Can you give examples of campaigns you've worked on that you think have been successful?

We worked with some groups in the north of Java on reforestation, replanting disturbed areas. Our street art projects—the murals, stencils and graffiti—these are quite successful. We work with a lot of independent groups, getting images and information out on a street level. We worked recently with a group of organic farmers on a scarecrow festival, trying to make a better scarecrow that might be able to communicate something as well. That project was partly responsible for some of the recognition organic farmer associations are getting right now, some support from government agencies.

Some things that haven't been successful?

A lot of the time we are guilty of being too optimistic. We'll make exhibitions of our print art and nobody will come, or nobody will come from the social realms we think would most enjoy or benefit from this artwork. We have to work, sometimes, at being satisfied with lesser results, being able to say "good enough."

Finally, can you explain what Taring Padi means in English?

Rice Fang. *Padi* is the word for rice in the field, and *taring* means sharp tooth. The *taring padi* are the sharp little spines sticking up from the end of the rice stalk as it matures. They'll stab you.

API KELAS PEKERJA

TAK PANTANG KERJA KECIL
TAK GENTAR KERJA BESAR
'AYO BERGERAK'

WOOD BLOCK   FIRE OF LABOUR   YUSUF

127 POET

This page: Yusuf, Fire of Labour, linocut, 2003. Translation: Spirit of the Workers; Don't ban the little jobs, don't fear the big job, 'Let's Move!' Previous page, from left: Yusuf, The Culture of Heroism is a Culture of Violence, linocut, 2003; Surya, Untitled, lithograph, 2004.

MOVING IMAGES AND INTERVENTIONS

A MAGICAL LAND OF ROVING SANTA CLAUS ARMIES, PIRATED ENERGY DRINKS AND A GIANT SQUATTED URBAN VILLAGE: POLITICAL ART ACTIVITIES IN DENMARK

BRETT BLOOM

Denmark is a tiny country of islands, fjords, and peninsulas cumulatively jutting out northward from the coast of mainland Europe, a veritable gateway to greater Scandinavia. Its population numbers around five million. Once a place where the people of the country decided to provide themselves with universal health care, free university education, housing for everyone, and other social services, Denmark is now a fading social democracy. In recent years, Denmark's democratic optimism has been darkened by a right-wing, nationalist, anti-immigrant erosion of the infrastructure of the welfare state and what was once a more open, welcoming society.

Denmark has a rich history of creative anarchistic and anti-authoritarian collective practices that have often sought to push the relatively progressive country further than what was acceptable to the mainstream majority. Very little of these activities are known outside of the country. They rarely have much presence in official national historical narratives either. I will discuss some of the actions of Palle Neilsen, Christiania, Solvognen, Den Eksperimenterende Kunstskole, Kanonklubben, Tøj Til Afrika Løgstør, YNKB, Blekingebanden, Superflex, N55, and Copenhagen Free University. Some of these groups have managed to circulate their ideas widely with a great deal of success, however, their work is not often enough linked into a historical narrative and cohesive set of ideas and practices.

The stories here begin in the late 1960s, though their roots reach further back and proceed through time and shifting attitudes to the present.

Shifts are very visible in the ways in which people did or did not record their activities. A lot of the earlier work is poorly documented because people believed that they were in the midst of a range of revolutionary, cultural and political struggles. They were living in the moment and not concerned about how their actions would be perceived in the future. It was common that people didn't consider their work as art, but instead felt that they were creating much needed change on the societal level. It was more important to people like the founders of Christiania, Solvognen, and Palle Nielsen to go out and do things that affected real change than it was to make a career out of their creativity. It also may have never occurred to some that documenting their activities might be highly valued today. This is contrast to more contemporary groups like Superflex and N55 that are well documented and move comfortably in and out of art and political contexts. One thing that binds all of the groups together over the generations is an acute understanding of how their ideas circulate virtually and symbolically.

This discussion of documentation opens a window into the perceived conflicts between creativity and politics. Art and activism are often framed in opposition to one another or as having separate sets of concerns and ends. But when brought together with the goal of trying to find new approaches to the problems facing society, the most powerful qualities of both can be joined for a greater impact. Political art is frequently dismissed for either not being political enough, or not being aesthetically detached from real world events; it often sits awkwardly in the middle of both more unabashedly political actions and overtly aesthetic ones. Political organizations demand that their visuals be in service of their stated goals, whatever these might be, but this art, created solely as propaganda, tends to be very conservative in form, even reactionary at times, rejecting more experimental approaches. This is a fundamental problem with the ways in which political organizations, particularly leftist and radical ones, instrumentalize art. The fight for new forms of social reality, ones that reject exploitation, war mongering, and unjust economies, should more openly involve art and creative activities that themselves are attempts to articulate new kinds of social formations or that try to envision the world differently. At the same time, the dominant social and economic sphere of art production and reception, the art world, is so thoroughly controlled by the market that most political art has been actively excluded from museums, galleries and histories.

We all exist deep inside a frenetic globalizing market economy. Capitalism has infected almost every square inch of the globe, and it is not just our material world that is affected—the social relationships that bind us together are deeply manipulated by capitalism. This leaves us no "outside of the system" from which to work. Whether willingly or not, every space we inhabit and every action we take is related to our complicit, if sometimes unconscious, participation in the machinations of capital. This means that no matter where we stand, it is a legitimate location of struggle. Working in museums and galleries can be just as important as working in the streets, department stores, rural farms, etc. There are no privileged places of resistance; every space can and should be contested.

There have been many highly compelling and imaginative political art works, initiatives, and movements in Denmark that sought to bring about new social formations through their very articulations.[1] Many of the stories told here are about attempts to rebuild or reorder the world in ways that are more just, more egalitarian or seek to dismantle abusive, hierarchical elements of society. Most have been subjected to the kinds of marginalization and dismissal by both the art world and the political realm discussed above. It is with a sense of urgency and excitement that these stories are recounted here.

Palle Nielsen[2]

Palle Nielsen dropped out of the painting class at the Royal Danish Academy of Art in the late 1960s. He then began worked alongside local activists, architects, and students from the Copenhagen University to surreptitiously build children's playgrounds. Nielsen designed playgrounds for the courtyards of buildings in underprivileged parts of Copenhagen and the surrounding suburbs. He would organize activists and the residents of the buildings to help make and install the playgrounds. Nielsen and his colleagues would arrive early in the morning at a public housing building, wake people up, tell them what they were doing, and by the end of the day they would all have collectively erected a hand-made, wooden playground.

Nielsen later was "invited to Stockholm [Sweden] to participate in the organisation of *Aktion Samtal* [Action Dialogue], a series of courtyard interventions with the purpose of expanding children's liberty of action."[3] This was in the late spring of 1968. While there, Nielsen met the head of the Moderna Museet, a museum of modern and contemporary art in Stockholm. Nielsen convinced the director to let him and a local activist network take over the museum for three weeks. They turned the museum into a giant social and pedagogical experiment with and for children, calling it *The Model for a Qualitative Society*. It ran from September 30–October 20, 1968. The installation was done with the intent of radically activating the children's imaginations and fostering the liberating social configurations the children could come up with in an environment that was as free as possible from the influence of adults.

At that time, the museum was a single large hall. Nielsen and his colleagues installed sheets of masonite on the floors and constructed walls for children to paint and modify in other ways. They built jungle gyms for the children to play on

---

1. The reader will notice a lack of discussion of Fluxus, COBRA, and the Situationist movements—except in relation to the activities of Copenhagen Free University (see below). They all had strong Danish iterations. They are mentioned briefly in this text, but only when necessary, as they are well documented elsewhere. Their strong international networks are one reason they have been given more attention. This text gives space to lesser known, but equally important activities, many of them happening simultaneously. It also starts at a point in time after Situationist activities had ceased.

2. This segment comes from many conversations over the years with Lars Bang Larsen, but most importantly his extensive research and the essay "Play and Nothingness: The Model for a Qualitative Society, an activist project at the Moderna Museet, Stockholm, Sweden 1968," in *Magic Moments: Collaboration Between Artists and Young People*, edited by Anna Harding (London: Black Dog Publishing, 2005.)

3. Ibid.

4. Ibid.

and covered the floor with chunks of foam in varying color, thickness, and hardness. The children were provided with paint, tools, and materials to build with. Other structures were built for the children to play on and change over the course of the exhibition. Turntables and loud speakers were put in each corner. An eclectic range of records was provided for the children to choose and listen to.

The exhibition was free for children, only adults had to pay. An enormous number of people attended *The Model for a Qualitative Society*. Estimates are that nearly 35,000 people came during those three weeks and 20,000 of them were children. The crowds were so large that an additional playground had to be built outside of the museum. Halfway through its planned run, Stockholm's fire chief shut down and removed the exhibit, claiming that the foam was a fire hazard endangering the children. Nielsen and company took this as a political provocation. They rebuilt the entire exhibit and reopened the show. After the exhibition ended at the museum, the playground was reinstalled in an inflated tent in the nearby city of Västerås, Sweden.

Nielsen saw the building of playgrounds as a direct alternative to street demonstrations. There was a huge lack of resources and imaginative spaces provided for children, and this was a place to concretely affect change. Instead of pressuring the city council or other local politicians for playgrounds, or protesting until such structures were provided, they took action into their own hands. Bang Larsen describes the liberatory potential that Nielsen saw for the playgrounds like this:

> Parents and the middle-aged, isolated in flats somewhere in the suburbs, were politically and existentially speaking, done for, lured into the ideological traps of consumerism and the nuclear family. However, as an act of revolution-by-proxy the adults could provide their children with a free space, unfettered by urbanism. Thereby the children could be empowered with the possibility of a freedom from which capitalist indoctrination had cut the adults off.[4]

Nielsen described himself to me when we met as an "ethical anarchist." This is useful for thinking about the work Nielsen and his colleagues

were doing with the playgrounds. They were not waiting for the bureaucratized numbness of "representational democracy" to give them permission to address their and others' needs, but took action with useful and potentially liberating results. Their goals took into consideration how their means would impact, and ultimately enhance, the lives of everyone involved, not trusting or waiting for the state or the market to create change.

Christiania

Copenhagen is a wealthy northern European city with a population of over one million people. It is one of the most expensive cities in the world to live in, given the combined high costs of housing, food and transportation. It is a bit jarring the first time one walks from Copenhagen into Christiania. One can easily feel a physical and ideological shift in the surroundings and goings-on.

Christiania describes itself as a "Free Town"—a place "free" from the dominant culture outside. It is located in the center of Copenhagen. It sits on an estimated eighty-five acres which served as a military base until 1971. It has been in use throughout Denmark's history and contains everything from World War II bunkers, old ramparts that date back to the twelfth century and even a medieval moat. Nearly one thousand people currently live there. The grounds are inter-

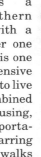

This page: *Christiana, you have my heart*, Christiania, 2006. Photo: Brett Bloom; next page: Slumstormers break through the fence to Bådsmandsstræde barracks and establish Christiania, 1971.

spersed with old military barracks and numerous experimental houses. Copenhagen's building codes have seemingly been left at the entrance, and the homes here range from the novel use of materials to frighteningly dilapidated shacks. One house has an entire two-story wall made of old windows and other repurposed materials. Another diminutive two-story house floats on one of the moats. Nearby is a house that looks more like a spaceship than a typical dwelling. The town boasts restaurants, bars, music clubs, bike shops, a bakery, horse stables, a recycling and reuse center, and more. Christiana has its own local currency and flag. The grounds are open to all visitors who are respectful. None of the gates to the numerous yards throughout the free town are locked. Another thing that distinguishes Christiania from the rest of Copenhagen is that it is entirely car-free.

Christiania started with exuberance and optimism, inspired largely by the youth movement of the late 1960s and an earlier squatter movement in the *Christianshavn* (Christian's Harbor) area. A visitor's guide to Christiana from 1999 tells the remarkable story that the town was started, in part, because a handful of people attended and participated in an art exhibition that greatly inspired them. The show was called *Noget for Noget* (Something for Something). The guide states that "all sorts of hippies, freaks, and people into macrobiotics showed themselves off, sold their goods, and exhibited their art including theater, pictures, and happenings."[5] Rather than displaying art objects, it was the exchange of ideas and goods that were at the heart of the show. It was

5. *Christiania Guide* (1999).

6. *Christiania Guide* (2005).

7. Ibid., 7.

8. Kim Dirckinck-Holmfeld and Martin Keidling, "Learning from Christiania." In *Learning From Christiania* (Copenhagen: Arkitektens Forlag, 2004), 11.

9. Ibid., 5.

10. Mercer Human Resource Consulting ranked Copenhagen as the eighth most expensive city in both 2005 and 2006.

mounted at Charlottenborg, currently a prominent place for artists to show their work. A magazine called *Hovedbladet* (Head Magazine) served as a catalog for the exhibition. The magazine included many proposals for what could be done with the then abandoned barracks sitting empty behind heavy-duty walls. In response, some people decided to break through the walls and occupy the barracks. The guide states "the article resulted in a massive immigration of people from all sectors of society, who came to create an alternative life based on communalism and freedom." These efforts to squat the military base and create Christiania began in late 1969, but it wasn't until 1971 that the efforts paid off and the town was born.

Christiania is governed by "consensus democracy." There are meetings to deal with all aspects of life in the free town. These include a Common Meeting, which all Christianites are invited to attend, as well as more specific meetings that cover business, economics, building, and more. Christiania is divided into fifteen regional areas and each one has a local monthly meeting to address localized concerns.[6] Christiania manages its own buildings, trash pick up, and other municipal concerns. They pay a price for greater autonomy:

> Christianites pay electricity, water, heating and taxes like everybody else. But we don't get as much for our taxes as everybody else, because we handle the task like kindergartens, youth clubs, renovation, postal services and maintenance of our whole infrastructure, green areas and much more ourselves.[7]

The free town used to be in charge of its own planning; a law from 1989 exempted Christiania from Copenhagen's strict zoning and planning regulations. A 2004 law rescinded the earlier one, removing the exemption so that all building and planning activities from that point on had to be done in accordance with that of all the rest of Copenhagen. This latter law is a part of a long cycle of attempts to "normalize" Christiania.[8]

Danish governments have attempted to reintegrate Christiania into the rest of Copenhagen several times since its inception. The future of the free town is increasingly uncertain as the most recent attempts, including the above-mentioned law, has been more prolonged and sustained than any others. Right-wing politicians and some citizens of Copenhagen harbor deep-held resentments against the inhabitants of Christiania. The place is:

> A nagging pain for the political right, which has never forgotten that the establishment of Christiania took place by those who took the law into their own hands in 1971 and with a judicious mixture of slum storming, flower power, free hash and loosely interwoven left-wing groups, broke through the Bådsmandsstrædes Barracks area...[9]

Christiania was a victory for the left in the culture wars of the 1960s and 1970s. Now that the right is in power, they want to take it away.

Those who want to dismantle Christiania have already won some victories towards normalization. Christiania had an open-air drug market for several years, charmingly referred to as "Pusher Street." Hard drugs, like heroin and cocaine, had been outlawed, but you could easily buy hash there. These days, locals using or selling hash in the open are routinely arrested and harassed by the Copenhagen police.

There are other forces exerting pressure on Christiania as well. Copenhagen is in the throes of a long term housing crisis, and is doing very little to adequately house its poorer citizens. They are being pushed to the outlying areas of the city—a phenomenon one can readily find in an increasing number of cities around the world. Efforts to preserve Copenhagen's medieval character have created an attitude that adversely limits the kinds of development and urban planning that are possible, with disastrous effects for poorer residents. For instance, high-rise housing is not allowed. New apartment buildings can only be built to the regulated height of five floors above the ground floor. The city has increasingly become a place for the wealthier inhabitants of the country. Several recent lists ranking the world's costliest cities put Copenhagen in the top ten.[10] The area around Christiana has seen an explosion in exorbitantly expensive luxury, which makes the land of the free town highly valuable and desirable. There are many who scheme ways to evict its inhabitants and make a lot of money through new development.

There is a need for more affordable places like Christiania. It costs each inhabitant 1000 Kroner (approximately $170) per month regardless of how large or small their living accommodations are. This money goes to meet the municipal needs of the free town. This fee is well below the market norm for Copenhagen, which various estimates put around 3500 Kroner per person per month. Christiania has served its inhabitants well by providing them with a very affordable housing option in a city that has done little to protect those most vulnerable. The free town is also a glaring reminder of this fact to the city government.

Christiania is important to many well beyond its borders. People come from all over the world to visit. Christiania boasts nearly one million visitors per year and spends no money advertising itself as a tourist destination. This undoubtedly brings money and revenue to both local businesses in Copenhagen, outside of Christiania proper, and tax dollars to the city government. It is interesting to compare the number of visitors to Christiania to that of Tivoli Gardens, a major Danish attraction and one of the oldest amusement parks in the world, in the center of Copenhagen with an estimated four million visitors a year. The contrast is quite impressive given the humble, counter-cultural roots of Christiania.

Solvognen

The Solvognen theater group existed from 1969–1983. Its motley players were lively and often cantankerous inhabitants of Christiania. The group took its name from an important Bronze Age object called the Trundholm Sun Chariot, which embodies pre-Christian Danish cosmology. Solvognen were an outward expression of Christiania's values. They used their theater activities to both critique the rest of Danish society and to suggest new social, historic, and economic relationships. In addition to more traditional theater performances, Solvognen took their activities into the streets of greater Copenhagen, and even rural Denmark, sometimes with infamous and hilarious results.[11]

11. An exhaustive history of Solvognen's activities exists, but only in Danish: Nina Rasmussen. *Solvognen: Tales From Our Youth* (2002).

12. Email to the author.

13. Several generic stories of anarchist Santas handing out goods from department stores have floated around activist oral histories for a long time. Interviewees for this essay believed that Solvognen's actions were inspired by those of King Mob, a group active in London in the 1970s. One former member of Solvognen, Nina Rasmussen, denied that there was any influence from King Mob or any group. It is difficult to either confirm or deny this. King Mob were anarchists inspired by a gritty, nihilistic Situationism (modeled loosely on the New York based group The Family—also known as Black Mask, and later Up Against the Wall Motherfucker). King Mob's Santa Claus action, which likely happened in 1967 at Selfridges department store in London, was met with brutal police repression and children were forced to give the items back. This King Mob action had in turn been inspired by The Family's "mill-in at Macy's."

14. Greenland is a self-governing territory of Denmark. It first became a Danish colony in 1953. Greenlanders are often of Inuit descent, an indigenous population that has second class status in Denmark and it seems like parallels were being drawn by Solvognen between the plight of Native Americans and indigenous Greenlanders.

15. *Christiania Guide* (2005), 4.

16. This account comes from Finn Thybo Andersen in an interview conducted at his apartment in Copenhagen in October, 2005.

17. The founding members were: Ole Sporring, Mogens Nørgård, Lene Adler Petersen, Susanne Hartig, Alfred Friis, Niels Nedergård Pedersen, Per Ehrenberg, Søren Keil, Jørgen Tang Holbæk, Lise Kragh, Birgit Diemer, Emma L. Nielsen, Carsten Nash, and Finn Thybo Andersen—from Lars Bang Larsen "Cannon Club Days," *NU* no. 3 (1999), 57.

One of their most notorious actions happened in the winter of 1974 with their *Julemandshæren* (The Army of Santas). Around one hundred people dressed as Santa Claus and took part in a weeklong series of activities trying, as Nina Rasmussen put it, "to do good things as a Santa should."[12] Originally conceived of as a campaign against unemployment, one of their activities just before Christmas received a great deal of attention throughout Denmark, and has become legendary beyond the country's borders. Around forty Solvognen members dressed as Santa Claus and went into Magasin, one of Denmark's most prominent department stores. They took items off the shelves and proceeded to hand out the items to the customers of the store as "gifts."[13] Both the employees of the store and the customers receiving gifts were very supportive of the action. They knew the Santas weren't real employees of the store, but the costumes, the generosity, and the sheer number of Santas created an atmosphere that made everything seem acceptable. For a short time the Santas turned the economics of Christmas upside down. Unfortunately the police were eventually called, and they dealt with the *Julemandshæren* severely. There are estimates that the police arrested thirty-five or more Santas. A photograph of one Santa being beaten by a police officer appeared in every Danish newspaper across the country. This propelled the troupe into instant notoriety and helped spread their radical Christmas cheer.

Another infamous Solvognen play was *Rebildaktion* in 1975. It was a large outdoor theatrical attack on the Danish celebration of the American Bicentennial. It took place in the Rebild Hills in northern Jylland. Solvognen dressed as Native Americans, African Americans, and Greenlanders[14] and crashed the staid official celebration. Some of the players rode in on horseback and were joined by several hundred protestors. They were demonstrating "against the American policy towards minorities, the poor, and the Third World."[15] Once again they were met with brutal hostility by Danish police. The violent arrests received international attention via news outlets all over the world. Solvognen were masters of creating spectacles that would rapidly snowball into a media storm that spread their message farther than their actual actions ever could.

Den Eksperimenterende Kunstskole

Den Eksperimenterende Kunstskole (Experimental Art School) began in 1961. It was posited as an alternative art school, a place to introduce foreign ideas and practices—at first these were the conceptual and minimalist works coming from New York. The first class started in 1961 and lasted until around 1966. It was never officially a part of the The Royal Danish Art Academy, which stubbornly only offered its students rigorous training in highly traditional forms of art making like painting and sculpture, each in their own separate schools within the university. The social structure of the school was patriarchal and old-fashioned; students were required to rise from their seats when their professors entered the room. The Academy was stodgy, inflexible and didn't even have a photography or film program at the time. It was ripe for change and questioning.

Julemandshæren passing Copenhagen's City Hall, 1971. Photo: Nils Vest

Some of the people involved in the first class of the Experimental School saw it as an extension of the Academy, while others saw it as an alternative to the Academy. The structure of the school was more open and was set up to foster discussion and the exploration of new ideas in contradistinction to the kind of training one would get at the Art Academy. Den Eksperimenterende Kunstskole eventually turned into something more akin to an artist group—often pejoratively referred to as the "Hard Boys" because of the severity in which they would engage those who didn't agree with their ideas and practice. Several of these artists went on to be highly commercially successful.

Not everyone was satisfied with what the Den Eksperimenterende Kunstskole had become. Poul Gernes and Troels Andersen, involved with the first class, helped start a second class in 1967. That class lasted one year. Classes were held in the evenings and still served to introduce new ideas. Each person was responsible for introducing new things to the others. This second class introduced its teachers and students to Situationism, Fluxus, Happenings, and other new developments in aesthetic and political practice. It was the only place these young art students could get access to any information about this work and have a place to discuss it. Situationist inspired *dérivés*, aimless drifts through different emotional zones of cities, were an important and frequent tool for aesthetic investigation at the school and many such walks were a part of their curriculum.[16] The Experimental School dissolved in 1968 due to "the political question"—the feeling that the times demanded more political forms of expression than the Den Eksperimenterende Kunstskole offered. Some of the members of the second class were instrumental in forming a new group that came to be known as the Kanonklubben.

Kanonklubben

Relatively inexpensive Super 8 cameras were commercially available by the end of the 1960s. In 1967, former members of the Den Eksperimenterende Kunstskole and other students from the Art Academy, 14 people total, pooled their money and purchased a camera.[17] They called themselves Kanonklubben (Canon Club) after the camera maker. Kanonklubben started largely because there were no facilities for making photographs or films at the Academy. They sought to establish their own school within the Academy, and opened it to all students and professors. The camera they purchased was collectively-owned and available to all the members of the group. They made many short movies, for which they established simple yet austere rules, most notably that all the editing of the films had to be done in-camera as the shooting took place. Editing after shooting the film was discouraged.[18] Everyone in the group eschewed more traditional forms of art making, though at least one person secretly continued to paint and draw at night.

In addition to their filmmaking activities, Kanonklubben did several other projects. Kanonklubben's membership was almost entirely women, with a handful of sympathetic men. Together in 1970, the group realized the first feminist exhibition in Denmark called *Damebilleder* (Lady Portraits).[19] Though they did not call it feminist at the time, they were concerned with women's issues and investigating different aspects of gender. The realization that they were doing feminist work came much later. The exhibition *Damebilleder* predates the more well known *Womanhouse* exhibition (Los Angeles, 1972), often lauded as the first feminist group show. For *Damebilleder*, Kanonklubben produced several "portraits," or tableaux, of what women were stereotyped to be. The components were: The Hooker, The Dishes, The Beauty, The Wedding Cake, The Defence, The Coats, The Camp, and The Party. The Hooker included all the female members of Kanonklubben taking turns dressing up as prostitutes and sitting in a store window at night for one hour each with a red light on in the fashion of the red-light district in Amsterdam. One tableau was a recreated beauty parlor. Another component involved the decoration of an entire small build-ing—an art space in a building from the WWII era that they rented—as a giant wedding cake complete with mannequins of a bride and groom perched on top. The group made short movies documenting each aspect of this project.

Later in 1970, two members of Kanonklubben, Finn Thybo Andersen and Per Bille, were singled out from the group and invited to Norway for the Young Biennial at *Kunstnernes Hus* (The Artists' House) a very prominent exhibition of the art work of young Scandinavian artists.[20] Kanonklubben decided that the two should accept the invitation, as well as take the production money that was being offered to them. At that time, only individual artists were invited to participate in exhibitions like this, not groups or collectives. Andersen and Bille accepted the invitation as individuals, but turned around and extended the invitation to some of the members of Kanonklubben,[21] as well as other political artists and radical activists. They bought fifty round trip tickets to Oslo for everyone. This larger loose knit group went to Norway

This page: Kanonklubben, *Osloturen (In Oslo)*. Previous page: Kanonklubben, *Osloturen (On the Boat)*, Oslo, Norway, 1970. Banner says "People of the World Unite." Photos: Finn Thybo Andersen.

18. Interestingly, this self-imposed austerity was echoed in the 1990s by the Dogma filmmakers (started in 1995 by the Danish directors Lars von Trier, Thomas Vinterberg, Kristian Levring, and Søren Kragh-Jacobsen), though there is no direct link between the groups of filmmakers. The Dogma collective, like Kanonklubben, operates by several austere, strict rules of filmmaking, which include: films must be shot with handheld cameras, natural sound and lighting must be used, filters aren't allowed on the cameras, and so on. A complete list can be found at <http://www.dogme95.dk/the_vow/vow.html>.

19. Rikke Diemer, Birgitte Skjold Jensen, Kirsten Justesen, Jytte Rex, Marie Bille, Jytte Keller, Lene Bille, Kirsten Dufour were the members of Kanonklubben that headed this project with support from the others.

20. Finn Thybo Andersen, in an interview, contends that they were singled out because the Biennial wasn't used to dealing with groups and chose him and Per Bille arbitrarily.

21. They didn't invite everyone from Kanonklubben as the group had already started to split.

22. "Cannon Club Days," by Lars Bang Larsen, in *NU* no. 3 (1999), 60.

23. This segment comes from an interview conducted with Finn Thybo Andersen and Kirsten Dufour in their apartment in Copenhagen, February 2006.

as Kanonklubben's contribution to the exhibition. The group travel itself became the art piece for the Biennial. They referred to it as *Osloturen* (The Oslo Trip). This was a highly experimental project for the time and was met with a lot of confusion by the Biennial's organizers. Initially the directors of the exhibit would not let everyone in, insisting that only Thybo Andersen and Bille were invited. They told Kanonklubben that they had to pay to see the exhibit, to which they received a chorus of: "We are the exhibit!" Several rounds of negotiations ensued and the board eventually allowed everyone to come into the exhibition. During the course of these negotiations, Kanonklubben occupied several city spaces with actions and banners. They occupied the rear entrance to the Oslo Stock Exchange and unfurled a banner reading, "People of the world unite!" They did this in multiple locations, creating a spectacle and disruption everywhere they went. Later in the evening, as an extension of their project for the Biennial, and as a compromise with the exhibition organizers of the Biennial, Kanonklubben held a large party in the countryside. They handed out fliers all over Oslo and got a huge turnout for the event. They made a Super 8 color film documenting the entire trip.

Kanonklubben only lasted for a short time. The *Osloturen* was a turning point for the group. A lot of young people in Denmark were dropping out of art and moving towards radical political work and the members of Kanonklubben were no exception. Some started putting their energy into squatting abandoned buildings, some in the group wanted to use it as platform for their careers, while others were more hard-line with their politics. This splintered the group into several directions:

> Kanonklubben split up into other project and work groups—among others, squatters and the production and painters collective Østen er Rød [The East is Red], the ragpicker group Tøj Til Afrika [Clothes for Africa], and feminist art groups.[22]

Some of those who went on to have successful careers actively denied that they were involved with Kanonklubben. Others weren't so embarrassed about their youthful exuberance and important experimentation.

Tøj Til Afrika Løgstør[23]

Two members of the group, Finn Thybo Andersen and Kirsten Dufour eventually dropped out of the art world altogether in favor of more direct political efficacy. Copenhagen was too expensive and they wanted to buy a house, so they left and moved to northern Jylland. They bought a farmhouse where they were visited by a steady stream of hippies and other travelers. Their move to the countryside was inspired by the back to the land movement, the advent of land art, and Mao Tse-Tung's call for people to move to rural areas. They were also interested in creating new audiences for their artwork and ideas. The artist Allan Kaprow highly inspired them to become "un-artists"—a term that he came up with. They were interested in giving up art practices, and as Kaprow said, creating new kinds of practices. Andersen knew Kaprow's ideas from discussions in Den Eksperimenterende Kunstskole and Kanonklubben.

They eventually helped form a group called Tøj Til Afrika Løgstør (TTAL) in 1975.[24] The group's main activity was ragpicking—collecting discarded and unwanted clothes that were then sent overseas to people working in revolutionary struggles in Third World countries—specifically the Eritrean revolution. They held giant flea markets up through 1986 as a way to raise money to send to revolutionary groups. TTAL claimed a Marxist analysis of the world and believed that they could strangle capitalism via solidarity with Third World resistance movements such as ZANU (Zimbabwe) and ERA (Eritrea). TTAL was typical of many revolutionary groups of the time, and was very authoritarian in structure, with a select inner group that provided leadership and direction for everyone else.

Over time the couple began to suspect that their ragpicking was a cover for a more radical set of activities. Andersen and Dufour increasingly wanted to do support work for their local political context and they increasingly became openly critical of TTAL and its authoritarian tendencies. The leadership wasn't concerned with the local situation, and once they learned that Anderson and Dufour had become critical of the group, the leadership told the rest of TTAL to be suspicious of them, not to talk to them, and that they could not be trusted.

TTAL blindly supported Stalinist dictatorship in the Soviet Union, and were equally uncritically opposed to American capitalism. Andersen and Dufour saw little difference between Soviet and US imperialism and were heavily criticized for this position. And it wasn't just a problem with the TTAL, they also became disillusioned with the movements they were working with in Africa. They, too, were extremely authoritarian and beholden to the Soviet Union.

As more people became increasingly critical of TTAL it began to unravel. Ragpicking was exhausting work and people were worn out from doing it for many years. As members split from the group they started doing yoga and focusing on their personal needs and not solidarity with others. They started having families and devoting energy to them. Andersen and Dufour decided to go back into the art world and start a small art school. They

began holding drawing classes with other artists as well as spending a lot of time doing their individual artwork.

YNKB

After roughly two decades outside of the art world, Finn Thybo Andersen and Kirsten Dufour Andersen returned to Copenhagen to re-engage, informed by the knowledge of experimental and radical ways of working they developed over the years. Around 2000, they put out a call to all the artists living in their local area to talk about making an art space and doing work collectively. They helped co-found a space in the Ydre Nørrebro (Outer Northern Bridge) neighborhood called YNKB (Ydre Nørrebro Kultur Bureau). They made *dérivés* through their neighborhood to look for parallel cultural and political initiatives that they could partner with and draw attention to.

YNKB is a space for meetings, film screenings, art projects, informal symposia, and campaigns. YNKB has published numerous small books related to their programming, research, and initiatives. The books chronicle a variety of projects and histories of work that haven't received much attention in the art or political worlds. One publication documents the adventure playgrounds in Copenhagen, and another documents a raid on a squatted house just down the street from YNKB.[25] The largest of these publications is about a conference and several actions that were done to agitate for the creation of a cultural center in an abandoned freight hall in the neighborhood.

The push to convert the freight hall is YNKB's most ambitious initiative to date. They have been fighting for the conversion of the old hall, which is owned by a Danish state-run company called DSB, into a multi-use art and cultural center. Ydre Nørrebro is one of Copenhagen's most diverse neighborhoods. The hall is on some of the only remaining open land in all of Copenhagen. In order to put pressure on local politicians, YNKB has held meetings, organized symposia, initiated letter-writing campaigns, and created guerrilla art projects. This included putting up giant speech bubbles made of painted wood on the building, making it appear as if the building itself is saying that it wants to be turned into something more than a site of land spec-

From top: The first Tøj Til Afrika Løgstør fleamarket, in an old dairy in Bislev, 1979. The bales are used clothes being prepared for shipping to refugees from Zimbabwe in Tanzania; TTAL participants in the fleamarket. Photos: Finn Thybo Andersen.

ulation. Their efforts have stalled DSB's attempts to sell the property to private developers who want to build luxury housing. The aforementioned book documenting their activities around the freight hall was also sent to local politicians and community leaders to push them to advocate for the art space. The building still sits open, rotting, waiting.

Blekingebanden[26]

Blekingebanden didn't directly arise out of an artistic practice, though it included many dropouts of the art and squatter scenes. An underground guerilla organization, they stand out for their highly creative approach to militant political action. They enjoy a legendary status—very similar to that of the better-known Baader-Meinhoff group in Germany—and captured the imagination of a lot of Danes. For a long time they received a great deal of public support due to the media's dissemination of news of their actions. They are most known for a series of daring bank robberies, the last one resulting in a police officer being shot and killed.

Blekingebanden got their start, before any of their high profile activities, in the Communist Labor Circle (KAK), a Maoist political splinter group from the Danish Communist Party (DKP). They left the DKP in 1963 over disagreements on issues of Third World independence. Danish anarchist and activist Rasmus Bjerre writes of KAK's split from the DKP:

KAK supported autonomy from Moscow and was of the opinion that as long as the industrialized countries oppressed the global south, the working class in the industrialized countries could always be bribed into passivity. This meant that until imperialism was forced back, no crisis could ever create a revolutionary situation in the privileged parts of the world. The anti-imperialistic struggles in the global south should thus have first priority—also in the political work in the privileged parts of the world. Because of the symbolic importance of China at the time, both as an example of a successful anti-imperialistic war and as an example of third world independence from Moscow, these quite widespread views were often somewhat confusingly dubbed Maoist at the time.

In 1978, this group split again and formed another group, calling themselves Kommunistisk Arbejdsgruppe (KA) (Communistic Labor Group).

KA was founded by seven people: five men and two women. KA didn't become known as Blekingebanden until a famous raid on one of their safe houses on Blekingegade (Blekinge Street) in Copenhagen. Later two more men joined the group. Around 1980 they began to withdraw from the rest of the anti-imperialist left. They were very smart about how to go about doing more militant work. Bjerre writes:

They all led normal lives and had normal jobs. They had also all quit all other activity on the left several years before engaging in their first money raising activity and were thus completely anonymous people.

They undertook the first robbery in March of 1983. That spring, they handed over the money to the Popular Front for the Liberation of Palestine while at meetings in Cyprus and Damascus, Syria. In fact they never kept any of the money they stole for themselves, but always put it towards causes they supported. All of their bank robberies were well planned so that they would avoid hurting anyone. However, their last robbery in November of 1988 went horribly wrong. They were in a gunfight with the police and a police officer was shot to death. The members of the group got away and were on the run for several months.

Four arrests of KA members were made on April 13, 1989. They had been under surveillance for a while and were aware of it. The police had been unable to track down evidence connecting the members of the group to the bank robberies. There was a stalemate. Those who were arrested would not talk to the police. The police couldn't find any evidence in their apartments, work places, or other areas of their normal lives.

24. TTAL was part of the larger TTA organization, which in turn was a member of the Kommunistisk ArbejdsKreds (KAK) (Communistic Labor Circle). See section on Blekingebanden below for more about KAK. TTAL separated themselves from the main TTA organization in 1979.

25. Adventure playgrounds are common throughout Northern European countries like Denmark, the United Kingdom and Germany. They are typically places where kids are given free reign—with some adult supervision—to build their own playgrounds out of scavenged wood and other recycled materials. These playgrounds are not to be confused with the ones Palle Nielsen was building. These were mainly built by children with the supervision of adults.

26. This segment is heavily indebted to the research of Ramus Bjerre, who conducted an interview with a former member of Blekingebanden upon my request. It is heavily paraphrased from an email that Bjerre sent to me. I have also included lengthy quotes from this email. Only Bjerre knows the identity of the interviewee. Many of the former members of the group want to put their past behind them, and won't talk about their activities in Blekingebanden. The interviewee is active with Bjerre in a political group in Copenhagen. The interviewee is still under surveillance by the Danish government and is considered a threat.

One of the free members of the group was in a mysterious car accident on May 2, 1989, in the countryside north of Copenhagen. The crash left him permanently blind. The police found keys in his possession, and suspecting his involvement in KA, they searched for a long time for the place they went to, eventually discovering the Blekingegade safe house. The police raided the safe house and found many documents connecting the group to the activities they were suspected of, as well as some plans for actions that hadn't been carried out. This included a several hundred page research document created in preparation for kidnapping the son of a Swedish billionaire who was the owner of the Tetra-Pak company. The plan was abandoned in 1985, because one of the group members was too nervous at the last minute to go through with it. Everyone else accepted this. In fact, if anyone ever wanted to back out of an action, the group accepted it with no reprimand.

Those who had been arrested were kept isolated from each other for two years. The police tried to play them off of each other, getting one to snitch on the others, but it didn't work. Ultimately the police were unable to establish who did and who didn't take part in the various activities of the group.

Eventually seven people were brought to trial. They were only convicted of one bank robbery, their final one and the biggest in Denmark's history. They had been charged with three other heists and planning another, but there wasn't enough evidence to convict them. Bjerre writes, "There is little doubt that some people connected with the group conducted these actions, but it was impossible to establish whom." The seven were convicted May 2, 1991 and the main actors received sentences of 10 years each. The authorities were unable to establish who had killed the police officer, so no one received a conviction for anything other than robbery. There was public outrage over this outcome. Bjerre concludes, "I don't think any of the former members of the group regret what they did, but they don't talk about it, and as far as I know, only one of them is active on the anti-imperialistic left today."

Superflex

Superflex is Bjørnstjerne Christiansen, Rasmus Nielsen, and Jakob Fenger. They began working together in school in the early 1990s. They chose to incorporate their art group as a for-profit corporation while still at the academy. They are both a group of artists and a legal business entity with all the social privileges both kinds of organizations enjoy. This allows them to move easily between both business and cultural realms. In an era of increased economic globalization, trade liberalization, and reductions in subsidized cultural spending throughout Europe and the West, this was both a timely decision and an understandable response to pressures of the historical moment.

Major global shifts were underway when Superflex formed. The European Union (EU) was established in 1992 as a way to compete with the market dominance of the US. Quickly it became a tool to enact a homegrown European neoliberalism, which meant a standardizing of goods, currencies, and anything else getting in the way of smoother trade. At this time, First World countries like Denmark were undergoing major shifts from manufacturing-based economies to service industries and

YNKB, *The Freight Hall Speaks*, Copenhagen, 2006. Word bubbles say: "I can be used for experiments. Good idea." Photo: Finn Thybo Andersen.

the production of immaterial labor. As information, rather than hard goods, became the commodity of primary value, who owned the information became increasingly important. With this shift, the importance of copyright and patent law increased exponentially.

Superflex saw that they could better enter the field and debate around neoliberalism and intellectual property if they were perceived and treated as a business rather than as a group of artists. Concomitantly, it was by choosing to continue to work as artists that their business dealings could more rapidly enter the world of symbolic combat and mass spectacle via the kind of media and cultural outlets the art world offers. Their decision to work as an incorporated art group reflects the near total encroachment of the market economy into all

This page: Superflex, meeting with farmers from Maués, Brazil discussing the production of *Guranna Power*. Photo: Superflex; next page: Superflex, Copyshop, Copenhagen, Denmark, 2005. Photo: Brett Bloom.

aspects of our lives. Their resistance to this is based in their counterproductive agenda in both the business and art realms. While they do produce art objects, installations, and other things to look at, this is usually done in a broader context of providing some kind of service or information.

Superflex formed before the Seattle protests in 1999 and the rise of global resistance to destructive corporate globalization, but their practice is a part of the sophisticated global resistance movement (whether they see themselves in this way or not). Their own type of resistance comes from their desires and willingness to figure out effective strat-

egies for contesting abusive corporate monopolies and intellectual property rights absurdities, even if that means looking and acting completely different from traditional leftist, activist organizations. Their activities aren't recognized as direct action or typical protest art and instead are disguised as business practices. It is because they are incorporated and use the language and form of business that they can infiltrate that world easily and avoid recognition as artists or protestors.

Superflex has been working against the strictures of profit-seeking intellectual property rights through a variety of projects and initiatives. *Guaraná Power* (2003) was initiated with guaraná farmers from Maués in the Brazilian Amazon rainforest. Transnational companies have had a destructive effect on the market for guaraná, driving the price for raw guaraná down by 80% while maintaining the price for their own retail products made from the fruit. Inspired in part by Mecca Cola, the anti-Coca Cola and anti-American soda developed in France, Superflex worked with the farmers to copy the formulas of the drinks produced by the conglomerates, and then to make their own drink. Superflex goes to great lengths to make their pirate activities clear and public. Their intentions are summed up by what Anupam Chander, a law professor at the University of California, Davis wrote about the process of designing a label for Guaraná Power:

Together with the community Superflex designed a label for the drink. The label reflects Superflex's belief that global brands can be used as the "raw material" for a "counter-economic position." Thus, the label slaps on top of the AmBev Antarctica logo a bold black-and-white "Guaraná Power" sticker, obscuring most of the Antarctica logo. In the background is a photo of members of the Maués community.[27]

for products that take copying as their point of origin and as a strategy for fighting global brands that establish exploitative relationships with their employees, suppliers of natural resources and historical knowledge, and consumers. Superflex writes this about the COPYSHOP:

> COPYSHOP challenges intellectual property. COPYSHOP is a place where you can photocopy everything from text to images. We use this name for a shop and information forum which will investigate the phenomena of copying. In COPYSHOP you will find products that challenge intellectual property. It can be modified originals, improved copies, political anti-brands—or a SUPERCOPY as the new original. COPYSHOP will discuss the control of value in the same place where it is produced and distributed: the market. As an active player the function of COPYSHOP will be as an ordinary shop. Furthermore, COPYSHOP will function as a gathering point and network for a diverse group who share a critical view on intellectual property.[28]

The new drink is produced directly by the farmers who are consequently able to get more out of their guaraná. It also contains more guaraná than the corporate soda giving an even stronger energy kick to anyone who drinks it. Guaraná Power is sold in several bars and cafes in Denmark, directly competing with the drink it has copied.

Superflex uses the strategy of copying to undermine the power corporations hold in the market and to try to create situations that are less abusive and more empowering for groups like the farmers in Maués.

Superflex has also set up COPYSHOP. Informed by the open source software movement and other challenges to the encroachment of copyright fanaticism into all aspects of our lives, it is both a physical store with products for sale as well as a platform from which to wage a symbolic battle against the corporate dominance that effects so many aspects of our lives. It is a clearinghouse

The COPYSHOP is one part of a larger headquarters the group has. They maintain a compound which houses an internet television studio, offices, working space for the group, and COPYSHOP. Sitting on the corner of a busy walking street filled with foot traffic, it looks and acts like a normal shop, but quietly insists on another way of doing things.

N55

In 1994 a small group of ten people started a non-commercial exhibition space and lab in a small storefront at Nørre Farimagsgade 55 in Copenhagen's Nørrebro neighborhood. Soon after, the group held an alternative to the Danish national elections called *Frit Valg* (Free Choice). Members of the group walked around Copenhagen with a megaphone, handing out ballots and encouraging people to come to their storefront. Another megaphone was affixed to the outside of the storefront, which was set up as a polling station where people could fill out the ballots. The questions on the ballots were related to discussions the group was having with the Danish philosopher and logician Peter Zinkernagel around issues of human perception and existence.[29] By posing a completely different set of ideas for the Danish public to discuss and vote on, *Frit Valg* was a challenge to the thinking behind the official elections. The group didn't believe that they would upend the election, but call into question the very ideological underpinnings of it. This was enough of a threat to bring the Danish Secret Police out to conduct surveillance on the group for several months.

Soon after *Frit Valg*, the group from Nørre Farimagsgade 55 reorganized and consolidated membership. Their smaller configuration allowed them to work in increasingly concentrated ways to the point of formalizing their group allegiance as N55 (shortened from the address of their space) in 1995. One of the first things the new group produced together, though work had begun on it before, was a terse and compact text formulated in conjunction with Peter Zinkernagel. The text is called *Art & Reality*.[30] It tries to think about the possibilities for discussions about art that are not subject to personal opinion or fashionable theory, and seeks to draw out the inherently political undertaking of making art. One challenge it offers us is to think about the "concentrations of power" that pervade every aspect of our existence:

> Concentrations of power do not always respect the rights of persons. If one denies this fact one gets: concentrations of power always respect the rights of persons. This does not correspond with our experiences. Concentrations of power characterize our society. Concentrations of power force persons to concentrate on participating in competition and power games, in order to create a social position for themselves. Concurrently with the concentrations of power dominating our conscious mind and being decisive to our situations, the significance of our fellow humans diminishes. And our own significance becomes the significance we have for concentrations of power, the growth of concentrations of power, and the conflicts of concentrations of power.[31]

From this, they conclude:

> It is clear that persons should be consciously aware of the rights of persons and therefore must seek to organize the smallest concentrations of power possible. Examples of concentrations of power which have interests in art include: Mass media (represented by journalists, critics, etc.), capital (represented by collectors, gallery owners, etc.), governments (represented by politicians, civil servants, etc.), and science (represented by historians, theorists, etc.). One can not permit these concentrations of power to have decisive influence and at the same time respect persons, the rights of persons or art.[32]

The text posits a central argument that it is impossible to not talk about art in relation to the objective conditions and logic of everyday life. The text asks several basic questions for the reader to consider,

relying on the concept of "logical relations." If one is to talk about art, she must take into consideration logical relations, which the group credits Zinkernagel with discovering. Logical relations are simply things that are so basic that one cannot meaningfully deny them. We can't deny that we have a body or that gravity affects a ball when we drop it. The text posits that we can't think about art without thinking about bodies, other persons, concrete situations and a range of other things. N55 sought to contest the prevailing postmodernist theory of the time that insisted everything was subjective and open to interpretation when this contradicts some of the fundamental things we have in common with one another. There are some basic things about being persons that we can't deny and N55 believed this was a starting point for building a different and more liberatory politics.

Logical relations are related to language through what Zinkernagel called "the conditions of description" upon which it is possible to talk rationally about the world. They are the presuppositions upon which all knowledge is built and how we collectively make meaning. *Art and Reality* puts it this way:

> Logical relations are the most basic and most overlooked phenomenon we know. Nothing of which we can talk rationally [about] can exist, can be identified or referred to, except through its logical relations to other things. Logic is necessary relations between different factors, and factors are what exist by the force of those relations. The decisive thing about logical relations is that they cannot be reasoned. Nevertheless, they do constitute conditions necessary for any description, because they cannot be denied without rejecting the factors of the relations.

N55 insists that if we pay closer attention to our logical relations to the world and to each other that we can begin to organize life in a completely different way. It is through an appeal to logical relations, rather than fashion or changing subjective whims of various concentrations of power, that we can begin to dismantle destructive societies.

Art & Reality exists as a challenge to its readers, and society in general, to think and act differently from the habitual conceptions—those things we do every day that keep us from paying attention

to logical relations and hence not changing abusive situations. At the same time, the text takes itself as if it were a set of logical relations, or some kind of expression of a fundamental reality, rather than as the ideological construction it is. Where the text is most powerful is in its inextricably linking art to the everyday production of life. One cannot think about art without taking into consideration persons, situations, significance and all the things that inform our daily experiences.

N55 concerned itself with the production of daily life, its myriad facets, and how it was possible to make art in a way that empowered people and brought them useful knowledge. Projects related to these considerations include: a clean air machine, home hydroponics systems, a vermi-composting soil factory, a hygiene system, tree houses, mobile bars, mobile houses that one person could roll by his or herself, giant elaborate public constructions that had multiple functions for living in public spaces and more. They would consider several formal and conceptual aspects simultaneously, such as efficient design, low cost production, low energy consumption, sharing resources and knowledge, and the ability to do it yourself. They produced manuals for every project and distributed them for free. This allows anyone, in theory, to replicate their projects.[33]

A great achievement of N55's activity of interrogating the conditions and the possibilities of their own production of daily life was their development of a modular housing system that they called N55 SPACEFRAME. N55 SPACEFRAME was inspired by Buckminster Fuller's designs for the Ford Rotunda in Detroit in 1953, which in turn were inspired by designs

27. Anupam Chander. "Guaraná Power to the People." (Guaraná Power), http://www.guaranapower.org.

28. A SUPERCOPY can be an item that is taken and modified making something "new". For example, SUPERFLEX took pirated Lacoste shirts, stamped "SUPERCOPY" on them claiming them as, they say, "a new original." http://www.superflex.net/projects/copyshop

29. Peter Zinkernagel was a Danish philosopher. He lived from 1921 until 2003. His published books include: *Omverdensproblemet*, 1957 (English version: *Conditions for Description*, 1962), *Virkelighed*, 1989, and *Tilvante forestillingers magt* (The power of customary views) in 2001. "All the work of Peter Zinkernagel concern fundamental problems in philosophy. In his doctoral thesis he formulated certain rules for using language, conditions for description, repudiating the classical philosophical problem of the existence of the material world ("How can we know for certain that there is a world which exists independently of human perception?") After the 1960s, Zinkernagel was primarily preoccupied with physics while also formulating the political and ethical consequences of his work on logic." ((N55), http://www.n55.dk.)

30. The full text, and the notes, which inform how this argument is to be better understood can be found on N55's web site: http://www.n55.dk/MANUALS/DISCUSSIONS/N55_TEXTS/ART_REALITY.html

31. Ibid.

32. Ibid.

for a similar system by Alexander Graham Bell in the early 1900s. N55 worked with an architect to develop a low-cost building system that was easy to construct, deconstruct and store. N55 SPACEFRAME can be built by hand with simple tools and assembled by anyone who can put a nut on the end of a bolt and use pliers, wrenches, and other tightening tools. Differently sized or shaped buildings can be made with the system and SPACEFRAME is easily modified to meet shifting needs. Prior to having a place or exhibition in which to put the SPACEFRAME, the group stored the materials for a small one-room building under a couch in their commercial loft.

Soon after the first SPACEFRAME was built, N55 was facing eviction from their loft in the center of the city. Gentrification was hitting their street hard, and it forced them to find new working and living conditions. Building a SPACEFRAME, or any other experimental building, is next to impossible in Copenhagen given the strict zoning laws, which cover building aesthetics and other concerns. Given this, N55 decided to build their SPACEFRAME on a floating platform in the harbor. They found a loophole in the rules for building on the harbor and created a floating platform that could take the pressures and strains of both being submerged and bearing the weight of another structure. The platform and the N55 SPACEFRAME link up perfectly and are easily bolted together.

Once the floating house was secured as a regular part of the neighborhood, N55 began to improve the immediate area. Together with others from the area they made a beach of trucked-in sand and built a pier from plastic shipping palettes. People instantly started using this new space. N55 was just beginning really interesting discussions around doing urban planning on a small, local level when the group split up for personal reasons. The N55 SPACEFRAME has been given a makeover and is now called Learning Site. Artists, architects, and others are invited to come and stay, give talks, present projects, conduct research, and contribute to the archive. There will soon be an island where people can garden and learn about topics that surround the production of food.

Info Centre, Copenhagen Free University, TV-TV

Henriette Heise and Jakob Jakobsen have been active in initiating and supporting several important initiatives both in Copenhagen and in London. They established the Info Centre in East London in 1998. It was simultaneously a project space, a bookshop, an archive, and their home. It was an extension of their practice as artists and fused art, politics, and their daily living conditions. Heise and Jakobsen decided that they would run the Info Centre for only one year. It quickly gathered a lot of momentum as it found a highly engaged audience and active political climate extending the Info Centre's life by six months. It was a clearinghouse for, as Jakobsen says, "art, architecture, technology and urban life."[34] He also says that the Info Centre "tied together the political fringes of the art world and the aesthetical fringes of the emerging social movement that was becoming very strong in London in the late nineties."[35] They did projects and worked with ideas of self-organization, autonomy, self-publishing, psy-chogeography and self-institutions.[36] They worked with many individuals and organizations like the London Psychogeographical Association (LPA) and the Association of Autonomous Astronauts (AAA).[37] The last thing to happen at the Info Centre was an exhibition called *Five Year Plan—Propaganda and Printed Matter from the Association of Autonomous Astronauts*. It happened in relation to the AAA's Intergalactic Conference Space 1999 in June of that year, which was in turn organized to coincide with the June 18th (J18) Carnival against Capital, which Jakobsen explains as:

> The first major manifestation of the global anti-capitalist movement. J18 was a huge street party stopping the financial district of London for a whole day. The police didn't know what to do

This page: Beer brewing, free beer and "The Five Year Plan - Propaganda and printed matter from the Association of Autonomous Astronauts," The Info Centre, London, UK, June 1999. Photo: Jakob Jakobsen and Henriette Heise; previous page, top: N55, N55 SPACFRAME and FLOATING PLATFORM, Copenhagen, Denmark, ongoing since 2000; bottom: N55, PUBLIC THINGS, Fort Asperen, The Netherlands, 2001. Photos: N55.

33. The group published a book, which I helped edit, that compiles the manuals and several discussions and exchanges they engaged others in. It is free for download at www.n55.dk/N55_BOOK_PDF/DOWNLOAD.html.

34. Email to the author.

35. Ibid.

36. Psychogeography is a Situationist idea articulated by Guy Debord in his essay "Introduction to a Critique of Urban Geography." It is: "Psychogeography could set for itself the study of the precise laws and specific effects of the geographical environment, consciously organized or not, on the emotions and behavior of individuals." Numerous psychogeographical organizations have started in the wake of the Situationists' practice.

37. The AAA formed to develop community-based plans for space travel. Numerous smaller groups and aligned individuals popped up all over the place under the aegis of AAA and sparked numerous events, conferences, exhibitions and actions.

38. Email to the author.

39. From an email to the author: "The Open University and the Manoa Free University in Vienna are important sisters. In London we had a project called the Club that was a discussion forum that met in public spaces once a month in 2000–2001; this was host to many important debates especially around the theme of the exodus. The Club included Johnny Spencer, Anthony Davies, and Howard Slater, among others."

because there were just so many people and no front line. Lot of groups did actions in many places at the same time.[38]

It was the Info Centre's work with the idea of "self-institution" that was to have a big impact in triggering the founding of many "self-institutions" or "free universities" in several cities throughout Europe and the United States. The Info Centre hosted regular discussions around this topic. Several persons who attended the discussion and the Info Centre's events went on to found their own self-institutions.[39] Jakobsen said the following about their decision to work with the idea of "self-institutions:"

> The Info Centre was the first time we worked with the idea of self-institution somehow to get beyond the dialectical oppositionality and the dependency of being alternative. We wanted to take power and define a situation that didn't mind the mainstream or the establishment or whatever.[40]

Self-institutionalization offered a way to think critically about the limits of autonomy. It asked the basic question of "Autonomy from what?" that implies a dominant power structure one must work against to be autonomous. Rather than replicating this power structure, the Info Centre sought to find a way where they defined the terms of the production of life, knowledge, and so on. It was a way to take power without repeating the same self-marginalization.

Heise and Jakobsen closed the Info Centre in 2001 and moved back to Copenhagen.

They found themselves in a much different social and political climate than London in the late 1990s, which had been a hotbed of anti-globalization organizing, creative street protest, and provided them with networks of people with similar concerns. Jakobsen says of Copenhagen at that time: "The situation in Copenhagen on the cultural scene was very depoliticized; most hype concentrated around the 'new marriage' between art and business that seemed to be a party that no one was critical of."[41]

Experience with the Info Centre helped Heise and Jakobsen in the founding of the Copenhagen Free University (CFU). Jakobsen connects the two initiatives:

> The whole debate about the knowledge economy and the info-capitalism that we engaged in came out of debates in London. And the idea to set up a new Free University within the knowledge economy would never have happened without the debates that we had been involved with in London.[42]

In addition, while they had begun to work with self-institutions at the Info Centre, it wasn't until starting the CFU that the idea became more articulated. CFU has a guide to the culture of self-institutions that they have established. It is called *The ABZ of the Copenhagen Free University* and includes many fascinating entries on everything from "mass intellectuality" and "fellow travelers" to "uneconomical behaviour" and "self-institution." This last entry gives insight into why the CFU articulates itself as a university and not some other kind of structure:

> The model of The Free University is one we have taken up and reworked, and is based on a direct unmediated exchange of knowledge between people as vehicle of social change. It is our hope that you instead of dreaming of the Copenhagen Free University or London Anti-University or the Free University of New York or the Spontaneous University, go where you live and establish your own university drawing on the knowledge in your networks.[43]

CFU hosts discussions, screenings, conferences, conducts research, as well as publishes small books and brochures. One of their research initiatives is the *Rise and Fall of the Situationists*.

40. Ibid.

41. Email to the author.

42. Ibid.

43. *The ABZ of the Copenhagen Free University* can be found at: http://www.copenhagenfreeuniversity.dk/abz.html.

44. Mikkel Bolt Rasmussen. "Situationist Map of Denmark," (Copenhagen Free University), http://www.copenhagenfreeuniversity.dk/sikortuk.html.

45. The TV-TV steering committee is Signe Skovmand, Kristina Ask, Stine Eriksen, Morten Goll, Joachim Hamou, Kent Hansen, Henriette Heise, Christian Hilleso, Ulla Hvejsel, Jakob Jakobsen, Jens Hultquist, Ida Grøn, and Kirsten Dufour.

46. TV Stop was formed in 1987 by people involved with Christiania, Ugeavisen København, and BZ bevægelsen (part of the international squatter movement active in Western Europe in the 1980s).

47. During the writing of this text, Jakob Jakobsen was working on a week's worth of airings of films that were made about various squatter struggles in the Nørrebro neighborhood, where TV-TV is located.

48. The full TV-TV manifesto is available at: http://www.tv-tv.dk/index.php/Manifest.

***

This essay would not have been possible without the generous help and support of Lars Bang Larsen, Rikke Luther, Cecilia Wendt, Jørgen Michaelsen, Judith Schwarzbart, Lise Nellmen, Finn Thybo Andersen, Kirsten Dufour, Åsa Sonjasdotter, Superflex, Mads Ranch Kornum, Rasmus Bjerre and Jakob Jakobsen.

It is both an archive of Situationist activities in Denmark as well as a critical analysis of the ways in which the Situationist movement has been historicized. Jakobsen says of this research:

> The image of the movement that is being reproduced is one of a male, analytical and theoretical movement. We have found many feminine, practical and artistic activities that happened especially in the Scandinavian part of the movement that we have brought back into history. The Situationists are good and bad examples at the same time; their avant-gardism and their organisation is not very useful, but their critique of commodification of our lives through the spectacle is still relevant, as well as their belief in play and change.

There is an extensive set of links and documents from Danish Situationists in addition to excellent essays like Mikkel Bolt Rasmussen's "Situationist Map of Denmark." Rasmussen's text recounts the rich and overlooked activities of Danish Situationists in both the capital Copenhagen and as well as a handful of tiny towns. Rasmussen describes an event at Galleri Exi in Odense, in 1963, where the first Situationist collective organized an exhibition:

> They turned the first room of the gallery into a shelter with sirens, stretchers and corpses. In the next room pictures of contemporary politicians like president Kennedy, Khrushchev, de Gaulle and the Danish foreign minister Per Hækkerup had been mounted on the wall as targets. The audience was told to use a rifle and shoot at them. If they managed to hit a politician's eye they would obtain a free copy of the catalogue. Adjacent to the targets hung a series of Debord's so-called directives. These were white canvases on which Debord had written slogans like: "*Abolition du travail alièné*" (Abolition of alienated labour).[44]

CFU is one of the coordinating organizations involved with TV-TV, an artist and activist-run television service that is on air three nights a week and has been in operation for over two years.[45] They inherited their space, equipment, and time slots on national television from TV Stop.[46] TV-TV's studios are located on the second floor of the last remaining squatted house in Copenhagen called *Folkets Hus* (People's House). TV-TV's programming runs the gamut from art videos to presenting activist strug-

gles.[47] Experimental in nature, the programming seeks to produce television that doesn't replicate mainstream TV's tropes and staid clichés. Their manifesto states:

> TV-TV is investigating TV. We want to experiment with TV, make time for an investigation of TV's possibilities and break with the rhythms offered by most TV channels. We will refuse ratings based generalizations of what people want, and rather investigate TV as a setting for communication. We want to break the monotony that characterizes TV today.[48]

TV-TV allows for a greater dissemination of art and activist activities to a broad audience.

Conclusion

The groups discussed here didn't wait for the dominant culture to decide that everything was going to change and that a more egalitarian society would be established. They took action themselves and achieved results. They built universities, houses, playgrounds, different economic exchange, experimental social and public spaces, and much more. Their projects remain open, even though some have long since ended, because we can learn from them and can apply them in new ways to open up our own possible courses of action to do and build things better. This will take a long time and a lot of people working together.

The choices for taking action to make the world into something other than what we inherit are varied and rich. We need not wallow in self-pity and feelings of helplessness, nor bother worrying about whether something is art or not. Similarly, there is little use in wondering whether any action you take is political. Inaction is just as deeply political as any action. Creative work, actions and activities that show us new possibilities and the potential for building new worlds are all too rare. When we do get them, we need to take care in what we do with this information. Replicating these actions without any attention to local conditions, needs, and politics will lead to frustration and formal repetition. We should share these stories and actions and build upon them, but not simply repeat them.

MCINTYRE 152

BLACK MASK

No. 4   FEB - MAR   1967   5 c

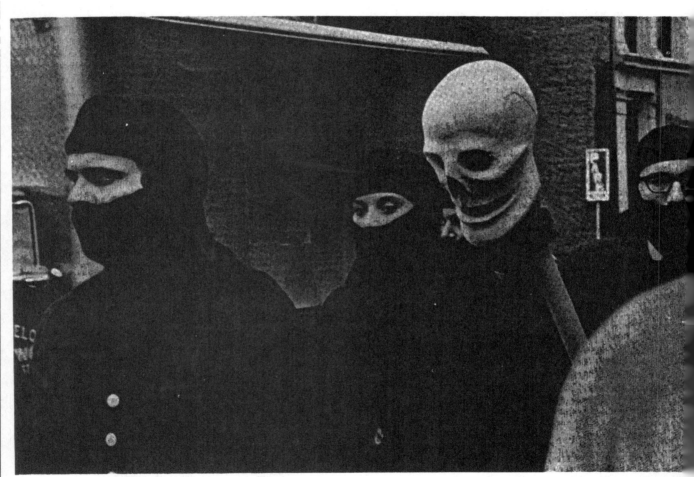

Photo: Laurence B.

BLACK MASK

A CONVERSATION WITH BLACK MASK

IAIN MCINTYRE

During the 1960s a number of radical groups emerged seeking to combine the energy of the artistic avant-garde and the revolutionary political movements, whilst simultaneously attempting to transcend the limitations of each. Following in the tradition of Dada, the Futurists, and the Surrealists these groups sought an end to the commodification of art through a revolution that would transform everyday life. Amongst those pursuing this goal were the Situationists, Provos, Diggers, and a small New York City-based group called Black Mask.

Starting out with an action that shut down the Museum Of Modern Art (MOMA) in 1966, Black Mask went on to disrupt art openings and lectures as well as play a role in the general anti-war and anti-racist ferment of the time. Always aiming to push themselves, and those around them further toward the concept of "Total Revolution," the group, through their actions, magazine *Black Mask*, and activities on the Lower East Side, moved their practice and critique beyond the art world to challenge the growing counterculture and student movements. Evolving into The Family (more widely known as Up Against the Wall Motherfucker), in 1968 members of Black Mask went on to play a provocative role in the sit-in at Columbia University before breaking into the Pentagon and cutting the fences at Woodstock. The following interview held with Black Mask founder Ben Morea and poet/historian/film critic Dan Georgakas traces the history, motivations, and tactics of the group.

"A new spirit is rising. Like the streets of Watts we burn with revolution. We assault your Gods… We sing of your death. DESTROY THE MUSEUMS… our struggle cannot be hung on walls. Let the past fall under the blows of revolt. The guerrilla, the blacks, the men of the future, we are all at your heels. Goddamn your culture, your science, your art. What purpose do they serve? Your mass murder cannot be concealed. The industrialist, the banker, the bourgeoisie, with their unlimited pretense and vulgarity continue to stockpile art while they slaughter humanity. The lie has failed. The world is rising against your oppression. There are men at the gates seeking a new world. The machine, the rocket, the conquering of time and space, these are the seeds of the future which, freed from your barbarism, will carry us forward. We are ready…"
Black Mask #1, November 1966

Tell us about your backgrounds and how you came to find yourselves involved in the radical scenes of New York City during the 1960s.

Ben Morea: I was raised mostly around the Virginia area. When I was ten years old my mother remarried and moved to Manhattan. I was basically a ghetto kid and got involved in drug addictions as a teenager spending time in prison. At one point, when I was in a prison hospital, I started reading and developed an interest in art. When I was released I completely changed my persona. In order to break my addiction I made a complete break from the kids I grew up with and the life I knew.

Black Mask newspaper no. 4, 1967.

In the late 1950s I went looking for the beatniks because they seemed to combine social awareness with art. I met the Living Theater people and was highly influenced by their ideas. Judith Malina and Julian Beck were anarchists and they were the first people to put a name to the way I was feeling and leaning philosophically.

I also met an American artist named Aldo Tampbellini who was very radical in his thinking and who channeled all of that into his art practice rather than social activism. He would only hold shows in common areas like churchyards and hallways in order to bring art to the public. He influenced me a lot in seeing that having art in museums was a way of rarefying it and making it a tool of the ruling class.

I'm self educated and continued my pursuit of anarchism and art through reading and correspondence. I became aware of Dada and Surrealism and the radical wing of twentieth century art, and sought out anyone who had information about it or who had been involved. I really felt comfortable with the wedding of social thought and aesthetic practice. I corresponded quite a bit with one of the living Dadaists, Richard Huelsenbeck.

At the same time, I became friendly with the political wing of the anarchists. I was meeting up with people who had fought in Spain, from the Durriti Column and other groups. They were all in their seventies and I was in my twenties.

I was also a practicing artist working at my own art and aesthetic. I was mainly painting in an abstract, but naturalistic form, as well as doing some sculpture. There was some influence from the American expressionists, but Zen practices were also an influence.

Dan Georgakas: I grew up in Detroit, Michigan at a time when it was the industrial centre of America. In 1945, half the cars in the world were built in the Detroit area. It was a very proletarian, liberal to radical city. Discussions around politics were common to everybody from factory line workers to college professors. Tough, often violent strikes were topics of the day and the general population was solidly pro-union. We were a diverse population. The majority was foreign-born or the first born in America. The other big segments were white

Appalachians and African Americans from all parts of the South. But Detroit was nearly as segregated in terms of housing as a Southern city and there had been a huge race riot in 1943. Just growing up in Detroit made me political. The older I became the more unhappy and distressed I was about conditions I saw locally and nationally.

As a reaction to the McCarthy era I became involved in the genesis of the New Left. I attended many political meetings and came in contact with the Trotskyist and post-Trotskyist movements in Detroit. For personal reasons I eventually left Detroit and went to New York. When I arrived in the mid 1960s I drifted to the Lower East Side in search of political and intellectual stimulation. I met up with Communists and Maoists, but was most attracted to anarchist thought. It suited my anti-authoritarian personality. In that I had been greatly influenced by my grandfather who had a disdain for organized government and organized religion.

"Each culture determines those forms which its art will take and we seek nothing less than the destruction of this culture. We have an art which is a substitute for living, a culture which is an excuse for the utter poverty of life. The call for revolution can be no less than 'total.' To change the wielders of power is not enough, we must finally change life itself."
Black Mask #7, August 1967

When did Black Mask come together as a group? How were you organized and who was involved?

BM: It's hard to say whether we started in 1965 or 1966, but the magazine definitely started in 1966. Black Mask was really very small. It started off with just a few people. As anarchists, and not very doctrinaire ones, we had no leadership although I was the driving force in the group. Both Ron Hahne and I had already been working together with Aldo doing art shows in public to promote the idea of art as an integral part of everyday life, not an institutionalized thing.

Ron and I became close friends and found that we had a more socially polemical view than Aldo in wanting to go closer to the political elements of Dada and Surrealism as well as to the growing unrest in Black America. We wanted to find a place where art and politics could coexist in a radical way. Once we started publishing *Black Mask* and holding actions, other artists and people on a similar wavelength were attracted to what we were doing. I've always favored an organic approach where you don't have meetings and people just associate informally rather than having a hierarchy and recruiting members.

Over time Ron became less interested in the political sphere and I became more interested in working with the people who were involved in fighting for civil rights and against the Vietnam war.

DG: Black Mask was a very loose entity. De facto there were three of us, but lots of people thought we were a much larger group and we never let on otherwise. That illusion held because whenever we sent a call out for an action many people would respond. I am sure some of them thought of themselves as being part of Black Mask and in a sense they were, but they were not in on the planning. This wider group numbered some women, but they were mainly girlfriends and sexual partners who came into the group via that connection rather than for strictly ideological reasons. Later on, when some of the Situationists got involved, there were women among them who were more politically motivated.

Ben was the real dynamo and power in the group. He'd come up with most of the ideas and the rest of us would toss in ours. Rather than using more organized forms like telephone trees, we'd go to the corner of 6th Avenue and 8th Street for every action, give out leaflets and then see what would transpire. It was very spontaneous and we'd often have no idea who would show up. Lots of the preplanning involved talking with like minded spirits in bars, coffeehouses, or political gatherings.

BM: I can honestly say that in both Black Mask, and then later in The Family, we never held a meeting where we consciously sat down to decide our direction or exactly how we would deal with a particular action or situation. It all developed as a very spontaneous, organic outgrowth of whatever we thought was appropriate at the time.

"On Monday, October 10 at 12.30pm we will close the Museum Of Modern Art. This symbolic action is taken at a time when America is on a path of total destruction, and signals the opening of another front in the world-wide struggle against suppression. We seek a total revolution, cultural, as well as social and political—LET THE STRUGGLE BEGIN."
Black Mask press release, 1966

One of Black Mask's first actions was to shut down the Museum Of Modern Art (MOMA). Tell us about what happened and the group's approach to direct action in general.

DG: I was not a founding member of Black Mask, but soon after I moved to New York I heard about a group that had sent a notification to the MOMA informing

them that they were going to shut them down. The police overreacted and surrounded MOMA with top security. One day this little guy [Ben Morea] just walked up and placed a sticker on the door reading "closed" and then walked away [laughter]. I thought that was really cool and wanted to meet these people.

One of the things I had learned in Detroit, and liked about Black Mask was that we had no interest in being martyrs or in playing by the other side's rules. Part of winning involves surviving to fight another day and planning your actions so that you set the agenda. You know what you want to do, you go and do it and then you leave. The authorities have a lot more power, a lot more money, and a lot more lawyers. So the courts are not the best place to do combat.

BM: We felt that art itself, the creative effort, was an obviously worthwhile, valuable, and even spiritual experience. The Museum and gallery system separated art from that living interchange and had nothing to do with the vital, creative urge. Museums weren't a living house, they were just a repository. We were searching for ways to raise questions about how things were presented and closing down MOMA was just one of them.

At other times we disrupted exhibitions, galleries, and lectures. Most of these actions were just thought up on the spot and a lot of what we did was part of a learning process. Things weren't completely thought out, but were a way for us to develop an understanding of our place in the ongoing struggle. A lot of political groups would have these big grandiose strategies and plans, but for us the actions were just a way of expressing ourselves and seeing how we could make a dent in society.

"We are neither artists or anti-artists. We are creative men—revolutionaries. As creative men we are dedicated to building a new society, but we must also destroy the existing travesty. What art will replace the burning bodies and dead minds this society is creating?"
Ben Morea, *Black Mask* #3, January 1967

In 1966 the group also targeted the Loeb Centre at New York University (NYU). What happened with that action?

DG: A lot of abstract expressionists were lecturing at NYU. Ben would go there and rather than sitting around quietly fuming about what was being said on stage, he would jump up and launch into a debate. This would disrupt the lecture as everyone would get excited and start arguing about what Ben was saying rather than the lecture topic. Finally we were challenged to go to an art gallery and have a serious discussion about our ideas.

We decided that rather than dignifying the other side by sitting around making boring points we would turn it into an action. There was an accelerating anger at the time and we felt we had to break out of the straightjackets we'd been put into like university classes and contained picket lines. We sent out a flyer announcing a free party with free booze and food. The only thing was that you

Motherfuckers poster, date unknown.

had to come in a mask or some sort of disguise and bring a noise maker. A few hundred people showed up making a huge racket and the gallery wouldn't let them in [laughter]. They eventually called the police.

BM: We had a strong sense of humor and of guerrilla theater. I remember that particular event seemed so pretentious that we had to do something. It was incredibly stratified and only meant for the elite and it seemed like they'd done everything possible to keep it away from the public at large. After we advertised it, they had to block off the streets all around because so many people showed up. We went down to the Bowery and handed out flyers so that all the street people would show up.

"WALL STREET IS WAR STREET. The traders in stocks and bones shriek for New Frontiers—but the coffins return to the Bronx and Harlem. Bull markets of murder deal in a stock exchange of death. Profits rise to the ticker tape of your dead sons… If unemployment rises you are given work, murderous work. If education is inferior, you are taught to kill. If the blacks get restless, they are sent to die. This is Wall Street's formula for the Great Society!"
Black Mask leaflet, February 1967

Tell us about the group's action on Wall Street.

DG: We decided to rename Wall Street so we put on black ski masks and carried a coffin with a skull that read "War Street." We marched down Broadway and since there is a law in New York against wearing masks the police kept stopping us. We'd pull down the masks a bit to show our faces before pulling them up again.
　　　When we reached Wall Street we did the action, but it didn't get as much "punch" as we thought it would. Unlike the people at MOMA the traders just laughed it off. There were so many demonstrations and things going on that this one wasn't dramatic enough to have an impact. There were two or three groups alone doing street theater

who would turn up in a laundromat or some other public place and start an argument that would draw in passers-by before it turned into a play. I remember one of those skits involved Capitalist Monster. Whatever you put into his mouth, he would just shit out money.

BM: The Wall Street action wasn't an exceptional event in terms of what it achieved or the attention that it elicited. It was just a way of us trying to broaden our approach from the arts. Our whole approach was really hit and miss. We'd just try things in order to find a way in which to make statements and get across to people that there was more to it than just the isolated, limited view that the artists should stay in the art community and the radicals amongst the radicals. We were trying to bridge the gap between these different arenas and different consciousnesses, to move between them. This was fairly unheard of back then.

"If the blacks [have] decided to get together with their brothers first, then the whites had better do the same: they can no longer ride the black panther. Yet revolution has no color barrier: if blacks can do it, whites better learn, for only then will Revolutionary power replace Black Power, revolution replace nationalism."
Black Mask #8, October 1967

Black Mask clearly drew inspiration not only from the Dadaists, Surrealists, and avant-garde movements of the past, but also from the contemporary black insurrections and youth movements of the 1960s. Tell us a little more about these influences and about your ideas and approach to politics and art, in general.

DG: I think the most important thing was that our inspiration started with our own reactions to the world. We were all unhappy with American society. We also all had ideas about the arts. Ben was more into visual arts, I was more concerned about literary forms. We certainly didn't think that there was a division between politics and art. We saw the two as fused together.

Black Mask action on Wall Street, February 1967. Photo: Dan Georgakas.

Looking around we saw that there were other people with similar views and of those the most dynamic were the Black groups. In Detroit I had known black artists and political activists so I thought it was natural that I would work with similar people in New York. We had some contact with Amiri Baraka, who had just changed his name from LeRoi Jones, and also Larry Neal. They were doing some theater-based things in Harlem. We planned some joint ventures that never materialized.

It wasn't like we were a bunch of white guys looking to ape or follow the Black Movement. It was more the case that we were angry and looking around to find other angry people. We weren't interested in being a support group. The Black Movement would soon be telling whites: "Organize your own communities, we don't need you organizing ours." We were trying to organize or at least stimulate other artists.

BM: From my perspective we saw a need to change everything, from the way we lived to the way we thought, to even the way we ate. Total Revolution was our way of saying that we weren't going to settle for political or cultural change, but that we wanted it all, we wanted everything to change. Western society had reached a stalemate and needed a total overhaul. We knew that wasn't going to happen, but that was our demand, what we were about.

It also meant seeing that you need all types of people involved, not just political activists. Poets and artists are just as important. Revolution comes about as a cumulative effect and part of that is a change in consciousness, a new way of thinking.

"[The] new establishment has all the mind sapping and anti-revolutionary characteristics of the old, with religion playing a dominant role... The most dangerous aspect of this establishment is the 'radical' mantle with which it seeks to cover itself and thus delude many dissatisfied youth with a false bourgeois sponsored 'rebellion.' The artists speak against the war for one week, but serve the capitalists all year. The poets clamour at the gates of the university while the real poets are in the streets crying 'Burn, Baby, Burn.'"
Black Mask #4, February 1967.

How did Black Mask fit into the New York political and arts scenes? It seems as if you went out of your way to ridicule and challenge ideologues of all stripes?

DG: What some people forget is that in the 1960s there were two parallel movements, which were not separate, but also not quite the same. There were a group of people who were very political and who tended not to be sensitive towards the arts. They gravitated towards Students for a Democratic Society (SDS), the Civil Rights movement, or one of the Old Left groups. Then there were the counter-culture people who were smoking dope, doing music and challenging society in a cultural way. Often the two would mesh, but many of the hard core political people thought that groups like Black Mask were silly and frivolous and that we should go hang out with the Ginsberg crowd, while the Ginsberg types would think, "Oh god, those Black Mask people are so political, what are they doing here." We liked to make fun of both [laughter].

You can see those tensions in the underground press of the time. Initially the two strains coexisted and were covered in the same newspapers. There was one of these papers on practically every campus and at one point there were more than a million copies of these papers circulating weekly. That's impressive. The political strain would break away in the late 1960s and become more rigid before dying, while the more cultural movement became very commercialized and fused into the dominant media.

BM: A lot of political people questioned what we did by saying we should only attack society on the political front, and that we shouldn't care about art. However we felt it was best to take action in the place where you were already at and that as artists these issues were important to us.

Many of the hippies distrusted us and the politicos hated us because they couldn't control us or understand what we were doing. As for the people in the art world, I'm sure most of them thought we were crazy.

"The irony is that Vietnam, which is waging a 'War of Liberation' (South) and one of defense against assault (North) is closer in many ways to what we seek, due to the nature of their struggle, than anywhere else. The North under the reality of American bombs has been forced to decentralize, placing control in many areas into the hands of the local population with a minimum of interference from Hanoi, whilst in the South the 'liberated' areas have been left under the control of the inhabitants with an almost complete lack of bureaucracy... We are sure this situation will change, for once the war is concluded, assuming the Americans have been prevented from carrying out the total destruction of Vietnam (North and South) the natural function of government to suppress (to govern) the masses will reassert itself."
Ben Morea, *Black Mask* #6, May 1967.

Black Mask seems to have issued various challenges to the peace movement, criticizing the moderates for their lack of militancy whilst also attacking the Left for its unconditional support of the National Liberation Front (NLF). Many radicals from the 1960s are now somewhat regretful or appear reticent to speak about their support for the North Vietnamese regime.

BM: We supported the right of the Vietnamese people to resist American invasion, but were not going to support the North Vietnamese government's own oppressive behaviour. I hated the knee jerk reaction of much of the Left who delighted in waving the NLF flag around. We didn't cheer the killing of American troops who were stuck over there as cannon fodder like some others did.

In a sense we didn't fit in anywhere and that meant we became a pole of attraction for all those other people who weren't interested in a dogmatic or pacifistic approach. Much of the later evolution of Black Mask into The Family came about through more and more of these people joining with us and affecting where we were going.

DG: One of the things we tried to do was to bring together people who were anti-authoritarian in their outlook and lifestyle, but who also wanted to be involved in radical art and activity outside of what most of the Left were doing. We were never able to coalesce in large numbers.

The closest we came was in 1967 when Martin Luther King came to New York to lead a march to the UN against the war. We were incensed that the organizers had allowed the police to set out the march route. We thought it took away from the protest to let the police tell us when, how, and where we could go. We formed an affinity group called the Revolutionary Contingent and had about 250 people with all sorts of flags—Black, National Liberation Front (NLF), Irish Republican, etc.

At one of the meeting points in Central Park we tried to stir up the crowd—with little success. Half an hour or so after waiting for the march to begin, we heard the chanting of a big contingent of black activists from Harlem. They'd marched about fifty blocks and were coming down a "forbidden" street, Central Park West, which was, and remains, a very chic thoroughfare.

There were a few hundred of them and our contingent stood up and began running towards them. Many of the people standing around assumed that the march was finally starting so they followed us and we wound up defying the police and taking our own route down Seventh Avenue, thoroughly disrupting business as usual. About 7000 people were involved. When we got to 42nd street, people began to turn to go to the UN. We tried to keep people going and disrupt the whole city, but the majority headed off to hear the speakers and finish the rally. Although that event didn't entirely work as we had hoped, we realized that there was a lot of anger and defiance waiting to be tapped and that's what we sought to do in many of our actions.

'We're looking for people who like to draw'

"But it is not enough to talk: we need to place dynamite at the very foundations themselves, not just tear off its branches. Art as alienation; the inevitable outcome of a culture (itself the result of a socio-economic system) which is divorced from real life. Nothing short of a complete social revolution can end the separation which exists between culture and life; the two are inseparable. Can we accept a regime as "revolutionary" which pays artists twice as much as workers and this in the midst of a 'cultural revolution' (Mao's China) or a regime that which celebrates its revolution (?) with a Tchaikovsky recital attended in full tails by the ruling class (Cuba). Can we accept any system as revolutionary which perpetuates one-man management as opposed to collective rule? Can any system which is economically based on hierarchal organization be free from the cultural hierarchy of artists and the tyranny of expert?"
Black Mask #8, October 1967.

Black Mask and later The Family were some of the first groups to encourage the concept of affinity groups as a way of organizing. One Family member famously defined an affinity group as a "street gang with analysis." How did this approach develop and the use of the term come about?

DG: At some point in the midst of all the things that were going on, activists began discussing the question of how we were going organize ourselves. What were we going to be if we didn't want to be a traditional vanguard party? Out of this the idea of organising as an affinity group emerged.

However there were many debates as to what an affinity group was, what was a gang, and what was a community? A huge question was that if you are anti-authoritarian you question actions that are out of sync with the community you want to reach even if you think those actions are the right ones to take. From my perspective you don't want to be command[ing] or adventuristic, but you also don't want to be timid like everyone else on the Left.

BM: Although we associated in similar circles with Murray Bookchin, our group was always very different because we were very visceral and he was very literate. Murray was keen on using the Spanish term *aficionado de vairos* to describe these non-hierarchal groupings of people that were happening. We said "Oh my god, can you really imagine Americans calling themselves *aficionado de vairos*? Use English, call them affinity groups."

"The false concept of art cannot contain us; what is needed is much more, a form that will embrace the totality of life. This false concept was not even satisfactory in the past. How many so-called artists were not accepted as such in their lifetime, only to be embraced later when man learned to widen his vision..."
Ben Morea, *Black Mask* #3, January 1967.

Tell us about the magazine you produced which ran from 1966 to 1968 and spanned ten issues.

BM: Ron and I mainly put the magazine together, but there was a wider group who helped produce, print and distribute it. We sold it for a nickel, which wasn't much money, but we figured if people had to pay for it then they would actually want it and read it rather than just take one look and throw it in the trash.

We tended to sell it on the Lower East Side, which was the most fertile ground for us as there were many artists and activists. We occasionally went up town as well although that was more to stir the pot.

DG: It was quite well thought out. We would put it together in Ben's studio. He came up with the idea of having it in black and white and using minimalism to make it powerful enough to appeal to many people. We generally only had four pages so it had to be pretty tight. As Mark Twain noted, "It takes a long time to write short."

We'd distribute them on the corner of 6th Avenue and 8th Street, which was a heavily trafficked and had bookstores and the like in the immediate area.

After a number of issues Ben began to question the whole concept of a magazine and began putting up flyers and artwork in the street. He felt that if you wanted to defy artistic conventions it was best to take it to the streets. The problem with that was that anyone could take it down and you had other constrictions on what you could do in terms of printing, what you could fit in, etc.

Cover of *Black Mask*, no.1, November 1966.

BLACK MASK

No. 1　　　　　　NOV. 1966　　　　　5 Cents

A new spirit is rising. Like the streets of Watts we burn with revolution. We assault your Gods - - We sing of your death. DESTROY THE MUSEUMS - - our struggle cannot be hung on walls. Let the past fall under the blows of revolt. The guerilla, the blacks, the men of the future, we are all at your heels. Goddamn your culture, your science, your art. What purpose do they serve? Your mass-murder cannot be concealed. The industrialist, the banker, the bourgeoisie, with their unlimited pretense and vulgarity, continue to stockpile art while they slaughter humanity. Your lie has failed. The world is rising against your oppression. There are men at the gates seeking a new world. The machine, the rocket, the conquering of space and time, these are the seeds of the future which, freed from your barbarism, will carry us forward. We are ready - -

LET THE STRUGGLE BEGIN.

"The weak willed and weak minded love to live in calm and beauty without participating in the struggle. Their favourite scene is peaceful existence behind the violence of a strong military and police force which they piously decry (with words), but never oppose (with deeds)... Even the revolt vs Viet Genocide too often becomes yet another career building gimmick. Rather than posing a threat to the status quo hippy culture furnishes whole new industries with unexpected profits. Capitalist promoters have showblitzed the Underground into a perversion of rebellion that is not even a reasonable facsimile. The pursuit of the perpetual High is nothing more than the velvet down on the inside of the imperialist iron glove."
Dan Georgakas, *Black Mask* #4, February 1967.

Black Mask was one of the first groups to take on countercultural figures like Timothy Leary and Allen Ginsberg for their timidity, orientation towards religion, and status seeking, labelling them at one point "The New Establishment." From 1967 onwards it seems as if Black Mask moved a lot of its critique away from the arts establishment and towards the growing hippy movement and New Left.

BM: Although we were critical of them, I was close to Allen Ginsberg and became close to Timothy Leary years later. What we were trying to say at that moment was that they were allowing themselves to be used as a safety valve. We wanted to attack the core of society and believed they weren't doing that. At the time we thought they were being used by the likes of *Time* and *Life* magazine although in hindsight *Time* and *Life* probably wish they had never covered them, especially Timothy.

We were always trying to shake things up, to push everyone else as well as ourselves. There was always a lot of interchange with all sorts of other radicals and sometimes there was fratricide in that we would strike out at people we otherwise liked just to make a point.

DG: We hated religion and pacifism. I would often be very provocative and say "Poetry comes out of the barrel of a gun" and countercultural types would get very upset. I wasn't saying go and shoot someone, but I was trying to point out that the military-industrial complex and the people who run America have immense power and that you weren't going to make them change by just singing a nice song.

A lot of our debates with these people were very physical and personal because if you lived on the Lower East Side you'd bump into them and argue things out. It was so cheap to live in the area and it was a huge hub of activist activity. Long before we put out a newspaper or leaflet we would have already been debating these points in the street and coffee houses.

Everything was happening very quickly and it's often hard to recall exactly what happened when. I remember that [Marxist philosopher] Herbert Marcuse would come to the Lower East Side to visit someone and word would get around and he'd soon find himself debating a whole crowd of people. He'd be upset on the one hand because here were twenty or thirty people disagreeing with him, but also thrilled because there were all these young people who had read his work and could argue at a sophisticated level.

I did a broadside that denounced Ezra Pound who the Hippy left and the campus poets both admired. We pasted that broadside up where people gave readings and at a few homes. I was accused of being "negative." In 1968, I also did a poem castigating a lot of hippy ideas. It was widely published and then a Persian anarchist made it into a huge poster and put it up on Telegraph Avenue as part of the anti-war struggle.

"We have no intention in writing off the student-left or casting them into a limbo of inactivity, but claim that it is only as non-students, non-consumers and non-spectators that they can realise a revolutionary role, since to be a student is ultimately to be a trainee for an inhuman social order; while it is by rejecting the role of spectator (student) and by realising that life must be played in its totality that they will become unable to accept anything less, bringing them closer to those 'with nothing to lose and a world to gain,' and therefore closer to revolution."
Ben Morea, *Black Mask* #5, April 1967.

What was Black Mask's connection to SDS?

DG: In 1967 some of the Black Mask people attended the SDS conference in Ann Arbor. At that point there was a lot of debate about what direction SDS should go in with the folks who eventually became the Revolutionary Youth Movement (RYM) and Weatherman arguing in one direction [anti-imperialist action direct action on the home front] and Progressive Labor in another [workplace recruiting].

We put forth the idea that SDS should go in an anarchistic direction and form affinity groups that were closer in spirit to how SDS had originated and best operated. SDS had been a very decentralized organisation where the central group would propose demonstrations for certain dates after which it was up to each local chapter to decide whether and how to participate. [Mexican revolutionary] Emiliano Zapata had organized his forces in a similar fashion.

Ben gave one of his impassioned talks, which drew in a few hundred people, and we went to one of the upper balconies to try to form a group within SDS that would go in an anarchistic direction. Unfortunately, as history shows, SDS didn't, and eventually imploded with various rumps that claimed the name going in authoritarian or adventuristic directions.

BM: We saw that SDS was becoming a real force for change and that all these traditional left groups and Maoists like Progressive Labor were trying to take it over and control its direction. We thought it was important for other kinds of people, like us, to get involved and show the students that there were many choices, many ways they could go.

I remember being at one of the SDS conferences and people were getting into a heated debate about the differences between the Yankees, the East Coast based establishment, and the Cowboys, the Texan based establishment. I got up and said "This is all bullshit, who cares about them, we're not the Yankees or the Cowboys—we're the Indians!"

With both Black Mask and later The Family we used guerrilla theater and actions to show that there was another approach on offer and the more volatile elements of SDS resonated with that. Some of the people who went on to form [US armed struggle organization] Weatherman hung out with The Family and, although it has never really been credited, borrowed a lot from our militant style and attitude. However they took it all in a very authoritarian direction.

"Life in this society being, at best, an utter bore and no aspect of society being at all relevant to women, there remains to civic-minded, responsible, thrill-seeking females only to overthrow the government, eliminate the money system, institute complete automation and destroy the male sex... The true artist is every self-confident, healthy female, and in a female society the only Art, the only Culture, will be conceited, kooky, funky, females grooving on each other and on everything else in the universe."
Valerie Solanas, *The Scum Manifesto*, 1966.

Tell us about Valerie Solanas, who was close to members of the group and for whom Ben wrote a defense following her attempted murder of Andy Warhol in 1968. There was a deafening silence in the underground press around her ideas and actions following the shooting. This seems a little odd given the fact that by this point the New Left had begun to increasingly glorify political violence.

BM: I actually met Valerie while selling *Black Mask*. This girl came up to me and said "I'd like one of those, but I don't have a nickel." I told her not to worry, she could have it for free because it was obvious that she wanted to read it. She said "No, no wait here," and went into a nearby bookstore and stole a copy of her own book, *SCUM Manifesto* to trade for *Black Mask*. I thought that was an audacious move and we quickly became very close friends.

I thought the film, *I Shot Andy Warhol*, made a cartoon of her life, but in all honesty the woman who played Valerie [Lili Taylor] really caught her spirit. There is a character in the film based on me and the film tries to show that we had some kind of sexual connection, but that was never the case. Valerie was a lesbian and we never had anything like that, but she was very sweet to me and I guess the only way the filmmakers could express our attachment was through a sex scene. I didn't mind that too much because that's just how straight people think.

There was a lot of parody and irony in Valerie's writing, but she was also, and I don't mean this in a bad sense, a fairly crazy person. She saw a need to raise a lot of issues around what happens to women and *SCUM Manifesto* was the best way she could express herself. I always loved people who were loose cannons, who didn't fit the mold.

Valerie used to stay with me quite a bit as she was often homeless and always on the move. One night when she was there I said "Valerie there is something I've been meaning to ask you. Your whole manifesto and output is about killing men so what about me? I'm a man, how you gonna deal with that?" She looked at me and said "I promise you now that you'll be the last man that we kill." [laughter] I asked for that in writing, but never got it.

Sometime later when Black Mask had wrapped up and The Family had started we were involved in the occupation of Columbia University [1968]. Valerie came up there and found me and asked, "What would happen if I shot somebody?" I said "It depends on two things—who you shoot and whether they die or not." A week later she shot Andy Warhol.

After she shot him I wrote a pamphlet supporting her. I may have been the only person who did that publicly. I went up to MOMA and handed it out there. Everybody I met was very negative about it, but, hey, I disliked Andy Warhol immensely and I loved Valerie. I felt she was right on and that he was way more destructive than she was because he was helping to destroy the whole idea of creativity in art. Some people dislike the term, but I feel that creativity is a kind of spiritual act, a profound thing for people to do. Warhol was the exact opposite, he tried to deny and purge the core of creativity and put it on a commercial basis. As a person he was really despicable as well and that's why Valerie hated him. He used and manipulated people.

The attack on Andy was met with silence on the Left and I think that was because it raised issues that no one could deal with. This wasn't violence occurring in some far off place. Andy had become a star, almost a sacred image, and here she was striking at it. Even the people who liked her feminist approach couldn't deal with the fact that she would harm Andy.

"We are the ultimate Horror Show... Hideous Hair and Dangerous Drugs... Armed Love striking terror into the hearts of plastic Mother and pig-faced Father.

The future of our struggle is the future of fear, FEAR!! The fear of free love, fear of not working, fear of Youth... We drink the magic potion and become the spectre that haunts Amerika. We are the WEREWOLVES baying at the moon and tearing at the fat. Fangs sharpened, Claws dripping. We are not afraid. We create fear. (The pig wanders from his sty...and the wolves descend)."
UAW/MF, International Werewolf Conspiracy broadsheet, 1969.

Black Mask continued as a magazine until mid-1968. What was the process by which the group began to evolve and change into what became known as Up Against the Wall Motherfucker?

BM: The Family/Up Against The Wall Motherfucker and Black Mask were related in that one grew into the other, but in reality they were very separate groups in terms of what they did and the people involved. There was no decision to start a new group, no blueprint, it was just an evolutionary thing where one died away and the next thing came to be. It's hard even to say exactly at which point one ended and the next began.

The Family went over the edge, was extremely volatile and didn't have as much inclination toward the cultural sphere. It included a lot of artists, but also people from all persuasions who wanted to live a life more real than that what was on offer. Something less limiting than just pursuing politics or art, something fiercer.

We never called ourselves Up Against The Wall Motherfucker, although we signed our posters and leaflets, which anyone in the group could produce, with that name. Amongst ourselves we were The Family, which might sound weird now because of the association of that name with Charles Manson, whom we had no connection and nothing in common with.

Graphic produced for the International Werewolf Conspiracy broadsheet, 1969.

Whereas I was the main figure in Black Mask, The Family was quite different because it involved a large group of people who were all equal in strength and in determining the direction of the group. It was essentially a loose confederation of affinity groups living across a series of crash pads who shared a tribal outlook and living style.

The first real action we did as The Family was to take garbage to the Lincoln Center in February 1968. There was a garbage strike in New York and there was tons of refuse piling up in the ghettos. The commercial and wealthier areas were able to hire private contractors to clean their streets so we decided to take some of the garbage from the Lower East Side up to the Lincoln Center. One of our members proposed this as a cultural exchange— garbage for garbage [laughter]. Although others tended to focus on our aggression and militancy we really had some beautifully witty people.

We put out a leaflet explaining why were doing this, but those of us involved realized that we weren't really Black Mask anymore and so we didn't want that name on it. There was a poem by LeRoi Jones with the line "Up Against The Wall Mother Fucker" in it and I suggested we put that on there. Somehow it stuck and from then on in everyone referred to us as that. It wasn't a deliberate thing on our part. It would have been fairly pretentious to just name ourselves "The Motherfuckers" [laughter]. Black Mask continued as a magazine for a little longer and then we started creating flyers and posters and doing things for papers like *The Rat*.

DG: Two things happened at this point for me. I was a little leery of some of the people who began to turn up on the fringes of Black Mask and who went on to the other group. Ben and some of the others wanted to stay in the streets and see how far that could be pushed. I thought that was a dead end. I became more interested in seeing if a mass unity organization of some worth could be created. It was a slow parting rather than an abrupt break. If each of the paths had been successful then that would have been great, but neither worked.

More significantly, on April 21st of 1967 a coup d'etat occurred in Greece when a junta of colonels seized power. This hit me in my ethnic gut and I became increasingly involved in the Greek

anti-junta movement which felt politically and personally healthier for me than what was going on in Black Mask. I put more and more of my energies into working with the Greek community.

"The present system of death and oppression cannot exist without waging war. US napalm is already falling in Latin America, and to be sure, the US government would not fall short of napalming its own black population. To bring 'peace' to Vietnam will only bring war elsewhere."
Janice Morea, *Black Mask* #8, October 1967.

With the US government on a permanent war footing overseas whilst simultaneously cracking down on civil liberties and dissent at home, it sometimes seems as if the left wing movements of the 1960s never existed. What do you see as the legacy of groups like Black Mask and the New Left in general?

BM: Part of the reason I re-emerged [after more than thirty years of anonymity] to talk about what we did back in the 1960s is the fact that things have gotten so bad in the US. It's at a point where you can't ignore it, it's worse than ever.

I figured that I'd start letting people know about our history and then go from there. All I can tell people is that when it looked pretty dismal in the past we took action and it did have an effect. A lot was achieved and yet a few years beforehand no one would have expected that we could take on the behemoth of American capitalism. It's counterproductive to sit back and say "You can't do anything." It's not my place to tell people exactly what they should do, but there is always some way to respond and take action, just look around.

DG: During that twenty years between 1955–1975, I never thought there was going to be a revolution like some of my cohorts did or even that we would be able to drastically alter the United States. But I did think, especially as we got into the late 1960s, that there would be enough critical mass to create a permanent alternative culture where dissident ideas would brew and one day create a mass movement. That didn't happen, but we did help bring an end to the Vietnam war and we began to address a lot of the prejudices in society so far as race and sexuality were concerned. That isn't Black Mask's legacy, but we were part of it.

There were some victories in that period and since, but the pendulum has swung so far the other way that you can't help but be dismayed. All of the 1960s activists are bewildered. Things are bad now, but then history is often cyclical and we are greatly overdue for a change. I take some solace, and I hope it's not just wishful thinking, from something [West Indian historian] C.L.R. James often said to me and others: "You never know what will happen next. Revolutionary change could begin tomorrow and when it hits you'll see all the build up that you don't see before."

I remember growing up in the mid-1950s, during the McCarthy era, and feeling so despondent because it seemed like nothing would ever change, but it did and partially because we got so sick of how things were and decided to take action. Some of the original activities I got into were not very dramatic or radical, but they began the process. People often ask if I think we wasted our time with all this anarcho-activism and I quote the great IWW poet Ralph Chaplin. He said that we need not mourn those who have rebelled and lost,

But rather mourn the apathetic throng—
The cowed and the meek—
Who see the world's great anguish and its wrong
And dare not speak!

Sources and further reading:

Black Mask and Up Against The Wall Motherfucker: The Incomplete Works Of Ron Hahne, Ben Morea and The Black Mask Group. London: Unpopular Press and Sabotage Editions, 1993.

Casey, C. *Up Against The Wall, Motherfucker: The Life and Times of a "Street Gang With Analysis."* Senior Thesis, Harvard University, 2003.

Gray, Christopher. "Black Mask." In *King Mob Echo: English Section of the Situationist International*, edited by Tom Vague. Edinburgh: Dark Star, 2000.

Hinderer, Eve. "Ben Morea, Black Mask and Motherfucker." http://www.16beavergroup.org/monday/archives/001031.php, 2004.

Mairowitz, David Z. and Peter Stansill, eds., *BAMN: (By Any Means Necessary): Outlaw Manifestos and Ephemera, 1965–70.* London: Penguin, 1971.

McMillian, John. "Garbage guerrilla." *New York Press*, May 4, 2005.

Neumann, Osha. "Motherfuckers Then and Now: My Sixties Problem." In *Cultural Politics and Social Movements*, edited by M. Darnovsky, E. Epstein, and R. Flacks. Philadelphia: Temple University Press, 1995.

Situationist International. "The Latest Exclusions." Statement, Paris, 1969.

Solanas, Valerie. *SCUM Manifesto*. Oakland: AK Press, 1997.

Black Mask, New York City, 1966–1968.

The East Village Other, New York City, 1968–69.

The Rat, New York City, 1968–69.

BLACK MASK
BLACK MASK

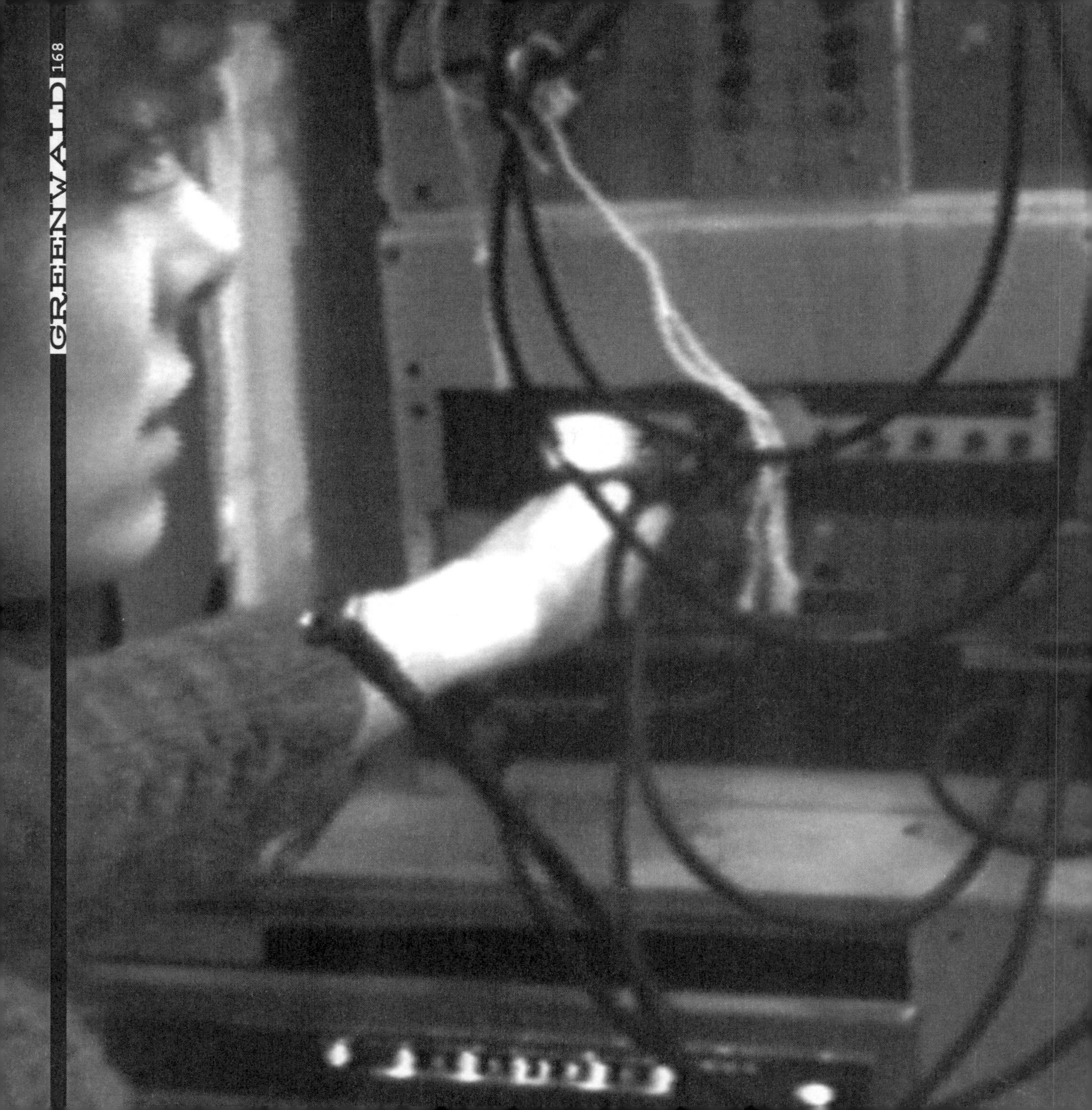

THE PROCESS IS IN THE STREETS: CHALLENGING MEDIA AMERICA

DARA GREENWALD

Images of street medics with home-made red crosses adorning their clothes, protest marching bands, cops in riot gear, tear gas in the streets; ideas and practices of decentralized organizations, anti-copyright, shared resources, networked communications, ecstatic experience, DIY media, pirate broadcasting, communal living, participatory culture, collective process. I'm not talking about the twenty-first century alternative globalization movement, but rather the documents and practices of the early 1970s video movement in the United States. These tendencies and images which, in recent years (since the 1999 "Battle of Seattle" and the birth of Indymedia.org) have emerged as an exciting aspect of current Left political movements were also here in the USA in the late 1960s and early 70s, and were documented and practiced by a little known, but highly productive media democracy and experimental art movement.[1] This movement focused its experiments with social relations and cultural production around the use of portable video technology.

I first became interested in video groups from the early 70s in 1999 when the Video Data Bank (VDB) in Chicago (where I worked) acquired the collection of the Videofreex, one of the early video collectives. This was an incredible collection made up of over 1300 videotapes, the majority of which were on obsolete tape formats.[2] These tapes were mostly raw footage shot between 1969–78 and some edited programs.[3] After seeing the first tape we preserved and converted to a viable format, an interview with Fred Hampton from the fall of 1969 just before he was murdered by the Chicago Police Department—it became apparent that this collection would have significance and resonate with today's media activists, as well as anyone interested in the history of radical culture.[4] Upon further investigation, I found that it wasn't just the video documents themselves that would resonate with anti-authoritarian media makers, but also the communal context and non-hierarchical process by which they were produced as well as the video movement's practice-based critique of centralized communication structures. They weren't just criticizing the media, they were making their own.

Videos origins are in radio and broadcast technologies, rather than in film or photography, thus early video users and critics were responding more to television than to cinema.[5] By the 1950s, televisions were becoming basic furniture in people's homes. By the late 1960s, when portable video equipment became available, many people in their early twenties had experienced TV both as ambient noise/images in their living rooms and as a focal point of their family and social development. Unlike cinema, rarely was there a focused viewing in a darkened theater surrounded by strangers; TV watching was an intimate experience in the private sphere. Unlike film, video was quick to process and easy to reproduce. When people shot video, they could immediately watch it, talk about it, and get feedback. Videotape's ability to be cheaply and infinitely copied, and thus distributed and screened in multiple contexts was crucial to the development of ideas about the medium's democratic potential.

Sony Corporation introduced the Portapak (its generic name was VTR for Video Tape Recorder) to the US market in 1965. By 1968, Sony was widely advertising the technology to educators, artists, and general consumers. The Portapak was one of the first portable and relatively affordable video cameras. Before that, video technologies were quite heavy, expensive, and only used by broadcast professionals and the military. But this was 1968, and counter culture and revolutionary thought and movement were gaining momentum. Quickly, these video technologies got into the hands of artists, activists, and participants in the counter culture. By 1969, several video collectives had formed, including: The Videofreex, Commediation, People's Video Theater, Raindance, Revolutionary People's Communication Project, Ant Farm, and Global Village. Some began using the technology as a focal point for their experiments in social organization as well as to document the changing world around them. Essential to many of the alternative video makers of the time was a critique of communication structures and a desire to challenge corporate TV broadcasting's tendency toward the centralization of information and one-way communication from the corporation to the viewer, but not vice versa. Some video users were also interested in challenging what was represented or rather excluded from representation on corporate television.

None of the groups or individuals from the early video movement made public statements about anarchism as a political philosophy. In fact, some made statements against any political solutions to societal problems, rather, they proposed "information solutions." However, many were explicitly interested in anti-authoritarian practices such as decentralized communication structures, self-organization, individual expression, anti-authorship, and collective ownership. Many also actively participated in mutual aid networks related to access to equipment, technical training, and the distribution of video. Contemporary anarchist theorists David Graeber and Andrej Grubacic might call this "little a" anarchism as it is not about an ideological naming of the philosophy, but rather a practice of the tendencies. In describing twenty-first century radical movements, they write: "...core principles: decentralization, voluntary association, mutual aid, the network model, and above all, the rejection of any idea that the end justifies the means..."[6] Certainly many of the video collectives ascribed to these values. Aesthetically they were more concerned with the process of production than the creation of a product. Their art, in many cases, was a means to a means.

Although video technology was cheaper than it had ever been (a Portapak was a few thousand dollars), it was still not accessible to most people, so a large amount of capital was necessary to invest in equipment for the development of this movement. The video collectives that formed in New York[7] were reliant on funding from the New York State Council on the Arts (NYSCA), another confirmation that they certainly weren't "big A" anarchists. At the time, NYSCA gave thousands of dollars to artists using new technologies with very few parameters on how they should use the money or what they had to produce. Without worrying about having to sell their cultural products, an experimental atmosphere arose and a certain level of freedom with form and process blossomed.

The fact that the State facilitated the development of a grass roots movement is perhaps a contradiction or an unexpected outcome of the State's granting process. A later problem with this relationship is that when State funding dried up, the different collectives began competing for money in a scarce funding environment and many just dissolved. Although groups received funding from the State, this did not make them immune to surveil-

---

1. For a short period in the early 70s, the experimental art and media democracy movements in the US seemed to be aspects of the same community. This merging had something to do with the necessity of shared resources/equipment. Through studying the early video movement, it's evident that both practices of media democracy and artistic experimentation have the potential to contribute to a liberatory politics and experience

2. Mostly 1/2-inch open reel, the format used with the Sony Portapak.

3. As of this publication, the VDB has attempted to preserve approximately thirty-three, of these tapes of which approximately twenty-five have had video and audio signals. All video formats disintegrate which makes preservation projects important endeavors since the evidence of our past dissolves each day.

4. On a personal level, as an activist/collaborative artist/counter cultural participant, I had a hunch that being able to see these videos and exploring both the context in which they were made, as well as how collective decisions were being made today about the future of the collection (twenty-five years after the collective disbanded) would be useful to my artistic and political practices, and also to the larger community. It also became apparent that working with dissolved collectives, and dissolving and fragile media formats is a formidable challenge, one which perhaps today's media collectives might have the foresight to think about when they break up, rather than thirty years after.

5. Throughout the world there were radical filmmakers and collectives prior to the 1970s. The Spanish CNT's film collective produced over one hundred anarchist films between 1936–37 alone. In this essay, I am focusing on video specifically. There is a lot of research still to be done on all forms of radical media and art. Video and film, although both capture moving images, are quite different technologies, and have historically lent themselves to different modes and qualities of production, reception, and distribution—as well as preservation.

6. David Graeber and Andrej Grubacic. "Anarchism, or the Revolutionary Movement of the Twenty-first Century," (*Znet*: January 6, 2004) http://www.zmag.org.

7. The focus of my research has been New York State, partly due to the explosion of activity facilitated by available funding.

lance by the State. A government informant even participated in the Videofreex experimental projects in order to provide info for the FBI.[8]

The Videofreex[9]

Three people (David Cort, Parry Teasdale, and Mary Curtis Ratcliff) founded the Videofreex in 1969 and their numbers quickly grew to ten (to include Skip Blumberg, Nancy Cain, Bart Friedman, Davidson Gigliotti, Chuck Kennedy, Carol Vontobel, and Ann Woodward). Although they did not share a defined ideology, they did share the belief that, "placing video cameras...in the hands of ordinary people would make the world a better, more just, and beautiful place."[10] In 1971, they moved from New York City to Maple Tree Farm in the upstate NY town of Lanesville to live communally and make videos. This context helped them continue to develop a collective support system to make individual and group video projects[11] (as well as to be more eligible for funding than in the competitive NYC environ-

ment). In *Guerrilla Television*, Michael Shamberg writes of the Videofreex,

> They have also the most collective lifestyle, sharing expenses and space for living. This is in no small part due to the nature of the videotape process and the Freex claim to get it off most when they're all plugged in together...and taping collectively. They also, of course, make tapes individually using the collective support system.[12]

At Maple Tree Farm, the Videofreex began a pirate TV station called Lanesville TV.[13] In the beginning, they broadcast three times a week, later reducing to one. Lanesville TV was on air from 1972–1977, making it the longest running pirate TV station in the US (I have been unable to find evidence of any other US-based pirate TV broadcasts.) The Videofreex programmed both their own experimental work and local content such as town hall meetings or news from the local farms. They believed media should be interac-

The Videofreex formally posed in front of the Hunter, NY American Legion Post, 1973. Photo: Videofreex.

From top: People's Video Theater, American Indian Action at Plymouth Rock, 1971; Peoples' Communications Network, Queen Mother Moore at Greenhaven Prison, 1973; Videofreex, Women's Lib Demonstration NYC, Aug 26, 1970. All images courtesy of the Video Data Bank.

tive and participatory, and broadcast their phone number so that viewers could call in and comment on the broadcast. They also had plans for a media bus—a kind of touring video production studio—but this remained unrealized. The collective's practice was informed by a do-it-yourself, self-sufficiency ethic and a belief that users of technology should be empowered to fix it. They did not want the movement to have to rely on Sony to repair their machines, so they published a book on how to use and repair video equipment called the *Spaghetti City Video Manuel*. They also had a production studio on their farm which was visited by up to 200 people a year. These visitors would come to learn video skills and contribute to Lanesville TV programming.

Each member of the Videofreex brought different skills and interests to the collective, and their documents reflect their diversity (from art to social action from community building to video erotica, among other things).[14] In addition to the TV station, they made their work available to viewers through screenings in NYC and through what was called "bicycling" the tapes, meaning trading tapes through the mail via a network of other collectives and through listings in the movement periodical *Radical Software*.

Their documents were often raw unedited footage, shot hand-held without voiceover. The footage is gritty, black and white—the technical limitations were incorporated into the style. Their aesthetics were influenced by learning the new technology while using it and by a belief in process over product. Some members saw themselves as artists with cameras who were making TV experiments.

I asked Parry Teasdale, a founding member of the Videofreex and author of *Videofreex: America's First Pirate TV Station and the Catskills Collective That Turned It On* (1999) about the politics of the video collectives. He responded:

> I think the Beatles, Stones, and possibly Dylan were far better known and more frequently quoted than Marx (except for Groucho). I can't claim to have read *Das Kapital* and certainly wasn't a Marxist. I had read McLuhan and did read Michael Harrington's *Socialism*, and later Wilson's *To the Finland Station*, but theoretical politics was not a topic of discussion at Videofreex or among the other groups that we knew, at least to

the degree I am aware of their internal dialogues. Certainly none of the video groups in and around New York City were modeled on any particular social experiment or based on a particular theory as I understand them. You should check with the others, though. This is not to say that we had no political outlook. But most of it was colored by a universal (among the groups) opposition to the war in Vietnam. I suppose we accepted the language of the political people that the war was in pursuit of American imperial ambitions. But anyone who went around spouting doctrinaire phrases like that would have been ridiculed or been made the subject of a tape. We did spend a lot of time in the early days taping Abbie Hoffman and other Yippies. And we had shot some footage of Tom Hayden, who was probably the most politically articulate of the anti-war movement people. But they were grist for tapes, and what we did we did in the service of furthering a more liberated television medium, not in service of a broader political purpose. Or so I see it.

Even in Teasdale's reporting of history he takes an anti-authoritative position—revealing his subjectivity, encouraging me to ask others for their version of the history.

I asked Skip Blumberg, another member of the Videofreex, if they were anti-authoritarian. He responded, "We were doing our own thing. Including lots of questioning. We did our share of protest videos, but concentrated on positive alternatives and our own imaginations." And if he knew if anyone in the movement was influenced by anarchist theorists? He responded, "That's an academic's question. Our crowd was too busy having adventures and keeping the equipment working." Regardless of what you label it, these tendencies of valuing the imagination, individuality, positive alternatives, and adventure all fall into historic and contemporary anarchist practice from Emma Goldman to CrimethInc.

Through working with the Videofreex in trying to assess, preserve, and distribute their work many questions arose.[15] Some of these questions are valuable for contemporary collectives to think about: What should happen to a cultural product that was intended only as part of a process? Who owns the materials produced in a context that resists ownership when that context no longer exists? When one believes information should be free, from where and how do funds emerge to pay to maintain access to the information? If there is money to be made from a collective project that is no longer functioning, who should profit? Given the challenging task of preserving obsolete formats of moving-image media and the possibility that it can't all be migrated to contemporary and viewable formats, who should get to decide what is saved for the public record? With the abundance of documents produced, where and how can they be maintained for future generations? When collectives dissolve, who has the authority to decide what happens to the work they have produced and who should get credit?

Other Groups and Tendencies

The Videofreex were just one group from this period, and they often collaborated with other video collectives. In 1971, the May Day Video Collective came together in Washington, DC to document the protests against the Vietnam War. People from around the country participated in the May Day Video Collective (including members of the Videofreex) by traveling to DC, shooting tape, and sharing footage. There was a cultural rejection of individual authorship; everyone was able to use any of the footage that was shot. This convergent and shared media practice to document the streets from an on-the-ground perspective evokes the atmosphere in Indymedia Centers during recent national protests (1999–2004). The documents created from these different historical moments not only overlap in their confrontational imagery of protest and repression, but also by the collaborative process in

8. Teasdale, Parry. *Videofreex: America's First Pirate TV Station and the Catskills Collective That Turned It On.* (New York: Blackdome Press, 1999), 140–149.

9. "Video Freak" was a common term for people in the video movement, and this group took their name, Videofreex, from that.

10. Teasdale, 47.

11. Smith, Pamela J, "Issues of Appraisal and Selection of Community Based Video: Assessing the Videofreex Collection," New York University, Master of Arts Thesis, May 2005, 9.

12. Shamberg, Michael and Raindance Corporation, *Guerrilla Television.* (New York: Holt, Rinehart, and Winston, 1971), 16–17.

13. Abbie Hoffman had given them a transmitter when they were still in New York City in order to create a pirate station there, but it didn't get off the ground until they moved upstate.

14. Smith, 12.

15. I met with several members of the original collective in the Spring of 2004 and 2005.

16. Boyle, Deidre, *Subject to Change: Guerrilla Television Revisited.* (New York: Oxford University Press, 1997), 8.

17. From an email exchange with Bob Devine, 2004.

18. You can view all issues of *Radical Software* at http://www.radicalsoftware.org.

19. *Guerrilla Television* is out of print but used copies can still be found.

20. http://www.radicalsoftware.org

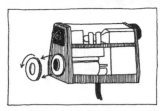
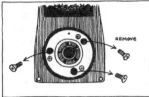
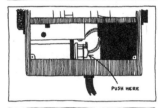
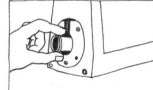
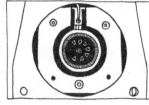
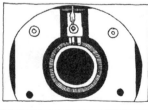
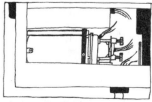

This page: Instructional camera repair images from The Videofreex, *The Spaghetti City Video Manual*, 1973. Next page: Covers of, from left, *Radical Software #1* (1970), *Guerrilla Television* (1971), *The Spaghetti City Video Manual* (1973).

which they were created.

Many of the 1970s groups worked in a style termed "street tapes," interviewing passersby on the streets, in their homes, or on doorsteps. The goal of street tapes was to create an "interactive information loop"[16] with the subject in order to contest the one-way communication model of network television. One collective, The People's Video Theater, were specifically interested in the social possibilities of video. On the streets of NYC, they would interview people and then invite them back to their loft to watch the tapes that night. This fit into the theoretical framework that groups were working with at the time, the idea of feedback. Feedback was considered both a technological and social idea. As already stated, they saw a danger in the one-way communication structure of mainstream television, and street tapes allowed for direct people-to-people communications. Some media makers were also interested in feeding back the medium itself in the way that musicians have exper-

imented with amp feedback; jamming communication and creating interference or noise in the communications structures.

Video was also used to mediate between groups in disagreement or in social conflict. Instead of talking back to the television, some groups attempted to talk through it. One example of video's use as a mediation tool in the early 70s was a project of the students at the Media Co-op at NYU. They taped interviews with squatters and disgruntled neighbors and then had each party view the other's tape for better understanding. The students believed they were encouraging a more "real" dialogue than a face-to-face encounter would allow because the conflicting parties had an easier time expressing their position and communicating when the other was not in the same room.

Groups were not only interested in making their own media but also in distributing it. At Antioch College, the Antioch Free Library (1966–1978) was set up so people could distribute their tapes by sending them in and requesting tapes in exchange. During its time, the Antioch Free Library copied thousands of tapes for free, sending out twenty-five to fifty a week.[17]

Theories of a Guerrilla Television

Many of the ideas these video groups were working with influenced or were influenced by the periodical *Radical Software*[18] started in 1970 and the book *Guerrilla Television*,[19] authored by Michael Shamberg in 1971. Both of these publications were developed by the group Raindance. Raindance got its name from R & D (research and development) and after the influential think tank, The Rand Corporation. They fancied themselves a think tank for the early video movement. Raindance was supported financially through the donation of $70,000 from a member's family money. Its mission was promoting video as a tool for change.[20] Raindance and other participants in the movement were heavily influenced by the theoretical work of Marshall McLuhan, Buckminster Fuller, and Gregory Bateson.

Eleven issues of *Radical Software* were published between 1970–1974.[21] The magazine acted as a networking tool for these media collectives. In the first issue alone, there was contact information for over thirty groups and individuals. Every issue included lists of available tape titles for sale and trade, contacts of video enthusiasts who had resources such as cameras or editing equipment to share, and articles crucial to the theoretical development of the community. Some of the ideas written about in the pages of *Radical Software* included: media ecology, the information economy, technological utopianism, media democracy, and video's therapeutic potential. In this space, art, cultural theory, community media, and activism all came together.

The term "guerilla television" came from Paul Ryan's 1970 article in the third issue of *Radical Software*, "Cybernetic Guerrilla Warfare." In this article he likens the use of video to guerilla warfare:

> Warfare...because having total control over the processing of video puts you in direct conflict with that system of perceptual imperialism called broadcast television that puts a terminal in your home and thereby controls your access to information. This situation of conflict also exists as a matter of fact between people using portable video for feedback and in situations such as schools that operate through withholding and controlling the flow of information. Guerrilla warfare...because

the portable video tool only enables you to fight on a small scale in an irregular way at this time. Running to the networks with portable video material seems rear view mirror at best, reactionary at worst. What is critical is to develop an infrastructure to cable in situations where feedback and relevant access routes can he set up as part of the process.

> Cybernetic guerrilla warfare...because the tool of portable video is a cybernetic extension of man and because cybernetics is the only language of intelligence and power that is ecologically viable...We need to develop biologically viable information structures on a planetary scale. Nothing short of that will work. We move now in this present information environment in a phase that finds its best analogue in those stages of human struggle called guerrilla warfare. Yet this is not China in the 1930s...In order to "win" in cybernetic guerrilla warfare, differences must he cherished, not temporarily suppressed for the sake of "victory."[22]

Michael Shamberg's *Guerrilla Television*, borrows heavily from different theories expressed in *Radical Software*, including Ryan's, but Shamberg expresses a less militant political view and, in several instances, claims that the movement is not political at all. He argues that, "In Media America, real power is generated by information tools not by

21. "Software" meaning the information/what was recorded on the videotape, "hardware" meaning the tools to make it.

22. Ryan, Paul, "Cybernetic Guerrilla Warfare," *Radical Software*, Volume 1, #3 (1971), 1–2.

23. Ibid., 2.

24. Ibid., 9.

25. Ibid., 12.

26. Ibid., 32.

27. Ibid., 21.

28. Ibid., 22.

29. Ibid., 36.

30. Ibid., 37.

31. Ibid., 24.

32. Ibid., 8.

33. Ibid., 53.

34. As video deteriorates quickly, there is a threat that certain time periods will have less and less visible evidence to view and learn from. Rick Prelinger of the Prelinger Archive spoke at a screening in Chicago in 2005 about how his generation, the Baby Boomers, were able to access tons of film made before 1964 to understand themselves and their world. He went on to say that my generation, people born in the 1970s, have very few ways to understand the context we were born into, due to the tightening of copyright laws around media. I want to extend the scope of this fear to the fact of the dissolving of the evidence itself, as video-based moving images quickly deteriorate and are not funded for preservation. There is another challenge related to these cultural artifacts: selecting what should be preserved from the huge amount of documents that these cheaper and more quickly processed video formats encouraged. VHS tapes, a familiar format to many of us, have a ten-year life expectancy. In our personal lives, some of us combat our fear of the loss of our memories of our families and friends through recording video. Quickly, we realize, it too will fade. And what then of documents of radical social movements and experimental cultures?

Today's even cheaper video and digital technologies allow us to amass a huge amount of documents of counterculture, everyday life, and social movements (among other things). Are we thinking about what will happen to them in five, ten, or thirty years? Are media collectives that have been documenting the alternative globalization movement cataloging their footage in translatable ways so that others might have access to it in years to come? Do they have a plan for what happens to the documents should the collective disband? Perhaps these are not useful questions to a movement trying to make useful media for the struggle right now, but studying the groups of the past makes me think perhaps they are questions worth thinking about.

opinion. The information environment is inherently post-political."[23] *Guerrilla Television* places a strong emphasis not on replacing content on broadcast TV (old structures) but actually transforming information structures of both production and transmission and building alternative support system for information. He states, "No social change can take place without new designs in information architecture."[24] And only through "radical re-design of its information structures to incorporate two way decentralized inputs can Media America optimize the feedback it needs to come back to its senses."[25]

Although, as already stated, no one from the movement claimed to be an anarchist, many of the ideas in *Guerrilla Television* critique societal systems from an anti-authoritarian perspective, including critiques of the education system, government bureaucracy, and, of course, television. Shamberg describes healthy systems as having diverse forms, complexity, symbiosis rather than competition, heterogenaity—all qualities that broadcast TV lacks.[26] I asked Paul Ryan where the anti-authoritarian tendencies in the video movement might have come from. He responded:

There was resistance to any ideology, particularly Marxism. For me it was another version of Catholicism with its emphasis on obedience. I distrusted authority...McLuhan pissed off the Marxists with his remark "Marx missed the communications bus." And McLuhan was very influential... I think the key turns around video perception undercutting the authority of language. Remember those in authority who were telling us what to do, were telling us to go kill in Vietnam.

I asked Ryan if he knew anyone in the movement who was influenced by anarchist political thought. He said he did not, but, "It was, however, 'in the air.' Kropotkin's name was known." I could not reach Shamberg for his input. He left the radical community to join the Hollywood movie industry and went on to produce over twenty-five major motion pictures including, *The Big Chill*, *Erin Brockovich*, *Pulp Fiction*, and *How High?* among others. Historians have attempted to interview him, but he thus far has not cooperated and seems to have distanced himself from his seminal text.

Regardless of Shamberg's life path, *Guerrilla Television* provides theoretical ideas and practical suggestions that are both sympathetic with, practiced by, and perhaps of use to contemporary anarchist media makers. One idea is around media literacy and education. Shamberg writes that, "tape was to television as writing was to language" and, "growing up on television...(without knowing how to make it) is like learning to how to read but being denied a chance to learn how to write."[27] He also suggests that using video might undermine the authority of teachers since schools want to promote the teacher's authority but, "video...allows students to generate their own knowledge."[28] This alternative vision for education was not just for children: "The new universities are any group of people functioning as a survival center, or who are learning by doing."[29]

The idea of survival centers seems particularly relevant in these precarious times. Survival centers would give people tools to survive in an information environment. "The true hope for success for an alternate culture is if it can become a valid information resource instead of a low variety parody of what it pretends to oppose."[30] Ideas about survival centers are connected to ideas about media ecology. "When our media only confirms their own product and don't move us to action, or at least pass

From top: Videofreex, Fred Hampton - Black Panthers, Chicago, Oct 1969; Videofreex, Women's Lib Demonstration NYC, Aug 26, 1970. Images courtesy of the Video Data Bank.

on survival information, they are no longer ecologically valid."[31] Media ecology criticized the overly-centralized, monoculture-producing dominant communications systems (similar to how ecologists critique factory farming and planting mono-crops). The ideas of media ecology ran parallel to environmental ecology in encouraging a diversity of form and the interconnectedness of systems.

The aesthetics of guerrilla TV documentary or "do-it-yourself TV" differed from broadcast news in that there was no spokesperson or mediator, it was mostly shot from inside events not outside, it included environmental sound, was from a first person perspective, and didn't have the traditional documentary "voice of god" voiceover (which was considered authoritarian).[32] There was an emphasis on a multiplicity of voices. There was concern with not exploiting the subjects and giving the subject the option to destroy any footage they did not want recorded. In Shamberg's words, "a participant should be given maximum control over his own feedback."[33]

Some of the concrete suggestions the book offers for decentralized communication projects include storefront information centers, wiring apartment buildings for closed circuit TV, pirate TV, micro broadcasts, mobile shows, taping police behavior, taping broadcast TV crews, having festivals in domes and inflatables (challenging dominant architectural structures), using tape to decode bureaucratic structures, multi-monitor juxtapositions, and using tape to analyze behavior for therapeutic purposes. There is also a section in the book that attempts to help the reader figure out how to access enough money to make videos, which includes, among other suggestions, "sell your car."

Connecting to Today

There seems to be some continuity in thought of the media democracy movement over the past thirty years. Tendencies in thematic content include that regular people's voices, countercultural voices, and social movements matter. Engaged media attempts to include the subject as a participant and allows the participant to have a say in how they are represented. Process is as important as content; it is not just that alternative media is being made that is important, but how it is being made. Sharing resources, technological knowledge, and video footage is crucial to the process. Distribution is important. Non-institutional spaces for communication and information sharing are crucial. These may include storefront theaters and infoshops, artist-run spaces or community centers, bicycling/mailing media through informal countercultural networks, and pirate broadcasting. Publishing journals and magazines also supports the alternative social networks. Media should be decentralized and both localized and internationalized—reflecting local lived experience and struggle, and at the same time being shared through a global network with other groups interested in survival.[34]

The media landscape has shifted dramatically since the introduction of the portable videotape recorder, but surviving in the information environment is no easier. The media democracy movement has grown alongside access to the tools of media production at lower costs (i.e. digital cameras, personal computers, copy machines, the World Wide Web, etc.), yet corporations still seem to have a hold on our media, and the art market often absorbs our experimental cultures. The dream of the early video collectives is far from realized but it is still informative. Flipping through the dozens of channels on cable TV, there are certainly more offerings than the 1970s, but nonetheless, a monoculture of expressive forms and commercial values persist. The one-way communication structure of mainstream television itself has not changed dramatically. The World Wide Web has been the strongest threat to corporate controlled, one-way communication structures, and anti-authoritarians have been quick to pick up and participate in this medium. Interactive communication structures on a global scale have finally seemed possible, yet currently a battle rages with corporations (and the State) attempting to control access and use of the Internet. Anarchists and anti-authoritarians must continue critiquing the coercive power of dominant media structures and representations while at the same time creating alternatives that prefigure a media world we want to live in. The documents left by the early video movement remind us that as long as corporate media input into society exceeds radical, grass roots media output, the survival of our liberatory ideas and cultures are threatened.

This page: Videofreex, *Lanesville Overview 1*, 1972; next page: Videofreex, *Davidson's Jail Tape*, May 2, 1971. Images courtesy of the Video Data Bank.

Bibliography

"Anarchist Film During the Spanish Civil War", Grupo Alavio, *Video and Direct Action*, Vol. 1 No. 3, November 2005, p. 20–21

Boyle, Deidre. *Subject to Change: Guerrilla Television Revisited*. New York: Oxford University Press, 1997.

Gever, Martha. "Like a Rolling Stone: Memories of TVTV." *The Independent*, Vol. 11, No. 7, August/September 1988, p. 16–17.

Graeber, David and Andrej Grubacic, "Anarchism, Or The Revolutionary Movement of the Twenty-first Century," January 6, 2004, *Znet*, http://www.zmag.org.

Hall, Doug and Sally Jo Fifer. *Illuminating Video: An Essential Guide to Video Art*. New York: Aperture, 1990.

Halleck, Dee Dee. *Handheld Visions: The Impossible Possibilities of Community Video*. New York: Fordham University Press, 2002.

Hill, Chris, "Bob Devine" and "Parry Teasdale." *Artist Interviews: Artists Interviewed* by Chris Hill. 1995.

Hill, Chris, ed. *Rewind: Video Art and Alternative Media in the United States, 1968–1980*, Chicago: Video Data Bank, 1995.

Mellencamp, Patricia. "Video Politics: Guerrilla TV, Ant Farm, Eternal Frame." San Francisco: Bay Area Video Coalition, http://www.bavc.org/preservation/dvd/resources/essays.htm.

Radical Software (1970–1974). Raindance Corporation. On-line at http://www.radicalsoftware.org.

Ryan, Paul. *Video Mind, Earth Mind*. New York: Peter Lang, 1993.

Shamberg, Michael and Raindance Corporation. *Guerrilla Television*. New York: Holt, Rinehart, and Winston, 1971.

Smith, Pamela. *Issues of Appraisal and Selection of Community Based Video: Assessing the Videofreex Collection from Product to Process*. New York: NYU Masters Thesis, 2005.

Surveying the First Decade: Video Art and Alternative Media in the US. [videorecordings]. Kate Horsfield, producer. Chicago: Video Data Bank, 1995.

Thompson, Patricia. "Collective Conscious: An Interview with Skip Blumberg and Linda Iannacone at the Republican National Convention 2000." *The Independent*, November 2000 from http://www.aivf.org.

Teasdale, Parry. *Videofreex: America's First Pirate TV Station & the Catskills Collective That Turned It On*. Hensonville, New York: Black Dome Press, 1999.

Troy, Maria. "Notes on a Lousy Dialectic," *P-Form*, Issue 34, from http://www.pfrom.org/archive/34lousy.html

Vasulka, Steina. "Kitchen Story." 1976. From http://www.vasulka.org/Kitchen/KP.html.

Webography

The Experimental TV Center
Experimentaltvcenter.org/history

The Early Video Project
208.55.137.252/index.html

Media Alliance
Mediaalliance.org (section on New York Video Collections)

Radical Software
Radicalsoftware.org

Paul Ryan's Site
Earthscore.org

Woody and Steina Vasulka have archived many documents from and on the history of video. They are available as PDF files at their site: Vasulka.org

Video Data Bank
Vdb.org

WHEN MAGIC CONFRONTS AUTHORITY: THE RISE OF PROTEST PUPPETRY IN N. AMERICA

MORGAN F. P. ANDREWS

Why was a cop knocking me off my bicycle on the afternoon of August 1st, 2000?

Maybe the cardboard goat head that I was wearing had something to do with it.

In July of 2000, a group of *puppetistas*—activist-artists who design, build, and perform with cardboard and paper mâché sculptures at political demonstrations and gatherings—had rented a large leaky warehouse in West Philadelphia for $500. The *puppetistas* would spend the next two weeks creating giant puppets and street theater in opposition to the Republican National Convention (RNC). They set to work storyboarding five days of public pageantry: July 28th centered around health care, July 29th focused on militarism and gun control, July 30th would highlight the shortcomings of the two-party system, July 31st featured a massive anti-poverty march, and August 1st was a day focusing on the prison industrial complex and the death penalty.

"I'm doing you a favor," said Michael Graves, a building contractor and arts patron who owned the warehouse. "You know the FBI is watching you. I'm putting myself at considerable risk."

Sure enough, on August 1st, 2000, the warehouse was besieged by a trio of helicopters and surrounded by 180 Philadelphia police officers. Michael Graves and the seventy-eight other occupants of the building were handcuffed and loaded onto armored buses, where they were detained for nine hours without food, water, legal counsel, or medical attention. Graves and his former tenants were each charged with ten misdemeanors and imprisoned with bails set at $10,000 apiece—the low end for the 420 activists arrested during the RNC.

"The police called the warehouse a 'nerve center of criminal activity'," chimed ABC network news. "The protesters say they were 'making puppets'." And the report went on, now referring to Michael Graves' building as "the nerve center."

The next day city employees visited the warehouse again, armed this time with three garbage trucks, into which were loaded the puppeteers' tools and paint, silkscreen equipment, musical instruments, and what one inspector from Philadelphia's Department of Licenses and Inspections later testified to be more than 300 pieces of "trash:" Trash that had been sculpted into enormous faces and hands united by brightly colored rivers of fabric. Trash in the form of banners and flags stenciled with poetically captioned illustrations that beckoned resistance. Trash that looked suspiciously like an array of tophatted peanuts making corporate campaign contributions to cartoonish animal parodies of political party mascots. Trash shaped like 138 eight-foot tall cardboard and bamboo skeletons, each bearing the name of a person that then Texas Governor George Walker Bush had executed to date. All this, and more, was unceremoniously hauled from the warehouse and compacted in the garbage trucks. Three volunteers from a local community garden came and sat down in front of the trucks in a last-ditch effort to stop the inevitable from happening. They were brought to jail and the puppets were taken to a landfill.

"The protestors had no clear message," chuckled Fox News reporters over images of shouting crowds.

"Yeah," said Ben Matchstick, a *puppetista* who had managed to not get arrested, "we had no message because the cops destroyed it."

Playing With Dolls

Most Americans don't get it. When I tell people that I'm a puppeteer, they usually assume that I work with either hand puppets or marionettes, and that the average age of my audience is 4 1/2. I've been openly laughed at for the work that I do. Puppeteers aren't taken seriously as workers (or even as artists) and earn little respect and even less money outside of the mainstream work of Julie Taymor's *Lion King* or Jim Henson's Muppets. The work is grueling and taxes all of a person's faculties. So why do it?

Today's adept puppeteer must be simultaneously skilled as a writer, architect, sculptor, painter, electrician, mechanic, musician, promoter, director, actor, modern dancer, political commentator, and manipulator of objects. Maybe this is why radical puppeteers are drawn to their medium: It presents a challenge on all fronts—artistic, social, political, economic, and logistical. To do it at all in the face of so many obstacles is itself an act of radicality. And to overcome these challenges and produce theater that moves an audience to action is rewarding—on every level.

You might ask, "What is radical puppetry? Where does it come from? Where can I see it? What and who is it for?" The history is vast, dating back to as early as humans began using art and theater to make fun of authority. As a kid did you ever dress up in funny clothes and mock your parents or teachers? Did you ever use dolls, toys, kitchen appliances, or furniture to enact stories where there was some kind of conflict or struggle? Well, that's what I'm talking about. Most of us did this. Some of us still do this. And we've found other people who still do this and we've formed connections, collaborations, and community with each other. An entire movement of artists has emerged consisting of subversive grown-ups who never stopped "playing with dolls." That, in a nutshell, is the radical puppetry of today.

This article focuses primarily on the modern continuum of massive "protest puppetry" that was birthed in North America during the movement to end the war in Vietnam, and eventually became a poster child for the anti-globalization demonstrations of the late 1990s and early 2000s. Protest puppetry is any kind of puppet theater that draws attention to the ironies and flaws in the way things are and hopefully illustrates a way that things could be instead. It predates the political and countercultural climate of 1960s, and some background will be given here to the artistic, community, and older protest traditions that parented it, as well as the social movements that shaped and were shaped by it. Thousands of people have done, and are still doing, this work, and tens of thousands of individual puppet shows have come and gone. Not all of them can be mentioned here, and so emphasis is given to a few groups, movements, and methods that have had a far-reaching effect on the history and culture of puppetry as protest.

The problem with puppet theater, and theater in general in this age of information, is that few people see it. Print, music, video and electronic media are so readily reproducible that live theater cannot compete in terms of numbers of spectators. Before the advent of all the modern entertainment technologies—computer, TV, radio, cinema, recorded music, etc.—theater reigned supreme and was widely discussed among the public. But today the wider public only flock to see live shows that are marketed to be familiar and expensive, and this limits not only who gets to see theater, but what kind of theater is made. There is a diminished desire to take risks on the part of the audience and therefore less incentive to make risks as a theater producer. It is in this low-risk environment of predictable, rehashed entertainment that the brazen upstart of modern radical puppetry rears its pointy little head. In case you may have missed it, here it is.

The Protest Parade

The shirtless man in the mask wears burlap pants and a twisted expression bordered by an explosive mane of straw. A semicircle of twenty drummers pound a path through the protest for the masked man as he struts down Pennsylvania Avenue, thrusting and tossing a huge hand-painted flag into the air. He is followed by 200 brown paper mâché bas relief figures, each between five and six feet in height, who choreograph themselves in clusters, swaying to the right and left, jumping up and down, laying themselves horizontally above their manipulators, or whooping and arcing from the back of the pack to the front. A giant mâché madonna-with-child bust hovers above this swirling sea of brownness, while a fifteen-foot tall skeletal horseman made from thick, wooden poles gallops behind on his matching skeletal steed. It is Death, sporting a pair of hand-painted signs that read "FREEDOOM" and "DEMOCRAZY," bringing up the rear in Bread & Puppet Theater's 2005 parade against the war in Iraq.

An onlooker points to the lumpy brown maelstrom of vaguely humanoid puppet figures and asks one of the drummers, "What are those supposed to be?"

"What do you think they're supposed to be?"

"I don't know..." He hazards a guess: "People?" (He's right.) "Iraqi people?" (Right again.) "American people?" (Of course.)

Whistles blow and the drummers quicken their beat, stirring samba rhythms up into a cacophony. The mâché population shakes and quakes and falls to the ground, their masked leader stumbles down dead in the road as the figure of Death cackles maniacally behind it all. Then a man runs around and wakes them all up with cymbal crashes and the parade resumes to the cheers of onlookers.

"Don't you get tired doing that?" asks a woman. She's holding one of the thousands of identical "US Out of Iraq!" signs. "I get so exhausted just carrying this sign around all day—I can't imagine doing all that falling down and then getting up and moving around with a puppet in my hands."

"That's exactly why I'm not tired," says one of the volunteers in Bread & Puppet's dance. "Because I *am* moving—I'm doing something."

Old World Roots

The Bread & Puppet Theater is the chief progenitor of modern protest puppetry in the United States. They began doing parades in New York City against the war in Vietnam in 1963. But Peter Schumann, Bread & Puppet's founder and director, really began building his theater in the aftermath of World War II.

"We were refugees in northern Germany after the War," recalls Peter. "We were hungry and had to steal food and we had to defend ourselves against the locals who wanted to beat us up, so

we had to form gangs and beat *them* up. And we did puppet shows. We went around to the soldiers in their tents who were imprisoned there, and to the houses in the village, and told them that we were doing a puppet show. We'd get some chairs and tables and turned them upside down and put the curtain over them and we started playing foolish—just doing puppets."

Puppetry was a commonplace affair throughout Germany. Roaming puppeteers traveled from town to town with a collapsible stage and a set of stock characters. The star of their public shows was the national comical hand puppet mascot Kasper, also known as Hans Wurst ("Jack Sausage") or Pickelhering ("Salted Herring"). Around the world he had many other names: In Czechoslovakia he was Kasparek. In Greece and Turkey, Karagiozis and Karagöz. Armenia and Iran had Karapet, while in Uzbekistan he was Palvan Katschal. Russia is famous for Petrushka, and Italy for Pulcinella. In France this was Puncinelle (before being replaced by Guignol) and in England he became the long-nosed Mr. Punch who had a wife named Judy. The list goes on: Panza in Spain, Pança in Portugal, João Redondo in Brazil, Semar in Indonesia, and Vindushaka in India—just to name a few.

A parade marshal guides nine paper mâché puppets mounted on backpacks around the bend on May Day of 1937 in Manhattan's Union Square. The puppets likely represented capitalists at odds with the marching workers in white berets and red sashes demanding a raise in pay. Photo: John Albok.

Regardless of his name, every national puppet protagonist played the same role in society. "He was the commoner's hero," says puppeteer K. Ruby in her *History of Radical Puppetry* slide-lecture. "He acted as a live news service for the people, satirizing local events, taking potshots at the government and spreading the gossip of the day."

"Punch and Petrushka and Guignol use nuance and innuendo," says theater historian John Bell. "So while the censors are listening or watching, you're not saying something outright, you're juxtaposing images that have four or five different levels of meaning and putting them together with other elements. You say, 'We're not doing a show where we make fun of the king,' but the real message becomes clear to the audience." And in the face of state oppression, these subversive puppet heroes resisted and survived. Throughout the repressive regime of the Ottoman Empire, Karagöz got away with everything from scathing social critique to absurd penis jokes. When the British dictator Oliver Cromwell shut down all of the theaters for eighteen years in the mid-seventeenth century, the roving Punch show could still be seen in public. While the Czech language was banned under Austrio-Hungarian rule in the nineteenth century, Karapet continued to spout anti-fascist remarks in his native tongue. Up until the twentieth century there were periods when Kasper and Guignol performances were monitored, censored, and even banned by European states, but as leaders came and went, the puppet lived on.

Another form of traveling public theater was the banner show, or *bänkelsang* (German for "bench-song"). Storytellers would stand on a bench and sing while pointing to painted banners that illustrated their tales. "The *bänkelsang* was quasi-news," says puppeteer Clare Dolan, "about murder, fires, death, affairs, sex. The bench-singers were vagrant people who were always getting arrested, censored, and exiled."

The banner show's history can be traced back to sixth century India when nomadic holy men eked out a living by knocking on doors and telling stories with painted scrolls depicting gods or the afterworld. Buddhism spread this art form to China, where it became *pien* literature, and to Indonesia, where it was transformed into the famous *wayang berber*, or scrolling shadowplay. Buddhist propaganda in Japan took shape as *etoki*, and the hanging scrolls were divided into panels or made into little booklets, paving the way for the popularity of *manga* (comics) centuries later. In Italy during the middle ages, the Church was using banner propaganda, and by the sixteenth century a secular tradition called *cantambanco* (bench-singer) or *cantastoria* (story-song) was sweeping the streets. Victor H. Mair writes of the bench-singers in his book *Painting and Performance*: "Their social status in the seventeenth century is determinable by their associations with magic, swindlery, skullduggery, quackery, charlatanism, puppetry, and even acrobatics."

"When I was a young kid *bänkelsang* was still in the market and on the fairgrounds just before it died," recalls Peter Schumann. "The Nazis killed that together with other folkloric forms."

The subversive puppets and performable artifacts of Europe weren't always small or concealable creations that a puppeteer could smuggle easily from place to place. Beginning in the fourteenth century, giants made of wicker began to crop up. Gog and Magog were the giant guardians of London who came to symbolize the end of the feudal system as they were paraded through the streets each year. Belgium's Guyant was a symbol of resistance to French domination that was banned and then rebuilt each time power changed hands. Catalonia gave birth to *gigantes y cabezudos* (giants and bigheads), fiesta figures depicting local personae or taking the forms of fantastical beasts. In Italy and southern France wicker statues made an appearance at Mardi Gras and Carnival festivities, which culminated in a mock trial of the king, who was always found guilty and burned in effigy. These giant puppet pageants were something for townspeople to rally around and bond over, as well as representations of common dreams of liberation.

Some of these dreams were sent overseas. "Many Italian anarchists who emigrated to the United States settled in Vermont," says Sara Peattie from the Puppeteers Cooperative in Boston. "With them came puppet theaters and town pageants. They used these as labor organizing tools." And sometimes these workers' pageants surpassed the scale of their humble village roots. In 1913, author John Reed collaborated with arts patron Mabel Dodge, painter John Sloan, and members of the Industrial

Workers of the World to mount a huge pageant to draw attention to the Silk Strike of 1913 in Paterson, New Jersey. The pageant brought 1,200 actual striking textile workers to perform at Madison Square Garden in nearby Manhattan, where they reenacted pickets, scuffled with *faux* police and sang union songs in front of a 90 by 200 foot painted backdrop depicting Paterson's silk mills. The show ended with triumphant speeches by labor leaders Elizabeth Gurley Flynn, Carlo Tresca, and Big Bill Haywood, though the actual strike ended in failure.

In the late nineteenth and early twentieth centuries, radical pageants grew less commonplace in the US as many cities and towns passed laws that restricted the number, size and content of public celebration. Often it was the elite that were permitted to parade and symbolically flaunt their power. St. Louis, Missouri's famed Veiled Prophet Celebration began after a trolley strike in 1878, with the prophet herself decked out in a white robe, white mask, and conical white cap, and packing a club, pistol, and two shotguns. "It will be readily observed," the *Missouri Republican* reported, "that the procession is not likely to be stopped by streetcars or anything else." The Pilgrim's Progress parade that takes place on Thanksgiving Day each year in Plymouth, Massachusetts, is a tradition rooted in a similar display of power, with the town's white populace marching gleefully to church with muskets and bibles in hand. Most town pageants in the US followed this trend, favoring patriotism and the histories that exalted the good-natured perseverance of the white race, whether based in fact or not.

"The basic battle in society is over how to tell different stories about what's going on in the world," says activist-artist David Solnit. It's a secret that the heads of state, religious and corporate institutions have been hording for millennia. "People who understand how to communicate with images and words and voices have the tools to catalyze people and reach people's hearts and minds, and tell different stories to combat the dominant control stories—to speak in the language of the heart and the gut."

A New World of Puppetry

In the 1950s the young Peter Schumann busied himself in the resurgence of the avant-garde in Germany.

"We rented a cellar in Munich and put posters all over the neighborhood, and we pretended to do a concert—improvisations with big titles, vocals, garbage sounds. It kept shifting. We did dance concerts and more people participated. I made big masks and figures and put people inside bags with or without holes in them, or just moved fabrics." He and his friends were continuing the work of the radical art movements that had been killed off by the Nazis. "It was in the air—the Expressionists, the Dadaists, the Abstractionists, the Bauhaus in Germany—all the radical turners of today's aesthetics had been extremely busy with different styles and mixings of media. It was learning from that, and also *protesting* that." Peter was both angered and ideologically shaped by the inaction of some of his forbearers. "Why did this not become a protest movement against Hitler? It was only wiped out."

Peter Schumann set out to start a dance company in New York. "First I'd tried to work with all these fancy dancers from the Merce Cunningham studio and they were non-responsive mostly." Peter's building superintendent (who called himself "The Ambassador of the Planet Uranus") had some friends who Peter recruited as his first volunteer performers. "I got all these dope addicts together and they were my company," he says. "And it was a great company." The incidental group performed a *Dance of Death* for the weeklong General Strike for Peace organized by the War Resisters League, the Greenwich Village Peace Center, and members of the Living Theater in February of 1962. Author Grace Paley, Catholic Worker founder Dorothy Day, and folksinger (and former puppeteer) Pete Seeger all spoke and performed throughout the week, alongside many others. All of New York's major daily papers refused to print ads for the strike or announce that there would be picketing at US Army recruiting offices and the New York Stock Exchange.

The Strike was the rekindling of a 1930s tradition. With fascism on the rise in Europe and in the midst of the Great Depression, there had been a General Strike for Peace in 1936, along with annual May Day parades in Manhattan's Union Square. Mexican muralist David Siqueiros, Works Progress Administration (WPA) puppetry director Remo Bufano, and the young painter Jackson Pollock joined scores of other artists to build floats and puppets, large and small, depicting African-American heroes, bulbous-headed politicians, or enslaved European workers being whipped by an SS officer as they towed Adolph Hitler and all of Germany's death camps down the street. The artistic wing of the WPA was an environment for people whose ideologies were as radical as their art, and puppetry was one part of that.

"Their point of view was, 'Puppets? Why not?'" says John Bell. The American puppeteers of the Depression Era were using puppets in the way that their Old World predecessors had used them. World War II and the subsequent rise of McCarthyism changed that. "The Cold War set in this idea that's still prevalent," says Bell. "That puppets are children's entertainment. This really dug

itself in and it's really an American idea." Perhaps that's why an un-American artist with un-American ideas is credited with igniting the radical puppetry revolution in America, as the 1960s ushered in a new era of rebellion and different thinking.

In 1963, Elka Schumann had a job teaching Russian at an alternative high school in Vermont, but her husband Peter was turned down when he wanted to teach dance. "They came to see that 'Dance of Death' and they were horrified," he laughs. "So I said, 'Oh, what about puppetry?' I just threw it out, just like that, and they said, 'Puppetry, yes. That's for children, right? Yeah. Good.'" The name for the Schumanns' puppet company came when another element was added to the theater. In addition to being a sculptor, dancer, printmaker, musi-

The Reaper claims the life of a labor leader in Bread & Puppet's *The Passion of Chico Mendez*, 1988. Photo: Bill Teel.

cian, and puppeteer, Peter Schumann was also a bread baker. He was heir to a century-old strain of Silesian sourdough culture—the key ingredient to his famous rye loaves that are dense, dark and not as easy to swallow as the white, pre-packaged Wonder Bread that most Americans are accustomed to. Peter slathers slices of his sourdough bread with a sharp aioli that is often so strong that it burns. He began serving this at every performance, and the audience went home with garlic on their breaths and politics on their brains, digesting both difficult bread and difficult theater—bread and puppet.

Bread & Puppet's earliest work was in the streets of New York City, staging scrolling *cantastoria* shows on top of garbage cans with Puerto Rican activists. They also worked in churches, transforming traditional Christmas, Easter, and Thanksgiving stories into anti-war shows. Peter Schumann made 100 puppets called "Gray Ladies"—narrow female figures that stood twelve feet tall, their hands clasped in prayer, and manipulated by a single pole—and used these in collaboration with a chamber music ensemble for a version of Bach's *Cantata #140* that also became a piece about Vietnam. "We borrowed kettledrums from some orchestra and during the Cantata movements the drums would

mow down people and the Cantata would [raise] them up. It was a very simple, big choreography. It came out wonderfully. Then we used the same Gray Ladies in parades—piles and piles of them." And the participants in these parades were the same people that performed in Bread & Puppet's shows all over the city. "It's something that grew very quickly to be for many, many people. We did parades where we needed virtually hundreds of people."

What Bread & Puppet was doing was completely unheard of. "Puppetry in America was Bil Baird and all the kitsch-makers of the world," says Peter. "I went to the Puppeteers of America festival in 1963—solid kitsch. We had to play outdoors because there wasn't enough space for us indoors. We strung people up by their necks in the show and all kinds of nasty things. Somebody wanted to kill me. And the fire department came."

Bread & Puppet's radicality stood alone in the puppetry community, but another kind of radical performance community was growing. "I participated with Kaprow and Oldenburg and other Happening-makers," says Peter. The Happenings were art events that arose in New York in the late 1950s in backlash against the dominance of abstract expressionism in the art world. The Happening-makers drew inspiration from the simultaneous performances conducted by the European Futurists and Dadaists a few decades before, and counted former Bauhaus professor Josef Albers and music composer John Cage among their mentors. Happenings happened in unusual locations—gymnasiums, garages, parking lots and abandoned hotels—and housed absurd performances with objects as everyday as typewriters, lawnmowers, and cement mixers, to the extraordinary, like cardboard firefighting uniforms or a nine foot tall boot that walked itself awkwardly around the playing space. These performances drew a variety of nervous responses from their willing audiences, distraught neighbors, and curious police detectives. "They were so similar to what I was doing in Germany," says Peter. "It was amazing."

Most of the Happenings' radicality was in form and not always in content, whereas Bread & Puppet's unwavering commitment to make theater whose message was as radical as its presentation was informed by Peter Schumann's close-up experience with war and time spent as a refugee. But with

increased US involvement in Vietnam impinging on American life, resistance to that involvement escalated. Some of this resistance came from artists. "In the late 1960s, street theater grew all over New York," Peter remembers. "Dozens of groups appeared all of a sudden, a lot of which had done workshops with us." Similar things were going on around the country, notably in California. "We also met with the west coast folks—the San Francisco Mime Troupe and Teatro Campesino. They came east and we went west. We did the Radical Theater Conference together. That was an exchange of ideas and similar things."

Bread & Puppet's *Fire* was an indoor show in remembrance of the first three Americans to die by self-immolation in protest of the war in Vietnam. *Fire* was a series of eight scenes revealed by a silent, masked narrator. A card displayed a day of the week, a small bell rang, and a curtain was drawn to display a dozen actors standing, sitting, or lying almost motionless, all wearing black garb and identical white masks molded from the face of Li Minh, a Vietnamese woman who was in the company. The scenes began as familiar, with the actors sharing a meal around a table, or poised to dance in pairs to sporadic music, or gathered around a deathbed while one of their number read another's last rites. The scenes grew more disturbing and dark, each hanging there for a few minutes that could feel like hours, before the curtain closed and the narrator moved through the ritual of presenting the next day. The play ended with a day called "FIRE" and a lone figure, enclosed in a cage of cinderblocks and barbed wire, entwined herself from foot to head by drawing strips of red tape up the length of her white robes.

Fire is cited as being the show that made Bread & Puppet famous, though not in America. New Yorkers appreciated it only as "weird protest theater" and not as art. The reaction in Europe was different. John Bell explains, "On an artistic level they saw Bread & Puppet's European sensibility and made connections to Futurism, Dada, Expressionism, and the Bauhaus." And on a political level, the European public had a cleaner conscience about the situation in Vietnam. "There was also this vision of the US as being at the center of youth culture and so Bread & Puppet appealed to young audiences." In 1968, the year that student demonstrations in Paris built into a weeklong general strike by two thirds of the French workforce, *Fire* played and there were crowds breaking down the door to see the show.

Bread & Puppet continued to make appearances in New York and abroad while taking a four-year residency at Goddard College in Vermont. The move from city to country affected Peter Schumann's output and he found himself working with a different set of players—Vermonters, not New Yorkers, and mountains, not skyscrapers. "What had worked in New York or DC didn't work in Vermont," says John Bell. John joined Bread & Puppet in the 1970s, after the residency at Goddard ended and the Theater had chosen to stay in Vermont, where there was more space to play with and store giant puppets and cheaper rent for the scores of puppeteers that it took to make giant puppet theater happen. "Elka's father had acquired this land in Glover, Vermont and on it was this huge gravel pit," explains Bell. "He had just sold the gravel to build the interstate and was going to have it smoothed over, but Peter said, 'Hey! This is an amphitheater!' and that became the setting for 'Our Domestic Resurrection Circus.'"

"Our Domestic Resurrection Circus" began as an annual event when Bread & Puppet first moved to Vermont. For two decades the circus drew crowds to Glover to camp out and wander the grounds, seeing sideshows around the field, in the forest, and under the barn before finding a spot on the hillside to watch the main event. Bread & Puppet's Circus transformed social critique into a series of quick acts with traditional circus figures. A lion would brandish a whip and command a pride of humans to stand on

buckets, jump through hoops and watch TV, while global warming or the National Debt could be a big, pink elephant that politicians would like to pretend isn't there. The Circus grew rife with plenty of puppet representations of Vermont life (cows, sheep, farmers, goats, a donkey) and actual aspects of local culture (like the use of traditional Sacred Harp singing, or sheaves of grain culled from a nearby field). Forms from the Old World showed up too: Germany's everlasting hero Kasper became the Circus' slapstick clown, and Bread & Puppet's output of *cantastorias* now numbers somewhere in the hundreds. And of course, there were giants.

Up through 1998 Bread & Puppet's summer staff would recruit volunteers from the Circus audience to be in a pageant that made full use of the rolling hills and expansive fields of their farmland. In earlier years the audience numbered a few hundred, but by the late 1990s there were an estimated 40,000 people coming from all over the country to see the Circus and partake in the spectacle that grew up around it. A lot of these people came primarily to party in the nearby campgrounds, many more just to see the shows, and quite a few to participate in any way possible. So when the call came for volunteer performers, hundreds of people responded, most of whom had never been in a puppet show before.

Volunteers were divided into teams, given costumes, taught their roles, and within an hour were performing in front of an audience of many thousands. The pageants were sparse, slow-moving, and far more abstract than the verbose antics of the Circus, pointing more to Schumann's roots as a choreographer. The pageant's climax was always the arrival of "Mother Earth," the largest puppet of

all, emerging over a rise to usher out the evils of the world.

It is this massive scale of participation that is the reason for Bread & Puppet's influence over arts and activism in North America. Many people who came and saw and participated wanted more—to run away and join the Bread & Puppet Circus. And a lot of them did by volunteering in Bread & Puppet shows in other cities, or by writing and requesting a summer internship in Glover. Some of these people stayed and became part of the community that grew up around the Bread & Puppet Theater and Farm over the years. Many others left to make their own work because they felt that the work they were doing at Bread & Puppet could never be their own—it was Peter Schumann's.

Aresh Javadi, an artist and organizer with New York's More Gardens Coalition, made the pilgrimage up to Glover after being told that his community arts work was reminiscent of Bread & Puppet. "I was very impressed by the joy and humor and smartness, and obviously the critique of administration that was lacking in other fun, celebratory, circussy things that I'd gone to. So I came back for the summer program and it was really exciting. You could just feel it building up as time went on because there's this big Circus day and a familial feeling of bringing everything together for the tens of thousands of people who are showing up to watch. The hierarchy was really obvious in that whole structure, coming from Peter down to the bottom, but it was really fun to put my hands into paper mâché and slop it and to have all this space to be able to be creative and to be around so many people who have high energy doing it full

on." When Aresh returned to New York, he began using puppetry in his activist work.

Gustavo Boada made masks for Peru's Yuyachkani theater group in the 1980s. He came to the US to work with Bread & Puppet. Peter Schumann was extremely impressed by Gustavo's craftsmanship, and Gustavo recalls how Peter expressed this. "He told me, 'I don't need a mask-maker—I am the mask-maker. You should be creating your own work.' So I did this." Gustavo moved to North Philadelphia to make masks, teach stiltwalking, and create street and puppet theater with members of the Latino community. "Peter inspired me to do the work I'm doing now. I wouldn't be doing this if he hadn't said what he said."

Matty Hart began making puppets with the Radical Færie community and was told that he needed to go up to Bread & Puppet. "It was a truly life-changing moment. I had never understood that that type of world existed, that that type of art got made, that people participated in anything on that scale. It completely changed the way that I understood how people got together, what art could be in the world, and the scale and function of participatory art." Matty reflects on being a young, queer puppeteer who founded Spiral Q Puppet Theater in Philadelphia partly in reaction to his experience at Bread & Puppet. "Bread & Puppet came to represent a paternal figure. I had to leave it. It was part of youth, to say, 'I'm not you, I'm something else.' And Spiral Q did it organizationally. 'We're not that, we're an urban public theater. We're street-based. We're younger, edgier, more radical.' And we were, but in a different way. Bread & Puppet had a political and capital capacity and a function and a breadth and an intelligence way beyond ours. But it was important to break away."

Graciela Monteagudo studied different forms of puppetry in Argentina and was looking for more serious training in street theater. She met Bread & Puppet in Brazil and worked as a translator for their show about Brazilian labor leader Chico Mendes. She says that many of the Brazilian volunteers took issue with Bread & Puppet arriving with a show about one of their national heroes that was already made. "They complained that it was not flexible. There were other problems, but in the end the show turned out good and everything was fine." Graciela moved to Vermont to join the company. "Bread & Puppet creates pieces at the farm in Glover, with Peter directing a small group of puppeteers. Once the show is finished, the group takes it on tour to different communities. Community members volunteer for roles, while the young Bread & Puppet people direct them into a fully scripted show. This is a process that opens a unique opportunity

for people who do not define themselves as artists to participate in a political artistic performance, but does not empower the community to tell their own story." Graciela went on to make street theater in Argentina and the US that incorporated collective input and community feedback into the creative process. "I still continue to work with Bread & Puppet because I have a lot to learn from Peter."

Matty Hart says, "It wasn't until much later that I realized that it was a European model of artist training: master and student. Peter was the master and there were students at different levels. You learn, you graduate through practice and production, and public humiliation and all this stuff, which is a part of that very old system. It's a cooperative hierarchy." Bread & Puppet's authority to do this is a testimonial to their ability as well as their longevity as a company. While most of their contemporaries from New York, San Francisco, and Vermont that were around in the 1960s and 1970s no longer exist, Bread & Puppet has continued to

be not just a theater company, but a theater school that has taught the art of making puppets and puppet shows, *cantastorias* and pageants to thousands of people worldwide. And it has served as a model for those wanting to make this kind of art and theater, as well as for those willing to teach it. In this way, radical puppetry has spread and taken on new forms and methods in its design and process.

Cooperative Beasts

It's the First of May 1977, and a few hundred people parade puppets and banners through the streets of Minneapolis. The imagery is a mishmash of purple-faced women, giant flowery dragons, majestic buffalo and other animals divided into four sections and representing the seasons of the year, each accompanied by its own musical sound. The procession makes its way toward Powderhorn Park for an annual maypole ceremony, until it is blocked by what looks like a group of people who should be in the parade. They have picket signs.

"They thought that we had stolen May Day from labor," says Sandy Spieler, artistic director for In the Heart of the Beast Puppet and Mask Theater. "I stepped forward and stated that our intention was to enact this procession as a way to celebrate the workers who build this community every day with the creativity of their hands, hearts, and minds."

Nixon was president and the National Guard had just killed four students at a campus protest in Kent, Ohio when Heart of the Beast performed its first show in 1973. Originally called Powderhorn Puppet Theater, Heart of the Beast was started by a handful of artist-activists who believed that society could be changed through art, and that public action in the form of theater could inspire people to take other forms of action. They had prior experience in agitprop protest theater that decried all the bad stuff in the world, issue by issue, with no end in sight. Powderhorn's founders had grown weary of agitprop's preachy and reactionary pitfalls, but struggled with trying to make something that went beyond the flatness of issue-based art. In the book *Theater of Wonder: 25 Years in the Heart of the Beast*, Powderhorn co-founder David O'Fallon writes about making a big militarized corporate puppet head that was plastered with bits of hardware, armed forces insignias and logos from IBM, Coca Cola, and Xerox. When he looked at the finished product, David realized that he had made something that was the physical embodiment of the didactic protest theater that he and his cohorts were trying to move away from. He threw it away and set about making a different kind of puppet theater.

Their first show, *A Boat, A Boot, A Book, A Ball of Yarn*, was made entirely from found materials and performed in a neighborhood park in front of a small lake on the Fourth of July, 1973. It was a simple, beautiful piece using puppets, giant masks, and cheap theatrical tricks. In the show, people struggle to reclaim the fruits of their labor (the objects in the show's title) that have been stolen from them by the forces of church and state. The people fall into subjugation before being awakened by a giant puppet named "Mama." They then realize that their power to create is in their own hands. About fifty people watched. Within thirty years, that number would swell to 35,000.

Heart of the Beast credits Bread & Puppet as a role model, as is evident in their use of clay-molded maché and specific images, such as the arrival of giant maternal liberator in their first show, or the stark Gray Lady-like figures in their wordless 1975 production *Magnificat*. Heart of the Beast had local influences too; the personality of Minneapolis, the Mississippi River, and the struggles of the American Indian Movement all had a major impact on their work. At one point Heart of the Beast was faced with the same choice that Bread & Puppet had made: stay in the city, or move out onto a farm.

"We consciously chose to ground ourselves in Minneapolis," says Sandy Spieler. "The issues that we took up were ones that affected us locally, but of course had global repercussions as well, because everything is interconnected." The theater's namesake reflects this ideology. "It's a phrase from Cuban poet José Marti, popularized by Che Guevara. When people from the US wanted to be part of the Cuban Revolution, Che said, 'I envy you. You North Americans are very lucky. You are fighting the most important fight of all—you live in the heart of the beast.' We take that to mean that wherever you are, that's your place of power—that's the community that you can affect from your own self, your own place of change, your own soul and heart and mind. From there you can go on to your immediate community, then the larger city, and eventually the nations of the world. You must work from where you are—that's the greatest challenge of all."

Working from where they were is exactly what Heart of the Beast did. In 1975 they held their first May Day Parade and Festival and have continued to do it every year. The Parade transforms ten blocks of Bloomington Avenue into a river of living images and music. Each section of the parade tells part of a story that unfolds into Powderhorn Park for a giant puppet pageant. The pageant has a different theme each year, but with recurring elements that give it a ceremonious quality to people who witness or take part in it repeatedly. The performance opens with "The Four Big Ones,"—giant puppets built in 1981 that represent Woods, River, Sky, and Prairie—and closes with the rowing of the Sun across the lake to lift the Tree of Life from its winter slumber. What happens in between is different every year, and pays tribute to both the "Green Root" (honoring nature) and "Red Root" (honoring labor) of May Day.

Tremendous planning goes into this day-long event. "We begin with a community brainstorm meeting in February," says Sandy Spieler. "We start thinking and talking and then break into teams who take artistic leadership for particular sections that they design, enact, direct and set music for. Each team brings their part back to the whole committee to see if it makes sense, or if anything is being repeated, or if it's going way way out. May Day's an interesting blend of individual artistry and collective brainstorming. It's never one exact process." The tail end of the Parade is called the "Free Speech Section" and anyone can participate. "We have rules in the storytelling part: no signage of individual groups. But in the free speech section each group *must* have a sign identifying who they are. There's no pre-meditated ordering to the lineup—it's first come first serve. So sometimes there's a really interesting flow of participants."

Heart of the Beast takes on issues and extends them beyond the limited scope of reactionary protest theater by exploring them on a committed, long-term basis. The speeches and struggles of the American Indian Movement (AIM) inspired a herd of giant puppet buffalo for the American Bicentennial, and a number of shows in tribute to the life of Anna Mae Aquash, a murdered AIM activist whose hands were cut off by the FBI. A three-year series of shows about water culminated in a thirty-person puppet circus tour that took the Theater from one end of the Mississippi River to the other by boat (or tried to—their boat, *The Collapso*, died en route and they had to complete the voyage by land.) In the three years leading up

Black banners bearing names of people killed in Iraq appear in Heart of the Beast's parades and May Day Ceremony, 2006. The banners are used by different groups for events in Minneapolis throughout the year. Photo: Liz Welch.

to the Quincentennial of Columbus' arrival in the Americas, Heart of the Beast produced a number of shows that, through collaboration with visiting puppeteers from Latin America and over a hundred community members, delved into the hemisphere's natural and cultural histories, conquest, exploitation, and possible futures.

Heart of the Beast was just one of several radical theater companies to emerge from their community in the early 1970s, and like Bread & Puppet, they continued while other groups came and went. The longevity of both Heart of the Beast and Bread & Puppet could be attributed to what they had that other performing groups didn't: giant puppets. "There's a centrality of big things," says John Bell. "What they attract is so different than 'actors' theater.'" And with giant puppets, a place is soon needed to store them. In 1990 Heart of the Beast purchased a former pornographic cinema to be their theater, workshop, and storage space. And then there's the Bread & Puppet Museum. "The Schumanns have a big barn," says John Bell, "and when you're a puppeteer you say, 'Here's the barn, fill it up with puppets!'"

Heart of the Beast and Bread & Puppet aren't the only long-standing participatory giant puppet institutions in North America. Sara Peattie and George Konnoff started the Puppeteers Cooperative in the 1970s when they began making "instant parades" with community groups. Sara is renowned for her handbook *68 Ways to Make Really Big Puppets* and still runs the Puppeteers Cooperative out of a church basement in Boston. "We try to be like the library," says Sara. "The library doesn't ask who you are or what you want it for. Our political stance is that it's a cooperative and people do a lot of different things." Part of the Cooperative's basement space is an organized workshop, equipped with tools, hardware, rolls of colored paper, and other materials used for making and maintaining giant puppets. The other part is the library itself— roomfuls of puppets that have been built over the years that anyone can borrow for whatever they want. Sara also works with a sister cooperative in Brooklyn and similar organizations have been cropping up around the country. "There's usually one in every city," says Sara. "It's an ecological niche. Once you have puppeteers, it's hard to get rid of them."

The Joker and the Fool

San Francisco is packed with pageantry. Annual celebrations honoring Chinese New Year, Carnival, Cinco de Mayo, LGBTQ Pride, and Day of the Dead all parade through a city whose buildings are adorned with hundreds of murals. These parades and works of public art reclaim space through culture that is rooted in the celebratory resistance of marginalized communities. In recent years, political demonstrations have joined the roster of public festivity with the presence of giant puppets, but back in 1990 there was no culture of protest puppetry to be seen in the Bay Area, or anywhere else on the West Coast. "There had been in the 1960s," says K. Ruby, "with the San Francisco Mime Troupe and Teatro Campesino, but there hadn't been since I began living in the city in 1981."

Ruby began making dolls at age seven, and as a young adult she was an accomplished maskmaker. "Masks are kind of dumb if you just want to be a visual artist and hang them on a wall," she says. "That doesn't seem very rich somehow." So in 1988 she landed a job performing with a troupe that brought the cathartic techniques of *commedia dell'arte* maskwork into prisons. The troupe also employed the *Theater of the Oppressed* techniques invented by Brazilian author and theatrical director Augusto Boal.

Boal criticized the legacy of what he called "formulaic tragi-drama." From tragi-drama's inception in ancient Greece and up through its modern-day reign in Brazil's televised *novelas* (soap operas), Boal argued that governments use tragic themes to keep people distracted, passive, and non-participatory, instead of working to solve real problems in society. He began making political theater in the 1960s with people in Rio's mostly black *favelas*, but as a white, middle-class man, Boal's effort to inspire poor people to rise up against race, class, and gender inequality was inhibited by his own position of privilege, which was only augmented by his designation as "director." So he threw away his scripts and replaced them with improvisation within the framework of theatrical games. The games had actors posing problems to an audience of "spect-actors" who could, at any moment, intercede to create and act out any number of potential solutions. In this "forum theater," any notions of rebellion and the impetus for change came from within the group Boal was working with, and he shifted from being a director to acting as facilitator—a role that he named "The Joker" after the playful and neutral nature of the wild icon from a deck of playing cards.

Brazil's military dictatorship responded to Boal's ideas by arresting, torturing, and finally exiling him, and so the *Theater of the Oppressed* spread throughout the world. Working in the global North, Boal found that though many participating spect-actors were dealing with different forms of oppression than those he had encountered in Brazil, the forum theater exercises still applied. And they were especially useful for people living in prison.

K. Ruby's troupe toured from prison to prison, making theater based on the inmates' stories. For $100 a month Ruby lived on the bus with the company, made masks of the stock *Commedia* characters, created theater with prisoners, and got her ass pinched by her boss. Within a year she left the troupe to seek out a project free from the paradoxical traps of patriarchy, hierarchy, and ass-pinching sexism.

Ruby ended up at Heart of the Beast and helped build their 1989 May Day Parade. "I worked twelve to sixteen hours a day for no pay," she says, "and I loved it." And she also loved working for a company that was run by women. She brought what she'd learned at Heart of the Beast back to the Bay Area, and joined forces with Amy Christian, an artist who had worked on "Mask-O-Rage"—a demonstration that had brought hundreds of people together to make masks and then parade with them to the gates of the Nevada Nuclear Test Site. The two women were approached by David Solnit, an activist who wanted visuals for an anti-nuke demonstration in remembrance of the Hiroshima bombing. "We built puppets in my basement," says Ruby. "I was still just learning and I was also trying to teach people. But we made four or five giant puppets and took them to this action." These puppets included a giant toxic waste monster pitted against an enormous bird, a huge root creature, and a big baby holding the world aloft, that called for clean air, clean earth, and a healthy future for our planet.

Amy and Ruby rented a larger space and spent a month working with people to build sixteen more giant puppets for another action against the Nevada Test Site. "People were excited," Ruby says. "There'd been a masked event the year before and now there was this bigger puppet event." Ten of these puppets wore matching happy faces and were choreographed to simultaneously flip around to reveal the apocalyptic expression from Edvard Munch's *The Scream*. What Amy and Ruby were doing was not entirely unheard of. Many people who came to the demonstrations assumed that this was the work of the Bread & Puppet Theater. Even though Vermont was located 3,000 miles away, Bread & Puppet's name had become synonymous with giant protest puppetry. The two women had not set out to start an organization, but with the question, "Are you Bread & Puppet?" being lobbed at them whenever their towering figures put in an appearance, they had to call themselves something. In the tradition of the court jester who spoke truth without censure and with a nod to Boal's Joker-facilitator, they named themselves Wise Fool Puppet Intervention.

Within a year Wise Fool had begun working with other activist and community organizations on issue-based puppet shows about alternative energy, white privilege, racial diversity, and living with HIV. The process of show-making began with group input and inviting people to come share their experiences. Several weeks later, people's stories came to life as large-scale, outdoor performances that used giant puppets, rod puppets, shadow puppets, *Bunraku*-style puppets, costumes, masks, and sculptural elements. Wise Fool also led free workshops in puppetmaking and stiltwalking—a skill that Ruby had picked up both in her stint making theater in prisons and via African stilting traditions used at Heart of the Beast. Wise Fool helped local artists and cultural workers to make living altars and parades for Day of the Dead and Carnival in San Francisco's Mission District. Wise Fool also brought their puppets to all the demonstrations. And there were a lot of demonstrations—George Bush (the first) had just launched a war in the Persian Gulf.

"We were getting up at 5:00 a.m. three or four days a week," says Ruby. Wise Fool would march their giant oilmen puppets, wearing dripping-red signs that read "Oil is Thicker than Blood," followed by fifteen costumed drummers walking on stilts. "For me that was the beginning of a new era of puppetry in the streets. We were doing it."

A Zapatista Theater

"I had been organizing for fifteen years on single-issue politics," recalls David Solnit of the early 1990s, "which is how most social movements in the United States were organized even though we all knew that the problems were systemic." David, like a lot of activists, was hungry for other forms of resistance and different ways of doing things. "I had organized demonstrations and marches and mass civil disobedience for years but they didn't feel adequate. I was looking for a new language. The shift for me was when the Zapatista uprising happened and told a different story about how to change the world."

The Zapatistas revealed themselves to the world on January 1st, 1994 as a counterweight to the implementation of NAFTA—the North American "Free Trade" Agreement, which threatened an accelerated marginalization and cultural homogeneity of Mayan peoples in Mexico. *Zapatismo* sought not to seize power via a party-line ideology, but fought to restore autonomy to civil society by submitting itself to the wishes of community, or "to lead by following." The cry of *¡Ya basta!* (Enough already!) was a "No!" that suggested multiple tangible forms of "Yes!" The Zapatista uprising called itself "a revolution to make revolution possible."

With manifestos that were poetry and speeches that told folktales, the Zapatistas invited outsiders to transcend antiquated models of token solidarity and imagine a new world where many different worlds fit. Visitors traveled to Chiapas to engage in *Zapatismo* through a series of meetings or *encuentros* (literally "encounters") in the Lacandon jungle.

At the First International Encuentro, the Zapatistas demonstrated their creative refusal to pander to elitism and hierarchy. An example of this is when they pulled the plug on the pushy and uncooperative corporate media. While waiting for the arrival of the EZLN at the onset of the Encuentro, several visiting news crews ignored a request to remove themselves and their gear from the stage, and so the electricity was shut off. All the power to run the cameras and recording equipment, as well as the lights for the entire Encuentro, was suddenly gone. There, in the darkness of the jungle, hundreds of international observers waited silently and could just barely make out a parade of tiny lights that flickered on a distant mountainside, descending slowly over the course of an hour before disappearing into the foliage at the mountain base. The gringo masses huddled in blackness until the procession of masked Zapatistas entered the clearing with torches aloft. The crowd erupted with cheers and applause, the Zapatistas ascended to the podium, and the lights were turned back on.

In the fullest embodiment of the Spanish verb *hacer*—to do, to make, to build, to perform—the Zapatistas are performance artists and theater-makers on a grand scale who, like Augusto Boal, propose questions on the stage of the world to be worked out by some six billion "spect-actors."

"The Zapatistas had a new language," says David Solnit. "I was very inspired by them. Looking around I thought, 'What do we have that we can create a new language with?'"

The Convergence Model

"It was the first time I ever saw people using cardboard for anything."

Four years before she hunkered down to pen portable murals for the Beehive Design Collective, Kehben Grifter was point-person for visual outreach and roller-skating at a ten-day gathering in Chicago called Active Resistance. Active Resistance was a counter-conference to the 1996 Democratic National Convention (DNC) envisioned by anarchist collectives from Chicago, Detroit, St. Louis, and other spots around the Midwest. It was more than just an anarchist gathering—it was for people wanting to organize with popular movements that didn't self-identify as anarchist. People participated in week-long workshops on alternative economics and community organizing that had a hands-on emphasis on sustainability and permanence, which many participants were experiencing for the first time. "It was formative for me to raise the standard for how things happened and try and make this historic event that was very hopeful," says Kehben. "It was very forward-looking....It was movement-building."

Kehben crafted posters and propaganda, but puppetry was strange terrain. "It wasn't on the radar screen for me," she says. "There had been a lack of creative stuff at anarchist gatherings. Visuals were a radical thing."

Well-established companies of giant puppet-makers existed in the Midwest—notably Chicago's Redmoon Theater and Minnesota's In the Heart of the Beast—with a history of running legally permitted puppet spectacles in the streets. But if puppets were "not on the radar screen" for the organizers of Active Resistance, then the idea of participating in an anarchist gathering that was to culminate in unpermitted demonstrations on the doorstep of the Democratic National Convention (DNC) would seem totally insane to professional puppeteers who sometimes relied on the support of the municipalities where they worked. Instead, experienced activist-puppeteers were called in from the West Coast to share skills with people who came to Active Resistance.

Artists didn't just build puppets, they organized the protest. "The whole logic was to step away from having cultural workers and performers there to just decorate a predictable demonstration," says David Solnit. "It was a participatory theater, not just a protest with a little bit of culture on the side." The "Festival of the Oppressed" pageant that attendees of the gathering brainstormed and built out of cardboard and paper mâché featured about 200 participants. Some carried puppets while others played roles indicated by placards worn on their bodies. The pageant's centerpiece was a four-sided corporate tower that manipulated gruesome likenesses of Bob Dole and Bill Clinton, looming over some thirty workers, consumers, taxpayers, and voters who

The Corporate Power Tower with puppets of presidential candidates, part of a 200 person theater pageant and march through Chicago's Wicker Park during the 1996 Active Resistance Conference. Photo: Susan Simensky Bietila.

dragged it down the street. A procession of as many shackled representations of immigrants, minorities, single moms and other marginalized people followed, all policed by puppet government operatives, politicians and bulbous porcine cops. Caricatures of reporters buzzed about toting oversized cardboard video cameras emblazoned with "EMPTY TV" and "SEE BS," randomly interviewing curious onlookers. The parade stopped at major intersections where, in the tradition of Boal's theatrical vision, the masses of oppressed people united to tear the walls from the tower to reveal costumed dancers and four positive visions of a future that Active Resistance participants had developed over a week of workshops.

The reaction from people on the street to this participatory theater differed greatly from the turn-offs that run-of-the-mill street protests normally offered the public. "I've seen these things not work," Kehben reflects, "but it was very well choreographed and there was a lot of engaging with people on the side of road."

Chicago's civilians weren't the only ones to respond strongly to the demonstration. As the pageant neared the DNC, the police presence flanking it grew, and, in tribute to Chicago's infamous DNC of 1968, many police hid their badges, then beat, stomped on, pepper-sprayed, and arrested a handful of demonstrators and independent journalists.

"I consider it 'state flattery,'" says David Solnit. "We've had a lot of flattery by the state where they consider our images so powerful and delicious that they feel obliged to try and arrest and repress them."

This unintentional flattery on the part of the state, coupled with positive reaction from the public, convinced organizers that this was a direction to go in. "Doing something with your hands was not going on at gatherings before that," says Kehben. "It was way more 'in-your-head' protest." It was a shift in the North American anarchist movement. A plan for a new model of organizing was being developed. "Active Resistance restructured the standard for what something like that should be. It set the bar. That was our goal."

The birth of Art & Revolution and a new connotation to the word "convergence" emerged at an event held at a tree farm north of Seattle in 1997. Building on the momentum from Active Resistance,

the Art & Revolution Convergence trained artists and organizers to use "culture as a weapon" through four days of sharing skills that culminated in a street action. "The goal was trying to shift what resistance and protest looked and felt like," says David Solnit. "To make it more of a festival and learn how to communicate not just through flyers and speeches, but through art and culture." Art & Revolution co-organized street theater actions with the United Farm Workers, Homes Not Jails, and Earth First! Similar convergences soon followed in Detroit, at the Headwaters Forest Reserve in California, and then again in Seattle the following year in tandem with Reclaim the Streets actions in England where the G8 were meeting. David says, "On a very small scale it was what the World Trade Organization protests would look like a year later." A downtown Seattle street was sealed off in an impromptu block party complete with puppet theater, dancers, music, a drum brigade, and general celebration. The Seattle police did not know how to respond.

Both Art & Revolution and Reclaim the Streets were operating on a decentralized model inspired by *Zapatismo*. This was different from more company-driven political street theater of groups like Bread & Puppet that had a director and a centralized structure of participation. Bread & Puppet would roll into town, put puppets into people's hands, make their theater happen, then pack up and leave. There was only one Bread & Puppet Theater. "But anybody who wanted to be Art & Revolution could be," says K. Ruby. "Art & Revolution is like Critical Mass, or Bikes Not Bombs, or Food Not Bombs—it's a repeatable structure that is free—free intellectual property." The creative, international network formed by these and other groups exploded into a popular mobilization that brought people to Seattle in 1999 to denounce the World Trade Organization (WTO).

"We took everything we'd learned about using art and theater as an organizing, educational, and mobilizing tool and we put it to use," says David Solnit. "We did puppet workshops for locked-out steelworkers, Unitarian youth groups, and local communities up and down the West Coast." Art & Revolution traveled with a union steelworker and a former sweatshop laborer who had been fired for trying to unionize. Their presentation articulated the pitfalls of corporate globalization from a variety of firsthand perspectives and was part of a growing network that led to events that would ignite a public dialogue throughout the world.

A Time Called Seattle

Q: "Where were you during Seattle?"
A: "I was being sworn in as a US citizen."

This was the exchange between a US Customs officer and Juan Martinez, a Colombian-born puppeteer with the Bikes Across Borders Cycle Circus who was returning to the US after a performance tour of Mexico. The odd thing about the officer's question is that "Seattle" isn't a point in time—it's a point in space—a city that has existed for over 150 years. The odder thing is that both Juan and the officer understood that "during Seattle" meant "during the 1999 demonstrations in Seattle where 50,000 people used direct action to shut down the ministerial meetings of the WTO."

Early in December of 1999, major newspapers ran a front-page photo of a mammoth banner sporting arrows labeled "Democracy" and "WTO" pointing in opposite directions. An activist stunt team had hung it from a crane high above the Seattle skyline and it sent a clear message to a media-gobbling public who had never heard of the World Trade Organization. The images delivered to people's homes via TV, newspapers, and the Internet made them wonder, "Why are these people risking their lives to hang a sign in front of the Space Needle? Why are people dressing like big sea turtles and blocking the streets? What is the WTO and why do so many people care?" It was Boal's model of forum theater set upon the American public: "Here is a problem—What can we do to solve it?" In the words of writer Paul de Armand, "The WTO protests were the Chiapas insurrection come to America."

Art & Revolution chapters from around the country converged and were joined by puppeteers from nearby Vashon Island and members of the Bread & Puppet Theater. Together they mapped out a pageant. "It was a step forward in that those of us who were artists and puppeteers were actually also organizers," says David Solnit. "We weren't just decorating and having other people do the organizing. The logic of the organizing was using art and theater logic. And puppet logic."

Though the actions against the WTO were an escalated continuation of the convergence model, the climate was different than it had been at previous gatherings. "Seattle was bigger and not about having conversations," says Kehben. "Our energy shifted to dealing with cops." The city and state government were underprepared for what they assumed would be a small protest. Martial law was declared, civilian defense against tear gas was outlawed, and police were ordered to arrest anyone who "looked like a protestor." The police also unwittingly took part in street theater.

"Anybody approaching the protest zone was stopped and had anything they were carrying taken away, including banners and puppets," says Jan Burger, co-founder of Paperhand Puppet Intervention in North Carolina. "Some people were wearing cardboard turtle costumes. The cops were so agitated from the previous day that they just came at us and threw us to the ground. And when they came at the turtles they actually tore the shells open and *de-turtled* them. It was incredible. It was an ironic, powerful moment because they actually had a plastron and a carapace and they pulled them apart." Ironic, too, that Seattle police were equipped with reptilian-looking anti-riot armor that earned them the nickname "mutant ninja turtle cops."

After the WTO meetings ended and the Seattle chief of police resigned, protest organizers licked their wounds, chalked up a victory for a revolution to make revolution possible, and asked each other, "What's next?"

The *Puppetista* Uprising

"Ten years ago when you heard the phrase, 'The Next Seattle' it meant that a city had a bunch of really hot grunge bands."

Author/musician Al Burian said this to an audience of hipsters in the spring of 2000. The nation's youth, along with people from grassroots social movements, plus a handful of hopped-up mayors and high-ranking law-enforcers were all talking about "The Next Seattle" now in terms of where the next mass mobilization was going to take place. Major international trade meetings that few people ever even knew about and even fewer people

had protested, were now slated to attract tens of thousands of demonstrators willing to travel across the country—even across the globe—to have their voices heard and their bodies counted. And a major attraction was the new wave of art that was happening in the streets.

In the spring of 2000, the Puppeteers Cooperative opened its doors to activists during BioDevastation, a conference and demonstration to counter an annual meeting of the biotech industry that was happening in Boston that year. At "BioDev," images by Maine's Beehive Collective were ubiquitous, Philadelphia's Shoddy Puppet Company shared stages with Vandana Shiva and Ralph Nader, and 3,000 people attended something that was as much of a festival as it was a rally. Several theatrical sideshows were situated around a major downtown park, and at one end a large stage served as a podium. The roster of speakers was broken up into twenty-minute segments, in between which people would go see a sock-puppet show about genetic engineering, or a theatrical basketball game where stilt-walking CEOs played "keep-away-from-the-people" with the Earth. The Bread & Puppet Theater arrived in their painted school bus full of puppets and announced, "We need 300 volunteers!" More puppeteers from the Dirt Palace and Big Nazo, both up from Providence, waltzed around in costume or on stilts. A throng of winged children and parents in monarch butterfly outfits fluttered around a nine-foot roller-skating Bride of Frankenstein and called for an end to GMO crops that killed beneficial insects. The Puppeteers Cooperative emptied its vaults to fill hands with beautiful beasts and gargantuan mutant tomatoes, and the mass of 3,000 seemed like twice its size as tourists and Sunday shoppers lined the sidewalks to watch and interact with an avenue awash with colorful figures. Protest transformed into parade.

BioDev 2000 launched a radical puppetry community on the East Coast. There were several pockets of puppeteers working in a variety of different ways: some ran puppetry lending libraries, others were in touring troupes, some were individual artists possibly playing at protest for the first time, and others had been organizing street theater with hundreds of people for thirty or forty years. All these came together with a common purpose and made something beautiful happen.

From top: The Face of Liberation spans a street in Washington DC, 2001. Photo: K. Ruby; The Flying Wrench Singers demonstrating against the IMF/World Bank in Washington DC, 2001. Photo: K. Ruby; "Hands Off Street Youth" puppet leading a 1998 march in support of Toronto's "squeegee kids," teens who earn money by washing car windshields. Photo: Scott Beibin, 1998)

Radical puppeteers needed a word to distinguish themselves in a country where "puppet" conjures up images of Howdy Doody, Lamb Chop, and other drossy icons of 1950s American kitsch-for-kids. Someone said, "We are *puppetistas*!" It was a fusion of the Germanic word *"puppet"* meaning "doll," and the Romantic suffix *"-ista"* meaning "one who does this" (e.g.: *dentista* and *taxista* translate from Portuguese or Spanish to dentist and cab driver). In North America this suffix bears an almost knee jerk association with Latin American leftist movements. "The *'ista'* part—it has a sort of revolutionary flair to it," says Argentinean puppeteer Graciela Monteagudo, "like *'anarquista'* or *'*Zapatista.'" It was the naming of an art movement whose ideals had indeed been funneled through the examples of Zapatismo. "I like it," says Graciela. "I like that it's spelled with a lower-case 'p'—that it has no center. Anybody who's working with giant puppets in the streets can claim to be a *puppetista*. I like the hybrid aspect of it—it's a great word."

Like many activist buzzwords, *"puppetista"* has the potential to stir up feelings of alienation outside of the countercultural communities where its meaning is understood. It was perhaps naïve for a group of radical artists, who were predominantly white, to appropriate a suffix from a language spoken mostly by people who are marginalized in the English-speaking world. Some *puppetistas* are people of color, but many more are not. K. Ruby speculates as to why this style of puppet theater appeals to some people and not others. "I believe that there is a way that we make puppetry that is distinctly European. It comes from that tradition and in part that's why it appeals to white people." Ruby also talks about working in a

prison system that's mostly populated by people of color. "The inmates would ask us about what we did, and they would say, 'Wow—this is really hard work! You must be getting paid a lot!' When I told them that we made a hundred bucks a month their jaws would drop. They just couldn't envision doing something that wasn't financially viable. As radical puppeteers, unless we kind of 'make it,' we're doomed to living off of pennies and I don't think that that has a big draw for most people of color."

"In this country white people are the most privileged," says puppeteer Jabari Jones, "while many black and Latino people are struggling to

obtain some form of status because we've been second-class citizens for so long. In order to become first-class citizens, one often adopts a posture of consumerism or anti-radicalism. Maybe the *puppetista* movement is overwhelmingly white because the people who do it see it as a rejection of privilege and normalized consumer values. And then there's this vicious cycle: when people don't see people like themselves doing something, they won't do it until someone emerges whom they respect, and even then that's not always guaranteed. My cousin has come to see me perform with Bread & Puppet and he tells me that it's not his thing, even though we're on the same page with the same issues."

"I think that it reflects on what the anti-corporate globalization movement was and is," says Graciela Monteagudo. "The *puppetista* phenomenon reflected this culture. But we were never really able to open up to communities outside of middle class white people in this country."

Trojans & Vikings

During their war with Troy, the ancient Athenians hid inside an enormous wooden horse and tricked the Trojans into accepting it into their city walls as a gift from the gods. Then forty Athenian soldiers popped out of the horse and opened the gates for an army of their friends who walked in, killed all the men, and took the women and children as slaves.

That's the story, circa 1200 BC, penned by Homer and Virgil, and literally the oldest trick in the book. Law enforcers knew the legend of the Trojan Horse and believed that giant puppets could be used in a similar manner. The *puppetistas* knew that if puppets were to be used as "Trojan Horses" that their legitimacy as objects of art and communication would be jeopardized and all puppets would suffer a demotion to "instruments of crime" and not be protected by the First, or any other, Constitutional Amendment. So the *puppetistas* adopted a "No Trojan Horse" tenet to their agenda.

It didn't matter. A conservative conspiracist think-tank calling itself the Maldon Institute (named for the Battle of Maldon, where Vikings surprised the Britons in 991 AD) was issuing reports to law enforcement agencies across the country suggesting that the *puppetistas* were "funded by the Federation of Former Soviet Republics [sic]," and also, "worshippers of Kali, the Hindu goddess of destruction." These claims, though absurd, amplified a growing fear of activists and protest culture among the police, and the information was used to justify raids and undercover police activity wherever puppets were being made or used.

Here's a sampling:

Two weeks before the 2000 Republican National Convention (RNC), Matty Hart was prep-

ping the studios of Philadelphia's Spiral Q Puppet Theater when he saw two men on a rooftop taking pictures of his building. He waved to them. "Hey guys! Where are you from?" Sarcastically, they said that they were from "Seattle" and left. Later that afternoon, Matty was running workshops with single moms from Kensington Welfare Rights Union and teenagers from Asian Americans United, plus a daycare center, when city inspectors dropped in to shut Spiral Q's studios down.

"It had been proven that puppets made a lot of sense and read real well in media," says Matty. "[They] created a fantastic environment that more people wanted to be a part of. They made protests fun. When there were these larger and larger demonstrations, there was a really powerful force from the government, and we were paying attention to what were the primary functions of that force. One of them was preemptive strikes and consolidation of all the art. We knew that this might happen, so we organized a few spaces that we were going to put stuff and had our legal stuff organized and had phone trees done, but also didn't really think that it was going to happen. There was a concern that people would disappear off the street, and later on, they did."

Philadelphia police harassed public puppet performances on numerous occasions. Agents photographed performers and audience members at a show in front of the Ethical Society building, and staged intimidating drive-bys at a Puppet Uprising cabaret, whose poster was critical of police harassment. During a rally in support of the puppeteers and other activists arrested during the RNC, thirty officers surrounded and searched a hand puppet show that was in progress in a park across the street from their headquarters. The show just continued while officers threw the props around. After finding nothing, the police hung back and watched the show as a hand puppet beat cop popped up and arrested the other puppets for conspiring to commit a crime.

On the eve of protests against the International Monetary Fund (IMF) and World Bank in Washington, DC, fire marshals declared the protest's convergence center unsafe and ordered everyone out. Then the DC police came in and confiscated all of the puppets, flags, musical instruments and kitchen supplies to determine their criminal nature. *The Washington Post* ran illustrated articles showing how water bottles could be made into explosives and detailing the ingredients for what they decided was a homemade pepper-spray: Onions, garlic and cayenne.

"I was making soup!" laughed one of the cooks.

"They wouldn't let us have any of our puppets back until the ACLU got on them and deemed the confiscation unconstitutional," says Jan Burger. "Then they gave us *some* of our stuff back. It was like a symbolic gesture. They didn't give back everything. Lots of our stuff got destroyed. We made these two fifteen-foot heads with the word 'Liberation' painted on them. They gave us one back and destroyed the other. It's just weird and bizarre." The police returned the puppets in what looked like a ceremony performed

by a team of unskilled furniture movers. "It was amazing seeing a high-ranking officer dragging this giant puppet labeled 'Democracy' through the street by her hair. It was beautiful in a horrific way."

Police have impounded puppeteers' trucks when they saw stilts or paper mâché figures strapped to the roof or stuffed in the back. David Solnit was invited to Windsor, Ontario for a teach-in prior to demonstrations against the Organization of American States. "They actually staked me out and followed me after the puppet workshop. They seized my truck full of puppets and threw me in jail for the duration of the protests." He was released on a legal technicality, and was told to be out of the country by sundown.

The Flying Rutabaga Cycle Circus was kicking off a cross-country bike tour in St. Louis, where the chemical company Monsanto was hosting the World Agricultural Forum (WAF) in 2003. The

Rutabagas' *Caravan Across the Cornbelt* was a puppet circus revue whose themes emphasized sustainable forms of transportation and agriculture. The *St. Louis Post-Dispatch* ran a front-page article that gave equal space to both sides of the agribusiness question. "That made Monsanto very nervous and they asked the police to intervene on their behalf," says puppeteer Jabari Jones, who was touring with the Circus. The St. Louis Police had teamed up with Allied Intelligence, a private agency hired to protect the WAF's interests, and raided the house where half of the Rutabagas were staying, arresting everyone inside. The other half of the Rutabagas were arrested in a park for "riding bicycles without a license"—a law that had been stricken from the books ten years prior to the arrest.

"Ironically, it was 'Bike to Work Day,'" says Dave Bailey, another puppeteer with the Circus. "We were arrested essentially for the 'intention to commit puppetry.'"

Though actual jail time served by most of these artists has been relatively short, the legal battles that follow are not. Many cases drag on for three years or more and drain thousands of dollars from people's pockets to pay travel expenses and lawyer's fees. And these people are artists—they live their lives out of love for what they do, not for money. By the time a case sees trial and some judge inevitably laughs it out of court, the city takes a moral and financial beating, while puppeteers are left with their lawyers' bill in one hand and the Maldon Report in the other, wondering, "Where's our check from the Federation of Former Soviet Republics?"

Clearly law enforcement has seen the effectiveness of art and theater as a form of action, and sometimes outlaws it altogether. At George W.

Bush's inauguration in 2001, puppets were banned, but cardboard signs were permitted, and these rules were enforced at a number of checkpoints around the city. One group of performers managed to side-step this by making a bunch of signs that unfolded and locked together into a giant puppet using a slot-and-tab system. In other cases, law enforcers carry the spirit of "state flattery" to the extreme by turning artists' own tactics against them.

In November of 2003, Jan Burger helped the Coalition of Immokalee Workers to orchestrate a three-day walking procession from Lake Worth, Florida to Miami where reps from every government in the western hemisphere were meeting to hash out details for the proposed Free Trade Area of the Americas (FTAA). Thirty people carried giant puppets for sixty miles in a pageant illustrating a history of globalization beginning with Columbus coming to America. Several towns along the route had passed temporary anti-puppet laws and Jan talks about an increased police presence that reached a critical mass upon entering Miami. "They had cleared out the entire downtown so that nobody saw the march. All we saw was cops. It was like trying to have a demonstration in the middle of a military camp."

The convergence space was under constant siege by the police, who had helicopters buzzing overhead shining searchlights down upon activists all night. They even turned the electricity for the entire block on and off just to interfere with spokes-council meetings. And law enforcers used theater as a weapon.

"There were agitators," says Burger, "undercover actors—just instigators of craziness. There was this one guy who was going around with his camera all up in people's faces, directly trying to create a provocation. Eventually these black bloc kids got up in his face, telling him to get the fuck out of there, and he said, 'I can do whatever I want. This is a free country.' Then a friend of mine said to the black bloc kids, 'Relax guys. He's just trying to get your goat.' They got mad at her and she said, 'Well, maybe you guys are the cops—who knows who the cops are?' That pissed them off to no end. They looked like they were going to go after her, so I said, 'Look guys, relax.' And they said, 'Don't tell us to relax!' And of course by then the guy with the camera was nowhere to be seen. Later on he handed out a card to somebody that read, 'AMBIENT MANIPULATIONS—Hire me for whatever job you want.'"

Another tactic used by agents is to exploit subculture through rudimentary clowning. Jan tells a story about a guy with a Band-Aid taped to his head, dressed in fatigues and wearing a floppy hat. He approached Jan, who was packing up his car, on the night before the big anti-FTAA demonstration.

"Where are you going?"

"Why do you want to know where I'm going? I don't know you."

"Can I go where you're going?"

"Why would you want to go where I'm going? You don't even know me."

"Look man, I lost my ride, I need to get out of here. Can you give a brother a hand?"

"What are you talking about?"

"Well, see, I got this package, you know? I need to take it somewhere. Can I put this in your car?" He showed Jan a mysterious four-foot long package covered in tape and stickers marked "FRAGILE".

"I thought, 'Holy shit! This guy is so bad!'" says Jan. "He was the most unbelievable cornball, and I was instantly freaked out, thinking, 'He's really going to try and put this thing in somebody's vehicle and then they're going to get busted with a felony for carrying an explosive or something.'" Jan ran into the convergence space and shouted, "There's this guy outside! He's trying to put stuff in people's cars!" The woman at the security desk told him that the Package Guy had been at it for hours and that there was nothing that they could do.

The disruption of activism by law enforcement is used like the tragi-drama of yore: it distracts us from the issues that we are working on. Instead we worry about the behavior of the police, and what ballistic and chemical weapons they are willing to let fly. The daily papers and nightly news play this up with shots of "protest porn"—skirmishes between demonstrators and police—instead of talking about why we are having a demonstration in the first place. Despite this divisive atmosphere, connections are sometimes attempted across the lines. At the IMF/World Bank protests in April of 2000, downtown Washington, DC looked like an enormous surrealist football game between protesters and police. A line of activists would span a street facing off with a line of helmeted officers who were ready to let loose with nightsticks and pepper spray, and then a ten-foot paper mâché monkeywrench would arrive escorting a secular Sacred Harp choir. Shouting gave way to singing, and the hostile situation would quickly calm. Another group tried a different tactic at the same protest: they locked themselves to a giant pink piggy bank made of wood, cardboard, and many layers of paper mâché. Anticipating arrest and confiscation by the police, the piggy's designers had left a surprise in the puppet's center: a big box of Krispy Kreme doughnuts. However, the piggy became the protest's media darling and, with added protection from millions of TV viewers, made it through the day unharmed.

The Puppet Horizon

Many *puppetistas* have taken a step back from the front lines of protest puppetry. After years of involvement in big puppet convergences, Ben Matchstick founded the Cardboard Teck Instantute in Montpelier, Vermont, and works locally touring his hand puppet shows and workshops by bicycle. "What was exciting for me is that we'd all come together and find out what we could all do collectively. It wasn't possible for us all to live in New York City or San Francisco—it would deprive our communities of the energy that we have. There was this macrocosm aspect that worked to a point but now needs to be rethought. Maybe it doesn't have to do with protests, but coming together and having art and culture and not necessarily rapid response to a perceived threat that's immediate. There's so much work to be done."

"Mobilizations are kind of like a sandwich," says David Solnit. "They're only as nourishing as what's in between the slices of bread. We have to have a lot organizing in our communities in between so that there's actually a demonstration of the power that we've built in our movements leading up to the mobilization."

"There's this big, big high to see these things happen at giant street protests," says Graciela Monteagudo. "But my favorite project was when I worked with other puppeteers in Buenos Aires in 2003 to build a show using ideas generated at the neighborhood *asambleas* (assemblies) about how people's money had been stolen from the banks in Argentina."

Argentina's economic crisis came to a head in December of 2001 when the policies of the IMF and multinational corporations began to affect the middle class. With half of the population living below the poverty line and one in four Argentine workers unemployed, people took to the streets, many making a musically theatrical statement with the banging of pots and pans—empty, for want of food. The popular uprising ousted five federal governments in two weeks and the general public began relating to one another "horizontally." A process of communication and discovery took root whereby people participate in ways that are directly democratic and nonhierarchical. People held public neighborhood *asambleas* on a regular basis, coordinated hundreds of micro-enterprise cooperatives, and more than 160 factories were occupied and run under workers' control. Graciela's theater took shape through horizontalism. "We brought it to unemployed workers' communities and performed it, and each time we got feedback, we reworked the script. Then we brought the show to Europe and the United States and used it as an introduction for activists to talk about their first-hand experience as workers in Argentina."

Graciela has also helped to apply the ideas of horizontalism to pageant-making for protests at Fort Benning in Columbus, Georgia. In many instances where giant puppets are seen as uninvited guests by a city government that has promised to play host to the GOP, WTO, WAF or whatever, puppeteers' artistic efforts have often been undermined by increased repression. The pageants of Bread & Puppet, Heart of the Beast, and Spiral Q emerged from similar traditions of protest, but grew into established annual ceremonies that are now ingrained in the social fabric of their regions. A middle ground between these unwanted guest protests and more accepted ritualized pageants can be found outside the gates of Fort Benning, where the Western Hemisphere Institute for Security Cooperation (formerly the School of the Americas, or SOA) attracts as many as 20,000 demonstrators every November. In the face of arrests, five year ban-and-bar letters, six month jail sentences, counter-protests by some of Columbus' residents, and infiltration by the FBI, the event continues to grow and puppets have become a large part of it.

Every year the pageant at Fort Benning focuses on an aspect of the SOA's role in promoting military dictatorships, torture and massacres, and on the Latin American social movements that have persistently resisted. The puppets add a beauty that runs counter to the horrors of the SOA, and also a meaningful, ritualized quality to the annual vigil. Catholic Worker Sue Frankel-Streit writes about bringing her three children with her to help create the pageant in her essay "Reflections of a *puppetista* convert:" "Being part of a puppet action gives participants a way to help write and live out the story. As we create each role, we challenge ourselves and each other to think about what that role means; how it looks, moves, sounds, how it plays into the bigger picture. Practicing this creative process helps us learn to analyze, challenge and change our own and others' roles in the real world."

Spiral Q Puppet Theater began as a place to build demonstrations with ACT UP and Kensington Welfare Rights Union, and then with schools, community groups, and residents of recovery houses, making puppet shows, pageants and parades. Matty Hart explains the name as a convergence of everyone who doesn't quite fit. "The Spiral is a universally recognized symbol of energy, a destination or source. It's kinetic—something's happening there. The Q is the queer, it's the other, it's the ghost in the back of the bus. It's the too fat, too kinky, too weird, too much to say, too dumb, or too far-out. The Q is the otherness that doesn't fit into the black box and doesn't have a role in traditional theater-making we see commercially in the US. The idea with the Spiral Q is that if all those people who actually aren't allowed to participate in contemporary theater, did their own public theater and performed in the streets, we would create a new vision for what theater could be: a real vehicle for a revolution that could be theatrical and based in community organizing. And it would look like us."

Spiral Q's Living Loft Museum is a weird mix of artifacts from the past decade: giant pink skulls from Day of the Dead parades, glittery gen-

der-bender puppets from the Philly Dyke March, a ballpark with fangs from Chinatown's victorious anti-stadium battle, some two-faced ex-mayors and district attorneys from a show built for the MOVE organization, a humongous Dracula head for the annual Halloween parade, and hundreds of diverse faces, houses, animals, trees, and representations of food products that reflect the lives and thoughts of the various kids and adults who made them. Every October all of the groups that Spiral Q has worked with over the year return to parade the contents of the museum through the streets in a citywide parade and pageant called Peoplehood.

New York's More Gardens Coalition began making puppets and street theater in 1999, specifically to defend community gardens from being destroyed. Aresh Javadi explains how the group managed to make giant things in a city where space is scarce. "Everything we had was foldable, crushable, squishable, and light. We made a wearable tomato out of metal rings connected by fabric that would squash into one big circle like a paper lantern. We had a carrot that was wearable and it would run around. We had birds, ladybugs—things that were beneficial and also very powerful. We also had the bad guys. We made a baby carriage into a bulldozer that was collapsible and could be carried around and then expanded and put together." More Gardens also made puppet vehicles—bicycles were welded together to form the innards of a giant ladybug that could transport four people, and a humongous jointed caterpillar that was pedaled by ten. The gardens themselves were watched over by twenty-six-foot tall metal sunflowers or an enormous Puerto Rican *coqui* (frog) that people could live inside of.

More Gardens' focus is on the positivity of their work and their street theater echoes this. Javadi says, "We didn't want it to be 'The garden gets bulldozed and these are the bad guys,' but to bring in a win-win situation so that people who were against us would join us, and they could see that vision as we performed it. There'd be a transformation where after a caterpillar was squashed by this gigantic auction mallet that said, "SOLD!" the caterpillar would then transform inside the mallet into a butterfly, come out and bring the people from the audience into this performance, and they would also help with turning the mallet into a pen that

would write, 'We are making community gardens permanent!' The bulldozer turned inside out and became a tool shed, again transforming things into something that is useful rather than something that's destructive. And oddly enough that's what happened. We have over 700 community gardens, and more than 600 are now permanent. A lot of real bulldozers we've had dig holes and come clean up empty lots to create new gardens and move old gardens into new locations. You create visions that you need through the puppetry and somehow people continually persist until it eventually happens. A lot of lawyers and politicians came out of their buildings and said, 'You know, it really lightens my heart and makes me happy to see these colors and butterflies and creatures out here in this cement courtyard.' So it does affect people who've been there just dealing with paper and all sorts of legislation that they know in their hearts is not something that is helping the people and is just helping some corporation and some rich person get richer."

Over the centuries radical puppeteers have moved through being wandering individuals with banners and hand puppet shows, to participants in small art movements that attempted to shape society, to being directed as untrained performers in puppet rituals on a massive scale, to horizontal relationships of making theater via spontaneous direct democracy. All of these forms and formats continue to exist and inspire others to take up the puppet as a voice for social change. In the process, art gets made, a show is performed, people watch and laugh and think. Dreams are shared, plans are concocted and carried out. Sometimes we achieve our goals, and sometimes we are utterly ignored, laughed at, attacked and defeated. And still we challenge and are challenged to tell our stories and create theatrical visions of a world we want to live in. We continue to work toward the horizon and what lies beyond it. We believe in forms that speak louder than words, that bring people together, that ask questions and stimulate dialogue. We believe in the power of play and of participation, of mockery and of the unique ability of the clown to laugh in the face of the king. We believe in magic, and offer up the words of some wayward *puppetista*: "When magic confronts authority, magic always wins."

INTERVIEW RESOURCES: Steve Abrams, Dave Bailey, John Bell, Gustavo Boada, Jan Burger, Amy Christian, Clare Dolan, Kehben Grifter, Matty Hart, Aresh Javadi, Jabari Jones, Xander Marro, Juan Martinez, Ben Matchstick, Graciella Monteagudo, Roby Newton, Beth Nixon, Sara Peattie, Erik Reuland, K. Ruby, Peter Schumann, Deb Shoval, David Solnit, Sandy Spieler, Lydia Stein, Rebecca Tennison, Paul Zaloom, Donovan Zimmerman.

Bibliography

Aria, Barabara. "Coming to a Street Near You: Puppetistas Create Hyphenated Art." *Arts International*, Fall 2002.

Beaumont, Keith. *Alfred Jarry: A Critical and Biographical Study*. Leicester: Leicester University Press, 1984.

Bell, John, ed. *Puppets, Masks, and Performing Objects*. Cambridge: The MIT Press, 2001.

Boal, Augusto. *Theater of the Oppressed*. London: Pluto Press, 1979.

———. *Games for Actors and Non-Actors*. New York: Routledge, 1992.

Brecht, Stefan. *The Bread and Puppet Theater*, 2 vols. New York: Routledge, 1998.

Cohen-Cruz, Jan, ed. *Radical Street Performance*. New York: Routledge, 1998.

Cook, Adam. *A Puppetista Manifesto: Itinerant Garbage Theater for Cultural Insurrection*. New London: Hozomeen, 2000.

Deller, Brian. "Dance of Dogs: The Radical Heritage of Folk Puppetry." *The Knowledge Bank at Ohio State University* (2005). https://kb.osu.edu (accessed August 15, 2006).

"El Teatro Campesino." *El Teatro Campesino Archives 1964–1988. California Ethnic and Multicultural Archives* (n.d.). http://cemaweb.library.ucsb.edu (accessed August 15, 2006).

Frankel-Streit, Sue. "Reflections of a puppetista convert." *SOA Watch* (n.d.). http://www.soaw.org (accessed August 15, 2006).

Goldberg, Rose Lee. *Performance Art From Futurism to the Present*. New York: Thames & Hudson, 2001.

Halleck, DeeDee and Tamar Schumann. *Ah! The Hopeful Pageantry of Bread and Puppet* (DVD). Austin: Liberation Video, 2001.

Hayden, Tom, ed. *The Zapatista Reader*. New York: Thunder's Mouth Press/Nation Books, 2002.

In the Heart of the Beast Puppet and Mask Theater, Will Hammeyer, director. *Out of the Mud* (Videocassette). Minneapolis: Blue Moon Productions, 1999.

Kirby, Michael. *Happenings*. New York: E.P. Dutton & Co., 1966.

Lyon, Raphael and Andres Ingoglia, directors. *i* (DVD). Providence: i Films, 2006.

Mair, Victor H. *Painting and Performance: Chinese Picture Recitation and Its Indian Genesis*. Honolulu: University of Hawaii Press, 1988.

Mogg, Kelly. "A Short History of Radical Puppetry." *Fifth Estate* (Spring 2000).

Monteagudo, Graciela. "PAR, Activism, and Art." Unpublished paper, 2006.

Peattie, Sara. *68 Ways to Make Really Big Puppets*. Boston: The Puppeteers Cooperative, 2000.

Perale, Andrew, ed. *Puppetry International*. (Spring 2001) Quilter, Laura. (1996). "Democratic Convention '96: The Iron Fist After All." *Spunk Library*. http://www.spunk.org (accessed August 15, 2006).

Ruby, K. "History of Radical Puppetry." *Wise Fool Puppet Intervention* (n.d.). http://www.zeitgeist.net/wfca/radpup.htm (accessed August 15, 2006).

———. *Wise Fool Basics*. San Francisco: Wise Fool Puppet Intervention, 1999.

Schumann, Peter. *The Old Art of Puppetry in the New World Order*. Glover: Bread & Puppet Press, 1990.

Senyer, Emin. "Traditional Turkish Shadow Theater Karagˆz Hacivat." *Karagˆz* website (n.d.). http://www.kara-goz.net/english (accessed August 15, 2006).

Sheehy, Colleen J., ed. *Theater of Wonder: 25 Years in the Heart of the Beast*, 1999.

Solnit, David, ed. *Globalize Liberation*. San Francisco: City Lights Press, 2003.

———. "Revolutionary Theater Takes to the Streets." *Groundwork Magazine*. http://www.groundworknews.org (accessed August 15, 2006).

Whitford, Frank. *Bauhaus*. New York: Thames & Hudson, 1984.

BEYOND AUTHENTICITY: AESTHETIC STRATEGIES AND ANARCHIST MEDIA

KYLE HARRIS

Anarchist media practitioners spend a great deal of time creating videos that explore problems of power, persuasion, and movement building. When sifting through independent, activist documentaries, their formal and conceptual problems become apparent.[1] Created with limited resources and training, the movies' technical and structural flaws undermine the power of the story. Viewers easily dismiss weak stories and poorly conceived films. Anarchism maintains its status as an esoteric subcultural practice rather than a dominant social force.

As anarchist media-makers fighting corporate giants with limited resources, we must develop sophisticated and low budget formal and conceptual strategies to create resistant, truthful, and revolutionary alternative media.[2] In order to turn our democratic alternative media networks into a viable rival of multinational media empires, we must use the priceless, costless tools of aesthetics and structure to win the war of ideas against the propagandists of state, corporate, and cultural tyranny.[3] Through curating media, writing, discussion, spectatorship, and production, we must work on determining what questions need to be asked, what strategies should be used, and what methodologies most successfully build viable movements.

Throughout the last century, anarchist producers have used avant-garde and DIY aesthetics to attack dominant culture. From Indymedia journalists to abstract expressionist painters, anarchists have been involved in movements of both stylistic innovation and democratic, grassroots storytelling. Unfortunately, gestural camerawork, punk aggression, and Surrealist and Dada explorations of the non-rational have paved the way for the pitfalls of DIY video production: sloppy camerawork, blown out sound, poorly lit images, and incoherent narrative. Modernist tendencies in art have trained us to tolerate visual and sonic decay in our activist journalism. This decay can be difficult for many to watch. Our democratic media is bordering on becoming an accidental postmodern theater of cruelty.

Anarchist artists have used a wide variety of aesthetics to critique dominant culture and reinvent the world according to their desires. Many of the most important anarchist cultural contributions involve aggressive and alienating aesthetics. In *The Theater and Its Double*, Antonin Artaud proposed that theater and subsequently art should replace political violence with cultural terrorism. The Situationist International and Situationist-inspired anarchist art movements like the Neoists have intervened in the psychogeography of daily life, challenging everyday social structures and public space with symbolic, graphic interventions and appropriations.[4] For these groups, art served a revolutionary function in everyday reality. Instead of imprisoning art in museums, these artists used popular cultural spaces, billboards, streets, and magazines for subversive alterations.

Musicians as varied in form as Crass and John Cage aggressively pushed the limits of music and performance by confronting audiences with chaotic noise, and sometimes an even more shocking silence. Movies such as Jeanne Liotta's *Muktikara* and Peter Hutton's *Landscape (For Manon)* take a "rear-garde" approach by rejecting the eternal push for technological progress and futuristic chaos.[5] They create meditative, hypnagogic landscape films designed to invoke the space between the conscious and unconscious. The Yes Men use the media to playfully prank the think tanks of global capitalism. Raphael Montañez Ortiz in *Cowboy and Indian*, Craig Baldwin in *Specters of the Spectrum*, and Martin Arnold in *Alone, Life Wastes Andy Hardy* work in traditions of collage by converting recycled found footage into cultural critique, violating the presumption of intellectual property rights sacred to the contemporary media industry.[6] All of these approaches are vital to expanding culture and challenging the ideological assumptions of capitalism and domination. In response to individualist, avant-garde modes of production and the "oppressive" dichotomy between the spectator and the artist, certain aesthetic strategies adopted by anarchists emphasize participatory creation and eliminate the spectators, by turning them into collaborators. The theaters of Jerzy Grotowski and Augusto Boal exemplify an inclusive, collective, and non-hierarchical practice where participants create a theatrical experience collaboratively, generating the performance as a group.[7]

Community television initiatives and open source websites like Indymedia provide any member of the community, who has access to certain technologies, the ability to report on current events. In these forms, at best, the audience is integral to the experience. In fact, the audience shapes the experience. At worst, these forms breed cultural carelessness and reinforce the notion that the signature of "authentic" egalitarianism and democracy is sloppiness.[8] Without a serious self-imposed editorial mechanism, these forms can become choice excuses for mediocre productions by creators who have neglected to take responsibility for the quality of their work. Anarchist media can empower collective creativity, but unchecked by constructive criticality, can also excuse and compromise the quality of the product in exchange for a meaningful process.

While there is social value in process-oriented forms of creation, and meaningful networks of artists and activists have been born from community media projects, the global media oligarchs continue to produce highly entertaining products. The entertainment value of such products has great appeal. While some people desire more interactive forms of communication, there is an incredible demand for passive entertainment. People like to watch, to be viewers, not creators. Despite the recent hype about interactivity and the democratic possibility of online distribution through sites like *YouTube*, and *Myspace*, the media oligarchs continue to dominate the online world by creating appealing movies with traditional narrative structures.[9]

Anarchist media makers cannot afford to abandon traditional, viewer-spectator product-oriented media and hope "the people" will organize themselves into an effective, decentralized network of citizen journalists who can organically feed the hunger for well-produced content. Rather, anarchists should consider the enormous importance of entertainment and education that high-quality media products create, and develop the institutions that can support the production of such work.

At this particular historical moment, the Right is dominating both capitalist and alternative media. In the marketplace of ideas, they are winning. Using binary, classical modes of thinking, defining clear protagonists and antagonists, and relying on what Leo Strauss calls "noble myths" to lead people towards destruction, the Right has prevailed against anti-authoritarians intent on thinking in terms of multiplicity, rhizomes, and what the Right correctly

This essay is based on a presentation I gave at the Renewing the Anarchist Tradition Conference at Goddard College, September 2005. The original lecture was titled 'Intentional Aesthetics: Anarchist Media and Movement Building."

***

1. Throughout the essay I use the terms "anarchist media," "activist media," "independent media," "alternative media," and "revolutionary media." While these genres frequently overlap, I am using each term in a particular way. When I am discussing media produced by self-identified anarchists, I use the term "anarchist." I use the term "Activist media" to describe a broader genre of media created by leftists, progressives, and anarchists to create social change. I use the term "revolutionary" to describe media used as a weapon in a larger Left, anarchist, and progressive social context for overthrowing and replacing dominant culture with an alternative social vision. "Independent" media describes media produced outside corporate economic structures. Independent media must be produced autonomously from corporate structures, funded by either individuals, within the non-profit context, or in educational contexts. Finally, alternative media describes projects that contrast dominant themes, structures, and aesthetics and attempts to be expressly different than mainstream media.

2. Of course, this article is based on the assumption that anarchist media-makers have an obligation to compete against corporate giants and have a desire to spread anarchist values.

3. All too often, critics of activist media dismiss movies because of their production values, the quality of the cameras, the experience of the crew, etc... More often than not, these movies would be greatly improved with a thoughtful structure. While a movie can certainly be improved with a bigger budget and anarchist media-makers have no obligation to work as cheaply as possible, this essay focuses on aesthetics and structure because a working knowledge of these skills can be applied without any expense at all. Regardless of whether a producer is working with a multimillion dollar budget or a ten dollar budget, structure and aesthetics can be achieved at no cost. There is no excuse for bad structure.

terms, "relativity." Many of the Right's most successful tactics come from their commitment to classical modes of thought. Through rigorously structured, binary, linear narratives that define "right" from "wrong," the Right has tactically overwhelmed the diversity of movements fiercely committed to the following priorities: broad participation over quality products, experimentation over reliable formal structures, and deconstruction over communication.

The Right has used classical narrative modes to attack the good intentions of the rest of us. Their tactics are not grounded in solving actual social problems. Rather, they construct fictional crises, dialectically opposing "good" versus "evil," "patriot" versus "terrorist," in the form of well-constructed protagonists and antagonists to sway mass opinion. Through deceitful, skilled narratives, they gain power at the expense of the common good.

As the Right has mastered the art of constructing noble myths to justify an oppressive social agenda to a diverse audience, the Left has invested its funds in participatory projects like youth media workshops, community-based production, and other forms of grassroots creation. Youth and community media projects like Video Machete, Paper Tiger Television, and the Global Action Project put cameras in the hands of young people and facilitate workshops where community-based producers learn to create their own media. The ambitious Argentinean video collective, Grupo Alavìo, provides equipment and training to the workers who have occupied factories in Buenos Aires. The workers document their own struggles. In addition, the collective has set up an Internet television station, ágora TV. Pepperspray Productions, Chicago Independent Television, and Blacked Out Media, all video collectives that program and produce media, offer collections of movies produced within the Indymedia movement and through other community-based initiatives.

This network of community-based media projects is most often economically independent from corporate structures, and produces media that address local issues and global issues as they affect local communities. These forms of media tend to value the individual and specific voices of people in local communities rather than figureheads, nationally revered progressive icons, and programmatic struggles. Instead of targeting the broadest audience possible, they often focus on appealing to the neighborhood viewer.

While this investment has certainly empowered many people to express themselves, the products produced in these educational and grassroots forums often lack the structural and aesthetic virtues of the menacing creations of the Right. Often the work is produced in creative traditions so far outside dominant culture that it fails to captivate a large audience. Furthermore, these products of the Left fail to compete in the broader media marketplace and therefore, consistently reach narrow audiences. The viewers are committed to watching formally weak products because of their condescending appreciation of, or their lack of expectation of, "community-based," "grassroots," and "authentic" producers. Their caustic benevolence reinforces the wrongheaded idea that locally-produced media is, inherently, structurally worse than corporate media.

While prioritizing product over process is not always appropriate, by having little to offer other than sloppy unappealing media, activists will fail to captivate a broad audience. If we want to compete with the Right, we must consider surrendering some of our structurally unappealing aesthetic tendencies. We must generously challenge the aesthetic carelessness often found in community media aesthetics and support quality, grassroots products, and producers whose work competes in the broader social arena. We must financially and culturally support producers whose quality of work and attention to structure evolves. We must also help sustain the work of media producers beyond their training, continuing to provide equipment and strategies for accessing equipment to the people involved in community-based projects. Training youth and community members to make media will only be fruitful when participants cultivate a sustainable expertise that extends beyond the educational experience itself.

Most importantly, anarchist media practitioners have an uncomfortable obligation to reconsider classical narrative strategies that may be our only hope for countering the cultural work of the Right. In order to demonstrate this point, let's examine anarchist protest videos intended to represent and build movements.

Montréal's Les Panthères Roses recently put together a collection of DIY videos called *Politically*

Erect, 2005. The video *Pink Bloc—Prague* demonstrates some of the pitfalls of DIY video strategies. This video documents the Pink and Silver Bloc, in the 2000 protests against the International Monetary Fund (IMF) and the World Bank in Prague. The grungy aesthetic demonstrates an uncompromising commitment to lo-fidelity and the virtue of the amateur. Using pop music, scant interviews with activists, and excessive montage of riot porn—footage glorifying police violence against protesters—the producer shows various conflicts between the police and the protestors and addresses the importance of creating spectacle to bring attention to an issue. Unfortunately, unless a viewer already appreciates the historical circumstances surrounding the protests against the IMF and World Bank, the images, spectacular though they may be, are not situated within a narrative of political and cultural struggle that makes sense to the uninformed. Instead of focusing on the problems with the IMF and the World Bank, the video documents throngs of strangely-clad white people, dressed in pink, dusting vicious cops with magic wands. As funny as these images could be, they fail to communicate the political ideas of the Pink and Silver Bloc. Beyond acknowledging that we live in a society of spectacle, the political analysis is weak. One of the only attempts at communicating the problems of capitalism comes in the form of a badly recorded, nerdy, white rapper rambling about his ecologi-

cally sound way of living and his criticality of global capital. The garbled audio and the irritating character fail to generate sympathy for what can be heard of his message. Scenes like this would be best found on the editing room floor.

Instead of focusing on a compelling character or several characters within a collective, it focuses on too many individuals for us to develop a clear identification with the actions we watch. The diversity of opinions regarding the issues at hand are never expressed. The politics of queer solidarity within the context of the global struggle against capitalism are hardly explored. Sadly, the viewer never gets a developed representation of the antagonist and therefore, never understands the conflict. No interviews were arranged with conference delegates. Instead, the video shows IMF and World Bank participants breezing by mobs of activists and citizen journalists. The footage attempts to demonstrate the participants' refusal to answer questions from the media. Instead, it shows the videographer's lack of skill at investigative journalism and unwillingness to go through the conventional channels of access to interview the enemies, or at the very least to find footage shot by people who gained access.

Far too often, activist media producers presume viewers are familiar with the social and historical context of their story. This is wrongheaded. The anarchist narrative we live and believe in, in which we are the protagonists and the capitalists are the antagonists, is an imaginary and false binary construct we create collectively with our storytelling. There is nothing objectively protagonist-like about our image or performance. Unless we clarify our heroism through narrative conventions, like character development, we can easily accidentally appear antagonistic. By not creating a compelling portrait of antagonists, video-makers lose a chance to demonstrate the magnitude of the capitalist enemy's ethical failures. Without an explicit narrative, our videos are incoherent rants devoid of a compelling struggle, confrontation, and climax. Frequently, they fail to demonstrate the value of our ideals.

Consider this hypothetical example based in the genre of anti-fascist, DIY documentaries about militant confrontations with hate groups. On the television screen: a pack of black-clad punks scream: "Racist go home! Racist go home! Racist go

4. For more information about the Neoists, see Stuart Home's *Neoism, Plagiarism and Praxis.* For information about the Situationist International, see the *Situationist International Anthology.*

5. For more information about Hutton's film see Scott MacDonald's *The Garden in the Machine: A Field Guide to Independent Films About Place.* Hutton's films can be rented from Canyon Cinema (Canyoncinema.com); Liotta's films can ordered from The Filmmakers Cooperative (Film-makerscoop.com).

6. Films by Baldwin and Arnold can be found through Canyon Cinema. Raphael Montañez Ortiz has had major retrospectives at the Whitney Museum of American Art in 1996. The New Jersey City Museum will feature a 2006 retrospective entitled "Unmaking: The Work of Raphael Montañez Ortiz." More information can be found about the Yes Men at http://www.theyesmen.org.

7. Grotowski's *Towards a Poor Theater* theorizes the function of the actor and describes the director's decentralized collaborative work. In an incredible scene in Louis Malle's *My Dinner With Andre,* Andre Gregory pontificates on his transformative experience with Grotowski's process.
   For more information on Boal's innovative theatrical processes, read *The Theater of the Oppressed* and *The Rainbow of Desire.*

8. Independent Media Centers frequently exemplify the cultivation of sloppy style. Without an editorial board or so-called "gatekeepers," an anything goes aesthetic replaces carefully created content. Quantity replaces quality. Aesthetic sloppiness reinforces itself and people fail to hold themselves to high standards of communication.

9. In *Desperate Networks,* author Bill Carter describes the entertainment industry's reliance on traditional narrative programs like *Desperate Housewives* to keep the edge on the market.

10. *Mise-en-Scène* literally means "put in the scene." In cinema, it refers to everything in front of the camera including costumes, set, props, character movements, textures, colors, etc.

home!" The distorted audio roars, peaks, pushes the microphone to the limit, and beyond. Every time the cameraman joins in the chanting, the audio drops out all together. The image fluctuates between blown-out clipped whites, figures lost, invisible, overexposed to crushed blacks, grainy, gritty chaos, occasional lights, occasional shapes, image underexposed. When faces and voices are clear enough to understand, we hear cursing, threats, idiotic jokes, and anti-fascists slipping into sexist, homophobic language. "You fucking pussy. You racist faggot." We hear racists mocking the anti-fascist's hypocrisy. We watch young men beat another man calling him a "fascist, violent fuck."

Watching the footage, having the privilege to fast-forward, slow down, study, pause, rewind, and play, the performance of the activists can be scrutinized. This is frequently the burden of the producer of the video who, while editing, witnesses the wild look in the eyes of angry activists, the wandering, distracted posture of the detached and bored, the tense communications between protestors, the ridiculous comments made to police, and the patronizing attempts to get bystanders to "join us." Sometimes the activist videographers see glimpses of true conviction, clarity, credibility, and gestures of kindness, dignity, and intelligence. At other points, they cringe at incoherent rants, humorless jokes, and wild gestures of violence without strategy. They study the legibility of banners, their humor, their ragtag, nostalgic sensibility, and the way they are held. Each and every element is scrutinized by the obsessive video activist, from the length, density, color, and design of hair, makeup, and clothes, to the quality of movement on the set, that is, the streets. The unsteady image, the crushed blacks, the clipped whites, and the peaking sound are deemed illegal for broadcast because they interfere with the quality of the signal. The videomaker cuts the unsalvageable footage together into a rambling, somewhat linear collection of unrelated images from the action. The result is messy, unstructured, and boring to all but narcissistic activists fascinated by their own sense of heroism.

Even after extensive editing, amiable viewers trying to grasp the state of the world turn away from activist media, unaccustomed to watching a bad signal, an unrecognizable image, and suffering through unbalanced distorted audio. The madness of it all, the poorly expressed ideology, the similarities in behavior between the fascists and the anti-fascists, the nausea-inducing handheld camera, and the utter disregard of narrative arc, beginning, middle, and end, succeeds only in alienating viewers. Rather than wading through unwatchable incoherence, they turn to capitalist and conservative media where well-lit patriarchs engage in aggressive and entertaining banter on screen while destroying the world off-camera. A chance to mobilize the viewer has been sacrificed by aesthetic carelessness and badly performed politics.

The aforementioned scenario is a grim hypothetical one based in several years of watching, programming, and producing activist media. It is a generalization based on an amalgamation of confrontational videos produced in good faith with little

Still from *Pink Bloc à Prague* created by the collective Les Lucioles, 2005.

means. At best, nobody will see this type of video and therefore it will not be harmful. When seen, it can injure our ability to build movements.

Movement Building

Anarchist video is in a crisis of representation because there is a crisis of production. Rarely have video activists taken the time to become skilled editors and shooters. Nor have we worried about assembling all of the ingredients for a delicious cinematic recipe. Nor do we care about story. Nor aesthetics. Nor broadcast standards, *mise-en-scène*, cinematography, or sound.[10] We don't seem to care about the audience either. Too much activist media is thoughtlessly created and too many stories effectively go untold because they are told incompetently, without intentional structure, character development, or style.[11]

The most compelling arguments for these rougher aesthetics suggest that within them lies a signature of the movement, a Do-It-Yourself sensibility, a self-reflexive, low-fidelity antidote to corporate finesse. When such arguments embrace bad, unintentionally alienating media, they are preposterous. When they begin to demand and defend well-structured narrative strategies, they pave the way for our signature DIY aesthetic to be taken seriously and improved upon. Of course, we shouldn't place much liberatory value in our aesthetics alone. Our handheld style has already been adopted by the mainstream media. Shows like *Cops* and *Cheaters* use this aesthetic to enforce the status quo by promoting policing, surveillance culture, and marital fidelity. Embarrassingly enough, the corporate handheld aesthetic is commercially superior to its anarchist counterpart, neither because its subject matter is more interesting and relevant, nor because the image is stronger, but because it applies classical narrative strategies that audiences can follow and enjoy.

Our tendency to value spontaneity and shun narrative has a historical precedent in the anti-rational romantic traditions that influenced anarchist dominated art movements like surrealism and abstract expressionism. These traditions honor the importance of individual creative expression and resist character driven linear narrative. While there is no denying the cultural and intellectual importance of these quests, they have deemphasized clarity and reason for chaotic emotionalism and incoherence. This interestingly dovetails with the ideas of John Zerzan and others in the anarcho-primitivist tradition, who see the symbolic order and representation as the root of oppression. They believe that to move away from the symbolic and representational pushes us away from the horrors of civilization towards a feral *telos*, a wild, utopian future, best exemplified artistically in the paintings of the abstract expressionists.

While their attempts to manifest pure expression are undeniable, their pragmatic application failed. Capitalists and government agencies appropriated their works in order to justify dominant, imperialist, American culture. Their aesthetics have become a dominant motif in capitalist marketing. The CIA promoted the abstract expressionists to the rest of the world as evidence of American tolerance and freedom. The artists' decision to abscond from language facilitated this process. As a result, they sacrificed the sustainability of anarchist values as part of their work. Within art, idealist politics that reject language fail to be persuasive because they refuse to acknowledge the indestructibility of the symbolic and fail to use systems of rhetoric and representation to illustrate and clarify their arguments. While many artists try, art cannot be divorced from language. It is forever trapped in the prison of representation. Popular audiences demand it, and as a result, no spiritually pure, creative realm exists that can be eternally isolated from the realm of popular discourse. Such isolation results in a downward spiral towards obscurity, irrelevance, and oblivion.

Much like how capitalist advertising has secured a place for abstract aesthetics by situating them within a larger rhetorical strategy, corporate media have used handheld aesthetics to aid its classical narrative tradition by supplementing glossy, studio productions with an immediate and "authentic" visual style. As critics of corporate media reveal that the industry is serving the wealthy through mind-numbing journalism, and is brainwashing the collec-

11. Here I am speaking of broad trends in the grassroots. There are many notable exceptions to this rule. Labor Beat, Democracy Now, Deep Dish TV, and Guerrilla News Network are amongst hundreds of others creating quality, appealing, and innovative activist media.

12. Such critics of corporate media include Noam Chomsky, Danny Schechter, and Robert McChesney.

13. Aristotle, *Poetics*, p. 37, 38, 51.

14. Ibid., p. 38.

15. Bakunin, Mikhail, *God and State*, p. 35.

tive psyche by successfully marketing products that kill, the producers of this media simultaneously use alternative, handheld, and DIY aesthetics to forge sincerity and develop an intimate relationship between media-networks and viewers.[12] What they never shun in their product, and what anarchist producers rarely use, is classical narrative strategy. One cannot confront a master narrative without better stories.

The neoconservatives' favorite philosopher, Leo Strauss, suggests that we look back to the classical texts of Western civilization and open our minds to our predecessors' immortal wisdom. Realizing that ignoring the strategies of conservatives is a tactical failure, take a moment to leap back through Western literary criticism and delve into Aristotle's systematic notes on poetry. Here we can immerse ourselves in nearly quantitative classical notions of tragedy, a formulaic, highly rational approach to art. Aristotle, in his *Poetics*, prioritizes the components of tragedy into a useful hierarchy of importance that can help us understand why a show like *Cheaters* is more successful than our own activist endeavors. For Aristotle, the "soul of tragedy" is plot-structure, the organization of events into a beginning, middle and end, containing moments of recognition, reversal and suffering. He defines plot as unity of action that involves (1) a complication, everything that occurs from the beginning to the moment before a transformation towards "prosperity or affliction," and (2) a dénouement, "the section from the start of the transformation to the end.[13] The second most important aspect of tragedy is characterization. Characters must be better than us, worse than us, or the same as us, and must undergo either a rise or a fall. For Aristotle, protagonists must be ethically good, appropriate, and consistent in behavior. The third most important aspect of tragedy is thought: "the capacity to produce pertinent and appropriate arguments."[14] According to Aristotle, in successful tragedy the ideas are less important than the structure and the characters. The fourth most important element is style of expression, followed by lyrical poetry and spectacle.

Cheaters follows this model precisely. Each show is narrated by a host who presents the same pattern every time. During the first act, a lover suspects the beloved of cheating. During the second act, *Cheaters*' spies follow the beloved and use video to prove the accusations. During the loudly announced confrontation, the host and the lover confront the beloved. The conclusion and dénouement occurs when the lover describes reconciling or permanently ending the relationship. When you sit down to watch *Cheaters*, you expect this pattern, this structure. No irrelevant material is shown. There is an Aristotelian unity of plot, a clear beginning, middle, and end, moments of recognition, when the lover realizes the accusations are true, and reversals when the beloved accuses the lover of nasty doings. The characters are well defined as victim and cheater. We follow the rise

Still from *Pink Bloc à Prague* created by the collective Les Lucioles, 2005.

and fall of both characters. The host is the voice of reason clearly explaining the plot. By prioritizing structure and character development over the "moral," the producers strategically communicate the show's argument against infidelity. Ironically, and in accordance with Aristotle's aesthetic hierarchy, if the show was a preachy documentary essay on the trouble with infidelity, valuing content over form, the show's persuasive value would be diminished. The handheld camerawork, the coercive music, and the spectacle of violence and seduction all contribute to the whole, but are insignificant compared to the plot. Without the structure and polarized characters, the rest would be boring.

To return to our hypothetical and all too familiar example of DIY video, anarchist media has the tendency to reverse Aristotle's formula. It prioritizes the spectacle of violent protest porn first. The articulation of ideas and arguments found in the chaotic chants comes second. The third most important component is lyrical poetry, the emotive garnishing, the standard anarcho-punk score. Style is fourth—that is, the handheld camerawork and the rapid cuts. Character is fifth, represented by the failed attempts to turn the anarchists into the protagonists and the fascists into the antagonists. Structure, of utmost importance to Aristotle, is prioritized last.

It is no wonder that *Cheaters* appeals to more people than our valiant activist media. We have neglected the classics. Capitalist media uses Aristotle well.

Failing amateur media-makers need to study the crafts they want to use. Bakunin writes, "In general, we ask nothing better than to see men endowed with great knowledge, great experience, great minds, and above all, great hearts, exercise over us a natural and legitimate influence, freely accepted, and never imposed in the name of any official authority whatsoever, celestial or terrestrial."[15] Do Leo Strauss and Mikhail Bakunin agree on this seemingly obvious point that people should learn from great minds? Could it be that corporate media follows this classical anarchist's advice more than anarchist media-makers, all too quick to dismiss the wisdom of antiquity? In our desire to liberate ourselves from the oppressive structures of Western civilization and tradition, have we rejected some of the best tools available?

By structuring their invasions of privacy, their destruction of individual lives and relationships, their jealousy-baiting, surveillance culture, and self-righteousness into the formulas of Aristotelian poetics, the corporate scallywags producing *Cheaters* and championing capitalist monogamy have triumphed over anarchist media makers.

Sadly, virtue and victory are not synonymous. To succeed, we need to accept the tools of Western antiquity alongside those provided by other cultures and times.

Activist media producers have an advantage over other types of documentarians. We are frequently part of the movements we are documenting. As a result, through organizing, we can help develop the look and feel of actions and interventions before they take place. If anarchist media producers can help design actions as media events, all aspects of action can become part of a well-defined cinematic vision. Consider the site of the protest a stage, the outfits of the protestors as costumes, and the behavior of protestors a form of acting. By orchestrating these elements of production design, we can create memorable, reproducible, and irresistible images of anarchist resistance that can be as effective after an action as they were at the time.

Many plot structures, models of characterization, and styles of action can excite an audience. The anarchist media practitioner's job is to determine which of those can activate an audience to revolt and create. A healthy suspension of singular models of articulation and a practice of experimentation can facilitate a diversity of entertaining and provocative structures for communicating anarchist visions. For this reason, our media, varied as it should be, must not subscribe to the notion of a singular anarchist aesthetic. While the DIY, Indymedia aesthetic signature still has great potential, a diversity of aesthetic tactics will appeal to a broader range of viewers. At this stage of movement building via media, the most important criterion when adopting an aesthetic is to have it be intentional. An intentional aesthetic targets a specific audience and uses form to affect the audience in a specific way. It adopts and adapts knowledge from the past and present to create effective, moving, and carefully designed structures, character relations, arguments, style, and spectacle.

Bibliography

Aristotle, *The Poetics of Aristotle*. Trans. Stephen Halliwell. North Carolina: The University of North Carolina Press, 1987.

Artaud, Antonin. *Antonin Artaud: Selected Writings*. Ed. Susan Sontag. Berkeley: University of California Press, 1976.

———. *The Theater and Its Double*. New York: Grove Press, 1958.

Bakunin, Mikhail. *God and the State*. New York: Dover, 1970.

Boal, Augusto. *Theater of the Oppressed*. Trans. Charles A. and Maria-Odilia Leal McBride. New York: Urizen Books, 1979.

———. *The Rainbow of Desire: The Boal Method of Theater and Therapy*. Trans. Adrian Jackson. New York: Routledge, 1995.

Carter, Bill. *Desperate Networks*. New York: Doubleday, 2006.

Chomsky, Noam. *Manufacturing Consent: The Political Economy of the Mass Media*. New York: Pantheon Books, 2002.

Grotowski, Jerzy. *Towards a Poor Theater*. New York: Simon and Schuster, 1968.

Home, Stewart. *Neoism, Plagiarism and Praxis*. Oakland: AK Press, 1996.

Kitwana, Bakari. *The Hip Hop Generation: Young Blacks and the Crisis in African American Culture*. New York: BasicCivitas Books, 2002.

Knabb, Ken, ed. *Situationist International Anthology*. Berkeley: Bureau of Public Secrets, 1981.

MacDonald, Scott. *The Garden in the Machine: A Field Guide to Independent Films About Place*. Berkeley: University of California Press, 2001.

McChesney, Robert. *Rich Media, Poor Democracy: Communication Politics in Dubious Times*. New York: The New Press, 2000.

Schecter, Danny. *The Death of Media: And the Fight to Save Democracy*. New Jersey: Melville House Publishing, 2005.

Strauss, Leo. *The City and Man*. Chicago: The University of Chicago Press, 1964.

Frances Stonor Suanders, *The Cultural Cold War: The CIA and the World of Arts and Letters*. New York: The New Press, 1999.

Zerzan, John. *Running on Emptiness: The Pathology of Civilization*. Los Angeles: Feral House, 2002.

Zuckerman, Laurence. "How the Central Intelligence Agency Played Dirty Tricks With Our Culture," *The New York Times*, March 13, 2000.

Webography

ágora TV
Agoratv.org

Canyon Cinema
Canyoncinema.com

Deep Dish TV
Deepdishtv.org

Democracy Now
Democracynow.org

Film-makers Cooperative
Film-makerscoop.com

Global Action Project
Global-action.org

Grupo Alavìo
Revolutionvideo.org/alavio

Guerrilla News Network
Guerrillanews.com

Independent Media Center
Indymedia.org

Labor Beat
Laborbeat.org

Les Panthères Roses:
Lespantheresroses.org

Pepperspray Productions
Peppersp.server312.com

The Yes Men
Theyesmen.org

Filmography

Alone, Life Wastes Andy Hardy. Dir. Martin Arnold. Film. 1998.

Cheaters. Bobby Goldstein Production. New York: MG Perin, INC. 1999–2006.

Cops. Creator and Executive Producer, John Langley. 1988–2006.

Cowboy and Indian. Dir. Raphael Montañez Ortiz. Film. 1958.

Landscape (For Manon). Dir. Peter Hutton. Film. 1987.

Pink Bloc á Prague. Les Lucioles. Video. 2005.

Specters of the Spectrum. Dir. Craig Baldwin. Film 2003.

THE DEPARTMENT OF SPACE AND LAND RECLAMATION

JOSH MACPHEE AND NATO THOMPSON

Ever wonder what would happen if the Department of Streets and Sanitation put up graffiti instead of removing it? What if the zoning board was run by mass consensus and decided that everything in the city was public space? The Department of Space and Land Reclamation (DSLR) was founded in Chicago in the spring of 2001 to answer those questions. A guerrilla city department, DSLR boldly demanded the reclamation of all space, land, and visual culture of Chicago by and for the people who work, live, and play in it. This took the form of a weekend-long, city-wide event which, at different points, resembled a political campaign, a conference, an outdoor traveling art exhibition, and a three-day-long party. Existing on the margins of both the art and political worlds—our art too political, and our politics too arty—we wanted to bring together as many disparate shards of our marginalized communities by exploring new ways of existing in the city.

DSLR was born during the upswing of the alter-globalization movement. It had only been a year and a half since November 1999 and the Battle of Seattle. Seattle had shocked and inspired all of us. The diversity of street tactics from puppet theater to graffiti, from organized marches to window smashing, and the democratization of protest organizing all informed the creation of new activist models. Pleasure and interventions had activated the dull chanting/marching culture of street activism. Spokescouncil organizing and the use of decentralized affinity groups had allowed long-held anarchist practices to gain popular use. And the embracing of technologies such as the Internet, cell phones, and video cameras found application in the form of Indymedia, flash mob, and protest videos. The dispersion of technology plus a little protester ingenuity provided a window for temporarily neutralizing the more repressive tools of capital and leveling the playing field of struggle.

Protest had broken from the shadow of the 1960s and begun to develop new cultural forms coalescing in opposition to the World Trade Organization, the World Bank, the International Monetary Fund and other manifestations of capitalist globalization. At the time, we felt part of a movement that directly confronted the most advanced aspects of capitalism, and we were possibly winning—or at least making a dent in the armor. For once we were struggling against capitalism and the unfettered market itself, not just the temporary behaviors of one section of the ruling class. Finally, a diverse yet unified front had appeared that agreed on a new form of action that took race, class, globalization, and power into account.

A critique of neoliberal capital had emerged as its pernicious effects increasingly encroached on daily life, not only halfway around the world, but more tangibly at home. Traveling across the world to large-scale protests had become part of the global protest formula, but we wanted to bring the struggle to the neighborhoods we knew best: Chicago, our communities, and ourselves. We had to merge strategies of anti-gentrification organizing, our critique of media culture, an appreciation of artistic activity and liberatory visioning, making tangible the privatization of urban space as well as the increasing encroachment of capital into our personal and collective subjectivities. We said it best in the materials we produced for the DSLR weekend:

> Global capital has reached such a point that both the physical and intellectual landscape have been completely purchased. To exist today means to tread

PROJECT #1
Ladder Mission Five
Curtis Oliveira

Curtis collected piles of scrapwood for weeks building dozens of rudimentary ladders of varying shapes and sizes. Over the DSLR weekend he drove around the city and placed the ladders alongside all types of barriers, fences, walls, and gates. This simple gesture, a ladder leaning against a barrier, inevitably invited the viewer to climb them, and thus overcome a construction designed to separate one space from another. These roughly hewn, almost toy-like ladders brought attention to one of the cardinal rules of our society, the inaccessibility of a majority of public space.

on the property of others. The city has increasingly become a space completely built around consumerism. The freedom of expression has come to mean the freedom to advertise. Like a minefield of manipulative codes, urban space has been designed to maneuver us from one point of sale to the next. Racist and classist anti-loitering and anti-gang laws have been instituted across the country as increasingly individuals and cultures are illegalized to protect rising property values.

The Event

DSLR had three primary manifestations. The first occurred in the streets of Chicago. Over sixty planned and dozens of spontaneous actions took place across the city on the weekend of April 27–April 29th, 2001. Second, these actions emerged from and retreated to our headquarters, or hub, which acted as a command center to prepare for and coordinate the street actions, communicate between all the participants, distribute information, and build community. The location of the third manifestation was more ethereal, carried by word of mouth and existing in myth, inspiring actions long after the event itself was over.

The DSLR street interventions were broad in scope, yet united in their appropriation of urban space. As we said at the time in our map/catalog, these were "reclamation projects…that actively trespass with the intent to resist." A brief look at some of the works include: a guerrilla gardener held workshops on local plant life, an artist placed dozens of ladders on fences and other barriers in the city, a lunatic did reverse donuts in his car until the police arrived, a poetry slam on gentrification occurred in the heart of Wicker Park (the gentrified neighborhood that had once birthed Chicago's political poetry slam community), and a giant ball of trash was rolled down Michigan Avenue. These disparate and bizarre actions coalesced into a carnival against capital that suddenly swept through the increasingly rarified, privatized, and homogenized Chicago. Six of these projects are described in detail in the sidebars to this essay, and they give a good overview of the kind of events taking place.

DSLR needs to be seen in the context of an experiment, an attempt at developing a new model for political and cultural engagement. Foremost, it was a campaign and not an exhibition. Unlike the static forms of artistic activities that highlight the end product of the art process, this project emphasized active engagement with social space and each other. The event occurred over seventy-two hours with participants eating, sleeping, drinking, and engaging in the same social space of the hub, as well as in the city at large. The project was as much about the social connections it produced internally as it was about reaching those who were an audience to the street interventions.

The campaign hub was a large warehouse turned into artist studios and band practice spaces. The Butcher Shop (named because of its life before artists ran it) made a perfect space, as it was centrally accessible yet not located in the middle of any of the well-worn cultural or political zones of the city.

The hub was split into numerous sections. The front distribution area housed leaflets, stencils, spraypaint, wheat paste, stickers, and posters that could be grabbed and dispersed outside the space. A back room contained a pirate radio station, a sound system, a space for lectures and discussions, and of course the dance floor for the on-going party. The kitchen provided space for the much-needed collective cooking of breakfast, lunch, and dinner (and ultimately, disparate communities gain a much fonder appreciation of each other through eating together). A chill-out space of couches and potted plants supplied a relaxed atmosphere to take some time off and get to know each other. A video editing bay allowed artists to edit the footage of their various interventions, which could be plugged into an accompanying wall of monitors installed so that video footage of a dozen actions could be simultaneously viewed. A large map of Chicago was hung on the wall so that participants could place numbered pins identifying their various interventions throughout the city and we could visually see our impact. Squeezed between all this were a small resource library and free photocopier, ongoing video and slide projections of other public space interventions, and a large-scale installation of hundreds of photographs of graffiti, illegal street art, and creative space reclamations. All the walls of the space were painted by three Chicago graffiti crews. In sum, we created the hub to provide a home to the community that emerged over the course of the weekend.

Largely because of its novelty within the city, as well as its focus on building social relations, DSLR quickly became a mythical entity. We had developed little or no plan to convert DSLR into a permanent grouping after the event, and although various collections of people that came together over the weekend ended up continuing to build on the work of DSLR, it never existed as a cohesive group after the event. This didn't stop various interven-

PROJECT #2
Trashball
by Men and Women

The project Trashball was as simple as it sounds: a 6' diameter ball of trash. The collective Men and Women donned plain white Tyvek jumpsuits emblazoned with the word "STAFF" on the back and proceeded to roll this stinking ball of trash down Michigan Avenue's Miracle Mile. As the area is often congested with eager shoppers, responses varied greatly. Some jumped out of the way, others looked confused or ignored it, and some managed to laugh unsure what the joke was. The action physically reorganized people's conceptions of space on the sidewalks, turning a quiet shopping day into a giant obstacle course. The trashball itself also confronted the sensory expectations which dominate this exclusive shopping district. On the ground this appeared to simply be a strange act, but with a map's eye view (available in the DSLR hub), one could see that the trashball began at 800 N. Michigan, the site of the Chicago Museum of Contemporary Art, and rolled south down Michigan Avenue to the Art Institute of Chicago, connecting the two of the largest art institutions to the stink of corporate excess and greed lying between them.

PROJECT #3
Kiosk Liberation
47ward.org

All along Lincoln Avenue, in the 47th Ward of Chicago, informational kiosks dot the sidewalks of the main shopping area. Typically kiosks are a community forum for discussing town matters, but these kiosks are a privatized space, only available for use to store owners and politicians. 47ward.org, a grassroots community group "liberated" the kiosks for public use over the DSLR weekend. Each kiosk gained a new banner describing it as a "Free Speech Area" and 47ward.org tabled next to them with a survey asking passersby how *they* would like to see the kiosks used. This simple act radically democratized the space, making visible one of the many systems of control.

tions happening in Chicago weeks and months later from being attributed to the "Department of Space and Land Reclamation," either by those that created them or those that saw them. This gave DSLR a decentralized and autonomous life of its own.

Rebuilding the City

Given that DSLR's declared objective was to reclaim all the "visual, spatial, and cultural space of Chicago and return it to those who live in it, work in it, and create it," we used the impossibility of the declaration to cast an aggressively wide net that we hoped would catch the disillusioned and autonomous agitators in Chicago. Besides its hyperbolic qualities, the goal also strategically combined the call for aesthetics with one for political change in the public sphere. In so doing, we drew a line connecting the private property of the outside world with the more internal privatization of cultural production. We will own our own city and our own lives, we will produce our own culture, and these are all intrinsically connected.

We knew the battle against capital could not simply be fought in Seattle, DC or Québec City (where a meeting to convene the Free Trade Area of the Americas was happening the week before DSLR). As manufacturing jobs left the city centers across the United States, the housing and factories for labor were abandoned, only to be reinvented as a potential home for the new urban upper middle class. The shift from manufacturing to service industries and the rise of the "global city" forced a massive restructuring of cities in the first world. Gentrification had severely sunk its teeth into Chicago by 2001, and every city corner could feel it. Neighborhoods like Wicker Park, Ukrainian Village, Rogers Park, and Pilsen had been targeted decades earlier by city planners as locations to re-urbanize in the image of the New Chicago, a playground for the moderately affluent. Youth of color were stigmatized as the locus of all urban ills (gangs, violence, drugs, and graffiti), while young white artists were scapegoated as the prime motivators of gentrification, an economic process most of them didn't even understand, never mind control. Working class communities fortified in a pitched battle to retain affordable housing, but unfortunately often blamed the recently arrived (often white) artists or their own youth for their problems, rather than attacking the root cause: the machinations of the city government, developers, and corporate business lobbies.

With property values skyrocketing, public housing being demolished, schools being privatized and youth, particularly youth of color, being blamed for all of the city's problems, we stepped into the picture. We wanted to bring together as many diverse communities affected by the city's transformation as possible and begin a dialogue about how to take the city back from the bottom up. In order to defeat what we faced, we needed to not only contest the city as it was, but build a new one. And that construction could not be simply physical, but had to be affective. We needed to rebuild our social relations in the image of the world we wanted to live in.

This is why we began with an "open call to public space modifiers, community garden enthusiasts, fringe neighborhood associations, chipper anarchists, nonfrothing leftists, culture-jamming slackers, alienated doodlers, spray-painting pirates, unproductive cultural producers, and monkey wrenching toddlers for a weekend campaign by the Department of Space and Land Reclamation." So our request for participation read—and admittedly there was a level of pleasure in the call itself. Engaging a broad audience was critical for DSLR's success, as everyone in a city needs to be involved in its reconstruction. We had to do an immense amount of one-on-one outreach to convince people that DSLR, a complex idea we barely knew how to explain ourselves, was something worth getting involved in. We had to tie the renegade autonomous productions of guerrilla gardening, pirate radio, and alternative food programs to the more ambiguous and resistant aesthetics of street art to the more traditional organizing of community groups and housing activists.

In producing a campaign that participated in open and often ambiguous nonpermitted actions in the public sphere, DSLR provided a context for anyone to get involved. Many projects included mass audience participation, often blurring the lines between producers and produced. In addition, in this context even the most apolitical actions can resist the overarching structure of the city itself. From wasps' nests made of electrical cords attached to stop signs to a campaign advocating jaywalking, the ambiguity of such projects provided a space to reflect and think. The ambiguous gesture resonates politically in a condition where its seemingly harmless existence is illegal. In contrast to the directed spectacle of advertising, road signs, and parking ordinances, these often absurd gestures—references without a referent—open a space of free floating desire.

These simple, nonpermitted actions resist the structure of the lived environment designed to commute a person to and from work, home, store, school or prison. And the coercive structure of Chicago became patently obvious when a visitor to the campaign headquarters saw these projects side by side. As the projects multiplied on our wall of monitors and the map of the city became inundated with pins marking each action, the city took on the character of a battlefield. Each square inch is constructed, but who gets to do the construction, and who does it benefit?

PROJECT #4
Bathroom Reclamation
Trans/Action

Overnight, dozens of gendered bathrooms became unisex! With a simple sticker which mixed up and fused the universal bathroom "men" and "women" signs, Trans/Action broke down the gender barriers of bathrooms throughout Chicago. Like most of the interesting actions that grew out of DSLR, it is a simple act—changing the sign on the bathroom—that raises deep questions, in this case about how our society perceives gender. But this wasn't a theoretical exercise, the stickers, for however long they stayed up, also acted as a concrete marker of meaning. They provided a sign of resistance for those uncomfortable with status quo gender binaries.

Chicago has developed a series of anti-gang laws designed in large part for the harassment of youth of color rather than an attempt to address conditions of gang violence. In 2001, the city banned small groups of teen-agers from congregating in "hot spots." Functionally this was an attempt at making it illegal for kids of color to hang out on the streets at all. Flotsam was interested in exploring both what "loitering" really means, and its current racist and classist judicial permutation. Initially the collective transformed an official city anti-loitering sign and changed it to say "LOITER." Then on a bright and shiny weekday morning in front of city hall, Flotsam installed an inflatable living room set (couch, chair, and coffee table with an appetizing box of doughnuts on the table) and hung the LOITER sign above the furniture. In addition they placed a pile of free business cards with the dictionary definition of "loiter" and "conversation" written on each side. Interestingly, the definitions of these words are remarkably similar.

Random passers-by soon took notice. Some rested their feet for a minute, others sat down and enjoyed a doughnut. In no time, a small crowd developed and began to talk, or more appropriately, loiter. City Hall security (the guys in the blue uniforms) quickly arrived on the scene to figure out what was going on, a task that was not easy. They were clearly confused and all they could think to do initially was to remove the sign. Then the next round in the hierarchy of security (the guys in the white uniforms) came out and turned all the furniture upside down and took away the doughnuts, much to the chagrin of the downtown business crowd. Finally the security guys in the suits and ties came out, and instructed the blue uniforms to haul away the furniture and scrub clean any vestige of the oasis, thus making visible one of the many systems of

Rebuilding Community

With our hearts set on the few hundred folks participating recreating ourselves as something altogether different and more cohesive together, we developed an environment that was conducive to that end. It was a social catalyst in the tradition of the Cabaret Voltaire, the Happenings, early hip hop street parties, Burning Man, and even DIY punk shows. Yet with an awareness of the culture industry snidely turning culture into marketing dollars, our politics were clearly set on the table.

The hub became a social space of becoming and this was the most effective part of the model. DSLR toyed with the political resistance of the outside world to produce new politically aware subjectivities—that is, everyone was doing something outside their comfort zone and developing new forms within which to interact culturally. Through the participation of a disparate collective willing to try something culturally new and radical, an energizing space of social production roared into life.

The ambiguity of the art projects (whether spoken word, dance parties, or graffiti) provided a fluid context to organize around. Attempting to organize across class, race, and gender boundaries is complicated, and often the worst place to begin is politics. People need to get to know each other, share moments; be more than a particular demographic, but thoughtful expressive individuals with a unique and valued history. Ambiguous aesthetic activity allows a language of communication that crosses multiple fields of identity and personal flavor. Personal and collective expression produces a psychological space where amazing activity can transpire. A zone of liberating individuality opens up and everyone can jump in. Watching people express themselves and having the space to do so can be an intimate and powerful moment, which can then give one strength for the larger political struggle.

A goal of DSLR was to use the guise of art as a way to get people to not only visualize the world they want to live in but also to attempt to actualize it. We chose one weekend to start, but it's a lifelong project. Not content to be a panel discussion on the hopes and dreams of a city, DSLR strived to put thought into action with as diverse a set of hands as possible. The social space produced did not simply rest in anyone's specific comfort zone, but was in many ways foreign to all. With everyone trying something new, we shared a vulnerable position where we found new radical forms to act together.

PROJECT #6
Neighborhood Sonification Module
FuZ FōN

FuZ FōN took on gentrification as an engineering problem: can we make a space so uncomfortable for developers and rich urbanites that they'll just leave? Their solution was fairly ingenuous. They developed extremely loud and shock resistant music players (small, nearly indestructable camp coolers with cd player and speaker inside) and placed on a continual loop, playing an earsplitting rumble of noise. These coolers were then installed in particular known sites of gentrification (in front of Starbucks, million dollar lofts, etc.) with bicycle u-locks. As they have themselves said: "In medicine, doctors break up kidney stones by focusing concentrated sound waves at the blockage. The waves break up the stones until the passage is clear. In much the same way, FuZ FōN proposes to break up the process of gentrification by aiming sound waves at a specific location where the tumor is visible."

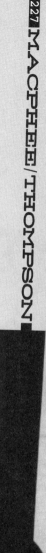

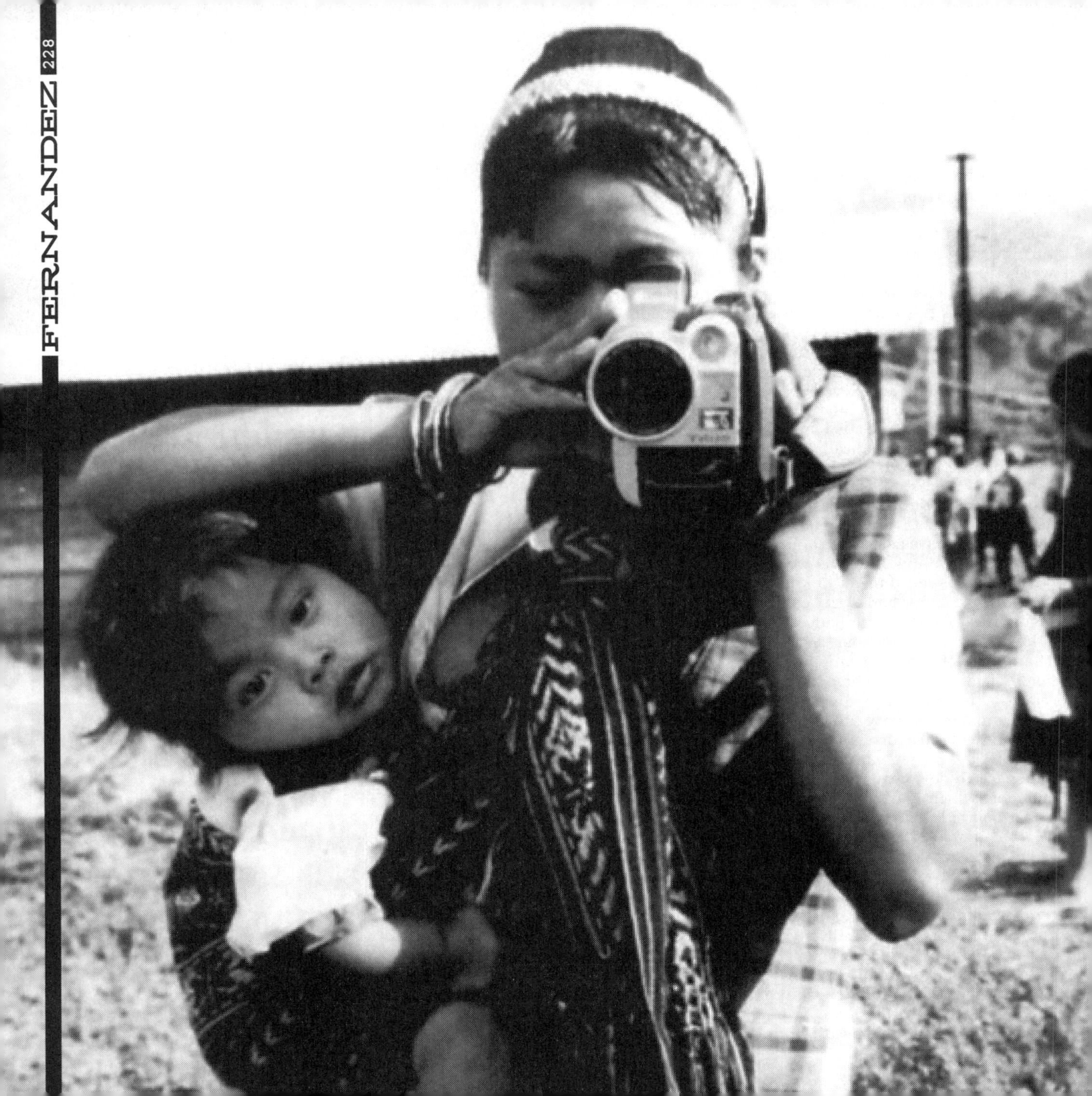

MOVEMENTS AND MILITANT MEDIA: COMMUNICATIONS TECHNOLOGY AND LATIN AMERICAN GRASSROOTS POLITICS

CARLOS FERNANDEZ

In 1998, four years into their insurgency and surrounded by the larger part of Mexico's military, the Zapatista movement took up a strategy of using video in documenting and communicating their struggle. With support from the Chiapas Media Project/Promedios, an outside organization, the Zapatistas set out to train their members, beginning with how to capture human rights abuses, and eventually to produce educational and creative works. This strategy sought to reverse the dynamic of the first years of their insurgency, in which outsiders recorded the Zapatistas' situation, keeping ultimate control of the technology and storytelling.

Since that start almost a decade ago, Zapatista video has joined a widespread adoption of communication technologies by the hemispheric movement for indigenous autonomy. Video is being used intensely by Andean, Mayan, Afro-Colombian, and other communities throughout Latin America. These communities use the medium in pursuit of the ability to determine for themselves their political and cultural place in the Americas as well as give their voices, previously rarely heard outside their immediate communities, more resonance.

For the Zapatistas, giving voice to the voiceless is one aspect of their goal of autonomy, along with redistributing resources and establishing political rights. Indigenous autonomy offers a path out of the marginalization suffered for centuries by Mexico's and Latin America's indigenous. The outlines of the Zapatistas' goal were seen in the San Andres Accords of 1996. Had the Mexican government implemented them, the Accords would have provided indigenous communities with some control and protections over their land, public life, and culture.[1] When the government reneged, the Zapatistas implemented some of their principles independently. Video was a part of this, with production and training based in the community centers now called *caracoles*. Their use of video immediately provided a greater degree of self-representation, but it would not remain a purely cultural tool.

Zapatista video has been a part of three concurrent transformations. The importance of video to indigenous movements has grown, as it has for Latin America's latest leftist and populist movements. These grassroots social movements in Latin America have continued to evolve in their shared responses to the disastrous experience of neo-liberalism.[2] At the same time, communication technologies have undergone ongoing, global changes as they have become more widespread and interconnected. Transforming together, media and social movements are experimenting with new ways of practicing the politics of autonomy, socialism, and democracy that motivate these recent movements. This experimentation has precedents in Latin America's history, but it has unprecedented possibilities for the integration of political and cultural practices.

The current closeness of video and politics in Latin America was preceded by the relationship between the New Latin America Cinema and the socialist movements from the Cuban revolution through the 1970s. Like today's movement video producers, filmmakers at that time undertook a cinema committed to the goals of their movements. In their work, the filmmakers tried to articulate practices that were not just expressions of socialist ideas but material realization of those ideas. The point of their filmmaking was to change its social context, starting with the making and dissemination of the films.

The films came out of the divergent situations that characterized Latin America at the time, from the cultural institutions established by Cuba's socialist revolution, to clandestine projects under a Chilean dictatorship. Filmmakers and critics identified links and similarities between these films, leading to a body of filmmaking theory. This theory was set out in the concepts of Fernando Solanas and Octavio Getino's "Third Cinema,"[3] Julio García Espinosa's "imperfect cinema,"[4] and Jorge Sanjinés' *cine junto al pueblo* (cinema with the people).[5] Over a number of essays, the three ideas described a new kind of cinema. Solanas, Getino, and Sanjinés described different aspects of films and filmmaking that conformed more closely to Latin American realities and sought the collaboration of their subjects and audiences in their production. Espinosa, writing in Cuba, imagined a cinema in process, an imperfect art because of its dedication not to the art of film but to the ongoing transformations of socialist revolution.

All of these concepts put cinema in the context of socialist movements. They proposed criteria of commitment, perspective, accountability, and authenticity for socialist cinema. Their work sought the deepest possible integration of art and its political goals. Also, these concepts recognized films' tactical nature. Their cinema was a process, always changing, but also a potent material instrument. Sanjinés called the camera a gun, a weapon crucial to a revolution. The film scholar Julianne Burton later wrote, "Latin American filmmakers' attempt to create a revolutionary cinema took as its point of departure...the transformation of the subjective conditions of film production and film viewing."[6] Rather than taking the role of watching and representing socialist movements, the filmmakers sought to bring the movements' transformative efforts to the context in which they worked. The filmmakers and theorists tried production collectives, new means of distribution, and other alternatives that would integrate their politics with their practices.

The impetus for this experimental integration has survived today. Zapatista videos, for example, are produced according to the principles of collectivity held in indigenous communities. The difference in today's experiments is the absence of one predominant ideology. The filmmaking of the New Latin America Cinema was held together by its period's unifying vision, a search in practice and theory for the ideal end-state of socialism. In that cinema's time, Cuba's revolution promised a common way out of the inequalities of capitalism and US imperialism. Many filmmakers practiced their craft in Cuba's ICAIC (Cuban Institute of Cinematic Art and Industry), and more watched films and other accounts of the country's economic, political, and cultural changes in pursuit of socialist ideals. Today, indigenous movements for autonomy co-exist or collaborate with leftist resistance to neo-liberal policies and populist movements that pursue democratic demands rather than ideological projects. Different bright spots of change in the Americas inspire different movements. The Zapatistas and Venezuela's Bolivarian Revolution have both been great spurs, though they are starkly different, while other movements such as Argentina's *piqueteros* and Brazil's landless groups have had narrower but significant influence. In this amalgam, experiments in the movement use of media are made with various, but intermixed motives. Just a few examples of Zapatista video and other recent productions from Mexico demonstrate the new possibilities opened by the shift from a unity of purpose to a proliferation of objectives.

The collaboration between the Zapatistas and the Chiapas Media Project/Promedios (CMP), a bi-national organization (based in the US and Mexico) that provides "video and computer equipment and training to indigenous and *campesino* communities in Chiapas and Guerrero, Mexico,"[7] has resulted in over two dozen videos created by indigenous filmmakers and distributed within indigenous communities by Zapatistas and other movements, and by the CMP across Mexico and internationally. The goal of the collaboration has been to allow the indigenous communities to tell their own stories. This project of self-representation, a part of the politics of autonomy, has expanded along with the Zapatistas' growing capacity to produce video. Their productions went from documentations of the low-intensity war they faced to later films for education, recording community events, and sharing stories. As Alexandra Halkin, founder of the CMP, wrote, "video making is part of community life."[8] In this development, Zapatista video production has revealed new paths by which other marginalized groups can bypass barriers that had made filmmaking irrelevant to their context, such as the priority of individual authorship or commercially viable audiences.

Most Zapatista videos are made for showing in Zapatista communities. This use, seen in isolation, appears to seek no transformation other than carving out its own unique space of self-representation. Other Latin American indigenous groups, such as Quechua communities producing video in Andean countries, have prioritized this use. However, the Zapatista-CMP videos circulate out into new contexts, and their significance is stretched further when they're seen in these contexts. Videos are selected for larger distribution, which the CMP undertakes in Mexico, the US, and internationally. In Mexico, they travel through grassroots channels, screened by political and cultural groups allied with the Zapatistas' national movement, as well as in universities and film festivals not linked to the Zapatistas. In the US and beyond, the videos are most often shown in academic circuits and film festivals, some with political affiliations, some not. Across these viewing contexts, the videos can be seen as efforts of self-expression first, but they also communicate their motivation as practices of the Zapatistas' politics of autonomy

In the 2005 Zapatista-CMP video, *The Land Belongs to Those Who Work It*, a community surprises a delegation of government authorities by documenting their entire unwelcome visit to discuss a property dispute. Watching this video in the US, one can guess that its primary motive is the defense of the community's autonomy. However, the video doesn't explicitly speak to foreign audiences, like the audience in Chicago with which I viewed it. While its distribution does seek to help support the Zapatistas

who made it, the video is not easily valuable to outside audiences, as either entertainment or information. In fact, its viewing breaks starkly with the tacit agreement of a normal screening, where the filmmaker promises to deliver satisfaction to the audience. While it appears to have been edited for length and possibly other issues of coherence, the recorded situation is presented without narrative, exposition, or other interpretive devices. The community's autonomy is defended in the recorded event, but why it is worth defending only gets expressed at the margins of the video's presentation. At its screening in Chicago, the host explained the video's content and connected it to the Zapatistas' politics and situation, including their struggle to secure common lands for cultivation.

Many of the Zapatista videos distributed by the CMP similarly forgo interpretation, leaving it to the distributor or presenter to help foreign audiences understand the video's motive. Videos are put in international distribution to generate solidarity with the Zapatistas and funding for the continued Zapatista-CMP collaboration. However, many of these videos are still principally for self-expression, one important part of the Zapatistas' efforts for cultural and political autonomy. When first viewed or viewed without extra explanation, this part of their politics of autonomy appears to be a gulf in communication, a muteness. However, the videos circulate accompanied by explanation, provided by the CMP or a Zapatista ally. The videos, when made by the indigenous producers, do not seek to either satisfy or convince foreign audiences. These goals lie outside their purpose of self-expression. However, in releasing videos for circulation, they do trust that sharing their efforts will be met with continued support from the CMP and the audiences who watch in good faith.

The trust and openness evident in the distribution of these videos breaks with the efforts of past socialist cinema. The videos do not seek to have their audiences join completely in the filmmakers' political project. The Zapatista-CMP use of video turns to external contexts for support, and accepts divergent values being grafted on to their work as it leaves their sphere. Part of this openness is a crucial feature of the Zapatistas' politics of indigenous autonomy, an active pursuit of intersections with movements that follow their own distinct goals, and in particular, movements for democracy and socialism in Mexico and Latin America.

The Zapatistas launched a new stage of social movements by linking their struggle for autonomy as indigenous people with movements in Mexico and internationally against the doctrines of neo-liberalism. They put forth a broad critique of the disenfranchisement and invisibility of indigenous Mexicans, as well as other excluded groups. They pointed to the neo-liberalism of the US and Latin American elite, exercised in free trade agreements and domestic economic policies, as responsible for the immiseration experienced broadly in the Americas. They have also been inclusive of alternative political programs in the discussions they have convened to find solutions to Mexico and Latin America's problems.

Early on in their movement, the Zapatistas invited the collaboration of other movements in Mexico and internationally. They reached out not only to other indigenous groups, but also to groups of workers, women, peasants, and other marginalized figures. Over their decade of engagement with allies and civil society, the Zapatistas have also articulated their take on socialist and democratic politics. These

1. http://www.globalexchange.org/countries/americas/mexico/SanAndres.html

2. The history and analysis of recent Latin American social movements are being written only now, and much of it only as journalism. Alma Guillermoprieto's *The Heart That Bleeds: Latin America Now* (New York: Alfred A. Knopf, 1994) covers some of their beginnings. Later, more scholarly treatments include *Cultures of Politics, Politics of Cultures: Re-visioning Latin American Social Movements* (Boulder: Westview Press, 1998) and *The Latin American Subaltern Studies Reader* (Durham: Duke, 2001).

3. Solanas and Getino were Argentinian filmmakers and critics. In their essay, "Toward a Third Cinema: Notes and Experiences for the Development of a Cinema of Liberation in the Third World," (In Michael Chanan, ed., *Twenty-Five Years of the New Latin American Cinema*. London: British Film Institute and Channel Four, 1983.) they suggested a Third Cinema as an alternative for Latin American filmmakers from the spectacle of "first cinema" typified by Hollywood and the auteurism of "second cinema" seen in European avant-gardes.

4. In his essay, "For an Imperfect Cinema," (In Michael Chanan, ed., *Twenty-Five Years of the New Latin American Cinema*. London: British Film Institute and Channel Four, 1983.) Espinosa argued for new criteria for the art of filmmaking in a revolutionary context. He sought to valorize the art for its reach outside art, even though this deviation would preclude its perfection as art.

5. Sanjinés and the collective of filmmakers, the Ukamau Group, wrote a number of essays, *Theory and Practice of a Cinema with the People* (Mexico: Siglo XXI Editories, 1979), explaining their approach in creating documentary and fiction films in Bolivia. Although they touched on many aspects of filmmaking, they emphasized the need to collaborate with the film's subjects (often Andean indigenous communities), serve the interests of those subjects, and practice socialist principles in production and distribution of the works.

6. Martin, Michael T., ed. *New Latin American Cinema*. Vol. 1. Detroit: Wayne State, 1997, 19.

7. http://www.promediosmexico.org/

8. Halkin, Alexandra. "Video Fuels a Cultural Revolution," *Smithsonian American Indian*: vol. 2 no. 3, 30.

sides of the Zapatista movement, exercised in their national consultations and engagement in public discourse, have brought them into different degrees of overlap with other social movements. Around these intersections, more uses of media beyond the Zapatista-CMP "autonomist" videos can be found, and new links made between media and movements for socialism and democracy.

In *La Otra Campaña* (The Other Campaign) held throughout 2006, the Zapatistas have undertaken a nationwide listening tour as an alternative to the concurrent campaign for Mexico's presidency. Subcomandante Marcos, as the Delegate Zero, set out to meet with groups in every state of Mexico who had joined the call to the Other Campaign. Adherents to the campaign belong to various ideological strands, and come from socialist, indigenous, labor, gender, and community-based groups. For hours at each stop, people have lined up to speak about their struggles. After each session, Marcos has commented on what he heard and connected it to other struggles in Mexico and a global struggle against capitalism. In these addresses and other communications, along with the adherents to the campaign, he has been elaborating a vision of a national anti-capitalist movement independent from Mexico's political class.

In this campaign, the Zapatistas and their allies have tried new uses of media, many of them packaged together through the Internet. The starting points for communications and documentation during the Other Campaign are two web sites, one for Mexico (enlacezapatista.ezln.org. mx) and one for other countries (zeztainternazional. org). Significantly, the first has a blog-like structure, with periodic updates, plus links, files, photos, and other resources, and the second has a companion blog (lazezta.blogspot.com). Another primary site is the home of the Zapatistas' radio show, *Radio Insurgente*, which provides weekly updates on the

Other Campaign, as well as interviews, music, and news from Chiapas. Numerous other sites have participated in a distributed coverage of the campaign, including Chiapas Indymedia (chiapas. indymedia.org), other Mexican Indymedias, and alternative news sites like Narco News (narconews. com). Connected to these sites are photographs and videos documenting the Other Campaign and related events.

The main sites and many of the connected sites are significant for their use of new publishing tools like blogs and RSS news feeds. From the start of the Zapatista insurgency, groups in Chiapas and Mexico have created web sites to help disseminate communications from the Zapatista. In the Other Campaign, the Zapatistas and their supporters have adopted advanced tools that most progressive organizations in the US have yet to utilize. Two important examples of the use of digital media by the Other Campaign are the regular production of *Radio Insurgente* shows and the campaign's adherents' use of the video-sharing site *YouTube* to publish their video of the campaign's events.

A search for "EZLN" on *YouTube* returns a list of over one hundred videos. Most of the videos seem to have been produced not by the Zapatistas, but by participants in the Other Campaign's events, who captured one part of Marcos' tour as it passed by. They then contributed their single perspective on this national undertaking to a flow of others' own videos. The collection of recordings provides only a shaky, irregular view of the Zapatistas' project, but offers many more choices of what part of the project to watch. With the adoption of digital publishing and sharing, along with inexpensive equipment, participants in the Other Campaign had the tools to produce work much closer to their personal experiences. They were able to go from the event to the production and finally to a substantial audience.

The *Radio Insurgente* website makes available archived radio programs since 2004. The shows are much more polished than the videos available on *YouTube*, and seek to be more comprehensive about the Zapatista movement and its Other Campaign. The shows are produced weekly for broadcast in Chiapas and by shortwave across Mexico. They are also archived and available for download online. The production of the shows follows well-scripted programs that regularly provide a mix of entertainment, news, and education. Tuning into a show, a listener will hear several songs, from indigenous music to Spanish-language pop, and then get an interview with a group or person participating in the Other Campaign. The radio hosts will also give updates from the campaign and from within Chiapas. These high-standard productions diverge greatly from both the amateur video and the Zapatista-CMP videos, because they seem to carefully seek a larger and broader audience and meet its expectations about content and aesthetics in order to connect with that audience. At the same time, the radio show producers are Zapatistas and keep production costs low by using new production tools, podcasting, and web-publishing tools.

It is important to note that these two sets of media, web and radio, were adopted by the Zapatistas and their allies during a campaign to reach out beyond their own movement. The Zapatistas have connected with other social movements since early in their insurgency, through encounters and consultations with their compatriots and international sympathizers. However, the Other Campaign has been easily their most thorough effort to interact with other struggles. Marcos' anti-capitalist ideas were crucial to tying together this campaign. The Delegate Zero sought to rally very different struggles around opposition to capitalism. In this effort, the media used in this campaign actively followed alternative modes of production and contribution. There may have been no directive from Marcos to prohibit commercialization of the campaign's media, but the tour's adherents seemed to follow his calls for Mexicans to organize themselves, both for their own struggles and as part of a unifying struggle against capitalism. In the use of blogs, podcasts, video sharing, and other tools, the media users directly managed their production and contributed their work to a media commons from which audiences could select freely.

Unlike the leftist movements of four decades ago, socialism was not proposed by the Zapatistas as an explicit organizing principle for the Other Campaign or its use of media. Socialism in this effort did not operate as a program or strategy toward an end-state. Instead, the emphasis in the campaign on the common struggle against capitalism elicited practical attempts to realize, in limited and experimental ways, alternatives to capitalism. The unevenness of this effort—the use of commercial websites for distribution or publishing, for example—only reinforces that the Zapatistas and allies were willing to make experimental efforts. This informal socialism, more an ethic than a program, fits better within the multiplicity of social movements and ideologies that characterize the current response to neo-liberalism, as well as with the variety of media by which it might express and realize itself.

While the Other Campaign's call for self-organization has spurred experimental adoption of media in Mexico's social movements, it has not generated a guiding theory or proposals comparable to that in the New Latin American Cinema. The absence of a unifying vision or goals might explain why no single technology has become crucial to contemporary social movements. This situation is not necessarily a problem, and while the determination to centralize efforts around a single medium might yet become apparent, for now the plurality presents an array of creative uses of media, especially as the social movements developing these uses grow and change.

The latest stage of social movements in Mexico exemplifies this situation. In the 2006 election year, the politics of democracy have emerged as primary motivator of two distinct movements: the effort to elect the charismatic presidential candidate, Andrés Manuel López Obrador, and the effort to remove the governor of Oaxaca. The first one, though tied to political parties, has some characteristics of a grassroots movement, especially when the close election led to challenges and street protests. Its most notable use of media was in the documentation of suspected electoral fraud, which spurred much of the massive support for López Obrador's denunciation of the election results. However, a fuller integration of media and movement politics has occurred in Oaxaca.

Starting with a teachers' strike in the spring, Oaxaca's urban, rural, worker, indigenous, and other groups joined in mass marches, work stoppages, and occupations that have demanded the resignation of the state's governor. This movement culminated in the establishment APPO (Popular Assembly of the People of Oaxaca), a coordinating body that has rapidly adopted media to communicate its positions, denounce moves against it, and reach out to other groups in Mexico. Its use of media has included the use of radio broadcasts—including a few takeovers of commercial stations—and video recording of violent attacks against the movement by the governor's allies. It has turned to local newspapers but also its own web site (www.asambleapopulardeoaxaca.com) and allied sites to provide updates on its struggle. None of its tools are exceptionally innovative, but their use of media is remarkable for its rapid adoption of a variety of technologies, and the context of its production. The Assembly has generated its wide range of media while operating as a populist movement that welcomes all ideologies and constituencies unified by their goal of replacing the state's administration along democratic principles, without the use of violence. Each instance of its use of media will be instructive for its creativity in a situation defined by heterogeneity and continual negotiation.

Improvisation appears to be APPO's approach to media in its rapidly evolving situation. This movement may endure and institute unique uses of media, but its current importance is that it epitomizes much of the recent integration of media and politics. Both movements and media have proliferated in the past ten years, appearing abruptly and in different contexts, and rapidly changing. In Latin America's past, socialist movements took up film and other media that were also changing—film, for example had become cheaper and more portable—but today's pace of change and multiplicity have made the quick and flexible links of improvisation necessary.

The lessons of Zapatista video, the digital media of the Other Campaign, and the multiple channels of movements for democracy have yet to point to some decisive strategy or theory for employing media. No particular tool, production process, or content has fit recent movements better than others. A conclusive approach might yet emerge, but it seems that improvisation and openness are also viable approaches. If the future of Latin America's social movement is a continued multiplicity of ideologies and politics, and changing media keep offering simple, flexible options, then we may see an open-ended integration. Movements may adopt and drop technologies as quickly as their situations change, and productions may include a variable mix of documentation, anecdotes, testimony, or polemic. This new set of possibilities promises to keep media relevant to struggles to change Latin America, as social movements like the Zapatistas continue to link and grow in pursuit of their political goals.

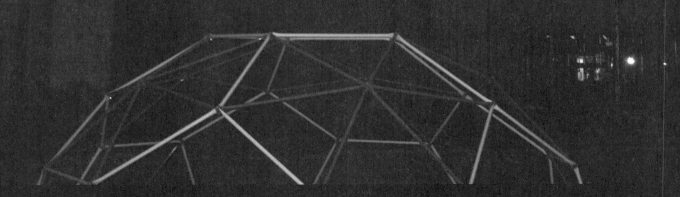

QUEER ART/QUEER ANARCHY: AN INTERVIEW WITH LUIS JACOB

ALLAN ANTLIFF

Luis Jacob was born in 1971 in Lima, Peru and grew up in Toronto, Canada. He attended the University of Toronto, and majored in Philosophy and Semiotics. Luis and I got to know each other at the Toronto Anarchist Free School (1998–2001) and since then we have collaborated on a number of projects.

An artist, curator, educator, writer, organizer and activist, Jacob's practice challenges categorization. His art production alone manifests itself as photography, sculpture, performance, artist multiples, public intervention, video, and installation. Jacob's pursuits are varied, but all are unified by his thoughtful concern for the philosophical and cultural possibilities of social interaction.

How did you come to identify as an anarchist?

I've been thinking about this question recently, thinking about my childhood and how I was brought up.

I've always felt somewhat disconnected from the society I was born into. I grew up in Peru, a country with a strong patriarchal, nationalist, and Catholic culture that, as a child, appeared as strange to me. I was sent to a Catholic school, but my family never inculcated me with a religious culture, with the result that I experienced the rites at school as something foreign and absurd. Coming to Canada as an older child I had to quickly learn the language and customs of my new home, without sharing the same popular referents as others here. And blossoming into my queer sexuality as a teenager, became for me another experience of feeling disconnected and like an outsider—the experience of what we call "the closet." These experiences of social disconnection are not, of course, nice experiences; alienation is not fun.

All my life I have been nourished, however, by the sense of inner strength I was given by my mother. In time and through my contact with "alternative" communities, I have come to regard what is normal as being neither natural nor even statistically more numerous, and to suspect that perhaps it is the experience of alienation that is statistically the "normal" situation.

I see alienation as the rather commonplace experience of disconnection that gives rise to the desire to conform to social norms. As social agents we reward one another when we conform to what we happen to envision as being normal, so that the promise of reward or the threat of its withdrawal are a means of control and coercion of each other's behavior. It's apparent to me that this coercion subtends all social experience—from everyday contact with family, friends, neighbours, and strangers, to the exceptional cases (which are everyday for some people) of encounters with the law and state force.

Violence, whether naturalized or not, whether normalized or not, is at the root of socialization. Society does not exist so that the experience of disconnection is done away with, but rather society must sustain alienation as the condition that binds it and the power that directs it. Those who most profit from this situation are of course inclined to reward others who work to ensure alienation remains in place.

The experience of alienation is uncomfortable and painful, but I do think there is something personally valuable in being able to see what is accepted as "normal" with some subjective distance. Alienation is personally valuable when it gives rise

Luis Jacob, *Flashlight* (nighttime installation view), LED signage, solar panels on steel pole, children's playground equipment, electrical generator, 2003–05. Commissioned by the Toronto Sculpture Garden as an outdoor public sculpture. Photo: Luis Jacob.

to a desire for a form of contact and community not founded on normalized coercion and violence. This desire is what we call anarchy. I began to identify as an anarchist (which to me is synonymous with identifying as queer) when I recognized that other people were also engaged in a long historical effort to create realms of communion not based on social coercion. Just as I said that violence is at the root of society, so too I'd say that the effort to counteract this violence is at the root of the history of society. Anarchy is woven into the fabric of society, and that is where I choose to devote my energies.

When did you start thinking about your art in relation to anarchist ideas—and what specific ideas within the anarchist tradition have you found most compelling for your art and life?

I recall the specific moment I started thinking of my art and its relationship to anarchist ideas. That was a moment in the process of working as part of the Anarchist Free School collective here in Toronto in 1998. At one point in the collective discussion about what to name the project, and about the pros and cons of using the word "anarchist," Alan O'Connor called anarchy "the politics that dares not speak its name."[1]

This paraphrasing of Oscar Wilde's famous definition of homosexuality struck a chord for me, since as an artist I have assumed responsibility for the cultural representations (or non-representations) within the society I'm part of. This lead me to reconsider the limits I impose on my own work when it comes to making explicit my politics, and to attempt to integrate my various activities as an individual by criscrossing the various communities I participate in.

The first realization of these aims was the installation *Anarchist Free School Minutes* (1998–99), that documents the process of germination of one collective community education project. This installation was first exhibited at the Artlab, University of Western Ontario, in 1999; and subsequently at Queens University in 2002 and at the Ontario College of Art and Design in 2006. Presented in the art gallery, it shares in the traditions of artist-run initiatives, do-it-yourself participatory ethics, and democratized cultural activities. In these exhibitions, *Anarchist Free School Minutes* has functioned as a kind of "counter-model" of an educational institution presented within the art galleries of three very large and established educational institutions. Visitors to the installation may read and peruse the activist and anarchist publications collected within the installation, and if they are so inclined, may take home with them duplicate copies of the publications as a way of personally extending the reach of this particular counter-model. In this way the gallery space becomes a kind of infoshop for the distribution of alternative information.

It is significant to me that my work had taken, at that time, a turn towards modes of collaborative and participatory practice that focus on education and collective pleasure.

A subsequent realization of my aim to crisscross the various communities I participate in is the outdoor installation *Flashlight* (2005). *Flashlight* was located at a City of Toronto park that has a public-sculpture program, and the project took the form of a children's playground of the type not uncommon in public parks (but certainly uncommon in sculpture gardens!). This playground contained a suspended mirrored disco-ball that connected the entire installation to the aspirations for self-transcendence and social union of "funk" culture from the 1970s. An LED sign further made this connection to funk culture within the park by containing a message from the Parliament song "Flash Light" that stated: EVERYBODY'S GOT A LITTLE LIGHT UNDER THE SUN.

Two sources of power were present in the installation. Solar panels provided electricity to the disco-ball's motor so that it rotated when the sun was out, in a revolution that was daily renewed. And the participatory energies of the park's visitors as they pedaled on two hidden electrical generators also provided electricity, this time to light up the LED sign and thus reveal its message to others present at the park. The project made the utopian proposition that playful interaction is a source of power parallel to the natural power of the sun under which we are all equal. Equally, we each carry within us an inner spark—an innate agency or power to manifest within that regulated and regimented terrain known as the public sphere.

Two ideas inform these art projects in ways that I see as belonging to the anarchist tradition: the idea of manifesting counter-models of social communion presented within society in its current form, here and now (not in some deferred revolutionary moment); and the idea of spontaneous participation as an overcoming of alienation and a liberation of energies of personal agency and collective pleasure.

These ideas are not the property of anarchist thought, of course, and one can experience versions of them elsewhere in society—in my experience they can also be found in the dance culture that is one of the great legacies of the African diaspora to the mainstream of culture in the Americas.

Lets discuss your activities at the Anarchist Free School and its successor, Anarchist U—how you got involved and so on. No doubt these have been very positive and affirmative experiences...

I attended the "Active Resistance" anarchist gathering in Toronto in 1998, and I was deeply impressed by many things I experienced there. These things can all be summed up by the idea of "participatory collective action"—which to my mind means not only actions that are done by people who form groups (collectivism), but which also means actions

that are conducive to the formation of more active and more embracing groupings (participation).

At the gathering I saw, for example, people offer their language skills to provide French and Spanish translation during all meetings (an instance of people pooling their skills and working collectively), and I recognized that this simultaneously became a way to respectfully acknowledge the presence—and actively welcome the participation—of people not fluent in English (an instance of people encouraging a more genuinely active collective). I saw how the Active Resistance event necessitated the work of a group of designated volunteers who went dumpster-diving each day (to provide lunch and dinner for each of the 700 people who attended during the six days of the gathering: an incredible responsibility!), and I saw how leaving unplanned the cleaning duties after each meal meant that those 700 people had to figure out on their own (without "organizers") how they were going to clean and dry and store the resulting pile of dishes, cups, and cutlery. I was struck by how profoundly the anarchist process involves not only collective action, but simultaneously action that encourages a genuinely participatory collectivism.

These things had a big impact on me, as part of my search for forms of interpersonal contact and community not founded on violence (the violence of exclusion, of making invisible, of making silent, but also the violence of disempowerment, of coercion, of pseudo-consent). I saw that the gathering was a way of creating a real realm of togetherness based on participation rather than coercion.

I think that once you taste this—once you experience what it is like to be treated as a real human being who possesses a real concreteness that deserves acknowledgment and respect—and once you experience what it is like to be served for free and to assist for free, and to enact your agency without the coercion of authority.... Well, I think there is no going back. A desire has been awakened!

A mere four days after the gathering ended, a meeting was called for people who had attended it to continue the discussions begun at the gathering, and to initiate a project that would put those discussions into action. The following series of planning meetings (averaging a very intense three meetings a week) became an amazing learning opportunity

Luis Jacob, *Flashlight* (daytime installation view), LED signage, solar panels on steel pole, children's playground equipment, electrical generator, 2003–05. Commissioned by the Toronto Sculpture Garden as an outdoor public sculpture. Photo: Luis Jacob.

Luis Jacob, *Anarchist Free School Minutes*, installation with twenty two framed sheets of typewritten paper, and reading area, 1998–99. This page: framed minutes; next page: reading area (installation view).

about anarchist process for all of us. During the month of planning the Free School, we had to figure out a process for speaking with each other, for forming a space where we could all feel comfortable to express our ideas, make collective decisions, reach agreements based on consensus, and work with disagreements without recourse to hierarchies. The installation *Anarchist Free School Minutes* includes the minutes of these meetings, which describe—in the voices of the various people who participated—this process of the collective's coming-into-being.

During the Free School's first semester, you and I facilitated the course "Art, Anarchism, Culture: History and Practice," and I participated in the course "The Conflict in Chiapas." During the second semester I attended the "Alternative Health Practices" course, and co-facilitated the "Art & Revolution" course. These remain very important experiences for me.

Have your anarchist art practices merged with and informed your anarchist educational practices in any way?

As an artist, I have been formed by the tradition of artist-run culture in Canada. This is an enormous and fascinating field, and much like anarchism itself, it has its own philosophy and ways of working. The idea of artist-run (or artist-initiated) culture is similar to the punk idea of do it yourself, which functions to encourage people to create rather than simply consume, to work with what you have

now rather than just feel frustrated that you don't have access to the wealth of resources of spectacle culture, and to establish networks of mutual support rather than wait for some institution or big guy to discover you.

For artists, this means that our role is not simply the creation of things called artworks, but that as artists we must also be responsible for the creation of the context for distribution and reception of our works. As artists we must therefore also be gallery organizers, or critics, or archivists, or art historians, or curators, or collectors, or publishers, or media technicians, or arts administrators. According to the idea of artist-run culture, it is all these things which make up the role—the task—of being an artist in society: artists must actively participate in the expanded context of their work (not simply the limited realm of their studios); and as collectively empowered agents, artists must engage with the social world around them (not simply the retreat realm of a pure, but hollow, art world). Needless to say, this philosophy runs counter to the given social context that steers artists towards individually produced and competitive work: the idea of the lonely, starving artist.

In 1999 during an artists' panel discussion at the University of Western Ontario, I described myself to the audience as "an artist working as curator, publisher of artists' multiples, writer, organizer, and studio artist." What I meant by this was that this range of activities is what constitutes my artistic practice. I see around me that at any given

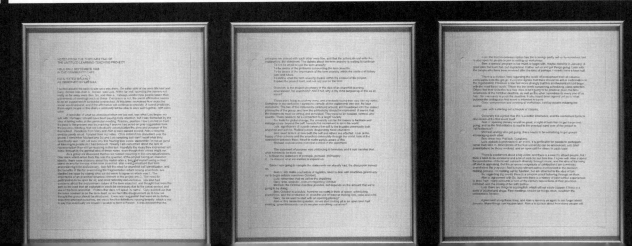

time, many of us work as publisher-as-artist, or curator-as-artist, or community-organizer-as-artist, or crate-builder-as-artist, or educator-as-artist, or archivist-as-artist, as well as being traditional studio artists—although these other functions are not usually recognized as legitimate artistic work. Running through all of these expanded functions is the idea that the work of an artist is not exclusively the production of objects, but the making dynamic of the culture in which we live.

My first real experiment in this philosophy was the project *Galerie Largeness World of Art* (1996–2001), a project to publish other artists' multiples and editions produced especially for the Galerie. In the span of its thirty issues, Galerie Largeness ambitiously presented work by some ninety artists—involving various solo and group exhibitions, five guest-curated projects, five audio-arts projects, one prayer project, one mail art project, and three separate events featuring video screenings and performances.

In 2002 I curated the exhibition *Golden Streams: Artists' Collaboration and Exchange in the 1970s*, at the Blackwood Gallery, University of Toronto at Mississauga. The exhibition and accompanying catalog focused on four artist collectives working in Toronto and Vancouver in the 1970s: Image Bank, General Idea, Banal Beauty Inc.,

and the New York Corres Sponge Dance School of Vancouver. I wanted to look at these historical precedents in Canada, of artists who pioneered many of the artistic strategies that younger artists in the 1990s were engaged in. These pioneering artists worked collectively as groups and collaboratively between groups, often engaging in a playful mutual appropriation of one another's imagery—challenging inherited ideas of originality and conceptions of visual—art production as individual, solitary work. They also created artistic personae and mythological narratives, wore costumes, and used props and other identifying devices, putting into question ideas of authorship, authenticity, and self-representation. And they engaged with alternative media and non-traditional artistic forms such as correspondence art, artists' publications, performance art, Super-8 film, television, and video. Exploring the potential in marginal art forms, new technical forms, and "non-artistic" media, I was very interested in how these artists engaged with society and mass culture.

It is this artistic and philosophical tradition which informs my work as artist, and which I can bring into my activities as an anarchist. But there is something crude in this way of talking about this process, since it implies bringing something from one realm into another one that is foreign to it. Rather, I see that what artists enact as artist-run

Anarchist Free School Minutes, 1999

culture, what punks enact as do-it-yourself culture, and what anarchists enact as an ethics of collective participation, all join within the same society to form multiple dimensions of one effort for a democratized culture.

Is there a tension involved when you work as an anarchist artist in the realm of the art gallery/art system?

I have the rather audacious attitude that as an artist I am completely entitled to participate in the art system. This means that at some level it is the art gallery, for instance, which must adapt itself to what I do as an artist, rather than me simply adapting my work in order to have it appear in an art gallery. This attitude is, I admit, rather audacious and a bit idealistic. But I must also say that

so far I've experienced a great deal of support and encouragement from the "art system" for what I do.

As I understand it, the key for this support to happen is the simultaneous presence in Canada of two art systems: a commercial system guided by profit and speculation, and a second, non-commercial system guided to a large extent by the philosophy of artist-run culture. This latter system is being threatened by neo-liberal cultural policies, but it remains surprisingly powerful and influential in Canada's art system. For example, it is common practice that the contemporary art curators at the largest public galleries in Canada (including the National Gallery in Ottawa, the Art Gallery of Ontario and the Power Plant in Toronto, etc.) all started as practitioners in the field of artist-run centers. As well, public funding for the arts

(in terms of individual grants to artists and grants to artist-run institutions) operate in Canada on the basis of two basic principles: that of arms-length and peer-review. This means that grants are distributed by arts councils with relative autonomy (at an arm's length distance) from political influence, and it means that within the councils, grants are awarded to artists according to the priorities established by other practicing artists (that is, grants are juried by our own peers and not by bureaucrats).

These very significant factors ensure the great influence of the philosophy of artist-run culture within the country—even at the highest institutional levels—and ensures the existence of a non-commercial system parallel to the commercial system of private dealers and collectors, where artists can obtain financial support and exhibition opportunities for their work. How astounding!

Having said that, there are several ideas present within the art system as a whole, which run in tension with this socialized and collectivized sub-system. One is the idea that artistic work can only ever be an individual achievement produced by a singular artist-author. Projects like *Galerie Largeness* and *Anarchist Free School Minutes* complicate this idea, since as art projects they clearly are the product of several people's work, not only my own. Their existence as artworks requires that they be identified by a single author—Luis Jacob. This art-system requirement for a singular artist-author, even in cases of obvious co-operation, raises the problem of the co-optation of collective or community creation whenever an artist chooses to locate their work as part of this broader creative process. In the case of documentary projects such as *Anarchist Free School Minutes*, this problem is obviously part of the work.

I have also tried engaging with this problem, rather than shying away from it in a move towards safely "disinterested" subject matter, in *Anarchist Sandwich Party; Bloor/Danforth Subway, Toronto #1–5* (2004). This project takes the form of a suite of five ballpoint pen drawings that documents a collaborative project: an anarchist "sandwich party" produced by the participants of the "Art and Collaborative Approaches" class held by the Anarchist Free University.

The Anarchist U is a second volunteer-run collective that followed from the Anarchist Free School in Toronto. Among the six weekly courses offered by the Anarchist U during its first semester in the Fall of 2003, I facilitated the "Art and Collaborative Approaches" class. As the last class of this course, the group decided to produce a collaboration of our own: an anarchist sandwich party held in Toronto's subway system.

On December 1, 2003, each course participant brought enough of one sandwich ingredient to make several sandwiches. The twenty people who attended this event assembled at Bathurst Station in downtown Toronto, boarded the subway train heading eastbound towards the suburb of Scarborough, and proceeded to form a sandwich-making assembly line. The first person brought out bread, then passed this bread to the next person, who added to it one ingredient. As it was passed from person to person in this way, the gradually growing sandwich was built until—filled with twenty different ingredients—it reached the end of the production line. In a mood of celebration, the sandwiches were enjoyed by the course participants and distributed to other passengers also riding the subway train.

Appearing somewhat like oversized ballpoint-pen sketches on high-school binders, *Anarchist Sandwich Party* documents this collective project in a process that was itself collaborative. I invited the participants of the original action on the subway to help produce the documentary drawings. Produced with the assistance of people who may or may not identify as artists, the variety of mark-making gestures and pen colours that were used become the manifest traces of the various hands at work in producing each drawing.

This series of drawings has been widely exhibited in Canada, touring to Montréal, Peterborough, Saskatoon, Calgary, and Toronto. Within the art system, the more exposure this project receives, and the more I personally gain in terms of "cultural capital" as a result of this exposure, the more likely it is to raise questions of co-optation. These are serious questions, especially if as a result of these exhibitions I, as "Luis Jacob," become a kind of "owner" of the sandwich party, or the Art and Collaboration class, or even of the Anarchist U itself.

Luis Jacob, Galerie Largeness World of Art, selection of publications, 1996-2001. Photo: Luis Jacob.

Luis Jacob, *Anarchist Sandwich Party; Bloor/Danforth Subway, Toronto #1–5*, ballpoint pen on paper, four out of a suite of five drawings, 2004. Produced with the assistance of Nick Ackerley, Christopher House, Peter Kingstone, Jeremy Laing, Scott McEwan, Amish Morrell, Will Munro, Yvonne Ng, Sandy Plotnikoff, Moh'd Shanti, Tina Shapiro, Fraser Smith, Catherine Stinson, and Netami Stuart.

We all enter into this process, as anarchists, when we take our values into realms that are antithetical in some way to our politics—of course the whole point is that we seek to transform these spheres and that is why we take on the risks of engagement. To my mind, questioning is part of the anarchist project: you assess your effectiveness on your own terms, as opposed to those of the status quo.

These questions are something I welcome. To this end, with the *Anarchist Sandwich Party* I decided to present an artist talk at each touring venue where I presented the drawings, so that the talks became a means of personal exposure to any possible objections to my use of the drawings. As well, as part of this touring exhibition (titled *Open Your Mouth and Your Mind Will Follow*), I asked the host galleries to organize a bread-baking workshop facilitated by a local baker at the gallery itself. Transforming the gallery as a place to prepare food, bread was baked that was offered later that day at the exhibition opening reception, which itself took the form of a large potluck party with food brought by attendees. In these various ways I hoped to make clear that the exhibition event (not only the objects on exhibit) can become an instance of co-operative, as well as authorial, creative processes.

The fact remains that at the end of the day it was "Luis Jacob" who originally proposed the exhibition, it was "Luis Jacob" whose name appears on the wall labels, it was "Luis Jacob" who receives the artist's exhibition fees, and it was "Luis Jacob" who is the responsible recipient of the success or failure of the exhibition. This is all built-in to the structure of the art system, even an "artist-run" system.

I am struck by how persistent the idea of the singular artist-author is within the art system and in society at large, and it seems that presenting the idea that an exhibition entails both co-operative and authorial creative processes can only be perceived in terms of a disturbing ambiguity. I am pursuing this ambiguity in subsequent work, and the strategies of educational and didactic forms (like artist talks, or reading groups) and forms of collective pleasure (like cooking/eating together, or playing together) have become especially fertile in this pursuit.

You mention that, for you, being queer and being anarchist are interrelated. I am interested in this. You are aware, of course, that there is a long history of anarchist artists, critics, and activists who were also lesbian, gay, or bisexual — Oscar Wilde, Margaret Anderson, Julian Beck, and so on, as well as strong supporters of sexual liberation—Emma Goldman comes to mind. Can you say more? And can you relate this to contemporary queer-anarchist movements—like the Radical Faeries,[2] for example?

With this excellent question, Allan, I think you will have me make explicit the mythopoeics by which I live. What an honour!

I'll begin by saying that my teenage years—the time when I had to begin making decisions about being or not being "in the closet"—were also the time of Queer Nation [founded in 1990] and ACT UP [founded in 1987], which ought better to be remembered by its full name: the AIDS Coalition to Unleash Power. The late 1980s was a time of an energetically militant queer community in North America, with the result that my identity as a "gay person" has become permanently connected for me with an "activist" identity. The cultural politics of Queer Nation and ACT UP—the wearing of your politics on your body, the organizing of kiss-ins at homophobic restaurants, the identification of SILENCE with DEATH—became for me what being "gay" was. This is not a matter of politics in an intellectual sense, but this was connected to sexuality, to desire. My sexuality was political. My inner yearnings were political. The risk of bodily harm for affirming my desires was political. And, with the reality of AIDS, whether I or others like me lived or died was itself political.

All this was connected to sex, or better yet, to the energy within me by which I manifest myself in the world and by which I connect to that corresponding energy in others. Drag queens have given all of us a very important word for what I'm trying to say, and that word is "fierce." When are you fierce? You are fierce when you are fully being who you are—then, you are unstoppable. Then, you have unleashed your power.

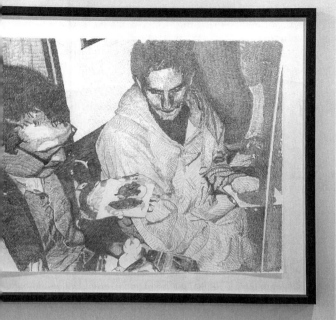

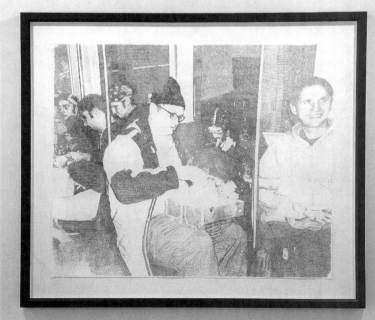

What I'm trying to describe is not precisely about sexual orientation (just like "sex" is not precisely about what you do with your genitals). I never really describe myself as "gay;" I identify as queer. Queer is a term that goes beyond sexual orientation, and describes something broader: one's identity-position in society with regards to what is normal, central, or validated, whatever that may be. And the term queer was an effort to connect gay liberation to a broader effort at sexual liberation.

This explains why queer cultural politics was not about affirming that gay people are the same as heterosexuals (except in our choice of partners), as important as this affirmation is within the horizon of possibility determined by "politics" proper. Queer cultural politics was not about having gay people also join in the benefits (such as equal marriage) of a society that would still organize itself by segregation and hierarchy, again, as important as this joining in is within politics proper. Because politics is never about liberation, but is about determination by power and accommodation to power.

To be queer is to regard politics—the measure by which those who are dispossessed of power are distinguished from those who are granted it, and the measure by which those who are dispossessed are deemed not-normal, marginal, illegitimate, sick, or invalid—with deep suspicion. The effort is therefore not for gay persons to become normal, to enter the realm of the acceptable, but rather to challenge the measure of normalcy itself. Queer will always remain, despite all the significant progressive gains made at the political level, the opposite of normal. Because normal itself is a problem. To identify as queer, whatever your sexual orientation may be, is to claim the space of not-normal as your source of personal power, rather than as the attempt to dispossess you of that very power. Queer is a defiance. It is fierce.

The Radical Faeries manifesto reprinted from "Queer Tapette/Queer Terrorist 2" in your book, *Only a Beginning: An Anarchist Anthology*, really is amazing.[3] The following words appear there, which I interpret in terms of creating a queer space:

> As faerie babes we were each born with a penis and (because of this penis) a burden of social expectation. As faeries we are sharply aware of the inappropriateness of society's gender expectations when applied to us. We faerie boys had queer ways of trying to throw a baseball. The boys (those who would grow up to be Men) told us we threw like the girls. But the girls, when we asked them, said we didn't throw like boys or girls—we threw like a sissy. There is the clue to our real gender. We are not-Men. We are other. We are sissies. We are faeries.

It's important to note here that faerie is a description of gender identity, not sexual orientation. Basically, a faerie is whoever identifies as not-Man; a faerie is a male person for whom society's gender expectations are inappropriate when applied to him: "We are other... We are faeries."

During my education as an anarchist at the Anarchist Free School, I was struck by learning that many of the strategies for organizing and consensus-building were being passed on from people who had themselves learned it from their involvement in queer cultural politics (in the *BodyPolitic* collective, to be precise).[4] It's amazing for me to imagine how the traditions of collective process, consensus, and non-hierarchic organizing can run through anarchist as well as queer spaces.

It's important to say that sexual orientation does not determine one's political stance. Far from it: there are plenty of right-wing, neoconservative homosexuals. The experience of marginalization for one's sexual orientation can make someone try to challenge this marginalization in all its forms (the radical position), or to simply join in the ranks of power that determine such marginalization (the conservative position).

In a text called, "Reasons Why Some of Us Call Ourselves Faeries," John Burnside writes:

> The term 'Faery' has for us a certain malicious charm, not lessened by the fact that it makes straight-identified gays squirm and scurry. But the positive meanings in 'Faery' really determines our choice of the word. It identifies us as a separate people."

This describes that even for gay men—for Conservative gays—faeries act as a sort of disturbing gadfly, a sign of the "otherness" which they wish to disown. According to this writer, there is something of a social leveling associated with this position of otherness—a non-hierarchy: "Faeries are not concerned with rank, place, and privilege among the mortals. We Gays, too, feel as easy with king as with scullery maid."[5]

So in my personal experience, being queer and being an anarchist are intimately linked. Broadening the scope of struggles for economic empowerment associated with the labor and socialist movements, anarchism has long identified that liberation must address our own fullness as human beings—not only our status in terms of social and economic class, but also in our various identities as persons who love and desire, persons who experience fear and shame, and persons with the capacity for pleasure and joy. For anarchism, liberation struggles must also entail liberation at the level of these dimensions of being human.

Burnside indicates this broadened scope for liberation, when writing: "Faeries are known to be devoted to music, dance, song, and merriment. For sharing these inclinations, we call ourselves Gay. Laughter is our first language, tears our second. A music, as of bells, underlies our sense of engaging reality." In my experience, anarchist culture asserts the idea that the struggle for liberation must itself entail the liberation of our capacity for pleasure, including sexual pleasure in its varied forms. There is something magical in this, as a politics founded on joy. There is also an ethics in this, because it runs counter to the idea (often summoned to support revolutions of all kinds) that the ends justify the means.

1. An important figure in the Canadian anarchist community, Alan O'Connor is author of *Raymond Williams: Writing, Culture, Politics* (London: Blackwell, 1989), and editor of *Raymond Williams on Television* (London: Routledge, 1989).

2. The Radical Faeries are an anarchist organization founded in 1978. See http://www.heathenharvest.com/index.php?topic=Radical_Faeries (accessed, August 14, 2006).

3. "Radical Faeries," "Queer Tapette/Queer Terrorist 2"(1990). In *Only a Beginning: An Anarchist Anthology*, edited by Allan Antliff (Vancouver: Arsenal Pulp Press, 2004), 378.

4. The *BodyPolitic* (1971–1987) was a collectively-run Toronto-based gay and lesbian magazine. See http://www.uwo.ca/pridelib/bodypolitic/bphistory/timeline.htm(accessed, August 14, 2006).

5. John Burnside, "Reasons Why Some of Us Call Ourselves Faeries" in *Who Are the Gay People? And Other Essays* (San Francisco: Vortex Media, 1989).

SECTION THREE

THEORIES

THE TWILIGHT OF VANGUARDISM

DAVID GRAEBER

Revolutionary thinkers have been saying that the age of vanguardism has been over for most of a century now. Outside of a handful of tiny sectarian groups, it's almost impossible to find radical intellectuals who seriously believe that their role should be to determine the correct historical analysis of the world situation so as to lead the masses along in the one true revolutionary direction. But (rather like the idea of progress itself, to which it's obviously connected), it seems much easier to renounce the principle than to shake the accompanying habits of thought. Vanguardist, even sectarian, attitudes have become so deeply ingrained in radical theory it's hard to say what it would mean to think outside them.

The depth of the problem really struck me when I first became acquainted with the consensus modes of decision-making employed in North American anarchist and anarchist-inspired political movements. These, in turn, bore a lot of similarities to the style of political decision-making in rural Madagascar, where I had done my anthropological fieldwork. There's enormous variation among different styles and forms of consensus building but one thing almost all the North American variants have in common is that they are organized in conscious opposition to the style of organization and, especially, of debate typical of the classical sectarian Marxist group. The latter are invariably organized around some Master Theoretician, who offers a comprehensive analysis of the world situation, and often of human history as a whole, but very little theoretical reflection on more immediate questions of organization and practice. Anarchist-inspired groups tend to operate on the assumption that no one could, or probably should, ever convert another person completely to one's own point of view, and that decision-making structures are ways of managing diversity, and therefore, one should concentrate instead on maintaining egalitarian process and on considering immediate questions of action in the present. A fundamental principle of political debate, for instance, is that one is obliged to give other participants the benefit of the doubt for honesty and good intentions, whatever else one might think of their arguments. In part this emerges from the style of debate consensus decision-making encourages. Voting encourages one to reduce one's opponent's positions to a hostile caricature, or whatever it takes to defeat them. However, a consensus process is built on a principle of compromise and creativity where one is constantly changing proposals around until one can come up with something everyone can at least live with; therefore, the incentive is always to put the best possible construction on other's arguments.

All this brought home to me just how much ordinary intellectual practice—the kind of thing I was trained to do in the graduate anthropology program at the University of Chicago, for example—really does resemble sectarian modes of debate. One of the things which most disturbed me about my training there was the way we were encouraged to read other theorists' arguments. If there were two ways to read a sentence, one of which assumed the author had at least a smidgen of common sense and the other that he was a complete idiot, the tendency was always to chose the latter. I had sometimes wondered how this could be reconciled with an idea that intellectual practice was, on some ultimate level, a common enterprise in pursuit of truth. The same goes for other intellectual habits: for example, that of carefully assembling lists of different "ways to be wrong" (usually ending in "ism:" i.e., subjectivism, empiricism, functionalism, all much like their sectarian parallels: reformism, hegemonism, leftism...) and being willing to listen to points of view differing from one's own only so long as it takes to figure out which variety of wrongness to plug them into.

Combine this with the tendency to treat (often minor) intellectual differences, not only as tokens of belonging to some imagined "ism," but as profound moral flaws, on the same level as racism or imperialism (or of actually being racist or imperialist arguments) and then one has an almost exact reproduction of the style of intellectual debate typical of the most ridiculous vanguardist sects.

I still believe that the growing prevalence of consensus and these new, and to my mind far healthier, modes of discourse among activists will have its effects on theorists, but it's hard to deny that so far, the change has been very slow in coming. Anarchist theory is clearly not impossible—though a single Anarchist High Theory in the style typical of university radicalism might be a contradiction in terms. One could imagine a body of theory that presumes and indeed values a diversity of sometimes incommensurable perspectives in much the same way that anarchist decision-making process does, but which nonetheless organizes them around a presumption of shared commitments. Clearly, it would also have to self-consciously reject any trace of vanguardism. This leads to the question: if the role of revolutionary intellectuals is not to form an elite that can arrive at the correct strategic analyses and then lead the masses to follow them, what precisely is it?

The History of the Idea of Vanguardism

Untwining social theory from vanguardist habits might seem a particularly difficult task because historically, modern social theory and the idea of the vanguard were born more or less together. On the other hand, so was the idea of an artistic avant garde ("avant garde" is in fact simply the French word for vanguard), and the relation between the three might itself suggest some unexpected possibilities.

The term "avant garde" was coined by Henri de Saint-Simon, a French aristocrat, political visionary, pamphleteer, and activist writing in the early-nineteenth century. It was the product of a series of essays he wrote at the very end of his life. Like his onetime secretary and disciple (and later bitter rival) Auguste Comte, Saint-Simon was writing in the wake of the French revolution and, essentially, was asking what had gone wrong. Why did the transition from a medieval, feudal Catholic society to a modern, industrial democratic one seem to be creating such

enormous violence and social dislocation? Could it be done right? At the time, Catholic and Royalist thinkers like Bonald and de Maistre were arguing that the Revolution had descended into The Terror because it had destroyed the divine principles of order and hierarchy of which the King had been merely the embodiment. Since the Middle Ages, the social system, they argued, had been upheld above all by the Church, which gave everyone the sense of having a meaningful place in a single coherent social order.

Saint-Simon and Comte rejected these reactionary conclusions—they didn't feel it would be possible to simply place the Medieval Church back in power. What was needed was to invent a new institution that would play the same role in the new world being created by the industrial revolution. Towards the end of their lives each actually ended up creating his own religion: Saint-Simon called his the "New Christianity," Comte named his the "New Catholicism." In the first, artists were to play the role of the ultimate spiritual leaders. In an imaginary dialogue with a scientist, Saint-Simon has an artist explaining that in their role of imagining possible futures and inspiring the public, they can play the role of an "avant garde," a "truly priestly function" as he puts it. In his ideal future, artists would hatch the ideas which they would then pass on to the scientists and industrialists to put into effect. Saint-Simon was also perhaps the first to conceive the notion of the withering away of the state: once it had become clear that the authorities were operating for the good of the public, one would no more need force to compel the public to heed their advice than one needed it to compel patients to take the advice of their doctors. Government would pass away into some minor police functions.

Comte is most famous as the founder of sociology; he invented the term to describe what he saw as the master-discipline which could both understand and direct society. He ended up taking a different, far more authoritarian approach: ultimately proposing the regulation and control of almost all aspects of human life according to scientific principles, with the role of high priests (effectively, the vanguard, though he did not actually call them this) in his New Catholicism being played by the sociologists themselves.

It's a particularly fascinating opposition because in the early twentieth century, the positions were effectively reversed. Instead of the left-wing Saint-Simonians looking to artists for leadership, while the right-wing Comtians fancied themselves scientists, we had the fascist leaders like Hitler and Mussolini who imagined themselves as great artists inspiring the masses, and sculpting society according to their grandiose imaginings, and the Marxist vanguard claiming the role of scientists.

At any rate, the Saint-Simonians actively sought to recruit artists for their various ventures, salons, and utopian communities—though they quickly ran into difficulties because so many within avant garde artistic circles preferred the more anarchistic Fourierists, and later, one or another branch of outright anarchist groupings. The number of nineteenth century artists with anarchist sympathies is quite staggering, ranging from Pissaro to Tolstoy to Oscar Wilde, not to mention almost all early-twentieth century artists who later became communists, from Malevich to Picasso. Rather than a political vanguard leading the way to a future society, radical artists almost invariably saw themselves as exploring new and less alienated modes of life. The really significant development in the nineteenth century was less the ideal of a vanguard than that of Bohemia (a term first coined by Balzac in 1838): marginal communities living in more or less voluntary poverty, seeing themselves as dedicated to the pursuit of creative, unalienated forms of experience, united by a profound hatred of bourgeois life and everything it stood for.

Ideologically, bohemian artists of this period were about equally likely to be proponents of "art for art's sake" or social revolutionaries. Contemporary theorists are actually quite divided over how to evaluate their larger significance. Pierre Bourdieu for example insisted that the promulgation of the idea of "art for art's sake," far from being depoliticizing, should be considered a significant accomplishment, as was any which managed to establish the autonomy of one particular field of human endeavor from the logic of the market.[1] Colin Campbell, on the other hand, argues that insofar as bohemians actually were an avant guarde, they were really the vanguard of the market itself, or more precisely, of consumerism. Their actual social function, much though they would have loathed to admit it, was to explore new forms of pleasure or aesthetic territory which could be commodified in the next generation.[2]

geoisie, who had—temporarily, at least—rejected their families' money and privilege. If they did not die young of dissipation, they were likely to end up back on the board of Father's company. One hears the same claim repeated today about activists and revolutionaries: most recently, about the "trust-fund babies" who supposedly dominate the global justice movement. In fact, Pierre Bourdieu has done the actual historical research and discovered that, in fact, a very large percentage of nineteenth century bohemians were the children of peasants. Bohemia was a convergence of a certain small number of children of bourgeois background in broad rejection of their parents' values, and a larger number of quite modest origins, often beneficiaries of new public educational systems. This latter group discovered, however, that simply attaining a bourgeois education was not enough to actually win oneself membership in the bourgeoisie. The remarkable thing is that this is consistently the demographic for vanguardist revolutionaries as well. One might think here of the meeting of Chou En-Lai (rebellious son of Mandarins) and Mao Tse-Tung (child of peasants turned school librarian), or Che Guevara (son of Argentine doctors) and Fidel Castro (son of modest shopkeepers turned unemployed lawyer). It continues to be true of revolutionaries and globalization activists to this day.

In the nineteenth century, the idea of the political vanguard was used very widely and very loosely by anyone exploring the path to a future, free society. For example, radical newspapers often called themselves "The Avant Garde." Peter Kropotkin was a frequent contributor to a Swiss anarchist newspaper called *L'Avant Garde* in the 1880s. There were periodicals of the same name (or local equivalent) in France, Spain, Italy, and Argentina. It was Marx who began to significantly change the idea by introducing the notion that the proletariat were the true revolutionary class—he didn't actually use the term "vanguard" in his own writing—because they were the class that was the most oppressed, or as he put it "negated" by capitalism, and therefore had the least to lose by its abolition. In doing so, he ruled out the possibilities that less alienated enclaves, whether of artists or the sort of artisans and independent producers who tended to form the backbone of anarchism, had anything significant to offer. The results we all know. The idea of a vanguard party dedicated to both organizing and providing an intellectual project for that most-oppressed class chosen as the agent of history, but also, actually sparking the revolution through their willingness to

Campbell also echoes common wisdom that bohemia was almost exclusively inhabited by the children of the bour-

1. Bourdieu, Pierre. *The Field of Cultural Production: Essays on Art and Literature.* New York: Columbia University Press, 1993.

2. Colin Campbell, *The Romantic Ethic and the Spirit of Modern Consumerism.* Oxford, UK; New York City: B. Blackwell, 1987.

employ violence, was first outlined by Lenin in 1902 in *What Is to Be Done?* This idea has echoed endlessly, to the point where the SDS in the late 1960s could end up locked in furious debates over whether the Black Panther Party, as leaders of one of the country's most oppressed elements, should be considered the vanguard of The Movement. All this had a curious effect on the artistic avant-garde, who increasingly began to organize themselves like vanguard parties. Beginning with the Dadaists and the Futurists, artists began publishing their own manifestos, communiqués, purging one another, and otherwise making themselves (sometimes quite intentionally) parodies of revolutionary sects. (Note, however, that these groups always defined themselves, like anarchists, by a certain form of practice rather than after some heroic founder.) The ultimate fusion came with the Surrealists and then finally the Situationist International. The Situationists were the most systematic in trying to develop a theory of revolutionary action according to the spirit of bohemia, thinking about what it might actually mean to destroy the boundaries between art and life. At the same time, in its own internal organization, the group displayed an insane sectarianism full of so many splits, purges, and bitter denunciations that Guy Debord finally remarked that the only logical conclusion was for the International to be reduced to two members, one of whom would purge the other and then commit suicide.

Non-Alienated Production

For me the really intriguing question is: why is it that artists have so often been drawn to revolutionary politics to begin with? Because it does seem to be the case that, even in times and places when there is next to no other constituency for revolutionary change, the place one is most likely to find one is among artists, authors, and musicians, even more so, in fact, than among professional intellectuals. It seems to me the answer must have something to do with alienation. There would appear to be a direct link between the experience of first imagining things and then bringing them into being (individually or collectively)—that is, the experience of certain forms of unalienated production—and the ability to imagine social alternatives, particularly the possibility of a society itself premised on less alienated forms of creativity. This would allow us to see the historical shift between seeing the vanguard as the relatively unalienated artists (or perhaps intellectuals) to seeing them as the representatives of the "most oppressed" in a new light. In fact, I would suggest, revolutionary coalitions always tend to consist of an alliance between a society's least alienated and its most oppressed. This is less elitist a formulation than it might sound, because it also seems to be the case that actual revolutions tend to occur when these two categories come to overlap. That would explain why it almost always seems to be peasants and craftspeople— or alternately, newly proletarianized former peasants and craftspeople—who actually rise up and overthrow capitalist regimes, and not those inured to generations of wage labor. Finally, I suspect this would also help explain the extraordinary importance of indigenous peoples' struggles in that planetary uprising usually referred to as the "anti-globalization" movement: such people tend to be simultaneously the very least alienated and most oppressed people on earth. Once it became technologically possible to include them in revolutionary coalitions (with the development of cell phone, the Internet, Indymedia networks), it was almost inevitable that they would take a leading role.

The role of indigenous peoples in turn leads us back to our earlier question—what would be a possible model for the non-vanguardist revolutionary intellectual? Maybe we can find some answers in ethnography and anthropology. Obviously what I am proposing would only work if it was ultimately a form of auto-ethnography, combined, perhaps, with a certain utopian extrapolation: a matter of teasing out the tacit logic or principles underlying certain forms of radical practice in communities, and then, not only offering the analysis back to those communities, but using them to formulate new visions (i.e. "if one applied the same principles as you are applying to political organization to economics, might it not look something like this?"). Offering these ideas not in the form of prescriptions, but as gifts. Here too, there are suggestive parallels in the history of radical artistic movements, which became movements precisely as they became their own critics (and of course the idea of self-criticism took on a very different—and more ominous—tone within Marxist politics). There are also intellectuals already trying to do precisely this sort of auto-ethnographic work. But I say all this not so much to provide models as to open up a field for discussion, first of all by emphasizing that even the notion of vanguardism itself is far more rich in its history, and full of alternative possibilities, than most of us would ever expect.

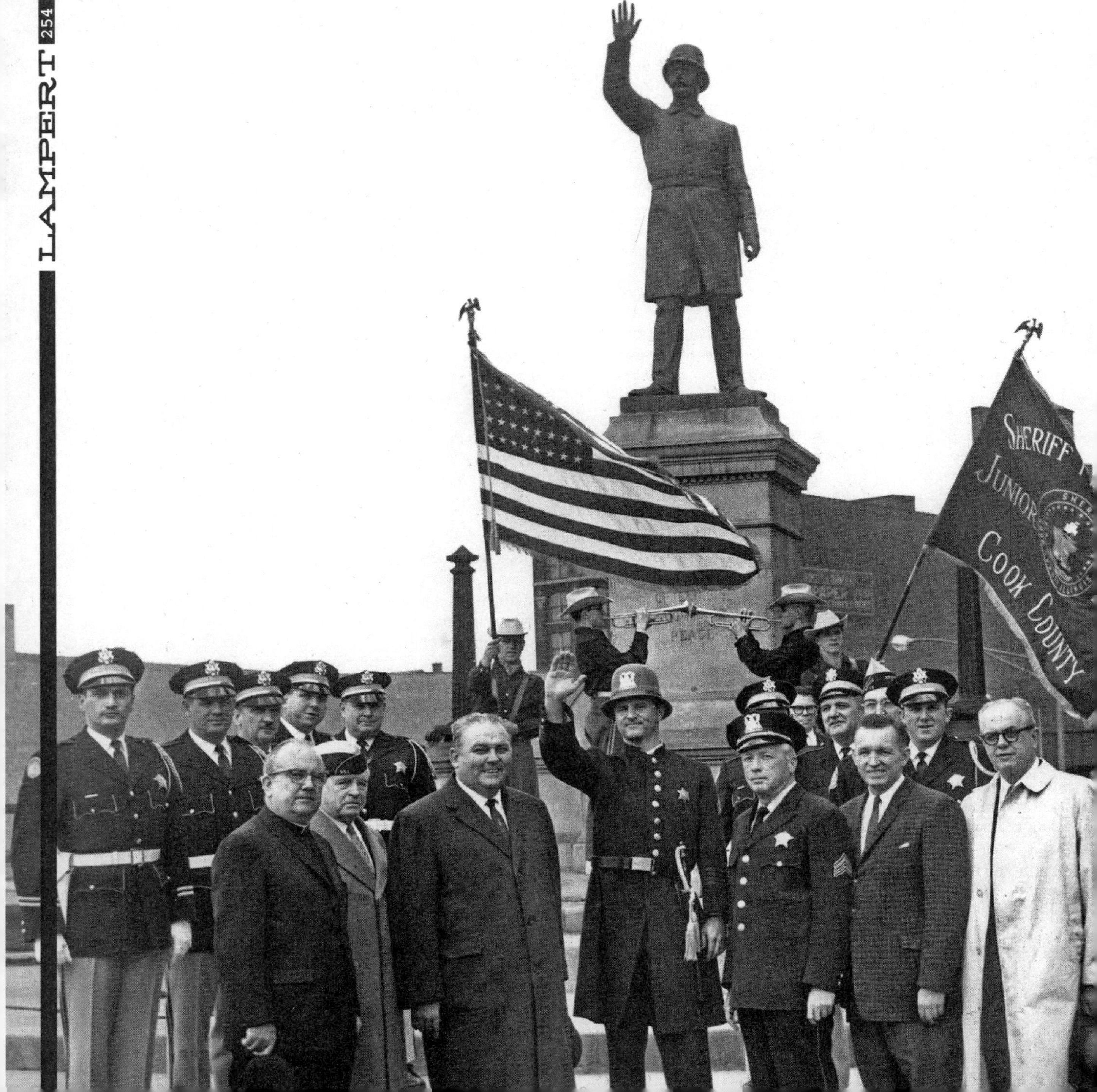
SHERIFF
JUNIOR
COOK COUNTY
PEACE

STRUGGLES AT HAYMARKET: AN EMBATTLED HISTORY OF STATIC MONUMENTS AND PUBLIC INTERVENTIONS

NICOLAS LAMPERT

On May 4th, 1927, a Chicago streetcar driver rumbled down Randolph Street. The driver had routinely passed by the Police Monument, the daunting statue of a policeman that had commemorated the Haymarket Riot solely from the perspective of the police. The monument had originally stood in Haymarket Square, the site of the riot, but due to congested traffic, it was moved by the city to Union Park, between Randolph and Ogden. Its new location did not calm the discontent that much of the public felt towards the statue, which was situated within a city with a strong working-class identity. It had been vandalized before, but anger towards it was about to be taken to a new level. Veering from his normal route, the driver suddenly jumped the tracks and directed his streetcar full speed ahead into the base of the monument, knocking the statue to the ground. The driver, whose name is only referenced in historical accounts as O'Neil, gave a simple reason: he was sick of seeing that policeman with his arm raised.[1]

In 1927 the memory of Haymarket still registered with much of the US public, yet as the decades passed, it began to fade, even within Chicago. The distance of time, the failure of schools to teach its history, and a concerted effort by the Chicago and the federal governments to erase its presence from public space all added to its steady disappearance, with consequences for future generations. For this erasure of Haymarket's history is part of a large pattern of leaving the public uninformed about its own labor history. Basic notions ranging from a shorter work week, to the existence of a weekend and child labor laws are now taken for granted, and are not understood as past struggles that were once fought for and won by radical and working-class movements. Negating these past histories also de-emphasizes the essential issue of class. Although it permeates every level of society, rarely does the concept of a class-based society become a topic of focus in American political and cultural life. Looking at the history of Haymarket shatters the notion of an equal society and informs us of the massive levels of class war and discontent that took place during the late 1880s. This type of historical awareness is a key reminder that we still live in a society that continues to be deeply divided by class. The actions of the past stand as inspiring, yet unfinished movements to continue to build upon and to adapt to present conditions. This multifaceted struggle also embraces the issue of public space and the contentious struggle over whose history is presented and whose is not, which is the central storyline of the Haymarket monuments.

Haymarket As Unresolved History

Historically, the events at Haymarket in 1886 grew out of the international eight-hour workday movement. On May 1st, Chicago was just one of many cities that participated in a national strike for the eight-hour day. The Chicago protest was massive and drew over 80,000 marchers in a parade up Michigan Avenue. At the same time, solidarity strikes were occurring throughout the city. At the McCormick Harvester Works, on the South Side of the city, trouble broke out during a skirmish between striking workers and replacement scabs. 1,400 workers had been on strike since mid-February and tensions were running high against the 300 strikebreakers who had crossed picket lines. On May 3rd, 200 police were called in to break up the skirmishes. The police opened fire on the strikers, killing four and wounding many others. August Spies, one of the prominent anarchist leaders in the city, had been addressing strikers at another plant just down the road when the massacre took place. Outraged, he rushed to the printers and issued a flyer that began with the inflammatory headline, "Revenge! Workingmen, to Arms!!!" A second flyer called for a protest demonstration the next day (May 4th) at Haymarket Square.

At this demonstration, Spies spoke to a crowd of 3,000, as did Albert Parsons, the editor of the largest anarchist newspaper in the country, *The Alarm*. Chicago was the epicenter of the anarchist movement in the US—a highly organized radical movement whose most prominent leaders addressed massive labor rallies and agitated on behalf of many of the poor, the unemployed, and immigrants within the city. At Haymarket Square, Spies, Parsons, and others denounced the police violence from the day before. Mayor Carter Harrison showed up at the demonstration and reported to the police that the

event was orderly and headed home for the evening. By 10 p.m., two-thirds of the crowd had left as rain began to fall. The event likely would have wound down without incident, but the police decided to show up in force with 180 officers marching toward the crowd demanding that it disperse. This type of police intimidation almost always exacerbates the situation; it's a rash tactic where one can likely count on police clubs descending down on people's heads, general panic and a host of unnecessary arrests. Yet something far more chaotic and deadly occurred as the police entered the crowd. A person, whose identity remains unknown to this day, threw a bomb in to the crowd of charging policemen. Was it thrown by a worker seeking revenge for the police violence from the day before? Was it an agent provocateur willing to use violence to disrupt the gains made by the labor movement? 120 years later, no one can say for certain. However, we do know that during the mayhem of the blast, police fired at will, killing many, including fellow officers. At least eight policemen died from the explosion and the spray of bullets and over 200 civilians were injured, including an uncounted number of deaths.

The ramifications of the blast would be profound. The police utilized the event to attack organized labor by shutting down their newspapers and arresting hundreds of individuals, essentially crushing the anarchist movement within Chicago. Throughout the city, as well as in many other regions of the country, immigrant populations were looked upon suspiciously and seen as trying to destroy the fabric of American society. Eventually, eight anarchists (the majority of whom were German immigrants) were brought to trial, including some who were not even present at the demonstration. The press focused its attention on Chicago and the trial, and much of the world watched in shock as the defendants were found guilty, and then four hung on November 11th, 1887—a date that became known as "Black Friday." August Spies, Albert Parsons, Louis Lingg, Adolph Fischer, George Engel, Michael Schwab, and Samuel Fielden had been sentenced to death on August 20 in a grossly unjust trial. Oscar Neebe was sentenced to fifteen years. Lingg would commit suicide in jail on November 10, while Schwab and Fielden had their sentences commuted that day to life. Even before the executions, all eight had become martyrs to radical labor and social movements throughout the world. Their memory was kept alive by many, including artists who created poems, songs, prints, and paintings to celebrate their lives. Yet in Chicago, the battle over the martyrs' memory, particularly over the building of monuments that addressed Haymarket, would be bitterly contested.[2]

Taking Sides: The Police Monument and the Haymarket Monument

Since 1886, organized labor, anarchists, and the police have clashed over opposing visions about how the Haymarket Tragedy should be remembered. Unions and labor historians have largely come to view Haymarket as part of the overall struggle for the eight-hour day and workers' rights, and have distanced themselves from the radical anarchist principles that the martyrs had called for in the late 1800s. Spies, Parsons and others had agitated for a collective society to replace capitalism and private property. They viewed the US government as a hostile entity that perpetuated a society based on inequality and a class system. Their call for a radical restructuring of society runs counter to the modern labor movement. Most modern unions seek to change very few systemic political or cultural elements within the US, viewing the government, instead, as a structure one can operate within and lobby for better working conditions.

The labor movement has long since argued that an official monument should exist at Haymarket that represents the history and concerns of workers from a vast range of professions and political viewpoints. Many anarchists, however, have argued that

the martyrs who died for their convictions would abhor any type of official monument that was sanctioned by the government. In the attempt to safeguard the memory and the ideals of the martyrs, anarchists today have often insisted that a monument that distorts the martyrs' memory is equal to a second death.

The police, on the other hand, looked at Haymarket through a different lens. To many police officers, Haymarket is remembered simply as the event during which an anarchist-led labor movement murdered their fellow police officers. In their view, if a monument should exist at the site where the bomb exploded, it should honor the police officers that died. Any type of tribute to the anarchists would be a bitter insult. For over a hundred years, the viewpoint favored by the police held sway in Chicago. Haymarket Square either featured a monument to the police or it remained bare without any notice of what had transpired. Labor and anarchists were completely barred from placing a monument representing their perspective of the Haymarket riot within city limits.

Anarchists responded to this ban by erecting a monument in 1893 in the nearby suburb of Waldheim (now Forest Park), at the Waldhiem (Forest Home) Cemetery—the gravesite of the executed martyrs. The Pioneer Aid and Support Association, an anarchist group that provided aid for the widows and the offspring of those executed and jailed following the Haymarket trial organized the monument campaign. Albert Weinert was selected to sculpt the Haymarket Monument, and in his design he depicted an allegorical figure of Justice placing a laurel wreath over the head of a dying worker. The female figure (also interpreted as Liberty, Anarchy, or Revolution) looks towards the distance with an intense gaze, and is portrayed as a protector of working class people.

The powerful monument would quickly become a focal point for the ceremonies of working class people and radical movements starting with its dedication on June 25, 1893. The date happened to coincide with the World's Columbian Exposition in Chicago, which allowed thousands of visitors in town from places around the world to attend the unveiling of the monument. Historian James Green explains the importance of the ceremony, along with the city's effort to neutralize its impact:

> The martyrs' families and supporters ritualized the act of remembering and began to do so immediately with a funeral many witnesses would never forget. After struggling with city officials who prohibited red flags and banned revolutionary songs, the anarchists led a large parade silently through Chicago's working-class neighborhoods on the long walk to Chicago's Waldheim Cemetery..."[3]

Over 3,000 people marched in the parade and 8,000 were present at the cemetery during the dedication. August Spies' final words before he was hung were chiseled on the base of the monument: "The day will come when our silence will be more powerful than the voices you are throttling today."

The day after the ceremony, Governor John Peter Altgeld pardoned the three men who remained in jail. He knew this action would ruin his political career, but Altgeld stood by his convictions, stating that the trial was a travesty of justice. His pardon would later be inscribed on the back of the monument. For his action, he was scorned by the power structure, but celebrated by labor, who tried in vain to have a monument built to him at Haymarket Square. But like the martyrs' monument, the city of Chicago would refuse.

In the years to come, the Haymarket Monument at the Waldheim Cemetery would continue to act as a symbol of resistance and sacred ground to the radical labor movement. The defiant monument has often been the site for May Day celebrations and remembrances of May 4th and November 11th. Likewise, the cemetery would become a burial ground to many of the country's most radical labor leaders and revolutionaries who desired to be buried in close proximity to the Haymarket martyrs. Emma Goldman, Lucy Parsons, Elizabeth Gurley Flynn, Joe Hill, Big Bill Haywood, and many others would either be buried there or have their ashes spread in the cemetery.

In comparison, the Police Monument, sculpted by Johannes Gelert, was dedicated in 1889, four years before the monument at Waldheim. It also had annual remembrance celebrations and was cherished by those it represented, the police. The *Chicago Tribune* and the Union League Club of Chicago had organized the fundraising drive for the monument, which was to be placed in the center of Haymarket Square, a working class section of town, home to farmers' markets and numerous union halls.[4] The placement of the monument, depicting a police officer with his hand raised in a "halt" pose was an overt message to the people of Chicago that if they rebelled and organized strikes, there would be consequences. While the monument of the police officer honored the officers who had fallen, it also proclaimed the distorted message to the public that the police had protected the city from the disruptive forces of the labor movement and the anarchists. It was fitting that the owner of the *Chicago Tribune*, Cyrus McCormick, also owned McCormick Harvester Works, where the police killings had led to the May 4th demonstration at Haymarket. Throughout the entire process of conceptualizing a police monument, the *Chicago Tribune* never hid its hatred for the anarchist movement. The paper's red-baiting tactics against anarchism and disdain for the radical politics of newly arrived Bohemian and German immigrant populations had helped ensure that a fair trial would be absent, leading to the guilty sentences and the executions.

It was no wonder that the monument received little fanfare from working people—the majority of the population in Chicago. After the Police Monument was first toppled in 1927, it was moved away from the streetcar lanes so renegade drivers could not destroy it so easily. Eventually it was moved to Jackson Boulevard, where it was ironically placed facing a statue of Mayor Carter

1. William J. Adelman. "The True Story Behind the Haymarket Police Statue." In *Haymarket Scrapbook*, edited by Dave Roediger and Franklin Rosemont (Chicago: Charles H. Kerr Publishing Company, 1986), 168.

2. For historical information on Haymarket, see: Avrich, Paul. *The Haymarket Tragedy*. (Princeton: Princeton University Press, 1984); Roediger and Rosemont, ed. *Haymarket Scrapbook*, 1986; Green, James. *Death in the Haymarket: A Story of Chicago, the First Labor Movement and the Bombing that Divided Gilded Age America*. (New York: Pantheon Books, 2006); Nelson, Bruce C. *Beyond the Martyrs: A Social History of Chicago's Anarchists, 1870–1900*. (New Brunswick: Rutgers University Press, 1988).

3. Green, James. *Taking History to Heart: The Power of the Past in Building Social Movements*. (Amhearst: University of Massachusetts Press, 2000), 129.

4. The Union League Club of Chicago (an exclusive club whose membership was limited only to European-American men through the mid-point of the twentieth century) was first established in 1879 and played a key role in establishing many of the city's elite cultural organizations and events, including helping to fund The Art Institute of Chicago, Orchestra Hall, The Field Museum, and the World's Columbian Exposition to Chicago in 1893. See: Nowlan, James D., *Glory, Darkness, Light: A History of the Union League Club of Chicago*, (Evanston: Northwestern University Press, 2004).

5. Adelman. *Haymarket Scrapbook*, 168.

6. "Police Groups Angered Over Haymarket Statue Bombing." *Chicago Tribune*, 8 October, 1969.

7. "Daley Asks for Law, Order at Haymarket." *Chicago Tribune*, 5 May 1970.

8. Harry Golden Jr., "We'll Rebuild Statue: Daley." *Chicago Sun-Times*, 6 October 1970.

THE DAY WILL COME WHEN OUR SILENCE WILL BE MORE POWERFUL THAN THE VOICES YOU ARE THROTTLING TODAY

Kehben Grifter, *Remember the Haymarket Anarchists*, hand-cut stone mosaic installed at the Haymarket site, 1996. Photo: Kehben Grifter.

Harrison, who had once testified against police corruption.[5] The two figures stared at each other, engaged in a silent dialogue.

In 1956 the Police Monument was moved once again, and returned to the Haymarket area, situated 200 feet west from its original location. The Chicago Police Department had lobbied for the monument to be moved back to Haymarket Square, but by the 1950s a new disruptive force—the construction of the Kennedy Expressway—had carved up the downtown neighborhood and the historical essence of the original site. Set amongst high-rise buildings (themselves monuments to capitalism) the monument rested on a special platform overlooking the freeway, situated on the north side of Randolph Street, a block west of Desplaines. On May 5th, 1965, the city council designated the monument a historical landmark, but this designation meant little to those set to start a new wave of attacks. The Police Monument soon fell prey to 1960s radicalism.

On October 6th, 1969 Weatherman, a radical, underground splinter of SDS (Students for a Democratic Society) stuck dynamite between the monument statue's legs and detonated it, sending the legs flying onto the freeway below.

Although Weatherman had yet to make a statement, Sgt. Richard Barrett, president of the Chicago Police Sergeants association, directed the blame towards SDS. In a statement, Sgt. Barrett (who was later reprimanded by his Superintendent) stated:

> The blowing up of the only police monument in the United States by the anarchists... is an obvious declaration of war between the police and the SDS and other anarchist groups. We feel that it is kill or be killed regardless of the Jay Millers [director of the Illinois ACLU], Daniel Walkers [author of a federal report that blamed the police for the rioting during the Democratic National Convention], and the so-called civil rights acts.[6]

In the midst of this tension between the police and anarchists, Mayor Richard J. Daley ordered that the monument be rebuilt. In his statements to the press, he asked for private donors to help with the costs and eventually received funds from many, including the International Brothers of Teamsters and a number of other unions. The statue was

rededicated on May 4th, 1970—the anniversary of the Haymarket riot. At the dedication ceremony, Daley told the crowd:

> This is the only statue of a policeman in the world. The policeman is not perfect, but he is as fine an individual as any other citizen. Let the younger generation know that the policeman is their friend, and to those who want to take law into their own hands, let them know that we won't tolerate it.[7]

Weatherman apparently ignored Daley's threat because on October 6th, 1970, exactly one year after they first toppled the monument, they blew it up again. This time the press received a call shortly after the blast from a Weatherman stating, "We

destroyed the Haymarket Square Statue for the second year in a row in honor of our brothers and sisters in the New York Prisons..."[8]

In what was clearly becoming a battle of sheer will and determination between the two sides, Daley ordered round-the-clock police security to protect the statue at a pricetag of $67,440 per year. The media ridiculed the twenty-four hour guard, noting that there were more important matters for the police to attend to. This dilemma generated a series of imaginative and incredibly humorous ideas on how to protect the bewildered monument. Some of the ideas thrown about included placing a large plastic dome over the monument or casting a series of disposable fiberglass police statues. According to this logic, each time the monument was blown up, it could easily be replaced.[9] None of these proposals came to fruition as Daley ultimately insisted that the monument stay true to its original form.

Realizing that it was inevitable that the monument would continue to be attacked as long as it remained in Haymarket Square, the Police Monument was moved in February of 1972 to a new location, inside the lobby of Central Police Headquarters on 11th and State Street. Yet this move proved to be temporary, and in 1976, it was moved again and placed within the courtyard of the Police Academy at 1300 W. Jackson, where it resides today. At this location, it is completely removed from the public sight and one needs a visitor's pass to even view it. However, the massive concrete base for the monument remained at Randolph Street for two more decades, acting as a visual reminder of how contested the space had been and continued to be.

The Temporary Monument: Public Interventions 1972–2004

I really don't trust monuments[10]
—Michael Piazza

The lack of a monument at Haymarket from 1972 to 2004 did not mean that the site was any less contested or active. For some, the empty site presented a opening to insert one's own perspective within public space. A monument, by its nature, is already defined, static, and rarely allows for participation.[11] A monument may allow for critique, for the viewer to respond to it, but it does not allow one to take an active role in adding to the dialogue and asserting one's voice into the landscape unless, of course, one does something drastic. In this manner, monuments often define a singular point of view that shuts out other perspectives. The lack of a statue at Haymarket, however, allowed for multiple perspectives through ephemeral monuments—temporary actions, performances, and other types of decentralized public interventions that many individuals and groups used to assert different "unofficial" versions of the Haymarket history into the physical space and collective memory. These actions, lacking any type of permission or government role, are in many regards much more closely aligned to the ideals of the Haymarket martyrs—they embrace autonomy and direct action.

At each of the locations significant to Haymarket—the Square, the location of the Police Monument, the Haymarket Monument at Waldheim, and McCormick Harvester Works—a multitude of separate actions, performances, guerilla landmarks and other types of public interventions have taken place over the years. The vast majority of these are divorced from one another, existing primarily in the memory of those who participated or those who happened to witness the ephemeral action. At times, a physical reminder would remain, perhaps graffiti or the remnants of a temporary monument. More than likely, only the documentation of the action would inform others of its existence.

One of the more recent creative actions took place in 1996 right before the Democratic National Convention that was held in Chicago. Kehben Grifter

9. Adelman. *Haymarket Scrapbook*, 168.

10. Nicolas Lampert, "Public Memories of Haymarket in Chicago: Michael Piazza Interviewed by Nicolas Lampert," *AREA* #2 (2006): 9.

11. Maya Lin's Vietnam Veterans Memorial (Washington DC) and Civil Rights Memorial (Montgomery, Alabama) counter this notion by encouraging the public to interact with the monument, often by touching the surface. As well, Jochen Gerz and Esther Shalev-Gerz' Monument Against Fascism, War and Violence—and for Peace and Human Rights (Harburg, Germany) invites the viewer to take an active role by carving words and marks into the surface of the monument.

12. The *Chicago Tribune* article featured quotes from Evan Glassman (a person Grifter was working with on a tile mosaic commission for a restaurant in Chicago at the time), who claimed in the article that he was the one who created and installed the mosaic—with Grifter as an "accomplice" who helped him with his project. However, in conversations that I have had with Grifter, she notes that the information that Glassman provided to the newspaper reporter was misleading and spiteful. Instead it was she who initiated the project, created the mosaic, and set it in the concrete. See: Blair Kamin, "Mystery Solved: Mosaic Artist Raises a Flag in Protest." *Chicago Tribune*, 13 August, 1996, 8.

For more information on Kehben Grifter's work with the Beehive Design Collective visit: www.beehivecollective.org

13. "Public Memories of Haymarket in Chicago: Michael Piazza Interviewed by Nicolas Lampert," *AREA* #2 (2006): 7.

(who works with the artist/activist Beehive Design Collective) created a small hand-cut stone mosaic to the anarchist martyrs and installed it within the sidewalk at the Haymarket site, without attempting to go through any official means of permission. At the time Grifter was working near the Haymarket site and noticed that the sidewalks were being redone, the wet cement in the process of drying, creating the perfect opportunity to install the mosaic. However, when she went to place the piece, she was spotted by city workers and questioned. Grifter quickly talked her way out of trouble by citing names in the city bureaucracy and falsely stating that the project had been given city approval. To verify her claims, the workers called their superior and described the mosaic and its content. Just her luck, the city official did not comprehend the illicit nature of the project, nor did he understand the mosaic's message or the significance of the Haymarket site. Better yet, the official insisted that the workers on site install the mosaic for her! For five weeks it remained at the Haymarket site and would likely have lasted longer had not a *Chicago Tribune* article brought attention to the mosaic, prompting the city to remove it.[12]

The pedestal of the Police Monument was also removed in 1996, right before the Democratic National Convention. The city must have also realized how inviting the site was and more than likely feared what would take place, anticipating a large amount of demonstrators. To many, the removal of the pedestal was a great loss, for it represented just how contested the history over the Police Monument had been and served as a grand stage for performances and other public interventions. However, when the cement slab was removed, it left a giant eighteen-foot diameter circle, clearly marking where the monument once stood. Although not as preferable as the pedestal, the circle still served as a stage.

Michael Piazza, a Chicago artist, utilized the location of the circle for a group project that he initiated in 2002 called the *Haymarket 8-Hour Action Series*. The year prior, Piazza got the idea for a series of performances after he saw the Chicago printmaker, René Arceo, perform an action on the circle during a May Day celebration. Arceo's performance was simple but poignant. He pulled up in a car, ran up, and started stomping on the circle as a crowd watched. Piazza's tribute to the "Arceo Stomp" involved putting out a call inviting other artists to do separate eight-hour actions at the site. Piazza notes that:

> Ever since 1986, I had been monitoring this blank pedestal and I realized that there was a division between a small group of people in town who knew what it represented, who had this local knowledge and memory, while there was a whole other group who just thought it was an empty pedestal. That always fascinated me.[13]

Piazza reasoned that artists, with their talents and creativity, could reclaim this history and make it more visible. Piazza surveyed the site and measured the diameter of the circle but before he put out the artist call, the city, either intentionally or coincidentally, paved over the circle, leaving no physical evidence of where the Police Monument once stood. Undeterred, the first project of the *8-Hour Action Series* involved Javier Lara and students from the School of the Art Institute who held a sewing bee at the site and constructed a large orange circle that became a

Haymarket 8-Hour Action Series, 2002, from left: Hay! Market Research Group (Lauren Cumbia, Dara Greenwald and Blithe Riley); John Pitman Weber's reenactment of a Eugene Debs speech; Javier Lara and students from the School of the Art Institute of Chicago hold a sewing bee and create a large orange circle that marks the location of the former Police Monument. Photos: Michael Piazza.

visual reminder of the monument's existence. In other performances, the circle served as a stage for a number of soapbox presentations, including William Adelman's historical presentation on Haymarket and John Pitman Weber's reenactment of a Eugene Debs speech.

Other performances that were part of Piazza's *8-Hour Action Series* used the circle as an end point. Larry Bogad did a project entitled, "The Police Statue Returns" for which he created a giant puppet that resembled the original police statue. In the performance, Bogad paraded the puppet along from the Daley Center, through downtown and eventually ending on Randolph Street. At the former location of the Police Monument, a large anarchist flag was placed over the circle in an act of reclamation. This type of creative street performance, unregulated and spontaneous, has an intrinsic beauty to it. Not only does it catch the public off guard, disrupting business as usual, but these types of actions, due to their atypical nature, encourage people to think and question not only their own daily routine, but the daily routine of the city's functions. In actions such as these, artists present other possibilities.

Likewise, Bogad's performance, either intentionally or inadvertently, touched upon a sense of nostalgia for the Police Monument—a seemingly contradictory desire for the monument to still remain near to the Haymarket site. Although his piece critiques the former monument, its brief "return," even as a puppet, reminds one of a time when the lines were more clearly defined. The Police Monument, with its authoritarian message, was such an obvious target that it became the perfect place to vent frustrations and to engage in symbolic acts of class struggle. Its removal obscured the issues and the subsequent removal of the monument's pedestal was akin to erasure, a means of publicly forgetting that any type of struggle had taken place at the site.

Another *8-Hour Action Series* project that spoke of the changing dynamics within Chicago was the "Hay! Market Research Group," a collaborative action by Lauren Cumbia, Dara Greenwald, and Blithe Riley. During the action, the group set up a table and a sign on Randolph Street at the location of the former Police Monument. The sign acted as a visual component, similar to a billboard, that first caught people's attention. Various slogans on the sign were interchanged, including: "What Happened Here in 1886?," "Guilt by Association: Who Died for Your Eight-Hour Workday?," "4 Hung, 1 Suicide, 3 Pardons," and "Public Hanging, Lethal Injection, Indifference?" Once people walked up to the information table, they could fill out surveys on Haymarket and issues that were connected to the present. The vital importance of the piece was utilizing art and street performances to get strangers to engage with one another in conversations about meaningful issues and histories that are not well known.

In nearly every intervention, the artists involved were responding to far more than just the Haymarket history. These actions responded to the entire city landscape and the culture at large. For some of these performances, Haymarket was simply a starting point. Brian Dortmund's project for the *8-Hour Action* was a May Day bike ride that traveled from Haymarket to the Waldheim Cemetery. In subsequent years, Dortmund continues to do the ride, but changes the route, so that the riders travel to different locations in the Chicago vicinity that are specific to labor and other radical struggles. In this manner, those who participated in the action formed a community, learned about various histories, engaged in dialogue, and had a shared experience. Sarah Kanouse, an artist and writer who took part in the bike rides, reflected upon the larger framework of the actions:

> Impermanent memorial events like political rallies, bike ride, pilgrimages, and picnics are new ways of inhabiting both the city and history... These events are not so much tours or lectures, with the implication of an omniscient guide, as encounters in which leadership is fluid and fleeting if it must be present at all.[14]

14. Sarah E. Kanouse, conference paper, "When Our Silence Will Be More Powerful: Haymarket's Ephemeral Memorials," 8 at: http://readysubjects.org/writing.html, March 3, 2006.

15. Ibid., 14.

16. Stephen Kinzer, "In Chicago, a Deliberately Ambiguous Memorial to an Attack's Complex Legacy." *New York Times*, 15 September 2004, A14.

17. "Putting Haymarket to Rest?" *Labor Studies in Working-Class History of the Americas*, Volume 2, Issue 2 (2005): 35.

18. In 1986, Mayor Harold Washington, the first African American mayor in Chicago's history, declared the month of May as "Labor History Month in Chicago" to commemorate the 100-year anniversary of the Haymarket Tragedy. Within his proclamation, Washington stated, "...on this day we commemorate the movement towards the eight-hour day, union rights, civil rights, human rights, and by remembering the tragic miscarriage of justice which claimed the lives of four labor activists." Washington in his speech also highlighted the program organized by the ILHS, the Chicago Federation of Labor, and the Haymarket Centennial Committee and urged, "all citizens to be cognizant of the events planned during this month and of the historical significance of the Haymarket Centennial. For a reprint of this statement, see, http://www.chicagohistory.org/dramas/

Kanouse did her own tactical bike ride in 2004 that involved biking twenty-seven miles from the Haymarket site to the former location of Fort Sheridan. Today, Fort Sheridan is an expensive suburban housing development north of the city, but in the 1880s the main purpose of the Fort was to protect wealth. In 1887, the year following Haymarket, the Union League Club (who also helped initiate the Police Monument) purchased the 632 acres, which became the Fort, for the United States Army. Troops could be stationed there and quickly deployed into the city to put down labor demonstrations and strikes. To help facilitate this, a military highway, Sheridan Road was constructed to allow for this rapid deployment.

Kanouse's bike ride, which she titled, "Unstorming Sheridan" traveled in the opposite direction, into the suburbs. During her ride, she brought with her radio transmission equipment that acted to jam other radio frequencies within close proximity, causing her broadcast to inter-rupt what others would be listening to on their car stereo as they passed her. Targeting the Clear Channel affiliated stations, she sent out bursts of "The Internationale" (a famous socialist/anarchist song that dates back to the Paris Commune) for a few seconds at a time. Her individual action spoke of a subtle and symbolic form of resistance against the massive corporate ownership of the airwaves, and was a means of both challenging that power and informing others that those systems are not as impenetrable and all-powerful as they appear to be. Whereas a street protest disrupts the usual cycles of the city causing those who see it to take notice, disrupting a powerful corporate radio station with radical content also startles listeners to imagine other possibilities, or at least to acknowledge that there are those who oppose these powerful institutions.

The *8-Hour Action Series* and Kanouse's bike ride, as compelling and creative as they are, come with limitations. Any action that is seen by such a small amount of people may be easily forgot-

Mary Brogger's Haymarket Monument on Desplaines Street, Chicago (c. 2006). Photo: Nicolas Lampert.

ten and its impact and ability to create widespread change may be minimal. Yet as Kanouse notes, "While it may be easy to critique the 'tactical' memorial as hopelessly romantic about (and even addicted to) its own ineffectiveness, lingering assumptions about the function of spatial monuments also need to be examined."[15] Mary Brogger's recently installed (2004) monument at Haymarket allows us to compare these two divergent approaches.

Mary Brogger's Haymarket Monument: The Monument That Forgot Class Struggle

> I think we're showing a new way to do monuments at historic sites. You make them open rather than pressing a precise meaning on people or directing them toward a specific feeling or reaction[16]
> —Nathan Mason, special projects curator of Chicago's Public Art Program

Nathan Mason's quote accurately describes the scope and the vision of the new monument sculpted by Mary Brogger that now resides on Desplaines Street. The historic location, which had been empty for so long, now features an abstract monument of bronze, genderless figures colored in a red patina, constructing and deconstructing a wagon. At the base of the monument, a series of cautiously worded plaques explains the history of Haymarket. Its mere existence, a monument to Haymarket within a city that had long since refused to acknowledge the history, except from the perspective of the police, is startling and leads us to wonder, why now?

To better understand how this drastic change came to be, it is important to first examine the complicated decade-long process that led up to the public artwork that was funded and approved by the city. When talking about the new monument's content, it is all too easy to focus attention on Mary Brogger, the sculptor herself. But it was the coalition of government agencies, labor organizations, and historians that first agreed upon a series of parameters that ultimately led to its realization and the content that the monument would project. A key player in this process was the Illinois Labor History Society.

The ILHS had lobbied the city government for a permanent monument at the Haymarket site since the organization's founding in 1969. Despite the fact that the city and the police had created a formidable obstacle to any type of monument to Haymarket from the perspective of labor or anarchism, there were some in Chicago who were willing to challenge this blockade. Les Orear, a Packinghouse union activist, and William Adelman, a labor historian, decided to pool their resources and energy together to form the Haymarket Worker's Memorial Committee. This project soon became part of a larger vision, and on August 5, 1969, the Illinois Labor History Society was formed. The IHLS, along with other local activists, including Bill Garvey, an editor of the newspaper *Steel Labor*, began the long process of lobbying the city government for a monument, representing the position of labor to be built at Haymarket. One of the first steps to revitalizing interest in a potential monument included a public performance in 1969 at the site where the bomb had exploded in 1886. At the event, Studs Terkel, the renowned author and radio host in Chicago, stood on top of a makeshift wagon and spoke of Haymarket's history. Terkel's performance, a public intervention in its own right, would foreshadow the many future actions that would take place in the ensuing decades as others reclaimed the history by means of temporary installations and performances.

Around the same time, the ILHS began organizing events at the Waldheim Cemetery for people to meet and listen to speeches in front of the Haymarket Monument on significant dates in Haymarket's history. The ILHS role of promoting Haymarket's labor history became even more "official" when the deed for the Haymarket Monument at Waldheim was transferred from the last surviving member of the Pioneer Aid and Support Association, Irving S. Abrams, to the ILHS in 1973. The ILHS assumed the role as its owner and became responsible for the monument's upkeep and annual commemorations. Yet, as Lara Kelland notes, this was not without opposition:

> Anarchists have responded in kind... A small group often appears at Waldheim during the ILHS events, jeering and interacting with the monument in an attempt to disrupt the proceedings in protest of the ILHS ceremonial work.[17]

19. Jeff Huebner, "A Monumental Effort Pays Off: After years of struggle and disagreement, a sculptural tribute to Haymarket is finally in the works—with almost everybody on board." *Chicago Reader*, 16 January, 2004. Section 2.

20. Tom McNamee, "After 138 years, Haymarket Memorial to be unveiled May Day, at last, for a cause." *Chicago Sun-Times*, 7 September, 2004, 51.

21. *Chicago Reader*, January 16, 2004. Section 2.

22. *New York Times*, September 15, 2004, A14.

23. *Chicago Sun-Times*, September 7, 2004, 51.

24. Michael Piazza interviewed by the author, in person, December 9, 2005.

25. *Chicago Reader*, January 16, 2004. Section 2.

26. The South Chicago Anarchist Black Cross is part of the larger Anarchist Black Cross Network. Their mission statement reads: "The stated purpose of the Anarchist Black Cross Network is to actively assist prisoners in their fight to obtain their civil and human rights, and to aid them in their struggle against the state/ class penal and judicial system. We believe the prison system in the US and internationally is the armed fist of the state, and is a system for state slavery. The prison system is not really for "criminals" or other "social deviants," and it does NOT exist for the "protection of society." The abolition of prisons, the system of laws and the capitalist state is the ultimate objective of every true anarchist, yet there seems to be no clear agreement by the anarchist movement to put active effort towards that desire. With that being said, the ABC exists to organize and network resources to support all political/class war prisoners." See: http://chicagoabc.tripod.com/

27. *Chicago Sun-Times*, September 7, 2004, 51.

28. Only a minute number of artists and others are informed or involved with city public art projects. More often than not, in most US cities, only a small handful of artists, often sculptors, dedicate themselves to applying for these types of grants and commissions. Their work usually graces public parks and the plazas of corporate buildings and grounds, but rarely do these artists engage themselves in art collectives, political art groups, or dialogues about the intersection of art and politics, all of which are deeply relevant to a project that focuses on Haymarket's history.

29. *Chicago Sun-Times*, September 7, 2004, 51.

30. *New York Times*, September 15, 2004, A14.

31. *Chicago Reader*, January 16, 2004. Section 2.

32 Donahue has voiced resistance to the proposed renaming of a city park to Lucy Parsons, wife of Haymarket martyr Albert Parsons. He also voiced objection to a street in Chicago being renamed after the late Fred Hampton, a Black Panther Party leader who was murdered in 1969 by the police during a raid. Donahue said, "It's a 'dark day' when city officials honor a man who called for harming police officers." See, "Union head blasts plan to name street after Black Panther," The Associated Press, 28 February, 2006, 7:50 AM CST.

Despite the constant jeers from many anarchists, the ILHS made inroads in lobbying the Chicago government to also have a monument to Haymarket commissioned at the original Haymarket site. This goal likely would have occurred had it not been for the untimely death of Mayor Harold Washington in 1987, who was one of the rare high profile politicians who advocated for the public recognition of Chicago's labor history.[18]

However, in the following decade, the ILHS, which had also teamed up with the Chicago Federation of Labor, found an unlikely audience in 1998 within Mayor Richard M. Daley's administration. Daley (the son of Richard J. Daley who held office from 1955–1976) gave the go-ahead to listen to various proposals for a monument, and in time the coalition grew to include representatives from the Chicago Historical Society and the Chicago Police Department. The success of the project had much to do with the proposed theme of the monument. Rather than focusing attention on either the anarchist martyrs, the police, the explosion of the bomb or the subsequent trial, the group settled on the broad-based theme of a speaker's wagon representing "free speech." The wagon alluded to what Samuel Fielden stood upon on May 4th, 1886 as he spoke to workers just before the bomb exploded, but the concept of free speech is much more elusive and abstract. Don Turner, who at the time was the president of the Chicago Federation of Labor, notes the significance of this choice for the proposal's eventual approval:

> I think the key issue was removing the focus from the anarchists and making it a First Amendment issue—though it's not like we still don't have anarchists.[19]

Turner further explained: "We brought everybody into the process—the police, the labor community, historians—and we came up with this idea of the wagon as the symbol of freedom of speech. That's how we really put our arms around it."[20] Everybody, that is, except the anarchists.

In 2000, with the concept established, funding was secured from the state program, Illinois FIRST, who designated $300,000 towards the project. By 2002, the project fell into the jurisdiction of the "Haymarket Tragedy Commemoration of Free Speech and Assembly Monument," under the direction of Nathan Mason, the special projects curator for Chicago's Public Arts Program. With the funding and theme in place, the next step involved selecting an artist to sculpt the vision that the committee had already established. Ten artists were selected to submit proposals, and an eight-member project advisory committee composed of representatives from labor, the police, historians, and community members chose the local sculptor Mary Brogger.[21]

Despite the fact that Brogger had yet to do a figurative public commission before, her Haymarket Monument satisfied the conditions of the committee's vision of a non-confrontational monument that focused upon the speaker's wagon and free speech. Brogger states:

> I was pretty adamant in my own mind that it would not be useful to depict violence. The violence didn't seem important, because this event was made up of much bigger ideas than one particular incident. I didn't want to make the imagery conclusive. I want to suggest the complexity of truth, but also people's responsibility for their actions and for the effect of their actions.[22]

In further explaining the symbolism and the message of the monument, she notes:

> It has a duality to it. From the standpoint of the wagon being constructed, you see workers in the lower part are working cooperatively to build a platform from which the figures on top can express themselves. And for the viewpoint of the wagon being dismantled, you see the weight of the words being expressed might be the cause of the undoing of the wagon. It's a cautionary tale that you are responsible for the words you say.[23]

Brogger's comments are as ambiguous as the monument itself, and could be understood as saying that the anarchist labor activists had it coming to them for directly challenging the power structure. Although she clearly seems more troubled by the speech of the anarchists than the indiscriminate gunfire of the police, a focus on the artist is not helpful here. Brogger is a minor player in the ongoing debate over the new monument. In the majority of public art projects today, the artist is simply hired to carry out the subject matter and the content that someone else has already pre-determined. The artist can add an aesthetic quality to the work, and in this regard, we can critique Brogger's efforts. Michael Piazza's humorous commentary of her sculpture is that it looks like a "Gumby version of a romantic Civil War memorial." That aside, the real issue of her Haymarket Monument is the nature of public art itself and the pitfalls of allowing a small group of individuals to decide what is placed within civic spaces.[24]

The small committee of government agencies, historical societies, and labor organizations (namely the ILHS, the Chicago Federation of Labor, the Chicago Historical Society and the Chicago Police Department) that agreed upon the monument's content is not a broad cross section of the population. A plan for a monument at the Haymarket site directed by any small group of individuals and agencies is inherently problematic and bound to alienate a vast amount of people. Thus the very concept of a top-down structure, which decides the monument for the Haymarket site, is an exercise in futility, if the goal is truly to represent the multiple meanings associated with its history.

As one might expect, the process-by-committee became guarded and exclusive. For example, the inviting of only ten artists to submit proposals for the design is clearly problematic. However, the biggest issue was the exclusion of voices that might have differed with the committee's opinions. From the start, anarchists were shut out of the discussion. Nathan Mason, Chicago's Public Art Program curator for the project, remarked in early 2004, "Who would they choose to represent themselves?"[25] This dismissive comment indicates a lack of serious effort on the committee's part to solicit the input of anarchists and also assumes that the committee itself was more qualified to visualize Haymarket's history.

The committee, with little effort, could have reached out to anarchists within Chicago and beyond. They could have learned about and contacted the A-Zone, a high profile center of anarchist culture and organizing that had been in existence for nearly a decade at the time of the process. Likewise they could have contacted the curators at the Labadie Collection at the University of Michigan, which houses the largest anarchist archive in the country, or any number of other academic collections with large anarchist holdings. Apparently a Chicago-area anarchist, Anthony Rayson, who is part of the South Chicago Anarchist Black Cross, was invited to a meeting in order to determine the text of the plaques that were attached to the base.[26] He declined to attend, but either way, inviting one person this late in the process—after the content of the monument was pre-determined—was far from sufficient.[27] Besides what would have inviting Rayson truly accomplished? It is equally problematic to assume that Rayson (or any single individual) could have represented the concerns of anarchists. The diversity of opinions amongst anarchists is as vast as any other type of political affiliation. This type of approach, of inviting a single person to speak for many, regardless of the affiliation, only reinforces the top-down structure of a project that was inherently flawed and undemocratic.

Considering the relatively closed process of selecting the monument, the dedication ceremony came as a surprise to many within the city and beyond who had no idea that a monument was even in the works.[28] On September 14th, 2004 the new monument was dedicated and not surprisingly, the public reaction to it was deeply divided.

During the official dedication ceremony, city officials, representatives of organized labor,

Graffiti on the plaque noting the National Historic Landmark status of the Haymarket Monument at Waldheim, 1997. Photo: Wikipedia Commons/posted by Bogdan Markiewicz.

and police officers congratulated themselves and each another. A central theme of many of their speeches was that of reconciliation, the notion that the wounds of the past and the divisions between labor and the police were beginning to heal. A small group of anarchists in the crowd held up black flags to voice their disgust with the entire proceedings. Anthony Rayson was quoted in the *Chicago Sun-Times* as saying, "This is a revisionist history thing. They're trying to whitewash the whole thing, take it away from the anarchists and make it a free-speech issue."[29] A *New York Times* article quoted another dissenting voice in the crowd, Steve Craig as stating,

> Those men who were hanged are being presented as social democrats or liberal reformers, when in fact they dedicated their whole lives to anarchy and social revolution. If they were here today, they'd be denouncing this project and everyone involved in it.[30]

They would have also heard Mark Donahue, president of the Chicago Fraternal Order of Police and a member of the monuments project advisory board, state, "We've come such a long way to be included in this... We're part of the labor movement now, too, and glad to be there."[31] The question remains, however, would Donahue have made such a statement had anarchists been part of the process of conceptualizing a monument? Would

he have stated this had the monument given a more pronounced focus to either the anarchist martyrs or the class conflict between labor and the police that had resulted in the Haymarket riot?[32] As the historian Lara Kelland notes:

> By polarizing the meaning of the 1886 event between free speech and labor in opposition to radical social critique of government and industry, the memorial effort becomes palatable for those officially involved.[33]

Donahue's notion of the police as now being part of the labor movement is also duplicitous. While it is true that police officers are "workers" and many are organized into unions, his comments promote the notion that the police and other workers in society share the same interests and class goals. While it is true that the police are no longer gunning down workers who are out on strike, the police still protect

First they took your life

HAYMARKET MARTYRS' MONUMENT

HAS BEEN DESIGNATED A

NATIONAL HISTORIC LANDMARK

THIS MONUMENT REPRESENTS THE LABOR MOVEMENT'S STRUGGLE FOR WORKERS' RIGHTS, AND POSSESSES NATIONAL SIGNIFICANCE IN COMMEMORATING THE HISTORY OF THE UNITED STATES OF AMERICA

1997

NATIONAL PARK SERVICE
UNITED STATES DEPARTMENT OF THE INTERIOR

Now they exploit your memory

the interests of capital and the state. At labor demonstrations, their batons and pepper spray fall squarely upon the heads of workers. Perhaps Donahue's biggest error was that he attempted to speak for a larger entity, when in fact he was speaking solely as an individual. Diana Berek, a Chicago-based artist and co-editor of *Chicago Labor and Arts Notes* explains, "Individuals can reconcile their wounds, but not classes, not institutions and certainly not the entities of organized labor and the police."[34]

If anything, Donahue's statements reinforce just how easy it is to oversimplify and blur history, especially events as complex as Haymarket. The new monument only adds to this confusion and the attempt to make it appear objective is one of its greatest flaws, for it is not possible to be neutral on the issue of Haymarket. As Berek notes, "Battles for social justice, conflicts around economic and political class conflict will never be easy to tidy up so that they can be objectified, sensitized and made emotionally uplifting to every point of view."[35] While much has changed in the 120 years since Haymarket, we do not live in a society where class conflict is a thing of the past. If anything, the division between the haves and the have-nots has become increasingly pronounced, and the methods to marginalize working class people, unions, and social movements have become increasingly sophisticated. A monument can proclaim that Haymarket was about free speech, but that does not make it necessarily true.

Others would disagree. Tim Samuelson, a cultural historian who was also part of the committee for the new monument, remarked, "It takes a while for people to get an objective perspective on historical events and see [Haymarket] as an overall tragedy and not a polarizing issue."[36] Samuelson, however, fails to mention how the public learns about historical events. He fails to qualify his statement by explaining who owns history. The new monument teaches the public to view Haymarket as a benign event where the most prominent issue was the right to free speech. In this regard, the committee who decided upon this content chose to ignore the history of the class conflict between the workers and the police. The past monuments, both of which represented their specific constituencies (The Police Monument representing the police, and the Haymarket Monument at Waldheim representing

anarchists and abstractly, the labor movement) did not shy away from defending their interests. The new monument, however, erases these interests and sets a dangerous precedent for a new generation to learn about Haymarket. The question remains if the new monument will, in fact, inspire people to learn more about the complex history of Haymarket, or if it will pacify people's interest in the history with its banal and abstract representation of the event.

In addition, why was the city so willing to act now when it had been so resistant in the past? Nathan Mason notes that, "Thousands of visitors come to the site. It speaks poorly of the city if we let it be a barren, littered concrete slab."[37] Yet this absence was not an issue in the past. Why now? Lara Kelland offers one possible explanation:

> The explanation for such a shift in preservation policy might be found in larger city forces. Chicago of the 1990s faced entirely different challenges than it did earlier in the twentieth century. Gentrification brought a middle-class base back into the city after a generation of white flight, and heritage tourism also now offered a tantalizing revenue stream to city leaders. It is at this moment that civic commemoration was finally in the city's interests, and the postindustrial environment offered a context in which organized labor was one interest group among many to be accommodated in the commemorative process.[38]

In this regard, is the new monument part of an overall tourism scheme? This notion perhaps helps explain one of the many complexities behind the monument finally coming to light. But arguably the most pressing issue remains the undemocratic nature of a small group of individuals deciding upon what is presented in public space and taking ownership of how Haymarket's history is represented in such an important location.

Where Do We Go From Here? Other Possibilities for the Haymarket Site

> I think [anarchists] would object to anything being put there by the city, the government[39]
> —William Adelman, labor historian, vice president of the ILHS

It is very doubtful that any type of monument on the Haymarket site that was funded, sanctioned and maintained by the city would be satisfactory to many anarchists. A singular monument by its nature counters the ideals of a directly democratic, collective society and is too closely related to the attitudes and actions of capitalist and communist societies where monuments to "great individuals" are abundant. Examining the past history of the Haymarket Monument at the Waldheim Cemetery is helpful in addressing this question. Emma Goldman spoke of this dilemma when she considered the merits of the martyrs' monument at Waldheim:

> My thoughts wandered back to the time when I had opposed the erection of the monument. I had argued that our dead comrades needed no stone to immortalize them. I realized now how narrow and bigoted I had been, and how little I understand the power of art. The monument served as an embodiment of the ideals for which the men had died, a visible symbol of their words and their deeds.[40]

Goldman's initial doubts over the need for a monument are refreshing and they are shared by many who have conflicting ideas over the positives and negatives of monuments. For each case is site-specific, and the issue of monuments to Haymarket's history is exceedingly complex, making it difficult to settle upon a rigid position. Yet to many anarchists, the monument at Waldheim becomes acceptable only because it was maintained by the martyr's families, including Lucy Parsons (widow of the slain Albert Parsons), under the direction of the Pioneer Aid and Support Association. The anarchist supported and initiated monument existed at the gravesite of the martyrs and was disconnected from direct government funding and control. Under these parameters, the Haymarket Monument at Waldheim has been widely embraced by anarchists and it is only in recent times that the monument has become contentious, especially since the ILHS took over its deed in 1973, and decided in 1997 to register the monument as a National Historic Landmark.

Connecting the martyrs' monument to the federal government was the last straw for many anarchists. The National Historic Landmark plaque is routinely vandalized with anarchist symbols in an act of protest and a reclaiming of the history. During the dedication ceremony of the landmark status in 1997, a group of anarchists disrupted the event and berated the crowd, labor speakers, and historians for selling out the memory of the martyrs by allowing the very government who executed them to give landmark status to their gravesite. At one point, the actress Alma Washington, dressed as Lucy Parsons, unveiled the plaque, only to have anarchists spit upon it. Clearly, the long-standing friction between anarchists and the ILHS is far from being resolved, if, in fact, it ever can be.

At stake is how the memory of Haymarket is projected. Does it belong to a broad-based labor movement or should it remain rooted within the anarchist principles of the martyrs? Likewise, does it belong to the police? And who represents each of these divergent groups? This divide complicates any discussion over the proposal and the manifestation of monuments to Haymarket, especially within Chicago. Yet this issue is not so black and white, and there exists a gray area, even regarding the new monument that was dedicated in 2004.

The new Haymarket monument gives just enough mention to the anarchists within the cautiously worded plaques that it is more difficult to vent out against compared to the obviously repressive symbol of the Police Monument. Nonetheless, the sculptor of the monument, Mary Brogger, expressed concerns that the monument would become a target. She noted, "The real challenge is to make a monument that people won't bomb," and she remarked that the surface patina was chosen so that it would be easy to clean up any graffiti written on it.[41]

To the new monument's credit, an element of participation, if extremely limited, was built in. The pedestal of the monument has room for a number of additional plaques to be installed connecting recent labor struggles to Haymarket. During the May Day 2005 ceremony at the monument, a delegation of union trade leaders from Colombia presented the first plaque to be added to the pedestal in honor of the 1,300 trade unionists that have been murdered in Colombia between 1991 and 2001.[42] Johnny Meneses, a union activist from Colombia, told the crowd, "You have one monument. But in Colombia, we would need many more than that."[43] In this case, the new monument served as an important location for solidarity campaigns, allowing US citizens to be informed of the troubling situation that is taking place within Colombia, and the static monument becomes more flexible. However, one should note that the pedestal is relatively small and only a certain number of plaques will be able to be installed. Who will select the plaques, which struggles will be deemed important, and which ones will be deemed unimportant?

The participatory aspect of the monument—arguably its most redeeming quality—raises the question of whether this should have been the monument's main focus. What if the monument on Desplaines Street was not a single monument on a pedestal, but a park that had ample room to explain the history of Haymarket from a variety of perspectives—be it labor's, the anarchists', the police's, or from the local and international community's? Within this park there could be a wall where eventually thousands of plaques could be added that spoke of global solidarity struggles. The park could include a museum that would be a place to learn about Haymarket's history and how it could be applied to the present. Lew Rosenbaum, a Chicago activist and co-editor of *Chicago Labor and Arts Notes*, suggested that a more ideal monument to Haymarket would also include an art center. He noted the idea of a living monument:

> Something that would attempt to envision what a group of revolutionaries today would be battling for. I'd want an art center that challenged artists to represent the polarities developing in our society, not the society of a century ago, and to carry the message out with them in their work. I somehow don't think today's Joe Hills are singing the same songs.[44]

To Rosenbaum, a single monument is problematic because it "crystallizes the past without allowing for a changing future."[45] This important critique relates to the majority of static monuments, but there is a common desire by many people to preserve past monuments as indicators of the cultural and political attitudes of the time. Many have objected to monuments and other symbols of state power being completely removed (such as the Berlin Wall and the monuments to Stalin and other communist leaders throughout Russia and Eastern Europe), because they still have the ability to educate us about a past history, however troubling they may be. In Budapest, Hungary, many of these didactic, authoritarian monuments were moved after the fall of communism to Statue Park, on the outskirts of the city, where visitors to the park can visualize the symbols of the oppressive dictators and culture of the recent past. This fascinating example of a collection of monuments representing various ideological viewpoints could be a model for Haymarket. Perhaps, if a park on Desplaines Street was created (which has been proposed in the past, including by the ILHS), a number of monuments could co-exist on the same space, and the public could decide their ultimate fate.

At present, there does not seem to be a critical mass of voices calling for either the creation of a more inclusive and honest marker at the Haymarket site or the removal of Brogger's Haymarket Monument. Is this because of the open-ended meaning of Brogger's monument or the fact that it attempts to appease all sides? Is it indicative of the present political climate of apathy towards the actions of the state? Are there simply more important things to advocate for? Amidst the consumer distractions and the long workweeks that most individuals endure, one wonders if monuments that address past historic struggles still matter and merit our attention? Back in 1890, Martin Lacher, then secretary for the Pioneer Aid and Support Association, in objection to the Police Monument, stated, "Perhaps not in this generation, [but] that statue will come down. Public sentiment will cause its downfall."[46] The question remains, will today's public demand the same?

33. "Putting Haymarket to Rest?" *Labor Studies in Working-Class History of the Americas*, 36.

34. Diana Berek interviewed by the author, by email, 20 February, 2006.

35. Ibid.

36. *Chicago Reader*, 16, January 2004. Section 2.

37. Ibid.

38. "Putting Haymarket to Rest?" *Labor Studies in Working-Class History of the Americas*, 35.

39. *Chicago Reader*, 16, January, 2004. Section 2.

40. Emma Goldman quoted in Melissa Dabakis, *Visualizing Labor in American Sculpture: Monuments, Manliness, and the Work Ethic, 1880–1935*, (Cambridge: Cambridge University Press, 1999), 50. See, Emma Goldman, *Living My Life*, vol. 1 (New York: Alfred A. Knopf, 1931), 221–22.

41. *Chicago Reader*, 16 January, 2004. Section 2.; New York Times, 15 September 2004, A14.

42. Green, James. "The Globalization of a Memory: The Enduring Remembrance of the Haymarket Martyrs around the World." *Labor Studies in Working-Class History of the Americas*, Volume 2, Issue 4 (2005): 22.

43. Ibid., 22–23.

44. Lew Rosenbaum interviewed by the author, by email, 20, February, 2006.

45. Ibid.

46. "Attempt to Wreck Monument, Mr. Lacher Says the Police Are the Conspirators-No Arrests," *Chicago Daily Tribune*, May 26, 1890, 3.

***

I am grateful for the edits, suggestions, conversations, and reviews of previous drafts of the essay by Josh MacPhee, Erik Reuland, Daniel Tucker, Sue Simensky-Bietila, and John Couture. This essay is dedicated to Michael Piazza, who passed away in 2006. His spirit, convictions, and dedication to art and activism will always inspire those of us who were fortunate enough to meet him.

H. H. 30.

BETTER A ONE-LEGGED MAN THAN A WOMAN

ERIKA BIDDLE

A Woman! comprising a man's anxious desires. Her sassy arm proclaims its debt to its male author—"I see...how she loves to be a straight line traced by a mechanical hand"; she is, naturally, "harebrained" (her "cerebral atrophy" a function of her brute physicality), and her dadaism is articulated through male desire: she "exists only in the exaggeration of her *jouissances* and in the consciousness of possession... I see her only in pleasure."

—Marius de Zayas, New York Dadaist

Dada was a male domain.
—Valerie Preston-Dunlop, "Notes on Bodies in Dada"

"Better a one-legged man than a woman." This old Japanese proverb resonates with much of the early twentieth century European and American avant-garde movements, but it is particularly striking with the dysmorphic and mechanomorphic works that characterized much of Dada's artistic production—works that spoke of the horrors and destructiveness of the First World War, the impact of modernity on the body and the psyche—and set the stage for an unprecedented break with the past. More often than not, Dada (fl. 1915–1923) is recognized as the first avant-garde art movement to embody a cultural resistance to the everyday life of the times and to reject artmaking as it was known. Dada was also the first real international art movement, and coalesced in the midst of World War I. It is said to have originated in Zürich, Switzerland, a neutral wartime refuge, and home to an expatriate community of artists and writers that included Hans Arp, Hugo Ball, Emmy Hennings, Richard Huelsenbeck, Marcel Janco, Hans Richter, Sophie Taeuber, and Tristan Tzara.[1] In slightly different manifestations and at different moments, Dada also surfaced in Paris, Berlin, Cologne, Hanover, and New York.

Although Dada may have been relatively short-lived, it has been written that Dada "supplied the alphabet for much of the innovative artistic thought of the Western world from the mid-twentieth century onward."[2] Its themes of nihilism, subversive humor, ruthless anti-authoritarianism, its use of unconventional media for the purpose of experimentation and to expand the idea of art, and its fierce critiques of the various political, economic, and aesthetic conditions and systems of the time in which it was active were manifest in all of its creative endeavors.

The dadaist strategy for life and art was absolute transgression, but in looking at the role of female artists within the movement it is notable that this avant-gardism did not extend to the conventional patriarchal socio-cultural reality of the times. In what can only be described as contradictory to the Dada stance on culture, the women involved in the movement were often treated as subordinates to their male contemporaries. In art and life, they were regarded as objects of desire, lovers, wives, muses, nurturers, or sometimes subservients, deviants, madwomen, and irritants. In many firsthand accounts of Dada, the women appear as secondary figures and collaborators, and not as contributors of strong artistic, intellectual, and ideological works in their own right. Even within the art of Dada, it was the female body that was subject to dysmorphic representations, to be chopped up and delivered to the viewer as the generic, war-torn and decontextualized body amputated of not only limbs but of agency. The mechanomorphic images were equally feminized, and created a visual metaphor of woman-as-machine, further stripping the female body of agency (however female and subordinate).

In the 1910s, the period in which Dada emerged, many European feminists claimed that a woman could become a whole person only through motherhood; it was her duty to repopulate the war-ravaged European continent. If this was the radical notion of the female in Europe in an epoch of bourgeois morality, she existed alongside the androgynous (read *emasculating*) figure of the "New Woman,"[3] the symbol of American industrial capitalism that was rising up as the answer to the "decadence" and "failure" of Europe. The change and anxiety of the times were often personified by the woman-as-machine: "bodies that appear human but are soulless, anonymous, and machine-like," or viewed more dangerously, "the machine has become more than a mere adjunct of human life. It is really a part of human life—perhaps the very soul" (Francis Picabia, 1915). This was partially a reaction to the upsurge of industrialism in the wake of the Great War, but at the same time, modern independent women were re-creating the age-old ideal of femininity on their own terms—by going to work in the factories to supplement the declining male population, waging the suffrage movement, demanding rights of their own bodies through

debates and demonstrations on birth control, among other battles for equal rights.[4] Perhaps partly owing to the transformative figure of the New Woman, but also to what was seen as the unique phenomenon of modernity that rapidly established the American spirit as the catalyst for the machine age, Dada women did much better in New York's avant-garde than in the earlier and even the contemporaneous European avant-gardes.

With the exception of a few works that are explicitly feminist, art historians have written about Dada as a masculine avant-garde, and in excavating the remains of this movement, have focused their attention (and consequently ours) on the lives and works of the male dadaists, highlighting them as Dada's leaders, and their works as exemplary of the ideas of Dada.[5] In Peter Bürger's *Theory of the Avant-Garde*, he writes that in studies of the avant-garde, the emphasis has been on movements rather than individuals.[6] Bürger argues that whereas bourgeois production is "the act of an individual genius," the avant-garde "responds with the radical negation of the category of individual creation," and not only individual creation but reception as well. Remarking on the "collective reception" accorded to Dada and Surrealist works, for example, Bürger observes that "Breton and Duchamp...lose their meaning as producers and recipients; all that remains is art as an instrument for living one's life."[7] This is a beautiful ideal, and yet paradoxically, in our cultural memory the "radical negation of the category of individual creation" dissolves; André Breton, or Marcel Duchamp, or Hugo Ball, etc. are heroized.[8] The 'great artists' of this period are never its female contributors.

While it is difficult to recover information from a movement whose nihilist attitude extended to its self-documentation, its compulsion to "*Verwisch die Spuren!*" ("Erase the Traces!")—a lot of what remains of early Dada, for example, are short-lived periodicals and the scraps of ephemera that announced performances, exhibitions, propaganda meetings, readings, actions, protests, etc.—it is even more challenging to conduct a search for what has historically been brushed under the carpet.[9] This is presumably where many of the women of the early avant-garde have been all these years.

In this brief history I am proposing, I would like to bring attention to several notoriously under-

---

1. At least this is where Dada received its name. There has been a long-term dispute amongst the Zurich dadaists about who to credit with its name—Ball, Huelsenbeck, or Tzara. It has also been written that what came to be known as Dada originated autonomously in the earlier works of Marcel Duchamp, who was based in New York City at the time.

2. From the forthcoming book *Provos* (working title) by Richard Kempton, to be released in Fall 2007 by Autonomedia. Among the art forms Dada has influenced are: Surrealism, Lettrism, the Situationists, Pop art, conceptual art, serial art, Minimalism, Fluxus, Happenings, Theater of the Absurd, sound poetry, concrete poetry, experimental writing, performance art, collage, and mixed media, in general.

3. Whereas the nineteenth century had the powerful *femme fatale* (supplied by European literature and art), who had an aura of distance and mystery to her credit, the New Woman (as utopian gender-equalizer), a figure also supplied by *fin-de-siecle* Romantics, became in America the public icon for the twentieth century "New World" in its first epoch of consumerism; this New Woman (think Mary Pickford) was displayed widely on billboards and in magazines, and thus, she was a living, breathing, very robust advertisement for capitalist culture.

4. I write this with a degree of ambivalence, as I deeply believe that to some extent, the New Woman was an image created to sell the death of the nineteenth century in order to make way for the progress (not progressivism) of the industrial-capitalist future.

5. Some notable examples of revisiting the early avant-gardes to draw out the contributions of female artists, writers, and thinkers include the works of art historians Shari Benstock, Mary Ann Caws, Whitney Chadwick, Irene Gammel, Naomi Sawelson-Gorse, Amelia Jones, Shelly Rice, Penelope Rosemont, and Susan Suleiman. Among these writers, there are mixed accounts on whether the underwritten histories of these women can be attributed to the misogyny of the movements' male counterparts, or the secondary role of women in society overall at the time.

6. Peter Bürger. *Theory of the Avant Garde.* (Minneapolis: University of Minnesota Press, 1984).

explored Dada women: Sophie Taeuber, Emmy Hennings, Hannah Höch, and Mina Loy.[10] I have assembled what amounts to a fragmentary history of their involvement in the movement and their lives beyond Dada. From there, I'd like to present a larger number of female artists from this period in even briefer form, in order to call attention to their contributions to Dada. While this is by no means a full recuperation, it is enough history, I hope, to provide a starting point for further exploration of Dada's female artists and writers.

Zürich Dada: Emmy Hennings and Sophie Taeuber

Only two women have been acknowledged as participants in Zürich Dada: Emmy Hennings (1885–1948), a German expatriate, and Sophie Taeuber (1889–1943), the group's only Swiss national. Both were linked to more famous male dadaist partners, Hennings to the German poet Hugo Ball and Taeuber to the painter/collagist Hans Arp, who was from Strasburg. The doings, writings, and artworks associated with this particular Dada phenomenon were largely collaborative and performative. Nevertheless, accounts of them are dominated by the powerful figures of Ball, Huelsenbeck, Janco, and Tzara. Hennings(-Ball) and Taeuber(-Arp) are primarily remembered as wives and cabaret performers—dancers, chanteuses, and puppeteers—who played supporting roles in the greater Zürich Dada activities. It has even been written, "neither [woman] made strong theoretical or ideological statements."[11] This is simply not true.

Emmy Hennings, a.k.a. Hugo Ball's Wife

Emmy Hennings is famously remembered as a singer and cabaret performer at the artist tavern *Simplicissimus* in Munich, where she met Hugo Ball in 1913. At the time, Hennings was also a widow and mother of two (though only one survived, and her mother raised the child), a gypsy-like performing artist, a prostitute, and "at one point sold bathroom supplies door to door."[12] Additionally, she was a published poet, a writer of short stories, and a journalist, whose works appeared in German left-wing publications such as *Pan* and *Die Aktion*. In 1913, she published her first poetry collection, *Ather Gedichte* (Ether Poems). In 1914, she was briefly imprisoned for forging passports for draft dodgers. With the full range of her own artistry and life experiences, Hennings joined Ball in Berlin later that year, and the couple fled Berlin for Zürich in 1915. In February 1916, they co-founded the Cabaret Voltaire, a nightclub that has come to be known as the birthplace of Dada. Hennings was its "star" singer, dancer, poet, and puppeteer. The *Züricher Post* wrote of Hennings on May 7, 1916:

> The star of the cabaret however, is Mrs. Emmy Hennings. The star of who knows how many nights and poems. Just as she stood before the billowing yellow curtain of a Berlin cabaret, her arms rounded up over her hips, rich like a blooming bush, so today she is lending her body with an ever-brave front to the same songs, that body of hers which has since been ravaged but little by pain.[13]

In spite of this recognition, in most of the firsthand accounts of Zürich Dada that are available (e.g., those of Huelsenbeck, Tzara, and Richter), Hennings' role is marginalized. By Ball's own account, he and Hennings were truly equal collaborators, and in each poster he made to advertise the recitals, dances, actions, poetry readings, etc. of the Zürich Dada group, the names of all participants, male and female, were included. Unfortunately, accounts by the other Dada males only address her participation as a cabaret performer:

> As the only woman in this cabaret manned by poets and painters, Emmy supplied a very necessary

note to the proceedings, although (or even because) her performances were not artistic in the traditional sense, either vocally or as interpretations. Their unaccustomed shrillness was an affront to the audience, and perturbed it quite as much as did the provocations of her male colleagues.

—Hans Richter

Except for Emmy Hennings, we had no professional cabaret performers. Her little voice was so meagre and boyish that we sometimes had the feeling it might break at any moment. She sang Hugo Ball's aggressive songs with an anger we had to credit her with although we scarcely thought her capable of it. Was this a child disseminating anti-war propaganda?

—Richard Huelsenbeck

There are a few elusive theories as to why the men in her inner-circle undermined Hennings, who in spite of her versatile contributions, which included poetry, was denied full-fledged membership into the Zürich Dada group. In some accounts, she is alluded to as a drug addict, and by this reading, her "morphine-induced" performances "betrayed" an emotional excess that was "terrifying." Other firsthand accounts of the period challenge her "true Dada spirit"—negating her Dada performances as just another cabaret role. These kinds of criticism are cloaked in gendered language. It is clear that in spite of their 'avant-garde' attitude to European culture, the Zürich Dada group maintained conventional early-twentieth century European ideas of gender, with the women circum-

scribed by the traditional feminine role assigned to them. Hennings most often recited Ball's monologues in her performances (rather than her own). She did not participate in a single Zürich Dada publication, nor was she invited to sign its manifestoes. Consequently, Hennings' contribution to Zürich Dada is principally remembered as the wife/lover/companion of Hugo Ball.

Hennings' partnership with Ball lasted beyond Zürich Dada, which, due to Ball and Tzara's "ideological" split, the couple had abandoned in 1918 for the nascent Dada group in Berlin. While there is documentation to support Ball's participation in Berlin Dada, there is no mention of any contribution made by Hennings. In 1919, Hennings signed Hans Richter's "Radical Artists Manifesto," the only female signature alongside Arp, Baumann, Eggeling, Giacometti, Helbig, Janco, Morach, and Richter. The "Association of Revolutionary Artists" as they were called, lasted only a few weeks, but its aim was to bring aesthetically revolutionary artists into the political revolution that had just broken out in Munich and Budapest. The same year, Hennings published her autobiographic novel *Gefängnis* (Prison). Later, Hennings was a collaborator to the magazine *Revolutions*, which was founded by Ball and Hans Leybold. From what I could glean from the spotty information available on her in English, both Hennings and Ball worked as journalists for *Freie Zeitung* in Bern. Hennings also worked as a correspondent for the *Neue Züricher Zeitung* [*New Zürich News*].

Ball and Hennings settled permanently in southern Switzerland at the end of the 1920s, and 'dropped out' of Dada. Here again they lived amongst an expatriate bohemian community that included the writer Hermann Hesse and dance theorist/choreographer Rudolf von Laban. Ball was employed on a biography of Bakunin, and just before he died finished work on a biography of Hesse entitled *Hermann Hesse. Sein Leben und sein Wer* (Herman Hesse. His Life and Work) (1927). Details of Hennings' activities at the time are hard to come by. After Ball's death in 1927, Hennings' financial situation deteriorated to the extent that she became dependent on the support of Hesse, the couple's longtime friend, who was then living in nearby Montagnola. In 1930 Hennings edited

7. Ibid.

8. Marjorie Perloff, "Dada Without Duchamp/Duchamp Without Dada: Avant-Garde Tradition and the Individual Talent," at http://epc.buffalo.edu/authors/perloff/dada.html.

9. See Bertolt Brecht's *Handbook for City Dwellers* (1926). See also: "We had lost confidence in our culture. Everything had to be demolished. We would begin again after the *tabula rasa*. At the Cabaret Voltaire we began by shocking the bourgeois, demolishing his idea of art, attacking common sense, public opinion, education, institutions, museums, good taste, in short, the whole prevailing order." Marcel Janco, "Dada at Two Speeds," trans. in Lucy R. Lippard, *Dadas on Art* (Englewood Cliffs: Prentice Hall, 1971): 36.

10. While it is by no means a remarkable gap, Höch and Loy have received more attention than Hennings and Taeuber.

11. "Zürich Dada and its Artist Couples" by Renée Riese Hubert in Naomi Sawelson-Gorse, ed. *Women in Dada: Essays on Sex, Gender, and Identity* (Cambridge, Massachusetts and London, England: The MIT Press, 1998): 517.

12. Thomas F. Rugh, "Emmy Henning's and the Emergence of Zürich Dada," *Woman's Art Journal*, Vol. 2, No. 1 (Spring–Summer, 1981): 1.

13. Available at http://www.peak.org/~dadaist/English/Graphics/hennings.html.

14. See Hans Richter's Letter (to Robert Motherwell), New York, January 26, 1949. Reprinted as a facsimile in Robert Motherwell's *The Dada Painters and Poets: An Anthology*, Second Edition (Cambridge, Massachusetts and London, England: The Belknap Press of Harvard University Press, 1979), 290.

15. Whitney Chadwick, ed. *Women, Art, and Society*, Third Edition (London: Thames & Hudson Ltd., 1990), 271.

the posthumous publication of Ball's *Sein Leben in Briefen und Gedichten* (His Life in Letters and Poems) (with a foreword by Hermann Hesse) and the 1931 *Hugo Ball's Weg zu Gott* (Hugo Ball's Way to God). According to Hans Richter in his *Dada X Y Z* (1948), in addition to publishing books about Hugo Ball and his posthumous works, Hennings wrote for magazines. She spent her later years working in a factory, and died alone in poverty in 1948.[14]

While some of Hennings' poems are available online or in rare book collections (in their original German), her writings are largely forgotten. Whereas Ball's *Flight Out of Time: A Dada Diary* is widely regarded as an important account of Zürich Dada, Hennings' own diary of her involvement with Dada, *Das Brandmal. Ein Tagebuch* (The Fire Mark. A Diary) remains both under-recognized and untranslated. Her autobiography, *Ruf und Echo. Mein Leben mit Hugo Ball* (Call and Response. My Life with Hugo Ball) was published posthumously in 1953 by the Swiss publisher Benziger. It too has not been translated. In 2001, German historian Bärbel Reetz published a biography of Emmy Hennings, *Ich bin so vielfach* (I am so multiple), which also remains to be translated from its original German.

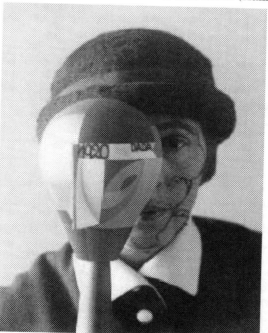

Sophie Taeuber, a.k.a. Hans Arp's Wife

> ...delirious strangeness in the spider of the hand vibrating quickly ascending towards the paroxysm of a mocking capriciously beautiful madness. Costume by Hans Arp.
> —Tristan Tzara

Far from a mere mannequin for the costumes of others, the Swiss painter, designer, and dancer Sophie Taeuber (1889–1943) was an active member of the Zürich Dada group from 1916 and 1918. She also participated in the Constructivist movement, and was an advocate of concrete art and geometric abstraction. Taeuber studied at the School of Applied Arts (St. Gallen, Switzerland) from 1908 to 1910 and at the experimental studios of Wilhelm von Debschits (Munich), a workshop of the *Blaue Reiter* epoch, in 1911 and 1913. In 1912 she attended the School of Arts and Crafts (Hamburg) and the Laban School of Dance (Zürich) in 1916.

Taeuber is best remembered as a painter. By 1915, she was producing abstract paintings that reflected her interest in the work of early modernist painters Wassily Kandinsky, Robert Delaunay, and Paul Klee, but probably derived their greatest influence from her training in textiles.[15] That same year she met the French sculptor, painter, and poet Hans (Jean) Arp in Zürich. Their first collaborations, embroideries and collages, were made within days of meeting each other. Her romance with Arp led her to contacts with the Zürich dadaists in late 1915.

By most accounts, Taeuber was recruited into Zürich's Dada group for her experience with dance to perform along with Emmy Hennings at the Galerie Dada, the new headquarters of the Zürich Dada group after the Cabaret Voltaire shut down. Dance was always an integral part of Taeuber's art and life; modern-dance pioneers Rudolf von Laban and Mary Wigman were not only her mentors, but also her close friends. Taeuber was a member of Wigman's ballet, and introduced a dialogue between Laban and Zürich Dada that has been substantially documented by her Dada peers, particularly Tristan Tzara. In addition to enriching the Dada performances, Taeuber also explored different media and techniques, producing puppets, theatrical designs, collages, embroideries, weavings, and sculptures.

From 1915 to 1932 Taeuber belonged to the Swiss Werkbund, an organization whose members believed that the applied arts could be used to create "an appropriate expression of the technological age," in line with the Swiss design ideal that function and aesthetics should be non-exclusive goals. She also taught textile design at the School of Applied Arts in Zürich from 1916–1929, which gave the period of her Dada activities the quality of a dual life—lecturer by day, Dada dancer by night. She performed in disguise—wearing "tribal" masks (designed by fellow dadaist Marcel Janco) and swathing, gender-obliterating costumes—to avoid losing her teaching post. Whereas Emmy Hennings had been recognized as the Cabaret's star performer, Taeuber was known as "the masked Dada dancer."

In 1918, Taeuber and Arp signed the Dadaist Manifesto. In late 1918, when the war ended and the borders reopened, Dada left Zürich for Berlin and Cologne, however, Taeuber remained in Zürich to retain her teaching post.[16] In 1922, Sophie Taeuber and Hans Arp married.

The period 1920–1926 marked a relatively inactive period in Taeuber's career during which she produced costume and set designs for theater companies, and for her own work she produced gouaches. In 1926 Taeuber completed a mural painting for Paul Horn, an architect in Strasbourg. The mural led to a commission for the interior of the Café de l'Aubette, the first realized Constructivist public space, designed to integrate art and function. The project was completed in 1928, in collaboration with Arp and de Stijl artist Theo van Doesburg.

In 1928, Taeuber and Arp moved to Meudon, a suburb of Paris. This marked the beginning of the most productive period in the artist's life. She joined a number of artists' organizations (Cercle et Carré group, the Abstraction-Création group and, later, the Vereinigung Moderner Schweizer Künstler Allianz—The Alliance of Modern Swiss Artists) and exhibited with them in Paris, edited and wrote for radical publications (such as the Constructivist review *Plastique/Plastic*), and exhibited her work throughout Europe. Taeuber is mostly remembered for the works she produced during this period.

Taeuber and her husband fled to southern France when the Nazis invaded Paris in 1940. In late 1942, they returned to Zürich, where she died the following year at the age of fifty-three—accidentally gassed by the stove in the house of the painter Max Bill. Although recognition of her abilities by her Dada peers was delimited to her dance performances, Taeuber's contributions as a visual artist have long established her as a leading precursor of concrete, serial, and minimalist art. After her death, numerous exhibitions, some of which included works by her husband Hans (Jean) Arp, were organized in both Europe and America. In 1981 the Museum of Modern Art (New York) mounted the one-woman show "Sophie Taeuber-Arp" which traveled to the Museum of Contemporary Art (Chicago), the Museum of Fine Arts (Houston), and the Musée d'Art Contemporain (Montréal). Most recently, Taeuber's *Dada-Köpfe* (Dada Heads) (1918–1920), portraits of her Dada peers constructed from hat stands, were on view in the major traveling exhibition of Dada that was at The Museum of Modern Art in New York City (June 18–September 11, 2006), and premiered at the National Gallery of Art in Washington, DC. She was one of the few female artists whose works were prominent in this very large survey of Dada objects and ephemera.

Berlin Dada: Hannah Höch

> She is certainly a whimsical observer of social conventions, but her ideological commitment is nil. What happened when both of them, presumably accidentally, used the same photograph of a listless, overworked and pregnant proletarian woman in 1930 is fascinating to note. In *Mothers, Let Your Sons Live!* Heartfield montages a photograph of a dead boy with his rifle, right behind the woman. The message is clear—agitate for change! Rouse yourself! Help prevent these kinds of atrocities! In contrast, Höch has no sense of mission. She cloaks the woman's face surrealistically, with a primitive mask, thereby deflecting the impact of the original photograph. *Le Mère* [Mother] is possibly an affecting but not a politically engaged image.
> —Manuela Hoelterhoff

The largest of several German Dada groups was formed in Berlin by Richard Huelsenbeck, John Heartfield, Raoul Hausmann, Hannah Höch, and George Grosz. During the period it lasted, 1918–

1922, Höch was the lone woman of the group. Owing to the dire political situation of Germany at the time, Berlin Dada manifested itself as a far more politically radical movement than it had been in Zürich.[17]

Hannah Höch (1889–1978) was born Anna Therese Johanne Höch in Gotha, Germany. In her early twenties, Höch studied graphic arts at the National Institute for the Museum of Arts and Crafts in Berlin, where she met Raoul Hausmann—who was to become her lover, though never her husband. By way of her "identification" (amongst the dadaists and art historians), the two were inextricably linked (in art and life) throughout the period that would come to be known as Berlin Dada. In 1918, Höch banded together with Hausmann and a group of contemporary writers and artists—including Johannes Baader, Richard Huelsenbeck, George Grosz, Franz Jung, Walter Mehring, and Gerhard Priess—to form Club Dada. She was the only female member of Club Dada and was often the only female performer at Club Dada events. The group also produced the publication *Dada Club*, edited by Huelsenbeck with the assistance of Hausmann, which was followed by *Der Dada*, the publication at the heart of the Berlin movement. As far as it is documented, Höch's work never appeared in either of these publications, in

spite of the innovative collages and photomontages she was producing at the time.

Höch was one of the first pioneers of the art form that would come to be known as "photomontage," to distinguish the technique from the painterly works of the Cubists, along with Max Ernst, George Grosz, Raoul Haussman, John Heartfield, and Kurt Schwitters. Hoelterhoff, in the above-quoted "analysis" of Höch's *Mutter* (1930) and the explicitness of the political content of Höch's work in general, misses the mark entirely with her criticism. To the naked eye, Höch's *Mutter* alludes to the artist's own advocacy of women's right to reproductive control. At the time, Höch was active in protests of Paragraph 218, a law in Weimar Germany at the peak of Germany's economic crisis (c. 1930–31) that called for the illegalization of abortion. The subject of *Mutter* is a photograph of a slumping, tired-looking pregnant working-class woman, with the eye of a stylish New Woman at a disproportionate size collaged over a tribal mask that covers her face. If it weren't for Heartfield using the same image, we wouldn't know the identity of this woman. Yet Höch's *Mutter* is a pretty explicit challenge to gender stereotypes and a call to liberate *Mutter* from her burdens: she collages the woman's face, obscuring her identity, so as to signify how unwanted pregnancy affects

Hannah Höch (1889–1978), *Cut with the Dada Kitchen Knife through the Last Weimar Beer-Belly Cultural Epoch in Germany*, 1919. Location: Nationalgalerie, Staatliche Museen zu Berlin, Berlin, Germany. Photo credit: Bildarchiv Preussischer Kulturbesitz / Art Resource, NY. ©2007 Artists Rights Society (ARS), New York / VG Bild-Kunst, Bonn.

all women, and the woman is disempowered to do anything about it except suffer it. Höch participated in the *Frauen in Not* (Women in Need) campaign to overturn Paragraph 218, and had two illegal abortions herself. Any way you look at it, the work has a clear political message—albeit, a feminist message.

Throughout her career, Höch bore oppression against her artistic statements and against her gender. She was often accused of not being as explicit and prescriptive with her political messages as her Berlin colleagues. In what might be described as overt patriarchy, Hans Richter described Höch's contribution to the Dada movement as the "sandwiches, beer and coffee she managed somehow to conjure up despite the shortage of money."[18] Hausmann even suggested that Höch get a job to support him financially. There is evidence that she collaborated artistically with Hausmann, although as in life, she was considered his lover and not his equal. Höch's work dealt with a variety of themes (including militarism, industrialization, allegories of femininity, feminism, reproductive rights, and race), but focused a great deal on critiquing stereotypical images and conditions of women in early twentieth century Germany. Perhaps the "depoliticalization" of her work by her Dada peers can be attributed to the fact that women played such prominent roles within it.

Höch addresses the hypocrisy of the Berlin Dada group and German society as a whole in her photomontage, *Da-Dandy*, in which she parodies the New Woman's fashion, but more acutely, her colleagues' ironic attitudes towards the modern female. Many of her works point out the faults of beauty culture, comparing reality to depictions of the *neue frau* (New Woman) in magazines. Her ten-year tenure as an embroidery designer at Ullstein, a publishing house, put her in a position where she was working with magazines targeted to women, making her acutely aware of the difference between women in media and reality. Marriage did not escape her criticism—she depicted brides as mannequins and children, reflecting the idea that women are not seen as complete people and have little control over their lives. This work was not only a broad societal critique, it was also autobiographical: Hausmann was married to another woman during their involvement, and refused to leave her for Höch. During the affair, Höch had her two abortions, one in 1916 and the other in 1918. In 1922, Höch and Hausmann separated.

From 1926–1929 Höch was involved in a lesbian relationship with Dutch poet Til Brugman, and she lived and worked in Holland. Höch exhibited her photomontages throughout Europe from the mid-1920s through the mid-1940s, but she had already been forgotten about as one of the founders of Berlin Dada and photomontage. In 1931 Höch moved back to Berlin (with Brugman), where she would ultimately spend the rest of her life. She had her first solo exhibition in 1934, in Holland. In 1938 she also committed her only marriage, with a much younger man, however the marriage only lasted until 1942. The last exhibition noted for her is a post-WWII show at the Museum of Modern Art in New York in 1945. Höch died in Berlin in 1978.

In the latter part of the century, many photographers and artists have looked back to her Dada works for inspiration. In fact, many of the concepts behind the "new feminist" artwork of the 1970s and 1980s had already been thoroughly explored by Höch sixty years earlier.[19]

New York Dada: Mina Loy

No one who has not lived in New York has lived in the modern world.
—Mina Loy

16. In 1919 Arp traveled to Cologne and founded the Cologne Dada group with Max Ernst and Johannes Baargeld. In 1920 he left Cologne for the even more exciting scene in Paris, where Tzara had already ignited Dada.

17. WWI had some of its fiercest battles in Germany. A naval blockade of Germany began during the war, and continued after the fighting ended. The signing of the Treaty of Versailles on June 28, 1919 officially ended the war. Included in the 440 articles of the treaty were the demands that Germany officially accept responsibility for starting the war and pay heavy economic reparations. It has been said that the aftermath of this economic crisis was the rise of Nazism and WWII.

18. Hans Richter. *Dada: Art and Anti-Art.* trans. David Britt (London: Thames & Hudson Ltd., 1997).

19. See in particular the uncanny similarities in the works of Martha Rosler.

20. Hans Richter. *Dada: Art and Anti-Art.*

21. Carolyn Burke. *Becoming Modern: The Life of Mina Loy* (New York: Farrar, Straus and Giroux: 1996).

22. Edited by Roger L. Conover (New York: Farrar, Straus and Giroux: 1996).

23. Conover is also the biographer of New York dadaist Arthur Cravan.

24. Extracted from the book jacket copy of *The Two of Us: Forbidden Tales of the French Erotique*, ed. & trans. Zalin Grant (Reston, VA: Pythia Press, 1999).

25. Penelope Rosemont, ed. *Surrealist Women: An International Anthology.* (Austin: The University of Texas Press, 1998), 93.

26. Beatrice Wood. *I Shock Myself: The Autobiography of Beatrice Wood*, ed. Lindsay Smith (San Francisco: Chronicle, 2nd. ed. 1988), 166. Reprinted in Paul B. Franklin's "Beatrice Wood, Her Dada... And Her Mama." In Naomi Sawelson-Gorse, ed. *Women in Dada: Essays on Sex, Gender, and Identity*: 105–06.

27. Linda Nochlin, "Why Have There Been No Great Women Artists?" (1971) reprinted in *Women, Art and Power and Other Essays*, ed. Linda Nochlin (Boulder, CO and Oxford, UK: Westview Press, 1988): 147–58.

28. Carolyn Burke, "Recollecting Dada" in Naomi Sawelson-Gorse, ed. *Women in Dada: Essays on Sex, Gender, and Identity* 562.

Not unlike Zürich, New York City was a refuge for European artists seeking to escape the war. The first pioneers were Marcel Duchamp and Francis Picabia, who arrived in 1915. Within a few months, the two artists, along with the American artist Man Ray, had become the center of radical anti-art activities in New York. Dada activities were held at Alfred Stieglitz's gallery, "291," or the nightly salons of the collectors Louise and Walter Arensberg, which became the "headquarters" for the New York dadaists. As Richter recalls, the origins of dadaist activities in New York "were different, but its participants were playing essentially the same anti-art tune as we were. The notes may have sounded strange, at first, but the music was the same."[20] Dada New York was the longest living manifestation of the movement, 1915–1923.

Mina Loy, the "New Woman"

> Stop looking to men to find out what you are not. Seek within yourself to find out what you are. At present you have the choice between Parasitism, Prostitution or Negation.
>
> —Mina Loy, "Feminist Manifesto"

Painter, poet, actress, playwright, feminist, mother, designer, and conceptual artist Mina Loy (1882–1966) was born Mina Lowy in London on December 27, 1882 in the lower echelons of the rigid British class system, to a Protestant mother and Jewish father. This is important to note because it means at birth she was already marginalized by religion, class, and sex. Loy attended art schools in London, Munich, Paris, and Florence. She achieved some success as a painter, but is much better known as the feminist voice of modernist poetry, a writer of content so shocking she was simultaneously celebrated and trashed by her contemporaries. Loy has been described as Futurist, Dadaist, Surrealist, feminist, conceptualist, modernist, and postmodernist. This inability to pin her down also extends to her artworks. She painted in oils and inks in the World War I years, then moved on to readymade sculptures featuring items collected from the streets of Manhattan. She always allied herself with her visual art more than her writing, claiming at the end of her life that she "never was a poet."

During her Dada years, Loy was married to the British painter/printmaker Stephen Haweis, who she had met in art school in London. In 1903, the couple moved to Paris to paint, and were married the same year. The couple had a child, but the girl died soon after her first birthday. While in Paris, Loy was introduced to the modernist "literary elite." By 1905 Loy was a frequent guest at the pre-Toklas Stein salon, and became lifelong friends with Gertrude and art patron Mabel Dodge (who later held a weekly salon at her apartment in New York's Greenwich Village). These contacts later gave Loy entry into New York's avant-garde circuit.

In 1905 Loy and Haweis moved to Florence, where they enjoyed a relatively open marriage until, after ten years, it soured. Nevertheless, the couple had two more children in 1907 and 1908. At the same time, Loy exhibited paintings in the First Free Exhibition of Futurist Art, but importantly, this is when and where Loy began to write. She became one of the only women involved with Italian Futurism, writing for the theater as well as poems and manifestos of futurist ideas. In January 1914, Loy's "Aphorisms on Futurism," a manifesto set like a long poem and her first modernist writing, appeared in Alfred Stieglitz's journal *Camera Work*. Loy's "Feminist Manifesto" (1914), which advocated the surgical destruction of virginity in pubescent girls and challenged "the social organization of gender," and particularly its encoding in avant-garde discourse, was never published until her poems were collected as *The Lost Lunar Baedeker: Poems of Mina Loy* in 1997.

Loy's involvement with Futurism lasted only two years (1913–1915), due to what she perceived of as Futurist 'leader' F. T. Marinetti's misogyny as well as his embrace of

Love Songs.
I.
Spawn of Fantasies
Silting the appraisable
Pig Cupid   his rosy snout
Rooting erotic garbage
"Once upon a time"
Pulls a weed   white star-topped
Among wild oats sown in mucous-membrane
I would   an eye in a Bengal light
Eternity in a sky-rocket
Constellations in an Ocean
Whose rivers run no fresher
Than a trickle of saliver

These are suspect places

I must live in my lantern
Trimming subliminal flicker
Virginal   to the bellows
Of Experience

Coloured glass

Mina Loy.

fascism. During the time she was involved with Futurism, she had "disappointing affairs" with Marinetti and Giovanni Papini, the political editor of *Lacerba*.

In 1916 Loy moved to the United States on her own and instantaneously became a participant in the New York Dada group, which was composed of artists and writers she had already met in Europe. She had already begun, and continued to publish poetry in *Camera Work*, Carl Van Vechten's *Trend*, Margaret Anderson's *The Little Review*, Alfred Kreymborg's experimental writing and poetry venue *Others*, and *The Blind Man*, edited by New York Dadaists Marcel Duchamp, Beatrice Wood, and Henri-Pierre Roché. While in New York, Loy also became well known as an emblematic figure of the New Woman for the mainstream media (less an honor at the time than a potent symbol for all that was threatening about urban industrialism), and married the Dada poet/boxer Arthur Cravan in 1918. It was a very brief marriage. Cravan, who refused to fight in World War I, spent many of the war years eluding active service by constantly being on the move—to various cities of Europe and then New York. He and Loy met at an Arensberg salon. They were married for eight months before he disappeared off the coast of Mexico as he prepared to sail to Buenos Aires to meet Loy, who was coincidentally eight months pregnant with their child at the time. This was November 1918, the month World War I ended.

For decades, Loy was virtually invisible among the Dada writers of this period, remembered primarily as the bride of Cravan—with the exception of Carolyn Burke's biography on Loy, and subsequent feminist accounts of Dada that reference this book. It has been said that her technique (free verse) and subjects (prostitution, menstruation, destitution, and suicide) shocked even some modernists, and she vanished from the poetry scene as dramatically as she had appeared on it. By the mid-1930s, most of her writings were out of print.

While she made colorful appearances in the biographies of many other writers and artists—including those of Djuna Barnes, Marcel Duchamp, Ernest Hemingway, James Joyce, Marianne Moore, and Gertrude Stein—Loy had no biography of her own until 1996, when *Becoming Modern: The Life of Mina Loy*[21] was released along with a new edition of her poems, *The Lost Lunar Baedeker*.[22] Many of these poems originally appeared in long-defunct and nearly forgotten avant-garde journals. Modernist historian Roger L. Conover, who provides sixty pages of editorial notes to accompany these lost and neglected works, views her as a pioneer who paved the way for the likes of Lucille Clifton, Sharon Olds, Adrienne Rich, and Ann Waldman.[23] Loy died on September 29, 1966, in Aspen, Colorado, leaving behind an unfinished biography of Isadora Duncan and an unpublished collection of poems she had written during the 1940s.

Some Other Survivors of the Early Avant-Garde's Patriarchy

Dada's contempt for traditional painting as a static, materialistic form found a pioneer in *Sonia Delaunay*'s (1885–1979) embroideries, as well as her fashion, textile, and furniture designs. She also collaborated on cloth-poems and dress-poems with the poet Philippe Soupault. Not only did she help introduce the marriage of arts and crafts to Dada, but she dressed the revolution. Tzara, René Crevel, and Louis Aragon all wore clothes she had designed and made. They wrote poems in exchange for her creations.

While frequently mentioned in accounts of New York Dada and in studies of her husband, the painter Albert Gleizes, *Juliette Roche* (1884–1980) was a painter, poet, and chronicler of the early twentieth century avant-garde. In a 1915 interview, she identified herself as anti-war, anti-bourgeois, anti-mass media, and revealed that she did not participate in women's suffrage because she never voted, and she and her husband "did not believe in politics." In the same interview she declared that she and her husband were feminists, "for we believe in equal artistic, industrial and economic opportunity for men and women." Roche distinguished herself amongst her Dada peers for her free verse poetry, and particularly the visual poetry ("ideoplastic poetry") or *"poésie fondée en peinture"* (poetry rooted in painting) she produced from 1917–1919.

Dadaist *Suzanne Duchamp* (1887–1968) was better known as the sister of Marcel Duchamp, and the wife of Swiss artist Jean Crotti. She had her first major exhibition at the Salon des Independents in Paris at the age of 22. After serving in WWI as a nurse, Suzanne Duchamp returned to Paris and made her first Dada works. In addition to paintings, she made mixed media works that drew on some of the same themes as her brother, such as machine allegories of the relationship between the sexes. Rather than Marcel's 'readymades,' Suzanne incorporated actual machine parts into her two-dimensional works, such as clock gears and plumb bobs.

Paris Dadaist *Gabrielle Buffet* (dates unavailable)—a musician, writer, painter, and activist—was better known in her time as the wife of Francis Picabia, or simply as "the painter's wife," and somewhat less often as the object of Marcel Duchamp's helpless crush, and possibly the inspiration for his erotic series of "Virgin" and "Bride" paintings. In 1941 she was a leader in the Résistance in Nazi-occupied Paris, giving refuge to those fleeing Nazi persecution and imprisonment and passing information to the Allies. In 1949 she wrote an essay on Pre-Dada for Robert Motherwell's seminal anthology *The Dada Painters and Poets*. She was the *only* female author who contributed to this volume. Today she is fairly well known as a prolific chronicler of Dada, "almost" equal to her male Dada peers.

Paris Dadaist *Renée Dunan* (1892–1936), a writer, critic, poet and activist, was the author of fifty novels. She published her erotic and science fiction novels under many pseudonyms: Marcelle the Pump, Mr. de Steinthal, Jean Spaddy, Louise Dormienne, and Renée Camera. "She was called an anarchist, individualist, and pacifist during her lifetime. Ms. Dunan was clearly a liberated woman who relished shocking her male colleagues by claiming complete equality in all matters, especially when it came to sex."[24]

The *Baroness Elsa von Freytag-Loringhoven* (1874–1927), was said to have *been* Dada; she surely out-Dadaed her male contemporaries, and this was evidenced by their abject fear of her. Her first published poems, collaboratively written with her then-husband Felix Paul Greve, appeared under the name Fanny Essler, the pseudonym Greve used in his novel about Elsa. In her time, she was mainly known for *doing* or *performing* Dada, and *dadafy-*ing downtown New York City, but the Baroness was also a sculptor and a prolific poet. Most of her poetry appeared at the time in the avant-garde journal *The Little Review*, which was run by the lesbian couple Jane Heap and Margaret Anderson. Two books have recently been published that detail the Baroness' works and her exploits: Amelia Jones's *Irrational Modernism: A Neurasthenic History of New York Dada* (2004) and Irene Gammel's *Baroness Elsa: Gender, Dada, and Everyday Modernity* (2002).

The Surrealist writer and collagist *Mary Low* (dates unavailable) was married to the much better known Cuban poet/revolutionary Juan Brea. From 1936–37 Low and Brea fought together in the Spanish Revolution as members of the *Partido Obrero de Unificacion Marxista* (Workers' Party of Marxist Unification) (POUM). Low edited the POUM English-language newspaper and helped organize the women's militia. The couple collaborated on poetry during this time that was published under the Editions Surréalistes imprint. They also collaborated on *The Red Spanish Notebook* (1937), the first full-length study in English on the Spanish Revolution, to which Low supplied the chapter "Women and The Spanish Revolution." At the outbreak of war, the couple fled to Cuba, and continued to collaborate on writings until Brea's death in 1941, at the age of thirty-five. One particularly striking work that they co-produced was the critical essay "Women and Love through Private Property," (1941), which was first published in Juan Brea and Mary Low's, *La Verdad contemporánea*, 1943, and appears in Surrealist historian Penelope Rosemont's anthology *Surrealist Women*. Low remained politically involved in Havana until 1964. After living briefly in Australia, she moved to the United States where she became an active contributor to the Surrealist Movement in the US. She is described by Rosemont as "one of the stalwarts of Surrealism for more than six decades."[25]

The gender-role revolutionary *Grace W. Pailthorpe* (1883–1971) served as a surgeon during WWI, worked as a physician in the wilds of western Australia after the war, and returned to England to study Freudian psychoanalysis, which she began to practice in 1922, with concentration on the study of female prisoners. A few years later, she opened the Institute for the Scientific Treatment of

Delinquency, the first of its kind, with a Board that included Sigmund Freud, Carl Jung, Alfred Adler and other analysts, as well as Havelock Ellis and H.G. Wells. In 1935, she began her explorations into automatic drawing and painting, and she helped found the Surrealist Group in London in 1936.

New York Dadaist *Beatrice Wood* (1893–1998) was the last surviving artist of New York Dada when she died at 105 years old. Wood was a painter, writer and illustrator whose early works received little critical attention. In her day, she was more famous for her affairs with Marcel Duchamp and the French art collector and writer Henri-Pierre Roché. In a 1978 lecture titled "Life as Dada" at the Philadelphia Museum of Art, Wood said herself, "What is Dada about this lecture is that I know nothing about Dada. I was only in love with the men connected with it, which I suppose is as near to being Dada as anything."[26] Wood also co-edited the short-lived journal *The Blind Man* with Duchamp and Roché. Her painting *Beatrice et ses douzes enfants!* (Beatrice and Her Twelve Children!) (1917), is an homage to her real (and imaginary) sexual forays with various members of the Arensberg circle. Her autobiography, titled *I Shock Myself: The Autobiography of Beatrice Wood*, was published in 1988.

De-Gendering Dada, or "Why Have There Been No Great Women Artists?"

Now the "Woman Problem," like all human problems, so-called (and the very idea of calling anything to do with human beings a "problem" is, of course, a fairly recent one) is not amenable to "solution" at all, since what human problems involve is reinterpretation of the nature of the situation, or a radical alteration of stance or program on the part of the "problems" themselves. Thus women and their situation in the arts, as in other realms of endeavor, are not a "problem" to be viewed through the eyes of the dominant male power elite. Instead, women must conceive of themselves as potentially, if not actually, equal subjects, and must be willing to look the facts of their situation full in the face, without self-pity, or cop-outs; at the same time they must view their situation with that high degree of emotional and intellectual commitment necessary to create a world in which equal achievement will be not only made possible but actively encouraged by social institutions.

—Linda Nochlin, "Why Have There Been No Great Women Artists?"

In 1971, feminist art scholar Linda Nochlin pioneered the field of feminist art theory with her essay "Why Have There Been No Great Women Artists?"[27] In this essay, she posits that when confronted with this question, "the feminist's first reaction is to swallow the bait, hook, line, and sinker, and to attempt to answer the question as it is put: that is, to dig up examples of worthy or insufficiently appreciated women artists throughout history; to rehabilitate rather modest, if interesting and productive careers…" This is often true. However, in re-examining Dada, there are clearly a number of women who were underappreciated whose output was anything but "modest."

In lieu of examining the Dada movement in its self-constructed binaries of "masculine" and "feminine," or tediously drawing out the "feminine" in these Dada artists' works, I believe that in looking back at a historical movement like Dada, the principal thing that needs to be done is to explore the socio-cultural circumstances of the time and place, and then to look at women artists and writers alongside the male artists and writers of their own period and particular outlook. As equals.

However, it is not really possible to ignore the issue of gender inequality when looking back at Dada, a movement that provided its own gendered language to describe itself and had the changing role of women in European and American society written into it. It doesn't take much digging to realize that female artists did provide great works and played important roles in making this movement the consummate rejection of art and life(style) it practiced at the time, and has come to be known as its signature. If Dada women were conscripted as eye-witnesses, what else can the feminist anti-art historian be than a many times removed witness? New York Dadaist Juliette Roche sums it up nicely in the fourth poem of her "La Tour Parle" (The Tower Speaks) (1919), where the speaker declares her willingness to settle for "the few bits and pieces, garbled fragments which suffice to amuse me." This is a feminist Dadaist's solution to life and art, or the "social, artistic, and emotional chaos" all around her.[28] Needless to say, I chose the same strategy in writing this essay.

BRANDING ANTI-CONSUMERISM: THE CAPITALISTIC NATURE OF ANTI-CORPORATE ACTIVISM
ANNE ELIZABETH MOORE

Selling Anti-consumerism

A preaching white man—loud, self-important, and filled with scorn for the decision-making abilities of the common folk—does not stand out much in 2005 when loud, self-important, preaching white men are abundant on every TV, from every radio, and at every street corner in town. This one, though, is standing in front of an international coffeeshop chain, counseling a boycott of the wares of this international coffeeshop chain, repeatedly mentioning this international coffeeshop chain by name to those he advises avoid it.

But this is not Reverend Billy's only strategic error, creating a large anti-advertising campaign that draws a great deal of attention to the stores he targets. This particular preaching white man has staked a career on telling people what not to buy, and where they should not buy it. He spreads his word with his actions, located at the stores he boycotts, and via videos he stars in, books he writes, and CDs he records, which are available for purchase at several national chain stores owned by companies he urges passersby not to support.

It's a disconcerting hypocrisy when viewed by the casual liberal, unaccustomed to the ironies of manic, late-stage capitalism. Reverend Billy Talen and the Church of Stop Shopping seem to be calling for a high-alert, all-product boycott. It is contradictory enough that the group creates products for which we can shop: are we to start shopping again, whichever chain store we may be in, when Billy appears on the package himself?

The paradox is so blatant it was pointed out by the Chicago *Redeye*, a paper no stranger to irony itself: this free tabloid version of the *Chicago Tribune* melds journalism and advertising so seamlessly it regularly runs news headlines such as, "Why You Should Buy the New X-Box." Yet the paper criticized the activist anyway, correctly positioning him within the consumerist framework from which he operates and against which he rails. "[Reverend Billy] Talen acknowledges the conflicts, saying he fears his own hypocrisy. And he admits he must sometimes dance with the enemy in an effort to spread his word."[1]

It is clearly dangerous to allow one's activism to become so rife with hollow sanctimoniousness that a free ad tabloid can find fault, yet the central problems of the Church of Stop Shopping arise from a fundamental misunderstanding of the boycott as an activist strategy, and not out of a personal hypocrisy on Reverend Billy's part. A full accounting of the elements involved in a successful boycott—and an investigation into the particular way the group has interpreted the practice—will lend us a more complete picture of what has gone wrong with contemporary activist strategies.

Named after Charles C. Boycott, the full practice involves the withholding of all support for a product, company, or government in the face of objectionable practices. An Englishman living in Ireland in 1880 as an estate agent for an absentee landlord, Boycott unfairly evicted several tenants of an apartment house. Charles Parnell, a politician and member of the Irish Land League working in land-reform issues, urged Boycott's servants and community to abandon him in punishment, and Boycott's entire family was additionally denied service in stores and did not receive mail for the length of the treatment.

As this first boycott shows, the practice may now be popularly understood as a way to coerce institutional change via withheld financial support, but there are clearly other modes of community support that contribute directly to the success of a boycott. In fact, on a personal level, these non-financial aspects of a boycott are probably much more effective, as they cannot be explained away by phrases like "whims of the market," nor erased by a bank loan. It is clearly not a cash-flow problem if you don't get mail and your neighbors ignore you.

It is true that boycott targets are most often corporations or the products of corporations. Targets may also be unsupportable arms of the government, although this type of boycott is a bit more difficult to strategize, as governmental support runs from tax paying to voting, which cannot be broken down into line items (making governmental support something of an all-or-nothing proposition). Boycotts can, therefore, be organized against three different targets: a company's product, method of production, or type of packaging; an entire company whose base practices or policies are offensive; and a government that is involved in objectionable practices. Withholding financial support—by refusing to buy certain products—is

important, certainly. That is the fiscal message the media can embrace and disseminate. Yet, while the loss of profit on certain products may be a contributing factor in a company's or government's decision to eventually change their methods, a boycott will enlist more backers and work more quickly if non-financial aspects of support are withheld, too. In fact, finding creative ways to withdraw such support and articulate its absence will be the ultimate point of this essay.

The problem for most people is that the issue of financial support must be considered fully. Reverend Billy's decision to allow a national music megastore chain to offer his product as one of several profit-making ventures for the company doesn't register with our call for a total absence of fiscal support; nor his regular repetition of the names of specific stores. These glitches in his message means that he has failed to note (or is choosing to ignore) the secondary financial and non-financial support lent, complicitly, to corporations. Therefore he is, perhaps accidentally, continuing to support them.

The message that Reverend Billy Talen and the Church of Stop Shopping preach is different from what is found in magazine advertisements, on billboards, in TV commercials, and on radio spots—but it's not that different. "Stop shopping (but if you need to buy something, purchase anti-consumerist propaganda)" is a new flavor of, "Buy this."[2] The structure of the message is basically the same, the players the same, the dialogue the same, the audience the same. It is no great leap to believe the message might ultimately be read the same as well.

"A Natural Response to a Mediated World"

Culture jamming, the process by which individuals revolt against the appearance of corporate interests in public space, is one of this decade's most fashionable activist trends. Methods range from the alteration of existing ads ("adbusting"[3]) to the organization of public-space reclamation parties; from the airing of TV "subvertisements"[4] to the performance of "cultural interventions."[5] Culture

Portions of this essay have been excerpted from an upcoming book called *Unmarketable*, due from The New Press in Spring 2007. Sections also appeared in *LiP* (Summer, 2004) and *Punk Planet* #69 (September/October, 2005).

***

1. Staff reporter, "'Shopocalypse' Coming?" *Redeye*. 9 December, 2005.

2. I worked for a short time at a newsstand in Seattle, and on one Buy Nothing Day was surprised to find a man in front of me about to purchase an *Adbusters* magazine. "You know it's Buy Nothing Day?" I asked him. It appeared to be all he was purchasing, and I thought I would suggest I hold his purchase for tomorrow. "Yes," he told me humorously. "But I think they would forgive me."

3. A combination of "advertisement" and, well, "busting" that describes a simplistic manipulation of existing corporate or governmental propaganda. It's a practice that's been around for decades, although it's unclear when the term was invented. Certainly, it's now branded and essentially owned by Kalle Lasn, who named his magazine for it.

4. Also popularized by Kalle Lasn, this combination of "subversion" and "advertising" describes a specific type of parodic "adbusting." To some degree, both of these terms go to show you how much you can control the debate if you're making up all the words with which to have it.

5. While on a global scale, this term generally refers to a some sort of forced imperialist conformity, when used in culture jamming circles it refers more to the situations supposedly created by adbusting: in other words, the situationist *detournement*.

6. Kalle Lasn, *Culture Jam*. (New York: Harper, 2000).

7. *Sonic Outlaws*, Other Cinema DVD. 1995–2005.

8. A musical genre consisting of the combination of the parts of more than one song. Generally, to create a successful mash-up, all original songs will be extremely popular and still recognizable, making them highly objectionable to strict defenders of intellectual property rights.

9. All McLeod quotations, unless otherwise noted, were taken from author interviews.

jammers claim to be changing the world already. Unfortunately, they're just promoting a different kind of consumption—and forging the way for a new kind of marketing.

Although this supposedly new activism has been popularized by Kalle Lasn, publisher of the magazine *Adbusters* and author of the book *Culture Jam,* it was art-noise band Negativland that originally coined the term "culture jamming" over two decades ago, when they titled an album with that phrase in 1984.[6] Before that, the same basic process had existed for decades under the names "collage," "graffiti," or "vandalism." (The term used depended entirely on how much you favored the resulting work, now an unintended collaboration.) Culture jamming as invented by Negativland, however, added an aural aspect to traditional collage work, which the artists attributed to the increased social reliance on television, radio, and film for entertainment and information. At its best, culture jamming is vandalism of mass media. In the 1995 Craig Baldwin film *Sonic Outlaws*, founding Negativland member Mark Hosler describes the process as a "totally natural response to growing up in a mediated world."[7]

Since then, popular culture jams have been perpetrated on high end clothing companies (such as the "skulling" of ads or the slight reworking of a name, i.e. "Calvin Klone"), major cigarette brands ("Joe Chemo"), fast food (the switch of part of their names with the word "murder") and several other widely recognized brands. Clever and hilarious reworked ads have captured the attention of a generation of liberals—including some keen entrepreneurs who have placed these images on T-shirts and postcards, making a buck from anti-corporate sentiment and underscoring the fashionable nature of such methods of cultural production.

It may be true that culture jamming at its most popular is not always culture jamming at its best. Yet it is also true that our public streets have been reclaimed, our culture intervened upon, and our consciousness repeatedly raised by antimarketing subvertising. And still, the widespread use of culture jamming doesn't seem to have prohibited corporate creep. In fact, we're being offered a whole new brand of activism to buy into. But we're accumulating no evidence that the product we're being sold even works.

Playing Fair

At the back of the mind of any budding culture jammer lie a few nagging legal concerns, and we'd best dispense with them before moving on to our more tactical ones. Because the question to be posed in the remainder of this essay is not: do artists, activists, and other cultural producers deserve the legal right to use all available images, sounds, objects, and experiences found in our culture? They—we—clearly do. The images and sounds we have grown up with are a part of our very brains—some more than others—and parcelling out space there that cannot be reused because it belongs to a popular clothing manufacturer, the creator of a video game system, or the ubiquitous producer of licensed children's products is a very ridiculous notion. Rather, the question posed here is: should we use all available images, sounds, objects, and experiences found in our culture? Or is culture jamming not worth the necessary reproduction of those aspects of our culture against which we revolt?

In other words, to get at the issue of what we want to portray in culture, it will be necessary to first make clear what is legally allowable to be portrayed in culture, and by whom. This is trickier than it would appear: the actual, on-the-books, legal limits of image reuse are widely misunderstood and misinterpreted. Even for those of us who work on the very fringes of culture, corporate influence has created an environment wherein it's become very difficult to remember exactly what is and is not legally actionable.

For example, it took a cease-and-desist letter (C&D) from a multinational record company for Kembrew McLeod, author of the book *Freedom of Expression*® (and the owner of the trademark on that phrase) to pin down how our intellectual-property policing system operates. He received it on Grey Tuesday—February 24, 2004. That day, copyright activists, McLeod included, had chosen to make DJ Danger Mouse's corporate-kiboshed *Grey*

Album, a mash-up of the Beatle's *White Album* and Jay-Z's *Black Album*, available for download on their websites.[8] The C&D contained a take-down demand and threats of swift, but painful legal battles. The author and copyright activists' actions might have been permissible under the fair use clause of the Copyright Act, but the letter contained no acknowledgement of this. The purpose of the C&D isn't to provide information; "The purpose is to scare people," McLeod says bluntly.[9] And it works.

"My first reaction was what a lot of people have, which was 'Oh, shit.'" McLeod says. Then he was hit with a thrill. "My second reaction was, 'Oh cool!'" he continues. But after a few moments of reflection on the time and energy a lawsuit takes—and on his new mortgage—the thrill passed. "There's nothing really exciting or sexy about [being threatened with a lawsuit], except that [the corporation] has taken the time to send a letter from their legal department."

While McLeod's initial fear is understandable, so too is his thrill at the C&D (which, by the way, he ignored). For a while a new artistic martyrhood seemed to be on the rise: receiving lawsuit threats in pursuit of creative expression was sexy and cool. C&Ds were an official register of complaints against The Man— as received by His legal department. However, the rapid accumulation of several high-profile cases against copyright transgressors including Jeff Koons,[10] the Girl Scouts,[11] and Napster downloaders[12] have put in motion a chilling effect throughout cultural production communities. Many artists now react to such well-publicized copyright scuffles with a complete avoidance of all things brand-specific and corporate-owned, which leaves beloved defenses like the fair use statute under-utilized and wasting away to valueless.

The Copyright Act of 1976 grants, under certain conditions, the publishing rights over a work of art to the creator, but it has always had limits. The original limits included both the fair use doctrine as well as a year, calculated from the author's death, into which works would enter the public domain. In theory, copyright is meant to protect the author of an original work. In practice, it has been rewritten to protect corporate licenses from comment and abuse by contemporary artists, mostly by a change to the date a work can enter the public domain.

Fair use, as defined by Nolo, respected publishers of D-I-Y legal guidebooks of all kinds, "authorizes the use of copyrighted materials for certain purposes without the copyright owner's permission. Generally, uses intended to further scholarship, education, or an informed public are considered fair use."[13] While it may be forgotten about, fair use still exists on the rulebooks. It remains an important part of the Copyright Act of 1976, which attempted to allow for the fact that releasing any product into the world necessarily gives that product a life of its own—one that can never be fully controlled, no matter how many lawyers are on your team. And, despite the climate of fear artists seem to operate in, the law continues to support the existence of fair use. McLeod writes in *Freedom of Expression*®, "in drafting and interpreting copyright laws, the Supreme Court, lower courts, and Congress...have consistently acknowledged that if we make some things totally off limits for comment, we undermine the founding principles of democracy."[14]

The point is that those original limits to absolute, permanent creative control were always considered a necessary part of authorial protection. The trick in reclaiming certain images from corporate control lies in publicizing exactly what those limits are. And since the issue of public domain seems to be left up to the courts, the potential for

10. Koons lost an extremely high-profile copyright infringement lawsuit when he admitted to using a black-and-white postcard image as the sole basis for a wooden sculpture called "String of Puppies," which he commissioned, painted brightly, and then sold three copies of.

11. In 1996, the American Society of Composers, Authors and Publishers (ASCAP) tried to collect royalties from the Girl Scouts for each time they sang "Puff the Magic Dragon" and "This Land is Your Land." Public outrage caused ASCAP to back down, but charges the group a nominal fee of $1 per year to perform the songs.

12. The feeding frenzy on Napster downloaders was initiated in 2000 when heavy-metal band Metallica decided to sue Yale, Indiana University, and the University of Southern California for allowing their fans to copy Metallica songs using Napster software. Shortly thereafter, A&M, Geffen, Sony, and others successfully sued Napster directly, which quickly forced the company to reconfigure itself as a legitimate enterprise. Strangely, several companies took out ads starring the innocent-looking children they'd "caught red-handed" and sued, probably as a warning to other potential downloaders (that practice still, obviously, thrives) but also in a weird and mean-spirited display of aggression toward youth and innovation.

13. See www.nolo.com. Often, although not always, scholarship and education are not seen to be present when commercial interests are represented. Meaning that if you are selling the work to which you feel the fair use statute applies, it will be difficult to argue for—although not impossible.

14. Kembrew McLeod, *Freedom of Expression*®. (New York: Doubleday, 2005).

15. McLaren's comments here were obtained in an author interview.

currently working artists seems to exist mainly in publicly exploiting the fair-use statute.

Brooklyn-based curator of the Illegal Art exhibition and *Stay Free!* editor Carrie McLaren agrees. "There is value to leveraging publicity against corporations who threaten artists over copyright claims," she says.[15] It's served her fairly well: her Illegal Art exhibition, which collects and highlights some recent visual art-based copyfights, has garnered quite a bit of (well-deserved) attention.[16]

It's a tactic rooted in art history. The radical group of cartoonists called the Air Pirates used it in 1970 when they created a comic book satire of a famous mouse couple and then dropped off copies at a board meeting of the corporation that owns these licensed characters. (They also listed their phone number and address in the yellow pages under "Air Pirates Secret Hideout" and then waited, for four months, until police tracked them down through less efficient methods.[17])

The logic of the C&D is clear. Corporations want to avoid expensive legal entanglements, just as much as Kembrew McLeod did. They'd certainly hate to lose an important case, an ever-increasing possibility as awareness grows of the vitality of the fair use statute. Just see the verdict against Mattel in favor of artist Tom Forsythe for proof: when the toy giant sued him for his popular Food Chain Barbie series of photographs, Mattel not only lost its 2004 case, but was also charged with fees and costs for, in the court's own words, "improper litigation tactics." The case was even called "objectively unreasonable" and "frivolous."[18] Had Mattel succeeded in scaring Forsythe into withholding his work from public view with a C&D, they could have saved themselves some money—and humiliation.

In fact, as the Air Pirates showed over three decades ago, deliberately calling for a lawsuit—incorporating copyrighted material into one's work as well as the publicity that could surround its discovery—is an established strategy in cultural production. It's served Negativland particularly well, ever since they caved in to Island Records' demand to pull their *U2* album from store shelves in 1992 for copyright infringement. The publicity surrounding that dispute allowed them the iconoclastic status to intervene on, and publicize, others'

disputes since—including Grey Tuesday. Their latest release *No Business*, in fact, practically begs for legal action: it's fully culled from entire, listener-recognizable sources from high-profile former litigants in copyright cases and comes with a 12,000-word essay defending the work as fair use.[19]

The need for cultural creatives to be reminded of the potential applications for fair use has recently been investigated by the Free Expression Policy Project (FEPP) of the Brennan Center for Justice at NYU School of Law. Marjorie Heins collected stories from cultural producers about the chilling effects of C&Ds in preparation for an FEPP report on the vitality of the fair use defense. "The purpose of the report," she tells me, "is to describe the copyright/trademark/fair use situation through some statistical analysis and lots of examples of conflicts between the 'intellectual property' claims of copyright and trademark owners and the free-expression or fair use rights of artists, scholars, and others who contribute to the culture."[20]

In truth, I stumbled upon these issues through the natural course of my own work. I was asked to interview with Heins for the report regarding my experience with copyright infringement issues. Following a project I had completed that criticized the American Girl series, I found myself so overly concerned about copyright infringement lawsuits— the only questionably ille-

16. Although it's been dormant for a few years, the exhibition will be back on the road in 2006. Check online at www.illegal-art.org.

17. Bob Levin, "The Pirate and the Mouse." *The Comics Journal* #238 and #239.

18. Find it online at www.aclu.org.

19. Not to be confused with their self-published book, *Fair Use: The Story of the Letter U and the Numeral 2.* This section on fair use originally appeared in *Punk Planet* and featured the work of a young Chicago artist named Chris Reilly, who collaged photographs together that he had collected through Google's image search function, and then emailed the copyright holders informing them of his right to use their work under the fair use statute. While many aspects of Reilly's project merit further discussion, his actual art work just isn't very interesting. In fact, he himself seemed to be using the works exclusively to promote his own name as an artist. Fundamentally, I don't feel there is anything wrong with promoting one's own work, but in an essay in which I am tracing back the tendrils of corporate promotion and discussing the inability of activists to shift the message of promotion when the message is the name, I became increasingly uncomfortable with re-forwarding Reilly's work—just as I did with the corporations I also discuss here. Their names, however, I prefer not to forward even in footnote, if possible.

20. Marjorie Heins's quotes are from author interviews prior to the publication of the report.

21. *In These Times*, for example, ran a version of an essay I wrote that described the intervention in their November 2004 issue. I refused to allow them to run the images, and instead of running my versions, they ran illustrations of the actual cards American Girl Place distributes freely in its stores. While this alleviated my concerns about follow-up action from American Girl's owner Mattel, it created the very odd situation I'm attempting to argue against throughout this essay: that it provided an actual, straightforward advertisement for a product I feel strongly should not be supported.

gal aspect to what I was doing—that I withheld the visual aspects of my project from appearing in certain contexts—thus invalidating the entire criticism for certain audiences, and keeping my criticism of the toy giant from appearing at all in certain venues.[21] I no longer withhold this work and now make it freely available and downloadable on my website, but I only felt safe in doing so after several discussions with Heins. (And after reading the Forsythe verdict.)

Artists, in other words—and I count myself among them—allow big copyfights to effectively curtail cultural criticism. I'm not, by far, the only one who has done so. Other artists have had remarkably similar experiences. In fact, as a preliminary report by Heins and Tricia Beckles on the FEPP website describes, "most disagreements don't get decided in court. Instead, copyright owners...send threatening 'cease and desist' letters to those they think are violating their copyright or trademarks. Needless to say, these letters do not advise recipients that their borrowing might be fair use."[22] In some cases, cultural producers cave to C&Ds even when the fair use statute can clearly be applied.

Heins and Beckles further find that recipients of C&Ds don't always possess an accurate understanding of the potential for a fair use defense—and even if they do, an accurate understanding of the law doesn't necessarily give them the courage to refuse to comply with the C&D sender's demands. Equally problematic is that under the Digital Millennium Copyright Act (DMCA), distributors and hosts of questionable material, like Internet service providers or search engines, can be held liable for copyright infringements if they fail to immediately comply with any take-down letters they may receive. Which means that the chilling ripple effects of lawsuit threats has also begun to influence the means of distribution for cultural products.

All of which leads to the strange situation we find ourselves in now—and that I've found myself in, personally. As intelligent, knowledgeable cultural producers, we may understand that, according to the letter of the law, we retain the right to parody, teach, or criticize the intellectual property of others. Yet we also understand that defending those rights takes more dedication, knowledge, money, and time than most of us have to work with. To many cultural creatives, it seems a waste of time to engage in copyright issues at all. So brash and irreverent takes on copyright issues—as that undertaken so blatantly by artists from the Air Pirates to Tom Forsythe and Negativland—may be the only ones we have left, until our right to reuse the language of our culture is secured.

And yet, demanding our right to use certain materials just because we want to, will only get activists so far. It is true that these images, logos, phrases, and ideas are now elements of our language: the corporations that put them into the world have no legal or moral right to control every aspect of their use. If we need a visual shorthand to communicate "oil," for example, we have several to choose from. While we could choose oil towers or barrels, however, we often fall back on easily recognized logos. Yet because corporate interests have commandeered aspects of our language, our communications, and our way of thinking about and describing the world, are we beholden to reclaim them? To reuse them? To accept the world as they describe it? Why would we want to?

Marketing the Antimarketing Movement

Naomi Klein presents an excellent description of the ethos of culture jamming as "go-for-the-corporate-jugular"[23] in *No Logo*, although she stops short of noting that the "jugulars" of corporations are not advertisements, brand names, commercials, or representations: the targets of culture jamming. She therefore fails to note an inherent irony to the practice: that the lifeblood of corporations is finan-

22. Located online at www.fepproject.org.

23. Naomi Klein, *No Logo*. (New York: Picador, 2002), 287.

24. Ibid.

25. Located online at www.anti-marketing.com.

26. This isn't so much an argument about incidents of hypocrisy, as Joseph Heath and Andrew Potter make in their snarky, yet insightful *Nation of Rebels*. It is, like our discussion of Reverend Billy and the Church of Stop Shopping, a reminder that failing to properly acknowledge our capitalist environment in your anti-capitalist work can lead to trouble.

27. Marketers, fortunately, have begun to move on. While strategies such as corporate-sponsored graffiti and *faux* spray-painted billboards peak, underground- and buzz-marketing has now become most desirable. Read more in a *Punk Planet* piece from November/December 2005 called "Black Market."

28. Online at www.guerillamedia.net.

29. Ibid.

cial profit, and financial profit comes from name recognition—the same currency trafficked in by culture jammers.

It is for this reason that activists have been voicing a secret fear that something about culture jamming doesn't work. Perhaps it is simply that the very popularity of culture jamming undermines its efficacy. The North American public, Naomi Klein writes elsewhere in *No Logo*, "delights to see the icons of corporate power subverted and mocked. There is, in short, a market for it."[24] A market is identified by an interest on the part of a certain demographic to spend money on certain goods. Cleverly, Klein here is acknowledging a market for antimarketing.

This might be funnier were there not already in existence a corporation that, in effect, already pre-co-opted antimarketing by naming themselves Anti-Marketing. The stated philosophy of this corporation could have appeared first in *Adbusters*: "If traditional marketing is lying, then antimarketing is telling the truth."[25] The mission of Anti-Marketing, which company will gladly offer its services to "help you enter the New Age of Marketing," is stated in the form of a non-rhyming poem, excerpted here:

People are becoming smarter.
They don't like to be deceived, or have their intelligence insulted...
People either ignore ads, or become annoyed by them...
It's easy to get lost in the crowd.
Everyone is selling something.
You need to be different, and draw your market to you...
Rise Above Your Competition!

"Technology, Business, and Life....All as Art," the company named Anti-Marketing promises in one slogan. Even culture jammers couldn't draw out hidden messages in such marketing. There aren't any. They know marketing sucks; in fact, they are against it. The suits at Anti-Marketing have read Lasn's *Culture Jam* and taken it to heart. Probably, they don't even wear suits.

In this post-ironic age, we don't need to dwell on the irony of a marketing company devis-

ing "antimarketing" campaigns. It is apparent and predictable, given capitalism's relentless appetite for new markets.[26] The co-optation of antimarketing techniques by marketers is also a simple survival technique. Marketing specialists struggle to appeal to the same public that culture jammers work to engage in their individual activist goals. Marketers have taught jammers some important new lessons, as jammers have done for marketing teams. The relentless consumption of new capitalist strategies into new capitalist endeavors simply must not surprise us anymore.

But what should continue to surprise us is our complacency. New marketing methods vary as widely as culture jamming techniques for good reason: both marketing and antimarketing work from exactly the same principles.[27] Much of what we call culture jamming achieves the same effect as traditional marketing. It's just being done by activists—for a fraction of the cost to corporate beneficiaries. Perhaps more startlingly, we're doing it ourselves.

Parody and Satire

At the heart of the failure to recognize the inability of culture jamming to institute social change seems to be a confusion on the part of activists over the differences between parody and politics. Consider the mission statement of one culture-jamming group, Guerilla Media: "Using satire as our main political tool, we primarily create and widely distribute parodies of daily newspapers, and government and corporate promotional materials."[28] Their projects have included "actions" on NAFTA, welfare reform, cuts to social programming, and environmental concerns. "We use humor as a means to expose powerful interests," the group's website states.[29]

Yet humor is not action. While the creation and dissemination of a newspaper of any kind, whether parodic in intent or not, is a difficult feat, humor can just as often be used to quell dissent as voice it. This has been demonstrated by David Letterman on a nightly basis, who pokes fun at the defense contractor who owns his network, but does not go so far as to criticize it. While satire can be a useful tool when properly applied, claiming that parodies of government documents expose powerful interests is akin to proclaiming that *The Simpsons* brought down television. Somehow, somewhere, we are confusing jokes with change.

It is a difficult misunderstanding to locate, as there are others that block its detection. Many cultural producers confuse parody and satire in the first place, the former being a mere imitation of a subject, while the latter is an imitation of a subject intended to amuse and point out folly. (And it should be clear that "pointing out folly" itself does not always—or even usually—incite action.) Parody and satire are used interchangeably, however, as both imitate subjects primarily for comic effect.

Adbusting, subverting, and many other activities employed by culture jammers, whether satiric or parodic are, at heart, reproductive. And this is where the methods of culture jamming begin to fail. Because a meaningful change to a system will not come about if it recreates the current system (even if, once recreated, it is more amusing).

The reproduction of that which culture jammers aim to unseat lies very deep within the strategies used. Lasn's discussion of memes in *Culture Jam* will provide us with only one example. Memes are bits of information (a catchphrase is an example he gives in his book) that compete against each other for popularity. They are a marketing tool, but they are also a natural occurrence, a thing that just seems to catch on and gain popularity, like certain toys, phrases, or Internet jokes. The most popular memes infect and shape our understanding of society in crucial ways. "Just Do It," is a meme put forth by an athletic clothing manufacturer, while "Just Stop It," is another put forth by the anti-sweatshop movement.

Such strategies are at the heart of culture jamming. Come the revolution, or as he calls it in *Culture Jam*, "World War III," Lasn suggests we "build our own meme factory, put out a better product and beat them at their own game."[30] Not far buried beneath the surface of Lasn's suggestion is the assumption that "beating them at their own game" means accepting the rules, the playing field, and the score-keeping system as they are presented to us. Lasn urges us to win a war we claim we never wanted to enter.

So, parody and satire, used to fight the meme war or as strategies in their own right, rely on representing the very subjects ridiculed. Culture jamming, adbusting, and parody in general, not only reassert the icons they half-heartedly attempt to dismantle, they encourage their continued survival. David Letterman, for example, is not a threat to his network nor the megacorporation that owns it. He is, in fact, their property. Losing his good-natured jibes, which do point, after all, to the obscene wrongness inherent in a corporation that makes a great deal of its money from defense contracts owning and operating a network of news and entertainment media, would harm both his owners and Letterman. Neither, surely wishes that. And Reverend Billy and the Church of Stop Shopping need shopping to continue—whether of Billy's products or a national coffeeshop chain's—to stay relevant. Or in other words, Larissa MacFarquhar writes in an extended criticism of Michael Moore's work in *The New Yorker*, "Satire doesn't unseat conventions; it reinforces them."[31]

Representational Politics

However, the reliance of parody and satire—and therefore culture jamming—on representation is highly problematic. The problem with representational politics is that one is always playing catch-up to new, improved representations. Sure, it was a problem that African Americans weren't, for a long time, depicted in ads experiencing many of the pleasures of everyday life, but now we have an even bigger problem: African Americans are being marketed to as heavily as anyone else (although, ridiculously,

30. Lasn, 124.

31. *New Yorker,* February 16 & 23 2004.

32. The sound artist who created *Plunderphonics*, an album made entirely of appropriated sound, and who works frequently in borrowed music.

33. A not-for-profit organization that offers more flexible alternatives to copyright law. This interview is located online at http://www.creativecommons.org/getcontent/features/rick.

34. It's true; it's the same image used on the cover of the first English edition of Guy Debord's *Society of the Spectacle*, the Situationists' most famous text. Black & Red, the anarchist publishers of this edition, of course stole the image.

35. Klein, 288.

36. Lasn, 123.

37 Peggy Phelan, *Unmarked*. (New York: Routledge, 1993), 11.

38. For the story behind this, see Zoneil Maharaj' interview with Riley at: http://www.alternet.org/wiretap/33867.

not always by the same companies). Gay life, a secret hidden in families for so many generations, now has the happy occurrence of *The "L" Word* and *Queer Eye for the Straight Guy* to prove the viability of the so-called lifestyle choice. Has the increased representation of gay people really improved tolerance in American culture or has the sinister force of capitalism simply popped up anew? Has it just become easier to market "black cigarettes" and "queer dairy products?" In other words, has the existence of anti-marketing just made it easier to market?

Demanding better representation is a never-ending struggle, which can conceivably only be brought about by a series of committees deciding how best their demographics should be presented. Accuracy, too, will present a similar problem, if we aim for ads or marketing that addresses our real, actual needs more directly. And this is the game we have been tricked into playing, the World War III that Lasn urges us to engage in so that we may win: better and more accurate representations of our lives and our culture can—and will—always be provided by a culture intent on production and consumption. More important, a culture intent on production and consumption produces representations—reproduces—in order to inspire further production and consumption. And if we take it into our own hands to shift the messages of advertising and marketing to more accurately depict society, we are merely playing into the hands of a cultural mechanism intent on furthering production and consumption. We are creating, for advertisers and marketers, the memes they will pillage and disseminate to spread their own messages.

Perhaps, for those of us whose ultimate aim is to decrease production and consumption, activists should start thinking about whether or not we want to participate in representation at all.

The Master's Tools

What we need to keep in mind when considering engaging in representational politics is that the rules, playing field, and scorekeeping system are already in place, as Lasn indicated: we just have to question whether or not we want to play that game. Consumers do not approach advertising or subvertising, that subset of advertising, expecting to be challenged. They expect to be marketed to. And they will receive even non-standard messaging in the way they have been trained to receive all messages, as an urge to consume. Projects such as Lasn's meme factory fulfill standard marketing expectations as well.

Participating in this system, however, instead of eliminating it, is a problem we can leave to address later. First we must turn to the insurmountable realization that re-using corporate-created images, logos, phrases, and ideas represents (and re-presents) those very images, logos, phrases, and ideas. Again.

In other words, even the most sophisticated billboard alteration in the world—those more intricate projects by Ron English or the Billboard Liberation Front that work from existing advertising messages to turn the intended message upside down—still provides product placement. It must, for that was both the subject of the intended message as well as the subject of the new, more accurate, activist message. Changing a pro-smoking cartoon character into a cancer-ridden one may shift the message from "smoking is good" to "smoking is bad," but there is still a message being conveyed about smoking. Which most health experts agree is something we can all pretty much live perfectly well without.

Moreover, with the recent, very smart move toward self-parody in advertising, marketers and the natural course of our cultural development have created a system that allows consumers to perceive an extremely high degree of negative messaging as straightforward advertising. This system is described in *Sonic Outlaws* by composer John Oswald, who explains that a work that mimics or quotes a known original "doesn't necessarily degrade or devalue the original. In cases of people like James Brown, it actually is of great advertising value to the original."[32] That is, when certain mimicked figures or products have achieved a certain status, parody no longer affects them negatively. The consumer retains the potential to read even parodied ads as legitimate advertising.

Rick Prelinger describes this very scenario on a larger scale in an interview with Creative Commons.[33] When he asked an associate at Time-

Life what the highest revenue-producing image they owned was, she indicated the ubiquitous image of the movie-theater crowd wearing 3-D glasses.[34] "You know this famous image," Prelinger tells Creative Commons. "It's kind of emblematic of the fifties. [Time-Life] makes a great deal of money selling that image...it's also pirated. It's been shot over and over again by people. People have set up people in theaters and then shot it on film, so they have a movie version of it. Repetition and ubiquity haven't lessened the value of that image: they've increased it... Ubiquity equals value." That's right. We've just described a popular aspect of contemporary activism as being, in John Oswald's words, "of great advertising value to the original."

The Master's House

In the worst-case scenario, culture jamming dismantles the master's house with the master's tools, and then provides the master with blueprints for a better house and better tools. This can be seen when tracing back the last few decades of marketing strategies, although it should be clear by now that this formula does not apply exclusively to corporate interests. Governmental propaganda, as well, has incorporated its own dissenting voices—politicians now place themselves regularly, and happily, on nighttime talk-show hosts' couches—from *Late Night* to *The Daily Show*—knowing that if they appear to be laughing at themselves, opposition will be somewhat muted.

Let's recap: Corporate and government follies happen; culture warriors mock them. Government and corporate officials see the value in the placement of their work, however ironically, before a new, ironic audience. The targets of this work allow such mocking to continue unabated, even adopting similar marketing methods themselves. Soon, ads come along pre-culture-jammed, already graffitied with a "subversive" message in Spraypaint™ font. As Klein notes in *No Logo*, "ads co-opt out of reflex—they do so because consuming is what consumer culture does."[35]

Culture jamming, or, more specifically, its definition as a political tool, has created an immediately co-optable antimarketing strategy that activists can no longer make effective use of. As a method of political action, culture jamming, because of its central reliance on parody and satire as politically effective strategies, has already failed. That is, because it reproduces the exact messages it claims to want to upend, culture jamming is necessarily ineffective.

All acts of representation ultimately fail as political tools because, in agreeing to use them, activists limit themselves to a pre-established set of symbols, each containing within it the very consumerist messages they work to combat. This is true on the small scale as well as the large. *Adbusters*' "Black Dot" campaign for example, in which logos are scribbled out with a black marker, doesn't eliminate the logo from the viewer's sight. By leaving the rest of the ad intact, in fact, visual theorists would argue that a partially covered image creates a compelling void in the visual plane that a viewer's mind struggles to fill with the appropriate, familiar logo. Which, of course, ultimately creates a situation where our brains are working that much harder to do the work of advertising for us. Yet Lasn's answer is to fight memes with more memes: "Whoever has the memes has the power," Lasn asserts with a meme of his own in *Culture Jam*.[36] But culture jamming never gets at the heart of the meme problem, which is that we are trained to use memes as pure, unreproachable information.

The co-optation of anti-advertising can't be quelled by bigger and better anti-ads, and it can't be stopped by mocking, parodying, or even becoming the media in the way that popular notions of culture jamming seem to suggest. If we can inspire genuinely critical responses to consumer culture, we might hope to end the representation of brands and the dogmas they stand for entirely. Then, while the playing field will be far from level, at least we'll have space in our brains to conceive of something that is unbranded, unrepresented, and uncontrolled.

Control, after all, is the central issue in matters of social justice, as well as in matters of free expression. The difference between control by Burger King and control by *Adbusters* seems negligible when you'd prefer to remain uncontrolled.

Politics Without Representation

Faults aside, culture jamming and adbusting, parody and satire have proven vital to our growth as political activists. The demand for and creation of improved representations have acted as developmental stages in the process of becoming critically engaged with our media. I would argue, however, that culture jamming and adbusting, parody and satire are not entirely useless. They are basic, reactionary acts that should be used to explore strategies, define targets, and play with materials. I am also not arguing that people stop culture jamming: I think more people should culture jam, and more often. Reacting in public space to public messages should be, as Mark Hosler described, a natural response to our mediated world. Culture jamming is simply not the useful tool for political change we believe it to be when we subscribe to it.

In other words, we cannot allow subvertising to be the end stage of our activist development. In the struggle to eliminate outmoded laws detailing what images can and cannot be re-used, parody, satire, and representation all continue to be important. We must retain the legal right to use the visual language of our culture whenever we wish to communicate, but we should not let that same, outmoded legal system dictate the bounds of what we say.

To conclude, I want to talk about two examples that start to articulate alternatives to the largely bankrupted culture jamming. First, struggling to right representational wrongs and depict—however fleetingly—the unacknowledged, Peggy Phelan writes in the great but largely unread political treatise *Unmarked: the Politics of Performance* that all representational works of art "are compatible with capitalism's relentless appetite for new markets."[37] For an audience of performance artists, Phelan attempts to locate and articulate the power in the unnoticed, the imperceptible, the unrevealed.

It's a difficult tactic to attempt to envision for the political realm, although the multimedia strategies of ACT UP in the mid-1990s come immediately to mind. A fully enacted boycott, in which financial, community-based, emotional, and all other aspects of support for an act of social injustice are withheld begins to give us clues as to how to formulate such an activist project.

And finally, the most brilliant example of this I have come across was Stetson Kennedy's infiltration of the Ku Klux Klan in the 1940s. A dedicated antiracist activist, Stetson went undercover in the Klan and, for a time, simply collected their secrets. When the authorities refused to act upon his information, Kennedy decided to approach the media. Not newspapers though: Kennedy went to the far more popular and universally beloved *Superman* radio program, and asked the producers to work the secrets of the Klan into their show. Klan members, regular listeners all, heard Superman expose their codes, hideout, and secret knock, all in this fictional radio fight with the Klan. Kennedy, who attended the Klan discussion, heard it all. And, when they changed all their passwords and secret handshakes, he heard that too. The next week, the *Superman* show reported it all. Shortly thereafter, that particular group disbanded—and, having been fictionalized and presented as pure children's entertainment, new Klan membership soon dropped to zero.

The important thing to keep in mind when considering this model, is that Kennedy's objectives were met without directly mocking the Klan. Their secrets, their proprietary membership information, was simply placed in an unusual and surprising context. They were given no weight as "factual"—in fact, they were relayed in the fantastical setting inhabited by 1940s superheroes—and did not—could not—visually represent the Klan's racist beliefs (which are, after all, based on visual difference).

Contemporary activists may wish to consider such strategies, and explore new or abandoned media for their work. Internet parodies and billboard alterations may be all the rage, but the denouncement is hollow. Pick, as poet Jessica Care Moore told hip-hop MC Boots Riley, a bigger weapon.[38] A plethora of social justice issues are rooted in the concerns of unacknowledged populations, dangers, and relationships. Articulating the unacknowledged in an artful, clever way doesn't have to include a play on the logo of a multinational corporation.

REAPPROPRIATE THE IMAGINATION!

CINDY MILSTEIN

United Victorian Workers, *Victorian Stroll* (public intervention), Troy, NY, 2005. Photo: Amy Scarfone.

An art exhibit, albeit a small one, is always housed in the bathroom of a coffeehouse in my town. A recent display featured cardboard and paper haphazardly glued together, and adorned with the stenciled or hand-lettered words of classical anarchists such as Mikhail Bakunin and Errico Malatesta. The artist's statement proclaimed, "I am not an artist." The show offered only "cheap art," with pieces priced at a few dollars. Undoubtedly the materials came from recycling bins or trash cans, and perhaps this artist-who-is-not-an-artist choose to look the quotes up in "low-tech" zines.

There is something heartwarming about finding anarchist slogans in the most unexpected of places. So much of the time, the principles that we anarchists hold dear are contradicted at every turn, never discussed, or just plain invisible. And thus seeing some antiquated anarchist writings scribbled on makeshift canvases in a public place, even a rest-room, raised a smile of recognition.

But only for a moment—then despair set in. Why is anarchist art so often a parody of itself, pre-dictable and uninteresting? Sure, everyone is capable of doing art, but that doesn't mean that everyone is an artist. And yet it is generally perceived as wrong in anarchist circles that some people are or want to be artists, and others of us aren't or don't want to be. Beyond the issue of who makes works of art, why can't art made by anti-authoritarians be provoca-tive, thoughtful, innovative—and even composed of materials that can't be found in a dumpster? More to the point, why do or should anarchists make art at all

today? And what would we want art to be in the more egalitarian, non-hierarchical societies we dream of?

This I know: an anarchist aesthetic should never be boxed in by a cardboard imagination.

Pointing Beyond the Present

The name of one radical puppetry collective, Art and Revolution, aptly captures the dilemma faced by contemporary anarchist artists. It simultaneously affirms that art can be political and that revolution should include beauty. Yet it also underscores the fine line between art as social critique and art as propaganda tool. Moreover, it obscures the question of an anarchist aesthetic outside various acts of rebellion. It is perhaps no coincidence at all, then, that Art and Revolution's logo design echoes the oft-quoted Bertolt Brecht contention that "art is not a mirror held up to reality, but a hammer with which to shape it"—with "ART," in this collective's case, literally depicted as the hammerhead.

Certainly, an art that self-reflectively engages with—and thus illuminates—today's many crushing injustices is more necessary than ever. An art that also manages to engender beauty against the ugliness of the current social order is one of the few ways to point beyond the present, toward some-thing that approximates a joyful existence for all.

But as capitalism intensifies its hold on social organization, not to mention our imagina-tions, efforts to turn art into an instrument of social change leave it all that much more open to simply mirroring reality, rather than contesting or offering alternatives to it. And short of achieving even the imperfect horizontal experiments of places like Buenos Aires and Chiapas, much less replacing statecraft with confederated self-governments, attempts to make art into a community-supported public good remain trapped in the private sphere, however collectively we structure our efforts. Artistic expression is fettered by the present, from commodification to insidious new forms of hierarchy, and hence creativity is as estranged from itself as we are from each other.

Such alienation isn't limited to the aesthetic arena, of course. But precisely because creative "freedom" appears to defy any logic of control—in "doing-it-yourself" (D-I-Y), one is supposedly crafting a culture that seems to be utterly of, for, and by us—it is especially seductive as a space of resistance. Our aesthetic tools should be able to help us build new societies just as much as demolish the old, but our renovations will likely be forever askew when set on an already-damaged foundation. And no matter how shoddily constructed, they will always be sold out from under us to the highest bidder. Still, we have to be able to nail down something of the possibilities ahead.

Art at its best, then, should maintain the dual character of social critic and social visionary. For the role of the critic is to judge, to discern, not simply beauty, but also truth, and the role of the utopian is to strive to implement such possible impossibilities. As Sadakichi Hartmann put it in a 1916 *Blast* article, radical artists should "carry the torn flag of beauty and liberty through the firing lines to summits far beyond the fighting crowds."[1]

This is perhaps art's greatest power, even when distorted by the present-day social order: the ability to envision the "not yet existent."

The Temporary and the Trashed

Since the 1970s, a series of interconnected phenomena loosely drawn together by the term "globalization" have transformed the world. One of these changes is the rise of "global cities" as nodes of control, and over time, this has become embodied in the designed/built aesthetic environment.[2] In *City of Quartz*, Mike Davis wrote of the "fortress effect" behind a free-market maneuver in the aftermath of the 1960s to reoccupy abandoned (read: poor because abandoned by capital, whites, and so on) downtowns. New megastructure complexes of reflective glass rose up in city centers, hiding elite decision-makers and their "upscale, pseudo-public spaces" inside.[3] Several decades later, with global capitalism seemingly triumphant, brazenly transparent architecture is replacing secretive one-way windows. Just take a peek at the revitalized Potsdamer Platz in Berlin, Germany. Corporate office-apartment buildings of see-through glass reveal lavish interior designs, and are ringed by airy public plazas featuring cheerful sculptures, artsy ecological waterways, and multimedia installations.

Since anarchists today are by and large neither city planners nor architects, nor those commissioned to produce public art, we've had to make do with temporary festivals of resistance decrying the environment that's been built to constrain the majority of humanity. Such carnivals against capitalism have succeeded in fleetingly reclaiming everything from facades to landscapes to outdoor art. And in those moments, libertarian leftists have become impromptu designers of place. The preferred artistic medium here is flexibility, with a dab of anonymity. A large stick of chalk, a homemade stencil, or strips of cloth are easily concealed, and just as easily used to transform a sidewalk, wall, or fence into a canvas. In these and many other ways, anarchist artists set up the circus tent of a playful urban renewal, bringing glimpses of the pleasure in reworking social spaces together, of integrating

1. Sadakichi Hartmann, "Art and Revolt," *The Blast* 1, no. 22 (December 1, 1916): 3; repr., *The Blast*, ed. Alexander Berkman, intro. Barry Pateman (Oakland, CA: AK Press, 2005), 181.

2. The term "global city" was first coined in Saskia Sassen, *The Global City: New York, London, Tokyo* (Princeton: Princeton University Press, 1991).

3. Mike Davis, *City of Quartz: Excavating the Future in Los Angeles* (London: Verso, 1990), 226, 229.

4. Obviously, many artists use free or discarded materials because they don't have the financial resources to buy art supplies, and hence their aesthetic can simply be chalked up to a lack of means. But also prevalent among anarchist artists is the notion that trash is valueless from the standpoint of capitalism, and so by utilizing such material, one is creating something of noncapitalist value. Or at least throwing capitalism's excess in its face as some sort of incriminating evidence. This reduces capitalism to economics, though, and ignores Karl Marx's great insight: that capital is first and foremost a social relation. Whether one uses expensive or free art supplies, the social organization behind them both remains the same. But of course, even on the level of economics, waste management is a multitrillion dollar industry, utterly dependent on recycling and garbage. So whether you take a materialist or social theory perspective, a "cheap art" aesthetic is perfectly compatible with present-day forms of domination. Today's junk can easily become—and has—tomorrow's boutique item; society's rejects (from punks to urban black youth) can become—and have—tomorrow's formula for hipster culture.

5. Contrast this to the project of anarchy *qua* primitivism, which is to somehow "forget" that we are imaginative, qualitative beings marked by our capacity for dialogue and hence reasoned actions, and instead "return" to passive receptacles foraging for our most basic needs, which seems to me exactly what capitalism and statecraft as forms of social organization strive to reduce us to. This is no digression: when we deny our very ability to think symbolically, the notion of art disappears too, not to mention us as humans along with it.

form as well as content into the everyday-made-extraordinary by creative cultural expressions.

On the other hand, when we've actually expropriated or "freed" spaces, we seem to re-create an aesthetic of deterioration in those places already destroyed by state and capital, racism and fear, almost reveling in the rubble. The degradation foisted on the poor, the marginal, and the forgotten is gleefully picked up as some sort of pirate sensibility. All too often, capitalism's trash is the blueprint for own trashed creations, as if artistic expressions modeled on a better, more visually pleasing world might just make us too comfortable to swashbuckle our way to revolution. Garbage, along with the shoplifted and the plagiarized, are all romanticized as somehow existing outside domination by anarchist artists who thoroughly inhabit a social structure (as does everyone) where the best of peoples' cultures are tossed aside, stolen, or plagiarized for profit and power.[4]

Whether conceived of as circus or chaos (or both), however, these types of civic artworks are as evanescent as the latest iPod updates; they merely frolic on built environments instead of collectively shaping them. Such artistic strategies are ultimately hollow, replicating the feeling of life under capitalism, whether one has material plenty or not. Instead of offering a challenge or a vision, both our joyful and joyless D-I-Y art ends up parroting the bipolar "choices" that most people struggle against daily: the lure of the ephemeral, unattainable spectacle, or utter rejection in the debris of its excess. And yet this reopening of social space via creativity brings with it a sense of inclusiveness, of democratic places remade and consented to by all—or at least the potentiality thereof.

Art as social critic/visionary, when doggedly and imaginatively placed in the commodified (non)commons of today, just might play its part in moving us toward a noncommodified commons: what we share and enjoy together, in the open, always subject to use by all, subject only to directly democratic structures, and always the vigilant sentry of a better and better society.

It's not that everyone needs to make art, nor should artists offer an aesthetic of revolt or a revolting aesthetic—that is, mere negation or else nihilism. That's not what makes art revolutionary. It's that everyone needs to routinely experience critical-utopian art as commons, commons as a critical-utopian art.

The Art of Value

To some degree, whether self-consciously or not, anarchists' artistic impulses get to the heart of what makes capitalism so deplorable. "Value" is determined by how much one has and can continually exchange as well as accumulate, whether in the form of money, property, or especially control over others. We anarchists, and billions of non-anarchists, know that value can never be measured by piling quantity on top of more quantity; that how we live our lives, and especially how we treat each other and the nonhuman world, is what matters.

As a political philosophy, anarchism aspires to the ongoing project of balancing individual subjectivity and social freedom—the qualitative dimensions of life—knowing that both are essential to the potentiality of the other. As a practice, anarchism engages in prefigurative politics, from forms of cooperation to institutions of direct democracy. This is what makes and keeps us human, in the most generous sense. And such a project will be forever necessary, whether within, against, or beyond capitalism.[5]

One way that anarchists attempt to reclaim

value is by carving out a cultural realm that allows everyone to participate, to be valued for what they can envision and/or create, and by redistributing the possibility of producing works of art through the use of affordable, accessible, indigenous materials. We use what's at hand, often lend a hand to whoever wants to make art, and attempt to do this in ways that are multicultural and inclusive. In isolation from the other realms of life—economics and politics, the social and the personal—and embedded within structures of domination and forms of oppression, however, the cultural effort to revalue value frequently reproduces the social system we oppose.

Examples abound here, sad to say. Puppets are among the easiest of targets, primarily because they became the poster kids for anticapitalist mobilizations. Devising a cheap and collective manner to produce artistic expressions of resistance isn't problematic per se; such creations have allowed us to prefigure a better life even as we protest present-day horrors. But when puppets all start looking alike—whether filling the streets of Seattle or Hong Kong; when they are mass-produced from the same materials, in the same manner; when they are something eco-entrepreneurs can fund to both create the appearance of grassroots protest and turn radical notions into the most liberal of demands[6]—then we are developing our own factory forms of creativity. Those we mean to empower—the everyone-as-artist—become near-assembly-line workers. So even when the production is fun or done in an edgy warehouse space, the profound recognition (of self and society) that comes from the creative act is lost. Art and the artists become unthinking, cranking out copycat rip-offs of the latest political art trend.

The distribution and consumption of such works can become equally debased. At a convergence in Windsor, Canada, to challenge free trade agreements several years ago, a prominent *puppetista* angrily insisted that thousands of anti-capitalists should pause their direct actions to watch her collective's street theater. "We're here to entertain you, and you need to stop and be entertained!"

It certainly isn't enough to make sure that more and more people are cultural producers (or consumers of free art)—the anarchist version of D-I-Y quantity piled on top of more D-I-Y quantity, somehow adding up to a new society. Indeed, "the people" making art might mean that there is no art at all, for quantity can

Corti monument, Hope Cemetery, Barre, VT, 1904. Elia Corti (1869–1903), a native of Viggiu, Italy, came to Barre in 1892. One of Barre's finest carvers, his accidental death occurred tragically at a gathering for the socialist leader Giacinto Serrati. A member of the crowd fired a pistol and Elia was fatally shot. His monument was carved by his brother and his brother-in-law. Grieving stone carvers from across Vermont helped carve the base, which includes carving tools (such as calipers, a square, and a chisel) and a palm branch (a symbol of peace). Photo courtesy of Marjorie Power/Barre Historical Society.

actually destroy quality. And without the qualitative dimension, there can be no appreciation of beauty or craft, or the self who crafted that beauty.

This Wal-Martization of resistance art—cheap, accessible, homogeneous, and everywhere—isn't the only conundrum we face. It is as hard for us, "even" as anarchists, as it is for "ordinary" people to resist the hegemonic forces at work: those dominant types of organization and ways of thinking that become naturalized, and hence almost unquestioned in a given time period. Perhaps the only bulwark against internalizing and thereby reproducing the current hegemonies we rebel against is our ability to simultaneously think critically and act imaginatively. Indeed, this is where anarchism as a political philosophy excels: in its ongoing suspicion of all phenomena as possible forms of domination, and its concurrent belief in nonhierarchical social relations and organization. This ethical impulse—to live every day as a social critic and social visionary—certainly infuses anarchist rhetoric. It also underscores all those values that anarchists generally share: mutual aid, solidarity, voluntary association, and so on. But for even the most diligent among us, acting on these ethics is much trickier than holding them in our hearts or jotting them down in a mission statement.

A British anarchist historian recently asked me for a tour of Hope Cemetery in Barre, Vermont. In Barre's heyday, at the turn of the twentieth century, socialists and anarchists worked together in the granite industry, living and dying (often and too young) as those who made tombstones. These Italian immigrants built an anarchist library and later a labor hall, established a food co-op and art school, published newspapers such as *Cronaca Sovversiva*, and hosted speakers like Big Bill Haywood, and rabble-roused. Yet, more than anything, they sculpted their communal aesthetics into the hard grey stones dotting the cemetery, a lasting commons to the good works of these radicals. "Look at the artisanal quality of each and every gravestone," to paraphrase my visitor. "This exemplifies the difference between the appeal of Marxism and anarchism back then. Factory workers could never see themselves in their work, but these stone carvers could recognize themselves in their designs; they could see their own potentiality."

Such recognition is the first step toward valuing our world, toward knowing we can self-manage the whole of our lives. But it can only come when our artisanal efforts are part of crafting a social beauty. This, in turn, can only be defined in the process of doing-it-ourselves (D-I-O), where we don't necessarily all produce art but we do all substantially participate in engaging with, debating, judging, and determining the place(s) of creative expression.[7] The qualitative would be that realm of social criticism and pleasure that comes in the full recognition of free selves within a free society.

Working at Cross-purposes

The creative act—the arduous task of seeing something other than the space of capitalism, statism, the gender binary, racism, and other rooms without a view—is the hope we can offer to the world. Such aesthetic expressions must also aim to denaturalize the present, though. And this dual "gesturing at and beyond" will only be possible if we continually interrogate this historical moment, and ask whether our artworks are working against the grain within that context.

For the pull of the culture industry is strong. No matter how subversive and cutting-edge we might remain in our creative works, global capitalism is always ready to recuperate our every innovation. Our rebellious ad-busting has become indistinguishable from advertisements employing rebellion-as-sales-pitch. For instance, just after Seattle 1999, an ad featured protesters running in their Nike sneakers from tear gas and police, with the familiar "just do it" tagline. Yet it was unclear whether this image was the brainchild of Nike or activists—and either way, it didn't matter. It sold a lifestyle; it mocked a movement.

Creative work and/or processes of collective art-making without an explicit politics that integrally and forever vigilantly incorporates critical thinking into its practice will almost necessarily, especially under the current conditions, become part of the problem. Some of this will be clear, as when our freely traded handmade patches become the inspiration for prefabricated "made-in-China" clothing in pricey boutiques. The less-obvious manifestations are more troubling: when the D-I-Y sensibility itself, so key to anarchist artistic creations, slowly but surely ingratiates itself into multiple mainstream commodities, from Home Depot's "You Can Do It" to the new Oreo kits that allow the consumer to "make" their own, with cookie tops and cream separated.

The flow, of course, doesn't simply go in one direction. As "products" of the dominant culture, we also are influenced before we ever cut a stencil or edit a video. Without constant awareness, we almost unwittingly take up the project of this society of control, with its fragmentation, insecurity, and shallow infotainment. Social isolation is mirrored by an anarchist art that asserts its anonymity, where we willingly erase our own subjectivity, and its temporariness and flexibility, where we willingly give up accountability and connectedness. The contemporary state's evisceration of human and civil rights, with its move from "the rule of law" toward "the rule of lawlessness," is reflected in an aesthetic that exalts in its own outlaw status. The art of cartography allows radicals to map out the constant fear of being watched by, in turn, surveilling others. And much of what anti-authoritarian artists produce replicates the culture of distraction that keeps people from acting and thinking for themselves—such as documen-

taries without a narrative, or screen prints that reduce social conflict to "us" versus "them."

The artist-as-social-visionary has to peer hard to separate potentiality from peril right now. As autonomist Marxist, Harry Cleaver commented in 1992 in relation to anarcho-communist Peter Kropotkin's method, "He had to seek out and identify, at every level, from the local workshop and industry to the global organization of the economy, signs of the forces of cooperation and mutual aid working at cross-purposes to the capitalist tendencies to divide all against all." Then and now, such cross-purposes are what gesture at "the future in the present," to again cite Cleaver, but discerning them isn't easy.[8]

Providing the Keys to Closed Doors

The artist-as-social-critic doesn't have to search far for subject matter these days, and yet many people seem to be "pushing against an open door," to borrow from Michael Hardt and Antonio Negri's formulation in *Empire*. That is, the social ills we're contesting have long since been superseded by even more horrific phenomena. As Hardt and Negri argue, we've been "outflanked by strategies of power."[9] Our countermove, then, must be based on imminent critique, working through the internal logic of what we're scrutinizing toward its own undoing and alternative potentialities. It must be a critique of the "real by the possible," as philosopher Henri Lefebvre asserted in 1958.[10]

One theme picked up and challenged by radical artists over a century ago was fragmentation, an emergent concern in their day. Now, social atomization is a fact of everyday life, and more frighteningly, is accepted and even celebrated. Contemporary artwork that portrays fragmentation only serves to mimic rather than decry our societal "breaking apart," precisely because the damage has already been done. So here comes one task for art: to depict resistance not as fragmentation per se, for mere description has lost all power of critique, but to illustrate how social acquiescence to it has become a valued commodity.

This ties into a related issue: alienation. Building on Karl Marx's work, avant-garde artists and intellectuals long ago moved the critique of

6. Some Vermont puppeteers, who certainly needed the money for their many unpaid projects, were commissioned to produce a puppet show for the 2005 Montreal Climate Control Conference. Yet there were strings attached. The eco-capitalist who financed these puppets had his own agenda in mind: make the art look like a self-initiated activist protest, but keep the theme in line with his own reformist political point. The artists were, in essence, paid to produce and think for their financial backer, not for themselves and their own political concerns.

7. As Erik Reuland noted in editing this chapter, "Many people would also argue that the whole definition of art should be exploded, and many things traditionally considered crafts or trades could be viewed—and invested with the same value—as artistic practices. They're not necessarily asserting that everyone can and should draw, write songs, and so on." Such a debate is complex, but at the risk of overgeneralizing for my present purposes, the notion that art's definition should encompass much more, and many more people could thus be considered artists, seems to often so water down what we mean by art and artists and makes both unrecognizable. Why does this matter? Precisely because of the concern articulated here about the recognition of our selves and each other as profoundly individuated humans, with wonderfully differing artistic and nonartistic things we might choose to excel in, embedded in a profoundly articulated community of our own ongoing self-determination.

8. Harry Cleaver, "Post-Marxist Anarchism: Kropotkin, Self-Valorization, and the Crisis of Marxism," 1997 extended essay (available from AK Press), 5, 8 (emphasis added).

9. Michael Hardt and Antonio Negri, *Empire.* (Cambridge, MA: Harvard University Press, 2000), 138.

10. Henri Lefebvre, foreword to *Critique de la vie quotidienne*, 2nd ed. (Paris, 1958), 16; cited in Richard Gombin, *The Origins of Modern Leftism* (1975; repr., Baltimore, MD: Insubordinate Editions), 47.

11. See, for example, Guy Debord, *Society of the Spectacle* (1967; repr., Oakland: AK Press, 2006); Raoul Vaneigem, *The Revolution of Everyday Life* (1967; repr., London: Rebel Press, 2001). For more on the Situationist International along with some downloadable texts, see http://www.bopsecrets.org/index.shtml.

12. David Harvey, *The Condition of Postmodernity: An Enquiry into the Origins of Cultural Change* (Malden, MA: Blackwell, 1990), 240.

alienation from (only) the realm of production to that of consumption, culminating most famously in the Situationist International's critique of everyday life and assertion of "all power to the imagination." Life had become a spectacle, with us as its passive spectators.[11] Today, this estrangement has gone one step further in a globalizing cyber-society, where people eagerly join the spectacle as active actors in the vain hope of feeling life again—through such things as reality television, hot dog-eating contests, and pieing prominent individuals—only to participate more thoroughly in their own removal from the world. And thus here's another aim for art: to capture the new forms of alienation that appear as active engagement, but that ultimately sap the very life out of us all.

A third area worthy of artistic scrutiny is what geographer David Harvey has called "time-space compression," pointing to "processes that so revolutionize the objective qualities of space and time that we are forced to alter, sometimes in quite radical ways, how we represent the world to ourselves."[12] Under globalization, temporality has become an ever-accelerating, just-in-time, simultaneous phenomenon, and spatial barriers have shrunk or even been overcome altogether. Yet anarchist art often still harkens back to a nostalgic time-space of "before," clinging to archaic forms and/or content—the pastoral black-and-white woodcut, say. Here's an additional artistic aspiration, then: to interrogate the dizzying "no-time" and displacing "no-place" of our present virtual reality and real virtuality.

This dovetails with the dilemmas raised by high technologies and excessive consumption/waste. During the industrial era, artists such as filmmaker Charlie Chaplin showed the "little guy" being dragged through the gears of *Modern Times*, yet in our informational age, the computer now bypasses the cog as emblematic, and the "programmer guy" is pulled into *The Matrix*. Moreover, the new forms of production made possible by digital technologies have filled houses with kitsch, dumpsters with food, and big-box stores with clerks. One anarchist answer to technological/production shifts has frequently been to use garbage as art material—a decades-old artistic choice that has lost any bite (especially since most commodities are now junk to begin with), but more crucially is unfeeling in light of the millions who are forced to use garbage as architectural (and often edible) material. Or else to supposedly avoid high tech—conveniently forgetting that nearly all commodities involve communications technologies in their design, production, distribution, and/or disposal. The task for artists here is to separate the wheat from the chaff: to critique the ways in which new types of technologies/production help facilitate, versus potentially diminish, pointless excess or new methods of exploitation as well as time-space compression, alienation, fragmentation, and of course top-down power.[13]

Which brings us to the question of maintaining power, or sovereignty: the possession of supreme authority. Wars, revolutions, and "peacetime" are all essentially waged in the name of seizing this ultimate power (with anarchists hoping to redistribute it horizontally), but the ongoing consolidation of sovereignty is where much of the terror is often done. An increasingly uneven balance of power is held in place today by nation-states inculcating a particular blend of fear, despair, paranoia, and hate, and if all else fails, returning once again to "improved" forms of torture as a last resort. Anarchist art frequently just pokes fun at anxieties, depicts its own hatreds and paranoia, or worse, lapses into portraying the ways that states retained control in the past—say, via a monopoly on violence (something that suicide bombings, 9-11, and other nonstatist acts of violence have shown to be false). Contemporary art should instead scrutinize and expose present-day mechanisms of power: how the mundane as well as the lovely—the bus to work, the toothpaste tube, or the nice new neighbor—are made into objects of anxiety-as-control; how explainable events become paranoiac fantasies of hate-as-control (the Muslim, the Jew, or the Mexican "is responsible"); and how one's private spirituality, sexuality, or diet (indeed, one's very personhood) become fair game as physical and psychological abuse in the faceless, nameless, hopeless Gitmoization of torture-as-control.

This list of aesthetic concerns could stretch out further, but let me wrap up with an area that art, from the start, has always tried to capture: remembrance. From bison hunts to biblical stories, from victories in battles or revolutions, from socialist realist to fascist art, artists have attempted to memorialize the past as a means to sustain or shape the present. At its best, such creative recollections have attempted to make sense of the past and the present in order to contemplate a better future—especially in the face of hegemonic representations. Strikingly, however, the current moment is marked by a reversal of aeons of art history: forgetting. Call it the postmodern condition, or blame it on the speed of daily life or efforts to escape harsh realities, but history seems to get lost almost before it's been made, and we're left with a hodgepodge art of immediatism. Such ahistoricism erases the developmental logic of domination and hence our ability to contest it, but also that of the revolutionary tradition and hence our capacity to nurture it, thereby helping to "disappear" hope. The artistic imperative here is simple: struggle against memory loss, including our own.

The above themes may seem amorphous. Worse, they may appear to be completely removed from the many pressing, often life-and-death issues people face—the numerous "isms" that most of us battle, from racism to heterosexism to anti-Semitism, and sadly on and on. But it is through such concerns that, for instance, racism operates in specific ways right now, and can therefore be illustrated and potentially fought. Today's form of fragmentation, for example, has turned many toward fundamentalisms—Islam, Judaism, or Christianity—as a means to regain community, often at the expense of women, queers, and indeed anyone dubbed as the transgressive other. Fear has an object, and in the contemporary United States that is frequently the young black male and the bearded Middle Eastern man. Spatial displacement brutally creates refugees, who then become targets of hate. You get the picture. Rather, you can paint, print, or perform the picture.

Lest I seem to be blaming artists for an inegalitarian world, or minimally for not doing enough to challenge it through their work, let me reiterate: I desire to encourage shifts in cultural production and cultural producers in order that both can contribute to the project of ever-freer societies. There are valid reasons for artistic choices—say, whether to sign a work or not—but all too often such choices seem already circumscribed or shaped by today's social ills. Art should instead aim to turn the tables: this miserable historical moment could be the raw material for artists to give shape to choices of our own construction—ones that might circumscribe domination.

As an anarchist whose creativity comes through the act of writing, I know all too well that penning words or printing a poster both become damaged in the context of a damaged world. And the world seems increasingly damaged at present. A lithographer friend recently told me, "I'm not making art right now, because I don't want to produce work that's nihilistic, and that's all I can feel these days." Despite these counterrevolutionary times, though, we must all try to work through our own fears and despair, in ways that allow our imaginations to run utopian. My hope is to instill hope in others by claiming that it is through our continual ability, together and alone, to understand and resist

The Troy Worker

UNITED VICTORIAN WORKERS · U.V.W. · LOCAL 518

LABOR CREATES ALL WEALTH

VOLUME ONE, ISSUE Nº ONE, DECEMBER 1886 · TROY, NY

FREE FOR WORKING PEOPLES

UNITY OF LABOR IS THE HOPE OF THE WORLD

COHOES, NY–Nothing could be more amusingly ridiculous than the frantic efforts of the anti-Labor press to drive wedges into the ranks of the Labor Party. The most absurd feature is that it is all being done allegedly to establish a "sane" Labor Movement. When the Labor Movement becomes "sane" in the opinion of its historic opponents, it will have forfeited the right to exist.

The workers have surely learned from experience that the objective of their opponents is always to divide and defeat. It is the only way to success for them. Labor's motto is: The Unity of Labor is the Hope of the World. It is the only hope too. There can be no other permanent unity and no other hope.

ATTENTION WORKINGMEN!

GREAT MASS-MEETING · TO-DAY, AT 2:00 O'CLOCK

TROY, Monument Square, Bet. 2nd and 1st. Good Speakers will be present to denounce the working conditions of our fellow-workmen. Workingmen Appear in Full Force! United Victorian Workers, Local 518.

OUR NATIONAL DISGRACE

Two million children in this country are at work, while other children play or go to school.

Two million children sacrificed to greed!

Here is the record. Read it.

10,000 Boys from 9 to 13 years old work in the Coal Breakers.

7,800 Children work in Glass Factories. Hundreds of them work ALL NIGHT.

60,000 little Children toil in Southern Cotton Mills. Little girls 8 years old work through a TWELVE-HOUR NIGHT.

Little Messenger Boys are ruined by NIGHT calls at Houses of Vice.

"The truth is, these child victims are working for us. The are working for me. They are working for you."—HON. CHARLES P. NEILL, United States Commissioner of Labor.

COLD AND WEARY

the emergent global order with clear eyes, and envision and prefigure humane alternatives with even clearer eyes, that we might just win.

Collectively Gesturing Toward Utopia

So how might we begin to clamber out of our boxed-in existence, precisely in order to "win," knowing that there will never be a final victory but simply better approximations of fundamentally transformed social relations?

One starting point might come from Emma Goldman, who in 1914 observed that modern art should be "the dynamite which undermines superstition, shakes the social pillars, and prepares men and women [*sic*] for the reconstruction."[14] Another might be found with anarchist artist Clifford Harper, who noted of his 1974 "utopian images" posters: "they depict an existence that is immediately approachable."[15] And yet another is hinted at by libertarian left social theorist Murray Bookchin, who in 2004, reflecting on his imminent death, wrote, "To live without a social romance is to see without color. Imagine what life would be like in black and white, without being able to hear—to be deaf to music. Step by step our potentialities like hearing became organized sound, and the Marseillaise was born."[16]

Other points of departure come from on-the-ground experimentation by contemporary artists, some anarchists and others not, that grapple with some of the concerns mentioned above. Such as provocateur street artist Banksy, who despite his growing fame and fortune, still manages to question how present-day sovereigns maintain their control. Whether painting giant windows to a better world on the separation wall being erected by the Israeli government, or placing a life-size figure dressed in Guantanamo Bay-orange within the scenery of a Disneyland ride, Banksy serves to startle, to act as a vigilant public eye. Moreover, he asks people to "imagine a city where graffiti wasn't illegal... A city that felt like a living breathing thing which belonged to everybody, not just the real estate agents and the barons of big business. Imagine a city like that and stop leaning against the wall—it's wet."[17]

Another example comes from installation artists Esther Shalev-Gerz and Jochen Gerz's attempt to deal with "'forgetting' in a place of 'remembering,' and thus establish, through the act of public participation, each person's memory." In 1986, they erected a twelve-meter-high lead column in a town square in Hamburg, Germany, and "invited passers-by to write their name on its surface." It became a "community board without restriction," and "mimicked the process of an ideal democracy—a public space open to unrestricted thought...and all-encompassing dialogue." Over seven years, which included the fall of the Berlin wall, the column was slowly lowered into the ground as sections filled up. A debate ensued during that time over public space/art, and especially the Nazi past and neo-Nazi present. But as this disappearing "countermonument" was also meant to illustrate, "in the long run," according to Shalev-Gerz, "it is only we ourselves who can stand up against injustice."[18]

To my mind, the best efforts are the ones that focus as much on horizontal social organization as on aesthetic questions, thereby highlighting the D-I-O art-as-commons dimension of anarchism that, again to my mind, really does distinguish an antiauthoritarian art. Novelist Ursula Le Guin, for one, imagined a utopia where museums might function like libraries. The Internet now facilitates open-source, interactive electronic museums. Other inklings of this can be found in those creative projects that play with, and work at, the notion of communal control of our now-privatized spaces and prefigure directly democratic, confederated social structures.

One compelling case study is the United Victorian Workers, Local 518, organized in late November 2005 by an artist/activist collective as a counterpoint to the Victorian Stroll in Troy, New York. The "official" stroll is a privately funded annual event designed to lure holiday shoppers to the "historic streets of downtown" by creating a "magical stage" peopled by the Victorian upper crust; the "unofficial" version "gave a presence to those whose labor built the city by dressing in Victorian-era working-class apparel and performing a period-inspired strike during the event."[19] Many of the bystanders as well as the participants, though, couldn't tell the difference, and the full history of nineteenth century Troy was reinserted into the public imagination. As one of the artists involved with this project remarked, "It was a collective

United Victorian Workers, newspaper created for and distributed at the *Victorian Stroll* (public intervention), Troy, NY, 2005.

intervention into public memory and Christmas shopping."[20] Certainly, "by making visible the class and labor struggles of the era," this interventionist art piece "obliquely points out the city's motives to present a selective history conducive to consumption," as *Shopdropping* observed.[21] But it also cleverly and clearly transforms the "Whose Streets? Our Streets!" of protest moments into a tangible lesson played out in the actual historical space—potentially sparking civic dialogue and action around contemporary injustice.

In a much more expansive effort in April 2001, the three-day Department of Space and Land Reclamation campaign involved sixty mostly illegal reclaimings of public space in Chicago, thereby explicitly linking artistic expression to vibrant conversations and decentralized self-management in the city's many distinct neighborhoods. As the weekend's catalog noted, "Artists/activists/radical citizens have once again found common ground" in multiple practices that "all resist the encroachment of top-down centralized control and private capital. Projects of reclamation situate the producer at a critical intersection of power." A central headquarters, open around-the-clock during the campaign, was designed "to connect various practitioners of reclamation as well as initiate a critical dialogue about the building of a radical aesthetic/arts movement in Chicago and beyond."[22] (For more on this campaign, see Josh MacPhee and Nato Thompson's piece on DSLR in this book.)

And in one final example, in summer 2006, CampBaltimore, in a surprising collaboration with the Contemporary Museum of Baltimore, encouraged people to debate urban design through the lens of social justice while building a network to transform art and society.[23] According to anarchist Mike McGuire, who participated in the project, CampBaltimore built "a trailer that could serve as a mobile convergence center," which included "a small infoshop, a place from which to serve meals, a mobile sewing workshop, and a place to do film screenings" within neighborhoods. Another part involved "Headquarters: Investigating the Creation of the Ghetto and the Prison-Industrial Complex," housed in the museum. Here, "blurring the lines between the practices of artists and activists," the museum also became "an infoshop and center of operations: a platform for activities that investigate Baltimore's program of uneven urbanism and a site to mobilize for local and global struggles."[24] "It's not like a traditional model of political activism or artistic models of political activism. It's both—and [it's] trying to offer an alternative way, seeing other ways...grappling with the evaporation of public spaces in the city and the privatization of everything," explained museum artist-in-residence René Gabri.[25] Rather than art on the walls, then, "Headquarters" featured short videos documenting grassroots struggles in Baltimore, a dry-erase map of the city that people could write on, a flowchart outlining socioeconomic interconnections, a mini library, and a meeting space, among other things. The trailer and museum became platforms for people to think and converse about their city—and hopefully change it.

In these instances and others, there is a sense of attempting to engage with the complexities of the present, and via a process of art-as-dialogue, working together to both critique and reconstruct our lived public places. Such imaginative projects indicate that centrally planned forms—whether

13. Josh MacPhee offered the following comment while editing this chapter: "The trouble is that *Modern Times* is a better movie than *The Matrix!*" I agree. And given that it's perhaps harder than ever to make artwork that isn't degraded from the start, Josh asks, "What is an artist to do, simply accept that degradation? Is not the woodcut a harkening to a time when craft mattered, and therefore a rejection of the made-in-China [or made-in-the-USA] aesthetics?" Sure. But what Josh and I are both getting at is this, to quote him again: It is "no longer about what we do (with capitalist globalization, everyone has access to everything, so skateboarding, noise music, tall bikes, and silk screening become fodder for Coke ads) but how we do it. This is a deceptively simple idea, but it can be easily misunderstood. It does not mean that there is a 'correct' way to do things (that is, a way to move into a neighborhood and not gentrify); we are still beholden to the larger systems we exist in. But it does mean that the ethics of how we do things matters, for the very reason that they are at the core of the new world we are trying to build." I appreciate the dialogue Josh and Erik added to this chapter in the editing process—a good example of "how we do it."

14. Emma Goldman, foreword to *The Social Significance of the Modern Drama* (Boston: Richard G. Badger, 1914), available at http://sunsite3.berkeley.edu/Goldman/Writings/Drama/foreword.html.

15. See http://www.infoshop.org/wiki/index.php/Clifford_Harper.

16. Murray Bookchin, "The Twilight Comes Early," November 2004, available at http://dwardmac.pitzer.edu/Anarchist_Archives/bookchin/twilight.html.

17. See http://www.banksy.co.uk/outdoors/tramp.html.

18. See http://www.shalev-gerz.net/ENG/index_eng.html; http://www.thephotographyinstitute.org/journals/1998/shalev_gerz.html.

19. For more on the official Troy Victorian Stroll, see http://www.troyvictorianstroll.com/about/index.cfm. For the unofficial version, see the "Action" section under the "Projects" header at http://www.daragreenwald.com.

20. E-mail to the author, October 19, 2006.

21. See http://www.rpi.edu/~scarfa/portfolio/project-pages/victorian-stroll.htm.

22. See http://www.counterproductiveindustries.com/dslr/dslrIdeas.html.

23. See http://www.campbaltimore.org.

24. E-mail to author, September 22, 2006; http://www.contemporary.org/past_2006_04.html.

25. Quoted in Bret McCabe, "Unite and Conquer," *City Paper*, July 12, 2006, available at http://www.citypaper.com/news/story.asp?id=12015.

capitalist, fascist, or socialist—cannot build a dailyscape that speaks to who we are and want to be. And that there also needs to be an integration—or reintegration in many cases—of what is now seen as art into those things now viewed as either material necessities, functional, or infrastructure. Mostly, though, they gesture, hopefully and often joyfully, at a time-space of "after."

What would such a time-space beyond hierarchy, domination, and exploitation look like, and what of an anarchist art then? That is something we need to dream up together, through our various acts of imagining, debating, fighting for, and deciding on that ever-dynamic time-space.

In the meantime, in this present awful time-space, I dream of an art that agitates even as it unmasks injustices; that educates even as it inspires; that organizes even as it models self-governance. That surprises and provokes, sometimes upsetting a few carts in the process, and that isn't identifiable as anarchist art by its look but instead by its sensibility. I long for a nonhierarchical aesthetic that isn't afraid of instituting imagination as a public good, which can also stand up to public involvement and interrogation, as well as directly democratic decision-making. That has an unending commitment to the notion that through creative expression, humans achieve a qualitative self- and social recognition that can, by breaking through the alienation we experience today, point toward self-determined social relations—not wealth or fame, but knowing that we are fully seen by and see others, "warts and all," as we shape a world of beauty together, all the while defining "beauty" by what upholds values such as cooperation, dignity, love, freedom, and other anarchistic ethics.

To hell with cardboard! Let's utilize whatever artistic mediums are necessary, toward endless, plastic possibilities in societies of our own, ongoing collective creation. That would be beautiful, indeed.

CampBaltimore's trailer being used for food service after a march in support of the United Workers Association, Baltimore, MD, 2006. Photo courtesy of CampBaltimore.

BIOGRAPHIES

Icky A. is a printmaker who lives in Portland, OR. He publishes the zine *Nosedive*.

Morgan F.P. Andrews has created over 50 original productions of radical puppet theater in under a decade and lugged them on buses across Brazil with the group Revolução de Papelão, by bicycle around Vermont in the Puppetual Motion Cycle Circus, and on foot in Philadelphia as Shoddy Puppet Company. When not engaged in the grueling drudgery of writing about, curating, producing, promoting, performing, tooling, tinkering, rehearsing, rehashing, and unleashing all things puppetry, Morgan builds community as a babysitter, cooperative housing organizer, gleaner, gardener, holistic healer, vegan chef, wacky music maker, and professional dream analyst to the rich and poor, famous and infamous dreamers in this overwhelming world.

Allan Antliff is Canada Research Chair in Modern Art at the University of Victoria. He edited *Only a Beginning: An Anarchist Anthology* (2004) and is author of *Anarchist Modernism: Art, Politics, and the First American Avant-Garde* (2001). He is a member of the *Alternative Press Review* editorial collective, art editor at *Anarchist Studies*, and art critic for *Canadian Art Magazine* and *Galleries West Magazine*.

Erika Biddle lives in NYC, is an active member of the Autonomedia editorial collective, a board member of the Institute for Anarchist Studies, and is trying to resuscitate the Artists in Dialogue (A.I.D.) collective. She writes, and makes videos and installations that address the concept of *zufall*.

Brett Bloom is an artist and writer living in Berlin. He works with the art group Temporary Services and co-runs an experimental cultural center in Chicago called Mess Hall. He has co-edited over five books. The most recent book, with Temporary Services, is called *Group Work* and investigates making art and music in groups. A forthcoming book, *UNHOUSED*, looks at creative resistance to global housing crises from the shanty towns of Delhi to the parks of Tokyo.

Carlos Fernandez is programs coordinator for Chicago Jobs With Justice. He can be reached at cf.thelos@gmail.com.

Christine Flores-Cozza is a visual artist, writer, and musician. Most recently she received international attention being in the top ten "Songs of the Times" on Neil Young's *Living with the War* website. You can read more about her and make contact at christinecozza.com.

David Graeber is an anthropologist whose fieldwork was originally in Madagascar. He has written extensively on value theory, and has been actively involved in the global justice movement and a variety of anarchist or anarchist-inspired groups since early 2000.

Dara Greenwald has participated in collaborative and collective cultural production and activism since the early 1990s. Participation includes the Pink Bloque, Ladyfest Midwest Chicago, Version>03, Pilot TV Chicago, and other groupings that resist being named. She worked as the distribution manager at the Video Data Bank from 1998–2005, where she distributed independent media and experimental video art and worked on the preservation of the Videofreex collection. She also writes, curates, and makes media art. Her writing has appeared in *Clamor*, Gurl.com, *the Journal of Aesthetics and Protest*, *Punk Planet*, and *Bad Subjects,* and her zine, *Educational Tourist*, is distributed by Microcosm Publishing. For a more detailed CV check out daragreenwald.com.

Kyle Harris currently resides in Denver, Colorado where he programs films and videos for Free Speech TV (Dish Channel 9415, www.freespeech.org). His videos and collective art projects have shown in festivals, museums, galleries, bars, living-rooms, and infoshops all over the world. He is finishing a feature-length queer-anarcho-eco epic film called "The Patriarchs" and is editing *Advertising Anarchism: The Pitfalls and Possibilities of Propaganda* (forthcoming, AK Press). For more information about these projects, contact Kyle at kyle@freespeech.org.

Nicolas Lampert is a Milwaukee-based interdisciplinary artist and writer. He was a co-editor for *Peace Signs: the Anti-War Movement Illustrated* (2004) and is currently co-authoring a survey text on radical art history in the US. His visual art website and contact information is at: machineanimalcollages.com.

Patricia Leighten, Professor of Art History & Visual Studies at Duke University, is author of numerous books and articles on anarchism, modernism and the visual arts. Her books include *Re-Ordering the Universe: Picasso and Anarchism, 1897–1914* (Princeton, 1989); *Cubism and Culture* (with Mark Antliff, Thames & Hudson, 2001); and *A Cubism Reader:*

Documents and Criticism, 1906–1914 (with Mark Antliff, University of Chicago, 2007). She is currently completing *A Politics of Form: Art, Anarchism and Audience in Avant-Guerre Paris* (University of Chicago, 2008), from which her essay in this anthology is drawn.

Erick Lyle is the editor of *SCAM* magazine. He lives in San Francisco.

Josh MacPhee is an artist, curator and activist currently living in Troy, NY. His work often revolves around themes of radical politics, privatization and public space. His other books include *Stencil Pirates: A Global Survey of the Street Stencil* (Soft Skull, 2004) and *Reproduce and Revolt: A Graphic Toolbox for the 21st Century Activist*, co-edited with Favianna Rodriguez (Soft Skull, 2007). More info at justseeds.org.

Iain McIntyre is a Melbourne-based author and community radio announcer who writes regularly about music and history and occasionally attempts to make a little of his own (with more success in the former than the latter). To check out his latest book *Tomorrow Is Today: Australia In The Psychedelic Era, 1966–1970*, visit 3cr.org.au.

Cindy Milstein is co-organizer of the annual Renewing the Anarchist Tradition conference, a board member of the Institute for Anarchist Studies, and a collective member of both the Free Society Collective and all-volunteer Black Sheep Books in Montpelier, VT. Some of her essays appear in *Globalize Liberation* (City Lights, 2004), *Confronting Capitalism* (Soft Skull, 2004), and *Only a Beginning* (Arsenal Pulp, 2004). She can be reached at cbmilstein@yahoo.com.

Dylan Miner is a Métis anarchist, artist, and historian living in New Mexico. He is a member of the Industrial Workers of the World and the Métis Woodland Tribe of Ontario. He frequently migrates between the US, Mexico, and Canada. Dylan helped found the Campesina/o Collective and can be reached at dylan@dylanminer.com.

Anne Elizabeth Moore is the co-editor of *Punk Planet*, the editor of the Best American Comics series, and the author of *Hey Kidz, Buy This Book: A Radical Primer on Corporate and Governmental Propaganda and Artistic Activism for Short People* (Soft Skull) as well as the upcoming *Unmarketable: Brandalism, Copyfighting, Mocketing and the Erosion of Integrity* (The New Press). She wishes sometimes it were true that print is dead, because then she might actually be able to get all her dishes done.

Bill Nowlin was a writer for the Canadian anarchist newspaper *Open Road*. Many authors for *Open Road* used pseudonyms, and no one from the paper actually remembers who Bill Nowlin was. We hope if he (or she) reads this, they will be happy to see their work reprinted here.

Roger Peet is a maker of shadow puppet shows, prints, and papercuts who lives in a log cabin far far away from you people. He does miss you sometimes, however. Please feel free to email mold2000@yahoo.com.

Erik Reuland, a.k.a. Erik Ruin, is a Minneapolis-based, Michigan-raised puppeteer and printmaker. He also at one time edited the zine *Trouble In Mind*, exploring the intersections of art, everyday life, and radical politics. He works and/or has worked with the UpsidedownCulture Collective, Street Art Workers, the Prison Poster Project and Barebones Productions.

Meredith Stern is a dancing and dj maniac who loves linoleum block printing. You can find her in Providence, RI where she currently drums for Teenage Waistband.

Nato Thompson is an activist, writer and curator currently working as Curator at MASS MoCA. He is deeply committed to the development of radical infrastructures that support the often unfunded fields of art and activism.

INDEX

Friends of AK Press

AK Press is a worker-run co-operative that publishes and distributes radical books, visual & audio media, and other mind-altering material. We're a dozen people who work long hours for short money, because we believe in what we do. We're anarchists, which is reflected both in the books we publish and in the way we organize our business. All decisions at AK Press are made collectively—from what we publish to what we carry for distribution. All the work, from sweeping the floors to answering the phones, is shared equally.

Currently, AK Press publishes about 20 titles per year. If we had the money, we would publish 40 titles in the coming year. New works from new voices, as well a growing mountain of classic titles that unfortunately are being left out of print.

All these projects can come out sooner with your help. With the Friends of AK Press program, you pay a minimum of $20 per month (of course, we welcome larger contributions), for a minimum three month period. All the money received goes directly into our publishing funds. In return, Friends automatically receive (for the duration of their membership), one FREE copy of EVERY new AK Press title (books, dvds, and cds), as they appear. As well, Friends are entitled to a 10% discount on everything featured in the AK Press Distribution Catalog—thousands of titles from the hundreds of publishers we work with. We also have a program where groups or individuals can sponsor a whole book. Please contact us for details. To become a Friend, go to: http://www.akpress.org.

Also Available from AK Press

CDs

MUMIA ABU JAMAL—175 Progress Drive
MUMIA ABU JAMAL—All Things Censored Vol.1
MUMIA ABU JAMAL—Spoken Word
JUDI BARI—Who Bombed Judi Bari?
JELLO BIAFRA—Become the Media
JELLO BIAFRA—Beyond The Valley of the Gift Police
JELLO BIAFRA—The Big Ka-Boom, Part One
JELLO BIAFRA—High Priest of Harmful
JELLO BIAFRA—I Blow Minds For A Living
JELLO BIAFRA—In the Grip of Official Treason
JELLO BIAFRA—If Evolution Is Outlawed
JELLO BIAFRA—Machine Gun In The Clown's Hand
JELLO BIAFRA—No More Cocoons
NOAM CHOMSKY—An American Addiction
NOAM CHOMSKY—Case Studies in Hypocrisy
NOAM CHOMSKY—Emerging Framework of World Power
NOAM CHOMSKY—Free Market Fantasies
NOAM CHOMSKY—The Imperial Presidency
NOAM CHOMSKY—New War On Terrorism: Fact And Fiction
NOAM CHOMSKY—Propaganda and Control of the Public Mind
NOAM CHOMSKY—Prospects for Democracy
NOAM CHOMSKY & CHUMBAWAMBA—For A Free Humanity: For Anarchy
CHUMBAWAMBA—A Singsong and A Scrap
WARD CHURCHILL—Doing Time: The Politics of Imprisonment
WARD CHURCHILL—In A Pig's Eye: Reflections on the Police State, Repression, and Native America
WARD CHURCHILL—Life in Occupied America
WARD CHURCHILL—Pacifism and Pathology in the American Left
ALEXANDER COCKBURN—Beating the Devil: The Incendiary Rants of Alexander Cockburn
ANGELA DAVIS—The Prison Industrial Complex
THE EX—1936: The Spanish Revolution
NORMAN FINKELSTEIN—An Issue of Justice: Origins of the Israel/Palestine Conflict
ROBERT FISK—War, Journalism, and the Middle East

FREEDOM ARCHIVES—Chile: Promise of Freedom
FREEDOM ARCHIVES—Prisons on Fire: George Jackson, Attica & Black Liberation
FREEDOM ARCHIVES—Robert F. Williams: Self-Defense, Self-Respect & Self-Determination
JAMES KELMAN—Seven Stories
TOM LEONARD—Nora's Place and Other Poems 1965–99
CASEY NEILL—Memory Against Forgetting
GREG PALAST—Weapon of Mass Instruction
CHRISTIAN PARENTI—Taking Liberties
UTAH PHILLIPS—I've Got To know
UTAH PHILLIPS—Starlight on the Rails box set
DAVID ROVICS—Behind the Barricades: Best of David Rovics
ARUNDHATI ROY—Come September
VARIOUS—Better Read Than Dead
VARIOUS—Less Rock, More Talk
VARIOUS—Mob Action Against the State: Collected Speeches from the Bay Area Anarchist Bookfair
VARIOUS—Monkeywrenching the New World Order
VARIOUS—Return of the Read Menace
HOWARD ZINN—Artists In A Time of War
HOWARD ZINN—Heroes and Martyrs: Emma Goldman, Sacco & Vanzetti, and the Revolutionary Struggle
HOWARD ZINN—A People's History of the United States: A Lecture at Reed
HOWARD ZINN—People's History Project Box Set
HOWARD ZINN—Stories Hollywood Never Tells

DVDs

NOAM CHOMSKY—Imperial Grand Strategy: The Conquest of Iraq and the Assault on Democracy
NOAM CHOMSKY—Distorted Morality
STEVEN FISCHLER & JOEL SUCHER—Anarchism in America/Free Voice of Labor
ARUNDHATI ROY—Instant-Mix Imperial Democracy
ROZ PAYNE ARCHIVES—What We Want, What We Believe: The Black Panther Party Library (4 DVD set)
HOWARD ZINN & ANTHONY ARNOVE (ed.)—Readings from Voices of a People's History of the United States

Contact & Ordering Information

AK Press
674-A 23rd Street,
Oakland, CA 94612-1163
USA

akpress@akpress.org
www.akpress.org

AK Press
PO Box 12766,
Edinburgh, EH8 9YE
Scotland

ak@akedin.demon.co.uk
www.akuk.com

For a dollar, a pound or a few IRC's, the same addresses would be delighted to provide you with the latest complete AK catalog, featuring several thousand books, pamphlets, zines, audio products and stylish apparel published & distributed by AK Press. Alternatively, check out our websites for the complete catalog, latest news and updates, events, and secure ordering.